COR

IN ITS

PICTURESQUE, SOCIAL, AND HISTORICAL

ASPECTS:

THE RECORD OF A TOUR IN THE SUMMER OF 1852,

.BY FERDINAND GREGOROVIUS.

TRANSLATED FROM THE GERMAN

BY RUSSELL MARTINEAU, M.A.

LONDON:
LONGMAN, BROWN, GREEN, AND LONGMANS.
1855.

TRANSLATOR'S PREFACE.

The Translator has endeavoured to enhance the value of this book to the English public by the verification of the references to classical and Italian authors, and the citation of the originals where any interest seemed to attach to them; and also by the addition of indices. All the notes, moreover, are added by him. He has received from the accomplished author encouragement in his task, and has been favoured with the correction of numerous errata in the German edition.

The Corsican Voceri the Translator considered to be so characteristic and original, that he did not feel himself justified in cutting down their number or curtailing their length. Cultivated Europe being obliged to M. Gregorovius for drawing these songs forth from their island obscurity, his Translator would be unpardonable if he shrunk from the labour of introducing them to an English public. Yet this is the part of the work for which the greatest indulgence is craved. An attempt to procure the Corsican book whence M. Gregorovius extracted them having failed up to the date of publication, the Translator has been forced to produce his version from the German translation, and has therefore reason to fear that it may be both harsher and farther from the Italian original than if translated at first-hand. In the slight metrical irregularities he has allowed himself, he is fully countenanced by the German version.

Over the original poems he is not so presumptuous as to fancy that he has shed any of the grace and poetic ease which form the charm of the originals, and have gained for them a comparison with Heine and even with Goethe. Enough if they serve to break the even tenor of the prose, and to raise a livelier and more poetical conception of the scenes that inspired them.

Finally, the Translator sincerely regrets to appear in an attitude of rivalry to an elegant and not unfaithful translation. But his work was almost completed at the time of the earliest announcement of Mr. Muir's projected translation; and his arrangements with his Publishers had been made many months previously.

PENRITH, *March*, 1855.

AUTHOR'S PREFACE.

It was in the summer of last year that I went over to the island of Corsica. Its unknown solitudes, and the legendary fame of its scenery and its people, urged me to make the trip. Yet I had no intention of entangling myself so deep in its pathless labyrinths as I have actually done. It fared with me as with the people in the story-book, who are decoyed by some strange wondrous bird into the mysterious forest, and then drawn deeper and deeper into the beautiful wilds. At the end of my tour I had pretty well traversed the island. The fruit of this summer's experiences is the present work, which I send home to my friends. May it not lack a sympathetic reception! This at least it hopes to deserve for the sake of the history and the popular poetry of the Corsicans.

The history of Corsica, all granite like its mountains, and wonderfully in unison with its scenery, bears quite a distinctive character; it is therefore capable of being presented briefly as a separate whole, while it awakens the same sort of interest as is possessed by the biography of a man of extraordinary organization. It would be worthy of our attention and admiration, even if it had not the glory of having produced a Napoleon. But it may well contribute something towards a complete understanding of Napoleon's character; and the fact that it culminates in this great phenomenon, enhances the interest attaching to it.

Observations in physical science lie beyond the scope of the work, as well as beyond the powers of the author. In other respects, the work is written with an earnest purpose.

I am indebted for much literary assistance to the learned Benedetto Viale, Professor of Chemistry at the University of Rome, himself a Corsican. It would be hard to say how ready with their help were my various friends in Corsica itself. But my warmest thanks are specially due to the Florentine exile and geographer, Francesco Marmocchi, and to Camillo Friess, the Recorder of Ajaccio.

F. GREGOROVIUS.

ROME, *April 2, 1853.*

CONTENTS.

HISTORY.

TRAVELS.

BOOK I.

BOOK II.

BOOK III.

viii   CONTENTS.

BOOK IV.

BOOK V.

BOOK VI.

BOOK VII.

BOOK VIII.

CORSICA.

HISTORY.—BOOK I.

CHAPTER 1.

THE earliest accounts of Corsica are found in the historians and geographers of the Greeks and Romans. We can form from them no distinct idea what races originally colonized the island, whether Phœnicians, Etruscans, Hispanians, or Ligurians. All these ancient races had been in Corsica before Carthaginians, Greeks from Phocæa, and Romans, migrated thither.

The position of the islands Corsica and Sardinia, in the great western expanse of the Mediterranean, made them the entrepôt of all the surrounding nations of the continent which practised commerce and founded colonies. Nearest, in a northerly direction, and one day's journey distant, lies Gaul; westwards, and three days' journey distant, Spain; to the east, and quite near, is the coast of Etruria;. and lastly, only a few days' journey distant to the south, stretches the coast-line of Africa. Thus the nations of the continent necessarily met upon these islands, and stamped their impress upon them, either simultaneously or one after the other. This composite character, curiously combined with a distinctness of national characteristics, and the multiformity of the traces left by such various peoples in buildings, sculptures, coins, language, and customs, which determine the gradual ethnographical formation of the island, as rock-strata its geological formation—these render Sardinia one of the most remarkable countries of Europe. The two islands lie on the border-line which divides that western basin of the Mediterranean

B 2

into a Spanish and an Italian half. So when the political, if not the physical influence also, of Oriental and Greek immigrations had passed away, these two countries began to assert their influence over the destiny of the islands. In Sardinia the Spanish element preponderated ; in Corsica the Italian. One may to this day recognise this fact simply in the language. In the case of Corsica, a third determining element was added in later times—the French; but this has only a political force. Even in the earliest times Celto-Gallic or Ligurian, as well as Spanish tribes, had passed over to the island. The Spanish nature, which struck even the philosopher Seneca as so remarkable in the Corsicans of his day, was overpowered, and has maintained itself only in the taciturn and gloomy, melancholy and choleric *naturel* of the people.

The oldest name of the island is Corsica, the later one Cyrnus. The former is derived from Corsus, a son of Hercules and brother of Sardus, the two brothers having led colonies to the islands named after them. Others make Corsus a Trojan, and tell how he carried off Sica a niece of Dido, whence the name Corsica arose. This is the story adopted by the earliest Corsican chronicler, John della Grossa.

The name Cyrnus was current with the Greeks. Pausanias says in his Phocian Geography,*—"There is an island not far distant from Sardinia, called by Greeks Cyrnus, but by the Libyans who inhabit it, Corsica." The appellation Libyans is common for Phœnicians, and Pausanias can hardly have meant primitive inhabitants. He meant immigrant colonists, like those in Sardinia. For in the same book he says,† that Libyans first of all came to Sardinia, but found inhabitants already there, and that after them Greeks and Phœnicians arrived. The word Cyrnus itself has been explained from the Phœnician Kir (*horn,* or *projecting cape of land.*) To cut the matter short, these are mere sayings, hypotheses, things that can never be determined.

But so much as this appears certain from the old traditions from which Pausanias drew his assertions; viz., that Phœnicians founded colonies in both islands in very early times—that they

* Paus. x. 17. 5.

† Paus. x. 17. 2.—Πρῶτοι δὲ διαβῆναι λέγονται ναυσὶν ἐς τὴν νῆσον Λίβυες . . . οὐ μέντοι τούς γε αὐτόχθονας ἐξέβαλεν ὁ τῶν Λιβύων στόλος. § 3. Ετεσι δὲ ὕστιρον μετὰ τοὺς Λίβυας ἀφίκοντο ἐκ τῆς Ελλάδος ἐς τὴν νῆσον οἱ μετὰ Ἀρισταίου. § 4. Μετὰ δὲ Ἀρισταίου Ἴβηρες ἐς τὴν Σαρδῶ διαβαίνουσιν.

found a population already there, which was either Ligurian or Etrusco-Pelasgian—and that, later, Hispanians also passed over thither.　Seneca, who lived eight years in exile in Corsica, writes from hence his Consolation to his mother Helvia, in the eighth chapter of which the following passage stands :*—" This island also has often changed its inhabitants.　Passing over the more ancient events which are incrusted with the rust of antiquity, I will only mention that the Greeks who now inhabit Massilia (Marseille) settled in this island first on leaving Phocæa.　It is uncertain what drove them hence—whether the harshness of the climate, the sight of the growing power of Italy, or the harbourless nature of the coast ; for, that the savageness of the inhabitants was not the cause, we gather from their placing themselves among the then particularly wild and uncivilized peoples of Gaul.　Afterwards, Ligurians crossed over to the island, and Hispanians also, which is rendered apparent by the similarity of their modes of life, since they have, the same head-dresses and the same kind of shoes as the Cantabrians, and even several words ; however, the language as a whole has lost its primitive national character by the frequent intercourse with Greeks and Ligurians."　It is to be regretted that Seneca did not think it worth while to investigate deeper the state of the island.　Even to him the oldest history of the Corsicans was shrouded in obscurity ; how much more must it be so to us !

But Seneca must be in error when he brings his Ligurians and Spaniards to the island *after* the Phocæans.　I have no doubt that Celtic tribes were the first and oldest inhabitants of Corsica ; even the physiognomy of the modern Corsicans appears to be Celtic-Ligurian.

CHAPTER II.

THE earliest historical event in Corsica is that arrival of the Phocæan exiles, lucidly related by Herodotus.　We know that these Greeks of Asia Minor had resolved rather to migrate from their native country into distant lands than to bear the inevitable yoke of Cyrus, and that, after a solemn oath sworn to the gods, they embarked on shipboard with all their goods and chattels.　They first treated with the Chians for a cession of

---

* Seneca, Consol. ad Helviam, § 8.

the islands of Œnussæ ; meeting a repulse they hereupon sailed
to Corsica, driven thither by no chance, but because they had
twenty years previously founded the town Alalia in that island.
They thus found here their own colonists, and remained five
years with them, building temples. "But," as Herodotus says,[*]
"as they visited their neighbours with plunder and rapine, the
Tyrrhenians and Carthaginians brought sixty ships against
them. On their side the Phocæans had equipped an equal number of ships, and sailed out into the sea in front of Sardinia to
meet them. They gained the victory, but it cost them dear ;
for forty ships were lost, and the remaining twenty rendered
useless, their beaks being turned. They returned to Alalia ;
and taking with them their women and children, and whatever
possessions besides their ships were able to convey, they abandoned the island Cyrnus, and sailed to Rhegium." That they
afterwards founded Massilia, the present Marseille, is well known.

Thus we have in Alalia, the modern Aleria, an undoubted
Greek colony, which subsequently passed into the power of the
Etruscans. That the latter must have sent out colonies to Corsica even before the Phocæans, the history of their flourishing
commercial nation might well induce us to believe. For how
should the powerful Populonia especially, situated close opposite
Corsica, have abstained from an attempt to make herself master
of the eastern coast of Corsica, when she actually had possession
of Elba ? Diodorus tells us in his fifth book,[†]—"Two towns
there are in Corsica worthy of mention—and of these the one is
called Calaris, the other Nicæa. Calaris the Phocæans founded ;
and, having dwelt there some time, were expelled from the island
by the Tyrrhenians. Nicæa was founded by the Tyrrhenians
when they were masters of the sea." Calaris is a corrupt reading for Alalia or Aleria. Nicæa is probably Mariana, situate
upon the same coast. We may suppose this colony to have
previously existed as well as Alalia, and the immigration of the
entire community of Phocæa to have excited fear and jealousy
in the Tyrrhenians, wherefore a hostile encounter took place
between the Greeks and the Tyrrhenians. Whether the Carthaginians had settlements in Corsica, is not quite certain. But
they possessed at this period colonies in its neighbour, Sardinia.

* Her. i. 165—6.

† Diod. v. 13.—Ὑπάρχουσι δ' ἐν αὐτῇ καὶ πόλεις ἀξιόλογοι δύο, καὶ τούτων ἡ μὲν Κά-
λαρις, ἡ δὲ Νίκαια προσαγορεύεται. Τούτων δὲ τὴν μὲν Κάλαριν Φωκαεῖς ἔκτισαν, καὶ χρόνον
τινὰ κατοικήσαντες, ὑπὸ Τυῤῥηνῶν ἐξεβλήθησαν ἐκ τῆς νήσου. Τὴν δὲ Νίκαιαν ἔκτισαν
Τυῤῥηνοὶ θαλαττοκρατοῦντες.

Pausanias mentions * that they subjugated the Libyans and Hispanians on this island, and founded two towns, Carabis (Cagliari) and Sulchos (Palma di Solo). The danger threatening them from the Greeks induced them now to make common cause with the Tyrrhenians, who had likewise settled in Sardinia, against the Phocæan intruders. Ancient authors mention also an immigration of Corsicans into Sardinia, where they are said to have founded twelve towns.

For a long period we hear nothing further of the fate of Corsica, whence the Etruscans continued to draw supplies of honey, wax, ship-timber, and slaves. Their gradually declining power yielded to the Carthaginians, who seem to have entered upon the complete possession of both islands—that is to say, of their emporia and harbours; for the tribes of the interior had never been subdued by an enemy. Then, in the Punic wars, the aspiring Romans wrested the two islands from the Carthaginians. But Corsica is not mentioned either in the Punic treaty of the Romans in the time of Tarquinius, or in the articles of peace of the first Punic war. Sardinia was ceded to the Romans. The proximity of Corsica could not but entice them to the conquest of this island also. Both, lying in the centre of the sea that washes Spain, Gaul, Italy, and Africa, were excellent stations, commanding the coasts of all those countries of the Mediterranean which Rome was then preparing to subjugate.

We are informed† that in the year B.C. 260, the consul L. Cornelius Scipio went over to Corsica and destroyed the town Aleria, making war at once upon the Corsicans and Sardinians, and upon Hanno, the Carthaginian. The mutilated epitaph of Scipio has the words HEC CEPIT CORSICA ALERIAQUE VRBE. But the subjugation of the wild Corsicans was not easy. They opposed quite as heroic a resistance as the tribes in the mountains of Samnium. We even find that the Romans were several times defeated, and that the Corsicans repeatedly rebelled. In the year 240, M. Claudius led an army against the Corsicans. Defeated and driven to desperation, he offered them favourable terms.

---

* Paus. l. c.—Καρχηδόνιοι δὲ, ὅτε ναυτικῷ μάλιστα ἴσχυσαν, κατεστρέψαντο μὲν καὶ ἅπαντας τοὺς ἐν τῇ Σαρδοῖ, πλὴν τῶν Ἰλιέων τε καὶ Κορσῶν, (τούτοις δὲ μὴ δε δουλείαν ὑπαχθῆναι τὸ ἐχυρὸν ἤρκεσε τῶν ὁρῶν) ᾤκισαν δὲ ἐν τῇ νήσῳ καὶ αὐτοὶ πόλιν οἱ Καρχηδόνιοι, Κάρναλιν τε καὶ Σῦλλουν.

† Livy, Epitome, lib. xvii. Arnold, Hist. of Rome, vol. ii. p. 579, who quotes Zonaras, viii. 11 ; Polyb. i. 24.

They accepted these, but the Senate would not ratify them. It ordered the consul C. Licinius Varus forcibly to chastise the Corsicans, and delivered Claudius up to them, to deal with according to their pleasure. This was a politic expedient of the Romans, which they sometimes employed when they wished to mitigate religious scruples about perjury. The Corsicans acted precisely as the Spaniards and the Samnites did on a similar occasion. They refused to take the guiltless general, and sent him back uninjured. At Rome he was strangled, and thrown out on the Gemonian Steps.

Though kept under by the Romans, the Corsicans always lifted up their head again; and, even in those early times, one may recognise in them that love of freedom and patriotism which in much later days has drawn the eyes of the world upon this little nation lost in the sea. They rose in arms together with the Sardinians; but, after the latter had been beaten, the Corsicans also suffered a bloody defeat from the consul C. Papirius on the Field of Myrtles. Yet they maintained a firm footing in the mountains, and seem to have forced the Roman general to an advantageous peace.*

They rose anew in the year 181.† M. Pinarius, prætor of Sardinia, crossed forthwith to Corsica with an army and defeated the islanders, killing 2000 of them in a battle of extermination of which Livy tells. The nation submitted, gave hostages and a tribute of 100,000 pounds of wax. Seven years later was a fresh rising, and again sanguinary contests; 7000 Corsicans fell on the field, and 2000 were taken prisoners. The tribute was raised to 200,000 pounds of wax. Ten years later, the valiant nation stands again in arms, and compels the Romans to send against them a consular army. Juventius Thalna, and afterwards Scipio Nasica, fully subjugated the island in the year 162.‡

Thus the Romans had to contend for more than a hundred years with this island people before they subdued it. They administered the government of Corsica, in common with Sardinia, by a prætor who resided in Cagliari, and sent a lieutenant or legatus to Corsica. But not till the times of the first Civil war did the

•

---

* B.C. 231. Arnold, Hist. of Rome, iii. 36, refers to Zonaras, viii. 28. Val. Max. vi. 3, 3.   Eutrop. iii. 3.

† Livy, xl. 19, 34. In Corsica pugnatum cum Corsis; ad duo milia eorum M. Pinarius prætor in acie occidit. Qua clade compulsi obsides dederunt et ceræ centum milia pondo.

‡ Livy, Epit. lib. xli.

Romans seriously think of sending colonies to the island. Then the renowned Marius planned the colony Mariana, on the splendid plain of the east coast, and Sulla later Aleria, on the same plain, restoring the old Alalia of the Phocæans. Corsica began now to be Romanized, to change its Celtic-Spanish language, and to admit Roman customs. We do not hear of the Corsicans ever venturing again to rise against their masters, and the island is named only once more in ancient history; when Sextus Pompejus, defying the power of the Triumvirs, cut out for himself a dominion on the Mediterranean Sea, and drew Corsica, Sardinia, and Sicily to himself. His kingdom was not of long duration.*

CHAPTER III.

That the state of the island under the long rule of the Romans was by no means so flourishing as people suppose, we gather from the condition of its interior, which they had probably never subjugated. They contented themselves, as it appears, with the two colonies and a few harbour settlements. The fair coast opposite Italy was especially chosen as a settlement. They had laid down only one single road in Corsica. According to the Itinerary of Antoninus this Roman road led from Mariana, southwards along the coast to Aleria, to Præsidium, to Portus Favoni, to Palæ, near the modern Bonifazio, on the Straits. Here was the place of transit to Sardinia, where the road was continued from a considerable town, Portus Tibulæ (castro Aragonese) to Caralis, the modern Cagliari.

Pliny† speaks of thirty-three towns in Corsica, but mentions by name only the two colonies. Strabo, writing not long before him, says on the other hand of Corsica,‡ "there are a few small towns there, such as Blesino, Charax, Eniconiæ and Vapanæ." These names are found nowhere else. Probably Pliny understood each castellum as a town. Ptolemy, however, mentions at length the localities of Corsica, and the tribes inhabiting them; many of his appellations are found to this day in Corsica, sometimes well preserved, at others easily recognisable.

Ancient authors have, moreover, given us a few notices besides

* See Merivale's Fall of the Roman Republic, pp. 511—517.
† Pliny, N. II. iii. 12, 80.   ‡ Strabo, v. 2.

on the character and nature of the country and people of Çorsica
if that period. I shall simply put them here side by side, as it
must be interesting to compare what they say with what is told
us of the Corsicans in the latter part of the middle ages, and to
this day.

Strabo says of Corsica,*—"It is poorly peopled, being rugged
and in most places quite impassable. Hence it comes that
those who dwell upon the mountains live by rapine, and are
actually more untameable than wild beasts. When the Roman
generals undertake an expedition against the island and assault
its strongholds, they carry off with them a great number of
slaves; and there one may see in Rome with astonishment, how
perfectly savage and like wild beasts they are. For they either
take their own lives, or weary their master by their insolence
and dulness; so that he rues his bargain, even if he has bought
them dirt-cheap."

Diodorus,†— "When the Tyrrhenians for some time held
sway over the Corsican cities, they took tribute from the
natives—resin, wax, and honey, which are produced in abundance in the island. The Corsican slaves are thought to be
superior to other slaves for the uses of life. The whole island,
which is of good size, has much of its surface mountainous,
covered with continuous wood, and watered by many little
rivers. The natives live on a diet of milk, honey, and meat, all
which the land produces for them abundantly. Towards one
another they live fairly and justly, above almost all other barbarians. For the honeycombs that are found in the trees, in the
mountainous country belong undisputedly to the first finder;
and the sheep, distinguished by marks, are preserved to their
owners even if no one guard them; and in all the divers economy
of life besides, they honour a just course of action to a surprising degree. But the most extraordinary is what happens with
them at the birth of children. No care is taken of the woman
in travail at her lying-in; but her husband lays himself up as
though ill, and lies in for a fixed number of days, as though he
were suffering some bodily evil. The box-tree grows here both
abundant and excellent; and from this cause the honey produced here is quite bitter. The island is inhabited by barbarians having a strange, and with difficulty intelligible, language.
Their number amounts to more than 30,000."

Seneca,*—" Now pass over from those places whose delightful situation, and the advantages of the district allures multitudes, go to desert places and the ruggedest islands, to Sciathus and Seriphus, Gyarus and Corsica; thou shalt find no place of banishment in which some one does not reside for pleasure. What can be found so bare, so cut off on all sides as this island of rock? What, if you regard its products—more starving; if you regard its inhabitants—more uncouth; as to its mere locality—more frightful; in the nature of its climate—less temperate? And yet here abide more strangers than natives."

From all accounts of the oldest authors, we must infer that Corsica was then but little cultivated, and was poor in natural products, with the exception of its original forests. Seneca's exaggerations are palpable, and resulted from his position. Strabo and Diodorus are of opposite opinions on the character of Corsican slaves. For the former speak history and the tried character of the Corsicans, who have ever shown themselves in the highest degree intolerant of slavery; and no fairer praise could Strabo have bestowed on them. What Diodorus, who speaks from greater knowledge, talks of the Corsican's sense of right, is so true that it is verified through all ages.

Among the epigrams on Corsica attributed to Seneca, one says of the Corsicans—" Their first law is to avenge themselves; their second, to live on rapine; to lie, their third; to deny the existence of gods, their fourth."

These are the most important statements of the Greeks and Romans about Corsica.

CHAPTER IV.

CORSICA remained in the possession of the Romans, from whom it in a later age received Christianity, until the fall of Rome rendered the island once more a prey to wandering tribes. Here then we have again a deluge of nations and a checkered medley of peoples, languages, and manners, as in the earliest ages.

Germans, Byzantine Greeks, Moors, and Romanesque tribes, overrun the island. But the fundamental and inalienable character of the Corsicans, impressed by the Romans and

* Seneca, Consol. ad. Helviam, § 6.

strengthened by hosts of Italian exiles, becomes Romanesque. The Vandals under Genseric came to Corsica and held the island for a long time, until Belisarius expelled them. After Goths also and Lombards had pushed in and been lords of the island, it, as well as Sardinia, fell into the power of the Byzantines, and remained nearly two hundred years in their possession. Many Greek names and roots, which the language and geography has to show even to this day, date from this period.

The Greek rule was a Turkish despotism. They seemed to regard the Corsicans as a herd of savages; they loaded them with impossible imposts, and forced them even to sell their children, in order to raise the necessary sums of money. Corsica now enters upon a time of unceasing contests, and its history, during long centuries, exists only as a constant battle for life and the freedom of their native soil.

In the year 713, appeared the first swarms of Saracens in Corsica. For when Spain had become Moorish, the Mohammedans spread their rapine and plunder over all the islands of the Mediterranean, and founded in several places durable dynasties. The Greek emperors, occupied in the East, abandoned the west, which found new protectors in the Franks. That Charlemagne had to do with Corsica, or with the Moors there, appears from his biographer Eginhard, who tells that the emperor sent out his Count Burkhard with a fleet to defend Corsica against the Saracens. So also his son Charles totally defeated them at Mariana. These battles with the Moors have been well preserved in the traditions of the Corsican people. The Roman noble, Hugo Colonna, especially figures in them, a rebel against Pope Stephen IV., who sent him to Corsica, in order to be rid of him and his companions, Guido Savelli and Amondo Nasica. Colonna first took Aleria from the Moors, after a chivalrous contest between three Paladins and three Moors, in the style of the stories of chivalry. Then Colonna defeated the Moorish king Nugalon at Mariana, and forced all the heathen people of the island to be baptized. The Corsican chronicler gives this Hugo Colonna a companion, Ganelon, a nephew of Ganelon of Mainz, and makes him come to Corsica to wash out the disgrace of his house in the blood of the Moors.

Now the story goes, that the Tuscan marquis Boniface, having annihilated the Saracens in a great naval battle near Utica, on the African coast, landed on his return at the southern point of Corsica, and built a fortress on the chalk cliff there, which received from him the name Bonifazio. This happened in the year 833. Louis the Pious made over Corsica to him as a fief. So, then, did the Etruscan coast for the second time assert its authority over the neighbouring island; and it is certain that the Tuscan marquises governed Corsica till Lambert the last of their number. Lambert died in the year 951.

After Beranger and Adalbert of Friuli had then ruled over the island, the Emperor Otho II. gave it to his adherent, the Marquis Hugo of Tuscany. Further historical events are obscure, and cannot be unravelled till the time of the dominion of the Pisans.

In this period, and till about the beginning of the eleventh century, a savage and defiant nobility grew up in Corsica, as in the countries of Italy, and spread over the island with many branches and seats of power. It was probably only in small part of Corsican origin. Italian magnates that had fled before the barbarians—Lombard, Gothic, Greek or Frank vassals, warriors, who had acquired castles, land, and feudal titles as rewards for doing battle against the Moors—gradually formed themselves into hereditary potentates. The Corsican chronicler derives all these Signori from that Roman Hugo Colonna and his adherents. He calls him Count of Corsica, and makes the most renowned family of Corsican signori, the Cinarchesi, to be descended from his son Cinarco, the Biancolacci from another son Bianco, and tries to derive the Pinaschi from Pino a son of Savelli, and similarly there are Amondaschi, Rollandini, descendants of Ganelon and others. In later times, a few families became prominent as the most powerful in this confusion of petty tyrants; on Cape Corso the Gentili and the lords Da Mare, and beyond the mountains the lords of Leca, Istria, and Rocca, of Ornano, and of Bozio.

CHAPTER V.

For a long time the history of the Corsicans is nothing but the bloody picture of the tyranny of the Barons and of their contests among themselves. The coasts were rendered waste, the ancient cities, Aleria and Mariana, gradually abandoned; the inhabitants of the seabord fled higher up into the mountains for fear of the Saracens, and built villages strong by nature and construction, calculated to ward off both sea-corsairs and barons. Perhaps there was in few countries so savage and ruthless a nobility as in Corsica. In the midst of a half barbarian and extremely poor population, in a rugged rocky country, not kept in bounds by the counterweight of civil functions or civil manners, uncurbed by the power of the church, cut off from the world and its civilizing intercourse—so we must picture to ourselves these lords, and as sitting on their rocks, spending the rage of a restless nature that demanded action, in sensuality and hectoring. In other countries, every thing positive, all law and human development, as opposed to the aristocracy, gathered together in the cities, and organized itself in guilds, rights, and societies, and strengthened itself by the union of the civil compact. This was infinitely more difficult in Corsica, where there were neither trade nor manufactures, neither towns nor a proper burgher-class at all. The more remarkable is the phenomenon presented by a nation of raw peasants, finding their own way to a democratic constitution peculiarly their own, one might say, in a patriarchal spirit.

The Barons, engaged in a constant war with the oppressed people of the villages, and striving among themselves for sole dominion, had, at the beginning of the eleventh century, yielded to the Lord of Cinarca, who intended to set himself up as tyrant of the island. Scanty though the accounts be, we may gather from them that the Corsicans in the interior had hitherto offered an obstinate resistance to the barons. Now, in danger of falling under the rule of Cinarca, the people assembled at a diet. This is the first national parliament of which we hear in the Corsican history ; it was held at Morosaglia. In this council the Corsicans elected a brave man, Sambucuccio of Alando, to be their chief, and with him begins the long series of Corsican heroes, who were great through their patriotism and heroism.

Sambucuccio defeated the Lord of Cinarca, and drove him back into his fief. To render this result secure, he established a league or confederation, as under similar circumstances, but in far later times, the Swiss did. All the land in a circuit from Aleria to Calvi and to Brando formed itself into a free community, and took the title of Terra del Commune, which it has retained till the latest times. The constitution of this community proceeded simply, and quite in a democratic spirit, from the natural divisions of the land ; for the land is divided by its mountain system into valleys like a tissue of cells. As a rule, all the localities comprised within a valley form an ecclesiastical district, which is still, as in the oldest times, called by the Italian name pieve (*plebs*). Thus every pieve included a certain number of communes or parishes (*paese*). Now every parish first of all elected in its assembly before the church-door a local head or *podestà*, and two or more fathers of the parish (*padri del commune*), probably for a year, as was the rule in later times. The fathers of the parish were to realize the intention of their institution, by caring in a fatherly spirit for the good of the parishes, establishing peace, and protecting the weak. They came together and appointed a separate officer with the title Caporale, who seems to have had the function of a tribune of the people, and was established expressly to defend by all means the rights of the people. The Podestàs again came together, and elected the Dodici or Twelve men, the supreme legislative council of the confederation.

However imperfect and confused as to dates are all these accounts of Sambucuccio and his institutions, yet this point is established beyond doubt, that the Corsicans at so early a period were able to create by their own unaided power a democratic community. These germs having been once planted, were never stifled again, but continued to grow through all storms and convulsions; they ennobled the raw force of a nation by nature passionate, maintained in it through all ages an unexampled love of country and a heroic love of freedom, and rendered Corsica—at a time when the great civilized nations of the continent lay enchained in the state-formulæ of depotism—capable of giving birth to the democratic constitution of Pasquale Paoli, which arose before North America liberated herself, or France began her revolution. Corsica had no slaves nor serfs; every Corsican was free, and concerned in the life of the nation, through the self-government of his parish and the national assembly; and this, taken in connection with the sense of law and the love of country, is the basis of all political freedom. The Corsicans possessed the sense of law, for which even Diodorus praises them; but the entanglements their island was subject to, and the foreign rule which, with their position and numbers what they were, they could never shake off, prevented the nation from thriving.

CHAPTER VI.

SAMBUCUCCIO the legislator suffered the fate of many another legislator. His institutions suffered a sudden shock on his death. The Signori came forth from their strongholds forthwith, and spread strife and war over the country. Then the people turned to the Tuscan marquis, Malaspina, seeking deliverance, and placed itself under his protection. Malaspina came to the island with an army, overpowered the resistance of the barons, and restored tranquillity. This happened about the year 1020; and the Malaspinas appear to have been the rectors of the Terra del Commune until the year 1070, while the Signori held sway in the rest of the country. The Pope also, who tried to derive rights of his own to Corsica from the Frank kings, interfered at this period with the affairs of the island. It even appears that he gave it away as fief, and that Malaspina was Count of Corsica by his consent. The Corsican bishoprics, of which six had been founded from time to time—Aleria, Ajaccio, Accia, Mariana, Nebbio and Sagona—next gave him a pretext for making himself master of the island.

Gregory VII. employed Landulph, Bishop of Pisa, whom he sent to Corsica to induce the people to determine to submit themselves to the supremacy of the Church. This having been done, Gregory, and after him Urban II., in the year 1098, put Corsica as a fief for ever under the see of Pisa, which was raised to an archbishop's see. Thus the Pisans made themselves lords of the island, which they maintained, though as a very precarious and constantly contested possession, for nearly a hundred years.

Their rule was wise, just, and beneficent, and is highly praised by all the Corsican historians. They exerted themselves to cultivate the land, fostered the growth of its natural products, restored the cities, built bridges and roads and towers on the coast, and transplanted to the island even their arts, at any rate in the architecture of the churches. The best old ecclesiastical buildings of the island are of Pisan origin, and may be at once recognised as such by their pleasing style. Every two years the republic of Pisa sent an officer to the island, who administered law and justice in the name of the city, and with the title of judge (Giudice). The parochial institutions of Sambucuccio remained in force.

Meanwhile Genoa had followed with jealous eyes the Pisan rule on the neighbouring island, and could not intend to leave to her rival so advantageous a station in the Mediterranean, and before her own gates. As early as when Urban II. put the Bishops of Corsica under Pisa as metropolitan, the Genoese entered their protest, and frequently compelled the Popes to take back this Pisan investiture. At length, in the year 1133, Innocent II. yielded to the urgency of the dispute, and divided the investiture, subordinating the Corsican bishops of Mariana, Accio, and Nebbio to Genoa, which had also been raised to an archbishopric, but leaving to the Pisans the sees of Aleria, Ajaccio, and Sagona. The Genoese were not to be put off by this makeshift; they aspired to the entire temporal dominion of the island. Constantly engaged in war with the Pisans, they seized a favourable opportunity to fall upon Bonifazio, just as the inhabitants of the town were making merry at a wedding. Honorius III. was obliged, in the year 1217, to confirm their possession of this important place. They fortified the impregnable rock, and made it the point d'appui of their dominion; then, by granting privileges to the town and freedom to its commerce, they induced a great number of Genoese families to remove thither. So Bonifazio was the first Genoese colony in Corsica.

CHAPTER VII.

CORSICA was now divided by factions. One part of the inhabitants was friendly to Pisa, another to Genoa; many Signori stood apart, and finally the Terra del Commune maintained its separate position. The Pisans, though assailed by their powerful enemies in Italy, and brought to extremities, were not inclined to abandon Corsica. They appointed a Corsican of the ancient family Cinarca as their lieutenant and Giudice, and committed to him the defence of the island against Genoa.

This man was named Sinucello, and became celebrated under the appellation Giudice della Rocca. His love of country and his heroism, his wisdom and justice, have given him a place among those men who have been prominent for personal virtue in barbaric times. The Cinarchesi, it is said, had been expelled

C

to Sardinia by one of the Papal marquises. One of their descendants was Sinucello. He had emigrated to Pisa, and distinguished himself in the service of the republic. Upon him the Pisans now rested their hopes. They named him count and judge of the island, gave him a few ships, and sent him in the year 1280 to Corsica. He succeeded in overcoming the Genoese party among the Signori by the aid of his adherents, and in restoring the Pisan supremacy. But the Genoese sent Thomas Spinola with troops. Spinola was signally defeated by Giudice. The war lasted many years, and was prolonged indefatigably by Giudice in the name of the republic of Pisa, even after the latter had lost the great naval engagement against Genoa near the rock of Meloria, in which Ugolino, of tragic fate, commanded, and in consequence of which the power of Pisa decayed, and Corsica also was no longer tenable.

After their victory, the Genoese made themselves masters of the eastern coast of Corsica also. They committed the subjugation of the island, and the expulsion of the brave Giudice, to their general, Luchetto Doria. But Doria, too, met with a humiliating defeat; and the extraordinary Corsican managed to maintain his position for many years in incessant contests with the Genoese troops and the Signori of the island, which appeared dissolved by total anarchy. The chroniclers have embellished with many stories the truly national Corsican figure of their favourite Giudice, and given a romantic character to his battles. However little this may concern history, it yet characterises the times, the ways of the country, or its inhabitants. Giudice had six daughters married to the six leading men of the country; and his bitter enemy, Giovanninello, had likewise six daughters, equally well provided for. The six sons-in-law of the latter, conspire against Giudice, and in one night kill seventy men-at-arms of his train. This becomes the cause of a division of the whole island between two parties, which now make war upon one another like Guelfs and Ghibellins, and prolong the contest for 200 years. But Giovanninello was expelled to Genoa; soon returning again, he built the fortress Calvi, which then gave itself up to the Genoese, and became the second Genoese colony in the island. Of the justice and of the mercy of Giudice the chroniclers have many a story to tell: as the following. Once having taken many Genoese prisoners, he promised freedom to as many as were married; only their wives must come in person to fetch them. The women came, and one of Giudice's nephews forced a fair Genoese to grant him her favours.   Giudice caused him to be immediately beheaded, and sent the prisoners home according to promise.   Thus this man bears the name Giudice, judge, *par excellence*, because in a barbarian nation and period the judicial power unites in itself all other power and virtue.

In extreme old age Giudice became blind.   The blind old man became involved in a quarrel with his natural son Salnese, who laid an ambush for him, took him prisoner, and delivered him up to the Genoese.   When the old man was being brought to the ship, he fell on his knees on the seashore, and solemnly cursed his son Salnese and his posterity.   Giudice della Rocca was thrown into a miserable dungeon in Genoa, and died there in the tower Malapaga, in the year 1312.   The Corsican historian, Filippini, says of him, that he was one of the most remarkable men that the island has produced; he was valiant and dexterous in arms, admirably quick in the carrying out of his enterprises, great in council, executing justice, very liberal towards his friends, and steadfast in adversity—characteristics which almost all distinguished Corsicans have possessed.   With Giudice fell the Pisan rule in Corsica.

CHAPTER VIII.

PISA formally ceded the island to Genoa; and thirty years after Giudice's death even the Terra del Commune, and the majority of the Signori, submitted to the Genoese supremacy. The Terra del Commune sent four ambassadors to the Genoese senate, and tendered its subjection upon condition that the Corsicans should pay no other impost than a hearth-tax of twenty soldi.   The senate accepted the condition; and thus the first Genoese governor went to the island in the year 1348.   He was Boccanera, a man whose vigour and prudence is praised, and who gave peace to the country during an administration of one year. But scarcely had he returned from his post, than the factions raised their head anew, and precipitated the land into the wildest anarchy.   For Genoa's right of rule was from the first not uncontested, as the pope Boniface VIII., as early as the year 1296, had, by virtue of the old feudal rights of the papal chair, assigned

Corsica and Sardinia to King James of Arragon. Thus a new foreign power, Spain, that had in ancient times been connected with Corsica, seemed about to assert its influence upon the island; and so, before there was any actual thought of conquest, those Corsicans who would not acknowledge the dominion of Genoa, were able to fall back upon the house of Arragon.

The next period of Corsican history shows the bloody contests of the Signori against Genoa. Immediately after Giudice's death so much confusion had arisen, and the people were driven to such distress, that the Corsican chronicler wonders that, in this wretched state of the country, the Corsicans did not rise and emigrate in a body. The barons, so soon as they no longer felt the heavy hand of Giudice, practised tyrannical violence, some purely by the right of the stronger, others strengthening themselves by paying tribute to Genoa. All sought to rule and to practise extortion. The utter dissolution of social order then produced an extravagant and fanatical sect of communists, a remarkable phenomenon on that wild island, but one which was seen in Italy also at the same time. This sect made itself renowned and fearful, under the name of the Giovannali. It arose in the small district of Carbini, beyond the mountains. Its authors were two brothers, Polo and Arrigo, lords of Attalà, and natural sons of Guglielmuccio. "In it," tells the chronicler, "were women as well as men, and its laws contained this, that all things should be in common, women and children, as well as the property of every one else. Perchance they wished to renew that golden age, which, according to the poets, existed in the time of Saturn. These Giovannali practised certain expiations after their fashion, and met by night in the churches to offer their sacrifices, on which occasions, following certain superstitious fancies and false ceremonies of theirs, they darkened the lights, and sported with one another in the foulest and most unseemly way, men and women, promiscuously as they lusted. Polo was the leader of this devilish crew, which began to increase extraordinarily, not only on this side the mountains, but also beyond."

The pope, then residing in France, excommunicated the sect; he sent a commissary with soldiers to Corsica, who signally defeated the Giovannali, strengthened by the accession of many Signori, in the pieve Alesani, where they had built a fort. And, wherever a Giovannalo was met with, he was slain. This phenomenon is assuredly a remarkable one; possibly the idea was brought over from Italy, in which case it is not surprising that among the poor distracted Corsicans, who regarded the equality of mankind as an original law of nature, it met with so extraordinary a dissemination, as the chronicler says. But never besides did ecclesiastical fanaticism, extravagant enthusiasm, or priestly rule, strike root in the Corsican people, and their island was spared at least this curse.

CHAPTER IX.

AFTER Boccanera's departure, the people, driven to desperation by the Signori, turned of its own accord to Genoa for aid. So the republic sent Tridano della Torre to the island. He vanquished the barons, and reigned vigorously and in peace for seven full years.

Here appears the second remarkable man of the house of Cinarca or Rocca, Arrigo della Rocca, young, vigorous, dashing, born to rule, obstinate as Giudice, quite as inexhaustible in expedients, and equally powerful in arms. His father, Guglielmo, had been engaged in battle with the Genoese, but been slain by them, the son took up the quarrel. Being unfortunate at the outset, he quitted his country and went to Spain, to tender his services to the house of Arragon, and to stimulate it to enforce its claim to those rights which the pope had awarded it. During Arrigo's absence in Arragon, Tridano was slain, the Signori rebelled, the island was split into two new parties, the Gaggionacci and the Ristagnacci, and the most sanguinary tumult had broken out.

Then, in the year 1392, Arrigo della Rocca appeared in Corsica at his own peril, and as good as totally unequipped; but no sooner did he show himself than the people flocked to his standard. Lionello Lomellino and Aluigi Tortorino were then governors, the urgency of the times demanding two at once. They called a diet in Corte, counselling and exhorting. Meanwhile, Arrigo had marched quickly upon Cinarca, had defeated the Genoese troops wherever he found them, stood before Biguglia, the governor's residence, stormed the place, assembled the people, and caused himself to be proclaimed Count of Corsica. The governors retired in consternation to Genoa, leaving the whole country in the hands of the Corsicans, with the exception of Calvi, Bonifazio, and San Columbano.

Arrigo now governed the island for four years unoppposed, with vigour and justice, though cruelly. He beheaded many, even his own relations. Perhaps these severities embittered people against him, or perhaps it was the inevitable Corsican party-spirit which estranged a part of the nation from him. The lords of Cape Corso rose first, having an understanding with Genoa ; but Arrigo put them down by force, and suppressed every insurrection with an iron hand. He bore on his banner a griffin above the arms of Arragon, a sign that he had put the island under the protection of Spain.

Genoa was at a loss ; she had fought so many years for Corsica and gained nothing. Circumstances tied the hands of the republic, so that she appeared likely to give up Corsica. Then five Nobili united to form a joint-stock company, and proposed to the senate to leave the island to them, saving the supremacy of the republic. They were Messrs. Magnera, Tortorino, Fiesco, Taruffo, Lomellino. They called themselves the Company Mahona, and each called himself governor of Corsica ; for the Genoese senate had agreed to the proposal.

They came to the island with a thousand soldiers, where Arrigo awaited them with the malecontents. They accomplished but little ;' on the contrary, they were driven into such straits by the valiant man, that they thought of coming to an amicable compact. Arrigo embraced the proposal ; but in a short time took up arms again, as he found that he had been deluded, and after a bloody battle he drove the Mahona out of the island. An expedition which Genoa next despatched was more fortunate. It forced Arrigo to fly for the second time.

He went once more to Spain to obtain support from John, king of Arragon. John readily gave him two galleys and some infantry, and with these the obstinate Corsican appeared again in Corsica after two months' absence. He vanquished and took Zoaglia, the Genoese governor, and made himself master of the whole island, except the strongholds Calvi and Bonifazio. This happened in the year 1394. The republic sent new commanders and new troops. What the sword could not accomplish, poison at last did. Arrigo della Rocca died suddenly in the year 1401. Just at this time Genoa became subject to the French king, Charles VI. Hence the fate of Corsica appeared to be taking a new turn ; but it was only for a time. The French king now appointed Lionello Lomellino as his feudal count of the island. He is the same who had belonged to the Mahona, and to whom Corsica is indebted for the foundation of her greatest city, Bastia. This city now became the seat of government, which had hitherto been the neighbouring castle of Biguglia.

CHAPTER X.

THE place of Arrigo della Rocca now began to be filled by a man of similar character. Formed by analogous circumstances of their country, the characters of these bold men have an astonishing family likeness; they form, down to Pasquale Paoli and Napoleon, a continuous series of valiant, indefatigable, tragic heroes, whose history, with a single exception, is as identical in kind, means, and fate, as the island's contest of centuries against the rule of the Genoese is one and the same. The beginning of the career of these men, who all come forth from exile, bears every time a romantic character.

Vincentello d'Istria was a nephew of Arrigo, son of one of his sisters and of Ghilfuccio, a noble Corsican. He also had gone in his youth to the court of Arragon, entered the service there, and distinguished himself by brilliant deeds of arms. Later he had conducted, with Arragonian ships, a successful Corsair war against the Genoese, and made his name terrible upon the Mediterranean. He resolved to profit by the position of affairs, and attempt a landing in his country, where Count Lomellino had made himself odious by his hard rule, and Francis of Rocca, a natural son of Arrigo, who governed the Terra del Commune as viscount in the name of Genoa, vainly contended with a powerful opposition.

Vincentello landed unexpectedly in Sagona, marched rapidly like his uncle to Cinarca, took Biguglia, assembled the people, and made himself Count of Corsica. Francis of Rocca immediately fell by assassination; but his sister Violanta, a masculine woman, took up arms, till she was overcome by Vincentello. Bastia also submitted. Genoa now speedily sent troops; after a two years' contest Vincentello was forced to abandon Corsica, because some of the selfish Signori made common cause with Genoa.

After a short time Vincentello returned again with Arragonian forces, and again rescued the whole island from the Genoese,

except the fortresses Calvi and Bonifazio. When he had succeeded thus far, the young king, Alfonso of Arragon, more
adventurous than his predecessors, set out in person with a well
equipped fleet to enforce by arms the presumptive claims of Arragon upon the island. He came from Sardinia in the year 1420,
sat down before Calvi, and compelled that Genoese town to surrender to him. Then he sailed before Bonifazio, and whilst the
Corsicans of his party stormed the impregnable fortress from the
land side, the fleet assailed it from the sea. The siege of Bonifazio forms a brilliant episode in these protracted contests, and is
distinguished as well for the valour of the besiegers as for the
heroism of the besieged. These, devoted to Genoa body and
soul, themselves for the most part of Genoese descent, remained unshaken as their rocks, and neither famine nor pestilence,
nor the fire and sword of the Spaniards, had power to bend their
resolution. All the storms were beaten off. Women, children,
monks, and priests stood in arms upon the walls, and fought
beside the citizens. For months long they fought, hoping
for relief, and humbled the Spanish pride, till at length Alfonso
got tired, and went away covered with shame, leaving to
Vincentello the continuation of the siege. But the Genoese
relief came, and delivered the exhausted town on the eve of
its fall.

Vincentello went back again; and as Calvi also had the same
time fallen again under the Genoese rule, the republic could still
rely on both fortresses. King Alfonso made no further attempt to
come into possession of Corsica. Vincentello, reduced to his own
resources, gradually lost ground, because the intrigues of Genoa
accomplished more than arms, and because the quarrels of the
Signori prevented any common rising.

The Genoese party was especially strong on Cape Corso, where
the lords Da Mare possessed the most power. With their help,
and that of the Caporali, who had gradually degenerated from
tribunes of the people into petty tyrants, Genoa repelled Vincentello, and confined him to his fief of Cinarca. The valiant
man fell partly by his own fault. He was addicted to voluptuous habits; and the rape of a maiden from Biguglia caused her
relations to take up arms, whereupon the place fell into the
hands of Simon da Mare. The unfortunate Vincentello now resolved to solicit again the aid of Arragon; but Zacharias Spinola
took the galley which was conveying him to Sicily, and brought
Genoa's terrible foe a prisoner before the senate. Vincentello

d'Istria was beheaded on the grand staircase of the palace of Genoa, in the year 1434. He was a glorious man, as the Cor-• sican chronicler says.

CHAPTER XI.

AFTER Vincentello's death, the Signori contended among themselves for the supreme power. Simon da Mare, Giudice d'Istria, Renuccio de Leca, Paolo della Rocca—each called himself in turn Count of Corsica. · On the part of Genoa, where the Fregosi and Adorni had split the republic into two factions, both these families sought to make Corsica a possession of their house. This occasioned new wars and new misery. The people had not a single year of peace. All were permanently in arms, either on the aggressive or on the defensive. The whole island was a scene of naught but fire, insurrection, and war, and was covered over and over with blood.

In the year 1443, a party among the Corsicans offered the dominion of their island to the Pope Eugene IV., perhaps that the church might constrain the factions, and establish tranquillity. The pope then sent his plenipotentiaries with troops, but they only made confusion worse confounded. Then the people assembled at a diet at Morosaglia, and elected a valiant and magnanimous man, Mariano da Gaggio, to be their lieutenant-general. Mariano first overcame the savage Caporali, drove them out of their rock-towers, destroyed many of these, and declared their dignity abolished. On their side, the Caporali called in Adorno, the Genoese. The people now put itself anew under the protection of the pope; but as the Fregosi had meanwhile attained to dominion in Genoa, and were favoured by Nicholas I., a Genoese, he transferred the government of the island, in the year 1449, to Lodovico Campo Fregoso. In vain did the nation under Mariano resist this appointment. To multiply still further the already boundless confusion, there appeared also an Arragonian viceroy, James Imbisora, demanding submission in the name of Arragon.

The people assembled hereupon in despair, at a diet on the Lago Benedetto, and here embraced the fatal resolution of putting themselves under the Bank of St. George, of Genoa. This society had been formed in the year 1346 as a company of capitalists,

who lent money to the republic, and in return received as
guarantee certain public revenues. Upon this proposal of the
Corsicans, the republic of Genoa made over Corsica to this bank,
and the Fregosi resigned their title for a compensation.

So the company of St. George entered into possession of
Corsica in the year 1453, under the supremacy of the senate,
regarding it as a demesne from which the greatest possible income was to be secured.

But years passed before the Bank was fortunate enough to
become master of the island. The Signori beyond the mountains,
united with Arragon, opposed a desperate resistance. The
governors of the Bank proceeded with indiscreet severity; many
were beheaded; other nobles went into exile, and rallied round
Tomasin Fregoso, a fickle man, who, his uncle Lodovico having
been doge, began to remember his family claims to Corsica. He
came accompanied by the refugees, overthrew the troops of the
Bank, and put himself in possession of a great part of the island,
being declared by the people Count of Corsica.

In the year 1464, Genoa fell into the hands of Francis Sforza
of Milan, and a power which had never had any thing to do with
Corsica, now regarded the island as its own. The Corsicans,
who liked any other master but Genoa, gladly took the oath at
the diet in Biguglia to the Milanese captain, Antonio Cotta.
But at this very diet a petty quarrel sufficed to put all Corsica
again in a blaze. A few peasants from Nebbio having got into
a sanguinary wrangle with the men of the Signori from beyond
the mountains, the Milanese commander had forthwith chastised
the guilty. The Signori, touched in their seignorial rights, sprang
on their horses and rode home full of resentment, without saying
a word. War was expected. To avert it, the people of the
Terra del Commune assembled in the Casinca, and appointed
Sambucuccio d'Alando, a descendant of the first Corsican legislator, to be vicar of the nation, and empowered him to employ
any means for the restoration of order. Sambucuccio's dictatorship inspired terror; he was obeyed, and tranquillity prevailed;
and a second assembly deputed him and others as ambassadors
to Milan, to represent to the doge the state of things, and pray
for the recall of Cotta.

Cotta gave place to the far worse Amelia, who occasioned a
war of many years. In all these tempests we see the democratic
Terra del Commune, like an island within the island, surrounded
by the Signori, but holding firmly together, and representing the

true Corsican people. And for almost two hundred years we have seen no decisive step taken without a national diet (*veduta*), and have often observed how the nation chose for itself counts and vicars.

Now when the war between the Corsicans and Milanese was at its height, Thomas Campo Fregosi appeared to try his fate once more. The Milanese sent him a prisoner to their city. But strangely enough, he returned thence in the year 1480, provided with diplomas promising him Corsica as a rightful inheritance. His rule, as well as that of his son James, was so cruel that it could not be of long duration, although they had connected themselves with Giampolo da Leca, the most distinguished man of the island.

In the meantime the people appointed Renuccio da Leca to be its leader, who immediately directed his attention to the Signor of Piombino, Appian IV., and offered him Corsica, under the condition that he would send adequate troops to deliver the island from all its tyrants. How miserable was the condition of the nation, when it had to turn to every side and call upon, now this, now that powerful despot, superinducing foreign to native tyrants ! The Lord of Piombino was glad to try his fortune in Corsica, having already part of Elba in his possession. He sent his brother, Gherardo di Montagnara, with a small army. Gherardo was young, handsome, of brilliant manners and a theatrical love of pomp. He came arrayed in costly robes, with a splendid suite, magnificent horses, dogs, musicians, and buffoons. He proceeded as though he meant to conquer the island with music. The Corsicans, who had barely the very bread of life, gazed at him as at a being from another world, led him to their popular assembly at the Lago Benedetto, and with great rejoicings made him Count of Corsica, in the year 1483. The Fregosi now lost heart ; abandoning their cause, they soon after sold their claims to the Genoese Bank for two thousand scudi of gold. The Bank now prepared energetically for war against Gherardo and Renuccio. The latter was defeated. This so terrified the Lord of Piombino, that he hastily left the island with less pomp than he came. Piombino renounced any further attempt.

CHAPTER XII.

AGAIN there arose two bold men, one after the other, to combat
Genoa; Giampolo da Leca had connected himself, as we have seen,
with the Fregosi. Though these lords had resigned their title
to the Bank, yet they could not endure the loss of their seigno-
rity. Accordingly, Janus in Genoa urged his relative to revolt
against the governor. Matthew Fiesco Giampolo began the war.
But, defeated and driven back by the troops of the Bank, and
having in vain applied to Florence for aid, he saw himself compelled to lay down his arms, and to fly, with his wife, child, and
friends, to Sicily, in the year 1487.

Scarcely had a year elapsed than he appeared again, invited by
his adherents. A second time unsuccessful, he escaped a second
time to Sardinia. The Genoese cruelly chastised the insurgents
by death, banishment, and confiscation of property. The fermentation multiplied. For ten years hatred against Genoa was on the
rise. So long Giampolo remained in his exile meditating revenge,
and with gaze fixed upon his country, oppressed by violence. Then
he returned. He had neither money nor arms; four Corsicans
and six Spaniards were his sole army, and with this he landed. He
was beloved by the people for his nobility, valour, and handsome
figure. The Corsicans thronged to him at once, those of Cinarca,
Vico, Niolo, and Morosaglia. He had soon 7000 Corsican infantry and 200 cavalry, a force that inspired the Bank of Genoa
with terror. They accordingly sent Ambrosio Negri, an experienced field-captain, to the island. Negri managed, by sowing
dissension and by tempting promises, to draw to himself some of
the party of Giampolo, and especially to entice Renuccio della
Rocca, an intrepid noble. Giampolo's forces melted away, and
the remainder was defeated at Foce al Sorbo. And, his son
Orlando having been taken prisoner, he concluded a treaty with
Negri, which allowed him to go freely into exile. He went again
with fifty Corsicans to Sardinia, in the year 1501, to end his life
there in bitter grief.

Renuccio della Rocca was the chief cause of Giampolo's fall.
This man, the head of the proud family Cinarca, perceived that
the Genoese Bank was pursuing with consistency the policy of
breaking for ever even the very last remains of the power of the

Signori, who had their chief seat beyond the mountains, and that the turn would come round to himself. Perceiving this, he suddenly stood up in arms in the year 1502. The contest was short and favourable to Genoa, whose governor was then one of the Dorias, who were distinguished for vigour and indiscreet cruelty, and were the sole cause of the final downfall of the Corsican nobility, aimed at by Genoa. Nicholas Doria forced Renuccio to a compact, and imposed on him the necessity of living henceforth with his wife and children in Genoa.

Giampolo still remained in Sardinia. Genoa feared him more than all, and made frequent attempts to come to an amicable agreement with him. His son Orlando had just fled from the prison at Genoa and gone to Rome, from whence he urged his father to shake off his silent inactivity. But the latter persisted in his silence, and listened neither to the insinuations of his son nor to those of Genoa. Then Renuccio suddenly disappeared out of Genoa in the year 1504 ; leaving his wife and children to the enemy, he went secretly to Sardinia to find Giampolo, whom he had in former days thrown into misery. But Giampolo refused to see him. He refused also the entreaties of the Corsicans, who all expected him. His own relations had meanwhile murdered his son. The viceroy had arrested the murderers, and was going to execute them as a sign of his friendship for Giampolo. But the noble man forgave them, and prayed for their release.

Renuccio in the meantime gathered eighteen resolute men round him, and landed in Corsica, undeterred by the fate of his children, who had been thrown immediately after his flight into a dark dungeon. Nicholas Doria, however, engaged Renuccio without delay, and overpowered him at the first onset. To shake his resolution he caused Renuccio's eldest son to be beheaded, and menaced the second with a similar fate, and only the submissive entreaties of the boy prevented the cruel deed. The unhappy father, beaten on every side, fled to Sardinia, and yet further to Arragon. But Doria persecuted with rage all who had joined him, and laid waste extensive districts of the island, burning down the villages and scattering the inhabitants.

Renuccio della Rocca returned in the year 1507. He would rather have died than see the rule of Genoa even from a distance. The inflexible man was quite the contrary of the reserved, resentful Giampolo. He landed upon his country with only twenty men. This time he was met by another Doria,

Andrew, afterwards the celebrated doge, who had served under his cousin Nicolò. The Corsican historian, Filippini, does not conceal the cruelties which Andrew perpetrated in this short contest. He succeeded in soon putting down Renuccio, and forcing him to take ship with a free escort to Genoa. When the Corsican landed there the people would have torn him in pieces; but the French governor hastily concealed him in his castle.

Three years had elapsed; Renuccio suddenly showed himself again in Corsica. Having fled from Genoa, he had vainly prayed for aid from all the princes of Europe, and, defying fate once more, had marched forth with eight friends and landed in Corsica. Former vassals in Freto received him with tears, moved by his accumulated disasters, and the unexampled boldness of the man's soul. He spoke to them, and conjured them to draw the sword once more. They followed him in silence. For a few days he remained concealed in Freto. Then by chance came Nicolò Pinello, captain of arquebusiers, on horseback from Ajaccio. The sight of him so enraged Renuccio that he fell upon him by night and slew him, took his horse, and now shewed himself openly. Upon the news of his presence the soldiers marched out from Ajaccio to take him. Renuccio fled to the mountains, chased like a bandit or a wild beast. But as the peasants were tormented by the persecutors on Renuccio's account, they preferred to put an end to their trouble by killing him. He was found in the month of May 1511, miserably slain on the mountains. He was one of the most manly of the noble house of Cinarca. "They say," says the Corsican chronicler, "that Renuccio remained his noble self to the last, and that he showed no less heroism in his death than in his life; which assuredly is greatly to his credit, for a noble-hearted man must never lose the nobility of his soul, even if destiny condemns him to an ignominious death."

In the mean time Giampolo had gone to Rome, to seek aid from the pope Leo X., and, being unsuccessful in his mission, died there in the year 1515.

CHAPTER XIII.

With Giampolo and Renuccio ended the resistance of the Corsican Signori, the nobility of the island decayed, and their castles crumbled, and now one rarely sees on the rocks of Corsica those black walls towering, which were formerly the castles of the Cinarcas, the Istrias, the Leccas, the Ornani. But Genoa, while prostrating this redoubtable enemy, had raised up a far more terrible one; and this was the Corsican people itself.

But when the rule of the Genoese Bank rested with its iron hand upon the island, many powerful men of action emigrated to gain glory and honour in foreign lands. They accepted military service in foreign countries, where they became re-nowned as field-captains and condottieri. Some were in the service of the Medici, others in that of the Strozzi, or they served under the Venetians, in Rome under the Gonzagas, or under the French. Filippini mentions a host of them, among whom are Guglielmo of Casabianca, Baptista of Leca, Barte-lemy of Vivario, surnamed Telamon, Gasparino Ceccaldi, Sam-piero of Bastelica. One Corsican, Arsano of Bastia, was especially fortunate, having raised himself from the position of a renegade to be King of Algiers, under the name of Lazzaro. This is the more surprising, as Corsica had just at this period so much to suffer from the Barbaresques, that the Bank sur-rounded the whole island with fire-beacons and towers, and converted Porto Vecchio on the southern coast into a fort.

After the wars with Giampolo and Renuccio, Corsica enjoyed at first a paternal government from the Bank, and rejoiced in the restoration of good order. This the Corsican chronicler asserts. The administration of the island, which remained essentially the same when the republic took the island again from the Bank, was as follows :—

The Bank annually sent a Governatore to Corsica, who re-sided in Bastia. He had as assessor, a Vicario, a doctor of laws. To the governor belonged the entire administration, the supreme judicial and military power. He had, besides, his lieutenants (*luogotenenti*) in Calvi, Algajola, San Fiorenzo,

Ajaccio, Bonifazio, Sartene, Vico, Cervione, and Corte. Appeal
could be laid from their judgment to the governor. All these
officers changed every year, or every two years. For the protection of the people against their transgressions, a syndicate had
been established, before which complaint might be entered
against any magistrate. If the complaint was found to be a
valid one, the acts of the culpable magistrate might be reversed,
and he himself deposed. The governor himself was answerable
to the Sindici. They were six in number, three from the
people, and three from the aristocracy, and were Corsicans as
well as Genoese. In special cases commissaries also appeared
to conduct investigations.

Moreover, the people had the right to nominate the Twelve
Men, which took place on every change of the supreme magistracy; there were twelve for the country on this side the
mountains, six for that beyond. The Twelve Men represented
the rights of the people in the government, so that nothing
on the island could be regulated, changed, or abridged without
their authority. One of them went as Oratore to Genoa, with
the view of representing in the senate the rights of the people.

The democratic basis of the constitution of the communes and
the pievi, with their fathers of parishes and podestàs, was not
changed, nor was the popular assembly (*veduta* or *consulta*)
abolished. The Governatore used to assemble it in Biguglia, as
often as any thing of general importance was to be ordained with
the sanction of the people.

It is evident that these arrangements were of a democratic
nature—allowed the people freedom of action and a share in the
government; gave it the support of protecting laws, and curbed
the caprice of officials. And so the Corsican nation might well
rejoice in them; indeed it might appear highly privileged in
comparison with other nations of Europe, if those laws were
really administered, and not merely a specious show. But that
they *were* a mere show, and that Genoa soon fell into an exe-
crable despotic system, and prepared to root out all Corsican
nationality, committing the same great error as Venice, of re-
pelling her foreign provinces by tyranny instead of attaching
them to herself by benefactions—we shall see in the sequel.
For now Corsica opposed to Genoa her bravest man, and one of
the most prominent characters of that age.

CHAPTER XIV.

SAMPIERO was born at Bastelica, a place lying in the wildest mountain scenery above Ajaccio; he was not descended from any old family, but was the son of obscure parents. Guglielmo, grandson of Vinciguerra, is named as his father. Others call his family the Porri.

Like other young Corsicans, Sampiero went early in life to the continent to serve in foreign armies. We find him in the service of Cardinal Hippolytus of Medici, in the Black faction at Florence; and soon his deeds in arms, and the nobility and force of his character, caused the world to speak of him. He was a sword and shield to the Medici in the contest against the Pazzi. He left their service for the standard of Francis of France, seeking a wider field for his active spirit as condottiere or captain of a free company. The king made him colonel of the Corsican regiment which he had formed. Bayard became his friend, and Charles Bourbon honoured his impetuous valour and military penetration. "On the day of battle," said Bourbon, "the Corsican colonel is worth ten thousand men." Sampiero distinguished himself in many battles, and before many a fortress; and his renown was equally great with friend and foe.

Though quite devoted to the war between France and Spain, he had yet eyes and ears for his native land, whence voices often called to him, which moved his heart. In the year 1547, he crossed over to Corsica, to take a wife from his native land; and he chose a lady of one of the oldest families beyond the mountains, the house of Ornano. Though he was himself without ancestors, yet his renown and manly vigour were admitted by Francesco Ornano as no contemptible patent of nobility; and the proud Corsican gave him his only child, the fair Vannina, and with her the inheritance of the Ornani.

Scarcely had the governor of the Genoese Bank seen Sampiero, who he foreboded would be his deadliest foe in his domain at Bastia, than he caused him to be overpowered and thrown into the dungeon, without a shadow of legality. Francis Ornano, fearing for his son-in-law's life, hastened to the French ambassador at Genoa. The latter at once reclaimed the French field-

D

captain. Sampiero was released. But the insult offered him, only added another personal stimulus to induce him to indulge his long-cherished hate of Genoa, and the ardent desire to deliver his country. The position of political affairs—the war between France and Charles V.—soon put him in possession of the opportunity to realize his wish.

Henry II., husband of Catherine de' Medici, who was deeply involved in the affairs of Italy, engaged in a violent war with the emperor, and, allied with the Turks, who were preparing to send a fleet into the western Mediterranean, took up the design of an expedition to Corsica. A double end appeared attainable by this course; on the one hand, Genoa was menaced in Corsica, and war levied against the emperor himself there, the republic having been closely allied with Charles V., since Andrea Doria had delivered her from the yoke of France; on the other hand, the island offered an excellent position in the Mediterranean, and a base of operations for the united French and Turkish fleet. So Marshal Thermes, who was in Italy when his troops occupied Siena, received the command to prepare for the conquest of Corsica.

He held a council of war in Castiglione. Sampiero was rejoiced at the turn of affairs; he desired nothing but to be the deliverer of his country; he urgently represented to Thermes the inevitable success of the enterprise, which was quickly put into execution. And its success was undoubted. The French had only to land, to call the Corsicans instantly to arms. Their hatred against the Genoese merchants had risen to its highest pitch since the fall of Renuccio. It had its roots not only in the nation's indestructible love of freedom, but also in material things. For as soon as the Bank seemed secured in its power, it made a despotic abuse of its authority. The Corsicans were deprived of all their rights,—the syndicate, the Twelve Men, the ancient parochial authorities. Law was venal, and murder free; or at least the murderer was protected in Genoa, and provided with letters of safe conduct. All the terrors of private revenge for bloodshed, therefore, took firm and ineradicable root. Authors agree that the demoralisation of the administration of justice was the deepest wound which the Bank of Genoa inflicted on Corsica.

Sampiero had sent a Corsican, Altobello de' Gentili, to the island, to catch the sentiments of the people; the letters he sent, and the eager expectation of him thereby excited, kindled a wild

delight. ₊ They awaited with trembling expectation the arrival ,
of the expedition. Thermes and Admiral Paulin, whose squadron had joined the Turkish fleet under Dragut, near Elba, now
sailed against Corsica in August, 1553. There was with them
the brave Piero Strozzi and his company, though not for long;
with them were the hopes of the Corsicans, Sampiero, John
Ornano, Rafael Gentili, Altobello, and other emigrants, all fired
with vengeance, and eager to bathe their swords in Genoese
blood.

They landed at Renella, near Bastia. Sampiero had scarcely
shown himself on the walls of the city, which they had surmounted by scaling-ladders, than the people tore open the gates.
Bastia surrendered. They now proceeded without delay to the
conquest of the other strong places, and of the interior. Paulin
posted himself before Calvi, Dragut the Turk before Bonifazio,
Thermes marched upon San Fiorenzo, and Sampiero upon Corte,
the important stronghold of the interior. Here also he had
scarcely shown himself before the people opened their gates to
him. The Genoese fled on every side, and all the country was
triumphantly conquered. Only Ajaccio, Bonifazio, and Calvi
defied them, trusting to their strong position. Neither Paulin
by sea, nor Sampiero by land, could shake the resolution of Calvi.
Its siege was raised, and Sampiero hastened to appear before
Ajaccio. The Genoese, under Lamba Doria, were equipping
themselves there for a desperate defence, but the people opened
the gates to the deliverer. The houses of the Genoese were
plundered ; yet even here the law of generosity and hospitality
even to enemies, implanted in the Corsican's nature, showed
itself so sacred, that many Genoese found protection with the
hostile peasants, into whose villages they went to entreat the
right of guests. Francis Ornano received Lamba Doria himself
into his house.

CHAPTER XV.

In the meantime the Turk was storming Bonifazio, laying
waste all the country round, and exasperated by the heroism of
the Bonifazines, who showed themselves worthy descendants of
their ancestors at the time of Alfonso of Arragon. Day and
night, despite hunger and fatigue, they stood on the walls, throwing back every assault—men and women being equally heroic.
Sampiero also appeared before Bonifazio. The town, though
incessantly assaulted, never wavered, but fought manfully, hoping for relief; for a messenger, Cattacciolo of Bonifazio, was
expected back from Genoa. The messenger came to announce
speedy relief, but fell into the hands of the French. They made
him a traitor, forcing him to carry forged letters into the town,
which destroyed all the commandant's hopes of relief. Wherefore the latter concluded a treaty, and delivered up the untaken
town, under the condition that it should not be plundered, and
that the garrison should be allowed to embark honourably for
Genoa. But the brave defenders had hardly moved from the
walls when the barbarous Turk, setting all humanity and his
oath at defiance, fell upon them and began to cut them to pieces.
Sampiero with difficulty saved as many of the Bonifazines as
could be saved. Not content with this vengeance, Dragut demanded the plunder of the town, and, when this was not granted
him, a large sum of money for desisting from it, which Thermes
could not pay, but promised to pay. Dragut embarked in a
rage, and set sail for Asia; Genoese gold had gained him.

After the fall of Bonifazio there remained to the Genoese not
a single spot of land but the "ever true" Calvi. There was
therefore no time to be lost if they wished to gain the island
back. The emperor had promised aid, and placed a few thousand Germans and Spaniards at the disposal of Genoa, and
Cosmo de' Medici gave an auxiliary corps. Thus a considerable
army was collected, and, to put the success of the enterprise quite
beyond question, the chief command was conferred upon their
most celebrated general, Andrea Doria, and the subordinate command upon Agostino Spinola.

Andrea Doria was then eighty-six years old. So urgent ap-

peared th**e** position of affairs, that the old general did not decline
the call made upon him.   He received the banner of the expedition in the cathedral of Genoa, from senators, protectors of the
Bank, clergy, and people.

On the 20th November 1553, Doria landed in the gulf of San
Fiorenzo, and in a short time the tables turned in favour of
Genoa. S. Fiorenzo, which Marshal Thermes had strongly
fortified, fell, Bastia surrendered, and the French yielded on all
sides.   Sampiero had fallen out with Thermes, and been removed
for a short time to the French court; but when he had conquered
the slanders of his enemies, he stood forth again more brilliant
than ever, and as the soul of the war, with whom the incapable
Thermes was ill-matched.   He was inexhaustible in defence,
in attack, in guerilla.   He decisively defeated Spinola on the
field of Golo; but a wound received in the battle rendered him for
a time inactive, during which time Spinola inflicted a bloody defeat
upon the Corsicans at Morosaglia.   Sampiero now left his wound
no time to heal, but appeared again in the field, and overbore
both Spaniards and Germans in the battle at Col di Tenda,
in the year 1554. The war continued with equal ferocity for
five years more.   Corsica seemed for ever secured for the protection of France, and appeared to regard herself as an inde-
pendently organized part of that country. Francis II. had already
appointed Jourdan Orsini his viceroy there, and the latter had, in
the national assembly, declared in his king's name the incorporating of the island in France, to the end that it might be impossible
to the end of time to sever the island from the crown of France ;
for only with his crown of France was the king to be allowed
to give up the island.   Thus the fate of Corsica seemed even
then bound up with the French monarchy, and the island withdrawn from the community of the Italian states, to which it
naturally belongs.   But scarcely had the king given this solemn
assurance, when the peace of Chateau Cambresis, in the year
1559, annihilated at one blow all the hopes of the Corsicans.

France concluded peace with Philip of Spain and his allies,
and engaged to give up Corsica to the Genoose. So, then, the
French delivered all places still occupied by them into the hands
of Genoa, and embarked their troops.   A desperate war of six
years had been conducted for nothing, and such streams of blood
had flowed for a political *game*/ The Corsican now saw himself
thrown back by a piece of paper, called a document of peace,
into his former misery, and exposed without defence to the

vengeance of Genoa. This breach of faith and this sudden blow drew from the country a universal cry of despair; but it was not heeded.

CHAPTER XVI.

HENCEFORWARD Sampiero showed himself in all his greatness; for only he is truly great, who, uncast down by fortune, is able to rise from adversity itself doubly strong. He departed an outlaw. Peace had deprived him of his sword ; the totally devastated island could by itself venture on no new contests, for it needed a respite, and the new contest a new support in a foreign power. So the indefatigable man wandered for four years over the world, applying for aid to the most distant European powers. He travelled to Catherine in France, hoping to find her still mindful of former services he had rendered to the house of Medici ; he went to Navarre, to the Duke of Florence, to the Fregosi, from one Italian court to another ; he sailed to Barbarossa at Algiers; he hastened to the Sultan Soliman at Constantinople. His earnest mien, that commanded respect, the power of his words, his penetrating understanding, his glowing patriotism, imbued all, whether Christian or Barbarian, with admiration ; yet they comforted him with vain hopes and empty promises.

While Sampiero was journeying over the world, instigating princes to an enterprise for the deliverance of Corsica, Genoa had not lost him out of her eyes ; she dreaded the possible success of his pains. Some attempt must be made to paralyse for ever the action of the fearful man. Poison and assassination, they say, had miscarried. They resolved, accordingly, to tame his soul, by bringing the natural feelings of the husband and the father into war with his passionate love of country. They wished to kill out his heart.

Sampiero's wife, Vannina, lived in her house at Marseille under French protection. Her youngest son, Antonio Francesco, she had with her; the elder, Alfonso, was at Catherine's court. The Genoese surrounded her with their spies and agents. Their object was to entice Sampiero's wife and child to Genoa. To this end they made use of Michael Angelo Ombroni, a priest who

had been-instructor of Sampiero's young sons, and enjoyed the
father's confidence in the highest degree, and a skilful agent,
Agosto Bazzicalupa. Vannina was of an impressible nature,
susceptible to insinuations, and proud of the ancient name of
Ornano. They represented to her the fate which awaited the
children of her outlawed husband. Suffering under their father's
outlawry, deprived of the fief of their renowned ancestors, poor,
not even their life secured—what would become of them? They
pictured to Vannina's impressible fancy these her beloved
children in the misery of a foreign land, eating the bread of
favour, or, still worse, if they followed in their father's steps,
chased as bandits on the mountains, taken at last, and chained
to the galleys.

Vannina was deeply moved, and the thought of going to Genoa
became less and less dreadful and objectionable. "There,"
Ombroni and Bazzicalupa told her, "the fief Ornano will be
restored to your children, and your gentle soul will succeed in
conciliating even Sampiero and the republic." The poor woman's
heart by degrees yielded. The natural sentiments turned the
scale, and they had no conception of the grand, rugged, fearful
character of the man who lived only in loving his country, and
hating her oppressors, and who yielded up every other possession
but his own great self, to feed the all-consuming flame of this
passion. Thus the blindness of her heart extorted from her the
resolution to go to Genoa. "One day," she said to herself, "we
may yet be happy, peaceful, and reconciled."

Meanwhile Sampiero was in Algiers, where the bold renegade,
Barbarossa, king of the country, had met him with brilliant
honours, when a ship came to land from Marseille, and brought
the news that his wife Vannina, surrounded by Genoese, was
preparing to escape with her child to Genoa. The moment
Sampiero began to comprehend the possibility of this flight, he
had fain thrown himself on shipboard, and hasted to Marseille ;
but then he came to himself, and requested his noble friend,
Antonio of S. Fiorenzo, to set out immediately, and to prevent
the step if it were possible. He himself, burying the sudden
grief in his inmost heart, remained, and treated with Barbarossa
about an expedition against Genoa, and then took ship for
Constantinople, to try his fortune there also with the Sultan,
and then at last to return to Marseille, to see after his wife.

Antonio of S. Fiorenzo hastened off without delay. Bursting into Vannina's house he found it unfurnished and empty.

, She herself, with her child, had left it secretly the day before on a ·Genoese ship, with Michael Angelo Ombrone and Bazzicalupa. Antonio hastily got together some of his Corsican friends armed, threw himself into a brigantine, and sailed under full canvass in the direction which the fugitives must have taken. Opposite Antibes he saw the Genoese vessel ahead. He gave a signal to heave to. Vannina in great terror begged them to put her ashore, and she knew not what to do ; but Antonio came up with her on the coast, and took the fugitive into his own keeping in the name of Sampiero and of the king of France.

The good man brought her, quite buried in grief, into the house of the Bishop of Antibes, to strengthen her by spiritual consolation, and to secure her refuge in a religious house. Terrible thoughts which he did not express, made this prudent. But the Bishop of Antibes, dreading the possibility of being called to account, delivered Vannina into the hands of ·the parliament of Aix. The parliament expressed itself willing to take her under its protection, and not to suffer any one to do her harm. But Vannina desired nothing, and declined the protection. She was, she said, her husband's wife, and whatever Sampiero might decree upon her she would accept with resignation herself. The recognition of her ·fault weighed heavy on her heart, and the penitence with which she was punished imposed upon her a mute and lofty resignation.

Sampiero having returned from Turkey, where Soliman, admiring the celebrated Corsican, had retained him for a time at court, now came to Marseille, and could give himself once more to the care that most nearly touched his heart. Antonio met him in Marseille, confirmed what had happened, and sought to suppress his friend's bursting resentment. One of Sampiero's relations, Pier Giovanni of Calvi, let fall the incautious remark, that he had long foreboded Vannina's flight. "And thou hast concealed what thou forebodedst !" cried Sampiero, and instantly he stabbed him with his dagger. He sprang on horseback and dashed away to Aix, where his wife was tremblingly awaiting him. Antonio was after him in an agony of fear and hope, whether he would yet be able to avert any dreadful deed.

Sampiero waited till morning under the castle-windows. Then he went to his wife and took her to Marseille. No one could read the thoughts of his dark soul. When he entered his house with her, which was unfurnished and desolate, then the insult and treachery offered him, fell convulsively with its full force , upon his heart; and as the thought once more pierced his soul, that it was his own wife who had basely given herself and his child into the hands of the hated foe of his country, the demon of distraction seized him, and with his own hand he gave his wife the death-blow.

Sampiero, says the Corsican historian, loved his wife passionately, but as a Corsican; that is to say, to the very farthest extreme of Vendetta.

He caused the deceased to be magnificently interred in the church of St. Francis; then he went to show himself at the court of Paris.   This was the year 1562.

CHAPTER XVII.

Sampiero was received with coldness at the French court; the courtiers indulged in whispers, avoided him, and scorned him under the garb of superior virtue.   Sampiero was not the man to be frightened by courtiers, nor was the court of Catherine of Medici the tribunal before which an atrocious deed, committed by one of the most remarkable men of his age, might be judged. Catherine and Henry II. soon forgot the murder of Sampiero's wife, but they would do no more for Corsica than see its liberation with pleasure.

When Sampiero had tried as diplomatist all possible means, and gained no prospect of any foreign support, he resolved to act as a man, and to trust solely to his own and his nation's strength.   So he wrote to his friends in Corsica, that he would come to deliver his country or die.   "It is ours," he said, "to try one last exertion to gain the happiness and the glory of complete freedom.   We have knocked at the cabinets of Paris, of Navarre, and of Constantinople.   If we are to grasp our arms only on the day when we shall be supported by the aid of France or Tuscany, oppression will, for a long time, yet be the lot of the country.   And, after all, what would be the value of a national existence owed to foreigners?   To free themselves from the Persian yoke, and save their independence, were the Greeks seen to go to their neighbours for aid?   The Italian republics afford us fresh examples of what the strong will of a nation can achieve, when it is combined with the love of country.   Doria delivered his country from the pressure of a haughty aristocracy, and shall we wait to rise till the soldiers of the King of Navarre come to fight in our ranks?"

On the 12th June, 1564, Sampiero landed in the Gulf of Valinco, with two ships and a band of twenty Corsicans and twenty-five French. He sunk the galley on which he had come. When asked why he did so, and where he would seek safety if the Genoese surprised him; he answered, " In my sword." He threw himself quickly with his little band upon the castle of Istria, took it, and dashed on to Corte. The Genoese came out to meet him before Corte with far superior force, while Sampiero's host counted as yet only a hundred men. But such was the terror inspired by his mere name, that they scarcely saw him coming but they fled without drawing a sword. Corte opened its gates to Sampiero, and so he had gained a first point of support. The Terra del Commune delayed not to make common cause with him.

Sampiero marched on to Vescovato, the richest land of the island, situated on the slopes of the mountains which sink to the fine coast-plain of Mariana. On his approach, the people of Vescovato assembled, fearful for their crops, dreading the storm of war, and acted upon by the historian of Corsica, Archdeacon Filippini. Filippini urgently advised them to keep quiet, and not to see Sampiero, whatever he might do. So, when Sampiero marched into Vescovato, he found the place surprisingly quiet and the people in their houses, until at last they yielded after all to their curiosity and sympathy, and came out. Sampiero addressed them, and accused them, as they deserved, of want of patriotism. His words made a deep impression. They offered him hospitality; but he punished the people of Vescovato by spurning it, and passed the night in the open air.

The place was, nevertheless, the scene of a bloody battle. Nicholas Negri led the Genoese to the attack. It was a murderous contest, all the more so because, from the small numbers of the combatants, it necessarily had the character of single contests. And Corsicans fought against Corsicans, as a corps of them had remained in the service of Genoa. When these were advancing, Sampiero drove them back again by the words, " That it was a shame to fight against their country." Victory was inclining to the side of the Genoese, as Bruschino, one of the bravest Corsican captains, had fallen; but Sampiero restored the ranks again, and, by gathering up their last strength, they succeeded in turning the Genoese, who spread themselves in disorderly flight in the direction of Bastia.

The victory of Vescovato immediately enlarged Sampiero's forces, and a second at Caccia, in which Nicholas Negri fell, called the whole inland country to arms. Sampiero now hoped for eager assistance from Tuscany, and even from the Turks; for in vanquishing Spaniards and Genoese step by step with such small resources, he showed what the Corsican love of freedom could do if it were supported still further.

After Negri's death, the Genoese speedily sent their best general to the island, Stephen Doria, worthy of this name from his valour, his wisdom, and his harshness. An army of 4000 German and Italian mercenaries accompanied him. Accordingly the flames of war raged afresh. The Corsicans suffered several defeats, but the Genoese more; and they were again driven back to Bastia. Doria had made an incursion upon Bastelica, and laid in ashes this the birthplace of Sampiero, and laid his house even with the ground. What was house and property to Sampiero, who had sacrificed his wife for his country? But the policy of Genoa is ever notable, of bringing the patriotism of the Corsicans into a tragic struggle with their personal feelings. What they had tried in vain on Sampiero, succeeded in the case of Achilles of Campocasso, a man of extraordinary heroism, of a highly respected house of ancient Caporali. They imprisoned his mother. The son wavered not a moment, but threw away his sword, and hastened to the Genoese camp to rescue his mother from the torture. But when the enemy exacted that he should be Sampiero's murderer, he slipped off and kept quiet at home. Sampiero was deprived more and more of powerful friends, since Bruschino had fallen, Campocasso gone over to the enemy, and also Napoleon of Santa Lucia been slain—a valiant man, and the first Corsican who rendered the name Napoleon illustrious by his deeds in arms.

If the entire hatred of Corsican and Genoese can be comprised in two names, they are those of Sampiero and Doria. Both these mortally hostile names are at the same time the most perfect representatives of their nationality. Stephen Doria surpassed all his predecessors in cruelty. He had sworn to annihilate the Corsicans; and these were his avowed principles—"When the Athenians, after a seven months' resistance, got possession of the capital of Melos, the ally of Sparta, they killed all the inhabitants above fourteen years old, and then sent a colony to people the town anew, and hold it in obedient subjection. Why do we not imitate this example? Is it because the Corsicans are less culpable than the rebels of that island? By these dreadful chastisements the Athenians wished to attain to the coquuest of Peloponnesus, of all Greece, Africa, Italy, and Sicily. By putting all their enemies to the sword, they restored the respect and the terror of their arms. It will be said, that by violating the law of nations we violate all laws of humanity and civilisation. But what is the odds, if they only fear us? That is all I care about. The judgment of Genoa is more to me than that of posterity, with which you try in vain to frighten me. This vain word 'posterity' hinders only weak and irresolute men. Our interest it is to extend the scope of our conquests, and to deprive the insurgents of all that can feed war. Now I see only two ways, destruction of the crops, burning the villages, and throwing down the towers where they fortify themselves when they can no otherwise keep up the contest."

These recommendations of Doria sufficiently declare Genoa's hatred, rising to desperation, towards the indomitable Corsican nation, and also instruct us as to the unspeakable misery which the latter had to endure. Stephen Doria laid waste half the island with fire and sword, yet without being able to vanquish Sampiero. The latter had held a national assembly at Bozio, to give a new, strength to the common cause by means of institutions, to put the Twelve Men and other popular functions upon a new footing, and to render possible a rising *en masse*. Sampiero was not a mere captain in war; his views were far-reaching. With his country's independence he wished to give it a republican constitution founded upon the ancient institutions of Sambucuccio of Alando. He wished to draw from the island's position, from its forests and produce, all the advantages which fitted it to become a maritime power; he wished, in union with France, to render Corsica free, powerful, and dominant, as in times of old Rhodes and Tyre were. Sampiero strove not for the title of Count of Corsica; he was the first who was called father of his country, and the times of the Signori were over.

He sent meanwhile messengers to the continent to apply to the courts, especially France, for aid; but the Corsicans were left to their fate. The messenger, Antonio Padovano, came back from France empty-handed; he brought with him only Alfonso, Sampiero's young son, 10,000 dollars in money, and thirteen standards on which was written, *Pugna pro Patria*. Nevertheless the Corsicans raised a cry of joy, and the banners, which Sampiero distributed to the captains, occasioned envy and a dangerous jealousy.

Here are letters written by Sampiero :—

"To Catherine of France. Our affairs have gone well so far. I can assure your Majesty that but for the support, secret and open, afforded to the Genoese by the Catholic King of Spain, in twenty-two galleys and four ships with a great number of Spaniards for a beginning, we should have driven our enemies to such extremities that they would be now without a strong position. Nevertheless, come what may, we shall never give up the resolution once formed, to die sooner than subject ourselves in any way to the dominion of the Republic. I therefore pray your Majesty in these circumstances, not to forget my devotion to your Majesty's person, and my country's to France. When the Catholic King has shown himself so inclined towards the Genoese, who alone are so powerful by themselves against us, deserted as we are by every one, will your Majesty suffer us to perish under the hands of our cruel enemies?"

"To the Duke of Parma. Though we should become tributary to the Porte, at the risk of offending all Christian princes, our resolution is yet irrevocable ; a hundred times rather the Turks than the Genoese. Even France has not respected the peace, which we were told was to be the guarantee of our rights and the end of our sufferings. If I take the liberty of troubling you with the affairs of the island, it is that your Highness in case of need may be able to defend its cause at the court of Rome against the assaults of our enemies. I wish my words at least to stand as a solemn protest against the cruel indifference of the Catholic Princes and an appeal to divine justice."

CHAPTER XVIII.

ONCE more ambassadors went to France. There were five ; but the Genoese intercepted them on the coast. Three jumped into the sea to save themselves, one was drowned, and the two that were taken were handed over to the rack and the headsman. The war assumed a terrible character, that of an unsparing Vendetta on both sides. Doria, however, got no forwarder. Sampiero had repeatedly totally defeated, and then almost annihilated him in the pass of Luminanda ; and only so bold a leader as Doria was could have succeeded in escaping. Bleeding, exhausted, despairing, Doria arrived at S. Fiorenzo, and soon left the island. The republic sent Vivaldi in his room, and after him the intriguing Fornari. But she now entertained no hope of annihilating Sampiero by open force in war. Against this man, who had come to the island an outlaw with a few outlaws, she had by degrees sent her whole force into the field—her own and a Spanish fleet, her mercenaries, both Germans and 15,000 Spaniards, her greatest generals, Doria, Centurione, and Spinola; and she, who had vanquished the Pisans and Venetians, could not subdue a poor and forlorn nation, that went to war hungering, ragged, unshod, and badly armed, and that found nothing when it returned home but the ashes of its villages.

Therefore they had come to the determination to murder Sampiero.

Differences had long been sown between him and the descendants of the old Signori. Some, as Hercules of Istria, had fallen off from him because Genoese pay excited their avidity, or their pride revolted at the thought of obeying the commands of a man sprung from the dust. Others had to avenge bloodshed upon him. These were the three brothers Ornani—Antonio, Francesco, and Michael Angelo, cousins of Vannina. Genoa had gained them by gold, and by the prospect of the fief Ornani, which belonged to the children of Vannina. The Ornani again gained over a monk named Ambrose of Bastelica, and Sampiero's own armourer, Vittolo ; and they then devised a plot for destroying Sampiero in an ambush. The governor Fornari approved their design, and entrusted the execution to Rafael Giustiniani.

Sampiero was in Vico when the monk brought him forged letters, pressingly urging him to come to Rocca, where a rebellion had broken out against the popular cause. Sampiero instantly sent on Vittolo to Cavro with twenty horses, and then followed him in person. With him were his son Alfonso, Andrea de' Gentili, Antonio Pietro of Corte, and Battista da Pietra. Meanwhile, Vittolo informed the Ornani and Giustiniani that Sampiero would be passing through the mountain valley of Cavro, whereupon they set out with many men on foot and horseback, and posted themselves in ambush near Cavro. So when Sampiero, with his little host, marched unsuspecting through the pass, he saw himself suddenly assailed on all sides, and the mountains gleaming with armed men. He then perceived that his hour was come. He immediately commanded his son Alfonso to abandon him, to fly and save himself for his country; his great soul thus recovering the sentiments of nature, which he had formerly revolted by the murder of Vannina. The son obeyed and fled. Whilst his men fell bravely fighting in the grey of morning, Sampiero threw himself into the thick of the fight, to force a passage, if it were yet possible. The three Ornani had never taken their eyes off him, and were first afraid to touch the terrible man, but then impelled forwards by vengeance, they pressed upon him, followed by Genoese soldiers. Sampiero fought desperately. He turned against Antonio Ornano, and wounded him in the neck with a pistol-shot. But his gun missed fire; for Vittolo, when loading it, had put in first the ball, and then the powder. Sampiero's face was streaming with blood; and while his left hand cleared it from his eyes, the right wielded the sword in defence. Then Vittolo shot him from behind through the back, and he fell. The Ornani immediately pounced upon him to butcher him when fallen. They cut off his head and carried it to the governor.

It was on the 17th January, 1567, that Sampiero fell. He had reached the age of sixty nine years, unweakened by age and war, undying for his greatness of character, loftiness of aim and love of country. He was great in arms, inexhaustible in council; without ancestors, and indebted for every thing to himself, and to an extraordinary soul, he gathered none of the fruits of success, which favours most upstarts, but all the bitter fruits of adversity, and fell like Viriathus by assassination. By his exalted example, he has shown us what a noble man can do when he remains true to one great passion.

Sampiero was of tall stature, of a gloomy warlike countenance, of haughty mien, with a dark beard and black curly hair. His gaze was piercing, his speech short, firm, and powerful. Though a son of nature and without education, he yet possessed a fine intellect, and an excellent judgment. His enemies accused him of striving for the crown of his island; but he strove purely for its freedom. He lived simply as a shepherd, wore the woollen smock-frock of the country, and slept on the bare ground. He had frequented the most voluptuous courts in the world, those of Florence and of Versailles; yet he had learned nothing of their false principles and corrupt morals. He was savage enough to be able to murder his wife, because she had betrayed herself and her child to his country's enemy; but he knew nothing of

those crimes which pervert nature, and convert its violation
into a refined philosophy of living.   He was simple, rude, and
great; desperately headlong and terrible; a man fresh from nature's workshop, cast in a single mould, and impressed with her
most powerful stamp.

CHAPTER XIX.

ON Sampiero's death, Genoa expressed her exultation by peals
of bells and illuminations.   But the murderers basely quarrelled
for the traitor's reward; Vittolo's share amounted to 150 gold
scudi.

Upon the land of Corsica fell a direful grief: its father was
slain.   They met on the square before the church at Orezza,
3000 men in arms, many weeping, all sad.   The silence was
broken by Leonardo of Casanova, Sampiero's friend and brother
in arms, who held the funeral oration for the deceased.

This man was bowed down by a heavy weight of grief, for
he had met with a lot utterly without example.   A short time
before he had fled from a dungeon, from which his heroic young
son had delivered him.   Leonardo had been taken prisoner by
the Genoese, who threw him into the dungeon of Bastia.   His
son Antonio pondered day and night how he could rescue his
father.   Attired in the clothes of a woman who used to bring the
prisoner his meals, Antonio entered the dungeon.   He conjured
his father to escape and leave him behind; for even should he,
the youth, die, his death would be honourable, and would preserve
to the cause of freedom the arm and the wisdom of the father.
This, he said, was the course prescribed by patriotism.   The
father wavered long in the terrible struggle; at last he knew
that he must act as his son had said, tore himself away from
him, and escaped attired in the woman's clothes.   The jailer
found the youth.   He yielded himself up to him, unarmed,
proud, and happy.   They led him into the governor's presence,
and by his command he was hanged at the window of his
father's castle, Fiziani.

Leonardo, with his son's sacrifice written upon his face, now
stood up like a holy man before the assembled people, and
tranquilly held the funeral oration for his brother in arms,
Sampiero.

"Slaves weep," said he; "free men avenge themselves. No pusillanimous lamentations! Our mountains shall ring again with nought but the din of war. Let us show by the vigour of our action that he is not quite dead. Has he not left us the example of.his life? Lo, of *that* the Fornari and the Vittoli could not deprive us. *That* escaped their plots and their assassin bullets. Why did he call to his son 'Save thyself?' Doubtless that there might yet remain to his country a hero, to the soldiers a head, to the Genoese a fearful foe. Yes, my faithful fellow-countrymen, Sampiero has attached to his murderers the infamy of his death, and to the young Alfonso the duty of revenge. Let us help him to achieve this noble work. Let us close our ranks. The spirit of the father revives in the son. I know the youth. He is worthy of the name he bears, worthy of his country's confidence. Of youth he has only the fire, not the inexperience. Maturity of judgment sometimes outruns the number of years. This boon has not been denied him by Heaven. For a long time he has shared the dangers and labours of his father. The world knows he is master of the rough profession of arms. The warriors are eager to march to his commands. You may rely on the sureness of his tact, which never fails. Masses of men intuitively know the worth of individuals. They seldom make a mistake in the choice of those whom they esteem capable of leading them. And further, what more brilliant homage can we render to the memory of Sampiero than by the election of his son? The hearts of those who hear me are strung to too lofty a pitch to be accessible to fear.

"If there are among us any who are base enough to prefer the ignominious security of slavery to the storms and perils of freedom, then let them go and separate themselves from the rest of the people. Let them tell us what their names are. When we have graven their names on a pillar of infamy, which we shall raise on the spot where Sampiero was assassinated, we will send them away covered with ignominy, to swell the court of Fornari with Vittolo and Michael Angelo. Or, let them know that the arms and the contests in which free and brave men find their most glorious portion, are also the safest for the weak. If they still waver, I would say to them, 'On the one side stands glory to our standard, freedom to ourselves, independence to our country; on the other, the galley, infamy, contempt, and all other evils of slavery. Choose!'"

When Leonardo had thus spoken, the nation by acclamation

E

elected Alfonso d'Ornano chief and general of the Corsicans.
Alfonso was seventeen years old, but he was Sampiero's son.
And so the Corsicans, so far from the death of Sampiero prostrating them as the enemy had hoped, opposed a child to the
proud republic of Genoa, deriding the old Genoese generals and
the name of Doria; and for two years, the youth, victorious in
many a battle, held his ground against the Genoese.

However, the long war had exhausted both parties. Genoa
desired peace; and the island, then disunited by the factions of
the Rossi and the Negri, was in a desperate condition, and inclined
to peace. The republic, which had in the year 1561 taken Corsica
from the Bank of St. George, now recalled the hated Fornari,
and sent to the island George Doria, the only one of his name
whom the Corsicans have preserved in friendly remembrance.
The first act of this moderate and wise man, was the proclamation of a general amnesty for the past. Many districts submitted,
many captains put down their arms. And the Bishop of Sagona
succeeded, too, in disposing the young Alfonso to a treaty, which
was concluded on the following terms, between him and Genoa.
(1.) Entire amnesty for Alfonso and his adherents; (2.) Free
permission to both men and women to embark for the continent;
(3.) Full disposing powers over their property, either to part
with it by sale, or to administer it by stewards; (4.) Restoration of the fief Ornano to Alfonso; (5.) Assignation of the Pieve
Vico to Alfonso's partisans till their embarkation; (6.) A term
of forty days for the disposition of their affairs; (7.) Licence to
every man to take a horse and some dogs with him; (8.) Remission of the debts of those who were debtors to the treasury;
for all other debtors, a respite of five years, in consideration of
the great national pressure; (9.) The release of some prisoners.

Alfonso left his country, with 300 companions, in the year
1569; he emigrated to France, where King Charles IX. received
him with honour, and made him colonel of the Corsican regiment which he was forming. Many Corsicans went to Venice,
and many the Pope took into his service, and formed from them
the celebrated Corsican guard of the 800.

HISTORY.——BOOK II.

CHAPTER I.

AFTER the conclusion of Sampiero's wars, the full misery of the island was revealed. It was like a desert, and the people, decimated by the war, and by forced or voluntary emigration, was totally impoverished and grown savage. To fill up the measure of its woes, the plague frequently appeared, and famine forced the inhabitants to feed like beasts on acorns and weeds. Moreover, the corsairs hovered about their coasts, fell upon their villages, and dragged people off into slavery. In such a condition of things, George Doria succeeded to the island as governor; and so long as he governed it, it rejoiced in his care, his mildness, and his conscientious observance of the treaty, which had especially guaranteed the statutes and rights of the Terra del Commune.

George Doria had no sooner resigned his post to his successor, than Genoa returned to her old bad courses again. Tyrants are generally so obstinate and blind, that they see neither behind nor before them. In time the Corsicans were dislodged again from all temporal, military, and spiritual offices, the least of which was occupied by Genoese; the statutes were suppressed, and a party government introduced. The island was regarded purely as a domain; impoverished Genoese Nobili procured appointment to offices there, to raise their finances. Involved in debt as the Corsicans were, they fell into the hands of usurers, mostly ecclesiastics, to raise the imposts. The governor himself was regarded as a satrap. On his arrival in Bastia, he received a sceptre as symbol of his power; his salary at the public expense was not small, and the country had besides to supply his table with purveyances in kind—with a calf, and a certain measure of fruit and vegetables weekly. His due was also 25 per cent. on fines, confiscations, and the prizes of contraband articles. And we must estimate his lieutenants and officers in proportion; for he brought to the island with him, a fiscal advocate, a master of ceremonies, a general secretary, a secretary in ordinary, a harbour commander, a captain of cavalry, a captain of police, and a chief jailer. All these officers were vampires, as even Genoese authors acknowledge. The imposts became more and more oppressive; all branches of industry were at a stand-still; there were no manufactures, and commerce there was none, because the law compelled all the produce of the country that was exported, to be exported solely to the port of Genoa.

According to the reports of all the writers who have spoken of this period of Corsican history, its condition was then the unhappiest of all countries of the world. Overcome by famine, the plague, and devastation in war, incessantly harassed by Barbaresque pirates, deprived by the Genoese of their rights and freedom, and afflicted by venal justice, drained and oppressed, internally rent besides by the Black and Red factions, bleeding at a thousand places with family wars and vengeance for blood, the whole land one single wound,—such is the picture of Corsica, an island blest by all the elements of nature. Filippini counts up sixty-one places perfectly suited for cultivation, which in his day were waste and deserted, with house and church still standing—a sight, as he says, that affects one to tears. Held together by no general moral spirit, the Corsican nation must have totally dissolved and fallen away into separate hordes, if the general sentiment of country had not taken such wonderfully forcible hold of them. And here the virtue of patriotism appears of a magnitude scarce conceivable, if we reflect what a wasted land it was to which Corsican hearts clove; a wretched land, but one saturated by their blood, and the blood of their fathers, brothers, and children, and therefore dear to them. The Corsican historian says in the eleventh book of his history, "If love of country has been seen, at any time and any place in the world, to exert any influence upon men, then may one assuredly say that it has been supremely powerful in Corsica; for I have been quite astonished that the attachment of the Corsicans to their country has in all ages been so great, as to hinder them from ever forming an energetic voluntary determination to abandon their island for ever. For if one traces their history from the earliest times to the present day, one may see that the people never in so many centuries, putting all together, had even as much as a hundred years of rest and recovery; and that they, notwithstanding, never resolved to go away and avoid the unspeakable ruin consequent upon so many, many cruel wars, teeming with famine, conflagration, private hatred, assassination, wrangling, violence from so many foreign nations, spoiling of their possessions, frequent incursions of those cruel barbarians the Corsairs, and finally with endless other unenumerated sufferings." In a space of only thirty years at that period 28,000 assassinations were perpetrated.

One great misfortune for Corsica, says the Corsican historian, is the great number of those infernal instruments, guns; for the Genoese government drew a considerable revenue from the oppressive tax upon the licence for the use of these guns. "More than 7000 licences," Filippini tells, "have been issued, and over and above many have guns even without licence, especially among the mountains, where one sees nothing but troops of twenty, thirty, or more arquebusiers. These licences raise annually 7000 lire from the poor and wretched Corsica; for every new governor on his arrival cancels the licences of his predecessor, in order to confirm them anew. But the purchase of the guns is a still worse burthen; for even the very poorest is found to have his gun, to the value of five or six scudi at least, exclusive of expenses for ammunition; and one who has no money at all, sells his vineyard, his chestnut trees, or other landed possession, to buy one, as if he could not live without it. It is really surprising; for the greater number of those people have not a coat on their backs worth half a scudo, and nothing in the house to eat, and yet they would hold themselves dishonoured were they to appear in others' presence without their gun. And hence it happens that the vineyards and fields are no longer in cultivation, and lie useless, turning into thicket, and the men are consequently driven to highway robbery and crime; and, where there are no facilities for this, they steal the ox, the cow, and other cattle, of those who do their work regularly to feed their poor family. Hence arises such misery that tillage, which was the sole source of a livelihood, and the sole skill of the islanders, is banished from Corsica. And now those who live so lawlessly, hinder the rest also from acting as well as they might be inclined to do. But the evil does not stop here; for over and above this, from the facility afforded by the arquebuses for doing mischief, assassinations are heard of daily, now in this village, now in that. For formerly, when these arms were not

in use, mortal enemies met openly upon the roads; and even if
the opponent had the advantage by three or four men, he could
scarcely venture upon the aggressive. But if any one now has
a little spite against another, though in the old way of fighting,
he would not dare to look him in the face, he hides in a thicket
or bush, and murders him without a thought, just as he would
shoot a beast; and nothing is said of it afterwards, for justice
dare not do her duty. Besides, the Corsicans have become so
skilful with these guns, that I pray God to preserve us from
war; for their enemies would have to take care of themselves, as
even children of eight or ten years old, who can hardly carry the
gun or leave the trigger alone, are used to stand all day long
before the mark, which they hit, though it be no bigger than a
scudo."

Filippini, Sampiero's contemporary, saw guns introduced into Corsica; till the year 1553 he says they had been unknown
on the island. Marshal Thermes and the French brought the
first guns to Corsica, and they must have been highly amused;
for the Corsicans, says Filippini, knew neither how to load nor
to shoot them, and, when they did shoot, they were as terrified
as savages. What the Corsican historian says of the fearful
consequences of the introduction of guns into Corsica, is as true
now after three centuries as then, and a chronicler writing now
could not alter an iota of what Filippini says.

The sudden appearance of a Greek colony in this frightfully
devastated island excites our wonder. To denationalize the
Corsican nation, by throwing in among them foreign and hostile
elements, was a long-cherished object of the Genoese. Perhaps
this policy had a good deal to do with the plan of settling a
colony of Greeks in Corsica, which was executed in the year
1676. Mainotes of the gulf of Colocythia, weary of the insupportable Turkish yoke, had formed a determination, like those
Phocæans of old who would not endure the Persian yoke, to
emigrate with their wives, and children, and possessions, and
find for themselves a new home. After a long search, their
deputy, John Stephanopulus, came to Genoa among other places,
and laid before the senate the wishes of his countrymen. The
republic heard with pleasure, and offered the Greeks the district
of Paomia, a strip of coast on the western extremity of Corsica,
between the gulfs of Porto and Sagona. Stephanopulus convinced himself of the favourable nature of the land, and then
the Mainotes concluded a treaty with the Genoese senate, ac-

cording to which this strip of coast, Paomia, Ruvida, and Salogna, was ceded to them as a colony. Their first necessities were supplied, and their religion and social institutions guaranteed to them; whereas they on their side swore fealty to Genoa, and had to subject themselves to a Genoese regent, who was to be sent to the colony. So in March, 1676, these Greeks, 730 in number, were seen landing from their vessels at Genoa, where they remained two months, and then took possession of their new country. Genoa was pleased by the rise of this colony; for in its brave men she had gained an irrefragably faithful host, a permanent outpost, as it were, in the enemy's country; and the Greeks could never make common cause with the Corsicans. The latter regarded the foreign new-comers with surprise. Perhaps they despised men who, having abandoned their country, could have felt no love for it; most surely the thought was revolting to them, that these intruders had been unceremoniously settled on their land. The poor Greeks were never destined to prosper in their new rude home.

CHAPTER II.

For half a century the island lay in its state of exhaustion, whilst the hatred of Genoa, fed by the universal and individual misery, at length stifled every other sentiment. The nation lived upon its hatred; this alone preserved it from destruction.

Many causes combined, meanwhile, to force the revolt to an outbreak. To sensible people like the Twelve Men, who still formally existed, the abuse of the sale of licences to carry arms appeared to be pre-eminently the source of the internal ills. In thirty years, as has been said, 28,000 assassinations were perpetrated in Corsica. The Twelve addressed urgent representations of the state of things to the senate of the republic, and demanded the abolition of these licences. The senate yielded the point. It forbade the sale of arms, and charged special commissioners with the disarming of the island. But as, with the abolition of the sale of the licences, a source of annual revenue was lost to the exchequer, a tax of twelve soldi was levied upon every hearth in the country, under the name of the *due seine*. The people grumbled, but paid it; and nevertheless the sale, both underhand and open, of the licences continued.

Another measure excited the resentment of the Corsicans in
the year 1724. The country was then divided into two govern-
ments, the lieutenant of Ajaccio being raised to the rank of governor ;—a double burthen and a double despotism. Both had
the irresponsible competence to sentence to the galleys and to
death without any form of proceedings, but, as it was expressed,
"from having informed their conscience" (*ex informata conscien-
tia*). Arbitrariness, illegality, and murder were the consequence.

In the meantime, a special occasion for the outbreak of revolt
was not long wanting. A Corsican soldier was ignominiously
punished in a small town of Liguria. A crowd of people stood
round the man, and scoffed at his disgrace, as he sat to public
exposure on a wooden horse. His fellow-soldiers, insulted in
their national feelings, fell upon the scoffers, and killed one or
two. The authorities had them beheaded for this violence.
When news of this reached Corsica, it set the national pride in
a blaze ; and when the day for the collection of the tax of the
due seine arrived, a spark falling in Corsica itself occasioned the
final explosion.

The lieutenant of Corte had gone with his collector to the
pieve of Bozio, when the people were out in the fields, and only
a poor old man of Bustancio, Cardone, awaited the officer, and
gave him his tax. There was a coin among it which was light by
the value of half a soldo. The lieutenant refused it. The old man
vainly prayed him to have regard to his bitter poverty. Repulsed, and threatened with an execution if he did not on the
morrow make up the farthing wanting, the old man went away,
pondering such harshness in his mind, and speaking to himself
as old people do. Others met him, stood, and heard his story,
as they came up one by one at the wayside. The old man
began to complain ; then going from his own case to the state of
the country, he carried his hearers away with a frenzy of rage,
eloquently representing to them the distress of the people and
the tyranny of the Genoese, and exclaiming at the conclusion,
" Now it is high time to put an end to our oppressors!" Straightway the crowd dispersed, and the old man's words flew through
the country, rousing every where the old cry of vengeance,
" *Evviva la libertà, evviva il popolo !*" From place to place the
blowing of the conch and the sounding of the alarm-bell was
heard. Thus a feeble old man had preached this crusade, and
a farthing had given the special occasion to a war that lasted

forty years. It was irrevocably resolved to pay no more taxes
of any kind whatever. This took place in October, 1729.

Upon the news of the popular movement at Bozio, the governor, Felix Pinelli, sent 100 men to the pieve. They passed the
night in Poggio de Tavagna, having been secretly received into
the houses of the village. But one of the inhabitants, named
Pompiliani, conceived the design of disarming them in the night.
This was put in execution, and they were sent back unarmed
to Bastia. Forthwith Pompiliani was the avowed head of the
insurgents. They armed themselves with axes, hatchets, and
vine-knives, fell upon the fort of Aleria, stormed it, cut the garrison to pieces, took arms and ammunition, and marched without
delay upon Bastia. More than 5000 men encamped in front of
the town, in whose citadel Pinelli fortified himself. To gain
time he speedily sent the Bishop of Mariana into the insurgents'
camp, to treat amicably with them. They demanded redress of
all the grievances of the Corsican people. But the bishop induced them to accept an armistice of twenty-four days, to return
to the mountains, and wait till the senate of Genoa should have
answered their demands. This took place. Pinelli used the
respite to reinforce himself, to fortify the surrounding forts, and
to disseminate discord. The people now, seeing themselves put
off and deluded, descended the mountains again, augmented to
the number of ten thousand, and encamped before Bastia. The
general rising was not to be stemmed, and in vain did Genoa
send her commissioners to pacify and negotiate.

An assembly of the people was held at Furiani. Pompiliani,
elected in their first need to be their leader, had shewn himself
incapable. He was set aside, and in his place two experienced
men, Andrea Colonna Ceccaldi of Vescovato and Don Luis
Giafferi of Talasani, were declared generals of the people.
Bastia was now assailed anew and more hotly than before; and
again the bishop was sent to the camp of the people to pacify
them. An armistice was concluded for four months. Both
sides employed it to arm themselves; plots also of the old sort
were devised by the Genoese commissioner, Camillo Doria, but a
murderous design upon Ceccaldi's life miscarried. The latter
had meanwhile traversed the interior of the island with Giafferi,
composed family feuds, and restored the authority of law ; then,
in February, 1731, they had opened a legislative assembly at
Corte. Laws were here issued, measures taken for a general
rising, and militias and magistracies organized. They bound

themselves by a solemn oath never more to endure the yoke of
Genoa. Thus the insurrection became legal, general, and
regulated. It was the whole people, of the nearer as well as the
farther side of the mountains, that rose inspired by one feeling.
The suffrage of religion was taken, too. The clergy of the island
had met in convocation at Orezza, and unanimously adopted the
resolution, that if the republic refused the people their rights,
war was a measure of self-defence, and the people released from
their oath of subjection.

CHAPTER III.

THEY had sent the canon Orticoni to the continent to entreat
the protection of foreign powers, and Giafferi to Tuscany to
procure arms and ammunition, of which they stood in need.
Meanwhile the armistice had expired. Genoa, conceding
nothing, demanded unconditional submission and the delivering up of the two chiefs. But as the war began to be kindled
at all points, and the Corsicans, after depriving her of several
strong places, were keeping Bastia, Ajaccio, and Calvi closely
invested, the republic perceived the imminent danger, and turned
to the emperor Charles VI. for aid.

The emperor granted aid. He assigned to the republic a corps
of 8000 German troops, concluding with her a formal contract
of sale, like one merchant with another. The time was then
beginning when the German princes sold the blood of their
subjects for money to strangers, that it might be spilled in the
cause of despotism. It was also the time when the nations
wakened into consciousness. A new spirit, the popular, was
going out through the world. The poor Corsican people has the
abiding glory of having ushered in this new period.

However, the Emperor disposed of the 8000 Germans on very
favourable terms. The republic engaged to maintain them, to
pay 30,000 florins a month, and to pay a compensation of 100
florins for every one slain or deserting. Hence the Corsicans
cried, whenever they killed a German, "Genoa, a hundred
florins!"

The mercenaries came to Corsica on the 10th of August, 1731;
not all, but only 4000 men at first; for the Genoese senate had
put off the other half, in hopes of doing without them. The

4000 Germans were under the command of General Wachtendonk. Immediately upon disembarking they fell upon the Corsicans, and forced them to desist from the siege of Bastia.

The Corsicans saw with grief and anxiety the emperor himself interfering to oppress them. They were in want of the merest necessaries. In their extreme poverty they had neither arms, nor good clothing, nor shoes. They ran to battle bareheaded and barefoot. Whom should they look to for aid to their side? They could reckon upon no one abroad save only their exiled countrymen. Accordingly they determined in a popular assembly to call upon these, wherever they might be living upon the continent; and they addressed to them the following summons :—

" Fellow-Countrymen ! our endeavours for the redress of our righteous grievances having borne no fruit, we have resolved to fight out our own freedom in arms. There can be no more wavering. *Either* we shall rise from the condition of humiliation and prostituted dignity, into which we had fallen ; *or* we know how to die, and to drown our sufferings and our chains in our blood. If no prince is to be found, who, touched by the story of our ills, will hear our lamentations, and defend us against our oppressors, yet there is an Almighty God ; and so we stand armed in the name, and for the defence of our country. Hasten hither, all ye children of Corsica, who are accidentally separated from our coasts, to fight beside your brethren, to conquer or to die. Let nothing hold you back ; take your arms and come! The fatherland calls you, and offers you a grave and immortality!"   •   •

They came, from Tuscany, Rome, Naples, Marseille. Not a day passed without the arrival of one or another; and they who could not bear arms sent what they could, money and arms. One of these returning exiles, Felician Leoni, of the Balagna, hitherto a captain in the Neapolitan service, landed one day at San Fiorenzo, just at the moment when his old father Geronimo was passing with a troop to assail the tower of Nonza. The father and son embraced weeping. Then the old man said, " My son, well is it that thou hast come ; go thou instead of me, and expel the Genoese from the tower." The son directly led on the troop ; the father remained awaiting the issue. Leoni took the tower of Nonza, but in the moment of victory was thrown down dead by a musket ball. A messenger ran with the mournful news to the father. The old man saw the messenger coming, and asked him how matters stood. "Sadly enough," said the messenger, "for thy son has fallen."—"Nonza is taken ?"—"It is taken."—"Ah! well," cried the old man, "long live the fatherland!"

Meanwhile Camillo Doria was devastating the island and destroying its villages, while General Wachtendonk marched into the interior, to quell the rising in the province of Balagna. But here the Corsicans encircled him in the mountains near S. Pellegrino, after having slain many of his men. The imperial general could stir neither forwards nor backwards, and was a lost man. Voices became clamorous for the total annihilation of these strangers. But the prudent Giafferi would not bring down the wrath of the mighty emperor upon his poor country, and therefore dismissed Wachtendonk with his army to Bastia uninjured, with the single reservation, that that general should intercede with the emperor for the grievances of the Corsicans. Wachtendonk gave his word to do so, and was astonished at the generosity of these people, whom he had come to restrain as a savage horde of rebels. An armistice of two months had been concluded. The grievances of the Corsicans were reduced to writing, and despatched to Vienna, but before an answer arrived the armistice expired, and the war began anew.

The second half of the imperial auxiliary force, 4000 men, now crossed the sea. The bold Corsicans vanquished them several times; and especially on the 2nd February, 1732, they defeated and annihilated the Germans under Doria and De Vins in the bloody battle of Calenzana. Hereupon the terrified republic begged the emperor a third time for 4000 troops. But the world began to testify a lively sympathy for the bold people who of themselves, independent of all assistance, and in the bitterest destitution, found solely in their patriotism the means of gloriously resisting two such formidable enemies.

The new imperial army was led by a celebrated general, Louis Prince of Würtemberg. He immediately proclaimed an amnesty on condition that the people would lay down their arms and submit to Genoa. But upon this basis the Corsicans would not negotiate. Accordingly the Princes of Würtemberg and Culmbach, Generals Wachtendonk, Schmettau, and Waldstein, advanced into the country according to a concerted plan of operations, while the Corsicans retreated to the mountains to wear out the enemy by guerilla. Suddenly arrived the answer of the imperial court to the complaints of the Corsicans, and commands to the Prince of Würtemberg to compound as amicably as possible with them, their rights being acknowledged to have been violated.

Hereupon a peace was concluded on the 11th of May, 1732, on the following terms : 1. a general amnesty; 2. abandonment of all claims to indemnification of the costs of the war; 3. remission of all taxes due ; 4. admission of all Corsicans to all civil, military, and ecclesiastical offices; 5. the right of founding colleges, and freedom of teaching ; 6. revival of the Twelve men and the Six men with all the privileges of an Oratore; 7. right of defence to accused persons; 8. the institution of a magistracy, whose duty it shall be to expose all abuses committed by public officers.

This compact, so favourable to the Corsicans, was to have the personal guarantee and ratification of the emperor. Accordingly most of the imperial troops left the island, after more than 3000 Germans had found a grave there. Only Wachtendonk remained behind for a time, to accomplish the consummation of the compact.

CHAPTER IV.

THE imperial ratification was awaited. But, before it arrived, the Genoese senate, embittered and revengeful, allowed itself to be seduced to an unrighteous act, which could only raise the Corsicans in revolt again. Ceccaldi, Giafferi, the Abbé Aitelli, and Rafaelli, the Corsican leaders who had signed the treaty of peace in the name of their nation, were suddenly arrested and dragged to Genoa under the pretext of treasonable designs. A cry of revolt rose hereupon in the island. They hastened to Wachtendonk, and made his honour responsible for this Genoese act of violence ; they wrote to the Prince of Würtemberg and to the emperor himself, and demanded the protection promised by the treaty. The result of this was, that the emperor ratified the treaty and reclaimed the prisoners. All four were restored to their freedom, but the senate tried to extort from them the obligation never to return again to their country. Ceccaldi betook himself to Spain, where he took military service ; Rafaelli to Rome ; and Aitelli and Giafferi went to Leghorn, to observe the course of events in the neighbourhood of their country, as from all appearances the present state of things could not be of long duration.

On the 15th June, 1733, Wachtendonk also, with the last of the Germans, left the island, which stood again alone with Genoa, though now possessed of the legally ratified treaty of peace. The two mortal enemies no sooner looked each other in the face than they seized their arms. Nothing but a struggle for life or death was now possible between the Corsicans and the Genoese. In the course of so many ages, hatred had become a second nature. The Genoese came breathing revenge, intriguing, cunning; the Corsican defiant, unconciliated, distrustful, and proud of his well-tried power, and in the full consciousness of his national self-dependence. A few arrests and assassins' plots, and the people rose and rallied at Rostini round Hyacinthus Paoli, an impetuous, resolute, and valiant citizen of Morosaglia. He was a man of remarkable talents—orator, poet, and statsman; for men had now been matured among the rude Corsican nation in the school of adversity and strife, who were to astonish Europe. The people of Rostini appointed Hyacinthus Paoli, and Castineta with him, to be their generals. Leaders, though possibly at first only provisional ones, were thus already found.

No sooner had the *émeute* of Rostini broken out, and the struggle with Genoa been taken up again, than the brave Giafferi embarked in haste and landed in Corsica. The first popular assembly was held in Corte, which had been taken by storm. Here war was unanimously proclaimed against Genoa, and the resolution adopted of putting themselves under the protection of the Catholic king of Spain, whose banner they erected in Corte. The canon Orticoni was sent to the court of Madrid to lay before it this desire of the nation.

Don Luis Giafferi was appointed anew general of the Corsicans, and succeeded, in the course of the year 1734, in depriving the Genoese of the whole country, with the exception of the strongholds on the coast. He then convoked a general assembly of the people at Corte. He here demanded to have Hyacinthus Paoli as his colleague; and this having been sanctioned, the advocate Sebastiano Costa was commissioned to draw up the statutes of the new government. Accordingly, this memorable assembly declared the independence of the people, and the eternal separation of Corsica from Genoa; and announced as the basis of the constitution, 1, self-government of the people in its parliament; 2, a junta of six men, appointed by the parliament, and renewed every three months, who were to represent the parliament in the council of generals; 3, a civil corporation of four men, commissioned with the administration of justice, finance, and the interests of commerce; 4, the assembled people was declared to be the sole fount of justice; 5, a code of laws was to be compiled by the supreme junta.

These were the fundamental articles of a constitution which the Corsican Costa drew up in the year 1735, and which, in the midst of the barbarism of the then European constitutions, a people formed for itself, of which the continent of Europe only heard in vague reports, few and far between, that it was dreadfully savage and barbarous. Here it is proved that it is not always knowledge, or wealth, or brilliant political events, that educates nations to freedom and independence; but perhaps oftener poverty, unhappiness, and love of country. And thus a little nation, without literature and without manufactures, had quietly, and by its intrinsic power, outstripped, in political wisdom and humanity, all the cultivated nations of Europe; its constitution had grown, not on the soil of philosophical systems, but on that of material necessity.

Giafferi, Ceccaldi, and Hyacinthus Paoli, were all three put at the head of the nation. Meanwhile, Orticoni also returned from his Spanish mission, and brought the reply, that the Catholic king declined to take Corsica under his special protection, but that he declared that he would never support Genoa with troops. So, as the Corsicans had no other princely protection to reckon on, they did in their forlornness what Italian republics in the middle ages had sometimes done ; they put themselves by popular decree under the protection of the Holy Virgin, whose image they received into the national banner, and they chose Jesus Christ their Gonfalonicro, or standard-bearer.

But Genoa, to whom the German emperor could render no aid on account of his entanglement with the affairs of Poland, was employing her utmost resources to subdue the Corsicans. The republic sent in succession, Felix Pinelli, the former cruel governor, and her bravest general, Paul Battista Rivarola, with all the troops that could be raised. And the position of the Corsicans was indeed desperate ; for they were in want of all necessaries, as the land was totally exhausted, and Genoese cruisers prevented all importation from foreign parts. To such extremities were they driven, that they now made proposals of peace, which however Genoa rejected. The whole island was blockaded, all intercourse stagnated, ships from Leghorn had been captured, their powder was at an end, and arms, especially fire-arms, were wanted. Now, when their need had risen to the highest pitch, it came to pass one day, that two strange vessels anchored in the gulf of Isola Rossa, and ·discharged a great quantity of provisions and stores of war, presents to the Corsicans from unknown and mysterious givers. The captains of the ships rejected all compensation, and asked only for a little Corsican wine, to drink to the success of the brave nation. Then they put to sea again, amidst the hearty benedictions of the people, who had assembled on the shore to see their strange benefactors. The Corsicans were now seized with unspeakable joy, and perfectly intoxicated by this little token of foreign sympathy. Joyous peals were rung in all the villages. They told one another that the Divine Providence and the Holy Virgin had sent their angel of deliverance to the poor country; they were now in hopes some foreign power would bestow its protection upon the poor Corsicans. The moral effect of this event was so great, that Genoa feared what the Corsicans hoped, and instantly negotiated for peace. But now the Corsicans rejected it.

These two ships had been equipped by large-hearted Englishmen, friends of freedom, and admirers of Corsican heroism. Soon after this, their patriotism was to be brought into conflict with their generosity by the North American revolution. The English ammunition assisted the Corsicans to the storming of Aleria, where they took four cannon. They now invested Calvi and Bastia. But their position became every instant more helpless and hopeless. All their means were expended, and yet no foreign power interfered. In those days the minds of the Corsicans were held on a strain of almost religious intensity. They resembled the Jews under the Maccabees when they were looking out for a Messiah.

CHAPTER V.

Now it came to pass, early in the morning of the 12th March, 1736, that a ship with British flag steered to the fine coast of Aleria. The people came thronging towards it, and greeted it with hurras, supposing it to be laden with ammunition. The vessel weighed anchor off the shore, and the most distinguished men of the island were soon seen going on board, and waiting upon a mysterious stranger who was in the ship. This stranger was of a kingly mien, of a pompous bearing, and attired in theatrical splendour. He was arrayed in a long caftan of scarlet silk, Moorish trousers, and yellow shoes; a Spanish hat with a plume covered his head; in a girdle of yellow silk hung a brace of richly inlaid pistols, and at his side a sabre, and in his right hand he held a long sceptre. After him, in an attitude of reverence, disembarked sixteen gentlemen of his suite, eleven Italians, two French officers, and three Moors. Thus this mysterious man entered Corsica with the mien of a king, and with the will to be one.

The Corsicans surrounded the mysterious personage with no small astonishment. They were convinced that he was, if not a foreign prince, at least the ambassador of a monarch who wished to bestow his protection upon the Corsicans. And the ship forthwith discharged its cargo before the eyes of the multitude: 10 cannon, 4000 muskets, 3000 pairs of shoes, 700 sacks of corn, a great quantity of ammunition, a few caskets of zechins, and no small sum in coins of Barbary. It seemed that the Corsican leaders knew of the arrival and the person of the stranger. Xavier Matra was seen to salute him with the reverence due to a king; and they were fascinated by the nobleness of the royal manners, and the solemnity of his bearing. He was led in triumph to Cervione.

This curious stranger was a German, the Westphalian baron Theodore of Neuhoff, of all the adventurers of his remarkable age the most talented and most successful. In his youth he had served as page at the court of the Duchess of Orleans, then gone into the Spanish service, and returned again to France. His brilliant mind had brought him into connection with all

F

the remarkable characters of the age, especially with Alberoni, Ripperda, and Law, in whose speculations on finance he had also engaged. Neuhoff had had experience of every thing, seen every thing, thought, endeavoured, enjoyed, and suffered every thing. Following his peculiar bent, he had run through all the possible forms in which happiness can appear to man, and had concluded with the idea, that it must be desirable to a mind of power to be a king. And this he thought, not with the crazed brain of Don Quixote, who rode out into the world and fancied the reward of his future deeds must be, at the least, the empire of Trebizonde; but his clear head took up casually the definite idea of a king's crown, and so he resolved really, and in a common-sense way, to become a king—and king he became!

Roving over Europe, Neuhoff had come to Genoa just at the crisis when Giafferi, Ceccaldi, Aitelli, and Rafaelli, were brought in prisoners. It appears that his attention was here first drawn to the Corsicans, whose valour impressed him greatly. He connected himself with those Corsicans who were in Genoa, especially those from the province of Balagna; and, as he gained an insight into the affairs of the island, the thought was matured within him of playing a part in this romantic land. He went forthwith to Leghorn, where Orticoni was staying, commissioned with the affairs of his country. He put himself into communication with this man, and succeeded by his talents in inspiring him with admiration and confidence in the large promises that he held out. For, intimately acquainted as he was with all the European courts, he said he could promise the Corsicans to procure, within the year, all the resources needed for expelling the Genoese for ever. He asked no other reward than that the Corsicans would crown him their king. Orticoni, carried away by the extraordinary genius of the man, the inexhaustibility of his calculations, and the cleverness of his diplomatical, financial, and political ideas, and perceiving that Neuhoff had the power to render his country essential services, addressed an inquiry to the generals of the island. They gave him, in their desperate position, full powers of treating with Neuhoff. So Orticoni concluded with the baron the compact, that the Corsicans should proclaim him their king so soon as ever he enabled them to deliver themselves fully from Genoa.

Now when Theodore of Neuhoff was certain of this prospect, he began to work at its realisation with an energy sufficient alone to bear witness of his genius. He communicated with the

English consul at Leghorn, and with such merchants as had commercial relations with Barbary; he procured letters of recommendation thither, and went to Africa; and at length, having moved heaven and earth there in person, and in Europe by means of his agents, he succeeded in putting himself in possession of all necessary resources, with which he then suddenly landed in Corsica.

He appeared there in the time of the highest need. On delivering to the Corsican leaders the stores of war, he declared they were only the smallest part of what was coming. He represented to them that his alliances with the European courts, even now powerful, would stand on a totally new basis from the moment the Genoese should be defeated, and he, wearing the crown, should be able to treat as a prince with princes. He therefore desired the crown. Hyacinthus Paoli, Giafferi, and the learned Costa, though men of undoubted good sense, and occupied by the most real problem that can be imposed upon men of action, the task of delivering their nation, and giving it a constitution, yet agreed to this demand. Obligations to the man, his services, the novelty of the event, which inspired the popular mind, the prospect of further aid, and in fine the extremity of necessity, rendered it imperative. Theodore of Neuhoff, King-elect of Corsica, entered his abode in the bishop's house at Cervione; and, on the 15th April, the people assembled at a general diet in the convent of Alesani, to pass a resolution about the establishment of monarchy. Two deputies from every commune in the island, and deputies from the clergy and the religious houses came together here, and more than 2000 people surrounded the congress. The following constitution was laid before this parliament: The crown of the kingdom of Corsica to be offered as a hereditary dignity to the family of Baron Theodore of Neuhoff; the king to have at his side a council of twenty-four men chosen by the people, without whose assent, as well as that of parliament, he can pass no resolution, nor raise any impost whatever. All offices to appertain to Corsicans alone; the legislation to abide with the people and the parliament.

These articles of the constitution were read out by Dr. Gaffori to the assembled people, who accepted them by acclamation; then Baron Theodore signed them with his autograph before the representatives of the nation, and swore upon the Holy Gospel, before the whole people, to abide faithfully by the constitution. After this act he was led into the church, where, after a solemn high mass, the generals put a crown upon his head. The Corsicans was so poor they had no crown of gold; so they twined one of laurel and oak boughs, and put it upon the head of their first and last king. Thus Baron Theodore of Neuhoff, who called himself already a grandee of Spain, a lord of Great Britain, a peer of France, a count of the Empire, and a prince of the Roman empire, became King of Corsica, Theodore the First of his name.

Though this curious event may be explicable in part from earlier events of Corsican history, and in part from the position of the Corsicans at that time, yet it must ever remain an astonishing one; for so great was in this nation the love of freedom, that to attain it, and save their country, they made a foreign adventurer their king, because he held out to them hopes of freedom, and their brave and experienced generals, the heads of the nation, without hesitation or envy, divested themselves of their authority.

CHAPTER VI.

THEODORE, now in possession of the royal title, wished to have also a royal court about him, and was therefore not sparing in the distribution of dignities. He appointed Don Luis Giafferi and Hyacinthus Paoli his prime ministers, and granted them the title of count; Xavier Matra became a marquis and grand marshal of the palace; Giacomo Castagnetta, count and commandant of Rostino; Arrighi, count and inspector-general of the royal troops. Others besides Theodore raised to be barons, margraves, lieutenants-general, and royal captains of the guard, and installed them as commandants of various districts. The advocate, now Count Costa, was appointed grand chancellor of the realm; and Doctor, now Marquis Gaffori, cabinet secretary to his majesty the constitutional king.

Ridiculous as these pompous arrangements must appear on the scene of the Corsican wretchedness, King Theodore nevertheless took up his task in sober earnest. In a short time he had restored order in the country, composed the family feuds, and raised a well-regulated army, divided into companies, with which he then, in April 1736, straightway took Porto Vecchio and Sartene from the Genoese. The Genoese senate had at first stared at the enigmatical event that was happening before its eyes, in fear it might cover the designs of some foreign power; but when Baron Theodore revealed himself, the Genoese hastened to render him ridiculous by pamphleteering, and to brand him as a knight of fortune deeply involved in debt. King Theodore replied to the Genoese manifestos with royal dignity, German plainness, and German wit. He then marched in person against Bastia, fought heroically and like a lion before its walls, and, not being able to take the town, invested it, and at the same time made an excursion into the interior of the island, destroyed some Genoese corps, and chastised places that had fallen off from him with impartial severity. The Genoese were soon reduced to their strong places on the sea-coast. They then, in their embarrassment, fell back upon an abominable means of strengthening themselves. They formed banditti, galley-slaves, and murderers into a company, whose numbers amounted to 1500 men, armed this refuse of society, and led them loose upon Corsica. These bands made inroads into the country, and perpetrated innumerable horrors. They were called Vittoli, from Sampiero's murderer, or Oriundi.

Meanwhile King Theodore wearied not of the care he bestowed upon the raising of the depressed country. He had established manufactories of arms, salt-works, and stuff-mills, and sought to enliven native industry, to draw strangers by commercial advantages, and to counterbalance the Genoese cruisers by the equipment of privateers of his own. The Corsican national banner was green and yellow, and contained the motto : *In te Domine speravi.* Theodore had lastly coined money, gold, silver and copper. These coins exhibited on the obverse a laurel-wreathed shield, over which is a crown, with the letters T. R.; on the reverse was, *Pro bono et libertate.* These coins were taken on the continent, from curiosity, for thirty times their value. But all these measures were of little avail ; the distress rose, the promised aid came not, and the people began to murmur. The king was constantly announcing the appearance of a friendly fleet ; which however stayed away, from the simple reason that the promise was an untruth. But when the voice of the country became more seriously formidable, Theodore assembled the parliament on the 2nd September at Casacconi ; there he declared that he would either resign his crown if the promised aid had not appeared by the end of October, or go to the continent to accelerate it. He thus was in the same desperate situation as Columbus was, according to the story, when the expected land would not appear.

As soon as the parliament, having accepted a new financial scheme proposed by the king, a property tax, had dispersed,

Theodore mounted his horse, to acquaint himself with his kingdom beyond the mountains also. In the land beyond the mountains had been the chief seats of the Signori of Corsica, and there aristocratic sentiments had still kept their ground. Luca Ornano received the monarch with an embassy of the principal gentlemen of those parts, and led him in a festive procession to Sartene. Theodore there lighted upon the princely idea of founding a new order of knighthood. The idea was moreover a politic one ; as indeed in general we discover that the German baron and Corsican king knew how to form schemes no less politic than other upstarts with power of larger dimensions before and after him have done. The new order was called the Order of Liberation, (della Liberazione). The king was grand master, and appointed the knights. They say the order counted in less than two months more than four hundred members, and that more than a fourth were foreigners, who sought the honour of membership for the curiosity of the thing, or for the sake of the brave Corsicans. It was an expensive privilege ; the statutes having fixed that every knight should pay on admission 1000 scudi, from which he was to receive an annuity of ten per cent. This was indeed the best object of the order, that it was at the same time a loan granted in return for the receipt of a certain honour, and a financial speculation. On occasion of his presence at Sartene, the king, by desire of the nobles of the district, distributed with lavish hand the titles of count, baron, and baronet, with which consolation the descendants of the Ornani, the Istrias, the Roccas, and the Lecas, returned home.

While the king was thus testifying his kingly nature, and filling the island with knights and counts, as though poor Corsica had become a splendid empire overnight, he was secretly oppressed by the bitterest cares of government. For, to confess the truth to himself, his kingdom was after all only a painted fiction, and he had surrounded himself with airy nothings. The fleet he had announced would not come, because it was likewise a fictitious fleet. And this chimera put the king into a state of greater apprehension than a real fleet of a hundred well-equipped hostile ships would have done. Theodore began to feel uncomfortable. A party had already been organized in the island, under the name of the Indifferents, comprising those who were dissatisfied with him. Aitelli and Rafaelli had formed this party, and Hyacinthus 'Paoli himself gone over to their side. The royal troops had already had one encounter with the Indifferents, and been defeated. Thus the kingdom of Theodore seemed about to burst like a soap-bubble; Giafferi alone allayed the storm for a short while longer.

Under such circumstances the king deemed it prudent to go out of the way of the storm, and leave the island; not, however, secretly, but as a prince hasting to the continent in person to bring the dilatory auxiliaries. He summoned a diet at Sartene, explained the fact, and the reason of his wishing to make this journey, arranged a regency, appointing Giafferi, Hyacinthus, and Luca Ornano, his regents; nominated twenty-seven baronets and counts to be governors of the provinces; published a manifesto, and betook himself, escorted by countless multitudes, to Aleria, on November 11, 1736, where he embarked under French colours, taking with him his lord chancellor, Count Costa, and a few officers of his household. King Theodore would have been caught up and delivered over to Genoa by a Genoese cruiser, actually within sight of his dominions, had not the French flag protected him. At Leghorn the king landed incognito, in the costume of an abbé; he then travelled to Florence, Rome, and Naples; and, leaving here his lord chancellor and his officers behind him, he took ship for Amsterdam, whence his subjects should, as he said, soon hear good news of him.

CHAPTER VII.

The Corsicans placed no faith in their king's return, nor in the aid which he had promised to send them. Pressed by necessity, the poor nation, intoxicated with its desire of freedom, had even taken up with the absurdity of an adventurer for their king. In their despair they had clung to a phantom, or seized upon a straw; and what would they not have done from hatred of Genoa, and from eager desire of freedom? Now they saw themselves not an inch nearer their goal. Many showed their displeasure. In this state of affairs the regents attempted to enter on negotiations with Rivarola, which however came to nothing, because the Genoese demanded unconditional submission and delivering up of arms. They convened the people to hear their opinion. The people, with resolution unshaken, insisted that faith must be kept with the king, to whom faith had been sworn, and that they would acknowledge no other suzerain.

Meanwhile Theodore had traversed part of Europe, forming connexions, entering on speculations, raising money, appointing cavaliers, enlisting Poles and Germans ; and although his creditors in Amsterdam had put him in the debtor's prison, the extraordinary man had succeeded, by his fertile genius, in getting together auxiliary troops, which he sent forthwith to Corsica. From time to time came a ship with stores of war sent by the king, and a proclamation exhorting the Corsicans to steadfastness.

This, and the fear that the active, never-resting man might at last after all succeed in gaining some continental power for his cause, kept Genoa in a state of anxiety.   The senate set a price of 2000 genuini on the head of the Corsican king, and the agents of the republic dogged his steps at all the courts.   Herself in pecuniary embarrassment, Genoa borrowed three millions from the Bank, and hired three Swiss regiments.   The petty war advanced.   It was conducted with extreme cruelty, as they had accustomed themselves to give no quarter.   Seeing no end to the exhausting war, the republic resolved to call in the aid of France. She had hitherto been loth to apply to a foreign power, as her treasury was exhausted, and previous experiences gave her no encouragement.

The French cabinet gladly seized the opportunity of at least preventing any other state from making its influence felt on the island, whose position opposite the coast of France was of such high importance.   Wherefore Cardinal Fleury concluded a compact with Genoa, on the 12th July, 1737, by which France engaged to send an army to Corsica to the end of subjecting the "rebels" to the republic.   Manifestos were sent off to apprize the Corsicans of this resolution.   They excited great surprise and deep grief, the more so that a power which in former times had stood in far different relations to the Corsicans, now declared its intention of making war on them.   The Corsicans answered this manifesto by a declaration, that they would never return under the dominion of Genoa, and by a despairing appeal to the mercy of the French king.

Five French regiments under the command of Count Boissieux landed in Corsica in February, 1738.   The general had distinct orders to attempt pacific negotiations, and Genoa hoped that the mere sight of the French would suffice to disarm the Corsicans. But the latter stood firm.   The whole land rose as one man at the approach of the French ; fire-signals on the mountains,

conch-horns in the villages, and bells in the monasteries, called
the population to arms. All who could bear arms assembled,
each man provided with bread sufficient for eight days. Every
village formed its company, every piece its battalion, every province its encampment. Thus they stood equipped and in waiting. Boissieux now entered on negotiations, which lasted six
months, till a proclamation came from Versailles, that the Corsicans were to submit unconditionally to the rule of Genoa.
The nation answered in a manifesto to Louis XV., that it
would well become him to cast a look of pity upon them, and to
remember the interest taken by his illustrious ancestors in Corsica ; and declared that they would rather shed their last drop
of blood than return under the murderous dominion of Genoa.
In the meantime they, under the pressure of bitter necessity,
gave the hostages demanded, and declared themselves ready to
trust the French king and to await his conclusive decision.

Things were in this state when Baron Droste, Theodore's
nephew, landed one day at Aleria, bringing a quantity of ammunition, and the assurance that the King of the Corsicans would
soon make his appearance. That extraordinary character did
actually land at Aleria on the 15th September, equipped more
splendidly and royally than the first time he came. He brought
with him three ships, one of 64 guns, the second of 60, and the
third of 55, besides bombarding shallops and a little flotilla of
transports. They were laden with considerable stores of war,
27 cannon, 7000 bayonet guns, 1000 large muskets, 2000
pistols, 24,000 pounds of coarse powder, and 100,000 pounds of
fine, 200,000 pounds* of lead, 400,000 pounds of flints, 50,000
pounds of iron, 2000 lances, 2000 grenades and bombs. All these
articles had been procured by the very man who had been thrown
by his creditors in Amsterdam into the debtor's prison. He had
succeeded by his talent of persuasion, in interesting the Dutch
for Corsica, and causing them to desire a connexion with this
island in the Mediterranean. A company of capitalists, comprising the wealthy houses of Boom, Tronchain, and Neuville,
had been formed, who advanced to the Corsican king ships,
money, and stores of war. Thus Theodore landed in his kingdom
under Dutch colours. But to his grief he found affairs in a
crisis which cast down all his hopes; and he experienced the
humiliation of discovering that he was only king as a knight of
fortune, and that the moment he came in royal style, and with
the real means of being king, he lost the power to be one. He

d the country divided between opposing views, and in full negotiation with France. The people did indeed lead him again in triumph to Cervione, where he had formerly been crowned; but the generals, his own Counts, gave him to understand that the circumstances that had transpired forced them to have nothing more to do with him, but to treat with France. General Boissieux had published a proclamation immediately after Theodore's landing, proclaiming any one a rebel and traitor who should listen to the outlaw, Baron Theodore; and thus the king saw himself abandoned by those whom he had so short a time previously raised to be Counts, Marquises, Barons, and Knights. The Dutch also, disappointed in their expectations, and menaced by French and Genoese ships, took a sudden resolution, and angrily made sail for Naples. Theodore of Neuhoff accordingly found himself compelled to depart likewise, and took ship, full of vexation, for the continent.

CHAPTER VIII.

In the last days of October came the decisive conditions of peace from Versailles, expressed in an edict published by the Doge and Senate of Genoa, and subscribed by France and the Emperor. The edict contained a few concessions, and explicit commands to lay down their arms and submit to Genoa. Boissieux gave the Corsicans fifteen days' time to accomplish these orders. The Corsicans assembled in a Convento at Orezza for deliberation and for exhortation to the people, and proclaimed in a manifesto: "We shall not lose heart, but, arming with the manly resolve to die, we shall prefer rather to end our lives with glory, and with arms in our hands, than to be miserable, idle spectators of the woes of our fatherland, or than to live in chains and entail slavery upon our posterity. We think, and we will say, with the Maccabees: Melius est mori in bello, quam videre mala gentis nostræ. 'Better is it to die in war than to see the woes of our people.' "

Hostilities began. The haughty and vehement Boissieux despatched 400 men to Borgo, to disarm the population there, even before the appointed day. The people were just holding their assembly at Orezza. Upon the news of the advance of the French upon Borgo, the old cry was raised, "Evviva la libertà, evviva il popolo." They dashed to Borgo, fell upon the French, and invested them. The commandant of the corps sent messengers to Boissieux, who marched up forthwith with 2000 men to rescue the menaced corps. But the Corsicans drove them down the mountains, scattered their battalions, and drove them before them into the walls of Bastia. Thereupon Boissieux sent despatches to France, to demand reinforcements; and, being himself afflicted with a mortal disease, he requested his discharge. He (who was a nephew of the celebrated Villars) died at Bastia, Feb. 2, 1739. His successor was the Marquis of Maillebois, who landed in Corsica in the spring with a considerable force.

Maillebois, severe and just, prompt and firm in action, was just the man to carry out his task. As soon as the time had elapsed that he had given the Corsicans to tender their submission, he caused his troops to advance at once in three different directions. Hyacinthus Paoli, having been assailed in the Balagna and forced to retreat, and being a better politician than warrior, despaired of resistance, and tendered his submission. The consequence of this was, that Giafferi also did the same. Maillebois then received the Corsican leaders at Morosaglia, and represented to them that the peace of the country demanded their expatriation. They yielded to the necessity, and accordingly twenty-two leading Corsicans left their country in the summer of the year 1739. Among them were Hyacinthus Paoli, with his son Pasquale, then fourteen years old; Giafferi with his son; Castineta and Pasqualini.

The country on *this side of the mountains was now subjugated; but beyond the mountains two brave relatives of King Theodore, his nephews, Baron Von Droste, and Baron Frederic of Neuhoff, still maintained their position, finding support especially from the men of Zicavo. After a courageous battle, and after Frederic had roved for some time over the mountains and in the bush, practising guerilla, they subjected themselves, and received honourable passports for foreign parts.

Maillebois now was the real ruler of the island; he thwarted the Genoese governor in his dishonourable intentions, and with masculine vigour preserved order, and a just and wise government. He united all those Corsicans who were deeply compromised and feared the vengeance of Genoa, and who had a mind to serve under the French flag, into a regiment. that bore the name Royal-Corse. Then events on the continent recalled him to France. He left Corsica in the year 1741, and the rest of the French troops soon followed him.

Scarce had the French evacuated the island than the hatred against Genoa again broke out into flame. It was now a heritage from the history of the country, a national quality. The governor, Domenico Spinola, made an attempt to levy the impost of the *due Seini.* In a moment, insurrection of the people, battle, and defeat of the Genoese. The war spread over the whole island.

Then, in January, 1743, the forgotten ex-king Theodore suddenly appeared again. He landed one day at Isola Rossa, with three English ships of war, provided as heretofore with a considerable supply of the materials of war. Though driven from his kingdom, Theodore had given up neither the wish nor the intention of being king; he went to England, and had his zeal once more rewarded here by the same success as had attended him at Amsterdam. He now anchored on the Corsican coast, distributed ammunition and arms, and sent proclamations throughout the country, punishing traitors in the tone of an offended and angered monarch, and exhorting his liege subjects to rally round his person. The people remained silent; and what the ill-fated ruler heard, convinced him that his power had melted away for ever. With a heavy heart he weighed anchor again and sailed away, never again to see his island realm. He retired to England.

The Corsicans and the Genoese had meanwhile become inclined to a fresh treaty. It was concluded on favourable terms, giving the island rights long demanded, but constantly violated. Now tranquillity seemed to be confirmed by two years of peace, though the island was torn by family feuds and blood-revenge. To abolish these evils the people appointed three men, Gaffori, Venturini, and Alerius Matra, protectors of the fatherland ; and these triumvirs appeared for the nonce as the national leaders. But others, exiled, enterprising men, perceiving that the flame continued to burn, and was only covered, resolved on a new assault upon the Genoese dominion.

There was then in the service of the king of Sardinia, Count Domenico Rivarola, by birth a Genoese of Bastia, but mortally alienated from the republic. Having got several Corsicans together, he represented to King Charles Emanuel the favourable issue of an enterprise on behalf of Corsica, received a few ships, and with English support conquered Bastia. The

Corsicans declared themselves for him, · and again the war became general. Giampietro Gaffori, a man of admirable heroism, now marched upon Corte, and assailed its citadel, perched on a rugged rock. The Genoese commander of ·the citadel foresaw its fall, if the Corsicans continued their steady fire, and opened another breach. So he seized the young son of Gaffori, who had been previously taken prisoner, and caused him to be bound to the wall of the citadel, to keep the father from firing. When the Corsicans saw Gaffori's son hanging on the wall, they were horrified, and in a moment the cannons were silent, and not a shot fell. Giampietro Gaffori shuddered, but then cried out suddenly after a deep pause, "Fire!" And the artillery began to fire with redoubled rage against the wall. The castle was broken open, but the boy was uninjured, and the heroic father had the reward of being able to clasp him living in his arms.

When Corte had thus fallen, all the interior of the island rose in arms, and a popular assembly, on the 10th August, 1746, pronounced anew the independence of Corsica. Gaffori, Venturini, and Matra were declared generals and protectors of the nation, and an exhortation was addressed to all Corsicans beyond the sea to return to their country. However, the hopes that looked to Sardinia were soon disappointed ; for her aid was insufficient. Bastia fell once more into the hands of the Genoese, and Rivarola had been forced to retire to Turin. But the Genoese senate had again had recourse to France, and entreated the minister to give them an auxiliary corps against the Corsicans.

Two thousand French went accordingly in the year 1748, under the command of General Cursay, to Corsica. Their appearance again gave the ill-fated nation a painful surprise. Now, as the peace of Aix-la-Chapelle had annihilated all hopes of Sardinian support, the Corsicans agreed to accept the mediation of the King of France. Cursay himself was a man of the noblest nature, humane, benevolent, and just ; the Corsicans had no sooner become acquainted with him than they loved him, and confidingly entrusted their cause to him. Thus a compact was concluded in July 1751, by French mediation, which was favourable to the Corsicans, guaranteed them more rights than they had hitherto obtained, and, above all, protected their nationality. But Cursay had become odious to the Genoese on account of this very compact, and got into open hostility with the republic ; bloody scenes were enacted, and the darling of the people would have lost his life in a tumult at Ajaccio, if the brave Gaffori had not hastened up to his aid. The Genoese now calumniated him at his court, called him the cause of continual disturbances, an intriguer and neglector of his duty, and gave it to be understood that he was aiming at royal power in Corsica. These calumnies worked their intended effect; France recalled the noble man, who was thrown as a state prisoner into the prison of Antibes, where he was to remain till his cause was decided.

The fate of Cursay put the Corsicans in a rage; all the people on the nearer and further side of the mountains rose and took up arms. A diet was held at Orezza, and Giampietro Gaffori was elected sole general and governor of the nation.

Gaffori now became the terror of Genoa. In the invincible spirit of this hero Sampiero himself appeared to have come to life again. He was no sooner at the head of his nation than he collected its forces and organized them skilfully; then throwing himself with lightning speed upon the enemy, he defeated him on all sides, and took all the island from him except the strong coast towns. Grimaldi was then governor; he, intriguing and cunning as Fornari had been in old times, saw no safety but in the murder of the powerful man. He made a plot against his life. Gaffori, as a Corsican, had mortal enemies or avengers, who were men of Corte, by name Romei. These the governor gained over; and, to make the deed more horrible, Gaffori's own brother, Anton Francesco, allowed himself to be drawn into the plot. The conspirators enticed Gaffori into an ambush, and murdered him there on the 3rd October, 1753. Punishment fell only on the unnatural brother; for, taken a few days after the perpetration of the guilty deed, he was tortured on the wheel, but the Romei had taken refuge with the governor. They tell how Giampietro's wife, long known for her heroic spirit, after the death of her husband, led her son of twelve years old to the altar, and made him swear to avenge his father's murder. The Corsican nation had lost in him its noblest patriot. Giampietro Gaffori, doctor of laws and a learned man, educated in an age of advancement, magnanimous, and of rare nobility of soul, ready to make any sacrifice for his nation, was also one of its bravest heroes, and worthy to be praised beside Sampiero in the history of his country. But a people that raised a continual succession of such men, was invincible. Gaffori had fallen;— Pasquale Paoli stood in his place.

After Giampietro's death the nation assembled, as of old after the fall of Sampiero, to pay funeral honours to its hero. They then resolved unanimously on war for life and death with Genoa, and declared all those guilty of a mortal offence who should dare to propose negotiations with the hereditary foe. Five men were put at the head of the government: Clement Paoli, the eldest son of Hyacinthus, Thomas Santucci, Simon Pietro Frediani, and Dr. Grimaldi.

For two years these five conducted the affairs of the nation and the war with the republic; but the necessity being felt of uniting the power of the nation in a single strong hand, they called in a man destined to become not only the glory of his nation, but also one of the fairest ornaments of humanity.

CHAPTER IX.

PASQUALE PAOLI was the youngest son of Hyacinthus. His father had taken him with him at the age of fourteen, when he went into exile at Naples. Here the striking endowments of the boy promised a man who should render great services to his country. The highly cultivated father gave his son a careful education, allowing him to enjoy the instruction of the most celebrated men of the city. Naples was then, and through the entire eighteenth century, strangely enough, a focus of that great Italian school of humanistic philosophers, historians, and political economists, which counted such men as Vico, Giannone, Filangieri, Galiani, Genovèsi. This last especially, the great national economist, was Pasquale's teacher; and he bore witness to the genius of his pupil. From this school then sprang Paoli, one of the greatest practical humanists of the eighteenth century, who sought to realize their principles as legislators and regulators of the body politic.

When the government of the five which had been established in Corsica failed to give satisfaction, it was Clement Paoli himself who directed the wishes of the Corsicans to his brother Pasquale. Pasquale was at that time an officer in the Neapolitan service, and had already distinguished himself by his valour in the Calabrian war, and endeared himself to every one by his nobility and his cultivated intellect. His brother Clement wrote to him one day that he must return to his island, because it was the will of his countrymen to put him at their head as

general of the nation.   Pasquale was deeply moved, and wavered.
"Go, my son," said the aged Hyacinthus to him; "do thy duty,
and be the deliverer of thy fatherland."

On the 29th of April, 1755, young Pasquale landed at Aleria
—the same spot where, nineteen years earlier, Baron Theodore had
landed.   In so few years what a different aspect affairs seemed
to have assumed !   It was now a young son of the soil, distinguished neither by brilliant actions nor by influential connexions and promises of foreign aid ;—no speculator, nor one
imposing by means of theatrical ostentation ;—he came with
empty hands, simple and modest, and brought naught with him
but his love for his country, his force of will, and his humanistic
philosophy, by which he desired to liberate and raise to a civilized
society a nation grown savage and torn by family hate, by the
system of banditti, and of revenge for bloodshed.   This problem
was strange, nay we may say unexampled, in the world's history;
and its success before the eyes of Europe, at a period when similar
attempts made by nations of culture were frustrated, gave a proof
that the raw simplicity of nature is more susceptible of democratic freedom than the refined corruption of culture ever can be.

Pasquale Paoli was then twenty-nine years old, of a noble, powerful figure, and a bearing that commanded respect ; his collected,
unassuming mien, the firmness and kindness of his countenance,
his fine voice, simple yet persuasive language, and clear head,
gained him people's confidence at once ; they saw in him the
Man of the People and the great Citizen.   When the nation,
assembled in Sant Antonio Della Casabianca, made a declaration
to the effect that Pasquale Paoli should be their sole general, he
in the first instance declined the nomination, pleading his youth
and inexperience : but the people would not listen even to the
proposition that they should give him a colleague.   On the 15th
of July, 1755. Pasquale Paoli took upon himself the supreme
direction of his native land.

He found his people in this condition : the Genoese confined
to their fortresses, and preparing war; the greater part of the
island free ; the people grown savage, entirely unused to laws,
torn by faction and revenge for blood ; agriculture, industry, the
sciences, neglected or non-existent ; every where unregulated raw
material, but full of healthy germs, planted by earlier ages, and
not stifled but improved by later ones.   In fine, he found a
people whose noblest qualities, love of country and love of freedom, were exalted almost into a passion and a mania.

The very first measures of Paoli went to the root of the evil. A law was published which punished the vendetta with the pillory, and with death by the hangman. Nor was fear alone appealed to, but also the sense of honour, and moral instruction. Missionaries and preachers against the revenge for blood, went about through the country, and preached in the open air the forgiveness of enemies. Paoli himself travelled through the country to reconcile families of mortal enemies. One of his relations, in defiance of his law, practised the revenge for blood : Paoli wavered not a moment; he caused the law to take its course against his kinsman, who was executed. This firmness and the sight of an impartial justice made a deep and wholesome impression.

In the midst of such occupations Paoli was surprised by the report that Emanuel Matra, having collected his adherents and taken up arms, was marching against him. Matra, descended from a noble house of ancient Caporali from beyond the mountains, was driven to this proceeding by ambition and envy. Having counted upon filling the highest post in the nation himself, he now rose in arms to wrest it from his rival. His power was formidable. Paoli wished to preserve his country from intestine war; he therefore proposed to his opponents to let their arms rest, and to refer to a national assembly the decision which of them should be general of the nation. The insolent Matra rejected this proposal, as was to be expected, and boasted of his valour, his experience in war, and even of support from Genoa. Having overcome Paoli's forces in several engagements, and been in his turn repulsed, he appeared again, at the beginning of the year 1756, with Genoese troops, and fell upon Paoli with great boldness in Bozio. Pasquale, who had only a few men with him, threw himself instantly into the convent, and fortified himself there. Great was the danger, tremendous the storm upon the convent; the doors were already on fire, and the flames had caught the interior of the building. Paoli gave himself up for lost, when conch-horns were heard on the mountains, and down came his brother Clement, and Thomas Cervoni, hitherto Pasquale's mortal enemy, but now armed by his own mother to save his opponent, with a valiant host. The contest now became desperate. They say that Matra, when his men were dead or fled, continued to fight with unexampled ferocity, even when a ball had already thrown him on his knees, till a second prostrated him in death. Paoli wept for grief over the corpse of his valiant

G

enemy, to see a man of such heroic power dead among, traitors, and lost to his country. The danger was now happily over, and the party of Matra annihilated; only a few of them fled to the Genoese at Bastia, to reappear at a favourable season.

However, it became manifest that Genoa was now exhausted. This republic, once so mighty, was now old, and on the eve of her fall. Alarmed by the progress of the Corsicans, whose national government continued to gain strength from day to day, she made attempts indeed to crush it by force of arms, but these attempts had no longer the same weight as in the time of the Dorias and the Spinolas. The republic frequently took Swiss and Germans into her pay, and assailed Paoli's head-quarters, Furiani, in the vicinity of Bastia, but without success. Hereupon she applied again to France. To prevent the English from occupying any strong place on the Corsican coast, the French cabinet sent garrisons to the strong towns of the island in the year 1756. But the French held themselves neutral, and did nothing but occupy the strong places, which they ultimately evacuated again in the year 1759.

Genoa was in despair. She saw the Corsicans growing a united and well-ordered state before her eyes, and the land thriving wonderfully in a short space of time. Their finance was regulated as well as their administration; agriculture became active, manufactures and even powder-mills were set on foot; a new town, Isola Rossa, had sprung up before the eyes of the enemy, Paoli himself had established a fleet, and Corsican cruisers made the sea dangerous for Genoese ships. All Corsica, cleared of family feuds, was well armed and equipped, the last strong towns which the republic still held were invested still closer, and their fall seemed at least not impossible. And the Corsican nation had, under a wise government and from innate power, received such a development that it no longer stood in need of foreign aid. Genoa now condescended to make proposals of peace; but the Corsicans declared that they would not enter upon any such till the Genoese should have entirely evacuated their island.

Once more, therefore, the republic tried the fortune of war. She applied to the Matras, Antonio and Alerius Matra, the latter of whom had been regent of the nation with Gaffori. Each in succession having been appointed as Genoese marshal, and provided with troops, raised an insurrection, and was overpowered after a short contest. Then the Genoese senate acknowledged that the Corsicans were no more to be conquered, unless it were by a serious attack on the part of France; and on the 7th August, 1764, concluded a new compact at Compiegne with the French king, by which the latter pledged himself anew to occupy the coast towns of the island for four years. Hereupon six French battalions landed in Corsica under the command of Count Marbœuf, who announced to the Corsicans that he should observe strict neutrality between them and the republic, seeing that his object was only the occupation of the coast-towns, in conformity with the compact. But to the Corsicans this occupation, which they could not prevent, was an act of hostility, and a neutrality was illusory which bound their hands against bringing to a successful termination the sieges already advanced so far. They protested, but raised the siege of San Fiorenzo, which was now near its fall.

Thus affairs remained in suspense for four years; the Genoese inactive, the French, in no wise dependent upon them, in possession of the strong places, and holding friendly intercourse with the Corsicans; the Corsicans, active and restless, strengthening their constitution, glad of their independence, and indulging the hope that, after the lapse of the four years of the compact, they should come into full possession of their island, and at length reach the goal of their heroic national contests.

All Europe was full of admiration of them, and praised the Corsican constitution as the model of popular freedom. And it certainly was praiseworthy in its simplicity and healthy spirit, and was the best monument erected by the political wisdom of the century of humanisation.

CHAPTER X.

WHEN Pasquale Paoli regulated the Corsican republic, he started from the simple principles, that the people is the sole fount of might and law, and the laws have the single aim of expressing and maintaining the good of the people. In regulating the form of the government, his idea was that it must form a kind of national jury, divided into as many branches as there are branches of administration or of rights; and that the administration must resemble a Crystal Palace, in which every one can see what is going on; for that mysterious obscurity favours the domination of caprice, and nourishes in the nation a want of confidence.

Paoli took as foundation to his constitution of the state, that popular communal system of the Terra del Commune, with its communi, pievi, mayors, and fathers of parishes.

All citizens of the parish above twenty-five years of age were electors to the general assembly (consulta). They met under the presidency of the Podestà of the place, having sworn beforehand to choose only such men as they should esteem the worthiest.

Every 1000 souls sent one representative to the General Assembly.

The General Assembly possessed the sole sovereignty in the name of the people. It was composed of the deputies of the communes, the deputies of the clergy, and the presidents of the provincial courts. It determined the imposts, decided questions of peace and war, and passed the laws. A majority of two-thirds gave validity to its measures.

From the General Assembly was composed the Supreme Council of state (consiglio supremo), a corporation of nine, representing the nine free provinces of Corsica, Nebbio, Casinca, Balagna, Campoloro, Orezza, Ornano, Rogna, Vico, and Cinarca. The supreme council had the executive, convened the general assembly, acted for it in foreign affairs, regulated the public works, and watched over the public safety. It was also privileged to be the last resort in the most important cases, and to lay its veto on the decrees of the general assembly until a new deliberation. Its president was the general of the nation; but without the advice of the councillors of state he could accomplish nothing.

Both powers, however, the president and the council, were responsible to the people or their representatives, and might be set aside and punished by a national decree. Moreover, the councillors of state were appointed by the general assembly for a year; they must be above thirty-five years old, and have been previously presidents of the province. The general assembly appointed likewise the five sindici or censors.

The Syndics were officers who traversed the provinces to hear the complaints of the people against the administration or the jurisdiction, and were competent to pass sentences which the general had no power to reverse. The general appointed all administrative officers and tax-collectors, who in their turn were subjected to the censorship of the five.

Justice was administered in the following form. Every podestà could decide causes up to the amount of ten lire; above this, and up to thirty lire, he had to take as assessors the two fathers of the parish. Whatever exceeded thirty lire went before the tribunal of the province, a court composed of a president and two assessors appointed by the general assembly, and a fiscal advocate appointed by the council of state. The tribunal of the province changed every year.

From this tribunal appeal could be made to the Rota Civile, a supreme court of three doctors of law appointed for life. The same tribunals had also criminal jurisdiction, always, however, supported by six heads of families, who had to discover the facts from the examination of witnesses, and to pronounce *guilty* or *not guilty*.

The members of the council of state, of the syndicate, and the tribunals of the provinces, could not be re-elected till after two years. The podestàs and fathers of parishes, moreover, were chosen annually by the citizens of the place above twenty-five years old, in the assembly on the open place before the church.

In cases of emergency, on occasions of insurrection and tumult at any part of the island, the general had the power to name a temporary dictatorship for the locality in question, called the Giunta of War (*giunta di osservazione o di guerra*). It was composed of three or more members, with a councillor of state at their head; and, invested with unlimited power of interfering, taking measures, and chastising, this momentary prevotal court was very formidable. It was called by the people the *Giustizia Paolina*. When its mission was fulfilled, it gave an account of its proceedings before the censors.

These are the fundamental features of Paoli's legislation and the Corsican republic. If we regard its leading ideas, self-government of the people, universal freedom of the citizen regulated by law, his interest in the life of the state, publicity and simplicity of administration, popular courts of law, we must surely allow that the Corsican state was ordered in a more human spirit than any other of the same age. If we regard, in fine, the period of its origin, which preceded by some tens of years the state of the great Washington, and the legislation of the French, there is yet more admiration due to Pasquale Paoli and his nation.

To a regular standing military system Paoli was averse. He

himself said: "In a country which wishes to remain free, every citizen must be a soldier, and hold himself always ready to arm himself for the defence of his rights. Disciplined troops act more in the interest of despotism than of freedom. Rome ceased to be free on the day on which she had paid soldiers, and the invincible phalanxes of Sparta were formed from a levy *en masse.* Lastly, as soon as there is a standing army, an *esprit de corps* is formed; people speak of the valour of this or that regiment, of this or that company. These are more serious evils than is commonly supposed; and it is good to avoid them as much as possible. We ought to speak of the firm resolve manifested by this or that commune, of the self-sacrifice of the members of this or that family, of the valour of the citizens of so-and-so; in this manner is the emulation of a free nation roused. When our manners shall be as refined as they ought to be, our whole nation will be disciplined, and our militia invincible."

Only under the pressure of necessity Paoli yielded so far as to allow of the creation of a small number of regular troops to garrison the strong places. They were two regiments of 400 men each, commanded by Jacobo Baldassari and Titus Buttafuoco. Each company had two captains and two lieutenants. They were exercised by French, Prussian, and Swiss officers. Every regular soldier was armed with a bayonet-gun, a pair of pistols, and a dagger. The uniform was the black woollen cloth of the country; the officer was distinguished merely by a little lace on the collar of his coat, and by his gun having no bayonet. All wore caps of Corsican boar-skin, and long gaiters of calf-leather reaching to the knee. The good service rendered by these two regiments was praised.

The militia was organized on the following system. All Corsicans between the ages of sixteen and sixty were soldiers. Each commune had to raise one or more companies according to its size, and to elect their officers. Every pieve again formed a camp, under a commander appointed by the general. The entire militia service was divided into three levies, each of which lasted fifteen days. It was the general rule to combine kindred, so that the soldiers of a company were mostly blood-connexions. Those who served in the strongholds received an annual pay, the rest only so long as they were in the field. The villages supplied them with bread.

All the expenses of state were covered by the impost of two.

lire on every family, and by the taxes on salt, the coral fishery, and other indirect taxes.

Nothing that can establish or augment the good of a people was overlooked by Paoli. To agriculture he devoted the most attentive care; the general assembly appointed annually two commissioners for every province, who had to foster agriculture. The olive, chestnut, and maize were planted; plans were designed for draining the marshes and making roads. What a remarkable position of affairs it was!—with the one hand the Corsican warded off his enemy, with the other he cast seed into the ground.

Science also, the highest guarantee and noblest consummation of all liberty and all prosperity, Paoli sought to give to his people. The iron ages had not permitted it to arise. The Corsicans remained children of nature, ignorant, but rich in mother-wit. They say Genoa had intentionally neglected education. Now national schools were every where to be seen springing up under the regimen of Paoli, and the Corsican clergy, brave and liberty-loving men, were zealous in the instruction of youth. A national press was established in Corte, which issued exclusively books devoted to instruction and the enlightenment of the people. The children found it written in these books, that the highest virtue of a noble man was love of his country, and that all who fell in battle for freedom were martyrs, and had their place in heaven among the saints.

On the 3rd January, 1765, Paoli opened the Corsican university at Corte. In it were taught theology, philosophy, mathematics, law, aAd arts. Medicine and surgery were put off till they should be able to procure the necessary apparatus. All the professors were Corsicans; the first were, Guelfucci of Belgodere, Stefani of Venaco, Mariani of Corbara, Grimaldi of Campoloro, Ferdinandi of Brando, Vincenti of Santa Lucia. Poor scholars were maintained at the public expense. At the end of every course a solemn examination was held in the presence of the members of the general assembly and of the government. The presence of the noblest citizens of the nation heightened the blame as well as the praise accorded. Standing in view of these, and of the nation in general, these young men knew that they were looked on as young citizens of the country, who would sooner or later be called to aid in the work of the deliverance of their fatherland. Growing up thus in the midst of the history of their nation, and actually among these stormy events, they had

the one single high ideal clearly realized before their eyes.   It
is, then, easy to see what a spirit breathed in these youths; and
the following fragment may prove it, extracted from one of the
speeches which used to be held by some scholar of rhetoric after
the public examination, in the presence of the representatives
and fathers of the country.   A scholar spoke in their and Paoli's
presence :—

"The nations that have striven for freedom, have suffered great
reverses ; there have been among them some less powerful and
less valiant than ours is.   Nevertheless they have in the end,
with firmness and perseverance, overcome all difficulties.   If
freedom were to be gained by mere speeches, all the world would
be free.   But it needs an unshaken steadfastness that clears all
obstacles ; and, because this virtue is rare among men, those who
have given proofs of it have ever been regarded as demigods.
Surely the privileges and the position of a free nation are so inestimable that they cannot be described adequately to their im-
port.   Yet enough is said when we remember that they excite
the admiration of the greatest men.   As to ourselves, may it
please Heaven to let us follow the course of our destiny !   But
our nation, whose heart is greater than its fortune—our nation,
poor though it be, and clothed in a coarse garment, is a reproach
to the whole of Europe, grown lazy under the burthen of heavy
chains ; and they feel the necessity of taking our existence
from us.

"Brave countrymen, the critical moment has arrived.   The
storm already roars above our heads ; danger threatens us on
every side ; let us know how we are to maintain ourselves in
these circumstances, and to gain new strength as the number of
our foes swells ; the question is the defence of our name, our
freedom, our honour.   In vain should we have shown heroic
feelings until this day, in vain would our forefathers have shed
streams of blood, and endured unheard-of woes ;—if we grow
weak, all is inevitably lost.   *We* grow weak !   Ye venerable
shades of our fathers, ye who have done so much to bequeath us
freedom as the richest heritage, fear not that we shall make you
blush for your sacrifice.   No, never ! your grandchildren will
imitate your example in all things, resolved as they are to live
free, or die fighting for the defence of their sacred and inviolable
rights.   We cannot make up our minds to believe that the King
of France will ever take the part of our enemies and turn his
arms against our land : no ! an event of this nature cannot take.

place. But yet if it is written in the book of bronze that the most mighty monarch of the earth shall make war on one of the smallest nations of Europe—we have still a just cause of pride; for we are sure either to live free for ever, and crowned with glory, or to render our fall immortal. May those who hold themselves incapable of such virtue, feel no alarm : my words are directed only to the true Corsicans, whose feelings are well known.

"As for us, brave youths! none of us—I swear by the Manes of our fathers !—no, none of us will wait for the second call to arms. We have to show, in sight of the world, that we deserve to be called brave. When the strangers land on our coasts prepared to give battle to support the pretensions of their confederates, shall we, who fight for our own weal, for the weal of our children, for the defence of our fatherland, for the maintenance of the just and magnanimous resolutions of our fathers— shall we waver, or hesitate to defy all perils, to expose or sacrifice our lives? Brave fellow-citizens, freedom is our aim ; and whatever noble souls there are in Europe, look with sympathy upon us, and raise their wishes for the triumph of our cause. May our steadfastness more than equal the general interest felt for us ! And may our foes, whatever be their name, learn by experience that the conquest of Corsica is not so easy as they think! There are free men in this land; and the free man knows how to die !"

CHAPTER XI.

THUS were all the thoughts and wishes of the Corsican people, of every age and sex, directed to the common end. This popular spirit was free and strong, ennobled by the purest love of country, by hereditary valour, and by the clear rationality of the constitution, which had been produced by no extraneous theorizing, but by the hallowed traditional institutions of home. The great citizen Pasquale was the father of his country. Wherever he showed himself, he was met by the love and the blessing of his people ; and women and old men might be seen to lift up their children and grandchildren in their arms, that they might see the man who had made the people happy. The coast towns also, which remained in the power of Genoa,

desired to share the benefits of the Corsican constitution.
Advances were made. Carl Masseria and his son, both of
heroic spirit, undertook by force or stratagem to bring the
castle of Ajaccio into the hands of the patriots. The attempt
failed; the son fell in the contest, and the father, mortally
wounded already, died on the rack without a groan.

But so much stronger had the Corsicans grown, that, so far
from anxiously looking for help from foreign powers, they
actually formed in themselves not merely means of resistance,
but also of aggression and conquest. Their flag already waved
on the Mediterranean; a Maltese knight, De Perez, was the
admiral of the little fleet, which already began to be formidable
to the Genoese. It was the talk in Corsica, that the island was
well qualified by its position to become a maritime power, as
of old Greek islands in the eastern Mediterranean had been;
and people even spoke of the possibility of the Corsicans effecting a landing on the coast of Liguria.

The surprising conquest of the neighbouring island, Capraja,
now gave greater probability to these dreams of possibilities,
and to the enemy more substantial grounds of fear. This little
island had in former times been a fief of the Corsican family of
Signori, Da Mare, and had thence passed into the hands of the
Genoese. It is unfruitful, but an important station in the
Genoese and Tuscan channel, difficult to be taken. A Corsican,
Centuri, embraced the idea of surprising it. Paoli readily
agreed, and so a little expedition of 200 regular troops, and a
band of militia, put off in Feburary, 1765, from Cap Corso.
They fell upon the town Capraja, which at first offered a
vigorous resistance, but subsequently made common cause with
them. But the castle was held by the Genoese commander,
Bernardo Ottone, with honourable valour; and Genoa, upon
the news of the event, hastily despatched her fleet under Admiral
Pinelli. It was thrice repulsed. The rage and the shame
of Genoa, at not being able to wrest Capraja from a handful of
Corsicans who had established themselves in the town, was so
great, that even aged senators burst into tears. Once more the
senate sent the fleet out against the island, forty ships of war in
number. The five hundred Corsicans, under Achilles Murati,
maintained their position in the town, and repulsed the Genoese
to the sea again. Then Bernardo Ottone capitulated in May,
1767, and Capraja, completely taken possession of by the
Corsicans, was declared a province of Corsica. Thus the

Genoese republic saw her commerce anew and dangerously menaced by a Corsican fortress almost at her very gates.

The fall of Capraja was a great blow to the senate, and accelerated the determination at last to give up the untenable Corsica. Yet the decrepit republic delayed to pronounce the bitter determination till she was driven to it by a mistake she made. To wit, the Jesuits had at that time been expelled from Spain as well as France; but the king of Spain entreated the Genoese senate to grant the exiles a home in Corsica. To oblige him Genoa had consented; and, accordingly, one day a great number of the society of Jesus was seen landing at Ajaccio. The French, who had sentenced the Jesuits to eternal banishment from France, took it as an insult on the part of Genoa, that the senate threw open to them those Corsican ports which were occupied by France herself. Count Marbœuf straightway received orders to remove his troops from Ajaccio, Calvi, and Algajola; but scarcely had this taken place than the Corsicans occupied the town Ajaccio in triumph—all but the citadel, into which the Genoese had entered.

Under these circumstances, and considering the dangerous variance that had arisen between France and Genoa, the Genoese senate foresaw that it would have to succumb to the Corsicans. So it came to the resolution of voluntarily selling to France its alleged rights to Corsica.

The French minister Choiseul accepted the proposition with joy. The acquisition of so important an island in the Mediterranean appeared a great gain, and a compensation at a time when they had just lost Canada. The compact was concluded at Versailles on the 15th May, 1768, and signed on the part of France by Choiseul, and on that of Genoa by Domenico Sorba. Genoa, in this instance, violating all international law, transferred a nation, over which she had no other rights than the long obsolete ones of conquest, to a foreign despotic power which had just been treating and holding intercourse with it as an independent nation; and thus was a free people, with a most moral and civilized political constitution, bartered away like a passive herd of cattle. Genoa had moreover made the dishonourable stipulation, that she might come into her rights to Corsica again, as soon as she were able to repay the cost which France, by the occupation of Corsica, had drawn upon herself.

Now, before the French expedition put off from the harbours of Provence, a report had already been spread in Corsica of the compact, which was at first kept secret. Paoli convened the National Assembly at Corte on the 22nd May, and they unanimously resolved on resistance of the French to the very last, and on a levy *en masse*. Carl Bonaparte, Paoli's secretary, spoke manfully, and full of fire.

In the meantime Count Narbonne landed with troops at Ajaccio. and the astonished inhabitants of the town saw the Genoese banner taken down, and the white flag of France put up in its place. Nevertheless, the French still denied the real object of their coming, and sought to deceive the Corsicans by false representations, till Marquis Chauvelin landed with all his troops at Bastia, commissioned with the command-in-chief in Corsica.

The compact of occupation, which had been concluded for four years, was to terminate on the 7th August of the same year; and on this day the commencement of hostilities was expected. But as early as the 30th July, the French, upon the command of Marbœuf, marched 5000 men strong from Bastia against San Fiorenzo, and, after an unequal contest, made themselves masters of some positions in the Nebbio. Thus it became patent. to all, that Corsica was to suffer the extremest of what she had dreaded. Fate, constantly adverse to her, had always thrown foreign despots betwixt her and Genoa, and forced her, on the eve of her deliverance, back into her old misery.

Pasquale Paoli hastened with a few militia corps to the Nebbio. His brother Clement had already taken position there with 4000 men. But the two could not hinder Marbœuf·from subjugating Cape Corso. Now Chauvelin also appeared with 15,000 French, sent out to subjugate the freest and bravest people in the world. He moved against the strongly fortified ·Furiani, accompanied by a traitor, Matthew Buttafuoco of Vescovato, the first who drew upon himself the infamy of earning reward and titles from the enemy. The struggle at Furiani was desperate. Only 200 Corsicans, under Charles Saliceti and Ristori, held the place; but they would not yield, even when the whole place was reduced to a heap of rubbish, and forced their way by night, with arms in their hands, to the sea-coast.

An equally murderous contest took place in the Casinca and at the Golo bridge. The French were repulsed at all points, and Clement Paoli was covered with glory. He and Pietro Colle are styled in history the most valiant heroes in the last Corsican war of independence.

The wreck of the defeated French army retreated to Borgo, a place lying high on the mountains of Mariana, and strengthened its garrison.   Paoli desired to gain this place at any price; he therefore began storming it on the night of the 1st October. This was the most brilliant deed in arms of the Corsicans. Chauvelin advanced from Bastia to the relief of Borgo; Clement threw himself in his way; while Colle, Grimaldi, Agostini, Serpentini, Pasquale Paoli, and Achille Murati, dashed against Borgo.   Every nerve was strained on both sides.   Thrice did the entire force of the French army make a desperate onslaught, and thrice was it repulsed.   The Corsicans, so inferior in point of numbers, with their militia here broke the close ranks of an army which, since the time of Louis XIV., was reputed to be the best organized in Europe.   Among the Corsicans, women might be seen in men's clothes dashing in with gun and sword among the French.   At length the French retreated to Bastia; many of them were slain, many, including Marbœuf, wounded; and the garrison of Borgo, 700 men, and their colonel, Ludre, laid down their arms, and yielded themselves prisoners to the Corsicans.

The battle of Borgo showed the French what a people they had come to subjugate.   They had now lost all the country again, except the strong towns.   Chauvelin wrote to his court, reported his losses, and demanded fresh troops.   They sent him ten battalions.

CHAPTER XII.

At this period sympathy for the Corsicans had become stronger than ever.   In England, especially, public opinion spoke loud for the oppressed people, and exhorted the government to interfere against the despotic principles which France was so shamelessly putting into execution.   It was said that Lord Chatham really took up the idea of expressing an authoritative opinion in favour of the Corsicans.   The Corsicans kept their eyes fixed upon constitutional England, hoping that a great and free nation would not allow a free people to be crushed; but they were deceived.   As in the year 1760, the British Cabinet forbade all intercourse with the Corsican "rebels."   The English people spoke out their opinion only in committees and in private, and went no further than these declarations and private subscriptions; but the cabinets sanctioned the stifling of a dangerous germ of democratic freedom in a heroic people.

Notwithstanding the successes gained by his people, Pasquale Paoli perceived all the danger of his position. He proposed to France a compact, which should give to the king the acknowledgment of his sovereignty, to the Corsicans their constitution, and to Genoa an indemnification. France rejected the compact, and prepared herself for a finishing blow. However, Chauvelin felt his weakness. They pretend he had learned intrigue from the Genoese; he intended Paoli to end his life, like Sampiero and Gaffori, by assassination. In the history of any brave and free people treachery is never wanting; for where human nature shines with the purest light, it appears necessarily to produce the shadow of deep vice. A traitor was found in the son of Paoli's own chancellor, Matthew Massesi; but letters lost by him revealed the secret purpose. When put on his trial before the council of state, he confessed, and was delivered over to the hangman. Another plot, concocted by the restless Dumouriez, who was then on service in Corsica, to arrest Paoli by night in his house at Isola Rossa, was likewise unsuccessful.

Chauvelin brought into the field the ten fresh battalions; but these also were repulsed by the Corsicans in the Nebbio. Covered with shame, the proud marquis despatched fresh messengers to France, to explain the difficulties that attended a conquest of Corsica. Thereupon the French government recalled Chauvelin from his post in December, 1768, and appointed Marbœuf the temporary commander-in-chief, till the arrival of his successor, Count de Vaux.

De Vaux, having served in Corsica under Maillebois, knew the country, and the best mode of conducting war there. Equipped with a great force of forty-five battalions, four cavalry regiments, and considerable artillery, he resolved to end the contest by a single blow. In the prospect of this danger, Paoli convened the people in the Casinca on the 15th April, 1769. They here resolved to fight to the last drop of blood, and to arm every man in the land. Lord Pembroke, Admiral Smittoy, and other English, German, and Italian friends of the Corsican cause, who were present, were astonished at the collected demeanour of the militia that poured towards the Casinca. Many foreigners enrolled themselves in the ranks of the Corsicans. On their side was also an entire company of Prussians, who from the Genoese service had passed into the Corsican. Yet no one could conceal from himself their desperate situation; and French gold now began to exert its influence, and treachery appeared; even Capraja had already fallen through the treachery of the commander, Astolfi.

But the fate of the Corsicans was to be fulfilled. England, on whom they hoped, did not interfere; and the French marched with their whole force upon the Nebbio. This mountainous province, traversed by a long and narrow valley, had often been the scene of decisive battles. Paoli had established his headquarters here, having left Saliceti and Serpentini in the Casinca. De Vaux, Marbœuf, and Grandmaison advanced into the Nebbio, to annihilate Paoli at one blow. The attack began on the 3rd May. After a contest of three days, Paoli was driven out of Murato, his camp. He now resolved to march over the Golo, and put this river between himself and the enemy. He established his head-quarters in Rostino, and entrusted to Gaffori and Grimaldi the defence of Leuto and Canavaggia, points by which the French might easily push forward. But Grimaldi became a traitor, and Gaffori, for what reason is uncertain, did not maintain his position.

Thus it came about that the French came down from the heights, and advanced towards Ponte Nuovo, the bridge leading over the Golo. The Corsicans stood extended along the Golo, and the Prussian company and more than 1000 Corsicans held the bridge. The French, descending unexpectedly from the mountains, drove the militias before them; and the latter, in confusion and seized with terror, dashed against the bridge, to get over it. But the Prussians, who were commanded to stop their flight, in their confusion fired upon their friends, whilst the French fired at the same time, and charged with bayonets. The terrible word *treachery* was heard. Gentili sought in vain to stem the disorder, which became general, so that no position was now tenable, and the militia corps scattered themselves in wild flight through the forests and the surrounding country. The unfortunate battle of Pontenuovo was fought on the 9th May, 1769; and on that day the Corsican people lost its freedom and its independence.

Paoli still attempted to hinder the enemy from penetrating into the province Casinca. But it was too late. The entire land on this side of the mountains fell under French dominion in a few days; and that instinctive feeling of helplessness which generally comes irresistibly over the minds of a people in disastrous moments, now took hold of the Corsicans. They needed such a man as Sampiero. Paoli was in despair. He hastened to Corte, and almost resolved to leave his country. The brave Serpentini did indeed still hold his ground in the Balagna, and Clement Paoli, as well as he, was resolved to fight to his last breath; and Abatucci maintained his position beyond the mountains with a band of bold patriots. All was not yet lost; they might at least retire to the mountains and keep up guerilla, as Renuccio, Vincentello, and Sampiero had done of old. But a man like Pasquale Paoli could not possess a defiant stubbornness of character, like those men of the age of bronze; nor would he, the legislator and Pythagoras of his nation, sink into a leader of banditti in the mountains. Dreading the blood that would be spilled in a prolonged contest, he yielded to his fate. His brother Clement, Serpentini, Abatucci, and others, joined him. The little band fled hastily to Vivario, and then, on the 11th June, to the gulf of Porto Vecchio. There they embarked, three hundred in number, in an English ship given them by Admiral Smittoy, and went by way of Tuscany to England, which from that time to our own days has been the abode of the refugees of unfortunate nations, and has never since received to hospitality nobler exiles than those Corsicans.

Those have not been wanting who, looking back upon the ancient tragical Corsican heroes, have accused Paoli of weakness. How Paoli judged himself, his words prove. He says in a letter: "If Sampiero had lived in my days, the deliverance of the country would have cost me less trouble. What we *attempted* for the establishment of our nationality, he would have *accomplished*. A bold and enterprising man was then needed, to spread terror into the very comptoirs of Genoa. France would never have meddled with the contest, or she would have found a more redoubtable adversary than were all those that I was able to oppose to her. How often have I lamented this! Assuredly it is not courage, nor heroic perseverance, that the Corsicans want, but a leader, who can effect combinations and guide the operations of war when opposed to experienced generals. We should have divided this noble work between us; whilst I should have worked at a code of laws, answering to the manners and needs of the island, his powerful sword would have undertaken to fortify our common work."

The Corsicans submitted to the French on the 12th June

1769. Yet in the midst of the great grief, that whole centuries of unexampled contests had after all not been able to save their beloved freedom, and amid the din of arms raised by the French occupying all the land on both sides of the mountains, the Corsican nation, with unexhausted heroic power, gave birth, on the 15th August, to Napoleon Bonaparte, the annihilator of Genoa, subjugator of France, and avenger of his nation. Such satisfaction did fate deign to give to the Corsicans in their fall, and so was the heroic tragedy of their history closed by a conciliation.

CORSICA.

FROM MY WANDERINGS IN THE SUMMER OF 1852.

Nel mezzo del cammin di nostra vita
Mi ritrovai per una selva oscura,
Che la diritta via era smarrita.
Ahi quanto a dir qual era è cosa dura,
Questa selva selvaggia, aspra e forte—
Ma per trattar del ben ch' io vi trovai,
Dirò dell' altre cose, ch'io viho scorte.

DANTE, *Inf.* i. 1.

CORSICA.

TRAVELS.—BOOK I.

CHAPTER I.

LANDING IN CORSICA.

Lasciate ogni speranza voi che'ntrate.

DANTE, *Inf.* iii. 9.

THE sea-passage from Leghorn to Corsica is beautiful, and more entertaining than that from Leghorn to Genoa. You constantly enjoy the sight of the picturesque islands in the Tuscan channel. Behind us lay the terra firma, and Leghorn, with its wood of masts, at the foot of Monte Nero; before us the solitary shattered tower on Meloria, that little rock in the sea, beside which the Pisans under Ugolino were destroyed by the Genoese, so that their naval power sank, and Genoa from that day came into the possession of Corsica; further off the rocky island Gorgona, and near it in the west the island Capraja. In view of it one recalls Dante's verses in his canto about Ugolino, (*Inferno*, xxxiii. 89.)

> Ahi Pisa, vituperio delle genti
> Del bel paese là, dove il sì sona;
> Poi che i vicini a te punir son lenti,
> Movasi la Capraja e la Gorgona,
> È faccian siepe ad Arno in su la foce,
> Sì ch' egli annieghi in te ogni persona.*

---

* Ah, Pisa! foul reproach of human kind
 In that fair land where *Sì* is heard to sound!
 Since slow to punish thee thy neighbour's mind,
Burst be Capraja's and Gorgona's bound,
 And let them pile 'gainst Arno's mouth a hedge
 Till every child of thine by him be drown'd.

Dayman's Translation.

The island Capraja conceals the western end of Corsica, but behind it the blue mountains of Cape Corso rise from the sea in far stretching outlines. Further still to the west is seen Elba, a rocky island rising boldly out of the sea, and sinking lower towards the terra firma of Piombino, which is indicated in faint outline.

The sea shone with the deepest purple, and the sun, sinking behind Capraja, tinged the sails of passing ships with a delicate rose-colour. A sail on this basin of the Mediterranean is in truth a sail through history itself. I fancied this beautiful sea peopled by the fleets of the Phœnicians and the Greeks, by the ships of those Phocæans who roved about here of old—then came Hasdrubal and the fleets of the Carthaginians, the Etruscans, the Romans, the Moors and the Spaniards, the Pisans and the Genoese. But yet more impressively does the constant view of Elba and Corsica remind one of the greatest world-drama of modern times, that bears the name Napoleon. The two islands lie in peaceful proximity, almost as near as a man's cradle and his grave. Corsica, which gave birth to Napoleon, spreads out far and wide before the eyes; Elba is small. That, then, was the rocky strait-waistcoat that they confined the giant in. He burst it as easily as Samson burst the bonds of the Philistines. Then came his fall at Waterloo. On starting from Elba he was only an adventurer, like Murat, who, emulating Napoleon, started from Corsica with a handful of men for the conquest of Naples, and met a tragic end.

The sight of Elba raises before the excited imagination a *fata morgana;* namely, the picture of the rocky island far away in the African seas, St. Helena. Thus four islands curiously determined the fate of Napoleon—Corsica, England, Elba, and St. Helena. He himself was an island in the ocean of the world's history; *unico nel mondo,* as the honest Corsican sailor beside whom I stood speaking of Napoleon within sight of Corsica, said to me. "*Ma Signore,*" said he, "I know all that better than you, for I am his countryman;" and then, with the liveliest gestures, he gave me a sketch of the history of Napoleon, that interested me more in this scene than all the volumes of Thiers.—"And the nephew?"—"I say the *Napoleone Primo* was also the *unico.*" The sailor was very familiar with the history of his island, and knew the life of Sampiero, as well as that of Pasquale Paoli, Saliceti, and Pozzo di Borgo.

In the meantime it became dark. The stars shone magni-

ficently, and the waves became phosphorescent. High above
Corsica shone Venus, the *stellone* or great star, as the seamen
called it, and toward which the vessel held her course. We
sailed between Elba and Capraja, and hard by the rocks of the
latter. There the historian Paulus Diaconus lived of old in
banishment, as Seneca before him had passed eight long years of
banishment in Corsica. Capraja is a bare granite rock. A Genoese
tower stands picturesquely on a precipice; and the only inhabited place in the island, called likewise Capraja, hides itself
timidly behind the gigantic rock crowned by the fortress. The
white walls and white houses, the dry reddish rock, the great
desolateness and separation from all the world, give the impression as of some Syrian rock-perched city. Capraja, which the
bold Corsicans conquered in the time of Paoli, remained in the
possession of the Genoese when they sold Corsica to France; and
with Genoa the island then fell to the share of Piedmont.

Capraja then, with its lights, vanished from our sight, and we
neared the coast of Corsica, on which fire-lights glittered here
and there, till at length the ship steered straight for the lighthouse of Bastia. We were in the harbour, which is surrounded
by the town, having the old Genoese fort on the left, on the right
the Marina, and an amphitheatre of dark mountains high above.
A boat came alongside, and took the passengers who wished to
land.

Thus then I stood, for the first time, upon the island Corsica,
which had a powerful attraction for me as a child, when I looked
at it on the map. The first entrance upon a strange country,
especially if it be veiled in the deep mystery of night, is extremely
exciting to the curiosity and expectation, and first impressions
generally last for whole days. I confess my state of mind was
none of the happiest, and it was long before I could get over it.
We in Germany know little more of Corsica than that Napoleon
was born there, that Pasquale Paoli fought there heroically for
freedom, and that the Corsicans practise revenge for blood and
hospitality, and are the most daring banditti. I had brought
the obscurest ideas with me, but the first events were of a kind
that seemed to justify them.

The boat landed at the quay, on which stood a group of
Doganieri and sailors, lighted up by the uncertain glimmer of
hand-lanterns. The boatman sprang ashore. I have seen few
men of so unprepossessing an appearance; he wore the Phrygian
cap of red wool on his head, and a white bandage over one eye;

he was a Charon incarnate; and the groundless rage with which he bellowed at the passengers, swearing and inspecting the faces by the lantern, gave me at once a proof of the choleric temper of the Corsicans.

Those standing on the quay were engaged in eager conversation. I heard them telling that, a quarter of an hour ago, a Corsican had murdered his neighbour with three stabs of a dagger (*ammazzato! ammazzato!* a word that I have heard countless times in Corsica; *ammazzato con tre colpi di pugnale.*) What for? "Only in the heat of conversation; the *Sbirri* are after him; he will ·be by now in the *macchia.*" The *macchia* is the bush. I heard the word *macchia* in Corsica quite as often as *ammazzato*, or *tumbato*. "He is gone into the *macchia*," is equivalent to "he has turned bandit."

I felt some little horror, and the excitement caused by the anticipation of adventures. I was just going to hunt up a *locanda*, when a young man came up to me, and said in Tuscan, that he would lead me to an inn. I followed the friendly Italian, a sculptor from Carrara. No lights but the stars of heaven burned in the steep and narrow streets of Bastia. We knocked in vain at four locandas; no one would open the door. We knocked at the fifth; no one heard. "They will not open the door here," said the Carrarese, "for the landlord's daughter lies on the bier." We wandered about for an hour in the deserted streets; no one would hear our knocking. Is this, then, the boasted Corsican hospitality? Methinks, I am come into the city of death, and to-morrow I will write over the gate of Bastia, "Ye who enter in, let all your hopes vanish."

However, we determined to make another attempt. Roaming on, we fell upon a party of passengers, who had been as unfortunate as I. There were two Frenchmen, an Italian emigrant, and an Englishman. I joined them, and we again made the circuit of the locandas. This gave me no great idea of the industry and the civilisation of Corsica; for Bastia is the largest town in the island, having about 15,000 inhabitants. If the stranger found no reception even in the town, what must he expect in the inland country parts?

Now a body of *Sbirri*, or Corsican gens d'armes met us, brawny fellows with black beards, in blue close coats with white shoulder-points, and with their double-guns on their shoulders. We preferred our complaint to them. One offered to lead us to an old soldier who kept a tavern; there, he thought, we might find quarters. He led us to an old desolate house opposite the fort. We knocked till we wakened the soldier-landlord, and he appeared at the window. At the same moment some one ran past us, our Sbirro was after him without saying a word, and both had vanished in the darkness of the night. What was the matter? What was the meaning of this race? After a while, the Sbirro returned; he had thought the man running might be the murderer. "But," said he, "he is on the mountains by this, or a fisherman has ferried him over to Elba or Capraja. A short time ago we shot Arrighi in the mountains, and also Massoni and Serafino. That was a dreadful battle, that with Arrighi; it cost us five men."

The old soldier landlord appeared, and led us into a large and very unclean room. We were glad enough to sit down to table, and heartily enjoyed our supper of good wheaten bread and fresh sheep's milk cheese, with excellent Corsican wine, which is fiery, like the Spanish. This Homeric traveller's feast was lightened up by a smoky oil-lamp, and cheered by good-humour. Many a good draught was quaffed to the honour of the heroes of Corsica, and one bottle after another brought out from the corner by the landlord. We were four nations together, Corsican, French, German, and Lombard. I once mentioned the name of Louis Bonaparte, and put a question— the company grew suddenly mute, and the sprightly Frenchmen put on a downcast look.

By degrees the morning grey appeared outside. We left the *casa* of the old Corsican, strolled down to the sea, and fed our eyes on the early morning brilliancy that rested upon it. The sun rose rapidly, and lighted up the three islands that are seen from Bastia—Capraja, Elba, and the small Monte Cristo. The fourth island of this series is Pianosa, the ancient Planasia, in which Tiberius caused the grandson of Augustus, Agrippa Postumus, to be strangled; it is flat, as its name says, and therefore not to be seen from hence. The constant view of these three blue island-mountains on the edge of the sea, makes the walks about Bastia doubly beautiful.

I sat down on the walls of the old fort, and looked down upon the sea and the little harbour of the town, in which hardly six ships lay at anchor. The picturesque brown coast-hills, the green heights, with their dense olive-groves, little chapels on the seashore, solitary grey towers from the time of Genoese rule, the sea in all the splendour of southern colouring, and the feeling of standing on a strange island lost amid that sea—all this left an ineffaceable impression on my mind.

When I left the fort, to remove now by the light of day into a locanda, I had a sufficiently strange, wild, and queer scene again before me. A crowd before the fort surrounded two carabineers on horseback, who had a man tied to a string, who was practising the queerest jumps and imitating all the movements of a horse. I saw that the man was crazy, and possessed by the illusion that he was a fine horse. None of the standers-by laughed, though the poor creature's capers were strange enough. All stood solemn and silent; and when I saw these people thus silent in the presence of misery, I took heart for the first time on this island, and said to myself that the Corsicans were no barbarians. The horsemen at length rode off with the madman, who travelled at the end of the line like a horse along the whole street, and appeared happy in mind. This method of getting him to his destination by making use of his fixed idea, seemed to me at once cunning and naïve.

CHAPTER II.

THE TOWN OF BASTIA.

IF not greatly distinguished by grandeur, the situation of Bastia is at least surprising. The town lies in an amphitheatre round the little harbour; the sea forms here no gulf, but only a landing-place or *Cala*. The right side of the harbour is closed by a gigantic black rock, popularly called Leone, as being like a lion. Upon it stands the dismal Genoese fort, or dungeon. On the left the quay runs out into a *molo*, bearing a little lighthouse on its point. The town rises in terraces above the harbour, with high tower-shaped, closely crowded houses, with many balconies: above the town tower the green mountains, with some abandoned convents and beautiful olive-groves; there are also orchards of oranges, citrons, and almonds in abundance.

Bastia has its name from the bastion built there by the Genoese. The town is not ancient; at least neither Pliny, nor Strabo, nor Ptolemy mention any town upon its site. Formerly there was there the little *marina* of the neighbouring village, Cardo. Then, in the year 1383, the Genoese governor Lionello Lomellino built the donjon-keep, or castle, round which a

division of the town, the Terra Nuova, soon clustered; the lower
original town was now called the Terra Vecchia. The two
quarters still form two separate cantons. The Genoese afterwards removed the seat of their Corsican government from
Biguglia to Bastia, and there resided the Fregosos, the Spinolas,
the Dorias (eleven Dorias governed Corsica during more than
400 years), the Fiescos, the Cibbàs, the Giustiniani, Negri,
Vivaldi, Fornari, and so many other nobles of renowned Genoese
families. When, under French rule, Corsica was divided in the
year 1797 into two departments, named after the rivers Golo and
Liamone, Bastia remained the capital of the department of Golo.
In the year 1811 the two divisions were united again, and the
smaller town of Ajaccio became the capital of the island. Bastia
cannot yet get over her vexation at having sunk into a *sous préfecture* after being the capital of the island; but in industry, commerce, and intelligence, she is without doubt the leading town of
Corsica. The mutual jealousy of the Bastinese and the citizens
of Ajaccio is almost absurd, and would appear the ridiculous
pettiness of cits, did one not know that the division of Corsica
into the land on the nearer and on the farther side of the mountains, is historical and very ancient, and the character of the
inhabitants of the two halves is also fundamentally different.
Beyond the mountains which divide Corsica into a northern and
southern half, there is far greater barbarism; there every one
goes armed;—on this side there is more civilisation, more agriculture, more gentle manners.

The Terra Vecchia of Bastia has now become, strictly speaking, a *Terra Nuova*, for it contains the best streets. The hand-
somest is the Via Traversa, a street only a few years old, of six
or seven storied houses, that are still being built, curving towards
the sea. Its position reminded me of the finest street that I
have ever seen, the Strada Balbi and Nuova, in Genoa. But the
houses, though palace-like, have no art nor noble materials. Corsica has the finest kinds of stone in almost incredible abundance,
marble, porphyry, serpentine, alabaster, and granite, of the most
precious kind, yet they are scarcely at all used. Nature lies
here neglected on all sides, as a fair spellbound princess.

A Palais de Justice at least is being built in the Via Traversa,
for the arcades of which I saw the columns hewn in the marble
quarries of Corte. Besides this, I looked in vain for marble
decorations; yet, who would believe it?—the whole town of Bastia is paved with marble, a reddish stone, that is quarried at

Brando. I know not if it be true, but I have heard say that Bastia has the most excellent pavement in the whole world.

Notwithstanding its length and breadth, the Via Traversa is the most lifeless of all the streets of Bastia. All public life is concentrated upon the Piazza Favaleui, the quay, and the fort in the Terra Nuova. Of an evening the *beau monde* promenades on the great Piazza San Nicolao, by the sea, where the *sous-préfecture* and the supreme court of justice have their buildings.

The stranger meets here not a single specimen of beautiful architecture, but finds his entertainment solely in the charming walks by the sea, and up to the olive-shaded mountains. The churches are often large and richly decorated, but externally heavy, and with no remarkable art. The cathedral, with many a Genoese lord's grave, stands in the Terra Nuova, and in the Terra Vecchia the handsome church of St. John the Baptist. I name it only on account of the grave of Marbœuf. Marbœuf ruled Corsica for sixteen years, and was the friend of Charles Bonaparte, the warm adherent of Paoli, and he opened the career of Napoleon, by procuring him admission to the military school of Brienne. His grave in the church has no inscription, the original one having been obliterated at the time of the Paolistic revolution against France. The Corsican patriots then wrote on Marbœuf's gravestone:—"The monument which infamous mendacity and venal flattery had raised to the tyrant of groaning Corsica, has now been destroyed by the true freedom and the free truth of united, rejoicing Corsica." After Napoleon had become emperor, Madame Letitia wished to grant to Marbœuf's widow the first rank of an imperial court-lady, but happily Napoleon avoided so great a want of tact, seeing it to be indecorous to offer Madame Marbœuf a servile position in the family which owed so much to her husband's patronage. He allowed the son of Marbœuf a yearly pension of 10,000 francs, but the young general fell at the head of his regiment in Russia. The little theatre of Bastia is a monument of Marbœuf, who had it built at his expense.

The grave of another Frenchman of note lies in St. John's, that of Count Boissieux, who died in the year 1738. He was a nephew of the celebrated Villars, but he had no success in the conduct of war.

But what had for me far the greatest interest in Bastia, was the life on the harbour, which to be sure is not large, and the doings on the markets.

Here the fish-market. I failed not every morning to pay my visit to the sea animals, and when the fishermen had caught any thing out of the common way, they kindly shewed it me, and said:—" This, signore, is called a *murena*, and this is the *razza*, and that the *pesce spada*, and the *pesce prete*, and the *triglia*, which is of such a fine red, and the *capone*, and the *gronyo*." In the corner there, not belonging to the fishmongers guild, sit the lagoon-fishers; the eastern coast of Corsica has great lagoons, partially separated by narrow sand-banks from the sea, with which they are however connected. The fishermen catch there, in rush baskets, large and well-tasting fish, lots of eels, and *mugini, ragni*, and *soglie*. The best of all fishes is the murena, which resembles a serpent formed of the finest porphyry; it follows the lobster (*legusta*), into which it sucks itself in; the lobster devours the *scorpena*, and the *scorpena* devours the murena. Here we have the clever puzzle about getting the wolf, lamb, and cabbage over a river. I am not diplomatist enough to solve this intricate war of the three fishes; the fishermen often take all three in one and the same net. Many tunny-fish and sardines are taken in the Corsican gulfs, especially about Ajaccio and Bonifazio. The Romans did not like Corsican slaves because they were too high-spirited; but the fishes of Corsica appeared on the tables of the great, and even Juvenal praises them.*

The market on the Piazza Favaleui affords in the morning a fresh, gay, and lively scene. There sit the vegetable and fruit women with their baskets, from which the beautiful fruits of the south peep smiling forth. You have only to go to this market-place to learn what fruits the climate of Corsica produces; there are apples and pears, peaches and apricots, and all kinds of plums; here green almonds, oranges and lemons, pomegranates, potatoes, and bouquets; there green or blue figs, and the never-failing *pomi d'oro* (pommes d'amour); there the finest melons, a soldo apiece; and in August also Muscatel grapes from Cape Corso. The women and girls come down in the early morning from the villages in the neighbourhood of Bastia, bringing the fruit to the town. One may see many a fair form amongst them. One evening, walking along the shore towards Pietra Nera, I met a young girl returning to her village with an empty fruit-basket on her head. "*Buona sera*"—"*Evviva, siore.*" We now fell into a brisk conversation. The pretty

* Juv. v. 92. Mullus erit domini, quem misit Corsica.

Corsican told me with the greatest simplicity her heart's secret;
her mother was pressing her to give her hand to a young man
whom she did not like. " Why do you not like him?"—
" Because his *ingegno* does not please me. Ah, Madonna!"—
" Is he jealous?"—" *Come un diavolo.* Ah, Madonna! I was
near running away to Ajaccio." As we were talking thus, a
man came towards us going to the well with a pitcher in his
hand. " If you would like to drink water," said he, " wait a
minute till I come back. And you, Paolina, come to me by
and by. I have something to say to you about your marriage."
" See," said the girl to me, " that is one of my relations.
They are all good to me, and wish me a good-evening whenever
I pass their way; and none of them will hear of my marrying
Antonio." We were now near the house where she lived.
Paolina turned to me suddenly and said in a grave tone, " Now,
Siore, you must leave me; for if you were to come with me into
my village, people would say what they should not (*faranne
mal grido*). But come to-morrow if you like, and be my mother's
guest, and then we will send you on to our relations; for we
have friends enough over the whole Cape Corso." I turned
homewards, and as I gazed at the unspeakably beautiful sea and
the still silent mountains, on which the herdsmen had just begun
to kindle their fires, a feeling quite Homeric came over me, and
I was reminded of the hospitable Phæacians of old and of
Nausicaa.

The Corsican women wear the *mandile*, a cloth of any colour,
covering the forehead, lying smoothly on the head and wound
round the back-hair, so that the hair is not to be seen. The
mandile is in use all over Corsica; it looks quite Oriental or
Moorish, and is extremely old, female forms on Etruscan vases
being represented as wearing it. It becomes young girls well,
but elderly women far less so, as it gives them the appearance of Jewish women. The men's head-dress is the pointed
brown or red *barretto*, the ancient Phrygian cap, worn by Paris,
the son of Priam. In marble representations of the Trojan
prince, he wears this barretto; so does the Persian Mithras in
the various symbolical representations that I have seen of the
sacrifice to Mithras. With the Romans, the Phrygian cap was
the symbol of barbarians in general; it is worn by the Dacian
prisoners on the triumphal arch of Trajan, who now stand on
the arch of Constantine; and by other barbarian kings and
slaves of the Sarmatians and Asiatic tribes, represented in.

triumphal processions. This same Phrygian cap was worn by the Doges of Venice as a badge of their dignity.

The Corsican women carry all weights on their heads, and it is almost incredible what weights they manage to carry; yet, when thus burdened, they often hold the spindle in their hand and spin as they walk along. It is a very picturesque sight to see the Bastinese women carrying their metal two-eared water-pitchers on their heads. These pitchers are almost like antique holy-water vessels; I only saw them in Bastia. Beyond the mountains they draw water in stone pitchers of rude shape, yet preserving a resemblance to Etruscan forms.

"Do you see that woman with the water-can on her head?" "I do; what is there remarkable about her?" "She might, perhaps, have now been a princess of Sweden, and consort of a king." "Madre di Dio!" "See that Paese on the hill, that is Cardo. The common soldier, Bernadotte, once fell in love with the daughter of a peasant of Cardo. The parents repulsed the poor starveling wretch. But the *povero diavolo* became king, and if he had married the lass she would have been queen. Now she goes about carrying water on her head, and grieving that she is not a Swedish princess." It was on the road from Bastia to San Fiorenzo, that Bernadotte worked on the roads as a common soldier. At the Ponte d'Ucciani he was made corporal, and highly pleased with his charge; he now inspected the workers as a road bailiff; then he copied the register-rolls for Imbrico, the *greffier* of the court. There are a great lot of these in his handwriting preserved in the archives of Paris.

It was at the Golo bridge, several miles from Bastia, that Massena was made corporal. Yes, Corsica is a wonderful island! Many a one roamed on the lonely mountains here, never dreaming that he should some time wear a crown. The beginning was made by Pope Formosus, in the ninth century, who was a native of the Corsican village Vivario; then, in the sixteenth century, came Lazaro, a native of Bastia, a renegade, and afterwards Dey of Algiers; the first Empress of Morocco, in the time of Napoleon, was a Corsican; and Napoleon himself was the first Emperor of Europe.

CHAPTER III.

ENVIRONS OF BASTIA.

How charming are the walks here in the early morning, or in the glow of evening! In a few steps you are beside the great element or in the mountains, and in either place away from the world, and in the most blissful loneliness of nature. By the sea there are thick olive groves. I often threw myself down there on a luxurious secret place, beside a little family burying-vault with a Moorish dome, and gazed at the three islands over the sea. The air is so sunny here, so still and healthy; and wherever the eye turns it meets every where holiday stillness and solitude; desolate brown rocks on the coast covered with prickly cactus, lonely watch-towers, neither man nor bird upon the water, and blue mountains right and left—warm and sunny.

I ascended the mountains nearest to Bastia. There is a charming view of the town, the sea, and the islands. Vineyards and olive-grounds, orange-trees, little country villas of the most fanciful shapes, here and there a fan-palm, graveyard-chapels under cypresses, and ruins quite overwhelmed with ivy, lie spread around you. The paths are toilsome and laborious; you walk over rolling stones between walls, bramble hedges, ivy festoons, or rank thistles. The views towards the coast, and south of Bastia, surprised me; for there the mountains, which, like almost all the mountains in Corsica, are of the finest pyramidal forms, recede further from the coast and sink into a smiling plain. The great lagoon of Biguglia lies picturesquely there, girded by sedge, still and dead, scarce furrowed by a narrow fishing-boat. The sun was just setting when I enjoyed this picture. The pool shone rose-coloured, and the mountains likewise, and the sea was overspread by the evening glow, with a single ship gliding over it. The stillness of a wide view tranquillizes the soul. On the left hand, I saw the convent of Sant Antonio beneath olives and cypresses; two monks were sitting in the porch, and some black-veiled nuns just then came out of the church. I once saw a picture representing a Sicilian vesper-hour, and recalled it in a moment when I found the reality here.

Descending now to the road, I came upon the way leading to Cervione; herdsmen were just driving home their herd of goats, and riders on red ponies darted past me, wild-looking fellows with bronzed faces, all with the Phrygian cap on their heads, the dark-brown woollen Corsican doublet thrown round them, and the double gun on their shoulder. I often saw two of them, one be-hind another, on the same pony, or man and wife together, and never without holding the great parasol over them. The para-sol is indispensable here; I often saw men as well as women sitting in the sea near the shore, the women clothed, and the men naked, and thus they sat comfortably in the water holding the parasol over them, as merry as a grig. The women ride here as well as the men, and are expert upon the animal. The man always has the *Zucca*, or round gourd-bottle slung round him, and often a *Zaino*, or small goatskin, too ; and round his waist the *carchera*, a leathern girdle, in which his cartouches are held.

A party of men returning to the town from their field-labour was walking before me.   I attached myself to them, and learned that they were not Corsicans, but Italians from the continent. More than 5000 labourers annually come over to the island from the Italian terra firma, especially from Liguria, the territory of Lucca, and from Piombino, to do the field-labour for the lazy Corsicans.   The Corsicans have to the present time maintained their well-founded reputation of shrinking from work, in which they are thoroughly unlike other brave mountain tribes, such as the Samnites.   These foreign labourers are universally called here Lucchesi.   I have had proof of the deep-seated contempt the Corsicans feel for these poor and industrious men, because they leave their homes and work in the sweat of their brow, ex-posed to the fever-bringing air, to take home some little savings to their families.   I often heard the word Lucchese employed as a term of abuse; indeed, in the mountains of the interior especially, all field-labour is hated, and deemed unworthy of a free man.   The Corsican is there a herdsman, according to the old usages of their fathers, and contents himself with his goats, the produce of his chestnut trees, the fresh draught of his spring, and the spoils of the chase.

I learned at the same time, that Corsica is at present the abode of many Italian democrats, who fled thither after the unsuccessful revolution. There were in the summer about 150 of them dispersed over the island—men of every rank ; most of them lived in Bastia. I had the opportunity of making the

I

acquaintance of the leading exiles, and accompanying them in their walks. Theirs was a company as varied as political Italy— Lombards, Venetians, Neapolitans, Romans, and Florentines. I discovered that, in a land of no culture, Italians and Germans feel immediately a mutual attraction, and have a home-feeling for one another on neutral ground. The universality of the fates of nations in the year 1848, too, has broken through many partitions, and fostered certain theories and views of life, in which the individual of whatever nation is equally at home. I found, among the exiles in Corsica, men and youths of all classes, as with us in a similar state of society, some with heads of exalted sanguine ideas, and others again men of positive experience, principles available in life, and clear intellect.

The world is now full of political exiles of the European nations; they are especially dispersed over the islands which are formed by nature for such refuges. Many exiles reside in the Ionian and Greek islands, many in Sardinia and Corsica, many in the Channel islands, and most of all in Great Britain. The fate that these exiles suffer is a universal and European one, the locality only varies; and the political fate of banishment is as old as the history of states. I was vividly reminded how, in older times, the islands of Mediterranean, such as Samos, Delos, Ægina, Corcyra, Lesbos, Rhodes, were the refuges of the political exiles of Greece, as often as they were driven by revolutions from Athens or Thebes, Corinth, or Sparta; I thought of the many exiles, banished especially in the Imperial time, from Rome to islands, as Agrippa Postumus to Planasia, near Corsica and the philosopher Seneca to Corsica itself. And Corsica has been in all ages a place of refuge as well as of banishment, and thus in the strict sense of the word, a bandit-island; which it is to the present day. Homeless in the mountains roam the avengers of blood; homeless in the towns live the political exiles. The ban rests upon both equally, and a prison, if not execution, would await them if the law could reach them.

Corsica fulfils towards these poor Italian exiles something further than her hallowed religion of hospitality—namely, the religion of gratitude. For the exiled Corsicans met with the most hospitable reception in all parts of Italy in bygone ages and her political refugees were seen in Rome, Florence, Venice and Naples. The French government has hitherto liberally tolerated these guests in the island. The retirement of the island forces the refuges to a contemplative, and dignified, quie life. For this they may after all be happier off than their brothers in misfortune in Jersey or London.

CHAPTER IV.

FRANCESCO MARMOCCHI, THE FLORENTINE.

Hic sola hæc duo sunt, exsul et exsilium.

SENECA ON CORSICA.

Οἱ προσκυνοῦντες τὴν Ἀδράστειαν σοφοί.

ÆSCHYLUS, *Prometheus*, v. 936.

THEY told me at the bookseller's Fabiani, to whom I went to look for a geography of the island, that one was now in the press, the author of which was an exiled Florentine, Francesco Marmocchi. I immediately sought out this gentleman, and made in him one of my most valuable Italian acquaintances. I found a man of prepossessing exterior, of an age verging towards forty; he was sitting in his study buried among books. Perhaps there are not many refugees' lodgings of this peaceable character. On his shelves there were the best classical works, Humboldt's Cosmos among others, which I saw with no small pleasure, and engravings on the walls representing Florentine views, and an excellent copy of a Perugino. I recognised in all this not the retreat of a merely learned man, but that of a Florentine of fine culture. There can hardly be a greater contrast than between Florence and Corsica; and it felt very strange to me at first, after a six weeks' life before Raffael's Madonnas at Florence, to be thrown immediately among the Corsican banditti. Yet Corsica is an island of enchanting beauty; and though banishment, were it in Paradise itself, would be banishment all the same, yet here a student of nature especially may find comfort in the natural glories, as Seneca did. Francesco Marmocchi may in full measure apply to himself all that Seneca writes from his Corsican banishment to his mother Helvia, of the consolations of science and the contemplation of nature ; and this former Florentine professor appeared to me, in his noble, dignified retirement, and in company of the Muses of his studies, as by far the happiest of all exiles.

Francesco Marmocchi had been minister of Tuscany with

Guerazzi in the revolutionary period, and subsequently secretary of state. He was more fortunate than his political friend; for he escaped from Florence to Rome, and from Rome to Corsica, where he had already lived three years. His never-resting activity, and the Stoical cheerfulness with which he bears up against his exile, afford a proof of his masculine vigour. He is one of the most distinguished and genial of the Italian geographers. Besides his great work, a Universal Geography in six quarto volumes, which is being reprinted, he has written a special geography of Italy in two volumes, a historical geography of the ancient world, the middle ages, and modern times, a natural history of Italy, and other works. I found him correcting the press of his small Geography of Corsica, an excellent hand-book, which it is pity he has had to write in French. This book is published by Fabiani in Bastia, and I owe to it many valuable notices about Corsica.

One morning we went before sunrise up to the mountains of Cardo. There, in the midst of verdant scenery, let us take the geographer himself as our guide and interpreter of nature, and receive instruction about the island from him. Here I follow his geography almost word for word.

Corsica owes its whole existence to a successive conglomeration of upheaved masses. During a long period of time there have been three great volcanic processes, which account for the bizarre and abrupt contour of the land. The three elevations are easy to distinguish. The first land-masses elevated are those that comprise the entire south-western side. The first elevation took place in a direction from north-west to south-east; signs of it are the great mountain-ridges running parallel to one another, in a north-easterly and south-westerly direction, down towards the sea, and forming the principal headlands on the western coast. Thus the axis of Corsica was then a different one, and the islands in the straits of Bonifazio, as well as some of the north-eastern part of Sardinia, stood in connexion with Corsica. The substance of this primal upheaval consists in great part of primitive granite; at the period, then, of this most ancient revolution, the island displayed no spark of life.

The second upheaval took place in a direction from south-west to north-east; and of this also a considerable part consists of granitoids. But the further you advance toward the north-east, the more does the prmitive granite pass into ophiolitic formations. However, the second upheaval is barely distinguishable.

It obviously destroyed in great part the northern ridge of the former; but Corsican geology has preserved barely any traces of it.

The almost total destruction of the southern part of the first upheaval, was the undoubted effect produced by the third and last upheaval, by which the island received its present form. It took place in a direction from north to south. As long as the mass of this last elevation did not come into contact with the masses formed by the proceeding elevations, it preserved a regular direction, as the mountain chain of Cape Corso shows. But the rocky ridges piled up to the south, had to be broken through with a tremendous shock; the upheaval overthrew them, altered their direction, and was interrupted itself in several places, as is proved by the mouths of valleys leading from the interior to the plain on the eastern coast, which have become the bed of streams flowing into the sea on this side, the Bevinco, Golo, Tavignano, Fiumorbo, and others.

The strata of this third upheaval are originally ophiolitic and calcareous, covered again in various places by secondary formations.

The 'primitive land-masses which occupy the south and west of the island, consist almost entirely of granite. They include on their boundary-line a few strata of gneiss and slate. The granite is covered almost everywhere; which is an evident proof that the period of its release preceded the time when masses were formed in the depths of the ocean, and deposited themselves in horizontal strata upon the crystalline granite masses. Layers of porphyry and eurite penetrated the granite; the mountains Cinto, Vagliorba, and Pertusato, the highest in Niolo, are crowned by a decided porphyry formation, which covers the granite. These porphyries again are pierced by greenstone of two or three feet thick.

The intermediate masses occupy the whole of Cape Corso and the east of the island. They consist of bluish-grey limestone, massy talc, stalactites, serpentine, euphotides, quartz, feldspar, and porphyries.

The tertiary stage shows itself only in isolated strips, as at San Fiorenzo, Volpajola, Aleria, and Bonifazio. These display many fossils of animals of low organization, as sea-urchins, pectens, polyps, and many other petrifactions in the calcareous strata.

As to the plains of the eastern coast, such as those of Bigug-

lia, Mariana, and Aleria, this formation is diluvial, from the
period when the floods destroyed a great number of animal
genera. In the vicinity of Bastia has been found among diluvial fossils, the head of a Lagomys—a little hare without tail,
that still lives in Siberia.

Corsica has no volcano, but traces of extinct ones near Porto
Vecchio, Aleria, Balistro, S. Manza, and other places.

It appears scarce credible that an island like Corsica, lying
so near Sardinia, so near Tuscany, and, above all, so near the
iron-island Elba, can be so poor in metals as it really is. Numerous signs of metal veins are indeed found everywhere; here
of iron or copper; there of lead, of antimony, magnesia, black-
lead; or of quicksilver, cobalt, gold, and silver. But they are
illusory, as Gueymard the engineer has shown in his work on
the geology and mineralogy of Corsica.

The only metallic veins of importance that can be worked,
are the iron veins of Olmeta and Farinole on Cape Corso, an
iron vein near Venzolasca, the copper vein of Linguizzetta, the
antimony vein of Ersa on Cape Corso, and the magnesia, near
Alesani.

On the other hand, Corsica is an inexhaustible treasure-house
of the rarest and most precious stones—a geological Elysium; yet
they lie unemployed; no one steals the treasure. It will be
worth while here to arrange these splendid stones in detail, as
geology has hitherto arranged them.

1. GRANITES.

    Red granite, like the oriental granite, between Orto and
        the lake of Creno.

    Coral-red granite, near Olmiccia.

    Rose-coloured granite, near Cargese.

    Red granite with light violet, near Aitone.

    Rosy granite of Carbuccia.

    Rosy granite of Porto.

    Rose-coloured granite, near Algajola.

    Granite, containing garnets (of a size of a nut), near Viz-
        zavona.

2. PORPHYRIES.

    Variegated porphyry, at Niolo.

    Black porphyry with rosy spots, near Porto Vecchio.

    Pale yellow porphyry with rosy feldspar, near Porto Vec-
        chio.

    Grey-green porphyry with amethyst, on the Restonica.

3. SERPENTINES.

Very hard green or transparent serpentines, near Corte, Matra, and Bastia.

4. EURITES, AMPHIBOLITES, AND EUPHOTIDES.

Globulous eurite, near Curso and Girolata, in the Niolo, &c.

Globulous amphibolite, commonly called orbicular granite (the globules consist of feldspar and amphiboles in concentric layers), in isolated blocks, near Sollucaro, on the Taravo, in the valley Campolaggio, &c.

Amphibolite, with crystals of black hornblende in a white feldspar, near Olmeta, near Levie and Mela.

Euphotides, called also *verde di Corsica*, and *verde d'Orezza*, in the bed of the Fiumalto, and in the valley of Bevinco.

5. JASPER AND AGATES.

Jasper (in granites and porphyries), in the Niolo, and in the valley of Stagno.

Agates (likewise in granites and porphyries), in the same situations.

6. MARBLE AND ALABASTER.

White statuary marble, of dazzling beauty, near Ortiporio, Casacconi, Borgo de Cavignano, &c.

Bluish grey marble, near Corte.

Yellow alabaster, in the valley of S. Lucia, near Bastia.

White alabaster, semi-transparent, foliated and veined, in a cave behind Tuara, in the gulf of Girolata.

CHAPTER V.

A SECOND LECTURE.

IT was an instructive lecture that Francesco Marmocchi, formerly professor of natural history, formerly minister of Tuscany, and now a *fuoruscito* and poor recluse, gave me, high up on the green mountain Cardo, in the very rosiest hour of morn, while we had the beautiful Mediterranean under our feet, whose colour was just as Dante said, *color del oriental zaffiro.*

" See," said Marmocchi, " the blue streak you see over there is beautiful Tuscany."

" O yes! I see Tuscany distinctly ; I distinctly see beautiful

Florence, and right into the *Uffizj*, where stand the statues of the great Florentines, Giotto, Orgagna, Nicola Pisano, Dante, Petrarch, Bocaccio, Macchiavelli, Galileo, and the divine Michael Angelo.   Three thousand Croats are just walking beneath the statues, the air is so clear one can see and hear every thing. Hear, Francesco, what an excellent verse the stone Michael Angelo speaks to the Dante :

> How I rejoice in stone to live and sleep,
> So long as these degraded times shall be ;   '
> To see naught, hear naught, this now comforts me ;
> Then wake me not; speak softly, ah! and weep !"

, But look how richly this brown rock has decked itself with flowers ! On its head it bears a glorious thicket of myrtles cover-ed with white blossom, and its breast is wreathed by a triple chain of favours, ivy, bramble, and white clematis.   There are no prettier garlands than these clematis wreaths make, with their white tufts of flowers and fine leaves ; the ancients loved them above all others, and liked in Horatian hours to wear them on their head.

In a circuit of a few steps, what a fulness of plants near one another !   There is rosemary and broom, here wild asparagus, beside it a tall clump of lilac-blossomed heath ; here again the poisonous spurge, which drops the milkwhite juice when broken ; and here the sympathetic rock-rose, with beautiful yellow flow-ers, which gradūally all fall off when you cut off a single branch. There again stands, strange and queer like a Moorish heathen, the prickly cactus, beside it the oleander, the cork-tree, the lentiscus, the wild fig ; and at their feet bloom the well-known children of my native land, the scabious, the geranium, and the mallow.   How fine, penetrating, and invigorating are the odours exhaled by all the flowering herbs, rue, lavender, mint, and all ' these labiates !   Did not Napoleon say in St. Helena, as his melancholy thoughts returned again to his beautiful island home, " All was better there, even to the very odour of the ground ; by its fragrance alone I should recognise Corsica with my eyes shut ? "

Hear we now something from Marmocchi relative to the bo-tany of Corsica in general.

Corsica is the most central province of the great vegetable kingdom in the Mediterranean zone ; a kingdom characterised by its fulness in fragrant Labiates and graceful Caryophylleæ.

These plants cover all parts of the island, and perfume its air at all seasons.

From its central position the Corsican flora connects itself with that of all the other provinces of that great vegetable kingdom. Through Cape Corso it connects itself with the plants of Liguria; through the eastern coast with that of Tuscany and Rome; through the western and southern coast with the flora of Provence, Spain, Barbary, Sicily, and the east; and lastly, through the very high and mountainous region of the interior, with the growths of the Alps and Pyrenees. What a wondrous richness, and what a surprising multiformity in the Corsican vegetation! It is a richness and multiformity that incalculably exalts the beauty of the various districts of this island, which are so picturesque even from their nature and soil.

Some of the forests on the mountain sides are as beautiful as the finest in Europe; the two best are those of Aitone and Vizzavona. Moreover, many provinces of Corsica are covered with immense chestnut woods, the trees of which are as gigantic and fruitful as the finest on the Apennines or on Etna. Olive plantations, in extent like forests, crown the hills and line the valleys that extend towards the sea, or lie exposed to its influence. Everywhere, even to the rugged and craggy sides of the high mountains, the vines and orchards climb and spread out to view their green leaves and purple grapes. Fruitful plains, golden with rich harvests, extend along the coasts of the island, and wheat and rye here and there adorn the mountain slopes with their fresh green, that contrasts so picturesquely with the deeper green of the thickets, and the cold tone of the stones and the bare rock.

The maple and walnut thrive, like the chestnut, in the valleys and on the heights of Corsica; the cypress and sea-pine love the less high regions; the forests are full of cork-trees and evergreen oaks; the strawberry-tree and myrtle become regular trees. The pyrus, and especially the wild oleaster, cover wide spaces on the hills. The evergreen privet and the Corsican and Spanish genista are mingled with various, but equally beautiful, heaths; among these may be distinguished the *Erica arborea*, which frequently reaches an extraordinary height.

In the tract watered by the overflowing of the rivers and brooks, grows the genista of Mount Etna, with its beautiful golden flowers, the cisti, lentisci, and turpentine-tree, wherever the earth is not disturbed by the hand of man. Lower down towards the plains, there is no dingle or valley but is over-shadowed by the graceful rose-bay, whose boughs, towards the sea-coast, fraternize with those of the tamarind.

The fan-palm grows on the rocks on the sea-coast, and the date-palm, probably imported from Afr.ca, on the best protected points of the coast. The *Cactus opuntia*, and the American *Agave*, grow everywhere in warm, dry, rocky places.

What shall I say of the splendid cotyledons, of the fine legu-mínous plants, the great verbenaceæ, the glorious purple fox-gloves that adorn the mountains of the island? and of the mallows, the orchids, liliaceæ, solaneæ, centaureæ, and thistles —plants which so well adorn the hot sunny, or the cool shady, districts in which their natural sympathies cause them to grow?

The fig, pomegranate, and vine, afford good fruit in Corsica, even if not tended by the husbandman; and the climate and soil of the coasts of this beautiful island are so favourable to the lemon and orange, and other trees of this family, that they form regular woods.

The almond, cherry, plum, apple, pear, peach, and apricot, and in general all the European fruit-trees, are common here. In the hottest parts of the island, the fruits of the carob and jujube trees, and of the medlar of several species, come to perfect matu-rity.

Lastly, the sugar-cane, cotton, tobacco, ananas, madder, and even indigo, might be introduced with success in the suitable districts for each respectively, without much trouble; in a word, Corsica might be to France a Mediterranean little India.

This very glorious vegetation of the island is favoured by the climate. The Corsican climate has three zones of temperature, graduated according to the elevation of the ground. The first climatic zone rises from the sea level to a height of 580 metres (1903 feet); the second, from thence to the height of 1950 metres (6398 feet); the third, thence to the summit of the mountains.

The first zone, namely, the sea-coast in general, is as warm as the parallel coasts of Italy and Spain. It has, properly speaking, only two seasons, spring and summer; the thermometer rarely descends here two or three degrees below the freezing-point, and then only for a few hours. On all the coasts the sun is warm even in January, but the nights and the shade are cool at every season. The sky is overclouded only at intervals; the south-east wind alone, the harsh scirocco, brings prolonged fogs, which are dispersed again by the violent south-wester, or libeccio. Upon the moderate cold of January follows soon a dog-day heat of eight months, and the temperature rises from 50° to 72°, and even 90° in the shade. It is a misfortune to the vegetation when it does not rain in March or April, and no unfrequent case either; but the Corsican trees have generally hard and tough leaves, which resist drought—as the oleander, myrtle, cistus, lentiscus, and oleaster. In Corsica, as in all hot climates, the watery and shady districts of the levels are almost pestilential; it is impossible to walk there in the evening without catching a long and severe fever, which, if total change of air be not resorted to, may end in dropsy and death.

The second climatic zone of the island corresponds to the climate of France, especially of Burgundy and Brittany. The snow that appears there in November sometimes lasts twenty days; but, remarkably enough, it does no damage to the olive up to the elevation of 1160 metres (3806 feet), but renders it yet more fruitful. The chestnut appears to be the characteristic tree of this zone; for it stops at a height of 1950 metres (6398 feet), and then yields to the green oaks, pines, beeches, box, and juniper. In this climate, the majority of the people live in scattered villages, on mountain slopes and in valleys.

The third climate is cold and stormy as that of Norway, during eight months in the year. The only inhabited places in this zone are the Niolo, and the two forts of Vivario and Vizzavona. Beyond these inhabited places, the eye can discern no other vegetation than pines clinging to grey rocks. There dwell the vulture and the wild sheep, and there is the storehouse and birthplace of the many streams that rush down to the plains below.

Corsica may thus be considered as a pyramid rising in gradations of three horizontal steps, of which the lowest is warm and moist, the upmost cold and dry, and the middle one partakes of both qualities.

CHAPTER VI.

LEARNED MEN.

On contemplating the series of remarkable men whom Corsica has produced in barely a hundred years, one cannot but be astonished that so small and so thinly peopled an island is so rich in the production of great men. The statesmen and generals are of European renown; less renowned certainly are her scientific talents, who, considering the nature of the island, and of its iron history, could not but occupy a secondary place.

But science also has, in these latter years, educated many excellent forces of native growth, and names such as Pompei, Renucci, Savelli, Raffaelli, Giubaga, Salvatore Viale, Caraffa, and Gregori, are the pride of Corsica. It is remarkable that most of the brilliant literary talent belongs to the profession of advocates. They have distinguished themselves especially in jurisprudence, and the history of their country.

Especially distinguished is Giovanni Carlo Gregori, one of the most meritorious men in Corsica, whose memory will never be extinguished. He was born at Bastia, in the year 1797, of a leading family of the island. Devoting himself to the study of the law, he became by steps auditor at Bastia, examining magistrate at Ajaccio, and judge first at the royal court at Riom, and then at the court of appeal at Lyons, where he was active also as president of the academy of sciences, and died on the 27th May, 1852. Besides his extensive studies on Roman law, he was incessantly occupied by his patriotic enthusiasm for the history of Corsica. He had intended to write it, made great studies in preparation, and collected materials, and then been overtaken by death. The loss of his labour cannot be too much deplored for Corsica. However, Gregori rendered good service to his country; he conducted the new edition of the national historian Filippini, whose work he had intended to continue; he also conducted the publication of the books of Corsican history of Petrus Cyrnæus; and, in the year 1843, he published a very important work, the Statutes of Corsica. In his younger days, he wrote also a Corsican tragedy, "Sampiero," which I have never got a sight of.

Gregori kept up brisk literary intercourse with Italy and Germany. His information was very extensive, and his industry of a pertinacity truly Corsican. He left in manuscript, at his death, part of his history of Corsica, and rich materials for a history of the commerce of maritime nations. Gregori's death filled not only Corsica with grief, but also the men of letters of France and Italy.

He and Renucci have also deserved well of the library of Bastia, which is in the large building formerly belonging to the Jesuits, and contains 16,000 volumes. Indeed they, properly speaking, created it, and it is the second library in the island, after that of Ajaccio. The scientific life of Corsica is in general very recent. As the historian Filippini, the contemporary of Sampiero, complains, indolence, the essentially warlike character of the Corsicans, induced by the constant wars, and the ignorance thence resulting, never allowed literature to arise at all. But it is remarkable that the Corsicans founded, in the year 1650, an academy of sciences, whose first president was the poet, advocate, theologian, and historian, Geronimo Biguglia. It was the fashion at that time to give to such academies the strangest names: the Corsicans named theirs the Academy *dei Vagabondi*, or vagabond academy; and they could not have chosen a better or more appropriate name. Marquis Cursay, whose memory is much cherished in Corsica, restored this academy; and Rousseau, himself a vagabond in his life, wrote for this Corsican institution a small essay, "What virtue is most essential to heroes; and who are the heroes in whom this virtue has been wanting." The very subject is truly Corsican.

Literary institutions (the just named academy having been broken up) are very poor in Bastia, as in Corsica generally. Bastia possesses a Lyceum, and other lower schools. I attended a distribution of prizes at the first girls' school. It took place in the court of the old Jesuits' college, which was gaily decorated, and in the evening well illuminated. The girls, all dressed in white, sat in rows before the leading citizens and authorities of the town, and those who had earned distinction received laurel crowns. The head mistress called the name of the happy victress, whereupon the latter came to the desk and received the laurel crown, which she took to one of the leading men of the town, silently giving him the favour of crowning her. This was then done in the prettiest fashion. Great numbers of these crowns were distributed, and many a lovely child bore off ten or twelve

of them for her immortal labours, and knew how to receive them
with an equal grace. But it seemed to me as though they
flattered wealthy parents or ancient families too much; for one
heard incessantly, "Miss Colonna d'Istria," "Miss Abbatucci,"
"Miss Saliceti," so that these young ladies carried home more
laurels than would suffice to crown the immortal poets of a
century. This graceful ceremony, which is surely nothing but
a French flattery of people's vanity, was concluded by a little
drama, which the little girls acted very prettily.

Bastia has but one newspaper, *L'ère nouvelle, Journal de la
Corse*, appearing only on Fridays. Its editor was, until this
summer, the advocate Arrighi, a talented man; but the new
prefect of Corsica, who was represented to me as a young official
without experience, and eager to cut a figure, as the Roman
prefects did in their provinces, menaced every displeasing utterance of the Corsican press, the most harmless in the world, with
a withdrawal of the licence, and thus forced M. Arrighi to retire.
The paper still exists as a regular Bonapartist journal. The
second Corsican newspaper is the government paper of Ajaccio.

Bastia has three booksellers' shops, of which the Libreria
Fabiani would do honour even to a German town. Its publi-
cations have many of them been well got up.

CHAPTER VII.

A CHAPTER OF STATISTICS.

I HAVE found the statistics of Corsica from the census of 1851,
in the Journal of Bastia of the 16th July, 1852, and will communicate them here.

Corsica had in the year 1740, 120,380 inhabitants.

"	"	1760, 130,000	"
"	"	1790, 150,638	"
"	"	1821, 180,348	"
"	"	1827, 185,079	"
"	"	1831, 197,967	"
"	"	1836, 207,889	"
"	"	1841, 221,463	"
"	"	1846, 230,271	"
"	"	1851, 236,251	"

According to the division into five arrondissements there were, in

Ajaccio,	55,008
Bastia,	20,288
Calvi,	24,390
Corte,	56,830
Sartene,	29,735

Corsica is divided into 61 cantons, and 355 communes, and has 30,438 houses, and 50,985 households.

. Males.	Single	75,543	
	Married	36,715	
	Widowers	5,680	
			117,938
Females.	Single	68,229	
	Married	36,916	
	Widows	13,168	
			118,313
			236,251

236,187 inhabitants are Roman Catholics, 54 Reformed Christians. French by birth (*i.e.*, inclusive of the Corsicans), 231,653.

Naturalized French	353
Germans	41
English	12
Dutch	6
Spaniards	7
Italians	3806
Poles	12
Swiss	85
Other Foreigners	285

2554 individuals were counted in the year 1851 as INVALIDS; of these 435 were blind of both eyes, 568 of one, 344 deaf and dumb, 183 idiots, 176 club-footed.

OCCUPATION. 32,364 men and women were possessors of land, 34,427 day-labourers, 6924 domestics. Artisans employed in building (masons, carpenters, locksmiths, painters, &c.), 3194. Dealers in fabrics, and tailors, 4517. Provision-dealers, 2981. Carriers, 1628. Dealers in articles of luxury (watch-makers, goldsmiths, engravers, &c.), 55. Rentiers, men and women, 13,160. Government officials, 1229. Communal officials, 803. Military and mariners, 5627. Apothecaries and medical men, 311. Clergy, 955. Advocates, 200. Teachers, 635. Artists, 105. Literati, 51. Prostitutes, 91. Vagrants and beggars, 688. Hospital patients, 85. The most original class of men in the island is not determined in this enumeration, the herdsmen.

The number of regular banditti is estimated at 200 ; an equal number of Corsican banditti may have fled to Sardinia.

I now give shortly the essential points about the general administration of Corsica, that my readers may have a clear idea of it also.

Since the year 1811 Corsica has formed one department, administered by a prefect residing in Ajaccio, and performing also the functions of an under-prefect for the arrondissement Ajaccio. There are four sub-prefects under him in the remaining four arrondissements. The prefect has as assessors the prefectian council of three members, which has to decide claims regarding taxes, public works, parochial and national property. The prefect is president of this council, from which appeal may be made to the council of state.

The general council is assembled every year at Ajaccio, and its members are chosen by the electors of every canton to deliberate on the public affairs of the country. It is competent to assign the direct taxes to each arrondissement. The general council can assemble only after an ordinance of the head of the state, who appoints the duration of its session. There is one representative for every canton, accordingly sixty-one in all.

Every arrondissement convokes in its chief town a district council of as many members as it has cantons. Those citizens, who are qualified electors according to the French electoral law, have also the right of electing to the legislative assembly. There are about 50,000 qualified electors in Corsica.

Mayors and adjuncts, appointed by the prefect, administer the communes; but the democratical privilege of electing the municipal council, which aids the mayor, has been retained by the people.

As to jurisdiction, the department stands under the court of appeal of Bastia, which is composed of one chief president, two chamber presidents, seventeen counsellors, one auditor, one procurator-general, two advocates-general, one substitute, five clerks of the court.

The court of assize holds its sessions in Bastia, and is composed of three judges of appeals, the procurator-general, and a clerk of the court; and its sessions are quarterly. There is a tribunal of the first resort in the chief place of every arrondissement. There is, moreover, a justice of the peace in every canton. In every commune exists a tribunal of municipal police, composed of the maire and his adjuncts.

In its spiritual administration, Corsica is subject to the diocese of Ajaccio, the bishop of which town is a suffragan of the Archbishop of Aix.

Corsica forms the seventeenth military division of France. The head-quarters are at Bastia, where the general of division has his residence. The gendarmerie, so important to Corsica, is formed by the seventeenth legion, and is likewise stationed at Bastia. It is composed of four companies, with four *chefs*, sixteen lieutenancies, and 102 brigades.

I will add a few words on agriculture and industrial relations. Agriculture, the foundation of all national wealth, is in a very low state in Corsica. This appears even from the single fact, that the ground subject to tillage amounts to but little more than three-tenths of the surface of the island. The exact surface is estimated at 2,159,254 acres. Great difficulties are opposed to the extension of cultivation by the existence of banditti, by the family feuds, the system of common lands, the deficiency of roads, the great distance of the fields from the houses, the unhealthiness of the air of the plains, and lastly, by the Corsican indolence.

Like the agriculture of Corsica, its manufactures also are in a very sorry state. They are confined to the most indispensable wants of trade and nourishment; the women almost every where weave the coarse brown Corsican cloth (*panno Corso*), also called *pelone;* the herdsmen make cheese and the cheese-cake, *broccio;* salt-works there are only in the gulf of Porto Vecchio. Sardines, tunnies, and coral, are taken on many parts of the coast, but the fisheries are conducted with no vigour.

The commerce of Corsica is likewise very inconsiderable. The chief export is oil, of which the island possesses such a quantity that, with more extended cultivation, it could produce it to the value of sixty millions of francs; but also lemons, wines, pulse, chestnuts, fresh and salt fish, timber, dyes, hides, coral, marble, much manufactured tobacco, especially cigars, for which the leaves are imported. The chief imports are, corn, grain, rice, sugar, coffee, cattle, silk, cotton, linseed, leather, iron-ore and hardware, tiles, glass, and pottery.

But the imports and exports are frightfully disproportioned to one another. The douane discourages all manufactures and commerce, and prevents foreign merchants from exchanging their produce for those of Corsica; so that the Corsicans pay a tenfold price for necessary imports from France, whereas wines

K

are imported from Provence free of duty, and the cultivation of
the Corsican vines is thus discouraged; for Corsica can under
ordinary circumstances export no wine to France, that being
itself a rich wine-country. Even flour and vegetables for the
troops are sent to the island from Provence. The exportation of
tobacco to the continent is prohibited. The tyrannical law of the
douane severely oppresses the poor island; and Corsica, which
is forced to buy from France articles to the annual amount of
three millions of francs, remits to France only a million and a
half. Yet she pays annually into the exchequer a million of
francs.

The chief commerce of the island belongs to the ports of
Bastia, Ajaccio, Isola Rossa, and Bonifazio.

However melancholy be the general condition of Corsica, she
is at least preserved by her thin population from the scourge of
an abject and perishing class, which has produced, in the great
centres of civilisation of the continent, far more terrible mysteries
than those of banditism and vengeance in Corsica.

The French have now been, with some inconsiderable interrup-
tions, eighty-five years in possession of Corsica; but they have
not succeeded in closing and healing over the great wound of
the nation, nor have they, with all the resources of their civilisation, achieved more for the island than a few lesser improvements. The island which has twice given France her Emperors,
and twice dictated laws to her, has gained nothing by it but the
satiation of her revenge. The Corsican will never forget in
what a shameful way France possessed herself of his country;
and a brave nation never learns to love its conquerors. When
I heard Corsicans even now railing bitterly at Genoa, I said to
them, "Let the old republic Genoa rest in peace; you have
accomplished your *vendetta* upon her; Napoleon, a Corsican, has
annihilated her: France deceived you, and deprived you of
your nationality; you have had your *vendetta* upon France too,
for you sent her a Corsican, Napoleon, who subjugated her; and
even now that great country is a Corsican conquest, and your
own province."

Two Emperors, two Corsicans, on the throne of France, keeping down the French nation with despotic power!—surely, if
an ideal sentiment can have the force of reality, we must confess
that a brave conquered nation never revenged itself more brilliantly upon its oppressors. It may be asserted that the name of
Napoleon is the only bond that attaches the Corsican people to

France; without this, their relation to France would be only that of other conquered nations to their foreign masters. I have read in many authors the assertion, that the Corsican people is at the bottom of its heart French. I regard this assertion as an error or an intentional untruth. I never convinced myself of the truth of it. The Corsicans and the French are separated by a deep gulf of nationality, innermost nature, and sentiments. The Corsican is a decided Italian; his language, avowedly, one of the purest Italian dialects; and his nature, his soil, and his history, still link the wandering son to his former home. Indeed, the French feel themselves strangers in this island, and soldiers and officials regard their period of service there as a cheerless banishment to the "isle of goats." The Corsican cannot even understand a nature like the French; for he is serious, taciturn, chaste, consistent, a man in the best sense of the word, and firm as the granite of his mountains.

There is still such a thing as Corsican patriotism; I saw it occasionally break forth. The resentment excited by the memory of the battle of Ponte Nuovo is still alive in them. As I was driving one day over the battle-field of Ponte Nuovo, and we saw the celebrated bridge, a Corsican countryman sitting beside me, nudged me, and exclaimed with passionate gesticulation, "This is the place where the Genoese murdered our freedom—I mean to say the French!" The meaning will be understood, when it is known that to the Corsicans the name Genoese is equivalent to mortal enemy; for their hatred of Genoa, as I was told by the Corsicans themselves, is eternal. Another time I asked an educated Corsican whether he was an Italian. "Yes," said he, "because I am a Corsican." I understood his meaning well, and shook hands with him. These are unconnected and casual hints; but often a living word caught from the mouth of the people casts a bright light upon its mind, and reveals a sudden truth not to be discovered from the books of literary officials.

I have heard it said often, and in all parts of the country, "We Corsicans should rejoice to be Italian (for we are really Italians), if Italy were but united and strong; as it now is, we are French, for we need a great power to raise us, who are so weak alone."

The government does all it can to supplant the Italian language by the French. All cultivated Corsicans speak French, and, they say, well; French is forced upon many by fashion, necessity, or the prospect of official situations. I was sorry to meet also with young men who evidently from vanity talked among each other in French. I could not refrain from expressing my surprise that they so lightly exchanged their beautiful mother-tongue for the language of the French. In the towns French is much spoken; but the people speak Italian only, even when they have learnt French at school, or by the intercourse of life. Into the interior and the mountains the French has not intruded at all; and there also the old cherished customs of the forefathers, the guilelessness of natural life, simplicity, justice, magnanimity, and love of freedom, have maintained themselves unimpaired. It were an evil day for the Corsicans, should they ever exchange the virtues of their rude but great forefathers for the refined manners of an effeminate Parisian society. The moral corruption of French society has destroyed the vigour of the French nation. Its infection has extended to the general society of other countries, and made an incapacity for action, as well as demoralization, general. It has shaken the most sacred foundations of human society, the family. But a people that has lost the spirit of the family is ripe for despotism. The entire heroic history of the Corsicans springs purely and singly from the natural law of the sacredness and inviolability of the family; and even their free constitution, which they gave themselves in the course of time, and concluded under Paoli, is only a further development of the family. All the virtues of the Corsicans spring from this spirit, and even the dreadful night-sides of their life, such as their blood-revenge, belong to this common root.

We look with horror upon the avenger coming down from the mountains to assassinate the kindred of his enemy, member by member; yet this bloody vampire may, in force of character, generosity, love of right and of his country, be a hero in comparison with the unbloody wretch who is always sneaking about in the *grand monde* of our civilisation, and secretly sucking out the souls of his fellow men.

CHAPTER VIII.

BRACCIAMOZZO THE BANDIT.

Che bello onor s'acqu'sta in far vendetta.
　　　　　　　　　　　　DANTE.

ON the second day after my arrival at Bastia, I was wakened in the night in my locanda in the Jesuit-street, by a tremendous noise. It was as though the Lapiths and Centaurs were engaged in a fray. I sprang to the door; the following scene was being enacted in the dining-room. The landlord, frantic and screaming, held his gun pointed at a man who lay on his knees before him; others joined their cries to the row, and endeavoured to appease him. The man begged for mercy—he was hustled out of the house. It was a young man who had pretended he was a traveller from Marseille, and played the fine gentleman, and at last could not pay his bill.

On the second day after this I crossed the square of San Nicolao, the public promenade of the Bastinese, in the early morning, to take a bathe in the sea. The hangmen were just erecting the guillotine close to the tribunal, not exactly in the middle of the square, but yet within its bounds. Carabineers and people surrounded this horrid scene, to which the bright sea and the peaceful olive groves formed the sharpest contrast. The atmosphere was dull and heavy with the scirocco. On the quay stood mariners and workmen in groups, smoking their clay pipes in silence, and gazing at the red post; and many a one in his pointed *baretto*, with his brown jacket thrown over him, and his brown breast open, and a red neckerchief negligently tied, looked as if he might have more to do with the guillotine than as a mere spectator. And, in truth, there may have been none among the crowd, who was secured from the fate that awaited this bandit, if he chanced to be driven by the hallowed custom of revenge for blood to murder, and from murder to the life of a bandit.

"Who is to be executed?"

"Bracciamozzo (the cripple-arm). He is only twenty-three years old. The sbirri caught him on the mountains; he de-

fended himself like a devil; they shot away one of his arms, and
was taken off, but he recovered."

"What is his offence?"

"*Dio mio!* He killed ten men!"

"Ten men! and what for?"

"For *Capriccio!*"

I hastened to the sea to enjoy my bathing, and then back to
my locanda, not to meet the procession. The impressions were
so frightful that a cold shudder came over me in this wild solitude. I took out my Dante; I felt as if I must read one of the
wild fantasies of his *Inferno*, where the pitch-devils push down
the poor souls with harpoons as often as they try to rise to
snatch a breath of air. My locanda was in the narrow and
gloomy Jesuit-street. An hour elapsed, and I was called to the
window by a hollow murmur and trotting of horses; Bracciamozzo was led past the house, escorted by the Capuchins in
their hooded cloaks, that leave no part of the face free but the
eyes, which peer out in a most ghostly fashion—corporeal
demon forms, gloomily murmuring to themselves, and awful,
seeming as if they had sprung into life from Dante's Hell. The
bandit walked with a firm step between two priests, one of
whom held a crucifix before him. He was a young man of
middle stature, with a fine bronzed head and curly raven locks,
and a pallor on his cheek, which was still further heightened by
the blackness of his whiskers. His left arm was bound on his back,
and the other was a stump. His eye, which must have been fiery as
a tiger's when the passion of murder thrilled through him, was now
still and tranquil. He was muttering prayers, as it seemed, as he
went. His step was firm, and his carriage erect. At the head
of the procession rode gens d'armes with naked swords; behind
the bandit followed the Capuchins in pairs; the procession was
closed by the black coffin—a white cross and a death's head were
delineated upon it. It was carried by four merciful brothers.
Slowly the procession passed through the Jesuit-street, followed
by the muttering crowd; and thus they led the vampire with
the maimed wing to the gallows. I never saw a more awful
scene, nor any whose smallest features have so daguerreotyped
themselves in my memory against my will.

I was told afterwards that the bandit had died without
flinching, and that his last words were, "I pray God and the
world for forgiveness, for I acknowledge that I have done much
evil.

This young man, I was told, was not an avenger of blood for personal reasons, but a bandit from ambition. His story casts much light upon the terrible state of the island. At the time of the fame of Massoni, who had avenged a kinsman's blood and then become bandit, Bracciamozzo, as the young Giacomino was called after the mutilation of his arm, used to bring him his food; for these banditti have always an understanding with their friends and the goat-herds, who bring them their provisions in their hiding-places, and receive pay whenever money is to be had. Giacomino, intoxicated by the renown of the brave bandit Massoni, got into his head that he would play a similar part, and gain the admiration of all Corsica. So he killed a man, and then escaped to the bush and became a bandit. One by one he killed ten men, and was called by the people *Vecchio*, the old one; probably because, though a young man, he had already spilt as much blood as an old hand. This Vecchio one day shot the universally beloved physician Malaspina, the uncle of a gentleman in the Balagna who was very hospitable to me; he took up his position in a bush, and fired right into the diligence as it came along from Bastia. The wild devil then escaped again to the mountains till he was overtaken by justice.

So fearful a life's history may a man have in Corsica. There no one despises the bandit, who is neither thief nor robber, but only a warrior and avenger, and free as the eagle on the mountain tops. Men with fantastical aspirations are excited by the idea of reaping glory by deeds of arms, and living in the popular ballads. The fiery temperament of these men, who are softened by no culture, who shirk labour as a dishonour, and who, thirsting for great actions, know nothing of the world but the wild mountains in which nature has confined them in the midst of the sea, seems, like a volcano, to demand an eruption. On another and a wider field, and in different circumstances, the same men who lurk for years in mountain caverns, and fight with the sbirri in the forests, would be mighty warriors, like Sampiero and Gaffori. The nature of the Corsicans is a warrior nature; and I can find no more suitable description of it than that which Plato applies to his class of warriors, namely, "full of passion" (θυμοειδής). The Corsicans are *passionate* creatures; jealousy, glory, ambition, vengeance—all these consuming passions are theirs, and they are born warriors in every sense of the term.

I was curious to learn whether, after Bracciamozzo's execution, the ladies would take their usual evening promenade on the square of San Nicolao, and I failed not to make my appearance there. And, behold, some Bastinese belles were walking in the square where the bandit's blood had flowed in the morning. Nothing betrayed the event of the morning, and it was as though nothing remarkable had occurred. I also took a few turns there, for the sea was most luxuriously tinted. The fishing boats then began to sail with their lights, and the fishermen to sing the beautiful fishing song—*O pescator dell' onde*.

There are in Corsica nerves of granite, and no smelling-bottles at all.

CHAPTER IX.

THE VENDETTA.

Eterna faremo vendetta.

CORSICAN SONG.

THE origin of the banditti is to be sought almost exclusively in the ancient custom of revenge for bloodshed, or Vendetta. Almost all the writers whom I have read on the subject, derive the Corsican revenge for blood from the ages when Genoese justice was venal, or actually encouraged murder. The constant wars, and the consequent stagnation in the administration of justice, doubtless did much to cause this barbarous custom to take root; but the root itself lies elsewhere. For this revenge for blood is found not in Corsica alone, but also in other countries; in Sardinia, Calabria, Sicily, Albania, and Montenegro; among the Circassians, Druses, Bedouins, &c.

These analogous phenomena must rest upon analogous conditions. These are easily discovered, as the social condition of all these nations is similar. They all live in a warlike state, and in wild and grand scenery; all, with the exception of the Bedouins, are poor mountain tribes, and live in districts not easily penetrated by civilisation, and most tenacious of ancient barbarous customs, as well as of their primitive or natural life. All, in fine, are penetrated by a like spirit of family, which forms the sacred groundwork of their society. In the state of nature, and in the dissolution of society caused by general war and insecurity, the family becomes a state in itself; the members of it hold firmer together; when one is injured, all the little state is injured. The family works out its own justice, which takes the form of revenge. And hence it appears that the revenge for bloodshed, a barbarity though it be, springs from the injured sense of right and the natural love of blood-relations, and that its source is a noble one; namely, the human heart. The Vendetta is a barbarous justice; and the Corsican sense of justice is acknowledged and praised, even by ancient authors.

The Corsican is governed by two great and noble passions, love of his family and love of his country. In a poor people, living on a solitary island of grand mountains, these passions must be very powerful, and make up for the want of the world at large. To love of country, that Corsican hero-story now known to us owes its birth, which is, properly speaking, naught but an ancient act of vengeance of the Corsicans against Genoa, propagated from generation to generation; and love of family has produced the no less bloody and no less heroic history of the vendetta, which still continues to enact its tragedy. One must indeed attribute an inborn force almost inconceivable to this little nation, which, while tearing the flesh off its own bones, actually possessed strength to strive in such incessant and glorious contests with their country's enemies.

Love for his relations is still a religion to the Corsican, as in the days of ancient heroes; the love of his country alone is a higher duty to him. Many examples from history prove this. As with the ancient Greeks, so with the Corsicans, the highest and purest form of love in general is esteemed to be that of brothers and sisters. The paternal relation is in Corsica regarded as the most sacred, and the names of brother and sister describe the purest bliss of the heart, its noblest treasure or its bitterest loss. The eldest brother, as the stay of the family, is from his very position an object of veneration. I believe nothing so clearly expresses the entire sentiments and moral being of a nation as its songs.

The Corsican song is, in all strictness, a dirge or song of vengeance; and most of these songs of vengeance are the laments of the sister for her fallen brother. I have always found that, in those songs, whenever the highest praise and love is to be poured upon the dead, it is said of him, "He was my brother." Even the wife, in the highest outpouring of love, calls her husband brother. I was surprised to discover the very same phase of feeling and expression in the Servian popular songs; for the Servian woman's highest term of endearment for her husband is brother, and the Servian swears his most solemn oath by the name of his brother. The natural religion of the heart maintains itself in its simplest forms of feeling among uncorrupted tribes; its sentiments are based upon that which is alone permanent in the relations of life, for the nation's feeling clings to what is simple and durable. The love of brothers and sisters, as of parents, is the simplest and the most permanent relation upon earth, because it is free from passion. And the history of human misery begins with the brother-murderer, Cain.

Wo, then, to him who has slain a Corsican's brother or kinsman! The deed is done—the murderer flies, in double fear, of justice which punishes murder, and of the deceased's kindred, who will avenge it. For no sooner has the deed become known, than the fallen man's relations seize their arms and hasten to find the murderer. He has escaped to the bush, and is perhaps scrambling up there to the eternal snows, and living with the wild sheep; his track is lost. But the murderer has relatives—brothers, cousins, a father; these know that they must answer for the deed with their blood. So they arm, and are on their guard. The life of those who suffer the vendetta is extremely miserable. Whoever has cause to fear the vendetta, shuts himself up in the house, and barricades the doors and windows, in which he leaves only loopholes open. The windows are stopped up with straw and mattresses—a proceeding which is called *inceppar le fenestre*. A Corsican house in the mountains, naturally high and narrow, almost like a tower, and with a very high flight of stone steps, is easily converted into a fortress. In this castle the Corsican always keeps on his guard, lest a ball through the windows should hit him. His kinsmen till the ground in arms; they set a watch, and are not sure of a single step in the fields. Cases were told me in which Corsicans had not left their fortified dwellings for ten or fifteen years, and had passed so large a part of their life under siege and in constant fear of death. For Corsican revenge never sleeps, and the Corsican never forgets. It happened a short time ago in Ajaccio, that a man who had lived ten years in his chamber and ventured at last into the road, fell down dead on his return before the threshold of his house. The bullet of the man who had watched for him ten years long, had pierced his heart!

I see a man going about here in the streets of Bastia, who

from his large nose is called by the people Nasone. His stature is gigantic, and his face disfigured by a lacerated eye. He lived years ago in the neighbouring village of Pietra Nera. He offended some one in the village. The latter vowed vengeance. Nasone fortified himself in his house, and blocked up the windows to protect himself against a shot. After a considerable time he ventured out into the road; his enemy instantly sprang upon him with a vine-knife in his hand. They wrestled desperately; Nasone was defeated, and his adversary, who had already given him a cut in the neck, was just about knocking off his head on a tree-stump, when some people came up. Nasone's wounds healed; his enemy escaped to the Macchia. Again a considerable time elapsed: Nasone then ventured again into the road, when—there came a ball that went through his eye. The wounded man was lifted up; and again his giant constitution conquered and healed him. The vengeful bandit then desolated by night his enemy's vineyard and fired his house. Nasone removed to the town, and now goes about there as a living example of Corsican revenge, horrible to the peaceful stranger who inquired his history. I saw the dreadful man one day by the sea-side, but not without his double-barrelled gun; his figure inspired me with dread, and he looked like the demon of vengeance incarnate.

To take no revenge is deemed dishonourable by the genuine Corsicans. The feeling of revenge is with them a natural sentiment, a consecrated passion. Revenge has in their songs become a worship, which is celebrated as a religion of natural affection. But a sentiment which the people have taken into their songs as a national and an essential one, is ineradicable; most of all when woman has ennobled it as *her* feeling. Most of the Corsican songs of vengeance are composed by girls and women, and are sung from the mountains to the seashore. This produces a perfect atmosphere of revenge, in which the people live and their children grow up; and thus they drink in the savage idea of vendetta with their very mother's milk. In one of these songs they sing, " Twelve souls are not enough even to avenge the deceased's—boots!" That is Corsican! A man like Hamlet, who strives, and is unable, to fill himself with the spirit of vengeance for blood, the Corsicans would account the meanest of mortals. Perhaps nowhere in the world is human life and human blood worth so little as in Corsica. The Corsican is ready to shed blood, but he is also ready to die.

If any one delay to avenge himself, or if perchance nature or philosophy have given him a touch of the milder feelings of a Hamlet, his relatives make insinuations, and others slander him for not having avenged himself. This reproach of having borne an insult without revenging it, they call *rimbeccare*. The *rimbecco* was punished by an old Genoese statute as an incitement to murder. The law is as follows (in the 19th Chapter of these statutes).

" Of those who reproach, or say *rimbecco*.

" If one reproaches another, or in his presence says *rimbecco* to others, for not having avenged the death of a father, brother, or other kindred, or for not having avenged himself for any other offences or insults done to himself; he shall be mulcted for every such offence in a sum ranging from 25 to 50 lire, at the discretion of the magistrate, and with due regard to the quality of the persons and other circumstances; and if he pays not the fine and cannot pay it within eight days, he shall be banished for a year from the island, or the *corda* (strappado) shall be administered to him once at the magistrate's discretion."

In the year 1581, the law was so far heightened that the person who said *rimbecco* had his tongue publicly pierced.

It is the women especially that instigate the men to revenge, by songs of vengeance over the body of the slain, and by displaying his blood-stained shirt. The mother often fixes a bloody shred from the shirt of the murdered father upon the son's dress, as a constant reminder that he has to avenge himself. The passions of these people are of a fearful demon-like heat.

In former times, the Corsicans had the chivalric and feudal custom of proclaiming the war of revenge beforehand, and even announcing to what degree of relationship the vengeance should extend. The custom is obsolete. From the close connection of the various kindred (*parentado*), the vendetta naturally crosses; and it is then called *vendetta trasversale*.

With this are connected, as a natural consequence, the Corsican family feuds, which are to the present day the scourge of the unhappy land. For the families who lie under the infliction of vendetta, immediately draw in all their relations, and even their friends into their quarrel; and in Corsica, as in other nations at a similar social stage, there is still the firm bond of the *tribe*. Thus arise family wars within one and the same village, or between village and village, or glen and glen; and the feud is kept up, and blood spilt, for years. Vengeance for blood, smaller injuries, or even casualties, give occasion to it; and with the choleric temperament of the Corsicans, any wrangle may easily cause bloodshed, as they are all armed. The feud extends even to the children; examples are known of boys of families that are at feud, having stabbed or shot one another. There are in Corsica certain vassalisms, as remains of the ancient feudal system subsisting in the time of the Signori, subsisting especially in the district beyond the mountains, where the descendants of the ancient Signori still live in their old *paesi*. They have now no feudal vassals, but dependants, friends, persons bound to them and rendering service. These are easily grouped together as a family retinue, and are in Corsican language the *patrocinatori*, or *geniali*. Family wars are still kept up in Corsica, as in the Italian towns in the middle ages, perhaps as a last remnant of the Signori's feuds. The granite island has obstinately held to its ancient renown, and its warlike history and constant civil strife, occasioned by the ambition and haughtiness of the Signori, has left on it the impress of party spirit, even to the present day.

In Corsica the fearful word enmity has still its full original significance. There the enemy is a mortal foe; and whoever lives at enmity with any one, goes forth to take his blood, and must in so doing risk his own. We too have received the original notion of mortal enemy from a state of such nature and unculture as the Corsicans, but it expresses with us something more abstract. Our mortal enemies will not murder us; they only do us evil behind our backs, calumniate us, and do us all manner of secret injuries; we often do not even know who they are. Enmities in a civilized state have generally something low and coarse; so the man of noble spirit in our social state cannot be an enemy, he can only feel contempt. But in Corsica mortal enemies assail one another's persons with arms in their hands; they vow loud and openly to revenge themselves with blood, and if they once meet, stab or shoot one another. There is in this something fearfully manly, unconstrainedly savage and imposing. Barbarous as such a social state is, it nevertheless constrains us to respect its natural vigour, especially as the Corsican avenger is often a truly tragic hero, driven by fate, because urged by consecrated usage, to commit murder. For there, even a naturally noble man may become a Cain, and many a one who roves as a bandit on the mountains of this island, bears the curse of barbarous manners, not of personal wickedness, and may be a man of such virtues as would honour and distinguish him in civil society.

One single passion, sprung from a noble source—revenge, and naught but revenge!—it is astonishing with what irresistible force it lays hold of men. Revenge is the fearful fate-goddess of the poor Corsicans, and forms the history of their lives. And so man here, through a single passion, becomes a dread demon, more relentless than the destroying angel, for he is not satisfied with the first-born. Yet, dark and benighted as the human form here appears, this very dread passion produces its brilliant opposite. Where there are foes to the death, there are also friends to the death; where revenge tears the heart with tiger's rage, brotherly love transports it to the sublimest resolves; there is a heroic forgetfulness of self, and divine clemency of forgiveness; and possibly one might nowhere find the Christian precept—Love thy enemy—realized in a more Christian spirit than in the very land of revenge.

Mediators, termed *Parolanti*, often interpose between the hostile parties, who take to them the oath of reconciliation. The oath is sacred as a religion; whoever breaks it is infamous, and proscribed before God and man. It is seldom broken, but *is* broken sometimes, for the demon has made his nest in the human heart.

CHAPTER X.

BANDIT LIFE.

Εἶεν· τόδ᾽ ἐστὶ τἀνδρὸς ἐκφανὲς τέκμαρ.
Ὅπου δέ μηνυτῆρος ἀφθέγκτου φραδαῖς.
Τετραυματισμένον γὰρ ὡς κύων νεβρὸν
Πρὸς αἷμα καὶ σταλαγμὸν ἐκμαστεύομεν.
ÆSCHYLUS, *Eum.* 244.

How the Corsican may be compelled to live as a bandit, to be suddenly launched from the quiet domesticity of his civil life into the mountain wilds, and converted into a man without a country, or an outlaw, will be evident from the account of the revenge for bloodshed.

The Corsican bandit is not, like the Italian, a thief and a robber, but what his name implies, one banned by the law. In the ancient statutes of the island all those are originally called Banditti who are banished from the island because justice has failed to get them into her grasp; they were proclaimed outlaws, and might be slain by any one with impunity if they showed their faces. The expression *banished* has been simply transferred to all who live in the *ban* of the law.

The isolation of Corsica, its poverty, and the Corsican's attachment to his country often prevent him, when proscribed, from leaving his island. In former times Corsican banditti sometimes escaped to Greece, where they fought valiantly; now some fly to Italy, but most to Sardinia, when they prefer to leave their country. Escape from the law is nowhere in the world easier than in Corsica. For no sooner has the blood flowed, than the perpetrator dashes to the mountains, which are never far distant, and conceals himself in the scarce penetrable bush. From the moment that he has entered the bush he is called a bandit. His relations and friends alone know his track; and as long as it is possible they supply his necessities, and even take him on many a still night into their houses. Reduced to the greatest straits, the bandit always finds goatherds who relieve his need.

The main hiding-place of the banditti is between Tox and Mount Santo Appiano, in the wilds of Monte Cinto and Monte Rotondo, and in the pathless regions of the Niolo. There deep shaded primeval forests that have never seen an axe, and densest thickets of shrubby oaks, of albatro, myrtles, and heath, cover the slopes of the mountains; dark ravines with wild roaring streams, where every path loses itself, and holes, caverns, and crumbling rocks, afford concealment. There, with the falcon, the fox, and the wild sheep, the bandit lives a more romantic and cheerless life than that of the American Indian. Justice takes its course; it has condemned him *in contumaciam;* the bandit laughs at it, and says, with his strange expression, " I have received the *sonetto*," that is, the sentence *in contumaciam.* The sbirri follow on his track; so also do the avengers; he is in perpetual flight; he is the wandering Jew of the desert mountains. Now there are fights with the gens d'armes, awful heroic fights; more blood is shed; but it is not blood of sbirri only; for the bandit is also an avenger, and it is not so much love of his own life as revenge that keeps him alive. He has vowed death to his enemy's kindred; and one may imagine how tremendously the sentiment of revenge must be heightened in the awful wilderness of the mountains, and the more awful personal isolation, under the influence of constant thoughts of death and dreams of the gallows. Sometimes the bandit comes

down from the mountains to slay his enemy; when he has
accomplished his revenge, he disappears again among the mountains. The Corsican bandit frequently sets up as a Carl Moor
of society.* The story of the bandit Capracinta of Prunelli is
still known in Corsica. His father had been unjustly condemned
to the galleys; the son went forthwith into the *Macchia* with
a few kinsmen, and these avengers descended from the mountains
from time to time, and assassinated or shot their personal enemies, soldiers, and spies; they once caught the public hangman
and executed him.

It is natural enough that the banditti often allow themselves
to be used as the tools of others who have a vendetta to accomplish, and apply to them for the loan of their dagger or their
ball. From the great ramification of families in so small a
country, the formidableness of the banditti must of course be
aggravated. They are bloody scourges of the land: the fields
lie waste, the vineyards are not kept; for who will venture into
the fields when menaced by a Massoni or Serafino? There are
moreover men among the banditti, who were formerly wont to
exert an influence over others, or to take part in public life;
banished to the wilds, they cannot endure to lose their entire
sphere of influence. I was assured that some still continue, even
in their caves and hiding-places, to read newspapers, which they
find means to procure. They often exert an intimidating influence upon the communal elections, and even upon the elections
to the general council, and they have not unfrequently menaced
the witnesses and the judges, and taken a bloody revenge upon
them. This, and the very mild verdicts of the jurymen, have
given rise to the desire frequently expressed for the entire aboli-

* The hero of Schiller's tragedy of "The Robbers," characterised by Schiller
himself in the following terms:—"A soul attracted to the extremity of crime
only by the *greatness* attached to its execution, the *force* it puts in requisition,
and the *dangers* attending it. A remarkable and important personage he is,
endowed with all possible force of character, and inevitably destined, according
to the direction given to this, to become either a Brutus or a Catiline. An
unhappy conjuncture of events decides for the latter, and it is only after an
awful aberration that he ultimately comes round to the former. False notions
of action and influence, and a fulness of power overriding all laws, were
naturally destined to run foul of social institutions; and let only some exasperation against the unideal world be superinduced to these enthusiastic dreams
of greatness and efficiency, and you have the curious Don Quixote ready made,
whom we abominate and love, admire and compassionate in the robber
Moor. I hope it is unnecessary to remark that I am as far from holding this
up as a picture of robbers only, as the Spaniard's satire was from lashing
knights-errant alone."

tion of trial by jury in Corsica. It is not to be denied that the Corsican juries may often be subjected to the influence of fear of bandit revenge; but if they be reproached with too great leniency in their decisions, the accusation will in many cases be unjust, for the life of banditti and its causes must be considered from the point of view of the conditions of Corsican society. I attended a sitting of the jury in Bastia, an hour after the execution of Bracciamozzo, and in the building before which he had been executed; the impression of the execution seemed to me sensible in the countenances of the jurymen and the public, but not in that of the accused. He was a young man who had shot a man; he had an obtuse stony face, and his skull looked like a negro's, as if it might be used as an anvil. Neither the execution just accomplished, nor the solemnity of the assize proceedings, made any moral impression whatever upon the young man; he showed not the slightest trace of confusion or fear, but replied with the greatest *sang froid* to all the judge's questions, expressing himself shortly and convincingly on the circumstances of his deed of blood. I forget to how many years of imprisonment he was condemned.

Though the Corsican bandit never disgraces himself by common robbery, he does not consider it beneath his knightly honour to extort money. The banditti levy contributions; they tax individuals, nay often whole villages and parishes, according to an assessment, and rigorously call in their tribute. As kings of the bush they impose their taxes; and it is said that taxable persons have paid these taxes more punctually and scrupulously than they ever paid the King of France his. It often happens that the bandit sends a note to some wealthy man, with the demand to deposit so many thousand francs for him at a certain place, else he will destroy him, his house, and his fields. The usual form of threat is, *si preparasse,* "Let him be prepared." Others fall into the bandit's power, and are forced to pay ransom. The insecurity of communication is thus increased, and culture rendered impossible. The banditti enrich their relations and friends with the money extorted by them, and purchase popularity for themselves in various ways, but money cannot improve their personal life; for, even though they could amass mountains of it, still they must live in the caverns of the rugged wilds, and in constant flight.

There are many cases of banditti who, having led a bandit life for fifteen or twenty years long, and hold their ground on

L

so small an area as that of their mountains, and been constantly
victorious in combat, have finally succumbed to the general fate
of banditti. The Corsican banditti do not form into bands,
which indeed the land would not be able to support; and the
Corsican nature feels a repugnance to obey the commands of a
captain. They live mostly in twos, in a kind of brothership in
arms. It is extraordinary that they also have their own blood-
revenge and mortal enmities among themselves; for so powerful
is the Corsican feeling of revenge, that a like lot and like misery
never reconciles one bandit with another, if vendetta has existed
between them. Many a case is known of one bandit having
hunted down and slain another on the mountains, for blood-
revenge. Massoni and Serafino, the Corsican bandit heroes of the
most recent times, had vendetta against one another, and shot
at each other whenever they met. Massoni had shot off one of
Serafino's fingers.

The history of the Corsican banditti is rich in heroic, demon-
like, and chivalrous traits of character. The people sing bandit
dirges throughout the whole country; it is their own fate and
their own grief that they express in these songs. Many banditti have immortalized themselves by their bold deeds; one
most of all, who is called Teodoro, and called himself king of the
mountains. So Corsica has had two kings of the name Theodore. Teodoro Poli suffered conscription one day about the
beginning of this century, and demanded time to procure the
money for a substitute, but the gens d'armes arrested him to enlist
him. Teodoro's pride and love of freedom were aroused. He
dashed to the mountains, and lived thenceforward as a bandit.
All Corsica was compelled to admire his boldness, and he became
the terror of the island; yet he was stained by no sordidness,
but rather praised for his magnanimity, and he even forgave
relations of his enemies. He was very handsome, and, like the
king his namesake, loved splendid and fantastic attire. His
mistress shared his lot, and lived merrily from the black-mail
(*taglia*) imposed by Teodoro upon the villages. There was
with him also a bandit, Brusco, to whom he had sworn eternal
friendship, and his uncle Augellone. The latter name signifies
Evil Bird, for it is the custom for banditti to give themselves
nicknames when they begin to play their part in the Macchia.
The Evil Bird was envious of Brusco, of whom Teodoro was so
fond, and he one day thrust the cold steel rather too deep into
his breast. Then he fled to the rocks. When Teodoro learned

his friend's fate, he uttered a cry of grief, like Achilles after the fall of Patroclus, and, as is the old custom with avengers, he let his beard grow, and swore never to shave it till he had bathed his hands in the blood of the Evil Bird. A short time elapsed, and Teodoro was seen again with shaven beard. These are the little tragedies enacted even among the banditti in the wilderness; for the human heart everywhere follows the bent of its ruling passions. At last Teodoro fell ill. A spy indicated the hiding-place of the sick lion. Then the wild wolf-dogs, the sbirri, came up the mountains and put him to death in a hovel; but he had first given the heads of two cause to remember him. The ballad boasts that he fell with the pistol in his hand, and the *fucile* by his side, *come un fiero paladino*, "like a haughty paladin." But such was the respect inspired by this king of the mountains, that they still paid his overdue taxes even after his fall. The persons who owed the tax that he had not yet collected, came and respectfully laid the money in the cradle of the little baby born to him by his queen of the mountains. Teodoro met his death in the year 1827.

Gallocchio is also renowned. His mistress had faithlessly left him, and he forbade any one to desire her hand. Cesario Negroni wooed her. Young Gallocchio gave one of his friends a hint to wound the bride's father. The wedding guests were merrily dancing, merrily went the fiddles and guitars—a shot! The bullet missed its intended course, and entered the heart of the bride's father. Gallocchio now turns bandit. Cesario fortifies himself; but Gallocchio drives him out of his house, hunts him through the mountains, comes up with him, lays him low. Gallocchio then fled to Greece, where he fought against the Turks. One day the news reached him that his brother had fallen in the vendetta in Corsica, which had been incessantly kept up to avenge the death of the bride's father and of Cesario. Gallocchio returned and killed two brothers of Cesario and others beside, and destroyed their entire family. The Red Gambini was his companion; in union with him he beat the gens d'armes, one of whom they tied to the tail of a horse and dragged over the stones. Gambini fled to Greece, where the Turks cut off his head; but Gallocchio died in sleep, for a traitor shot him.

Renowned are also Santa Lucia, Giammarchi (who kept his ground in the bush for sixteen years), Camilla Ornano (who maintained himself in the mountains for fourteen years), and Joseph Antommarchi (who was bandit for seventeen years).

A short time before my arrival in Corsica, the noted bandit Serafino was shot; he was betrayed, and met his death in sleep. Arrighi also, and the dreaded Massoni, had met their end a short time before; it was as wildly romantic as their life.

Massoni was a man of the boldest spirit and unexampled energy; he was the son of a family in good circumstances, in the Balagna. It was blood-revenge that drove him to the mountains. There he lived for many years, supported by his relations and favoured by the herdsmen, and he killed in many contests a great number of sbirri. With him was his brother and the brave Arrighi. One day he was visited by a man of the province Balagna, who had a kinsman's blood to avenge upon a powerful family, and who asked his assistance. The bandit received him hospitably, and having nothing to offer for a meal, went to a herdsman on Monte Rotondo, and asked him for a lamb. The herdsman gave him one out of his flock. But Massoni refused it, saying, "You are giving me a lean lamb, though I have a guest to honour to-day; see, there is a fat one, I will take that;" and in a trice he shot the fat lamb dead, and carried it to his cave.

The herdsman was enraged at this arbitrary proceeding. He hastily descended the mountains meditating revenge, and indicated Massoni's hiding-place to the sbirri. He was avenging the lamb's blood. The sbirri ascended the mountains in great force. These Corsican gens d'armes, familiar with the nature of the country, and practised in fights with banditti, are no less brave and daring than the game they hunt. Their life is in constant danger when they venture up to the mountains; for the banditti are on their watch, and keep a look-out from their hiding-places with the telescopes which they always carry with them; and when danger appears, they are up and off, more nimbly than the Muffro or wild sheep, or they let the bailiffs come within shot, and never miss their aim.

So the sbirri came up the mountains, the herdsman leading the way; they crept up the rocks on paths known to him only. The banditti lay in a cave, which was almost inaccessible, and concealed by a bush. Arrighi and Massoni's brother lay in this cave, and Massoni sat on the look-out behind the bush.

The sbirri crept up on a path above the cave, and others commanded its mouth. Those above looked down upon the bush, to see whether they could see any thing. A sbirro took a stone and threw it into the bush, in which he thought he observed something black. Instantly a man jumped up behind the bush and fired off a pistol to rouse those in the cave. But at the same moment the reports of the bailiffs' guns were heard, and Massoni fell down dead before the cavern's mouth.

As the shots fell a man darted out of the cave—Massoni's brother. Like the mountain goat he sprang wildly from rock to rock, with bullets whizzing round him: one wounded him mortally, so that he fell down the rocks. Arrighi, who saw all that passed, kept in the cave. The gens d'armes pushed on cautiously, but no one durst penetrate into the cavern, until at length the most dare-devil of them ventured in. No one was visible there; nevertheless the bailiffs were not to be deceived, and persisted that the cavern still concealed a man. They occupied the entrance.

Night came. Torches and camp-fires were kindled; they resolved to starve out Arrighi. In the morning some went to the adjacent spring to draw water. A shot fell, and another,—and two sbirri fell. Their companions, screaming with rage, fired off their guns towards the cave. All was still.

Now they had to fetch the two dead or dying men. They hesitated a long time, and then a few resolved to risk it ; and this again cost the life of one. Another day passed. One then hit upon the idea of smoking out the bandit like a badger, a means that had been successfully employed in Algiers. So they piled up dry wood before the entrance of the cave, and kindled it, to drive out the bandit, but the smoke diffused itself through the crevices. Arrighi heard every word that they said, and held regular conversations with the sbirri, who could neither see nor reach him. He refused to give himself up, though they had promised him pardon if he would. At last the Procurator, who had been summoned from Ajaccio, sent to the town of Corte for military and an engineer. The latter was to give his opinion whether the cave could be blown up with gunpowder. The engineer came, and declared it possible to throw petards in. Arrighi heard what was being arranged, and the thought of being blown up and buried under the ruins of the cavern, filled him with such horror that he resolved upon flight.

He waited till nightfall, and then rolled down some stones in a false direction and sprung from rock to rock, to reach another mountain. Behind him, the sbirri popped off their guns with no certain aim; but one hit him on the ankle. He bled profusely, and his powers were fast failing. By daybreak his blood-stained track betrayed him like the wounded hunted deer. The sbirri are off on the track. Arrighi had crouched exhausted under a block of rock. A sbirri clambered up this block with his gun ready to fire. Arrighi put out his head to look round; a report—and the bullet had blown out his brains.

Thus died these three avengers of the mountains, happy not to meet their end on the gallows. But so great was the respect that they had enjoyed from the people, that none of the dwellers near Monte Rotondo would lend his mule to help to bring away the bodies of the fallen men. " For," said these people, " we will have no share in the blood that you have shed." As soon as they had beaten up the requisite mules, they piled the dead banditti and sbirri upon their backs, and thus the train of sbirri descended the mountains to Corte—eight corpses hung over the saddles of the mules, eight men slain in bandit warfare.

If the island of Corsica could disgorge again all the blood that has been shed in it in the course of time in battle and in vendetta, it would flood its towns and villages, and drown its people, and dye the sea red from the island's shore to Genoa ! Here red death has truly established his empire !

One can scarcely believe what the historian Filippini relates, that in his day, in thirty years 28,000 Corsicans were murdered in revenge. By the calculations of another Corsican historian, I find it stated that in the thirty-two years, up to the year 1715, 28,715 murders were perpetrated in Corsica. The same historian estimates the sum of persons murdered through the vendetta, during the period from the year 1359 to the year 1729, to be according to this computation 333,000. An equal number, he thinks, may be allowed for wounded persons. This would give us 666,000 Corsicans struck by a murderer's hand. This people is like the hydra : though all its heads be struck off, they grow anew.

According to the address of the Prefect of Corsica, held in August 1852, before the assembled departmental general council, 4300 murders (assassinats) have been perpetrated in Corsica since 1821; in the last four years of this period 833, in the last two years 319, and in the first seven months of the year 1852, 99.

The island has 250,000 inhabitants.

The government tries to extirpate this blood-revenge . and

bandit-system by a general disarming. Whether, and how, this will be capable of execution, I know not. It will cost mischief enough in the execution; for they will not be able to disarm the banditti at the same time, and their enemies will then be exposed unarmed to their bullets. The system of banditti, the family feuds, and the vendetta, which the law has not been able to overcome, have hitherto made it necessary to permit the carrying of fire-arms. For if the law cannot protect the individual, it must leave him the power of protecting himself; and thus it happens that Corsican society stands in a manner beyond the domain of the state, on the footing of natural rights, and arming for personal defence. In our century such a phenomenon is strange and frightful in a European country. The carrying of pistols and daggers has long been abolished; yet here every one carries double-barrelled guns, and I found half villages under arms, like barbarians advancing against one another; a sight of fantastic savageness, to see about one these haughty men in the *pelone* and Phrygian cap, in lonely, dismal, rocky districts, all with the leather powder-belt slung round them, and the double gun on their shoulders.

There is probably no other means of certainly putting down the blood-revenge, murder, and bandit-life, than culture.* But culture advances in Corsica but slowly. Colonisation, laying

---

* Among the Jews the Mosaic laws expressly forbade the acceptance of a pecuniary compensation for murder (Num. xxxv. 31). Among the Arabs, " Mohammed did not abolish, but endeavoured to mitigate this custom; he permits the murderer's life to be spared in return for a pecuniary fine (which has become very usual in Persia); and he desires to put an end to cruel and torturing modes of taking life. But the Bedouins seldom or never admit a compensation; for they think they would then seem to have abetted the murderer in his crime. They hold sacred the right of demanding the blood of the murderer; and they neither desire the murderer to be killed by judicial authority, nor to take his life themselves, because in the latter case they would have relieved the hostile family from a wicked member; but they reserve to themselves the power of declaring war against him and his family, and killing any of them whom they may choose—even the most exalted, and the stay of the family, because he ought to have a watchful eye over the conduct of all its members. The popular belief of the Arabs, and even of the Hebrews, contains many indications of the conception that innocent blood spilt calls for revenge,—namely, that no dew or rain falls upon the spot of such bloodshed; that charcoal is set on fire by it, and that a bird flies out from the head of the slain man, and cries incessantly, ' Give me to drink!' till the blood be avenged."-- (Ersch and Gruber's *Encycl.*) " It is ordained [in the Koran] that murder shall be punished with death, or that the perpetrator shall pay to the heirs of the person whom he has killed, a fine, which is to be divided according to the laws of inheritance; and it is optional with the said heirs to decree whether the murderer shall be put to death or the fine accepted."—(Lane's *Modern Egyptians.*)

down roads through the interior, increase of commerce, and productiveness, which would also put a new life into the port-towns—all this would, probably, be a general disarming of the country. The French government, totally powerless against Corsican insolence, deserves most righteous reproaches for allowing Corsica to become a Monte Negro, or an Italian Ireland—Corsica, an island possessing the finest climate, fruitful districts, a position commanding the entire Mediterranean between Spain, France, Italy, and Africa, and splendid gulfs and roadsteads—which, moreover, is rich in forests, minerals, medicinal springs, and fruits, and is inhabited by a brave, bold people, capable of great things.

TRAVELS.——BOOK II.

CHAPTER I.

THE IMMEDIATE NEIGHBOURHOOD OF CAPE CORSO.

CAPE CORSO is the long narrow peninsula which runs out into the sea, and terminates Corsica towards the north. The rugged mountain chain called the Serra traverses it, rising in Monte Alticcione and in Monte Stello to a height of more than 5000 feet, and descending in lovely valleys towards both coasts.

I had been told much of the beauty of the valleys of this little district, of their productiveness in wine and oranges, and of the gentle manners of the inhabitants, so that I started with real pleasure upon my wanderings. The very first approach, too, to the canton of St. Martino is imposing, as a good road leads through olive-groves along the coast. Chapels buried in foliage, family vaults surmounted by a dome, solitary cottages on the seashore, here and there an abandoned tower, with the wild fig-tree nestling in its chinks, and the prickly cactus multiplying at its base, give a picturesque aspect to the landscape. All Corsica is beset with these towers, built by the Pisans and Genoese to protect the coasts against the predatory Saracens. They are round or quadrangular, built in lonely situations of brown granite, and of a height of not more than from thirty to fifty feet. A corps of guards was stationed in them, and gave the alarm in the district on the approach of the Corsairs. All these towers are now abandoned, and falling to decay. They give an exceedingly romantic character to the Corsican seacoast.

It was a charming ramble in the brilliant early morning, the eye embracing the sea with the beautiful forms of the islands Elba, Capraja, and Monte Cristo, and being rejoiced again by the contrast of the mountains and valleys in immediate proximity to the sea. The heights here form an amphitheatre, enclosing little verdant shady valleys with streams gurgling through them. Round about stand the black villages with taper church-steeples and old convents; upon the valley-meadows the shepherd world are carrying on their avocations; and wherever a valley opens out to the coast, there stands a tower, and a little out-of-the-world fishing-village, with a few boats lying at anchor.

Every morning at sunrise, groups of women and girls come from Cape Corso to Bastia, to carry their fruit to market. A neat blue or brown gown is put on for the town, and the gayest cloth wound round the hair as a *mandile*. It is a charming sight to see these figures trudging along the seashore in the morning light, with their bright baskets on their head, holding a cheering burden of gold-red fruits; and there could scarcely be a more gracious sight than a fair, slender lass carrying a basket full of grapes on her head, and tripping lightly along like a Hebe, or Titian's daughter. They all passed me, chatting and joking, and with the same beautiful greeting, *Evviva*. There is nothing better that one human being can wish for another, than that he may live.

But let us on; for the sun is in Leo, and will in two hours be tremendous. Beyond the tower of Miomo, and near the second pieve, Brando, the carriage road ceases, and now one must clamber like a goat, for there are passable driving-roads in few places only about Cape Corso. I ascended from the little Marina di Vasina, which is quite buried out of sight on the shore, to the mountains on which are the three communes that form the pieve of Brando. The way was steep and rugged, but refreshing from dashing streams, and from the luxuriance of the gardens. The entire coast is covered with them, full of vines, and oranges, and olives, in which Brando is particularly rich. The fig-tree bends down with its ripe fruit, and does not draw back from the mouth that waters at it, like the tree of Tantalus.

In one of the rocks on the coast is the beautiful stalactite cave of Brando, which was discovered no long time ago. It is in the garden of a retired officer. A refugee from Modena had given me a letter to this gentleman, and so I visited him on his estate, which is quite glorious. The colonel has transformed the entire coast into a garden, which hangs dreamily over the sea, kept cool by quiet olives, myrtles, and laurels; there are cypresses and pines, single and in groups, flowers everywhere, ivy clustering on the walls, the vines laden with grapes, trees upon trees of oranges, a summer-house concealed among green, a cool grotto deep in the earth, solitude from the world, quiet, a sight of the azure heaven, and the sea with its hermit-islands, a searching look then into one's own happy heart!—I know not when one ought to live here, while one is still young, or when one is old and matured.

An elderly gentleman looked out from the villa on hearing me ask the gardener for the colonel, and beckoned me in. Who he was the garden had already told me, and now the little room too that I entered told me the same. The walls were decorated with significant emblems; I saw the fraternisation of the various estates represented by a countryman, a soldier, a priest, and a scholar joining hands. There sat the five races, European, Asiatic, Negro, Australian, and Red Indian, in harmony round a table, with glasses in their hands, drinking to good fellowship, and gaily encircled by vine festoons. I saw directly that I was in the fair land of Icaria, and had come to none other than the excellent uncle in Goethe's "Travels of Wilhelm Meister." And so it was; this person was single, and quite like the uncle, a humanistic socialist, and a country gentleman of great but silent influence for good.

He came to me with a cheerful tranquil mien, holding the *Journal des Débats* in his hand, and joyously smiling at what he had been reading in it.

"I have read in your garden and your parlour, Signore, the *Contrat Social* of Rousseau and a bit of the Republic of Plato. You prove to me that you are a countryman of the great Pasquale."

We spoke all manner of things about the world, humanity, and barbarism, and how theories prove so ineffective. But these are old stories that every thinking man has perhaps meditated and conversed about.

With thoughts thus excited I descended into the grotto, after having bade farewell to this remarkable man, who had so surprisingly converted into reality what I had beheld only in fiction. How strange this island is!—Yesterday a bandit who had murdered ten men from *Capriccio*, and was led to the scaffold; and to-day a practical philosopher, a devotee of the brotherhood of man!—both being equally genuine Corsicans, the product of their nation's history. Walking under the blooming trees of the garden, I said to myself that it would not be difficult in paradise to love men. I believe the wonderful power of the primitive

Christianity sprang from the fact, that its teachers were poor and often unhappy men.

St. Paul, so says Corsican story, landed on Cape Corso, the Promontorium Sacrum as it was called in ancient times, and preached the gospel. It is indubitable that the Christian religion was first introduced on Cape Corso, whenever it came to the island. Thus this district is even from ancient times a soil consecrated to human progress.

A gardening girl led me to the grotto, which is neither very lofty nor very deep, and is a series of chambers, through which one walks at one's ease. Lamps hang from the roof. These the girl lighted, and then left me alone. The pale half light now illuminated this beautiful crypt with such fantastic stalactitic formations as only a Gothic architect can imagine, in pointed arches, capitals, tabernacles, and rosettes. The grotto is the oldest Gothic cathedral in Corsica; nature built it so in her most enchanting whimsical humour. While the lamps flickered and lighted up the bright yellow transparent stalactites, it was exactly like a crypt. While left alone in this twilight, I saw the following vision portrayed in stalactites.

A wonderful maiden sat perfectly still on a throne of the clearest alabaster, covered with a white veil. On her head she wore a lotus flower, and on her breast a carbuncle. The eye could not take itself off the veiled maiden for the feelings she excited. Before her knelt many little dwarfs; the poor little wretches were all of stalactite, and wore yellow crowns of the most beautiful stalactites. They moved not, but all held out their hands towards the white maiden, as though they would lift her veil, and bitter tears dropped from their eyes. I fancied I ought to know some of them, and address them by name.

"This is Isis," said the toad satirically, sitting on a stone, and with her eyes apparently holding all spellbound. "Who knows not the right word, and yet would lift the veil of the fair maiden, shall be petrified like these. Stranger, wilt thou speak the word?"

I was here just falling asleep, being much fatigued, and finding the air in the grotto so cool and dark, and the falling of the drops so melancholy, when the gardener's girl entered the grotto and called, "It is time!"—Time? to lift the veil of Isis, O ye eternal gods! "Yes, Signore, time to come out again to the beautiful sun and the living garden." So said the girl, and said well, methought; wherefore I followed her immediately. •

"See this *fucile*, sir ; we found it in the grotto, quite encrusted with stalactite, and human bones beside it.   It was most likely the gun and the bones of a bandit.   The poor fellow probably skulked in this hiding-place, and died there like the wounded deer."   Nothing was left of the gun but the rusty barrel.   It may have directed the avenging bullet into many a heart.   I now hold it in my hand here, dug up to the light like the fossil remains of a barbarous history, and it opens its mouth, and tells me Vendetta-stories.*

CHAPTER II.

FROM BRANDO TO LURL

Πῇ δ' αὖτ', ὦ δύστηνε, δὶ ἀκρίας ἔρχεαι οἶυς,
Χώρου ἄιδρις ἐών;

ODYSSEY, x. 281.

I NOW descended to Erba Lunga, a seaside village of rather more life, from the harbour of which fishing-boats put off daily for Bastia.   The terrible heat compelled me to rest there a few hours.

Here was formerly the residence of the most powerful Signori of Cape Corso, and the ancient castle of the Signori Dei Gentili still looks down upon Erba Lunga, its mighty black walls towering up from a rocky hill.   The Gentili held sway over Cape Corso, together with the Da Mares.   To the family of Da Mare belonged also the adjacent island of Capraja, which, greatly oppressed by these violent lords, delivered itself from their rule by an insurrection in the year 1507, and put itself under the Bank of Genoa.   Cape Corso always had the reputation, confirmed by its very position, of Genoese sentiments, and its inhabitants were deemed unwarlike.   Even at the present day the Corsican mountaineers look down with contempt upon the gentle and stirring people of the peninsula.   The historian, Filippini, says of the inhabitants of the cape, "They dress well, and are from their commerce, and the vicinity of the continent, much more domestic than the other Corsicans.   There obtains among them great integrity and good faith.   Their industry is

* These stories appear to be put off till Book vii. chap. 4.

employed solely on wine, which they export to the continent."
As early as Filippini's time, the wine of Cape Corso was
renowned, and mainly of a white colour. The wines of the
greatest repute are those of Luri and Rogliano; these are among
the most excellent growths of Southern Europe, resembling those
of Spain, Cyprus, and Syracuse. Cape Corso is, however, also
rich in oranges and lemons.

Rambling further on these heights, at a distance from the seashore, one sees little of the charms of the beautiful district, which
lie concealed in the valleys. All Cape Corso is a system of such
glens towards the sea on both sides. But the mountains themselves are rugged and destitute of shade; for their bushes are no
protection against the sun. Limestone, serpentine, talc-slate,
and porphyries appear. I at length came late in the evening,
after a fatiguing walk, to the valley of Sisco. A *paesano* had
promised me hospitality there, with which cheering prospects I
descended into the valley. But which was the commune of
Sisco? There were, round about at the foot of the mountains,
and stretching higher up them, several little black villages, all
comprised under the name Sisco. This is the Corsican way, to
call all the localities of a valley by the one general name of the
pieve, though each bears its peculiar name also. I directed my
steps towards the nearest village, where an old convent under
pine-trees seemed to attract me and say, "Pilgrim, come, taste
the delights of my good wine." But I was disappointed, and had
to go uphill for a couple of miles more, till at last I reached the
house of mine host of Sisco. The little village lay picturesquely
beneath uncouth black rocks, with a tearing stream foaming
through them, and Mount Stello towering up above.

My host's house was a new establishment, and comfortable. Some
men were just come in from the mountains with their guns, and
there was a little party of country people assembled. The
women took no part; they only prepared the meal, served it,
and disappeared. The evening was passed in conversation.
The people of Sisco are poor, but hospitable and friendly. On
the morrow my host waked me at daybreak; he accompanied
me a few steps from his house, and then gave me to the care of
an old man, who was to guide me over the labyrinthine mountain
tracks into the right road to Crosciano. I had a few introductions for other villages of the cape, given me overnight. This
is the excellent and praiseworthy custom in Corsica, that the
host gives his parting guest a letter to his relations or friends

to use on his journey, and these then receive him to a like hospitality, and on his departure furnish him with a like introduction to others. Thus one may be entertained as a guest from day to day, and meet great attention every where. As there are scarcely any inns in the villages, travelling would otherwise be hardly possible.

Sisco has a very ancient church dedicated to St. Catherine, which is a noted place of pilgrimage, standing high on the sea-coast. A strange ship being once cast on this coast, the crew vowed offerings to the church for their deliverance, which they subsequently really devoted. They are rare relics indeed, and the people of Sisco may feel some pride in professing such fine things as a bit of the clod from which Adam was modelled, a few almonds from Paradise, Aaron's rod that blossomed, a bit of manna from the desert, a bit of the hide worn by John the Baptist, a bit of Christ's cradle, a bit of Christ's reed, and the celebrated rod with which Moses parted the Red Sea.

There are many picturesque views in the mountains of Sisco, and the country becomes more charming the further you go north. I went along the side of Monte Alticcioni through many villages, Crosciano, Pietra Corbara, and Caguana ; but I found also the wretchedest villages, in which even the vineyards came to an end. As I had declined a breakfast in the house of my host, not to drive the good people at sunrise into the kitchen, and it was now close upon midday, I began to feel extremely hungry. There were neither figs nor walnuts by the road-side, so I determined to appease my hunger at any cost in the next *paese* that I should pass through. In three houses they had nothing—no wine, no bread; it was all gone. In the fourth house I heard the tones of a guitar. Two old men in ragged smock-frocks sat here, one on the bed and the other on a stool. The former held the *cetera* on his arm, and played, gazing contemplatively into vacuity ; perhaps recalling his long bygone youth. The old man opened a drawer and took out a half loaf, wrapped carefully in a cloth, and presented me the bread to cut myself a piece. Then sitting down again on the bed, he struck the guitar and sang a *vocero*, or dirge. I sat by, eating the bread of the bitterest poverty, and fancied myself in the presence of the old harper in Wilhelm Meister, who sang,

> " Who ne'er his bread in sorrow ate,
> Who ne'er the mournful midnight hours
> Weeping upon his bed hath sat,
> He knows you not, ye heavenly Powers."

Heaven knows how Goëthe came to Corsica! but this is already the second character from Goëthe that I have met on this wild cape.

So my hunger was more than appeased, and I passed on. As I descended into the vale of Luri, the country around me became a perfect paradise. Luri is the most charming valley in Cape Corso, and the most extensive too, although it is only six miles long and three broad. Towards the land side it is enclosed by fine mountains, on the highest summit of which stands a solitary black tower, called the Tower of Seneca, because, according to popular story, Seneca passed there the eight years of his exile. Towards the sea, the valley gently sinks as far as the Marina of Luri. A copious mountain-stream waters the whole valley, and is conducted in channels through the gardens and orchards. Here are the communes that form the *pieve* of Luri, looking wealthy and comfortable, with their taper church-steeples, convents, and towers, in the midst of the most luxuriant southern vegetation. I have seen many a glorious valley in Italy, but I remember none that presents so smiling and joyous an aspect as this vale of Luri. It is quite full of vineyards, shaded by orange and lemon trees, and fruit-trees of every kind, rich in melons and garden plants; and the higher you mount, the thicker become the groves of chestnuts and walnuts, and of fig, almond, and olive trees.

CHAPTER III.

PINO.

A GOOD carriage road leads up from the Marina of Luri. One enjoys the balmy air of a never-ending garden. Houses, in an elegant Italian villa-style, give evidence of prosperity. How happy must man be here,—spared the raging of the elements and of human passions! A vine-dresser, who saw me coming along, beckoned me into his *vigne*, and I waited for no second invitation. Naught of vine-disease to be heard of, but plenty and geniality every where. The wine of Luri is fine, and the citrons of this valley are said to be considered the best in all the Mediterranean countries. It is principally the species of citrons with thick peel, called Cedri, that is grown here, and especially on the whole western coast of the cape, but most of all at Centuri. This tree, which is extremely tender, demands careful training. It thrives only in warm sunshine, and in the valleys that are sheltered from the wind Libeccio. Cape Corso is a perfect Elysium of this precious tree of the Hesperides.

I now started on my journey again, to cross the Serra to Pino, on the other sea. For a long time I walked through woods of walnut-trees, whose fruit was ripe; and I must here confirm what I had heard, that the Corsican walnut-trees are unequalled. Fig-trees, olives, and chestnuts, alternate with the walnuts. It is delightful to roam through a dark-shaded German forest of beeches, oaks, or pines; but the woods of the south are also glorious, for their trees form a most noble company. I climbed up the tower Fondali, which stands quite embosomed in green, close to the little village of the same name, making a very picturesque effect in the midst of this fresh foliage. From its battlements one looks into the beautiful valley and down to the blue sea, and upwards sees green hills upon hills, darkly crowned by abandoned convents. And upon the highest crag of the Serra is seen the Tower of Seneca, frowning down like a Stoic standing wrapped in thought, far into the land and sea. The many towers that stand hereabouts (for I counted several) give proof that this vale of Luri was richly cultivated, even in ancient times. They were built to protect its civilisation; and even Ptolemy, in his Corsican geography, knows the vale of Luri: he calls it Lurinon.

I climbed up through a shady grove and flowering creepers to the ridge of the Serra, close under the foot of the mountain-cone on which the Tower of Seneca stands. From this point both seas are visible, to the right and to the left. Now the path descended to Pino, where some Carrarian sculptors awaited me. The view of the western coast, with its red roofs and little indented rocky bays, and of the densely wooded piève of Pino, was quite a surprise. Pino has a few chateau-like houses and beautiful parks, where a Roman Duca would not disdain to dwell. There are millionnaires even in Corsica, and especially on the Cape they reckon up about a hundred wealthy families, among whom are a few inordinately opulent, whose wealth has been gained by themselves or their relations in the Antilles, Mexico, and Brazil.

One of these Crœsuses of Pino has inherited from his uncle in

St. Thomas an estate of ten millions of francs. Uncles are, after all, the most capital people. To have an uncle is as much as to be always putting into a lottery. They are excellent people; they may make any thing of their nephews: millionnaires, immortal, historical characters. The nephew at Pino has built a chapel of Corsican marble to his uncle for his deserts—a charming Moorish family-vault on a knoll near the sea. The Carrarese sculptors, who were just working at it, took me into the chapel. Above the uncle's grave is written, " Under the protection of God."

In the evening we visited the curé. We found him strolling up and down before his gloriously situated parsonage, in a brown Corsican jacket and with a Phrygian cap of liberty on his head. The hospitable gentleman showed us into his parlour, sat down on a wooden chair, and ordered the donna to bring wine. While the glasses were coming, he took down his guitar from the wall, and began to strike the strings with a free, bold, and joyous hand, and to sing the Paoli March. The Corsican clergy were ever free-souled men, and fought in many a fight beside their parishioners. The parson of Pino now cocked his Mithras-cap, and commenced a serenade to the fair Mary. ·I shook hands with him heartily, and thanked him for the wine and the song, and went to the bed that was prepared for me in a *paese.* We intended to ramble about early on the morrow, and then visit Seneca upon his tower.

On this western coast of Cape Corso, beyond Pino, is the fifth and last *pieve* of the Cape, called Nonza. Near Nonza stands that tower that I mentioned in the ·History of Corsica, when telling of a trait of heroic patriotism. The tower may boast of another deed of heroic audacity. In the year 1768, the old captain Casella was stationed in it with a small corps of militia. The French had already brought the Cape to submission, and the other captains had capitulated. Casella would not do the same. The tower had one cannon and sufficient ammunition, and the militia had their muskets. With this, the old man said, they could defend themselves against a whole army, and if the worst should come to the worst, they must blow themselves up. The militia knew their man, and that he would do what he said; they therefore made off in the night, leaving their arms behind them, and the old captain found himself alone. So he resolved to defend the tower entirely alone. The cannon was loaded; he loaded all the muskets, distributed them at the loopholes, and awaited the

CHAPTER IV.

THE TOWER OF SENECA.

Melius latebam procul ab invidiæ malis,
Remotus inter Corsici rupes maris.

SENECA, *Octavia*, ii. 1.

THE Tower of Seneca is visible even on the sea, and many miles off. It stands on a bare gigantic block of granite, which towers up solitary from the mountain-top, and supports the black and weatherbeaten walls. Solitary stand these also, awful and melancholy, with mists hanging about them. Desolate mountain heaths all round, and the sea far below on both sides.

If the exiled Stoic really passed eight years of banishment here, enthroned high among the clouds, in the silence of this rock-wilderness, as a significant tradition maintains, the locality was not amiss for a philosopher to indulge in sage meditations on the world and destiny, and to contemplate with wonder the eternal elements. The spirit of solitude is the best instructor of the wise. It may then have revealed to Seneca the secrets of the universe and shown him the vanity of the great Rome, in silent nights when he would have lamented his lot as an exile. When he returned again to Rome, he may, in the midst of the horrors of Nero, have often wished the solitary days of his Corsican life back again. There is an old Roman tragedy, Octavia, having for its subject the tragical fate of the wife of Nero. In this tragedy, Seneca appears as the moralizer, and utters the following verses of lamentation :*—

* Seneca, Oct. ii. init.

> Quid me, potens Fortuna, fallaci mihi
> Blandita vultu, sorte contentum mea
> Alte extulisti, gravius ut ruerem edita
> Receptus arce, totque prospicerem metus ?
> Melius latebam procul ab invidiæ malis
> Remotus inter Corsici rupes maris :
> Ubi liber animus et sui juris, mihi
> Semper vacabat, studia recolenta mea.
> O quam juvabat (quo nihil majus parens
> Natura genuit operis immensi artifex)
> Cœlum intueri, solis alternas vices,

Wherefore, with guileful visage flattering me,
Thou, potent Fortune! hast exalted high
Me with my lot contented? that my fall
Be so much deeper, and with fears beset?
Better by far away from envy's ills
Among the rocks of Corsican seas I lurk'd;
My mind was free and self-controlled, and aye
Had leisure olden studies to rehearse,
O how I joy'd—the grandest pleasure 'tis
Dame Nature 'mong her countless gifts bestows—
To observe the heavens, and watch the changeful sun,
And Phœbe's orb, by wandering stars begirt,
And then the glittering pride of air's expanse!
And when this universe grows old, anon ___
To chaos blind it shall relapse; e'en now
Draws on the last great day which shall o'erwhelm
A godless race beneath the heaven's collapse.

Rough was the shepherd's path that led us over crumbled
stones to the summit. Concealed among the bushes and rocks
below the tower, and about half-way up, stands a deserted
Franciscan monastery. The herdsmen and the wild fig-trees
now dwell in its porches, and the raven croaks the *De profundis*.
Yet the morning and the evening come to celebrate their silent
worship, and to enkindle in sacrifice the wild myrtle, mint, and
broom. What a fragrance of plants all about, and what a
morning stillness upon the mountains and the sea!

We now stood at the Tower of Seneca, having scrambled up
on hands and feet to reach its walls. One can hold on by ledges
of the wall, and so, hanging over the precipice, climb to a window; for there is no other way into the tower. Its outworks
are entirely destroyed, and it can only be discovered from their
remains that there was here a castle either of the Signori of the
Cape or of the Genoese. The tower is round, and built of
astonishingly firm materials; its cornice is shivered. Seneca
can hardly have lived on this Avernus, which is at any rate unattainable to the flight of the moral philosopher—a genus that
loves the flats. Seneca surely lived in one of the Roman colonies, Aleria or Mariana, where the Stoic, accustomed to Roman
comfort, may have furnished a nice house near the sea, from
whence the favourite mullus or tunny had no long journey to
his dinner-table.

Orbemque Phœbes, astra quem cingunt vaga,
Lateque fulgens ætheris magni decus!
Qui si senescit, tantus in cæcum chaos
Casurus iterum, nunc adest mundo dies
Supremus ille, qui promat genus impium
Cœli ruina.

An idea from the terribly beautiful world of imperial Rome
passed through my mind as I sat upon Seneca's tower. Who
can understand this world fully and correctly ? I sometimes imagine it to be Hades, and fancy the human race to be holding a
great fool's carnival in its obscurity, dancing a giant ballet before
the emperor's throne ; but the emperor sits on the throne
gloomy as Pluto, and occasionally breaks out into a foolish
laugh : for this carnival is really too mad for any thing. Ancient Seneca, too, plays among the *pulcinelle*, and enters the stage
with his bathing-tub.

Even a Seneca may have something tragicomic. See him in
the half-touching, half-ridiculous form of that ancient statue
which bears his name. He stands undraped, with a cloth round
the loins, in the bath in which he intends to die ; the figure is
so perfectly miserable, lean, and bent-kneed, and the countenance
laments so very lamentably ! He looks like St. Jerome, or like
an emaciated penitent, pitiful, and yet provoking laughter, in the
same way as many pictures of martyrs are tragicomic, from the
form of their sufferings being generally so strange.

Seneca was born of a knightly family in Corduba in Spain,
three years before Christ. His mother was Helvia, a woman
of uncommon *esprit*, and his father a well-known *rhetor*, Lucius
Annæus, who went with his family to Rome. Seneca the son
flourished at the time of Caligula as an orator and Stoic philosopher of immense learning, in which he had been aided by an
extraordinary memory. He says himself that he could repeat
in the same order two thousand names that were given him, and
that he found it easy to repeat accurately more than two hundred
verses after one hearing.

Becoming distinguished at the court of Claudius also, he was
overthrown by Messalina. She accused him of having had illicit
commerce with the notorious Julia, the daughter of Germanicus,
and the most shameless woman in Rome. The accusation is
doubly comic, both as proceeding from a Messalina, and because
we have to imagine the moral philosopher as a Don Juan. What
truth there is in the scandalous story we cannot know; but
Rome was a queer place, and there could be nothing more eccentric than the characters of its inhabitants. Julia was set aside,
and the Don Juan Seneca banished among the barbarians of
Corsica. So Seneca now became in the strict sense of the word
a Corsican bandit.

There was then scarcely a more terrible punishment than

exile, because exile from Rome was an expulsion out of the world. For eight long years Seneca lived on the wild island. I cannot therefore forgive my old friend that he has said nothing, noted down nothing, about its natural features, and the history and manners of the then population. A single chapter by Seneca on the subject would now be of great value. But it 'is characteristic of the Roman, that he had nothing to say about the barbarous country. Man was at that time haughty, confined in his views, and unloving towards the human race. How differently do we now look at nature and history!

To the exiled Seneca the island was only a prison to be hated. The little that he says about it in his letter of consolation, shows how little he knew it. For if it was then less cultivated than nowadays, yet its size was always the same. Yet he composed the following epigrams upon Corsica, which are among his poetical works :*—

Corsican island, thou erst by Phocæan colonists dwelt in,
　　Corsica, whom they call'd　　Cyrnus in language of Greece ;
Corsica, shorter than great Sardinia, longer than Elba,
　　Corsica, crossed and recrossed　　by many streams full of fish ;
Corsica, terrible isle when summer's first heat 'gins to burn us,
　　Fiercer yet, when his face　　Sirius shows in the sky
Spare then the exiles—rather the buried already I'd style them ;
　　O'er poor living men's dust　　soft be thy covering soil.

A second epigram has been declared spurious ; but I know not why the complaining man should not have written it as well as any of his contemporaries or successors in Corsican exile. The epigram says :—

*Seneca, *Epigr.* i. et ii.

Corsica Phocaïco tellus habitata colono,
　　Corsica, quæ patrio nomine Cyrnus eras;
Corsica, Sardinia brevior, porrectior Ilva ;
　　Corsica, piscosis pervia fluminibus;
Corsica terribilis, quum primum incanduit æstas ;
　　Sævior, ostendit quum ferus ora Canis ;
Parce relegatis, hoc est, jam parce sepultis.
　　Vivorum cineri sit tua terra levis.

Barbara præruptis inclusa est Corsica saxis :
　　Horrida, desertis undique vasta locis.
Non poma autumnus, segetes non educat æstas ;
　　Canaque Palladio munere bruma caret :
Umbrarum nullo ver est lætabile fetu,
　　Nullaque in infausto nascitur herba solo ;
Non panis, non haustus aquæ, non ultimus ignis :
　　Hic sola hæc duo sunt, exsul et exsilium.

N

Barbarous, and by rugged rocks is Corsica guarded
   Desert and vast are her fields   barren on every side.
No fruits autumn matures. nor corn the summer doth ripen,
   Nor by Pallas' dear gift   is the dark winter cheered
Never is spring there blest by the growth of shadowy leafage;
   Never a plant that will thrive   in the poor hapless soil.
Here is nor bread nor water, nor life's last boon, even fire, seen;
   Here is the Banished alone,   lone with his Banishment.

If *exsul* be translated "bandit," the verse is strikingly applicable, even at this day.

The Corsicans have not spared Seneca their revenge. Because he has said such abominable things of them and their country, they have fixed a tale of scandal upon him. The popular legend, namely, tells this one only event of the time of his Corsican residence. As Seneca sat in his tower, and looked down upon the frightful island, he saw the Corsican maidens, and they found favour in his eyes. The son of the gods came down, and began to flirt with the daughters of the country. He deemed a fair shepherdess worthy of his embraces. Whilst he was partaking with her of a joy remarkably human, he was surprised by the relations of the fair one, who took him and scourged his lust out of him with nettles. Ever since the nettle has grown ineradicably at the foot of the Tower of Seneca as a warning symbolical plant for moral philosophers! The Corsicans call it *ortica di Seneca.*

Poor Seneca! he cannot escape from tragicomic situations. A Corsican asked me, "You have read what Seneca said of us; *ma era un birbone*" (but he was a great rascal). Seneca morale, says Dante: Seneca birbone, says the Corsican. That again is a sign of Corsican patriotism.

The unfortunate man breathed out other sighs in verse; a few epigrams to his friends, and one to his native town of Corduba. If Seneca ever wrote any of the tragedies that bear his name, he certainly wrote the Medea in Corsica. Where was there a locality that could inspire him more to this poem on the Argonauts, than the seagirt isle? There he might well make his Chorus sing the remarkable words which prophesy Columbus: *—

---

* Seneca, *Medea,* ii. 374.

      ......venient annis
    Secula seris, quibus Oceanus
    Vincula rerum laxet, et ingens
    Pateat tellus, Tiphysque novos
    Detegat orbes; nec sit terris ultima Thule.

......" In the latter days
Is to come an age when the ocean shall
The bonds of the universe loose ; and huge
Lie open to view the earth, and new worlds
Shall Tiphys discover ; nor longer be Thule the farthest of lands."

But the mariner Columbus was born in the Genoese territory, in the vicinity of Corsica. The Corsicans make him a native of Calvi, in Corsica, and they still maintain this.

CHAPTER V.

SENECA MORALE.

—— e vidi Orfeo
Tullio e Livio e Seneca morale.
DANTE, *Inf.* iv. 140.

SENECA gathered many excellent fruits in his exile, and perhaps was indebted for some part of his noble contemplation of the universe rather to his Corsican solitude than to the doctrines of an Attalus and Socio. At the end of his letter of consolation to his mother, Helvia, he writes thus:—"I fear how you may think of me: brisk and joyous, as in the best days of my life. Those are, indeed, the best days of a man's life, when the mind is freed from all cares, and has leisure for its own activity, and he amuses himself one while with lighter studies, another while, in his eager search for truth, rises to the contemplation of his own nature and that of the universe. He first investigates countries and their position, then the nature of the surrounding sea, and the laws of its alternate ebb and flow ; then he examines all that tract, rife in terrors, that lies between heaven and earth —a space disturbed by thunder, lightning, blasts of wind, and the falling of rain, snow, and hail ; then, having passed all lower things, he takes his flight to the highest, and enjoys the grandest view of the divine ; and, mindful of his own eternity, he enters upon all that has been or shall be throughout all ages."

When I took up Seneca's letter of consolation to his mother, I was not a little curious to see how he would console her. How would any of the thousand exiles of culture, who are at this present day scattered over the world, console a mother ? Seneca's letter to his mother is a treatise in seventeen chapters, arranged according to the most approved models of the schools.

It is an exceedingly instructive contribution to the psychology
of those Stoical characters. The son thinks less of consoling his
mother than of writing an excellent and elegant treatise, the
style and logic of which shall be admired. He is quite proud
that his treatise will form a new class of literary composition,
and writes to his mother as an author deliberately weighs his
subject with a critic. " Though I have perused," he says, " all
works composed by the greatest minds with a view of checking
or moderating grief, I could not find an instance of any one
offering consolation to his friends while he was himself deplored
by them. So I was at a loss in so new a case, and feared I
might open old sores instead of healing them. But would not
a man, who should raise his head even from the funeral pile to
give a last consolation to his friends, require new forms of speech
not taken from common daily conversation ? And every great and
excessive grief must necessarily deprive one of a choice of language,
as it often even stops the voice itself. Be it as it may, I will
strive to succeed, not through confidence in my talents, but
because I, as a consoler, may be equivalent to the most cogent
arguments for consolation. And I hope that to me, to whom
you can deny nothing, you will not refuse even this (howbeit
all mourning is stubborn), that I fix a limit to your grief."
    He then begins to console after the new fashion, by counting
up all that his mother has already endured, and drawing thence
the inference that she must be hardened to suffering. Through
the entire treatise peeps out the skeleton upon which it is constructed—that, first, his mother must not grieve for his sake; and,
secondly, she must not grieve for her own sake. The letter is full
of the finest Stoical contempt of the world.
    "'But it is dreadful to be deprived of one's native land!'
But pray consider that crowded population, for whom the countless
dwellings of the great city are barely sufficient ; the greater part
of those multitudes is without a native land ; from their municipal towns and colonies, and the whole world besides, they have
come streaming to Rome. Some are attracted by ambition,
others by the claims of public life, others by the duties of an embassy, others by luxury seeking a wealthy place convenient for
excesses ; some by desire of liberal studies, others by the thea-
tres ; a few by friendship, or by speculation, seeking a wider
field for the display of its abilities ; some bring the beauty of
their person to market, others the eloquence of their tongue.
Then leave this city, which may in a manner be called the com-

mon fatherland of all; go the round of all other cities; there is none in which a large part of the population is not foreign. Now pass from those cities which attract many by their delightful situation or the advantages of their position, and go to desert regions and rugged islands, to Sciathus and Seriphus, Gyarus and Corsica; you will find no place of banishment where there is no one living for pleasure. Even here in Corsica there dwell more foreigners than native inhabitants. For a stirring and restless mind has been given to man; which you will not be surprised at if you regard its first origin—that it is not congealed from a gross and earthly body, but is deduced directly from the Celestial Spirit, and that celestial things are always in motion. Regard the heavenly bodies that enlighten the world; none of them stands still; they move incessantly and change their places." This fine thought has been suggested to Seneca by his poetic talent. Our well-known "Wanderer's song," says :—

> The sun he ne'er tarries there up in the heaven,
> To wander o'er land and o'er seas he is driven.*

"Against the actual change of place," Seneca continues, "Varro, the most learned Roman, considers it a sufficient remedy to remember that the nature of things is the same wherever we go. Marcus Brutus finds solace in the consideration, that those who go into exile can take their virtues with them. And how little it is after all that we lose! two glorious things follow us wherever we move, universal nature and our individual virtue. Let us measure the length of any countries whatsoever, we shall find no soil in the world where man could not set up his home. Every where the eye raises itself equally to heaven, and equal intervals separate all divine abodes from all human. Accordingly, so long as my eyes be not drawn off from that sight, of which they can never drink their fill; so long as I can behold the sun and moon, and fasten my gaze upon the stars, investigate their rising and setting, their distances, and the causes of their moving—now quicker, now slower—and see so many stars twinkling through the night, some immoveable, others moving in no large circle, but coming round upon their own track again—some bursting into light suddenly—some dazzling the sight with streaming radiance as if they were falling,

---

* The song alluded to will be found in most collections of German *Volkslieder.* It commences, Wohlauf! noch getrunken den funkelnden Wein.

or flying past with a long train and much light ;—so long as I
be with these, and mixed up with the things of heaven, as far as
man may ; and so long as my mind, ever striving after the contemplation of things kindred to itself, remains above ground,
what care I what ground my foot treads ?   This island is not
productive of pleasant or fruit-bearing trees, nor is it watered by
large navigable rivers ; scarce fertile enough for the sustenance
of its own inhabitants, it produces nothing desired by other nations ; no precious stone is quarried here (*non pretiosus hic lapis
cæditur*), nor veins of gold or silver worked.   But narrow is the
spirit that is delighted by earthly things ; it should be led to
those things which appear equally every where, and are equally
brilliant every where."

This also is beautiful and clever, " The longer porches they
build, the higher they raise their towers, the further they spread
out their suburbs, the deeper they dig their summer grottos, the
more massive the pinnacles of the dining-halls that they raise,
so much the more have they to hide the heavens from their
sight.   Brutus, in his book on virtue, says that he saw Marcellus in exile at Mitylene, and that he was living most happily,
as much so as the nature of man permitted; nor had he ever
been more devoted to the fine arts than then.   So, he adds, that
when he had to return without Marcellus, it seemed to him as if
he were rather himself going into exile than leaving the other
in exile."

Now follows a eulogium of poverty and contentedness, in
opposition to the gormandizing of the wealthy, who rake all seas
for their treasures to tickle their palate, who fetch their game
from beyond the Phasis, and their fowls from the Parthians, and
who eat in order to vomit, and vomit in order to eat.   "The
Emperor Caligula," says Seneca, "whom Nature seems to me to
have produced in order to show what the extreme of crime has
it in its power to do when conjoined with the extreme of prosperity, dined on one day for ten millions of sesterces; and,
though in this he was assisted by the talents of all the clever
people, he yet scarcely discovered how to consume the tribute of
three provinces in a single meal."   Seneca, like Rousseau, preaches
the return of men to the simple condition of nature.   The times
of the two moralists were analogous; they themselves are similar
in their weaknesses of character, though Seneca was a Roman
and a hero compared to Rousseau.

" Scipio's daughters received their portion from the public

treasury because their father left them nothing. O happy husbands of these two girls!" exclaims Seneca, "to whom the Roman people acted the part of father-in-law! which do you consider happier—the fathers of ballet-girls, whose daughters marry with a dowry of a million sesterces, or Scipio, whose children received from the Senate, their guardian, clumsy copper coins for their portions?"

After Seneca has consoled his mother with regard to his own sufferings, he consoles her also on her own account. "Thou needest not to regard the ways of some women, whose grief, when once it has entered into them, only death can terminate: Thou knowest some who never put off again the mourning they assumed for the loss of their sons. From thee, whose nature is fundamentally stronger, more is expected: no feminine indulgence can be allowed to one from whom all feminine faults are far. Thou hast not been drawn to the side of the many by the greatest evil of our age—immodesty; thee, no gems nor pearls have corrupted; thee riches have not dazzled as the highest good of the human race; thou, who wert well brought up in an ancient house of strict virtue, hast not had thy judgment distorted by imitation of the bad, a thing fraught with danger even to the upright. Thou hast never been ashamed of the number of thy children, as though it reproached thee with thy advancing age; nor concealed the bliss that awaited thee as an unseemly burden, after the fashion of other ladies, whose sole commendation is the beauty of their figure; nor renounced thy hope of a numerous progeny. Thou hast not polluted thy face with rouge and cosmetics; nor ever been charmed by a dress made more to expose than to veil the person. The only real adornment and greatest comeliness thou hast judged to be modesty, which is the fairest kind of beauty, and one upon which years have no power." So writes the son to his mother, and methinks we may trace in it the genuine philosophic phlegm.

He reminds her of Cornelia, the mother of the Gracchi; yet he will not conceal from himself that grief is a stubborn and unyielding thing. Tears will break forth, after all, from the face that puts on a look of sternness. "We sometimes try to engross ourselves with games and gladiatorial exhibitions; and, in the midst of the very means used to distract our morbid thoughts, they are invaded by some silent prompter of our grief. Therefore it is better to overcome than to evade grief. For that grief which has been cheated, and drawn off by pleasures and distrac-

tions, rises again, and gains through the very interval of rest
fresh force to harass; but that which has yielded to reason is
allayed for ever." Here the voice of a sage declares beautiful,
simple, and true, but bitterly hard rules of living. Therefore
Seneca does not advise his mother to employ the usual means of
getting over grief (here we are again forced to smile), namely,
to take a delightful journey, or to seek distraction for the thoughts
in domestic affairs; no, he advises intellectual employment.
He here laments that his father, an excellent man, but one who
clove too strictly to the customs of his fathers, could not resolve
upon giving her a philosophical education. Here we have, on a
small scale, a capital picture of old Seneca, the father. We know
now what he looked like. When the modern gentlemen and
ladies in Corduba, having caught up the emancipation and higher
position of women from Plato's Republic, represented to the old
man that his young wife would indeed do well to attend the
lectures of a few philosophers, he blustered out, "Humbug! my
wife shall be no spoiled princess, and no silly blue-stocking; she
shall know how to cook, get children, and bring up children."
So said this excellent worthy, and added in the best Spanish,
"Basta!"

Seneca then speaks much of greatness of soul, of which woman
too is capable; but he little thought then that he was to see it
exemplified on occasion of his death, in his own wife, Paulina.
A noble man, then, and a Stoic of the most exalted sentiments,
has spoken in this consolation to Helvia. Is it possible that the
same man could think and write as a common cringing flatterer?*

CHAPTER VI.

SENECA BIRBONE.

Magni pectoris est inter secunda moderatio.
                                        SENECA.

HERE is a second letter of consolation, written by Seneca in
the second or third year of his exile in Corsica, to Polybius, the
freedman of Claudius, a common courtier. Polybius was
associated with the overlearned Claudius as his scientific adviser,
and was himself labouring at a Latin translation of Homer, and
a Greek of Virgil. Seneca's letter of condolence to the courtier

_* Seneca, Cons. ad Helv., 1, 6, 8, 9, 12, 16.   ₥

was prompted by the loss of his talented brother. He wrote the treatise in the conviction that Polybius would read it to the emperor; thus he hoped to appease the wrath of Claudius, and the essay became a model of low flattery towards princes and their influential chamberlains. In reading it, one must not forget what sort of people Claudius and Polybius were.

"O Fate!" exclaims the flatterer, "how unerringly thou hast discovered that this part alone was exposed to thy darts! For what else couldst thou have done to such a man? Shouldst thou have taken his money? to that he never was a slave, and now he even throws it away whenever he can.—Life?—the fame of his genius promised him immortality. He himself took care that his better part should live on, and that by the composition of splendid oratorical works he should exempt himself from the common lot of mortality. So long as any honour is paid to literature, so long as the Latin language maintains its power, or the Greek its grace, his name will live coupled with the greatest men, whose talents he has equalled, or, if his modesty will not allow that, has come near to.—Unworthy deed! Polybius mourns, and has some grief, while the emperor continues his favour! It was doubtless this, inexorable Fate, that thou wert aiming at— to show that no one can be defended against thee, not even by the emperor.—Thou must not complain of fate, Polybius, so long as the emperor is saved to thee, who thou always sayst is dearer to thee than thy life. If he is safe and well, thy friends are safe, and thou hast lost nothing; then thy eyes ought to be not only dry, but sparkling with joy. In the emperor thou hast every thing; he stands in the place of every thing besides.—So long as thy gaze is fixed on this thy deity, sadness will find no entrance into thy mind."

"Keep thy hands off the emperor, Fortune, and exhibit not thy power on him, unless it be thy power of blessing; suffer him to heal the long diseases of the human race, and to restore to its place and amend all that was shattered and destroyed by the fury of the former emperor. This sun, that has enlightened a world hurled into the abyss and sunk in darkness, ever may it so shine! May he give peace to Germany, unlock the unknown wilds of Britain, and celebrate triumphs like his father's, and new ones beside! The clemency that holds the first place among his virtues, gives me hopes that I shall be allowed to witness these; for he did not cast me down in such a way that he would be unwilling to raise me again; he did not indeed cast me down

at all, but upheld me when stricken by fortune and falling to the
ground, and set me gently down by the guidance of his divine
hand.   He supplicated the senate on my behalf, and not only
gave me life, but even besought it for me.   He will soon see how
he deigns to think of my cause, whether his justice perceives it
to be good, or his clemency makes it good.   In either case his
benefit to me will be the same, whether he knows that I am
innocent, or determines that I shall be.   In the mean time, it is
a great alleviation of my misery to see his mercy pervading the
whole world; and since from this very nook of the world to
which I am bound he has dug up and brought back to the light
many who were buried under the rubbish of many years, I have
no apprehensions that I shall be the only one passed over.   And
he himself best knows the time to succour each sufferer; I shall
use every effort to prevent his being ashamed of coming to me.
All hail to thy clemency, Cæsar! which causes exiles to lead
under thee a more tranquil life than under 'Caligula lately the
first men of the empire did.   They tremble not, nor hourly expect
the sword, nor turn pale at the sight of every arriving ship.
By thee they have both a limitation of the horrors of their
present fortune and tranquillity under it, and likewise the prospect of a better.   Know that only those thunderbolts are the
most absolutely just, which are worshipped by the persons they
strike."

O nettles! more nettles, noble Corsicans—*era un birbone!*

The letter of consolation concludes with these words: "These
thoughts I have put together as well as I could with a mind
rendered dull and long incrusted with the mould of inactivity;
if they seem either too little in accordance with your mind, or
a feeble remedy for your grief, consider how little leisure for
consoling others he can command who is preoccupied by his
own ills; and how difficult it must be to find the appropriate
Latin words, when one has constantly dinned into one's ears an
uncouth barbarous jargon, offensive even to the more polished
barbarians."

This flattery bore no fruit for the man of trouble; but the
changes that took place in the Roman court recalled Seneca from
exile.   The head of Polybius had fallen; Messalina had been
executed.   Claudius was so obtuse that he forgot the execution
of his wife, and asked at supper a few days after why Messalina
did not come to table.   All these horrors have this kind of
tragicomic character; and in the midst of them returns the

prime consoler in affliction, the Corsican bandit. Agrippina, Claudius's new wife, had him recalled to educate her son Nero, a boy eleven years old. Can one fancy any thing more tragi-comic than Seneca in the capacity of instructor to Nero? He came thanking the gods that they had imposed on him the vocation of training a boy to be ruler of the world. He now hoped to fill the earth with his spirit, by imparting it to young Nero. What a task, at once tragical and ridiculous! He was hoping to educate a tiger's whelp on Stoic principles. Still, Seneca found this promising pupil to be as yet utterly unspoiled by false school methods; for he had grown up in right royal ignorance, and enjoyed the closest intimacy with a barber, a coachman, and a rope-dancer. From their hands Seneca received the boy who was destined to rule over gods and men.

As Seneca was banished to Corsica in the first year of Claudius, and returned in his eighth, he could rejoice in "this deity and this celestial star" for more than five years longer. But Claudius died suddenly, Agrippina having given him poison mixed by the notorious Locusta, in a gourd that served as drinking-vessel. The death of Claudius brought Seneca the longed-for opportunity of giving vent to his vengeance. He took terrible reprisals for his banishment, by writing upon the deceased the Apocolo-cyntosis, a pamphlet of astonishing wit and incredible audacity, fully equal in genius to Lucian. The very title is an invention of genius; it parodies the notion of the apotheosis or translation of the Emperors to the gods, and signifies the *translation into the society of gourds*, or *gourdification* of Claudius, who was poisoned by a gourd. This satire is well worth reading. It is characteristic of the Roman times, when, under unrestricted despotism, a man's tongue durst yet speak such things, and a recently deceased emperor might be openly derided by his successor, by his family, and by the people, as a harlequin, saving the imperial dignity. Every thing in this Roman world is an ironical accident, tragicomic and grotesque—a regular fool's paradise.

Seneca speaks with a masquerader's freedom, and commences thus: "I wish to record what happened in heaven on the 13th of October, in the consulship of Asinius Marcellus and Acilius Aviola, in the new emperor's year, and the commencement of a most felicitous era. I shall yield neither to revenge nor to favour. If any one shall ask me how I know the truth of my statements, I shall in the first place not answer, unless I please:

who can force me to it? I know that I have become a free man
since he went the way of all flesh, who made true the proverb,
'One must be born either king or fool.' If I choose to answer,
I shall say whatever comes into my head." Seneca then says
decisively, he has received what he is going to tell from the
senator who saw Drusilla (the sister and mistress of Caligula)
ascend to heaven on the Appian way (for this barefaced declaration, Livius Geminus actually received from Caligula
250,000 denarii reward); that the same senator saw all that
passed on Claudius's ascent to heaven.

" I believe I shall be better understood," proceeds Seneca, " if
I say the month was October, the day the thirteenth. The
hour I cannot tell for certain; philosophers will sooner agree
than clocks. However, it was between the sixth and seventh
hour." " Claudius began to pant for breath, and could find no
outlet for his departing soul. Then Mercury, who had always
delighted in his talents, took one of the three Fates aside, and
said, ' Wherefore, cruel woman, sufferest thou a wretched man
to be in tortures? he should never have been so long tormented;
for the last sixty-four years he has been struggling for breath.
What spite hast thou against him? Suffer the astrologers for
once to say a true thing, when they bury him every year and
every month, since he has been emperor; and yet it is no wonder
if they 'err, for no one knows Claudius's hour, for nobody considers him to have been ever born. Do thy duty,

And let him die: his empty court a better man shall rule.'"

Hereupon, the Fate cuts Claudius's life-thread, but Lachesis
spins another bright-shining thread, that of Nero. Phœbus accompanies on the lyre, and Seneca flatters his pupil, his new sun,
with fine, good-for-nothing verses: *—

Phœbus hath spoken : he shall transcend the span of life mortal,
Bearing my likeness upon his brow, my beauty resembling,
Neither in song nor in voice a whit worse ; to wearied mortals
Happy the age he shall bring, of laws first breaking the silence.
Like as Lucifer scatters the starry army of heaven,
Or as Hesperus rises to greet the return of the starlight,
Or as when rosy Aurora, first dissolving the darkness,
Leads on the day, and earth is beshone by the radiant sunlight,
And his golden wheels the sun brings forth from their prison :
Such is Cæsar, and such shall Rome admiring behold soon
Nero. whose beaming countenance glows with a gentler refulgence,
And on whose beauteous neck rich waving curls are diffused.

---

* Phœbus ait: vincat mortalis tempora vitæ,
Ille mihi similis vultu, similisque decore,
Nec cantu, nec voce minor: felicia lassis

"Claudius meanwhile bubbled out his soul, and thereby ceased to be supposed to live. He expired while he was hearing the comedians, so you see I do not fear these without cause."

So Claudius is dead. "Now news is brought to Jupiter of the arrival of a man of good figure, rather bald, who utters some sort of menaces against him, is always shaking his head, and trails his right foot. On being asked of what nation he was, he replied with some confused sound; they did not understand his language, which seemed to be neither Greek nor Roman, nor of any known nation. Then Jupiter bids Hercules, who had vagabondized over the whole world, and was supposed to know all nations, to go and discover what sort of man this was. When Hercules saw his extraordinary figure, and his unheard of gait, and heard his hoarse voice, more resembling some sea-monster than any terrestrial animal, he thought there was a thirteenth labour in store for him; but, on looking more attentively, he thought he discovered resemblance to a man. So he approached him, and accosted him in Greek, the easiest thing in the world for a Greek—

'Say, who, and from what men thou art, and where thy city lies?'

"When Claudius heard this, he was rejoiced to find philologians in heaven, and had hopes of finding some readers for his histories." He had written in Greek twenty books of Tyrrhenic, and eight of Carthaginian history. So he answered at once in another line of Homer, foolishly—

"From Ilium the winds have cast me 'mong Ciconians here." *

Fever, who alone of all the Roman gods had accompanied Claudius to heaven, gives him the lie, and calls him a regular Gaul. "Therefore he did what a Gaul must do, made himself master of Rome." (As I write down this sentence of the old Roman here in Rome, and actually hear French trumpets, its correctness is curiously verified). Claudius directly gives orders to have Fever's head cut off. "But you would have thought they were all his freedmen, so little did they mind his command." He gains over

---

Secula præstabit, legumque silentia rumpet. .
Qualis discutiens fugientia Lucifer astra
Aut qualis surgit redeuntibus Hesperus astris,
Qualis quum primum tenebris Aurora solutis
Induxit rubicunda diem, sol adspicit orbem
Lucidus, et primos e carcere concitat axes:
Talis Cæsar adest, talem jam Roma Neronem
Adspiciet: flagrat nitidus fulgore remisso
Vultus, et effuso cervix formosa capillo.

* Od. i. 170, and ix. 39.

Hercules, however, who introduces him into the hall of the gods. But the god Janus brings forward a motion, that none of those who " eat the fruits of the field" shall henceforth be deified, and Augustus reads a written resolution, by which Claudius must evacuate Olympus within three days. The gods approve the decree, and Mercury then hustles them off by the collar into the lower world.

On the Sacred way they are met by the funeral procession of Claudius, which is thus described:—" It was most beautiful, and full of such pomp and expense, as showed clearly that a god was being buried. There was such a multitude of flute-players, horn-blowers, and trumpeters of all sorts, that even Claudius could hear them. All were joyous and lightsome; the Roman people walked about as though it felt free again. Only Agathon and a few advocates wept, but their mourning was truly heart-felt. The jurisconsults came forth from darkness, pale, thin, and only half alive, as if they were just coming to life again. When one of these saw the advocates putting their heads together and deploring their lot, he approached them, and said, ' I told you the Saturnalia would not last for ever.' When Claudius saw his funeral, he discovered that he was dead. For the following anapæstic dirge was being sung with great bombast :—

" Stream forth, ye tears of woe !
Of counterfeit mourning,
Let echo the forum.
Nobliest hearted,
Over the wide world,
He in the swift race
He the rebellious
And with his light darts
And with a sure hand
Foes in flight headlong
He could transfix, and
Shield of the flying
He too the Britons,
Shores of the Ocean,
Tribe of Brigantes,
Fetters of Romulus ;
Tremble before new
Fasces and sway.
Quicker than others
Lawsuits decide,
Hearing but one, or
Who as our judge
Through the whole year?
Yield up his place,
Dead giveth laws,
Cities in Crete.
Palms on your breasts, ye

Sound, lamentations
With the sad clamour
Fallen is he, the man
Braver than whom there was
Never another.
Conquered the fleetest ;
Parthians routed ,
Followed the Persian ;
Strained the bowstring ;
With but a small wound
Pierce through the painted
Cowardly Mede.
Dwelling beyond known
And the blue-shielded
Forced to submit to
And bade old Ocean
Masters, the Roman
Weep for the man, who
Could at an eye-glance
Of the two parties
Oft hearing neither.
Now will hear causes
He will to thee now
Who to the silent
Ruling a hundred
Beat with your mournful
Pleaders special, ye

Venal race.　　　　　　　　Ye too, new poets,
Weep and be downcast;　　　Ye too above all,
Who have gained lucre　　　Princely and glorious,
　　　　　Shaking the dice-box."*

A band of singers meets Seneca on his entrance into the lower
world with the exclamation, "We have found him ! rejoice
greatly !" the cry by which the Egyptians proclaimed the discovery of the ox Apis. These were all whom Claudius had had
executed, Polybius and his fellow freedmen among them. Æacus
now examines the deeds of Claudius, and finds that he had
judicially murdered "thirty senators, three hundred and fifteen
Roman knights or more, and other citizens as many as the sand
or dust" ὅσα ψάμαθός τε κόνις τε). So he decrees him the punishment of
playing at dice with a perforated dice-box. Then suddenly
appears Caligula to claim him as a slave. He brings witnesses
to show that he had often given his uncle Claudius a box on
the ear, and beaten him with rods and whips, which no one
being able to gainsay, Claudius is assigned over to Caligula. The

* Fundite fletus,
Fingite luctus :
Clamore forum :
Cordatus homo,
Fuit in toto
Ille citato
Poterat celeres,
Fundere Parthos,
Persida telis,
Tendere nervum :
Vulnere parvo
Pictaque Medi *
Ille Britannos
Litora ponti,
Scuta Brigantas
Colla catenis
Nova Romanæ
Tremere Oceanum.
Quo non alius
Discere causas,
Parte audita,
Quis nunc judex
Audiet anno ?
Sede relicta,
Jura silenti,
Oppida centum.
Pectora palmis,
Venale genus.
Lugete novi :
Qui concusso

Edite planctus,
Resonet tristi
Cecidit pulchre
Quo non alius
Fortior orbe.
Vincere cursu
Ille rebelles
Levibusque sequi
Certaque manu
Qui præcipites
Figeret hostes,
Terga fugacis.
Ultra noti
Et cæruleos
Dare Romuleis
Jussit, et ipsum
Jura securis
Deflete virum,
* Potuit citius
Una tantum
Sæpe et neutra.
Toto lites
Tibi jam cedet
Qui dat populo
Crotura tenens
Cædite mœstis
O causidici,
Vosque poëtæ,
Vosque in primis
Magna parastis
　　Lucra fritillo.

latter bestowed him upon his freedman Menander, to whom he
was to render aid in commissions of inquiry.

Such is the remarkable Apocolocyntosis of Claudius. Seneca,
after meanly flattering the living emperor, was base enough also
to throw dirt upon him when dead. A generous man takes no
revenge on the corpse of his enemy, were he ever so ridiculous
a monster : the coward insults it. The Apocolocyntosis is the
truest mirror of the Roman Imperial times when sunk in
baseness and servility.*

CHAPTER VII.

SENECA EROE.

Alto morire ogni misfatto amenda.

ALFIERI.

OUR Pasquino, Seneca, straightway metamorphoses himself
again into the noble moralist. He writes his treatise " Of grace,
to the Emperor Nero,"—an absurd contradiction, Nero and grace;
it is, however, known that the young emperor, like all his predecessors, ruled for the first few years without cruelty. Seneca's
treatise is once more excellent, wise, and full of noble sentiments.

Nero loaded his instructor with riches, and the author of
the tract on poverty possessed a princely fortune—gardens, fields,
palaces, villas before the Nomentan gate, in Baiæ, and on the
Alban mountains, and more than six millions of money. He
carried on the business of a usurer in Italy, as well as in the
provinces, avariciously scraped together money upon money, and
cringed like a dog before Agrippina and her son, until the tables
were turned.

In four years Nero had shaken off every restraint. The timid
Seneca could not prevent his perpetration of matricide, and the
high-minded Tacitus speaks of him with blame. But at last
even the philosopher became inconvenient to Nero. When the
latter had murdered his prefect Burrhus, Seneca hastened to
place all his possessions at the madman's disposal, and lived
thenceforward in complete retirement. But his enemies accused
him of being privy to the conspiracy of Calpurnius Piso, and his

* Cons. ad Polyb. 21, 26, 32, 37.

nephew, the celebrated poet Lucan, was involved, not without cause, in the same charge. Lucan conducted himself on this occasion with incredible pusillanimity, pleading guilty, demeaning himself by the most abject entreaties, and, under cover of the august example of Nero's matricide, actually denouncing his innocent mother as a party to the conspiracy. When, this hideous conduct being powerless to save him, he was condemned to a voluntary death, he went home, wrote a few lines to his father, Annæus Mela Seneca, on certain emendations in his poem, dined magnificently, and then with perfect composure opened a vein.

The feeble Seneca appears in his death noble, great, and venerable, with almost the cheerfulness of a Socrates and the tranquillity of a Cato. He chose to bleed to death, and allowed his heroic wife Paulina to die the same death. They were living among friends and attendants on their estate, four miles from Rome. Nero sent his tribune uneasily to the villa and back again, to see how matters stood there. Being hastily informed that Paulina also was bleeding to death, he sent a hurried command to prevent her death. The slaves bound up their mistress's veins, and stopped the flow of blood, and Paulina was saved against her will; she lived some years longer. But the blood of the aged Seneca flowed but feebly, subjecting him to a slow torment. So he begged Statius Annæus for poison, and took it, but without result. He then had himself put in a warm bath. He besprinkled the attendant slaves with the water, and said, "To Zeus the deliverer I pour this libation." Not being able to die even here, he had himself transferred from the warm bath into a hot vapour-bath, and was suffocated in the vapour. He was sixty-eight years old at his death.[*]

Who will now quarrel any more with this sage, who indeed was a man of his degenerate time, but in whose nature a divine talent, and love of truth and wisdom, were coupled with the basest weaknesses? His writings exerted a great influence throughout the middle ages, purifying many a mind from passions, and attuning it to all that is good and noble. Let us then part good friends, Seneca.

[*] Tacitus, *Ann.* xiv. 52-56, 65, xv. 56, 63, 64.

CHAPTER VIII.

A BRIDE'S THOUGHTS.

——σοὶ δὲ γάμος σχεδόν' ἐστιν· ἵνα χρη καλὰ μὲν αὐτὴν
ἕννυσθαι, τὰ δὲ τοῖσι παρασχεῖν, οἵ κέ σ' ἄγωνται.
ἐκ γάρ τοι τούτων φάτις ἀνθρώπους ἀναβαίνει
ἐσθλή· χαίρουσιν δὲ πατὴρ καὶ πότνια μήτηρ.
                                    ODYSSEY, vi. 27.

EVERY valley or *pieve* of Cape Corso has its Marina, or seaport,
and there can scarcely be any thing more desolate than these
little hamlets on the quiet shore.   It was sultry noon when
I came to the strand of Luri—the time when Pan used to take
his sleep.   The people in the cottage where I wished to wait
for the boat seemed to be all asleep.   But a lovely maiden was
sitting at the open window, dreamily stitching at a *fazoletto*
with a mysterious smile, and all manner of secret flowery
thoughts.   She was embroidering something on the stuff, which
I perceived to be a little poem that her happy heart had made
for her approaching wedding.   The blue sea, to which the
sailor's daughter had confided all her secret, laughed joyously
through the window behind her back.   The girl wore a sea-green
dress, a flowered boddice, and the mandile neatly wound round her
hair ; the mandile was snow-white, with narrow red stripes, three
together.   To me also Maria Benvenuta confessed her open
secret, and entertained me with all manner of chat about
wind and waves, and the beautiful Musica at the wedding dance
in the valley of Luri.   The wedding will be in a few months,
and no fairer one will have ever been celebrated in all Corsica.
On the morning when Benvenuta is to leave her mother's
house, a charming Trovata, or green triumphal arch, gaily decorated with ribbons, will be erected at the entrance of the seaside
hamlet.   Friends, neighbours, and relatives will assemble on
the Piazetta for the *corteo*, or bridal procession.   Then a youth
comes up to the bride in her bridal dress, and complains that
she is going to leave the place where she has grown up from
childhood in kind keeping, where she has never wanted for corals,
flowers, or friends.   But, as she now wishes to depart, he heartily
wishes her in the name of her friends all happiness, and gives

her his farewell. Then Maria Benvenuta bursts into tears, and
presents the youth with a gift for the commune as a remembrance of her. A gaily caparisoned pony.is led before the
house, on which the bride mounts, and well-armed youths
ride by her side, crowned with flowers and ribbons, and the
corteo passes through the triumphal arch. A youth carries the
freno, or symbol of fruitfulness, a distaff surrounded at top by
many spindles, and adorned with gay ribbons. A handkerchief
waves above it as a banner. With this *freno* in his hand the
freniere heads the procession, proud and joyful.

The procession approaches Campo, where the bridgroom lives,
into whose house the bride is now to be introduced. There
stands another fine *trovata* at the entrance of Campo. Here a
youth advances, holding high in his hand a ribbon-decked olive
bough, which with fine words he presents to the bride. Then
two youths from the *Corteo* of the bride dash off in mad haste
towards the bridegroom's house, to ride for and gain the *Vanto*,
that is, the honour of being the first to bring the bride the keys
of the bridegroom's house. The keys are represented under the
symbol of a flower, which the rapidest rider gains, and holds
triumphantly in his hand, and then dashes back to deliver to the
bride. The procession now advances towards the house. On
all the balconies stand women and girls, who strew flowers, rice,
and grains of wheat upon the bride, and throw fruits of the
season among the procession, with joyful exclamations and
blessings. This they call *Le Grazie*. But the shooting with
guns, the sound of the mandolines, and the playing upon the
Cornamusa, or bagpipe, is incessant. What a jubilee for Campo,
a popping, hurraing, twanging, and fiddling like mad, and the
air full of spring-swallows twittering, larks singing, flowers
flying, wheat-grains falling, motes hovering in the sunbeam; and
all this for this little Maria Benyenuta, who is sitting at the
window here, and embroidering the whole story into the *fazoletto!*

Then the old father-in-law will come out of the house and
speak seriously to the strange *corteo* thus : " Who are ye, men in
arms? friend or foe? Are ye the escort of a *donna gentile*, or
have ye carried her off by force, though your appearance seems
to me to betoken you noble and brave men?" " We are friends
who may claim hospitality," says the leader of the bridal train,
" and are escorting this fair and excellent damsel, the pledge of
our new friendship. We plucked the fairest flower on the
strand of Luri to bring it as a present to Campo."

" Be then welcome, my friends, and step into my house and
enjoy the feast." Thus says the old man, who then lifts the
maiden from her horse, embraces her, and leads her into his
house. There the happy bridegroom clasps her in his arms, to
the tune of the sixteen-stringed *cetera*, and the noise of the
cornamusa.

Then they go to the church, where the tapers are already
lighted, and myrtles are plentifully strewn about. And when the
couple have been united and again enter the house of the wedding, two chairs are set in the banqueting room, on which the
happy pair seat themselves. Now comes a woman smiling
roguishly, and carrying on her arm a baby in swaddling clothes,
and decked with ribbons, which she puts into the arms of the
bride. Little Maria Benvenuta, without blushing in the least,
takes the child and caresses it to her heart's content. Then she
puts a little Phrygian cap on its head, charmingly decked
out with gay ribbons. After this the relatives embrace the
couple, and each speaks the good old wish:

" Dio vi dia buona fortuna
Tre di maschi e femmin' una; "

that is, " God give you fortune, three sons and one daughter."
The bride now distributes little gifts to her husband's relations,
the next of kin receiving a small coin. Then follows the banquet
and then the *ballo*, in which they will dance the *Cerca*, the
Marsiliana, and the *Tarantella*.

Whether they will further observe the more antiquated usages
mentioned by the chroniclers, I know not. Formerly it was the
custom for a young kinsman of the bride to go before her into
the bridal chamber, to jump and roll several times over the
bridal bed, then seat the bride upon it, and untie her shoestrings
with the same decorum as Anchises loosens the sandals of the
reclining Venus, as represented in old pictures. The bride would
prettily shake off her shoes and let them fall to the ground, and
give a present in money to the sandal-loosening youth. In a
word, there will be merry doings on Benvenuta's wedding-day,
and there will be talk of it for many years after in the valley
of Campo.

We chatted seriously on all these matters in the little room
of the Luri sailor; and I have also the lullaby with which
Maria Benvenuta will rock the little baby in her arms to sleep.

NANNA.

Ninniná, my heart's beloved,
  Ninniná, my only joy;
Thou'rt my dancing, dear little ship,
  Dancing on the blue waves, my boy,
Fearing not the rising billow,
  Fearing not the winds at sea.
    Sleep awhile and slumber, darling,
    Do thy *ninni nani*.

Darling ship, thou heavy with jewels,
  Silks thou bearest, stuffs of great fame.
And thy sails are of brocade,
  From an Indian port they came;
And thy rudder is of gold,
  Costly is the work thereon.
    Sleep awhile, &c.

Darling, when thou were just born,
  To the font they carried thee soon;
And the sun was godpapa,
  And thy godmamma the moon;
And the stars of heaven did rock thee
  In a golden cradle fair.
    Sleep awhile, &c.

Brightly shone the heaven, my darling,
  Blue and laughing was his eye;
Also, even planets seven
  Brought thee offerings lovingly.
All the herdsmen on the mountains
  Held an eight days' festival.
    Sleep awhile, &c.

Heard was nought but citherns, darling,
  Seen was nought but dancing rare
In the dale of Cuscioni,
  Far and wide, and every where.
Boccanera and Falconi
  Bark'd for joy as it listed them.
    Sleep awhile, &c.

When thou art grown bigger, my darling,
  Thou shalt ramble over the lea;
All the flowers shall spring into blossom,
  Dew shall turn to oil for thee,
And to finest balm be converted
  All the water in the sea.
    Sleep awhile, &c. .

Cover'd shall the mountains, my darling,
  Be with sheep as white as snow;
Then shall run close after thee, darling,
  Horned chamois, goat, and roe,
But the hawks and kites and foxes
  Flee away from this our dale.
    Sleep awhile, &c.

> Darling mine, thou art my primrose,
> Dearest, thou art heart's-ease fair,
> Growing in the vale Bavella,
> Or Cuscioni's native air,
> Thou, my leaf of sweetest clover,
> That the kids delight to pluck.
> Sleep awhile, &c.

Should the child be too much excited by this fanciful song, its mother will sing to·it the following little *nanna*, which will send it to sleep directly :—

> Ninni ninni, ninni nanna,
> Ninni ninni, ninni nolu,
> Allegrezza di la mamma
> Addormentati, o figliuolu.

CHAPTER IX.

A GHOSTLY VOYAGE.

MEANWHILE sounds·were heard on the shore. The sailors were come; so I took leave of the pretty Benvenuta, wishing her all sorts of good things, and stepped into the boat which was sailing to Bastia. We sailed along the coast, and close to the shore. The boat came to land at Porticcioli, a small seaport with a dogana, to have its four passengers registered. Some sailing boats also anchored here. The ripe figs on the trees, and the fine grapes in the vineyards, were very tempting; so they brought us half a vineyard full of the most delicious Muscatel grapes, and figs of the sweetest flavour, for a few soldi.

Sailing on in the evening, I was greatly delighted with the moonlit sea and the curious shapes of the coast, where I saw many towers on the rocks, and here and there a ruin, church, or convent. We sailed past the old church of St. Catherine of Sicco, which stands up high and splendid on the coast.· But the weather was growing wild, and a storm threatening. When within sight of St. Catherine's, the old steersman took off his *baretto* and prayed aloud, "Holy Mother of God, Mary, we are sailing to Bastia, grant that we come safely to port!" The sailors all took off their *baretti*, and crossed themselves devoutly. The moonlight, suddenly breaking forth upon the sea from black thunder-clouds, the fear of a storm, the coast in an awe-inspiring moonlight, and lastly St. Catherine, suddenly excited in the

whole boat's company one of those irresistible moods of mind
that find vent in the narration of ghost-stories. The sailors
began to tell of all kinds of witchcraft. Now one of the passengers, who would not have his countrymen appear superstitious
in the foreigner's eyes, kept shrugging his shoulders, vexed that
I should hear such things; but another of them always confirmed
his own and the sailors' opinion with the argument, " I have
never seen witches with my own eyes, but devil's arts there
must be." I myself maintained that I believed firmly in the
streghe and witches, and that I had had the honour of knowing
some of the best of them. The partisan of the devil's arts, an
inhabitant of Luri, had however given me an insight into the
depth of his mysterious studies, by throwing out the question, on
occasion of a conversation about London, whether London was
a French place. So it seemed to me excellent policy to keep
the fire burning in this witches' kitchen.

The Corsicans call the witch *strega*. She draws children's
blood like a vampire. One of the sailors, having once come upon
one in his father's house, described her appearance: she is pitch
black upon the breast, and can change herself into a cat, or from
a cat into a young woman. These *streghe* are especially noxious
to children, looking at them with the evil eye, and committing
all manner of *fattura*. They can also enchant weapons so as to
make them miss their aim. In this case, one should make a
cross on the gun-stock; the cross is indeed in general the best
protection against all magic. It is always good to carry relics
and amulets; some of these will protect against bullets, and
against the bite of the venomous spider, *malmignatto*. Among
these amulets, they formerly had in Corsica a travel-stone, which
was found only near the Tower of Seneca, and was four-cor-
nered, and contained iron, like what frequently occurs in the
northern mythology. Whoever bound such a stone above his
knee, had an easy and prosperous journey.

Some few heathen usages have been retained in Corsica, especially among the herdsmen of Niolo. The most remarkable
is divination from bones. The diviner takes the shoulder-blade
of a goat or sheep, polishes it, and reads from it the destinies of
the person in question. It must, however, be the left shoulder-
blade, because by the old proverb, *La destra spalla sfalla*, " The
right shoulder-blade is fallacious." We hear of many celebrated
Corsicans having their fate prophesied to them by diviners. It
is said, that while Sampiero was sitting at table with his com-

panions on the eve of his death, an owl screeched on the house-top the whole night through; and a diviner then read the scapula, and to the horror of all discovered Sampiero's death in it.

Napoleon's fate also was prophesied upon a *spalla*. There was an old shepherd of Ghidazzo renowned for his reading of shoulder-blades; inspecting a scapula one day, when Napoleon was a child, he found clearly delineated upon it a tree, that shot up high towards heaven with many branches, but had only few and small roots. Hence he inferred that a Corsican would be ruler of the world, but only for a short time. This prophecy is popular in Corsica; it has a remarkable similarity to the dream of Mandane, respecting the tree which signifies Cyrus.

Many superstitious ideas of the Corsicans, testifying of a very poetical fancy, are connected with death, who, having his mythic house so peculiarly in this island of blood-revenge, is the true genius of the Corsican popular poetry. I could call Corsica the island of Death, in the same way as other islands were islands of Apollo, Venus, and Jupiter. When any one is about to die, his death is often announced by a pale light shining on his house. The owl screeches the whole night, the dog howls, and often is heard a little drum, beaten by a ghost. The dead often come by night to the house of a person about to die, to announce it. They are attired precisely like Capuchins, in long white-hooded cloaks with pointed hoods, from which the eyes look out in a most ghostly manner; and they act all the gestures of the Capuchins, who stand round the bier, lift it, carry it, or precede it. And so the ghosts keep haunting the house till the cock crows. When the cock crows, they glide away to their grave, some to the churchyard, the rest into the church.

The dead love society. If you go to the churchyard by night you may see them come forth; then make the sign of the cross on the stock of your gun, and shoot right among them. Such a shot has power over ghosts, and they will disperse, and cannot come together again till after ten years.

The dead occasionally come to the bed of the survivor, stand before him, and say to him "Lament no more, and cease thy weeping, for I have the assurance of being soon blessed!"

In the silent night, when you are sitting on your bed, and your sad heart will not let you sleep, the dead often call your name; "O, Marì! O, Josè!" Answer them not for your life, however plaintively they call, and however near your heart is breaking. Answer not; for, if you answer, you must die.

"*Andate, andate!* the storm is coming! see the *tromba* there, how it drives past Elba!" And mightily did the black sea-spectre spread its robes over the sea, an awfully beautiful sight; the moon's light was extinguished, and sea and land were overspread by a lurid storm-light. God be praised; here we are at the tower of Bastia! The Holy Virgin had helped us, after all; and the storm began to rage as soon as we had landed from the boat: but we were in port.

TRAVELS.——BOOK III.

CHAPTER I.

VESCOVATO AND THE CORSICAN HISTORIANS.

On the heights of the eastern coast, and a few miles south of Bastia, lies Vescovato, a place celebrated in Corsican history. Having reached the tower of Buttafuoco on the road, you ascend towards the mountains, passing through glorious chestnut forests that cover all the hills in the vicinity. This beautiful district is called the Casinca, and the environs of Vescovato bear the special name Castagniccia, or chestnut country.

I was intent upon seeing this Corsican paese, in which Count Matteo Buttafuoco once offered Rousseau a refuge. I expected to find such a place as I had seen plenty of on the mountains. So I was astonished when I saw Vescovato before me, surrounded by green hills, concealed among the most magnificent chestnut-groves, wreathed round with oranges, vines, and fruit-trees of every kind, watered by a mountain stream, and built in original Corsican style, yet not without some elegant architecture. I said to myself, that of all retreats a misanthropic philosopher could choose for himself, Vescovato is by no means the worst. It is a mountain retreat in a shady wooded solitude, with charming walks for undisturbed reverie, now leading among the stones by the wild mountain burn; now passing under a bush of thick-flowering erica, close by an ivy-covered convent; now climbing a mountain-side, from which the eye looks down into the paradise of the Golo valley and to the sea.

The place was founded by a bishop, and was in later times the residence of the bishops of the old town of Mariana, which lay in the plain below.

•Vescovato is an oasis of historical reminiscences and names,

adorned first and foremost by three Corsican historians, all of
the sixteenth century—Ceccaldi, Monteggiani, and Filippini.
Their houses are as well preserved as their memories. The curate
of the place took me to Filippini's house, which is a wretched
peasant's cottage. I could not forbear smiling when they showed
me a stone taken out of the wall, on which the most celebrated
historian of Corsica had in the joy of his heart engraved the inscription, " Has Aedes ad suum et amicorum usum in commodi-
orem Formam redegit, anno MDLXXV. cal. Decemb. A. Petrus
Philippinus Archid. Marian." Certes, the requirements of these
honest men were modest in the extreme. Another stone displays
Filippini's coat-of-arms—his house, and a horse tied to a tree.
The archdeacon had the custom of writing his history in his
vineyard at Vescovata, which they still show. When he had
ridden up from Mariana, he tied his horse to a pine-tree, and sat
down to meditate or to write, protected by the high wall of his
garden; for he was never secure against the bullets of his enemies
all ·his life through, and so he wrote the history of the Corsicans
under truly dramatic and exciting influences.

Filippini's is the chief work of Corsican history, and is a national production of which the Corsicans may be proud. It grew
up quite on popular ground, and is formed of songs, chronicles,
and lastly, self-conscious history. The first worker at it was
Giovanni della Grossa, a lieutenant and secretary of the valiant
Vincentello d'Istria. He collected the old legends and traditions, and followed the same plan as Paulus Diaconus in his
history; and he brought the history down to the year 1464.
His pupil Monteggiani continued it to the year 1525, rather
scantily and insufficiently; then Ceccaldi brought it down to the
year 1559, and Filippini to 1594. Of the thirteen books of the
whole, he thus wrote only the last four, but as he revised the
entire work it now bears his name. It appeared first at Tournon
in France in the year 1594, in Italian, with this title:—

" The History of Corsica, in which all things are told that
have happened since it began to be inhabited, till the year 1594.
With a general description of the whole island; disposed in thirteen
books, of which the first nine were commenced by Giovanni
della Grossa, and continued by Pier·Antonio Monteggiani, and
subsequently by Marc' Antonio Ceccaldi; and they were collected
and enlarged by the Very Rev. Antonpietro Filippini, Archdeacon of Mariana, and the last four made by himself. Diligently
revised and given to the light by the said Archdeacon. In

Turnon. At the press of Claudio Michael, printer to the University, 1594."

Though Filippini was an opponent of Sampiero, and suppressed some facts, and wrested others in his book from fear or untruthfulness, yet he told the Genoese so many bitter truths that they hotly persecuted his history. It became very scarce; then Pozzo di Borgo earned great thanks from his country by setting on foot a new edition of Filippini, conducted by the learned Corsican, Gregori, and enriched by an excellent introduction. It appeared at Pisa in the year 1827, in five volumes. The Corsicans are worthy of having the sources of their history cared for. Their modern historians blame Filippini greatly for receiving all the legends and fables of Grossa into his work. I commend him for it; for one must not measure one's own early history according to laws of severe historical science, and just as it is it has for us the high value of a national dress. Nor do I agree with these censurers when they depreciate Filippini's talents. He is somewhat broad, but copious, and possessing a sound philosophy, drawn from a moral contemplation of life. One must hold him in honour; he did much for his nation, notwithstanding that he was an unfree partisan of Genoa. But for Filippini a large part of Corsican history would be now buried in obscurity. He dedicated his work to Alfonso d'Ornano, Sampiero's son, in the pleasure that he felt when the young hero reconciled himself with the Genoese senate, and even visited Genoa.

" When I undertook to write the history," he says, " I confided more on the gifts with which nature has endowed me, than on the art which is expected from him who writes such a book. In my own case, I considered I was absolved in the eyes of my readers, when they see how great is the deficiency of all literary means in this our island (in which it hath pleased God that I live), so that one cannot even apply one's self to sciences of any kind, to say nothing of writing in a pure and perfectly immaculate style." In other passages, also, Filippini complains bitterly of the ignorance of the Corsicans, and their total want of scientific knowledge. Even the priests he will not except from this condemnation; for he says there were hardly twelve of them who had learnt grammar, and among the Franciscans, who possessed twenty-five monasteries, hardly eight literati; and so the whole people grows up in ignorance.

He never conceals the faults of his countrymen. " Besides

their ignorance," he says, "one cannot find words to express
how great is the idleness of the islanders in tilling the ground.
Even the finest plain in the world, of Aleria and Mariana, is
desert, and they do not even chase the wild-birds. But if they
chance to become masters of a single carlino, they imagine they
shall never be in want again, and so they sink down into idleness, and doing nothing." This strikingly describes the nature
of the Corsican at the present day also. " Why do they not graft
the countless wild oleasters?" asks Filippini; "why not the
chestnut ? But they do nothing, and therefore are they all poor.
Poverty leads to crime, and there are daily robberies. They
perjure themselves, too. Their hostilities and their hate, their
want of good faith and love, are almost eternal; hence that proverb
becomes true, which people are wont to say—The Corsican never
forgives. And hence arises all the reviling and calumniations
that we are always beholding. The Corsican tribes are (as
Braccellio has written) more innovating and rebellious than
all other tribes; and many are devotees of a certain superstition
that they call Magonie, for which men are employed as well as
women. A kind of divination is also in vogue here, practised
by the observation of the shoulder-blades of dead animals."

This is in brief the moral outline of the picture sketched by
the Corsican historian of his nation; and he has spared it so
little, that he has really said nothing else of the Corsicans than
what Seneca is said to have expressed about them with the following lines :—

> Prima est ulcisci lex, altera vivere raptu,
> Tertia mentiri, quarta negare Deos.

In his dedication to Alfonso, on the other hand, he most
zealously defends the virtues of his nation, which had been
assailed by Tomaso Porcacchi Aretino da Castiglione, in his
description of the most celebrated islands of the world. " This
man," Filippini complains, "treats the Corsicans as assassins.
This fills me with no little astonishment and surprise at him ; for
I can truly say that there is no nation in the world by which
foreigners are more cherished, nor where they can travel more
securely ; for in every part of Corsica they find the choicest
hospitality, without having to disburse a single *quatrino* for
their sustenance." This is the case ; a foreigner herewith attests
the lasting truth of the Corsican historian's remarks, even after
the lapse of three hundred years.

Whilst we are standing here in an oasis of historians, I will cast a glance also upon the other Corsican historians. An island nation of such wealth in historical events, heroic contests, and great men, and of such almost unexampled love of country, must surely be rich in historians; and in fact the number of them is astonishing, taken in connexion with the smallness of the population. I shall here name only the principal.

Next to Filippini, the most eminent historian of Corsica is Peter of Corsica, or Petrus Cyrnaeus, Archdeacon of Aleria, the other old Roman colony. He lived in the fifteenth century, wrote, besides his "Commentarium de bello Ferrariensi," also a history of Corsica in Latin, bearing the title, "Petri Cirnaci de rebus Corsicis libri quatuor," and coming down to the year 1482. His Latin is among the best of the period, and his style vigorous and in bold strokes, like that of Sallust or Tacitus; but his treatment is utterly unartistic. He pauses longest at the siege of Bonifazio by Alfonso of Arragon, and at his personal adventures. Filippini neither used nor even knew of his work at all, as it existed only in one manuscript, and was first brought to light from the library of Louis XV. Muratori incorporated this manuscript in his great work in 1738; and Gregori conducted an excellent edition of Peter of Corsica, published at the expense of Pozzo di Borgo, Paris 1834, in which he gave an Italian translation beside the Latin text.

Peter speaks still more aptly and with deeper insight, of the character of his countrymen; and we will consider also what he says, to ascertain whether the modern Corsicans still preserve much or little of the nature of their ancestors of that age.

"They are eager to revenge an insult; and it is esteemed disgraceful not to take revenge. When they cannot reach him who has committed a murder, they chastise one of his relations. Therefore, so soon as a murder has been perpetrated, all relatives of the murderer immediately take up arms and defend themselves." The offensive and defensive armour of the Corsicans of that age he describes thus: "They wear pointed helmets called cerbelleras, or round-topped ones, and carry daggers, spears four ells long, two to each man, and a sword; the dagger is on the right side, the sword on the left."

"In their own country they are disunited, but out of it most closely bound together. Their souls are prepared to meet death (animi ad mortem parati). They are all poor, and hold commerce in contempt. They are eager for glory; gold or silver they scarcely use at all. Drunkenness is held to be peculiarly disgraceful. They hardly learn to read and write; few hear orators and poets; but they are so practised in controversy, that, when a dispute comes, one would suppose they were all excellent conductors of causes. I have never seen a bald head among the Corsicans. The Corsicans are, of all men, the most hospitable. Even for the first men of the nation the wife prepares the food. They are naturally taciturn, made more for action than for speaking. They are also most religious.

"It is customary to separate the men from the women, especially at table. The women and their daughters draw water at the wells; for servants there are scarcely any. The Corsican women are hard-working; they may be seen going to the well carrying the pitcher on their head, leading the horse (if they have one) after them, and turning the spindle. They are also very chaste, and not long sleepers.

"The dead are buried with considerable circumstance; for they never inter them without exequies, without *lamento*, without panegyric, without dirge, or without prayer. For their funeral celebration is very similar to that of the Romans. One of the neighbours raises the cry, and cries towards the nearest village, 'Oh thou, call in that direction, for he has just died!' Then they assemble whole villages, towns, or communes, as the case may be, approaching one by one in a long train, first the men and then the women. When the latter come up, they all raise a cry of weeping and lament, and the wife and brothers of the deceased rend their clothes on their breasts. The women, disfigured by weeping, beat their breasts, lacerate their faces, and tear their hair. All Corsicans are free."

It will have been noticed that this picture of the Corsicans bears resemblance in many points to the image Tacitus presents to us of the ancient Germans.

The heroic fifteenth and sixteenth centuries were the flourishing period of Corsican historical composition; which kept silence throughout the entire seventeenth century, because the people were in a death-like state of exhaustion. From the start that the nation took in the eighteenth century, the writing of Corsican history also received a fresh impulse. Here we have the books of Natali, "Disinganno sulla guerra di Corsica," and of Salvini, "Giustificazione dell' insurrezione" useful but not extraordinary works.

A history of Corsica was written by Dr. Limperani, extending to the end of the seventeenth century, a work copious in matter, but enormously spun out. A very useful work, indeed indispensable especially for the documents it contains, is the history of the Corsicans by Cambiaggi, in four quarto volumes, dedicated to Frederick the Great, an admirer of Pasquale Paoli and of Corsican heroism.

Now that the freedom of the Corsican nation is lost, its learned patriots—and Filippini would not now have to complain of the deficiency of men of literature and science—have taken up its history with laudable zeal. They are mostly advocates. Pompei wrote a book "L'etat actuel de la Corse;" Gregori edited Filippini and Peter, and collected the statutes of Corsica, a most deserving work. These laws sprung from old Corsican legal and penal decisions, received, adopted, and completed, even by the old democracy of Sambucuccio, gradually multiplied and arranged under the Genoese dominion, and finally collected by the Genoese in the sixteenth century. They had become very scarce; and the new issue of them is a splendid monument of Corsican history; whilst the code itself does high honour to the Genoese. Another talented Corsican, Renucci, wrote "Storia di Corsica" (2 vols., Bastia 1833), which shortly touches upon ancient times, and treats at length of the eighteenth and nineteenth centuries down to the year 1830. This work is rich in matter, but very weak as a history. Arrighi wrote lives of Sampiero and of Pasquale Paoli. The work that enjoys the most extended circulation is Jacobi's history of Corsica, in two volumes, which extend to the end of the war of independence under Pasquale Paoli; another volume being expected as conclusion. Jacobi has the merit of being the first to give a general view of the history of Corsica from all available sources; his book is indispensable, but not of the best school of criticism, and not nearly objective enough The most recent author of an excellent small compendium of Corsican history, is the recorder of Ajaccio, Camillo Friess, who told me he contemplated writing a larger history of Corsica. I wish him all success in it, for he is a man of undoubted talent. I wish he may not write his work in French like Jacobi, but, from a feeling of duty towards his country, in Italian.

P

CHAPTER II.

ROUSSEAU AND THE CORSICANS.

I WENT to the house of Count Matteo Buttafuoco, which was to have been the abode of Rousseau; it is a sightly, chateau-like building, the grandest at Vescovato. At present part of it is occupied by Marshal Sebastiani, whose family are natives of the neighbouring village of Porta.

Count Buttafuoco is the same against whom Napoleon, as a young democrat at Ajaccio, hurled a fiery pamphlet. When the count was an officer in the French service, he invited Jean Jaques Rousseau to Vescovato; for the philosopher of Geneva had expressed himself in the "Contrat Social" in the following prophetic manner about Corsica.* "In Europe there is still one country capable of legislation, I mean the island of Corsica. The vigour and the perseverance with which this valiant people has found means to attain and to defend its freedom, well deserve to be rewarded by some wise man teaching them how to preserve it. I have a presentiment that this little island will some day astonish Europe." On occasion of the last French enterprise for the subjugation of Corsica, Rousseau had written:—"It must be confessed, your French are a very servile people, a people easily bought by tyrants, very cruel, and like hangmen towards the unfortunate; if they knew of a free man living at the end of the other world, I believe they would march thither purely for the pleasure of destroying him."

I will not assert that this, too, was a prophecy of Rousseau's; but *that* was, and has been fulfilled, for the day has come on which the Corsicans have astonished Europe. It was Rousseau's favourable declaration about the Corsican nation, that induced Paoli also to invite him to the island in the year 1764, so that he might withdraw from the persecutions of his enemies in Switzerland. Voltaire, the bitter envier and derider of Rousseau, had disseminated a rumour, that they had offered him a refuge in Corsica to play him a malicious trick; thereupon Paoli himself wrote an invitation to Rousseau. Buttafuoco went still

* Du Contrat Social, liv. ii. ch. 10.

farther; he asked the philosopher to compose a legislation for the Corsicans, in the same way as the Poles begged him for a constitution. Paoli seems not to have opposed this request, perhaps because, though holding such a labour to be useless, he regarded it as still in some respects serviceable to the renown of the Corsicans. So the vain misanthrope saw himself in the flattering position of a Pythagoras; and he replied with delight, "that the very idea of engaging in this task exalted and inspired his soul, and that he should consider the remainder of his unhappy days to be laid out nobly and virtuously, if he could expend them to the advantage of the brave Corsicans." He now in good earnest requested materials for his task. But his work was never finished, as the toils and vexations of his life hindered its completion. What could have come of it? and what should the Corsicans have done with a theoretical system, when they had given themselves their living national constitution, based upon material necessity?

Circumstances, meanwhile, diverted Rousseau from his intention of going to Corsica; and a pity it was. He might here have put his theories to the test, for the island appears like the realized Utopia of his ideas on the normal condition of society, eulogized by him especially in the treatise, "Whether the arts and sciences have been salutary to mankind." In Corsica, he would have found to the full what he wished; natural men in woollen blouzes, living on goat's milk and a few chestnuts; neither science nor art; equality, valour, hospitality, and blood-revenge at every step. I think the warlike Corsicans would have heartily laughed to see Rousseau walking about under the chestnut trees with his cat on his arm, or twining his basket-work. O no! the din of *vendetta, vendetta!* and a shot or two from a *fucile* would have soon chased away again poor Jean Jaques. Yet Rousseau's connection with the island of Corsica is still memorable, and essential to the internal history of his life.

In the letter declining Count Buttafuoco's invitation, Rousseau writes:—"I have not lost my sincere desire to live in your land; but the total prostration of my powers of body, the cares I should subject myself to, the fatigue I should suffer, and other obstacles arising from my position, compel me to give up, at least for the present, my intention, which still, despite these difficulties, my heart will not yet quite despair of carrying out. But, my dear sir, I am growing old and failing; my strength is leaving me; the wish excites me, and the hope vanishes. However it be, accept yourself and present to M. Paoli my sincerest and tenderest thanks for the refuge he has deigned to offer me. Brave and hospitable people! No, I shall never forget, as long as I live, that your hearts, your arms, your hands, have been opened to me at a moment when scarcely any other refuge was left me in Europe. If I have not the good fortune to leave my bones in your island, I shall endeavour at least to leave behind me a monument of my gratitude there, and I shall do myself honour in the eyes of the whole world if I name my friends and protectors. What I promise you [the count], and what you may reckon upon from this time, is, that I shall be occupied for the rest of my life only with myself or with Corsica; all other affairs are entirely banished from my soul."

This last promises a great deal: but it is only Rousseau's exaggerated rhetorical language. How curiously and strangely this language and the Rousseau nature contrast with the gloomily taciturn, manful and strong, savage and bold-acting Corsican! Rousseau and Corsican seem to be two immeasurably separated notions, the antipodes of one another; and yet they have their point of contact, like the corporeal and the incorporeal, being brought together by union in time and sympathy of ideas. It is remarkable how, beside Rousseau's prophetic dreams of a democracy, there resounds the Corybantine dance in armour of the Corsicans under Paoli, proclaiming the new age which their heroic contest ushered in. With their din of steel they were to deafen the ear of the old despot-gods, what time the new god Jupiter was born in their island—Napoleon, the revolutionary god of the iron age.

CHAPTER III.

THE MORESCA, CORSICAN DANCE IN ARMOUR. .

The Corsicans, like other brave nations of fiery nature and poetical feeling, have a dance in armour, which they call Moresca. There is a dispute about its origin, some deriving it from the Moors, others from the Greeks. The Greeks called these dances of warlike youths with sword and shield Pyrrhic dances, and ascribed the invention of them to Minerva and Pyrrhus, the son of Achilles. It is uncertain how they spread to the western countries; suffice it to say, that after the contests of the Christians

and Moors they were called Moresca, and they appear to be still
in use wherever nations are rich in traditions of the old gigantic
contest between Christian and Heathen, between Europe and
Asia; as in Greece, Albania, Servia, Montenegro, Spain, and
other countries.

I know not what other meaning may be attached to the
Moresca, as I saw this very fine dance only once danced at
Genoa; in Corsica it has always preserved a crusading character,
constantly representing a contest against the Saracens, whether
the deliverance of Jerusalem, the conquest of Granada, or the
taking of the Corsican towns Aleria and Mariana by Hugo
Count Colonna. The Moresca has thus, like many solemn
dances of the ancients, assumed a semi-religious character, and
been impressed, through the historical style of its representation,
with a remarkable national stamp.

The Corsicans have at all times enacted this entertainment,
especially in the troubled times of national contests, when such
a national game of arms inflamed the spectators, while it
reminded them of the great deeds of their fathers. I know of
no nobler amusement for a free and manly nation than the
spectacle of the Moresca, which is the flower and the poetry of
all battle ardour. It is the sole national drama of the Corsicans,
who, having possessed no other enjoyments, had the exploits of
their heroic forefathers represented to them by dancing, on the
very ground which the latter watered with their blood. It
would often happen that they went from the Moresca straight
away to battle.

Vescovato was frequently the theatre of the Moresca, and
even Filippini mentions it as such. It is recorded to have been
danced there to the honour of Sampiero; and it was executed
also in the time of Paoli. The last representation took place in
the year 1817.

Especially popular was the representation of the conquest of
Mariana by Hugo Colonna. A village represented the town,
an open place formed the stage, the green hills served as an
amphitheatre, on which reclined the thousands upon thousands
who streamed together from the whole island. Fancy this
audience—these rugged, haughty men all in arms, lying beneath
the chestnut-trees, and following the steel-clad heroic dance with
their eye, words, and gesture. The actors, sometimes two
hundred in number, are divided into two companies, all wearing
the Roman toga. Each dancer holds in his right hand a sword,

and in his left a dagger; the colour of the crest and the breast-plate alone makes the Christians and the French distinguishable. A single fiddler rules the time of the Moresca.

He commences. A Moorish astrologer comes riding out of Mariana in a caftan, and with a long white beard; having observed the heavens and interrogated the stars, he foretells evil fortune, and then hastens back with gestures of terror into the city-gate. When, lo! a Moorish messenger, whose look and bearing express sudden fear, comes running to Mariana, bringing news that the Christians have already taken Aleria and Corte, and are advancing against Mariana. As soon as the messenger has disappeared under the gateway, the horns sound, and Hugo Count Colonnà advances with the Christian army. Endless applause greets him from all the hills round.

> Hugo, Hugo, Count Colonna,
> O how he of all most nobly
> Dances, like the royal tiger
>   Sporting up the rocks and hills!
>
> Then his sword Colonna raises;
> On its hilt the cross he kisses,
> And to his bold band of warriors
>   Thus he speaks,.the noble Count:
>
> "Up, in God's great name, and storm it!
> Dance up Mariana's bulwarks,
> E'en today we'll let the heathen
>   Feel the edge of Christian's sword.
>
> Know ye, whoso falls in vict'ry,
> He today, to heaven translated;
> Shall with quires of angels blessed
>   Dance the dances of the spheres."

The Christians put themselves in position. The Moorish king, Nugalone, with his army, marches out from Mariana.

> Nugalone, O how finely
> Lightsome limbs to dance he beareth,
> Like the brown bespeckled panther
>   When he dances from his bush.
>
> Nugalone twirls his whiskers
> With his left hand, bracelet-gilded,
> And to his bold band of warriors
>   Thus he speaks, the haughty Moor:
>
> "Up my men, i' the name of Allah!
> 'Gainst the Christian's host prevailing,
> Prove we by a vict'ry glorious,
>   Allah is the only God!
>
> Know ye, whoso falls in battle,
> E'en today in Eden's garden
> Shall he dance voluptuous mazes
>   With the fairest Houri blest!"

Both armies now defile; the Moorish king gives the signal for the attack, and the figures of the dance begin, of which there are twelve.

Clear and sharp sound strokes of fiddle:
Nugalone and Colonna
Dancing near each other hover;
    Dancing on advance their hosts.

Graceful they to music's guidance
Sway their young limbs hither, thither,
Like the slender stems of flowers
    When the evening breeze doth sing.

Scarcely yet they meet, the warriors'
Lightly brandished swords bright gleaming: —
Swords are they, or rays of sunshine,
    Beams of sunlight in the hand?

Fiddle-tones grow fuller, louder!
Clink and clank of swords now crossing
Backwards, forwards, whirl they lightsome,
    To the sound of fiddle-bow.

In a ring tight-locked they dance now,
Moor and Christian firm enlaced;
With their swords' clear silvery clangour
    Oft their armed chain resounds.

Clink and clank of swords now crossing!
Changed the tune, and changed the motion,
Now the armed chain is broken,
    And they form two crescent lines.

Wilder, wilder the Moresca
Rushes on, with ardour dashing,
As the wave of ocean dashes
    When the storm pipes o'er the rocks.

Keep up bravely, thou Colonna!
Dance them down to earth, and smite them!'
For with sword in hand our freedom
    Dancing we shall gain to day.

Thus then Vescovato's mountains
We'll descend with stormy dances!
Thus then we'll dance down thy armies,
    God-accursed Genoa!

New figures one after the other, till at length they dance the last, called *resa*, when the Saracen yields himself defeated.

When I saw the Moresca danced in Genoa, it was executed in honour of the Sardinian constitution, and on the anniversary of that event, May 9th: for this beautiful dance has a revolutionary significance in Italy, and is therefore prohibited in the despotic states. It was a glorious spectacle; for the open place by the harbour was completely thronged by the people in their picturesque costumes, especially the women with their long white veils. Some thirty young men, all in close-fitting white dresses, with green and red aprons tied round their waist, danced the Moresca to the accompaniment of horns and trumpets. They all held a paper in each hand; and while dancing the various figures, they clashed their swords together. The Moresca displayed no historical allusions.

The Corsicans, like the Spaniards, have also kept up the old plays in Passion-week, which, however, have likewise become very rare. In the year 1808, an entertainment of this kind was given at Orezza in the presence of 10,000 people. There were tents to represent the houses of Pilate, Herod, and Caiaphas. Then there were angels and devils who rose up from a trapdoor. Pilate's wife was acted by a young man, twenty-three years old, with a raven-black beard. The captain of the guard wore the French national-guard uniform, with a colonel's gold and silver epaulettes; the second commander wore an infantry uniform, and both had the cross of the legion of honour on the breast. Judas was represented by a priest, the curé of Carcheto. When the play began, the spectators from some unknown cause got into a fray, and began to bombard one another with pieces of rock that they tore up from the natural amphitheatre. Hereupon Jesus, who had just entered the stage, would not play any more, and retired in a tiff from this earthly vale of wo. But two gendarmes took him under the arms and forcibly brought him back to the stage, so that he had to play on. This absurd story is told by the engineer Robiquet, in his historical and statistical investigations on Corsica.

CHAPTER IV.

JOACHIM MURAT.

Espada nunca vencida!
Esfuerço de esfuerço estava.

ROMANZA DURANDARTE.

THERE is a third very memorable house at Vescovato, that of the family Ceccaldi, from which two well-known men are descended, viz., the above-mentioned historian, and the brave general, Andrea Colonna Ceccaldi, one of the heads of the nation, and a triumvir with Giafferi and Hyacinthus Paoli.

But another reminiscence attaching to this house interests yet more. It is the house of General Franceschetti, or rather

of his wife, Catharina Ceccaldi, and it was here that the ill-fated
king, Joachim Murat, found a hospitable reception when he
landed in Corsica on his flight from Provence; and here he
formed the plan of reconquering his beautiful kingdom of Naples
by a knightly *coup de main*.

Again, then, the living image of a brave cavallero passes before
our eyes on this wonderful island of stories, where crowns grow
wild on the trees, like the golden apples in the garden of the
Hesperides.

Murat's end is as touching as that of any other man who ever
dashed through the world for a time like a splendid meteor, and
then ended with a crash and a miserable fall.

After his last ill-considered war, Murat had gone to France.
He kept himself concealed for a time on the coast of Toulon,
roaming about at the risk of his life in vineyards and thickets:
an old grenadier saved him, and preserved him from dying of
hunger. The identical Marquis de Rivière, whose life Murat
had generously spared after the conspiracy of George Cadoudal
and Pichegru, now sent out soldiers to bring the fugitive dead
or alive. In this dreadful position Joachim hit upon the idea
of seeking hospitality in the neighbouring island of Corsica.
He hoped to find protection among a generous people, who hold
the rights of hospitality sacred.

So he fled from his hiding-place, reached the coast, and fortunately found a boat which brought him safe to Corsica, despite
of storm and tempest, and extreme danger of drowning. He
landed near Bastia, August 25, 1815; and hearing that General
Franceschetti, who had formerly served in his body-guard at
Naples, was at Vescovato, he repaired thither. He knocked at
the house of the *Maire*, Colonna Ceccaldi, the general's father-in-
law, and asked to see the general. Franceschetti relates in his
memoirs about Murat's stay in Corsica, and his end: "A man
presented himself to me wrapped in a hooded cloak, with his
head buried under a black silk cap, with a thick beard, and in
the trousers, gaiters, and shoes of a common soldier. He was
emaciated with misery. What was my astonishment when
under this coarse disguise, I recognised King Joachim, that till
lately magnificent prince! A cry escaped from my mouth, and
I fell at his feet."

On the news of the landing of the king of Naples, there was
a movement at Bastia in his favour, and many Corsican officers
hastened to Vescovato to tender him their services. Count

Verrière, the commander of Bastia, was alarmed, and sent an officer with a detachment of gendarmes to arrest Joachim on the spot. But the people of Vescovato instantly seized their arms to defend the sacred rights of hospitality, and the person of their guest, and the troop returned without effecting their object. But as the rumour spread that King Murat had appealed to the hospitality of the Corsicans, and was in personal danger, the people streamed to Vescovato, in arms, from all the surrounding villages, and formed an encampment there to protect their guest, so that, on the very next day, Murat found himself at the head of a small army. Poor Joachim was in raptures at the *Evvivas* of the Corsicans. He had it in his power to make himself King of Corsica, but he had no thoughts but of his beautiful Naples. This last view he ever enjoyed of an applauding multitude, gave him the feeling of being a king again. "And if even these Corsicans," said he, "who have nothing to thank me for, are so devoted to me, how will my own Neapolitans receive me, on whom I have lavished so many benefits ?"

The resolution of regaining Naples became irresistibly fixed in his soul; and he was not deterred by the example of Napoleon, who had adventurously reentered France from the neighbouring island of Elba. The son of fortune could not but venture his last throw, and stake it upon a crown or death.

The Ceccaldis' house, meanwhile, became the rendezvous of many officers and gentlemen from far and near, who wished to see and to serve Murat. He had laid his plan. He summoned from Elba, Baron Barbara, a Maltese, who had been an old naval officer of his, and consequently was well acquainted with the coasts of Calabria, to discourse with him of the precise measures to be pursued. He sent a Corsican secretly to Naples to form connections and raise money. He bought in Bastia three vessels, which were to take him up on the coast at Mariana; but the French in Bastia, being informed of it, laid an embargo on them. Sensible people vainly tried to dissuade Murat from his foolhardy adventure: the idea was firmly fixed in him, that the Neapolitans loved him, and that he had only to set his foot on Calabrian ground, to be triumphantly led back to his capital. And people coming from Naples told him, that King Ferdinand was hated there, and that they bitterly longed for Murat's rule again.

Two English officers coming from Genoa, repaired to Vescovato and made King Joachim an offer to conduct him safely to England. But Murat rejected this offer with righteous indignation, remembering how England had behaved to Napoleon. Meanwhile his position at Vescovato grew more and more perilous, both for himself and for his generous hosts Coccaldi and Franceschetti; for the Bourbonist commander had published a proclamation, declaring all to be traitors and enemies of their country who should follow or harbour Joachim Murat.

Murat resolved, therefore, upon leaving Vescovato as soon as possible. He was still negotiating for the restoration of his sequestrated vessels, in which affair he applied to Antonio Galloni, the commandant of the Balagna, whose brother he had formerly loaded with favours. But Galloni sent word to Murat that he had no power of acting in this business, but, on the contrary, had received orders from Verrière-to march against Vescovato on the following day, with 600 men, and take him prisoner; yet, from consideration of his misfortunes, he said he would wait four days first, and gave a solemn promise not to molest him if he should have removed from Vescovato within that period.

When Captain Moretti returned to Vescovato with this message, and with no prospect of the recovery of the vessels, Murat shed tears. "Is it possible," he exclaimed, "that I am so unfortunate? I bring ships to sail away from Corsica, and they are put under embargo; I burn with impatience to leave the island, and every road is cut off from me. Well! I will send back the brave men who are so magnanimously guarding me; I will remain alone, and oppose my breast to the hostility of Galloni, or else I shall find means to release myself from the bitter and cruel destiny that presses upon me;" here he glanced at the pistols which lay on the table. Hereupon Franceschetti entered the room, and said to Murat with emotion, that the Corsicans would never suffer any harm to befall him. "Nay," replied Joachim, "I shall never suffer Corsica to undergo the least annoyance on my account: I must be off!"

The respite of four days having elapsed, Galloni appeared with his troops before Vescovato. But the populace was prepared to give him battle: a fire was opened upon him, and he retreated; for Murat had just left the place.

He departed from Vescovato on the 17th September, in the company of Franceschetti and a few officers and veterans, and escorted by more than five hundred men-at-arms. He resolved to go to Ajaccio and embark there. Wherever he showed himself, in the Casinca, in Tavagna, Moriani, Campoloro, and beyond the mountains, the people thronged his steps, and received him with *Evvivas*. The people of each commune escorted him to the boundary of the next. At San Pietro di Venaco, Muracciole, the priest of the parish, went out to meet him with a numerous train, and brought him a beautiful Corsican horse as a present. Murat instantly mounted the horse, and galloped along on him, as proud and ardent as he had been when he dashed through the streets of Milan, Vienna, Berlin, Paris, and Naples. and over such countless battle-fields.

At Vivario he called at the house of the aged priest Pentalacci, who for forty years had given hospitality to the most various exiles, alternately English, French, and Corsican, and who had once sheltered the young Napoleon at his house, when the Paolists were seeking his life. At breakfast, Joachim asked the old man what he thought of his designs upon Naples. "I am a poor clerk," said the priest, "and I do not understand affairs of war or diplomacy; but yet I should question whether your majesty will be able to regain now the throne that you formerly were unable to keep when at the head of your army." Murat replied with animation, "I am as sure of regaining my kingdom as I am that I hold this napkin in my hands."

Joachim sent Franceschetti on to Ajaccio to see how matters stood with regard to his reception. For, ever since he had been in Corsica, Napoleon's relations at Ajaccio had taken no notice of him; and so he thought of remaining at Bocognano, and not going to Ajaccio till all the arrangements for his embarkation were completed. But Franceschetti wrote him word that the citizens of Ajaccio were beside themselves with eagerness to see King Murat again within their walls, and that they sent him a pressing invitation to come.

On the 23rd September, at four in the afternoon, Murat entered Ajaccio for the second time in his life ; for on the first occasion he landed there with Napoleon, decorated with glory, and celebrated through the world as a hero, when Napoleon was returning from Egypt. On his entry, all the bells rang a peal, the populace thronged him with acclamations, bonfires blazed in the streets, and the houses were illuminated. The city authorities, however, instantly withdrew from the town, and Napoleon's relatives, the Ramolinos, likewise retired ; Signora Paravisini alone had the courage and the affection to remain to embrace her relative, and offer him hospitality in her house. But Murat deemed it advisable to stay at a public locanda.

The garrison of the citadel of Ajaccio was Corsican, and therefore attached to Joachim. The governor confined them in the citadel, and put the town in a state of siege. Murat now made the necessary arrangements for his departure. He also composed a proclamation to the Neapolitans, under thirty-six heads, which was printed in Ajaccio.

On the 28th of September, Maceroni, an English officer, arrived, and demanded an audience of Joachim. He brought passports for him from Metternich, signed by the latter as well as by Charles Stuart and Schwarzenberg, and drawn out for the Count of Lipona, under which name (an anagram of Napoli) a secure refuge was guaranteed him in German Austria or Bohemia. Murat kept Maceroni to dinner, and they conversed on Napoleon's last deeds of arms, and the battle of Waterloo. Maceroni gave a circumstantial description of it, and praised the cool intrepidity of the English infantry, whose squares the French cavalry was unable to break. Murat took him up, "Had I been there, I should assuredly have broken them." Maceroni replied, "Your majesty would have broken the Prussian and Austrian squares, but never the English." Murat exclaimed with fire, "And I should have broken the English, too: for Europe knows that I have never met with any square whatsoever that I have not broken."

Murat accepted Metternich's passports, and seemed at first as if he would enter into the plan proposed; but he declared subsequently, that he must go over to Naples to conquer his kingdom. Maceroni entreated him with tears to hold back as long as there was yet time. But the king dismissed him.

At midnight of the very same day, the ill-fated Murat embarked; and as his little squadron was leaving the harbour of Ajaccio, the governor of the citadel fired a few cannon-shots at it, which however were said to be only feint shots. The little fleet consisted of five vessels and the *scorridore* (which was a fast sailing *felucca*), under the command of Barbara; and conveyed about 200 men including the inferior officers and twenty-officers, besides a small number of sailors.

His voyage was full of disasters, and utterly unattended by the fortune that still accompanied Napoleon when he sailed off from Elba with his six ships and 800 men, to regain his crown. Seven months before Murat's departure from Corsica, the Emperor had put to sea from the neighbouring island. It is touching to observe how Murat hovers about the coast of Calabria, with his heart racked by doubt and uncertainty; how he is abandoned by the other vessels; how the warning hand of destiny seems now to repel him from the hostile coast; how he is already forming a resolution to sail to Trieste, and go to Austria; and how finally the dreamer, over whose head the deceitful image of a crown was always hovering, is after all suddenly possessed by the fantastic, chivalrous idea of landing at Pizzo.

"Murat," said a man who told me much of his last days at Ajaccio as an eyewitness, "Murat was a great knight, and a small intellect." This is surely true. He was the hero of a historical romance, a genuine Paladin; and, on laying down the book of his life, one feels for long after an agitation of mind as from a novel. He had a better seat on his horse than on his throne. He had never learnt how to rule; he had only, what born kings are often without, a princely demeanour and courage to be king, which he was most of all when he descended from his throne. And this whilom waiter in his father's tavern, abbé, and expelled inferior officer, stood before his executioners more royally than Louis XVI. of the house of Capet, and died with no less dignity than Charles of England, of the royal house of Stuart.

A servant opened for me those rooms of Franceschetti's in which Murat had lived. Views of the battles in which he shone, such as Marengo, Eylau, Borodino, and the land-battle of Aboukir, adorn the walls. His portrait caught my eye at the first glance. The dreamy eye, the locks of brown hair falling over the forehead, the soft romantic features, the fantastic white attire, the red scarf, were surely Joachim's. Beneath the portrait I read these words: "1815. Tradito!!! abbandonato!!! li 13. Octobre assassinato!!!"—ejaculations of grief uttered by Franceschetti, who accompanied him to Pizzo. Beside Murat's portrait hangs the general's, a tall soldierlike figure with a physiognomy firm as iron, and a lively contrast to Joachim's troubadour countenance. Franceschetti entirely renounced himself, and left his wife and children for Murat; and though disapproving of the enterprise of his former king, he followed him, and never left his side to the very last. I was told a fine instance of generosity, and I read it also in the memoir of the general. When the roving bands of soldiers at Pizzo were pressing on against Murat to maltreat and insult him, Franceschetti sprang forward crying, "I am Murat!" A sabre-cut prostrated him to the ground, and at the same moment Murat sprang forward and•

declared himself. All the officers and soldiers taken with
Murat at Pizzo were thrown into a dungeon, wounded as they
were. After Joachim's execution, they and Franceschetti were
conducted to the citadel of Capri, when they lay in prison for a
long time expecting death, till at length King Ferdinand
awarded them an unexpected pardon. Franceschetti then
returned to Corsica, but he had hardly landed when the French
arrested him as guilty of high treason, and carried him off to
the citadel of Marseille. The unhappy man passed several years
in the prisons of Provence, and was at length set at liberty, and
allowed to return to his family at Vescovato. His estate was
ruined by Murat; and the general who had exposed himself to
death for his king, found himself necessitated, first to allow his
wife to travel to Vienna to Murat's wife to recover a part of his
disbursements; and when this proved fruitless, to conduct a
long action at law with Caroline Murat, which he lost in every
instance. Franceschetti died in the year 1836. His two sons,
retired officers, are among the most respected men in Corsica, and
distinguished for their zeal for agricultural improvements.

His wife, Catherine Ceccaldi, still lives at a great age in the
house where she gave a hospitable reception to Murat. I found
the fine old lady in an upper room employed in rural occupations, and surrounded by doves, which fluttered out of the
window on my entrance—a scene that showed me, at a glance,
that the healthy and simple nature of the Corsicans has been
preserved not only in the house of the peasant but also in that
of the gentle folk. I thought of the dazzling period that this
lady had passed through in her youth at beautiful Naples, and
at the court of Joachim; and, in the course of conversation, she
herself alluded to the time when General Franceschetti was in
the service of Joachim, together with Coletta, who has also
published a pamphlet on the last days of Murat. It is inspirit-
ing to see a strong nature that has withstood victoriously
many storms of life, and remained constant while fortune
changed. So I regarded this old matron with veneration; while
she, in the midst of conversation about the great events of bygone times, was carefully splitting beans for her children's and
grandchildren's dinner. She also spoke of the time when Murat
lived in this house. "Franceschetti," she said, "represented the
affair to him in the plainest colours; he did not shrink from
telling him he was bent upon impossibilities; but then Murat
would exclaim with bitterness, 'You, too, will abandon me? Ah,

my Corsicans will leave me in the lurch!' He was not to be gainsaid."

When I travelled on from Vescovato into the Casinca, the image of Murat would not leave me. I could not think of him without comparing him with the adventurer, Baron Theodore of Neuhoff, who landed on this very coast seventy-nine years earlier, strangely and fantastically attired, like Murat, who also loved fantastic costume. Theodore of Neuhoff was the precursor of all those men in Corsica who have won for themselves the fairest crowns the world had to bestow. Napoleon gained the Imperial crown, Joseph the crown of Spain, Louis that of Holland, Jerome that of Westphalia, the country of Theodore King of the Corsicans; and besides these, the adventurer Murat gained the Norman crown of the Two Sicilies, and Bernadotte the crown of the chivalrous Scandinavians, the most ancient knights in Europe. A hundred years before Theodore, Cervantes had, in his Sancho Pansa, cast ridicule upon a chevalresque island-kingdom;—and, behold, a hundred years after Cervantes, this story of Arthur and the knights of the round table is enacted again off the frontiers of Spain, in the island of Corsica, and goes on through the broad daylight of the nineteenth century, down to the very times in which we live.

Don Quixote and the Spanish romances often came into my mind in Corsica; and I seemed to see the worthy knight of La Mancha again riding through the world's history. Surely ancient Spanish names are now actually becoming historical—names which have been as romantic and unknown to the real world as Theseus, Duke of Athens, in the Midsummer Night's Dream.

CHAPTER V.

VENZOLASCA, AND AN OLD CONVENT.

Que todo se passa en flores
Mis amores,
Que todo se passa en flores.
SPANISH SONG.

NEAR Vescovato is the small village of Venzolasca, reached by a magnificent walk over the hills and through chestnut groves. I passed the abandoned Capuchin convent of Vescovato, situated on an enchanting elevation, built of brown granite and roofed with black slates, and looking serious, like the Corsican history itself, but original and highly picturesque in the midst of the verdure.

On these wanderings through the land of chestnuts one forgets all fatigue. The luxuriance of nature, the smiling mountains, the view of the Golo plain and of the sea, rejoice the heart; while the proximity of many villages enliven the picture, and afford many *genre* scenes. I saw many fountains of hewn stone, at which women and girls were drawing water in their round pitchers, some of them also holding the spindle, as Peter of Corsica says.

Outside Venzolasca is a beautifully situated monument of the family of Casabianca, by the roadside. This family also is a native of Vescovato, and one of the most distinguished of the island. The immediate ancestors of the present senator Casabianca made their name renowned by deeds of arms. . Raffaello Casabianca, governor-in-chief of Corsica in the year 1793, senator, count, and peer of France, died at Bastia at a great age, in the year 1826. Luzio Casabianca, a deputy from Corsica at the Convention, was captain of the admiral's flag-ship Orient in the battle of Aboukir. When Admiral Brueys was shot to pieces by a cannon-ball, Casabianca took the command-in-chief of the ship; the ship took fire, but he made all possible arrangements for the rescue of the crew, and would not abandon his ship. His young son Giocante, a boy of thirteen years, could not be prevailed upon to stir from his father's side. The ship might blow up any moment; father and son held themselves fast locked in each other's embrace, and were thus blown up to the sky with the fragments of the ship. Go where one will in Corsica, one breathes an atmosphere of heroism.

Venzolasca is a small place, with a gaily decorated church, gay at least in the interior. They were just painting the choir, and complained that the master workman who was to gild the wood carving had cheated them abominably; for he had pocketed the gold they had given him for his work. The only luxury in which the Corsicans indulge is in the decoration of their churches; and there is scarcely a *paese*, however small, that does not pride itself on having bright and varied colours and gold decorations in its church.

From the plateau on which the church of Venzolasca stands, there is a ravishing distant view over the sea, and on the other side a view of the indescribably beautiful mountain basin of the

Q

Castagniccia. Few regions of Corsica gave me such delight as these mountains in their connexion with the sea. The Castagniccia is an imposing circle, enclosed by mountains of a beautiful fresh green, and the finest forms. They are all covered with chestnut trees to near the summit, and have at their feet olive groves, whose silvery grey contrasts picturesquely with the deep green of the chestnut foliage. From the midst of the foliage solitary hamlets look forth, such as Sorbo, Penta, Castellare, and Oreto, perched high among the clouds, dark, and with slender black church spires.

The sun was sinking as I ascended these mountains, and I had some delightful hours. I again passed an abandoned convent, one belonging to the Franciscans. It lay quite buried beneath vines and foliage, and the fruit-trees could hardly bear their produce. As I entered the court and the convent-chapel, I was surprised by this picture of desolation, which smiling nature concealed with her growth of plants. The stone flags of the graves were opened, as though the dead had burst them in order to fly heavenwards; skulls lay about in the verdure, and the Christian symbol of all grief was concealed in a sea of flowers.

THE CONVENT OF VENZOLASCA.

Into a shady leafy wood
　My erring steps me led aside;
The sun low in the west then stood,
　When convent walls afar I spied.

The ivy round the grey old gate
　Entwined a fair triumphal arch;
In front, an olive old and great,
　Which on patrol appear'd to march.

To enter in the cloister's rest
　He asks me with his silent boughs.
As he were porter, who the guest
　Invites to prayer, or to carouse.

Dead is the monk who here was housed,
　And here the juicy grape who press'd,
And with his brethren who caroused
　'Midst flowery bowers in fragrance dress'd.

With gentle hand the vine-shoot traces
　Upon the walls, in letters green,
Inscriptions lovely, full of graces,
　Of what order has the convent been.

The crucifix—O, wonderful!
　A Christ has fallen from the cross,
Of heavenly joys and rapture full,
　Into the midst of vines and moss.

A vine-shoot tender saw I there
  Cling close around the Master's feet;
'Twas Mary Magdalene the fair,
  And that her kiss, the sinful-sweet.

And John too at his master's head,
  Upon his knees his posture keeping,
In ecstasy he gazed, and said
  To Mary, to the willow weeping:

"O wring thy hands not in thy wo!
  What can be better than such death,—
From ardent, loving friends to go,
  After a life of love and faith?"

Then whispering said the lovely vine:
  "I have pour'd forth my pains and smart,
Outpour'd the rapture that was mine,
  Unbosomed deep my inmost heart."

I ponder'd well the mystery o'er,
  To Christian hearts obscure in meaning :
The rose then utter'd this sweet lore:
  "O man! Love was in the beginning!"

THE CROWNED SKULL.

Into the cloister did I pass;
  A skull there lay before my feet,
Which laughing peep'd from out the grass,
  And did me hospitably greet.

No common dust its figure mangled;
  For round its bare and ample brow
Protectingly its shoots entangled
  The blooming clematis did throw.

Meseem'd as though the skull then said:
  "An Abbot Corsican I was;
The gospel text full oft I read
  To them, my brethren in this place.

"I taught them from an allegory:
  Ye are the branches, I the vine;
This ever was my constant story,
  Its meaning simple to define.

"And simple was my sacrament,
  My doctrine of communion;
The highest gifts to mortals lent
  Are fruit of vine and ear of corn.

"These gave I forth to many a guest,
  God's blessing to the poor I gave;
Was blithesome through life's earthly rest,
  And laid me cheerful in my grave.

"See here, my son, the foliage young;
  My life I could retain no more;
Yet now upon my skull is hung
  The chaplet green that oft I wore.

" Be now my guest, enjoy my wine,
And mayst thou relish convent fare;
And may thy head in death, like mine,
. Be crowned, and a green chaplet wear."

CHAPTER VI.

HOSPITABLE FAMILY LIFE AT ORETO.

Πρὸς γὰρ Διός εἰσιν ἅπαντες
Ξεῖνοί τε πτωχοί τε δόσις δ' ὀλίγη τε φίλη τε.

HOMER, *Od.* vi. 207.

I NOW went between orchards, whose walls were quite covered with festoons of the beautiful climbing clematis, and through chestnut groves, for two hours more uphill as far as Oreto, the highest *paese* of the Casinca.

Oreto has its name from the Greek ὄρος, *mountain;* the village stands high and picturesquely on the summit of a green hill. A monstrous block of granite towers with its grey head out of the midst of the village, like a basement formed to set a colossal Hercules upon. To reach the *paese* I had to climb toilsomely up on a narrow path, over which at many places a stream gushed down.

Arrived at the top, I entered upon the village green, the largest I had yet found in a *paese.* It is the plateau of the hill, overlooked by other hills, and surrounded by houses which look like peace itself. The priest was walking about with his sexton, and the *paesani* were leaning against the orchard walls, enjoying the repose of the Sabbath. I went up to a group, and asked whether there was a *locanda* in the village? " No !" said one, " we have no locanda; but I can offer you my house, and you shall take pot-luck with us." I accepted the invitation with joy, and followed my host. Before I entered his house, Marc Antonio wished me to inspect the village fountain, the pride of Oreto, and to taste the water, the most excellent in the whole land of Casinca; so I followed him, for all my fatigue. The fountain was capital, and even architecturally elegant. The icy water streamed forth in inexhaustible plenty from five pipes in a little stone temple.

Arrived at Marc Antonio's house, I was welcomed by his wife without many words. Having wished me good-evening, she went into the kitchen directly to prepare the meal. Mine host led me into his best room, where I was astonished to find a little stock of books; they were religious books which he had inherited. "I am unfortunate," said Marc Antonio; "for I have learnt nothing, and I am very poor. Therefore I must stick to this mountain, instead of going on the continent and getting an official situation." I observed closer this man in the brown smock and the Phrygian cap. He had an unconfiding countenance of truly iron hardness, and furrowed by passion; and what he said was short, decided, and in a bitter tone. I never once saw this man smile; and in him I discovered among the lonely mountains a soul struggling to rise, and tormented by ambition. Such phenomena are not rare in Corsica; the example of many families allures people away from their villages, where one may often find in the dingiest cabin the family portraits of senators, generals, and prefects. Corsica is the land of upstarts and of natural equality.

Marc Antonio's daughter, a pretty young girl of fine blooming figure, entered the room. Taking no other notice of the presence of a guest, she merely asked quite aloud and naïvely, "Father, who is the stranger? is he a Frenchman, and what does he want at Oreto?" I told her I was a German, which she did not understand. Giulia then went to help her mother to prepare the meal.

It was served up, and was the richest meal a poor man can command,—vegetable-soup, bread, and peaches, and in honour of the guest a little bit of meat. The daughter served up the food, but, according to Corsican custom, neither she nor her mother shared the supper, and the man alone helped me and ate at my side.

He afterwards led me into the little church of Oreto, and to the edge of the rock, to enjoy the incomparably beautiful distant view. The young curé and no small party of *paesani* accompanied us thither. It was a gloriously fresh evening, with golden sunlight. I stood astonished at such unimagined glories of nature; for at my feet I saw the chestnut-covered mountains sink into the plain—this plain stretching out, like an endless garden, to the seashore—the rivers Golo and Fiumalto meandering through it—and bounding all, the sea in its glory, on the horizon-line of which the islands Capraja, Elba, and Monte Cristo appeared in a row. The eye embraces the entire coast-line as far as Bastia, and southwards to San Nicolao—landwards again, mountain upon mountain crowned with villages.

A little congregation had now assembled at this spot, and I was delighted to praise the island, which is rendered so remarkable as well by its natural features as by the history of its heroic people. The young curé took up this eulogy with great enthusiasm, the peasants echoed it, and every one knew how to honour his country. I remarked that these good people were capitally at home in the history of their country. The curé excited my admiration by his *esprit* and his humorous mode of expression. Once speaking of Paoli he said, "Hark ye, his time was a time of action; the men of Orezza spoke little, but they acted much. Had our day produced a single man with the great and self-sacrificing soul of Pasquale, it would now be otherwise with the world. But now is the time of chimeras and pens, and yet man is not made to fly." I followed the curé with pleasure to his parsonage, a poor-looking house of black stone. But his little room was smart, and possessed a neat library of a few hundred volumes. I passed a pleasant hour conversing with the cultivated and enlightened man over a bottle of the most delicious wine, while Marc Antonio sat by mute and shut up in himself. We came to speak of Aleria, and I asked after Roman antiquities in Corsica. Marc Antonio suddenly took up the word, and said very short and seriously, "We need not the glory of Roman antiquity; we have enough in that of our fathers."

Returning to Marc Antonio's house, I found both mother and daughter in the room, and we sat down together in a cosy family circle. The women were mending their clothes; they were chatty, unconstrained, and naïve, like all Corsicans. The restless activity of the Corsican women is well known; subject to the men, and in society modestly taking a serving part, on them rests the whole burthen of the labour. They share this fate with the women of all warlike tribes, as especially the Servians and Albanians.

I described to them the great cities of the continent, their festivals and usages, as also some customs of my own country. They never expressed any astonishment, although what they heard was entirely strange to them, and Giulia had never seen any town, not even Bastia. I asked the girl her age. "I am twenty years old," said she. "Impossible! you are barely seventeen." "She is sixteen," said the mother. "Why, don't you know your own birthday, Giulia?" "No, but it is in the register, and the Maire will know it." "So the Maire is the only happy being who can celebrate the birthday of the pretty lass;

namely, when he puts his great horn-spectacles on his nose, and refers to the great register."

"Giulia, how do you amuse yourself? youth must have its enjoyments." "I have enough to do; my brothers are wanting something every minute; on Sunday I go to mass." "How shall you adorn yourself to-morrow?" "I shall put on the *faldetta*." She brought the *faldetta* out of the cupboard, and drew it on; she looked very pretty in it. The faldetta is a long garment, generally of a black colour, the hinder end of which is thrown over the head, so as to resemble a nun's robe with a hood. To elderly women the faldetta gives dignity; young girls it surrounds with a mystery and charm.

The women asked me who I was. This was a difficult question to answer. I brought out my unartistic sketch-book, and, showing them a few leaves of it, I said I was a painter. "Are you come into the village," asked Giulia, "to paint the rooms?" I laughed out; this question was so sharp a criticism on my Corsican sketches.

Marc Antonio said very seriously, "Never mind; she does not understand it."

Of the fine arts and sciences, these Corsican women have no idea; they read no novels; in the hour of twilight they play the guitar, and sing a melancholy *vocero*—a beautiful dirge, which they perhaps improvise themselves. Yet in the narrow circle of their observation and feeling, their soul remains strong and sound as nature itself,—chaste, pious, self-relying, equal to any sacrifice, and capable of such heroic resolves as the poetry of civilisation sets up for all time as the noblest images of human greatness of soul, as in the characters of an Antigone and an Iphigenia. These children of nature have, in their history or legends, a parallel to every single heroic deed of antiquity.

In compliment to Giulia, the young Corsican maiden, I will tell the following Corsican story, which, like every other that I shall present, is historical.

THE CORSICAN ANTIGONE.

It was towards the end of the year 1768. The French had occupied Oletta, a considerable village in the land of Nebbio. This post being from its position extremely important, Pasquale Paoli had established secret combinations with the inhabitants, for the purpose of falling upon the French garrison and

taking them prisoners. The garrison amounted to 1500 men,
under the command of the Marquis of Arcambal. But the
French were on their guard; they proclaimed martial law in
Oletta, and held so watchful and severe a rule, that the men of
the village could not attempt nothing.

Stillness, as of the grave, now reigned in Oletta.

Now a youth named Giulio Saliceti left his village one day
without permission from the French sentinels, to go out on the
Campagna. On his return he was arrested and thrown into
prison; his freedom however after a short time was restored
to him.

The young man went from the prison to the house of his
kinsmen, resenting in his heart that the enemy had put an insult upon him. He muttered something to himself, which must
have been a curse against the hated French. A sergeant who
heard what he was muttering, gave him a blow on the face.
This happened before the window at which Giulio's kinsman,
Abbot Saliceti, was just then standing, called by the people
Peverino, that is, *pepper*, from his passionate and choleric temperament. When Peverino saw the blow fall upon his kinsman's
face, his heart burned within him.

So when Giulio rushed into the house beside himself with
wrath, Peverino took him into his chamber. After a while, both
men were seen to come out, tranquil, but with a grave look that
foreboded no good.

In the night other men entered Saliceti's house, and sat
together deliberating. The matter of their deliberation was, that
they intended to blow up the church of Oletta, which the French
had converted into their barracks. They were for revenging
and delivering themselves.

They dug a mine from Saliceti's house to underneath the
church, and having crept through to the end of it, they filled
it with all the powder which they had been able to keep
concealed.

On the 13th February of the year 1769, towards nightfall, the
church was to be blown up.

Giulio's heart burned with rage and resentment. "To-morrow,"
he said shuddering, "to morrow! Let me lay the match. They
gave me a blow in the face. I will give them a blow that shall
send them up sky-high; I will thunder them out of Oletta with
a shot like the lead from a grenade."

"But the women and children, and they who know not of it?

the explosion will destroy the next houses and the whole neighbourhood."

"They must be warned. They must be bidden, under some pretext, to go at the appointed hour to the other end of the village,
and this with all possible secresy."

Thus the conspirators proceeded.

Now when the fearful hour of the following evening came,
men, women, the young and the old, might be seen going silently,
quick, and timid with an undefined fear, to the other end of the
village and assembling there.

Then the French began to suspect something was in the wind;
and a messenger from General Grandmaison came dashing up,
who gave sudden news of what had already been disclosed to
the general by a traitor. On the instant, the French threw
themselves into Saliceti's house and into the mine, and prevented
the infernal undertaking.

Saliceti, with a small portion of the conspirators, cut his way
through with desperate bravery, and escaped safe out of Oletta:
but others were seized and put in chains. The court-martial
condemned fourteen to death upon the wheel, and on seven
miserable wretches the punishment was actually put into
execution.

Seven corpses were seen publicly displayed on the open place
before the convent of Oletta. No interment was to be granted
them. The French commander had issued the order, that whoever should take from the scaffold and bury one of the dead
should be condemned to death.

Horror lay upon the village of Oletta. A deadly awe had
seized every heart. No human being shewed himself on the
roads; the fire was extinguished on the hearth; every voice dead
but that of wailing. They sat in the houses, and their thoughts
were fixed unceasingly on the convent-square, where the seven
corpses lay on the scaffold.

The first night came. In her chamber sat Maria Gentili
Montalti, on the bed. She wept not; she sat with head bent
upon her breast, her hands in her bosom, her eyes closed. Often-
times her soul found vent in sobs.

It was as though a voice called to her, though the stillness of
the night, " O Mari!"

In the silent night the dead often call the name of the person
they have loved. Who answers them must die.

" O Bernardo!" cried Maria ; for she wished to die.

But Bernardo lay on the scaffold before the convent, and was
the seventh and youngest of the dead. He was Maria's lover, and
the wedding should have been in the following month. Now he
lay dead on the scaffold.

Maria Gentili stood still in the dark chamber ; she listened
towards the side where the convent square lay, and her soul held
converse with a spirit. Bernardo seemed to entreat her for
Christian burial.

But the penalty of death awaited him who should take from
the scaffold and bury any one of the dead. Maria wished to bury
her lover, and then die.

She opened gently the door of her chamber, to leave the house.
She passed through the room in which her aged parents slept.
She stepped up to their bed, and watched their breathing in
sleep. Then her heart began to tremble, for she was her parents'
only child and stay ; and when she considered that her death
by the hangman would bring down her father and mother with
sorrow to the grave, her soul wavered in great anguish, and she
took a step back towards her chamber.

Then again she heard the voice of the dead wail, " O Marì !
O Marì ! I have loved thee so, and thou wilt now forsake me !
In my broken body lies the heart that has died true to its love
of thee ; bury me in the church of St. Francis, in the tomb of
my fathers. . . . . . O Marì!"

Maria opened the house-door and stepped out into the night.
She tottered to the convent-square. The night was gloomy;
stormy gusts often swept the clouds away, so that the moon shone
down. When her light fell on the convent-square, it was as
though the light of heaven refused to see what it did see, and the
moon put on her veil of black clouds again. For on the blood-red
scaffold before the convent lay seven corpses, one beside the
other, and the seventh was the corpse of a youth.

The owl and the raven screeched on the tower ; they sang the
dirge, the *Vocero*. But a grenadier was pacing up and down
near the square, shouldering his musket. He had drawn his
cloak over his face, and walked slowly up and down, shuddering
into the very marrow of his bones.

Maria had shrouded herself in the black *faldetta*, that her
figure might lose itself the easier in the surrounding darkness.
She sent a prayer for help to the Holy Virgin, the Mater dolorosa,
and then advanced quickly towards the scaffold. It was the
seventh body—she loosed Bernardo ; her heart, and a gleam that

lighted up his lifeless features, told her, even in the dark, that it was he. Maria took the dead man on her shoulders—she grew as strong as a man. She bore the body into the church of St. Francis.

There she sat down exhausted on the steps of an altar, over which burned the lamp of the Virgin. The dead Bernardo lay on her knees, as the dead Christ on the knees of Mary! This picture is in the south called Pietà.

Not a sound in the church. The Virgin's lamp flickers—without, a gust of wind hisses by.

Then Maria raised herself. She let the dead Bernardo glide down on the steps of the altar. She went to the spot where the tomb of Bernardo's fathers was situated. She opened the grave. Then she took the dead, kissed him, and let him down into the grave, and closed it up again. Maria knelt long before the image of the Virgin, and prayed that Bernardo's soul might have peace in heaven, and then she went quietly back to her house and her chamber.

When day broke, Bernardo's corpse was missed from the bodies in the convent square. The news fled through the village that it had disappeared, and the soldiers beat an alarm. No one doubted but that the family Leccia had taken down their kinsman by night from the scaffold; and their house was immediately entered, and they arrested and thrown, hung with chains, into the dungeon. Condemned to death by the law, they were to suffer death, although they denied the deed.

Maria Gentili heard in her chamber what had happened. Without saying a word, she hurried out of the house to Count De Vaux, who was come to Oletta. She threw herself at his feet, and prayed for the release of the prisoners. She avowed the deed. "I have buried my lover," said she; "my life is forfeit—here is my head; but leave in freedom those who suffer innocently."

The Count would not at first believe what he heard; for he considered it equally impossible that a weak maiden should possess such heroism, as that she should have the power to accomplish what Maria had. When he had convinced himself of the truth of her assertion, he was deeply affected, and moved to tears. "Go," said he, "magnanimous girl, and thyself release thy bridegroom's kinsmen, and may God reward thy heroism!"

On the same day they took the six bodies from the scaffold, and gave them all Christian burial.

CHAPTER VII.

A RIDE THROUGH THE LAND OF OREZZA TO MOROSAGLIA.

I WISHED to go from Oreto, through the land of Orezza, to Morosaglia, the native place of Paoli. Marc Antonio had promised to accompany me, and to engage good horses. So he called me early in the morning, and got ready to start. He put on his best suit, and wore a velvet jacket, and had shaved very smooth. The women gave us a good breakfast by way of preparation for the journey; and we then mounted our Corsican ponies, and rode off in style.

My heart leaps for joy even now when I recall that Sunday morning, and the ride through this beautiful romantic country, over the verdant mountains, through the cool glens, past dashing streams, and through gloomy oak forests. As far as the eye can reach, it meets every where these shady, fragrant chestnut-groves, and mighty gigantic trees, such as I never saw any where else. Nature has done every thing here, and man—how little! The chestnuts are often the only treasure man possesses here; and the Corsican frequently possesses nothing but his six goats and six chestnut-trees, which give him his *polenta*. The government has sometimes had an idea of cutting down the chestnut-woods, in order to drive the Corsicans to agriculture, but this would starve them downright. Many of these trees have trunks twelve feet thick; the thick, fragrant foliage, the long, broad, and dark green leaves, and the fibrous light-green capsules, present a beautiful spectacle.

Beyond the *paese* of Casalto we came into a perfectly romantic glen, watered by the Finmalto. There is serpentine and the valuable marble, *Verde antico*, all about here. The engineers call the district of Orezza the very elysium of geology; the valuable stone is carried down by the waters of the river. We rode on and on through balmy groves, up hill and down hill, to Piedicroce, the chief place of Orezza, renowned for its medicinal waters. For Orezza is rich in mineral waters as well as in minerals.

Francesco Marmocchi says in his geography of the island,

" Mineral waters are every where the characteristic indications of countries elevated by internal forces. Corsica, wonderfully displaying in a small compass the thousandfold workings of this old battle between the heated interior and the cooled-down crust of the earth, forms no exception to this general rule."

Corsica has, then, its cold and warm mineral springs ; and, though the springs of this kind that have been counted are numerous, there are undoubtedly many more as yet unknown.

As to natural history, and especially mineralogy, this large and beautiful island has not been any thing like completely investigated.

Only fourteen mineral waters, both warm and cold, are as yet accurately and completely known. The distribution of these beneficial waters over the surface of the island is very unequal, especially in respect of their degree of warmth. The region of primary granite has eight, all warm, and more or less sulphureous except one ; whereas the region of the primary ophiolitic and calcareous formations possesses only six, of which not more than one is warm.

The wells of Orezza, breaking forth at many places, are situated on the right bank of the Fiumalto. The main well alone, which is cold and chalybeate, is used. It gushes out with great strength from a stone basin in a mountain below Piedicroce. No steps have been taken to provide any accommodation for the visitors to the waters, who have to walk or ride down the mountains, under their parasols, into the shady woods where they have set up their tents. After a ride of many hours in the burning sun without a parasol, this sparkling water tasted excellent.

Piedicroce lies high. Its slender church-steeple looks down free and airy from the green hill it stands upon. The situation of the Corsican churches in the mountain-villages is often enchantingly beautiful and bold. They seem to stand at the very entrance of heaven ; and when the church doors are opened, the clouds and the angels can walk in among the congregation.

A majestic thunder-storm lowered over Piedicroce, and the thunder echoed with mighty tones from the mountains around. We rode into the *paese* to escape the rain. A young man in spruce town attire darted out of a house, and invited us to dismount and step into his *locanda*. There were two gentlemen there besides, with cavalier beards and very adroit demeanour, who immediately asked for my orders. They were brisk too in

carrying them out ; one beat up eggs, another put wood on the
fire, and the third minced the meat. The oldest of them had a
finely chiselled but fevered face, and a long Slavonic moustache.
So many and such gentlemanly cooks for a humble meal I had
never seen, and I was utterly bewildered till they told me what
they were. They were two exiled Modenese and a Hungarian.
Whilst the Magyar was cooking the meat, he informed me that he
had been a first lieutenant for seven years. "And now I stand here
and cook," he added ; " but so things go in the world. When one
has become a poor devil without a home, one must take things
easy. We have set up a locanda here for the season of the water-
cure, and have hardly laid by any thing." I was deeply touched
by the aspect of this wan-faced man, who had caught a fever
at Aleria.

We sat down together—Magyar, Lombard, Corsican, and
German—and discoursed on many old topics, and mentioned
many a name renowned in the most recent times. How many
of these names must keep a reverential silence before the
single great name of Paoli ! I may not mention them together ; the noble citizen and the strong man of action must
stand alone.

The storm had blown over, but the mountains were still suspended in dense mist. We mounted our horses again, to ride on
over the ridge of San Pietro to Ampugnani. The thunder still
growled and rolled in the misty glens, and the clouds drove along
with the wind. The mountains seemed to have put on a wild,
dismal, and tearful air, startled by an occasional flash ; some appearing immersed in the sea of clouds, others working themselves
out of it like giants. Wherever the veil was rent, appeared a rich
landscape, with green woods and black villages ; and all this flies
past the rider like a dream, peaks and valleys, convents and
towers, mountains, and mountains hanging in the clouds. The
wild elemental forces that sleep enchained in the human soul
would now fain burst their bonds and break forth. Who has
not known such moods of mind when sailing on the tempestu-
ous sea, or travelling through the storm ? What we feel at such
seasons is the same natural chaotic force, which, when crystalliz-
ed into a certain definite form, we call a passion. On goes
Marc Antonio, and on we gallop on our bay ponies along the misty
mountain side, young and vigorous as we are, and clouds, mountains, convents, towers, every thing flies past us. Oh ! it is glorious to fly ! There is a black church-tower poised high in the clouds

up yonder, and the bells are pealing and pealing Ave Maria, to compose the soul to peace.

The hamlets are very small here, dotted picturesquely over the mountains on all sides, lying high or in charming green dales. From one spot I counted seventeen around me, with as many slender black church-towers. We met many men from the old historical region of Orezza and Rostino, powerful heroic-looking figures. Their fathers of old formed Paoli's guard.

Near Polveroso there was a glorious view into a gorge, in the middle of which lies Porta, the chief place of the district of Ampugnani, quite surrounded by chestnut-trees, now dripping with rain. Here lay the old bishopric of Accia, which has disappeared without leaving a trace. Porta has an uncommonly smart aspect, and many of its houses resemble elegant villas. The little yellow church has a neat façade; and a remarkably graceful bell-tower stands beside it, according to the Tuscan custom, as a separate campanile. From the mountain San Pietro one looks down into these streets and rows of houses grouped around the church, as into a gay theatre. Porta is the native place of Sebastiani.

The mountains now become more bare and *laconic*, and lose the chestnut-trees that set them off so beautifully. I found immense thistles on the path, with splendid broad leaves, and bearing the character of arboreous shrubs, with hard woolly stems. Marc Antonio had relapsed into total silence. The Corsicans, like the Spartans, speak little; mine host of Oreto was generally as mute as Harpocrates. I had ridden over the hills with him for a whole day, from morning till evening, and yet I could keep no conversation afloat. He only occasionally threw out a naïve question, "Have you cannon in your country?"—"Have you bells?"—"Do fruits grow with you?"—"Are you rich?"

At length, after vespers, we reached the canton of Rostino, or Morosaglia, the native place of the Paolis, the most glorious scene of Corsican history, and the centre of the old democratic Terra del Commune. Marc Antonio took leave of me in the Campagna; he intended to pass the night in a house in the open country, and to return with the horses on the morrow. He gave me a fraternal kiss, and then turned back, silent and grave; and I, rejoiced to be in this land of free men and heroes, wandered on alone to gain the convent of Morosaglia. It is a walk of an hour, over a rather desolate plain; so before I reach Paoli's house, I will take up his and his country's history where I broke it off.

CHAPTER VIII.

PASQUALE PAOLI.

Il cittadin non la città son io.

ALFIERI's *Timoleon.*

WHEN Pasquale Paoli, with his brother Clement and his friends, had left Corsica, the French easily made themselves masters of the whole island. Only some single bands of guerilla carried on the struggle on the mountains. Among these, one noble champion of freedom especially deserves the love and admiration of posterity; I mean the poor priest of Guagno, Domenica Leca, of the ancient family of Giampolo. He had sworn upon the gospel to remain true to the cause of freedom, and to die rather than leave off the contest. So when the country was all subjected, and the enemy called upon him to lay down his arms, he declared that he could not break his vow. He let go those of his congregation who would not follow him any longer, and dashed to the mountains with his brave men and true. For months he kept up the contest there, fighting however only when assailed; and whenever wounded enemies fell into his hands, he cared for them with Christian compassion. He never hurt any one but in honourable fight. The French vainly urged him to come down, giving him assurances that he should live without molestation in his own village: the priest of Guagno still roved over the mountains, for he would not lose his freedom. When all his followers had forsaken him, the goatherds sustained him in life, but one day he was found dead in a cave, whence he had passed into the presence of his Lord, worn out and full of sorrows, and as a free man. Giuseppe Ottaviano Savelli, a kinsman of Paoli, and friend of Alfieri, has celebrated the memory of the priest of Guagno in a Latin poem entitled *Vir nemoris,* the man of the forest.

Other Corsicans also, who had gone into exile in Italy, landed here and there, and endeavoured, as their forefathers Vincentello, Renuccio, Giampolo, and Sampiero had done in the olden times, to deliver the island; but they were never successful. Many were barbarously thrown into dungeons, and many were condemned to the galleys of Toulon, as if they had been Helots rising against their masters. Abbatucci, one of the last to lay down arms, being convicted of high treason by false accusations, was sentenced at Bastia to be branded and sent to the galleys. But when Abbatucci was on the scaffold, the hangman had not the heart to apply the redhot iron. "Do thy duty!" cried a French judge; and the hangman turned and stretched out the iron towards the latter, as if he would fain brand the judge. Abbatucci was subsequently acquitted.

In the mean time Count de Vaux had been succeeded in the command of Corsica by Count Marbœuf. His administration was in the main beneficial; the old Corsican civil laws and statutes were retained; the committee of Twelve instituted anew, and steps taken to ensure a better jurisdiction. He also endeavoured to raise the manufactures and agriculture of the totally impoverished island. After governing Corsica for sixteen years, he died at Bastia in the year 1786.

As soon as ever the French Revolution broke out, that immense movement swallowed up all special Corsican interests; and these lovers of freedom threw themselves enthusiastically into the current of the new age. The Corsican deputy, Saliceti, made a proposal of incorporating the island of Corsica with France, that it might take part in the French constitution. This took place by virtue of a decree of the Legislative Assembly of November 30, 1789, and there was general rejoicing in Corsica on the event. This was an extraordinary reversal of the posture of events: the same France who, twenty years before, had sent out her armies to annihilate the freedom and the constitution of the Corsicans, now raised this very constitution to the throne.

The revolution recalled Pasquale Paoli from exile. He had been first to Tuscany, and thence to London, where the court and the ministers had received him with honour. He lived in London in complete retirement, and little was known of his life and his occupation. Paoli came to England quite noiselessly; the great man, who had pioneered the new career of Europe, relapsed into obscurity in his house in Oxford Street. He held no pompous declamations. He knew only how to act as a man, and how to keep a dignified silence when he could no longer act. Indeed, a school-boy of Corte had said in his presence, "If freedom were to be gained by mere speeches, all the world would be free." We may learn something from the wisdom of

R

this school-boy. When Napoleon, on board the Bellerophon,
implored the hospitality of England—he, as a true Corsican,
finding hospitality his last resource and hope—he compared himself to Themistocles when seeking protection : but he had no
right to compare himself to the great Athenian citizen ; Pasquale
Paolo alone was the banished Themistocles.

Here are a couple of letters of that period.

PAOLI TO HIS BROTHER CLEMENT,

(Who had remained behind in Tuscany.)

"London, *Oct.* 3, 1769.—I have received no letters from you;
I fear they have been intercepted, for our enemies are on the
alert. . . . I have been well received by the king and queen.
The ministers have visited me. This reception has given displeasure to some of the foreign ministers ; I hear that they have
complained of it to this court. I have promised to go down to
the country next Sunday, to visit the Duke of Gloucester, who
is very favourable to our cause. I hope to obtain something
here for the support of our friends, if Vienna will do nothing.
These people's eyes are now opened, and they see the importance
of Corsica. The king has spoken urgently with me on the subject ; with regard to my own person, his kindness quite
bewildered me. My reception at court has almost drawn down
upon me the anger of the opposition, so that a few of them have
begun to hurl satires at me. Our enemies endeavoured to
stimulate them by throwing out mysteriously, that I sold my
country ; that I bought an estate in Switzerland with French
gold ; that our estates were not meddled with by the French;
that we are on terms of good understanding with the present
ministers, because they too have sold themselves to France.
But I think every one will now be enlightened on the subject;
and every one approved my resolution to meddle with no party
dealings,. but to further the principles which I approve, and in
which all may combine without any sacrifice of their individual
views.

"Send me an exact list of all our people who have gone into
exile ; we must not fear expense ; and send me news of Corsica.
Letters must go under the address of private friends, or they will
not reach me. I enjoy perfect health. This climate seems to
me as yet very mild.

"The country is always quite green. No one who has not

seen it can have any idea of spring and loveliness. The ground
of England is undulating, like the sea when raised by the wind
into gentle ripples. People here, though excited by political
faction, live, as regards private quarrels, as if they were the
closest friends; they are philanthropic, intelligent, and generous
in all their dealings; and they are happy under a constitution
which could not be better. This city is a world of itself, and it
is undoubtedly the finest of all cities. A whole fleet seems to
be sailing up the river every minute; I believe Rome was neither
larger nor richer. But what we reckon by pauls, they reckon
here by guineas, that is louis d'ors. I have written for money;
I would not hear of any contributions for my own support, till I
know what they have decided about the other exiles; but I
know they have good intentions. In case they should be unable,
and we should have to tack about, they will be prepared on the
outbreak of the first war. I greet you all heartily; live happily,
and think not of me."

CATHERINE OF RUSSIA TO PASQUALE PAOLI.

" M. le Général de Paoli,

" St. Petersburg, *April* 27,1770,—I have received your
letter of Feb. 15, from London. All that Count Alexis Orloff has
given you to understand of my good intentions towards you,
is a consequence of the feelings inspired in me by your greatness
of soul, and the noble manner in which you defended your
country. The details of your residence at Pisa are known to me.
They contain among other things the expressed respect of all
who had an opportunity of knowing you. This is the reward of
virtue, in whatever situation she may be placed. Be assured that
I shall ever feel the most lively sympathy with your virtues.

" The impulse that occasioned your journey to England, was
a natural consequence of your sentiments towards your country.
Nothing is wanting to your good cause but propitious circumstances. The natural interests of our empire, closely united as
they are to those of Great Britain, and the mutual amity of the
two nations consequent thereon—the reception that my fleets
have therefore met with, and that which both my ships in the
Mediterranean and the Russian commerce may expect from a
free nation standing in a friendly relation to mine—these are
so many momenta that can only be favourable to you. So
you may be assured, Sir, that I shall not leave unimproved

the opportunities which may offer for rendering you all the good services that the conjuncture may permit.

"The Turks have declared against me perhaps the unjustest war that ever was declared. I can only defend myself at the present crisis. The blessing of Heaven, which has hitherto accompanied my good cause, and which I pray God to preserve to me, shows sufficiently that justice is not defeated for long, and that perseverance, hope, and courage in the end reach their goal in this world full of trying situations. I accept with pleasure, Sir, the assurances of the attachment you are willing to bestow on me, and I entreat you to be assured of the esteem with which I remain   CATHERINE."

* * * * *

Paoli had lived in London as an exile for twenty years, when he was recalled to his country. The Corsicans sent a deputation to him, and the French National Assembly invited him by a pompous letter to return.

On the third April, 1790, Paoli entered Paris for the first time. He was fêted here as the Washington of Europe, and Lafayette was constantly at his side. He was received with deafening acclamations and magnificent declamations by the National Assembly. He addressed to the Assembly these words :—

"Gentlemen, this day is the fairest and happiest of my life. I have passed my life in struggles for freedom ; and the noblest spectacle of freedom I find here. I left my fatherland in slavery ; I now find it in freedom. What have I to desire more ? After an absence of twenty years, I know not what changes oppression will have wrought upon my countrymen ; it cannot, alas ! have been other than deleterious, since oppression always degrades its victims. But in taking the chains off the Corsicans, as you have done, you have given them their old virtues back again. You must not doubt my sentiments on returning to my fatherland. You have been magnanimous towards me, and I was never a slave. My past course of action, which you have honoured by your approval, is a guarantee for my future conduct. My whole life, I may say, has been an unbroken oath of fidelity to freedom ; so it is just as if I had sworn to the constitution you have established before it existed. But it remains for me to perform this oath to the nation that adopts me, and the monarch whom I now acknowledge. That is the favour that I demand from this august assembly."

In the club of the friends of the constitution, Robespierre said to Paoli, "Oh! there was a time when we endeavoured to suppress freedom in its last places of refuge. But no! this was the crime of despotism. . . . the French people has exploded it. What a great atonement for conquered Corsica, and injured humanity! Noble citizens, you defended freedom at a time when we did not venture even to hope for it. You have suffered for it; you triumph with it, and your triumph is ours. Let us unite to preserve it for ever, and may its venal opponents grow pale with fear on beholding this our holy alliance."

Paoli could not yet foresee in what a relation the course of events would put him towards this very France, and that he would once more oppose her as an enemy. He departed for Corsica. At Marseille a Corsican deputation awaited him, among which were the two young club-leaders of Ajaccio, Joseph and Napoleon Bonaparte. With tears Paoli stepped on to the land at Cape Corso, and kissed the soil of his country; he was conducted in triumph from canton to canton. The *Te Deum* was sung throughout the country.

From that time Paoli devoted himself entirely to the affairs of his country, as President of the National Assembly, and as Lieutenant-general of the Corsican National Guard; and in the year 1791, he undertook also the command of the division of the island. Now although the French Revolution had silenced the special interests of the Corsicans, yet these interests began to work, and most of all in the soul of Paoli, whose uppermost virtue was patriotism. Paoli could never convert himself into a Frenchman, nor ever forget that his nation had once had its independence and its own constitution. A variance soon took place between him and some parties; some were aristocratically disposed, and friendly to France, such as Gaffori, Rossi, Peretti, and Buttafuoco; the rest were enthusiastic democrats, who saw the happiness of the world only in the whirl of the French Revolution, as the Bonapartes, Saliceti, and Arena.

The execution of the king, and the desperate conduct of the men of the people in Paris, wounded the humanist Paoli. He gradually broke with France and the revolution; and this breach was publicly visible after the unsuccessful enterprise undertaken by France from Corsica against Sardinia, the frustration of which they laid at Paoli's door. His adversaries formally accused him and Pozzo di Borgo, the attorney-general, of being particularists, and desirous to separate the island from France.

The Convention summoned him to answer these accusations, and sent to the island as its commissioners, Saliceti, Lacombe, and Delcher. But Paoli did not mind the decree, but sent a firm and dignified letter to the Convention, in which he repelled the accusations, and complained of their summoning before a court an aged man, and a martyr to freedom. Should Paoli present himself to the opposition of criers and mountebanks, and then have to lay his hoary head, after all, under the knife of the guillotine? should this be the conclusion of so eventful and so noble a life?

The refusal to follow the command of the Convention occasioned the complete secession of Paoli and the Paolists from France. The patriots equipped themselves, and published distinct declarations, that they desired to consider Corsica as separated from France. The commissioners hastily took their departure, and on their reports the Convention declared Paoli guilty of high treason, and put him out of the pale of the law. The island separated into two hostile armies, the patriots and the republicans, which were already approaching a collision.

In the mean time Paoli had resolved to place the island under the protection and the government of England. Nothing could be a more natural wish for him; he had already concerted measures with Admiral Hood, who commanded the English fleet lying before Toulon; and Hood set off with his ships in the direction of Corsica. He landed at San Fiorenzo, February 2, 1794. This fortress fell after a brisk bombarding, and Bastia was taken likewise, by the capitulation of General Antonio Gentili.

Calvi alone, that had withstood so many storms in so many ages, still held out; the English bombs committed dreadful devastation in the little town, which almost sank into ruins. On the 20th July, 1794, the fortress surrendered; the commander, Casabianca, capitulated, and embarked with his troops for France. Bonifazio and Ajaccio being already in the hands of the Paolists, the republicans had no tenable post on the island left. They emigrated; and Paoli and the English were the undisputed masters of Corsica.

A Corsican national assembly hereupon proclaimed the total separation of the island from France, and placed it under the protection of England. But England was not satisfied with the mere right of protection, but laid claim to sovereignty over Corsica; and this occasioned a breach between Paoli and Pozzo di Borgo, whom Sir Gilbert Elliot had gained over to his side. On the 10th June, 1794, the Corsicans declared that they were willing to unite their country with Great Britain; but that it must retain its independent existence, and be governed by a viceroy, according to its own constitution.

Paoli had counted on the King of England making him viceroy, but he was disappointed; for Gilbert Elliot was sent to Corsica in this capacity. This was a great mistake, both because Elliot was utterly unacquainted with the condition of the island, and because Paoli could not but be deeply wounded by it.

The aged man immediately retired into private life, and when Elliot perceived that the difference between him and the English must become dangerous, he wrote to George III. to beg that he would endeavour to remove Pasquale. This was done. The King of England invited Paoli, by a friendly letter, to repair to London, to pass the remainder of his days in honour at court. Paoli was in his house at Morosaglia when he received the letter. He repaired sorrowfully to San Fiorenzo, where he embarked; and thus he left his country for the third and last time, in October, 1795. This great man shared the fate of most of the legislators and people's men of antiquity: he died, requited by unthankfulness, unhappy, and in a foreign land. The two greatest men of Corsica, Pasquale and Napoleon, hostile to one another, were both to die and be buried on British ground.

But the dominion of the English in Corsica, perverse and bad from ignorance of the country and people, lasted not long. As soon as Napoleon had conquered in Italy, he despatched Generals Gentili and Casalta with troops to the island; and no sooner did these appear than the Corsicans, already exasperated at the banishment of Paoli, rose against the English. The latter gave up, with almost unaccountable haste, an island, from whose people an unbridged chasm of national contrast separated them; and in November, 1796, there was not an Englishman left in Corsica. The island returned under the supremacy of France.

Pasquale Paoli lived to see the empire of Napoleon. This satisfaction at least, that of seeing a fellow-countryman at the head of the history of Europe, was vouchsafed him. Having again lived in exile in London for twelve years, he died a peaceful death, February 5, 1807, at the age of eighty-two years, falling asleep with thoughts of his people, which he had loved so ardently. He was the oldest legislator of the times of European liberty, and the patriarch of liberty. In his last letter to his friend Padovani, the noble old man says, when reviewing his life with humility: "I have lived long enough, and could it be granted to me to begin my life again, I would decline the boon, unless accompanied by the rational cognition of my past life, to correct the errors and follies that have attended it."

One of the Corsican exiles announced his death in these terms, in a letter to his native country:—

GIACOMORSO TO M. PADOVANI.

"LONDON, *June* 2, 1807.—It is true, alas! that the public papers are guilty of no error about the death of the poor general. He lay down on Monday, February 2, at half-past eight o'clock in the evening; and at half-past eleven o'clock on the night of the following Thursday, he died in my arms. He bequeaths to the school at Corte, or to the university, an annual salary of £50 sterling for each of four professors; and a new mastership to the school of Rostino, which is to be established at Morosaglia.

"He was buried on the 13th of February, at St. Pancras, where almost all Catholics are interred. His funeral must have cost nearly £500. About the middle of April last, Dr. Barnabi and I went to Westminster Abbey, to find a place where we can erect a monument to him, containing his bust.

"Paoli said when dying, 'My nephews have little to expect from me, but I will bequeath to them, as a memorial and consolation, this Bible-saying: I have not seen the righteous forsaken, nor his seed begging bread.'" *

CHAPTER IX.

FROM THE NATIVE PLACE OF THE PAOLI.

IT was late when I reached Rostino or Morosaglia. These names designate not a single *paese*, but a collection of hamlets scattered over the solemn rugged mountains. I found the right road, with difficulty, through several of these adjoining hamlets, to the convent of Morosaglia, mounting upon difficult rocky paths, and descending again into the valley, under gigantic chestnut-trees. Opposite the convent is a locanda, a rarity in Corsica. I found there an enlightened young man, who an-

* Psalm xxxvii. 25.

nounced himself as the director of the Paoli-school, and promised me his assistance for the morrow.

In the morning I went to the little village of Stretta, where the three Paolis were born. One must see this Casa Paoli fully to comprehend the history of the Corsicans, and to admire yet more these extraordinary men. It is a wretched, blackened village-hovel, standing on a granite rock. A fresh mountain-spring wells up immediately before the door. The house is composed of stones put together without art, ragged and unhewn like a tower, and with frequent gaps; and has few and unsymmetrical windows, without glass, but with wooden shutters, as in Pasquale's time. When Pasquale was chosen by the Corsicans to be their general, and was expected to arrive from Naples, his brother Clement had panes of glass put in the windows of the sitting-room, to make the paternal abode more comfortable for his brother. But no sooner had Pasquale entered and noticed the luxurious alteration, than he smashed all the panes with his stick, saying that he would not live in his father's house as an 'arl, but as a plain native of the country. The windows have remained paneless now, as then. You may survey from them the grand panorama of mountains from Niolo as far as the heaven-towering Monte Rotondo.

A simple country lass, a relative of Paoli, took me into the house. Every thing in it bears the stamp of a peasant's cottage; you ascend by a steep wooden staircase to the mean-looking chambers, in which Paoli's wooden table and chair are still standing. I was delighted to stand in the little room in which Paoli was born, and felt more pleasurable emotions there than in the chamber of Napoleon's birth.

Pasquale's fine figure presented itself to me here once more— plastic, grave, and dignified as he used to appear, associated with the figure of a noble father and a heroic brother. In this little chamber Pasquale came into the world, April, 1724. His mother was Dionisia Valentina, an excellent woman, from a place near Ponte Nuovo, which was pregnant with such fatal events to her son. With his father, Hyacinthus, we are already acquainted; he was originally a physician, and was made general of the Corsicans, together with Ceccaldi and Giafferi. He was distinguished by exalted virtues, and worthy of the glory of having given two such sons to his country. He was an excellent orator, and known also as a poet. Amidst the din of arms, these powerful minds found time and buoyancy enough to keep

themselves superior to the shackles of passing events, and to
sing steel-clad sonnets like Tyrtæus, such as the following, which
Hyacinthus wrote to the valiant Giafferi after the battle of
Borgo, in the year 1735.

TO DON LUIS GIAFFERI.

May Mars crown Cyrnus' hero unsubdued!
  Before him Fate itself shall lowly bend;
The sighs by him from Genoa forced in feud,
  Fame's trump shall echo to the wide world's end.

Before the foe cross Golo scarce he stood,
  Than in a dance of death he 'gan contend;
His numbers few, with vict'ry yet indued;
  He won where'er his sword he did but lend.

Her contest great, whose end all Europe bides,
  To his good sword and his heroic stand
Hopefully Fate and Corsica confides.

And what though walks dread Fear through Genoa's land,
  If o'er the hair of her head his sword but glides—
The sceptre he will lay in Cyrnus' hand.

All these men are like statues cast from Grecian bronze.
And they were men of Plutarch, worthy compeers of Aristides,
Epaminondas, and Timoleon. They could deny themselves, and
sacrifice themselves; they were plain, strong citizens of their
country. They became great by Things, not by Theories, and
the nobility of their principles was grounded on positive actions
and experiences. Do we desire to comprise the entire nature of
these men in a single word, that word is Virtue; and the fairest
flower of virtue is Freedom.

Here my gaze lights on Pasquale's portrait. I would not
fancy him different from what I here see. His head is powerful,
and his expression clear; his forehead high and arched, and his
hair long and free; his eyebrows thick, and rather falling over
the eyes, as if they were quick to contract in anger. But his
blue eyes are bright, large, and free, expressive of a clear intellect; and over the open beardless countenance reigns gentleness,
dignity, and human kindness.

It is one of my greatest enjoyments to contemplate the portraits and busts of great men. Four periods of human history
here mainly attract and engage our attention—Greek heads,
Roman heads, the heads of the great fifteenth and sixteenth
centuries, and those of the eighteenth. One would never come
to an end, if one were to try to place beside one another the

busts of all the great men of the eighteenth century; but such a museum would be a very rewarding one. When I see a certain group of them together, I fancy I trace in them a certain family likeness—the likeness, namely, of one and the same intellectual principle: I mean the group of Pasquale, Washington, Franklin, Vico, Genovesi, Filangieri, Herder, Pestalozzi, and Lessing.

Pasquale's head bears a striking resemblance to Alfieri's. Though Alfieri, being aristocratically proud and stiffly egotistic, like Byron, is far removed from his contemporary Pasquale, the quiet humane citizen, yet he was a mind of admirable energy and abhorrent of tyrants. He was capable of understanding a nature like Paoli's better than Frederick the Great did. Frederick presented Paoli with a sword of honour, with the inscription, LIBERTAS, PATRIA. The great king of far distant Prussia supposed Pasquale to be an extraordinary soldier. He was no soldier at all; his brother Clement was his sword; he was a thinker, a citizen, and a strong and noble man. Alfieri understood him better; he dedicated his Timoleon to him, and sent him a copy.

Here is Alfieri's letter to Paoli:—

"TO M. PASQUALE DE PAOLI, THE MAGNANIMOUS CHAMPION OF THE CORSICANS.

" To write tragedies of freedom in the language of an unfree nation, will perhaps with justice appear an absurdity to him who sees nothing but the present. But whoever, from the continual changes of past events, draws inferences for the future, cannot form so random a judgment. Therefore, I dedicate this my tragedy to you as one of the few; one who, because he possesses the truest conception of other times and nations, and of all high thoughts, were worthy to be born and to act in a less enervated age than ours. It was not vouchsafed to you to set your country free: but I estimate men not by the measure of their success, as the common herd do, but by their works; and I deem you fully worthy to listen to the sentiments of Timoleon, as sentiments which you will quite appreciate and sympathize in.

" VITTORIA ALFIERI."

Upon the copy which Alfieri sent to Pasquale, he had inscribed the following verses:—

" To the noble Corsican, who made himself
The master and compeer of new-born France.
Thou with the sword, and I with my poor pe l,
O Paoli! strove fruitlessly from sleep
Sooner or later Italy to rouse.
Now see if here my hand hath power to trace
The workings of thy heart.

" Paris, *April* 11, 1790.   " V. A."

Alfieri displayed refined feeling in dedicating to Paoli his
Timoleon, the tragedy of a republican of old, who in the neighbouring island, Sicily, gave wise democratic laws to his liberated
people, and then died a simple private citizen. Pasquale was
fond of Plutarch, like most of the great men of the eighteenth
century. Epaminondas was his favourite hero; they were kindred spirits, both scorning splendour and prodigality, and living
as citizens inspired by love of their country. Pasquale was fond
of reading; his library was select, and his memory extensive.
An aged man told me that, when a boy, he was once going along
the road with a schoolfellow, reciting a passage of Virgil; Pasquale, happening to come up behind him, tapped him on the
shoulder and continued the passage.

Many details of Paoli's life still live here in the mouths of
the people. Old people have seen him walking beneath these
chestnut-trees, in his long green coat with gold stripes—the Corsican colours—and in a vest of brown Corsican cloth. Whenever he showed himself, he was surrounded by his peasant
friends, whom he treated as his equals. He was accessible to
all, and he vividly remembered a day in the last war of liberation, when he had bitterly repented of having shut himself up
against intrusion for an hour's time. He was at Sollacaro,
overwhelmed with business, and had told the sentinels to admit
no one. After a while there came a woman, accompanied by a
youth in arms. She was in mourning, and wrapped in the
faldetta, and wore round her neck a black ribbon, with a Moor's
head in silver, the arms of Corsica. On requesting admission,
she met with a repulse from the sentinels. On hearing the
noise, Pasquale opened the door, and asked her sharply and im-
periously what she wanted. She said in a calm and mournful
tone, " Sir, have the goodness to hear me. I was mother of
two sons; one fell at the tower of Girolata, the other stands
before you, and I come to offer him to his country, that he may
fill up the place of his dead brother." She turned to the youth,
and said to him, " My son, forget not that thou art more thy

country's son than mine." She went away. Paoli stood for a minute as if thunder-struck; then he ran after her, embraced her and her son with deep emotion, and presented them to his officers and functionaries. He afterwards said he had never been so dumbfounded as in the presence of that magnanimous woman.

He was never married; his people was his family. He married his only niece, the daughter of his brother Clement, to a Corsican named Barbaggi. Yet Pasquale, who possessed all the virtues of a friend, was not without a connexion of tender friendship with a noble woman, a talented and ardent patriot, to whom the greatest men of the country confided their political plans and ideas. But this Corsican Roland held no *salon;* she was a nun, and a noble lady of the house of Rivarola. What a zealous interest she took in the war of liberation, is evinced by the single fact, that after the heroic conquest of Capraja by Achilles Murati, she, in the joy of her heart, actually went over to the island, as if to take possession of it in the name of Paoli. There are many letters of Pasquale addressed to the Signora Monaca, which are entirely political, as if written to a man.

The immensity of Paoli's activity appears from the mere collection of his letters. The most important of them have been collected into a thick volume by the talented Italian, Tommaseo, now living in exile at Corfu; they are highly interesting, and display a clear and powerful masculine mind. Paoli did not like writing, but he dictated, like Napoleon; and he had an aversion to sitting down, for his mind never left him sufficient ease. It is said of him that he never knew the date; and that he could read the future, and often had visions

Paoli's memory is sacred among his people. Napoleon fills the breast of the Corsican with pride, as being his brother; but if you mention the name Paoli, his eye glistens as that of a son when you speak to him of his noble father called home to his rest. It is impossible for a man to be more honoured and loved by a whole nation after death than Pasquale Paoli. If posthumous fame is a second life, then this greatest of the sons of Corsica and Italy in the eighteenth century still lives a thousand-fold, nay, in every Corsican heart, from the old man who actually knew him, down to the child whose mind is imbued with his great example. There is no higher title than "Father of one's Father-land." Adulation has often abused it and rendered it ridiculous; but in Corsica I discovered that it may be the plain truth.

Paoli is a fine contrast to Napoleon—the contrast of the love of one's kind and the love of self. No dead rise up against Paoli to curse his name. On Napoleon's nod millions of men were murdered for the sake of glory and possession : the blood Paoli allowed to flow, was shed for freedom's sake ; and the country gave it freely. like the pelican who rends her breast to rear her starving brood. Pasquale's memory is adorned by the name of no battle, but is here at Morosaglia cherished for the foundation of a national school, and this glory seems to me fairer and more human than that of Marengo and the Pyramids.

I visited this school, the endowment of the noble patriot; it is established within the old convent. It consists of two classes, the lower containing 150, and the upper about forty scholars; but two masters are not sufficient for these great numbers. The master of the lower class was so kind as to hold a little examination in my presence. There I discovered the Corsican freedom from constraint even in the boys. There were more than a hundred, of ages ranging from six to fourteen, divided into corps,—wild, brown little fellows, ragged, torn, unwashed, and all with their caps on their heads. Some wore crosses of orders attached to a red ribbon; these appeared ridiculous enough on the breast of a little tawny rascal, who, resting his head on both fists, looked with a free and independent gaze out of his black eyes, proud perchance of the glory of being a Paoli scholar. Such marks of honour are given out every Saturday, and worn by the scholar for a week—a foolish, and at the same time pernicious French custom, which may nourish bad passions, and encourage too early a false ambition in the Corsican, naturally endowed with a more than ordinary desire of distinguishing himself. These young Spartans were reading Telemachus. Upon my request that the master would make them translate the French into Italian, that I might see how well at home the children were in their mother-tongue, he excused himself by pleading the express prohibition of the government, which " will not suffer Italian in the schools." The subjects of instruction were reading, writing, arithmetic, the elements of geography, and biblical history.

The lower class meets in the chapter-house of the old convent in which Clement Paoli dreamed away his life. The large airy Aula in which these Corsican boys study, and the view out of the window, over the mighty mountains of Niolo and the battlefields of their forefathers, might be envied by many a German university. Next to their historical reminiscences, the heroic

nature of the Corsicans seems to me to present the most powerful means for their education. And the mere sight of that
portrait of a Corsican boy hanging on the wall of the school-
room there, is worth a great deal; for it is the portrait of
Pasquale Paoli.

CHAPTER X.

CLEMENT PAOLI.

Blessed be the Lord my strength, which teacheth my hands to war, and my
fingers to fight.—PSALM cxliv. 1.

THE convent of Morosaglia is perhaps the most venerable
monument of Corsican history. It looks like a hoary legend
petrified, brown and gloomy, with a dismal high-towering
campanile by its side. At all periods of the history national
parliaments were held in this old Franciscan monastery. Pasquale
had rooms and offices here, and was often seen in the summer
with the monks, who carried the crucifix into battle at the head
of the army whenever necessity offered. His gallant brother
Clement was fond of residing in the same convent, and died in
one of its cells in the year 1793.

Clement Paoli is a highly remarkable character, perfectly
resembling one of the Maccabees, or a crusader glowing with
religious fervour. He was the eldest son of Hyacinthus. He
served with distinction as a soldier in the Neapolitan service, and
subsequently became one of the generals of the Corsicans. But
public affairs had no charm for his fanatical spirit; and, when
his brother had come to the head of the affairs of Corsica, he
retired into private life, donned the dress of a lay brother, and
relapsed into religious contemplation. He knelt, like Joshua,
entranced in prayer to the Lord, and on rising from prayer
dashed into battle, for the Lord had given his foes into his hand.
He was the mightiest in fight, and the humblest before God.
His gloomy nature has something prophetic, glowing, and yet
self-abasing about it, like that of Ali.

Where the danger was greatest he appeared like an avenging
angel. He delivered his brother from the convent of Bozio, when
besieged by Marius Matra; he drove the Genoese out of the
province of Orezza after a terrible battle; he carried the assault
upon San Pellegrino and San Fiorenzo; he was victorious in

innumerable battles. When the Genoese were storming the fortified camp of Furiani with all their force, Clement remained unshaken in the ruins for fifty-six days, though the whole place was battered down. A thousand shells fell all around him; but he prayed to the God of Armies, and quailed not; and the victory was his.

To Pasquale Corsica owed its freedom, from his leading mind, but to Clement solely from the achievements of his sword. He achieved most brilliant feats of arms also after the French had proceeded to assail the Corsicans, in the year 1768. He gained the glorious battle of Borgo, and he fought desperately at Ponte Nuovo, and when all was lost hastened to rescue his brother. He dashed to Niolo with a small and valiant band to oppose General Narbonne, and cover his brother's flight. As soon as ever this movement was crowned with success, he flew to Pasquale at Bastelica, and then embarked with him sorrowing for Tuscany.

He did not accompany his brother to England, but remained in Tuscany, for a strange language would have made his heart sad. In the delightful lonely convent of Vallombroso, he relapsed again into fervent prayer and severe penance, and no one who saw this monk kneeling in prayer, would have seen in him the terrible warrior and the mighty hero of freedom.

After a convent· life of twenty years in Tuscany, Clement returned to Corsica shortly before his brother. Once more he glowed with hopes for his country;· but events soon discovered to the aged hero that Corsica was lost for ever. He died in penance and grief in the December of the year in which the Convention had cited his brother Pasquale on a charge of high treason.

In Clement the love of his country became a worship and a religion. A great and holy passion in its highest excitation is in itself religious; when it seizes upon a nation, especially in times of fearful distress, it becomes like a worship. In those days priests were heard preaching the contest from every pulpit ;.monks went into battle, and crucifixes supplied the place of banners. Parliaments were held mainly in convents, as though they were, thus under God's immediate presidency; and in former times the Corsicans had actually by national decree placed their country under the protection of the Holy Virgin.

Pasquale was also devout. I saw the chapel which he had contrived in a dark closet in his house; it has been left undis.

turbed there.   He prayed daily to God.   But Clement knelt in prayer full six or seven hours every day: he prayed even in the midst of battle; and it was terrible to see him standing, with his rosary in one hand and his musket in the other, clad like the meanest Corsican and distinguishable only by his large fiery eyes and thick eyebrows.   They say he could load his gun with furious quickness, and that he was so sure of his aim that he used to bless the soul of the man he was going to shoot, and to exclaim, " Poor mother!" He then sacrificed the foe to the God of Freedom.   After the battle he was gentle and kind, but always grave and deeply melancholy.   His words were: " My blood and my life are my country's: my soul and my thoughts are all my God's.

Pasquale's prototype must be sought among the Greeks, but Clement's among the Maccabees.   The latter was a hero not of Plutarch, but of the Old Testament.

CHAPTER XI.
THE OLD HERMIT.

THEY told me at Stretta that a countryman of mine, a Prussian, was settled there, an old eccentric man on crutches; and they had told him also, that a countryman of his had arrived.   So as I was returning from Clement Paoli's death-chamber, absorbed in thoughts of this old religious hero, my old countryman came hobbling up on crutches, and gave me a German shake of the hand.   I ordered breakfast, and we sat down to it; and I listened for hours to the extraordinary stories of old Augustine of Nordhausen.

" My father," he said, " was a Protestant clergyman, who wished to educate me in Lutheranism; but even as a child I could not like the Protestant church, and I soon discovered that Lutheranism was a blaspheming of the sole true church, as it exists in spirit and in truth.   The idea of turning missionary passed through my head.   I attended the Latin school at Nordhausen, and got as far as logic and rhetoric.   And when I had learned rhetoric, I went to the beautiful land of Italy, to the Trappists at Casamari, and was silent for eleven years."

" But, friend Augustine, how could you keep that up?"

" Why, to be sure, any one who is not cheerful cannot stand it long; a melancholy person becomes crazy among the Trappists.

B

I could joiner, and I joinered the whole day, and secretly
hummed a tune to my work."

" What had you to eat?"

."Vegetable soup, two plates full, bread as much as we would
and half a bottle of wine. I used to eat little, but I never left
a drop in the bottle. God be praised for the good wine! My
brother on the right was always hungry; he always ate two
plates of soup and five pieces of bread to it."

" Have you ever seen Pope Pio Nono?"

" Yes, and spoken to him as a friend. He was at Rieti in
the capacity of bishop, and I went there in my cowl, when I
was in another convent, to fetch the consecrated oil on Good
Friday. I was then very ill. The pope kissed my cowl when
I came to him in the evening; and on taking leave of me he
said, ' Fra Agostino, you are ill; you must eat something.'
' Sir Bishop,' I said, ' I have never seen a brother eat any thing
on Good Friday.'—' No matter;. you are absolved, for you are
ill.' Then he sent to the first hotel for half a fowl, some meat-
broth, preserve, and wine, and I sat at his table."

" What, did the Holy Father eat, too?"

" He ate only three nuts and three figs.—I now became more
and more ill, and I went to Tuscany. Suddenly I took a dis-
like to the works of men, and abominated them fundamentally.
I resolved to turn hermit. So, taking my tools with me, and
buying what I needed, I sailed to the little island of Monte
Cristo. It is a little island of nine miles in circuit, uninhabited
but by wild-goats, snakes, and rats. In ancient times the
Emperor Diocletian kept St. Mamilian, Archbishop of Palermo,
in exile there; the saint built himself a church upon the heights,
where a convent was subsequently founded. There were once
fifty monks there, first Benedictines, then Cistercians, and then
the Carthusians of St. Bruno. The monks of Monte Cristo
erected many hospitals in Tuscany, and did much good; they
founded the hospital of Maria Novella at Florence. Now the
Saracens carried off the monks of Monte Cristo, with all their
servants and oxen; but the goats climbed up the rocks and could
not be caught, and so they became wild."

" Did you live in the old convent?"

" No, it is in ruins. I lived in a cave, which I fitted up with
my tools, and closed up by a wall in front."

" How did you pass your long days? I suppose you were
always praying?".

"O no! I am no Pharisee. One cannot pray much. What is God's will happens. I had my flute. I went out to shoot the wild-goats, or sought for stones and plants, or watched how the sea came up against the rocks. I had also books to read."

"What sort of books?"

"The whole works of the Jesuit, Paul Pater Segneri."

"What grows upon the island?"

"Nothing but heath and wild-cherries. There are some little dells that are pretty and green; all the rest is rock. A Sardinian came to the island and gave me some seed, so I got vegetables, and even planted trees."   .

"Is there good stone upon the island?"

"Yes, fine granite and black tourmalin, which is found in the white stone; and of black garnets I discovered three kinds. At last I fell dreadfully ill in Monte Cristo; and luckily some Tuscans came and brought me away. Now I have been here eleven years on this accursed island among its rogues; for they are all rogues alike. The physicians sent me here; but when a year is over I hope to see the land of Italy again. Such a life as that in Italy there is not in all the world besides: and the people are agreeable. I am getting old, and walk with crutches; and being old and having thought to myself, 'I shall soon have to give up my joinering, and yet desire not to go a-begging,' I went to the mountains and discovered the Negroponte."

"What is Negroponte?"

"It is the earth of which they make tobacco-pipes in Negroponte; at home they call it Meerschaum. It is a perfect flower of a stone. This Negroponte is as good as that in Turkey; and, when I have brought it out, I shall be the only Christian that has manufactured it."

Old Augustine would have me go into his workshop. He has fitted it up in the convent, underneath the rooms of poor Clement; there he showed me with delight his Negroponte, and the pipe-bowls he had already made and laid out in the sun to dry.

I fancy every one has once in his life a time when he would be glad to go into the green-wood and turn hermit; and every one has once in his life a time when he would like to keep silence, like a Trappist.

This picture of old Augustine's life I have recorded because it made such an impression on my imagination; and I think it is a genuine piece of German nature.

CHAPTER XII.

THE BATTLE-FIELD OF PONTE NUOVO.

Gallia, vicisti! profuso turpiter auro,
Armis pauca, dolo plurima, jure nihil.
THE CORSICANS.

I STARTED from Morosaglia before vespers, to go down the hills
to the battle-field of Ponte Nuovo. There is placed also the
post-house of Ponte alla Leccia, where the mail from Corte ar-
rives after midnight, and by it I intended to return to Bastia.

The evening was fine and clear, and the calm mountain solitude disposed one to think. The twilight is short here; the
Ave Maria is scarcely over before night is come.

How often, when I hear the bells sound for Ave Maria, I am
reminded of Dante's beautiful verses, in which he has described
the evening frame of mind on both land and water!

Era già la ora che volge il disio
Ai naviganti, e intenerisce il core,
Lo dì che han detto ai dolci amici a dio,
E che lo novo peregrin di amore
Punge, se ode squilla di lontano,
Che paja il giorno pianger che si more.*

There is a single cypress on the mountain there, enkindled by
the evening glow like a vesper candle. It is a regular Ave
Maria tree, monumental like an obelisk, black and mournful.
It is beautiful, the way in which alleys of cypresses are used in
Italy to lead up to the convents and the churchyards. We
have the weeping willows instead. Both are regular grave-
trees; but how contrasted to one another! The willow points
downwards with its drooping shoots to the grave; the cypress
rises upwards like a candle, and points from the grave to the
skies. Thus they express inconsolable grief for the bereavement,
and hopeful faith. The symbolical language of trees is a significant indication of the unison of man with nature, whom he is
always drawing into the circle of his feelings, to make her share
his sentiments or expound them. So also the fir, the laurel, the
oak, the olive, and the palm, have a human significancy, and
poetical language.

* Dante, *Purgatorio*, viii. 1.

I saw but few and small cypresses in Corsica; yet they ought to belong particularly to this island of death. But the Tree of Peace grows every where about; the war-goddess, Minerva, to whom the olive is consecrated, is likewise goddess of peace.

I had to walk fifteen *miglia* over wild and silent mountains, with my eye constantly fixed upon the heaven-towering mountains of Niolo yonder, the snow-clad Cinto, Artiga, and Monte Rotondo, the highest mountain in Corsica, 9000 feet high. Monte Rotondo was now violet in the evening glow, and his fields of snow glistened with rose-colour. I had been on his summit, and distinctly perceived the highest pinnacle of rock, on which I had stood with a goatherd. I was delighted to see this. When the moon rose above the mountain there was an enchanting picture.

It is delightful to walk thus by moonlight in the still mountain wilds. There is not a sound, unless it be the gurgling of a spring; the rocks shine in many places, and the stone then looks like solid silver. Nowhere is a village to be seen, nor a human creature. I went at a venture in the direction where I saw the Golo exhaling vapour deep below in the valley. But I fancied I had taken a wrong path, and was just about to cross a ravine to the other side, when some muleteers came up, who told me I had chosen not only a right road, but the very shortest.

So I came to the Golo at last. This river flows through a wide valley, whose air is full of fever, and is shunned by the people. It is the air of the battle-field of Ponte Nuovo. At Morosaglia they warned me against walking through the night mists of the Golo, or remaining long at Ponte alla Leccia; whoever walks about there, may hear the dead beat ghostly drums or call his name, or at least he will get the fever and see visions. Somewhat of the latter I fancy I could verify in my own case; for I saw the entire battle of the Golo before me, and the terrible monk, Clement Paoli, with the large fiery eyes and thick eyebrows, with the rosary in one hand and the *fucile* in the other, blessing the soul of him whom he is just going to shoot. Then pell-mell flight; and dying men.—"The Corsicans," says Peter Cyrnæus, "are men prepared to die." The following trait is characteristic: A Frenchman found a Corsican mortally wounded, awaiting death without a moan. "What do you do when you are wounded," he asked him, "without surgeons and without hospitals?" "We die," said the Corsican, as laconic as a Spartan. A nation whose character is so plastic, and possesses such a mas-

culine greatness as the Corsican, gains nothing by comparison
with ancient heroic nations. Yet Lacedæmon is always hovering before my eyes here. If it is allowable to say that the spirit
of the Hellenes has been once more quickened in the wonderfully
endowed Italian people, then this applies, in my opinion, mainly
to the neighbouring provinces of Tuscany and Corsica. The
former displays all the richness in ideas of the Ionian mind; and ·
while her poets, from Dante and Petrarch, down to the time of
Ariosto, sang in their melodious language, and her artists, in
painting, sculpture, and architecture, renewed the days of Peri-
cles, whilst her great historians rivalled the glory of Thucydides,
and the philosophers of her academy filled the world with Pla-
tonic ideas, here in Corsica the rugged Dorian mind was revived,
and Spartan battles were fought.

In the year 1790, young Napoleon visited the battle-field of
the Golo. He was then twenty-one years old, but he had probably seen it as a boy. There is something demonic in the
thought. Napoleon, on the first battle-field he ever saw, as a
youth without formed prospects and without guilt,—he who was
to redden half the world from the ocean to the Volga, and from
the Alps to the Lybian desert, with the blood of battles!

It was just such a night as this that young Napoleon was
roving over the Golo field. He sat down by the river, which on
the battle-day, so the people tell, was blood-red for a distance of
twenty-four miles to the sea, and carried corpses along with it.
The fever-mist made his head heavy and dreamy. A ghost
stood behind him with a red sword in his hand. The ghost
touched him, and carried his soul flying through the air. They
paused over a field where a bloody battle was being fought; a
young general galloped off over thousands of corpses. "Montenotte!" cried the spirit; "and thou art he who fights this
battle!" They pause over another field, where a bloody battle
is being fought; a young general dashes over a bridge with
the banner in his hand, in the midst of the smoke of cannon.
"Lodi!" cried the spirit, "and thou art he who fights this
battle!" And on goes their flight from battle-field to battle-field;
the spirits pause over a great river, which is carrying down
corpses, while ships are burning upon it, and endless desert
bounds the scene. "The Pyramids!" cries the spirit, "and this
battle too thou wilt fight!" And so they fly on and on from
one battle-field to another, and the spirit calls in quick succession
the terrible names, "Marengo! Austerlitz! Eylau! Friedland!

Wagram! Smolensk! Borodino! Beresina! Leipzig!" Till at
length he pauses over the last battle-field, and exclaims with a
voice of thunder, "Waterloo! Emperor, thy last battle, and thy
downfall!"

Young Napoleon sprang on his legs again beside the river Golo,
and shuddered; in a fearful dream he had dreamt frenzied fancies.

But this entire fantasy was a consequence of the unhealthy
Golo mist that surrounded me. On this vaporous Corsican
battle-field, and on a night of pale moonshine, it is surely excus-
able to have visions. And what a wild, misty, awfully beautiful
moonlight night! Above yonder gigantic black granite mountains the red moon is poised—no! it is no longer the moon; it
is a great head, pale as a corpse, yet horrible with blood, hanging
over the island of Corsica, and mutely looking down upon it—a
Medusa head, a Vendetta head, awful and with serpent locks.
Whoever dares to behold this head is not transformed to stone,
but driven like Orestes by the fury, the double fury, that he
must first commit murder under the influence of raving passion,
and then roam from mountain to mountain, from cavern to
cavern, tracked by vengeance and the law, which stick close to
his heels. . . . I saw the spirit of vengeance riding through the
air on a winged horse, holding the dread Medusa's head by
the hair, tearing along and screaming, "Vendetta! vendetta!"

What fancies! and there is no end to them. But, God be
praised! here is the post-house of Ponte alla Leccia, and the
dogs give the alarm. Some men are sitting at the table in the
large desolate room, round the smoky oil-lamp, with their heads
drooping on their breasts, heavy with sleep. A priest, in a black
coat and hat, is pacing up and down the room, waiting for the
mail. I will start a conversation on spiritual subjects with
this holy man, that he may dispel all my cobwebs of ghosts'
drumming and demons' tricks.

But although this man's orthodoxy was firm as a rock, I could
not exorcise the evil Golo spirit in me, but arrived at Bastia
with a throbbing and aching head. I uttered my complaint to
my landlady, saying that the sun and the mists had occasioned
it, and that I feared I should die unlamented on foreign soil.
She said nothing would be of any avail in this case but having a
wise woman to say an *orazion* over me. I declined the *orazion*,
and asked to be allowed to sleep; and I slept the deepest sleep
during a whole day and night, and when I woke the god of day
stood high and glorious in the heavens.

TRAVELS.—BOOK IV.

CHAPTER I.

THROUGH THE DISTRICT OF NEBBIO TO ISOLA ROSSA.

BY ascending from Bastia the Serra, a range which connects itself with Cape Corso, you enter the land of Nebbio, on the sea at the other side of the island. An excellent road first climbs the sides of Monte Bello for a couple of miles. You look down on your left into the plain of Biguglia and Furiani, and into the large lagoon into which the river Bevinco empties itself. When the summit is reached, you behold the sea on either side. The road now descends towards the western coast, the eastern being lost from sight; and the enchanting picture of the gulf of San Fiorenzo suddenly opens out before your eyes. Reddish cliffs curiously indented, almost destitute of vegetation, and sinking down towards the coast, enclose the deep blue bay. The sight was grand, foreign, and southern.

On the side of the mountain ridge lies the gloomy village of Barbignano, which the road passes in the midst of groves of chestnuts and olives. This road was laid down by Count Marbœuf, and it was here that Bernadotte laboured on the roads. It describes an M with its immense zigzags, as the conductor of the diligence bade me observe.

We approached the glorious gulf of San Fiorenzo, which appeared radiant with smiles in the midst of the encircling solitary and monotonous red banks. It is an old and very apt image of the gleaming surface of the sea, to say that it *laughs*. I recalled a passage of Æschylus, in which he says: "O thou countless laughter of the ocean waves!"* And this gulf

* Æsch. Prom. 89. ποντίων τε κυμάτων
ἀνήριθμον γέλασμα.

laughed with innumerable little purplish-blue waves and ripples; and a valley with a brook meandering through it, laughed too, with thousands and thousands of rosebays, or oleanders, which luxuriated far and wide around, covered with their red flowers. In our country a stream is happy if it can deck itself with alder and willow bushes; here, in the beautiful south, it glories in graceful oleanders.

The district is little cultivated, indeed scarcely at all. I often saw solitary, deserted, and half-ruinous houses, looking very picturesque, with the ivy quite overrunning them and burying them in its shoots, which spanned the doors and windows. In such ivy houses one might fancy the elves to have their abode, chuckling when a sunbeam or moonbeam steals through the green leafy casements, to see what rogueries the wights are at. The history of the men who once lived there, may have been very bloody and horrible; perhaps they were driven out by the invaders from Barbary, or by the murderous war against Genoa, or by blood-revenge.

Here and there stands an old Genoese tower on the coast.

The country became more and more picturesque in the neighbourhood of San Fiorenzo. On the right the gulf now opened out in its full size, and on the left, far in the background, the eye scanned the high towering amphitheatre of mountains, which descend in a semicircle towards the sea-basin. They are the proud mountains of Col di Tenda, at the foot of which the Romans of old were defeated by the Corsicans. They surmount the district called Nebbio, which encompasses the gulf of San Fiorenzo, and open out only towards that district. Nebbio is a mountainous province of great aridity, but rich in wine, fruits, olives and chestnuts. From the earliest times the Nebbio was regarded as a natural fortress; wherefore all conquerors, from the Romans to the French, have endeavoured to force an entrance into it and gain a firm footing in it, and innumerable battles have been fought there.

The Nebbio at the present day contains four cantons or *pieves*, San Fiorenzo, Oletta, Murato, and Santo Pietro di Tenda. San Fiorenzo is the chief place.

We reached the small town, of a few houses and 580 inhabitants, about the heat of midday. It is a seaport, perfectly gloriously situated on one of the finest gulfs in Corsica. The only extensive valley of the Nebbio, the valley Aliso, traversed by the river of the same name, lies before the town. The river creeps sluggishly through a morass, which renders the whole district pestilential. On its brink I saw a solitary fan-palm, which in the glowing mid-day air gave the whole landscape a tropical character. Women and children were lying round a cistern chatting, with their bronze water-pitchers beside them—a *genre* picture that agreed charmingly with the fan-palm. The universal character of the gulfs on the Corsican coast is idyllic, half Homeric and half Old Testament.

A quarter of an hour suffices to walk through the town. A small fort with a tower surmounted by a cupola, and looking more like a Mecca chapel than a castle, protects the harbour, in which a few boats lay at anchor. The situation of San Fiorenzo is so glorious, and the gulf, one of the most beautiful on the Mediterranean, so alluring to a more considerable maritime settlement, that one cannot but wonder at its desolation. Napoleon mentions this place, in Antomarchi's Memoirs, in these words:—
" S. Fiorenzo is one of the happiest situations I know. It is the most favourable for commerce : it touches France and is adjacent to Italy; its landing-places are secure and convenient, and its roads could receive whole fleets. I would have built a fine large town there, which should have been a capital."

According to Ptolemy the ancient town of Cersunum must have stood somewhere on the gulf. In the middle ages the considerable town of Nebbio was situated here, whose ruins are half a mile distant from the present San Fiorenzo. The old cathedral of the Bishops of Nebbio, considerably decayed, but still venerable, still rises on a hill, displaying the Basilica style of the Pisan architecture, and probably of the eleventh or twelfth century: it was consecrated to Santa Maria dell' Assunta. Beside it stand the ruins of the former bishop's house. The Bishops who dwelt there were not less warlike than the proudest of the Corsican Signori : they called themselves Counts of Nebbio, and are said to have appeared with swords at their sides at the Corsican national assembly of the Terra del Commune, and to have always had two loaded pistols lying on the altar when they said mass. The town decayed, like other considerable towns and bishoprics in Corsica, Accia, and Sagona. At the present day many Roman coins and sepulchral urns are dug up there.

The later town, San Fiorenzo, was one of the first Corsican places that gave themselves to the Bank of Genoa in the year 1483. On this account the town received many liberties and privileges: and the Bank annually sent a castellano and a Podestà, who administrated the laws in company with four Consuls. In subsequent wars the castle of San Fiorenzo was often of importance.

There was excellent fish in the town, fresh from the gulf, which I had roasted, and then went on my way. For some distance the road now leaves the coast, and ascends a mountain range which does not always leave the view open towards the sea. It is an unfruitful coast and mountain region from hence into the Balagna, and as far as Isola Rossa. The Plutonic forces have scattered many great masses of rock about, which often cover the mountain sides with their gigantic blocks or small debris: slate, limestone and granite, are seen every where.

The cultivation of the olive and chestnut now becomes infrequent; but on the other hand the wild olive (oleastro) covers the hills, and the strawberry-tree, rosemary, myrtle, and heath, enjoy their heyday. The sun had parched these shrubs; and the reddish-brown hue of their shoots, the green of the olive, and the crumbling rocks, gave the country a melancholy tone as far as the eye could reach. The air alone quivered with heat in this silent scene; no bird was singing, and only the grasshopper chirping. Occasionally, a herd of black goats was seen reposing under an olive, or leaping over the rocks, seized by a panic fear.

From time to time we came to a small solitary road-side tavern, where the mules of the diligence were changed, or to a well encased in stone, which was immediately rapturously assailed by both man and beast.

I saw in some places small corn-fields, both barley and wheat. The corn was already reaped, and was being trodden out in the field. This process is very simple: in the middle of the field is a circular stone floor walled in, on which the husbandman shakes down the reaped corn, and has it trodden out by oxen, who drag a heavy stone behind them. I found the oxen every where muzzled, contrary to the injunctions of Moses. Innumerable treading-floors of this kind were scattered over the fields, with no villages visible near them; but in the vicinity of the floors were small barns, cubic stone buildings with flat roofs. The circular treading-floors and these grey huts, standing every where about, far and wide, looked very curious in the deserted landscape, like dwellings of grey earth-dwarfs. The Corsican laughs when we tell him how corn is threshed among us; such galley-slave labour he would for no consideration perform.

On the whole journey I saw not a single conveyance. Now and then came a Corsican on horseback, with his double gun slung over his shoulders, and an umbrella over his head. Here they shoot a great many wild pigeons and men. At length we again approached the seashore, after passing the little river Ostriconi. The land on the coast is often elevated only 100 feet above the sea, and then it rises again in the boldest shapes. The nearer you come to Isola Rossa, the more mighty are the mountains; they are the romantic peaks of the Balagna, the Corsican promised land, which flows in truth with oil and honey. Some of the mountains wore caps of snow, and shone with a dazzling crystal whiteness.

There lies Isola Rossa on the seashore before us! There are the two grey towers of the Pisans! There the blood-red island-cliffs which give the town its name. What a little charming seaside idyl in the evening light! Silent mountains above, the still sea here, grey olives that stretch out their boughs of peace to the pilgrim, hospitable smoke ascending from the hearth—verily, I swear I have reached the magic shore of the Lotus-eaters.

CHAPTER II.

SEASIDE IDYL OF ISOLA ROSSA.

'Αλλ' αὐτῷ βούλοντο μετ' ἀνδράσι Λωτοφάγοισιν
Λωτὸν ἐρεπτόμενοι μενίμεν, νόστου τε λαθίσθαι.
                                        HOM. *Odyss.* ix. 96.

THERE is a large rural space at the entrance of the little town, and enclosed by its walls, which look like garden-walls. In the middle rises a fountain, on the cubic granite pedestal of which stands a marble bust of Pasquale Paoli, erected two mouths ago. Paoli is the founder of Isola Rossa; he founded it in the year 1758, in the midst of war with the Genoese, who held their ground in the neighbouring strong town of Algajola. He said at the time, "I have set up the gallows on which I will hang Algajola." The Genoese came with gun-boats to interrupt the work; but the walls rose amidst the rain of their shot, and Isola Rossa is now a place of 1860 inhabitants, and the important port and emporium of the oil-raising Balagna.

I found some children playing around the fountain, one of whom was a beautiful child, six years old, with the blackest locks and large black thoughtful eyes, and lovely as an angel. " Do ye know," I asked, " who is the man standing on the fountain before us?"—"Yes, we know," said they; "it is Pasquale Paoli."—The children asked what country I came from; and when I bade them guess, they guessed all imaginable countries, even Egypt, but not Germany. They now will follow me here on all my walks, and I cannot get rid of them. They sing me songs and bring me coral dust and brilliant shells from the shore; they are always by me, and many others with them. Like the rat-catcher of Hameln, I draw a train of children after me, and they follow me even into the sea. The earth-shaker Poseidon, Nereus, and the azure-footed Nereids, suffer us all in their presence; and I see many a dolphin sporting joyously through the crystal waves.

And this is just the place to be a child among children.

It has a soothing effect upon the mind to be so world-lorn here on the white sands, or in the greenwood. The little town lies still as in a dream ; the flat-roofed houses, with their green Venetian shutters, the two snow-white towers of the little church, and every thing besides, look so tidy and homelike. In the sea are the three red cliffs, on which an old tower keeps guard, and tells in the still air of evening old tales of the Saracen. Blue wild-pigeons and martlets were fluttering round it. I climbed these cliffs in the evening ; they can now be reached by land, being connected with the shore by an embankment. They are rugged and steep rocks ; and there is a scarcely accessible cave into which the waves of the sea find entrance. Near these cliffs they are now sinking a new mole, and French workmen were just then occupied in heaving by cranes, moving along, and letting fall into the waves, the great cubes for the mole, which are formed of a congeries of stones baked together into a mass.

The evening view is beautiful from these red islands. On the right, the sea and the whole peninsula of Cape Corso veiled in haze ; on the left, a red tongue of land, with the sea curving round it ; the little town in the foreground, with fishing smacks, and a few sailing boats in the harbour ; in the background, three glorious mountains, Monte di Santa Angiola, Santa Susanna, and the ruggy rocky Monte Feliceto, with olive groves and many black villages on their sides. Here and there, one sees the glow of the godlike goatherds' fires.*

Nowhere could the people live more quietly and patriarchally than here. The land and the sea both yield their produce : the people have enough. They sit of an evening on the mole and gossip, or they angle in the still water, or stroll in the olive groves and orange-orchards. By day the fisherman gets his nets out, and the artisan sits under the mulberry-tree before his door, and works diligently. Here the song and the guitar are never out of place: the young landlady of a little coffee-house where I had made myself at home, sang very pretty songs ; so by my desire a party assembled in the evening, and we had many a charming ditty sung, and many a pretty air strummed on the guitar.

The children also sang me songs as they ran after me—the Marseillaise, the March of the Girondins, and Bertram's Adieu, adapted as a eulogy on the President of France ; the refrain always concluded with the words, *vive Louis Napoléon!* Little Camillo sang the Marseillaise the best.

We looked for shells on the seashore: there are plenty of them if you pass the little nunnery that stands in a garden by the sea, inhabited by the sisters of the Madonna alle Grazie. The sisters in this villa have the choicest view of the sea and the mountains, and many a one of them may dream over again her blighted romance of love, when the moon's crescent of gold gleams over Mount Reparata as it did to-night. The shore is snow-white for a great distance, and the sands are variegated by red coral dust, and the prettiest shells. Little Camillo helped me bravely in looking for shells, but he was more taken by the little living *leppere*, shells that adhere to the stones by suction, than by the pretty ones. He broke them off in the water, and ate the animal with great gusto, and was surprised that I would not join him. In the evening we enjoyed the phosphorescent waves, and bathed, swimming through millions of sparks.

Charming world of children ! It is well when its long unheard voices begin to speak again. These lotus-eaters will not let me alone ; they fancy me a rich baron, and propose that I should buy lands and settle at Isola Rossa. It were no bad idea to forget the world here.

" Yes, blood-revenge is 'the death of us !" said a citizen of

* The author uses Homer's epithet for the honest herdsman, Eumæus: δῖος ὑφορβός, *Odyss.* xiv. 3, *et passim.*

Isola Rossa. "See the little *Mercato* there, our market, with
the white pillars. One day last year, a citizen was walking up
and down there : suddenly a shot was heard, and he collapsed
and fell dead. It was Massoni, who had come down into the
town in open day, and aimed a ball at his enemy's breast ; and
off he was again to the mountains, and all this in open day."

There is the house where Paoli was surprised, when the
celebrated Dumourriez had contrived a plot against him. And
here Theodore of Neuhoff, King of the Corsicans, landed for the
last time, and put to sea again when his dream of royalty was
over.

I went one day with an Alsacian of the tenth regiment, which
is at present distributed over Corsica, up Mount Santa Reparata,
and into the *paese* of the same name. It is difficult in words
to paint the picture of such a Corsican mountain village ; one
would come nearest to it by fancying rows of blackish towers,
cut through in the middle, and having windows, gaps, and loopholes. The houses are often built of quite unhewn granite,
generally covered only by a mud roof, upon which plants often
grow ; very narrow steep stone steps lead up to the door. I
found poverty and uncleanliness every where; men and swine together in cave-like rooms, lighted only through the door. And yet
these poor people, high on the mountains, live in an ocean of
air and light ; but they are housed like the Troglodytes. From
one of these caves issued a pale young woman with a child in
her arms ; I asked her whether she could feel well here, as she
always sat in the dark. She looked at me and laughed.

In another house I saw a mother putting her three children to
bed. They all stood naked on the floor, and looked sickly and
starved. The beds on which these poor little creatures slept were
poor indeed. This stout-hearted mountain people grows up in
wretchedness. They are hunters, herdsmen, and cultivators at
once. Their only wealth is the olive, the oil of which they sell
in the towns ; but not every one is equally rich in olives. Here
then life is wretched, not from the evils of civilisation, but from
the evil of the retention of the natural state.

I went into the church, whose black façade pleased me—the
white bell-tower is new. The Corsican church-steeples have no
points, but end in an abrupt belfry. The interior of this church
had a pulpit and a high altar, a very queer affair of white-
washed stone, with many extravagances. Above the altar was
an inscription in Latin, "Holy Reparata—pray for thy people,"

populus, in the true old democratic style. On the walls were some crude beginnings of painting, and some niches enclosed by half pillars, some of the Corinthian and some of the Composite order. An interdict now lies upon St. Reparata, and no mass is said there. After the death of the last priest, the parish refused to accept the successor sent by the Bishop of Ajaccio, and split into two parties, who kept up a deadly feud. The interdict laid in consequence upon the church has not yet allayed the strife.

I went through the narrow, dirty lanes to the outer border of the valley, whence an extensive view is enjoyed of the mountain range, closed by the distant Balagna. Many brown hamlets stand among the circle of mountains, and many olive groves. The dryness of the rocks contrasts powerfully with the green of the gardens and groves. A man had conducted me thither who stammered, and had his face flushed with St. Anthony's fire, and I think he was imbecile. I made him tell me the names of the places in the Balagna valley. He told me in a guttural tone much I only half understood ; but I well understood him to point to this place and that, and mutter, *ammazzato, ammazzato col colpo di fucile*. He was pointing out places on the rocks where human blood had been shed. I shuddered, and got away from my unpleasant companion as soon as I could. I returned by the Paese of Oggilione, descending on narrow herdsman's paths through olive groves. Armed Corsicans passed me on horseback, their horses climbing rapidly from rock to rock. Evening came on; the lonely Feliceto glowed with the tenderest of hues; a bell on the mountains pealed for Ave Maria, and on the hill side a herdsman was playing on the shepherd's pipe. This all accorded delightfully together, and by the time I reached Isola Rossa I had worked myself up again into an idyllic mood.

Awfully sharp are the contrasts that here meet—a world of children, a world of herdsmen, and blood-red murder !

CHAPTER III.

VITTORIA MALASPINA.

Ed il modo ancor m' offende.
FRANCESCA DA RIMINI.

I HAD made the acquaintance in Bastia of a man of station in the Balagna, Signor Mutius Malaspina. He is a descendant of the Tuscan Malaspinas, who governed Corsica in the eleventh century; and by his wife Vittoria, he became connected with the family of Paoli, she being a great granddaughter of Hyacinthus, a granddaughter of the celebrated Clement, and daughter of the universally popular Councillor Giovanni Pietri, one of the most meritorious men in Corsica.

Signor Malaspina had given me an invitation to his house at Monticello, a *paese* lying above Isola Rossa, and a few miles distant from thence; and I had joyfully promised to be his guest at a house once inhabited by Pasquale, whence many of his letters are dated. Malaspina gave me a note to his house, which I should find open to me at all times, even before he had himself returned to it.

So I arrived at Isola Rossa with the intention of going up to Monticello, and passing a few days, there. But on my way thither I was told, what I had not had an inkling of, and what Malaspina himself had concealed from me—the awful affliction that his family had suffered not three years ago. I knew not which to be more astonished at—the enormity of the calamity, or the character of the Corsican who, in spite of it, offered hospitality to an unknown stranger. I could not now bear to enjoy this hospitality in a house where hospitality herself had been murdered. Still I went up to Monticello, to pay the tribute of human sympathy to suffering.

The house Malaspina stands at the entrance of the *paese*, on the plateau of a rock encircled by woods—a large, solemn, strong, and castellated house of the olden times. Mournful cypresses surround its terrace, and prepare the traveller while yet at a distance for the tragedy that was enacted there. A small waste space lies before the entrance of the house, with

young plane-trees upon it, spreading their green round a cemetery chapel.

Passing through the entrance arch, I mounted a dark narrow
stone staircase, and looked about for the inhabitants. The house
appeared dead and deserted. I passed through dismal bare
chambers, from which the spirit of home had departed, until at
length, I found an old dame in mourning attire, who was the
housekeeper, and a child of eight years, the youngest daughter
of the family. It cost me some trouble to win a gracious look
from the old dame, till she, little by little, opened out towards me
more confidingly.

I put no questions; but little Felicina herself asked me to see
her mother's rooms, and told me in her innocence more than
enough.

The old lady, Marcantonia, sat down beside me; and what
she told me I will faithfully repeat, only concealing the sur-
name and native town of the miserable man.

"In the summer of 1849, many Italians fled from their native
country and sought refuge in Corsica. Among them was one
who was to be given up; but Signor Pietri, who is kind to
all men, took compassion on him, procured him the power
of remaining here, and took him into his own house at Isola
Rossa. The stranger, who was called Giustiniano, stayed a month
with Signor Pietri down at Isola Rossa; and then, as that gentleman had to attend the council of Ajaccio, Signor Mutius and
my lady Vittoria took him into their house here. Here he had
all the pleasure he could desire, hunting and horses, a good table,
and no end of guests who came to the house in his honour. The
Italian was very agreeable and sociable; but he was sad at
living in a foreign land. Signora Vittoria was loved by every
one, and most of all by the poor; she was indeed like an
angel."

"Was she beautiful?"

"She had a delicate complexion, blacker hair than Felicina,
and extremely beautiful hands and feet; and she was tall and
full-built. The Italian, instead of feeling at ease in a house
where he received all possible friendliness and kindness, grew
sadder and sadder. He began to speak and eat little, and looked
as pale as death. He walked for hours on the mountains, and
often sat looking troubled in his mind and without speaking a
word."

"Did he never betray his passion for the Signora?"

"He once went into her room after her; but she thrust him out, and told the maid to be silent about it, and say nothing to her master. A few days before the 20th of December, nearly three years ago, Giustiniano became so miserable that we thought he was going to be seriously ill. He was to leave Monticello and go to Bastia for change of scene; he himself wished it. During three days he ate not a morsel. One morning I was taking his coffee to him as usual, but the door was locked. After a while I came again, and called him by his name; he opened to me. I was shocked at his looks. I asked him, 'Signor, what ails you?' He laid his hand so upon my shoulder, as I lay mine upon yours, and said to me, 'Oh, Marcantonietta! if you knew how my heart aches!'—Not a word more he said. On his table I saw a pistol lying, and powder heaped up in a paper, and also bullets. These he had sent Felicina's elder sister to the *boltega* for, on the previous evening. He now wished to go back to Bastia, and there take ship for another country. He took leave of all and rode down to Isola Rossa; this was the 20th of December. On the morning of that day Signora Vittoria had said to me, 'I had a bad dream last night. I thought my sick *compare* (godmother) was dying. I will go to-day and take her some refreshment.'—For that was her way; she often went to the sick, and took them oil, wine, or fruit."

Here old Marcantonia wept bitterly.

"Signor Malaspina had gone out riding to Speloncato. I was away, and no one was in the house but the sick Madamigella Matilda, a relation of my mistress, the youngest children, and a maid. It was afternoon. As I came back to the house, I heard a shot. I supposed they were hunting on the mountains, or blasting. But soon after there came a second shot, and methought it came from the house. I was trembling in all my limbs as I came to the house, and in great terror I asked the maid, 'Where is the mistress?' and she said also trembling, 'O God! she is upstairs in her room changing her dress, to go to the sick woman.' 'Run,' said I, 'and see after her!'

"The maid dashed down the stairs again, pale as a corpse.— 'Something must have been doing,' said she; 'for my mistress's door stands wide open, and the room is all in a mess, and the visitor's room is locked.' I ran up—so did the maid, Felicina, and her sister. It looked horrible in my poor mistress's room: the door of the Italian's room was locked. We knocked, we screamed, we tore it at length off its hinges—there, sir, we saw it before our eyes——But now I will not tell you a word more.'

No, not a word more, Marcantonia! Greatly shaken by the narrative, I rose and went out. Little Felicina and the house-keeper came after me, and took me into the chapel. The child and the old woman knelt before the altar and prayed. I took a myrtle branch from the altar, and cast it on the spot beneath which Vittoria is buried. And then I wandered sadly back to Isola Rossa.

It is hard for the thought to grasp such a terrible thing, and words are reluctant to tell it. Giustiniano had suddenly returned after leaving Monticello. He silently ascended the staircase again. The rooms occupied by him and by Vittoria are on the same upper floor; they are separated by a sitting-room. Vittoria was just then in her room, engaged in changing her dress. Giustiniano burst in upon her, armed with a pistol and a dagger, and bereft of sense through the madness of his love. He wrestled fearfully with the strong woman: he threw her to the ground, and dragged her to his room; she was already dying, pierced by the stabs of his dagger. Her beautiful hair was found torn and scattered about, and the room thrown into confusion by the struggle. Giustiniano laid down the hapless dying woman on his bed—shot her through the temples with his pistol—drew the rings from her fingers, and put them on his own—then lay down beside her, and blew his brains out.

Thus they were found by the old woman and poor Felicina, then a child of five years, who cried and exclaimed, "That is my mother's blood!"—an awful sight, and a cruel experience impressed for life upon the soul of a child. The people of Monticello would have torn in pieces Giustiniano's corpse; but Malaspina, who returned unsuspecting from Speloncato, prevented it. It was interred among the rocks of the mountain of Monticello. Vittoria was thirty-six years old, and mother of six children; Giustiniano scarcely twenty-five.

I found Mutius Malaspina a simple plain man, with features expressive of iron steadfastness and calmness. I should have hesitated to tell the sad story here, but it is in every one's mouth, and told even in a little book printed at Bastia, con-taining sonnets to Vittoria. The memory of Vittoria will live as long as the island lasts. Some centuries hence the noble woman's sad fate, which I heard from the mouth of a member of the family, and in her very rooms, will have become a legend.

Even now I perceived how rapidly a real event begins to transform itself among the people into the legendary. The very same person, the housekeeper, told me that poor Vittoria's spirit had appeared to some sick people in the *paese*. And it will soon be said that the murderer rises by night from his rocky grave, pale and restless as he was in life, and glides to the house where he perpetrated the horrible deed.

*   *   *   *   *

Angry with human nature, I descended the hills, pondering the narrow boundary, the transgression of which may transform the noblest passion, love, into the most frightful fury. How near together are God and the devil in the human soul, and how comes it that one and the same feeling is the matter from which both are produced? I saw neither the mountains nor the calm and merry sea; I cursed all Corsica, and myself that I had ever set my foot upon its bloody soil. Just then the pretty Camillo came running up; he had run over all the rocks after me. He had gathered a handful of blackberries, which he held out to me, his friendly eyes expressing that I must eat them. The sight of this innocent child instantly cheered me up. It seemed as if he had put himself in my way on purpose, to show me how fair and guileless man issues from the hand of nature. Camillo now kept running along beside me, and springing from stone to stone, until at length he said suddenly, "Now I am tired, and I will sit down a little." So he sat still on a piece of rock. I never saw a more beautiful child. When I told his elder brother so, he replied, "Yes, all people love Camilluccio; and at the procession of *Corpus Domini* he was an angel, and had a snow-white robe on, and held a great palm-branch in his hand." I beheld him with delight as he sat upon the rock, with his fine raven locks flying wildly over his face, and his large eyes looking fixedly before him. His dress was tattered, for he was the child of poor people. All at once, of his own accord, he set up singing the Marseillaise, "Allons, enfants de la patrie . . . contre nous de la tyrannie l'étendard sanglant est levé." It was curious to hear the Marseillaise in the mouth of such a lovely boy, and to see his grave face in singing it. But how historical this bloody song sounds in the mouth of a Corsican boy! And when little Camillo sang, "Against us is Tyranny's bloody standard raised," I thought, "Poor child! Heaven preserve thee, that thou fallest not by the bullet of revenge, nor be forced to roam over the mountains as an avenger of blood."

As we approached Isola Rossa, we were alarmed by a red glow over the town. I hastened towards it, supposing a fire to have broken out ; but it was a fire of joy. In the Paoli square the children had kindled a mighty bonfire, and were dancing round the flame, joining hands in a ring, and laughing and singing. They sang countless little verses invented by themselves, a few of which I still remember :—

Amo un presidente,	I love a president,
Sta in letto senza dente.	He is in bed and has no teeth.
Amo un officiale,	I love an officer,
Sta in letto senza mâle.	He is in bed and has nothing amiss.
Amo un pastore,	I love a shepherd,
Sta in letto senz' amore.	He is in bed with no one to love.
Amo un cameriere,	I love a chamberlain,
Sta in letto senza bere.	He is in bed with nothing to drink.

The little flock never flagged with their verses, and they whisked merrily round the fire the while. The air was charming, naïve, and childish. This extempore juvenile fête delighted me so much that I too volunteered a verse or two, on which the little folk burst out into a laugh of joy that echoed through all Isola Rossa.

The next day I drove by a *char-à-bancs* to Calvi. Little Camillo stood by the carriage and said sorrowfully, "Non mi piace che tu ci abbandoni." The wanderer takes notes of many things, mountains and rivers, cities, and occurrences in the fine— nay, and in the ugly—world ; why not paint for once also the picture of a beautiful child ? Like a lovely song, it will be a delight to the memory after the lapse of years.

CHAPTER IV.

FROM ISOLA ROSSA TO CALVI.

MY *vetturino* told me by way of greeting, that I had the honour of riding in an extraordinary carriage. "For last year," he said, "I drove in this carriage the three great bandits, Arrighi, Massoni, and Xaver. As I was driving along the road, they happened to come this way, all armed to the teeth, and they commanded me to take them to Calvi. I did so without more ado, and then they suffered me to return unharmed. Now they are all dead."

The road from Isola Rossa to Calvi leads along the coast all the way. On the mountains are seen many ruins of places destroyed by the Saracens, and above Monticello are situated also the ruins of a castle of the celebrated Giudice della Rocca, the Pisan lieutenant. This just judge of his people still lives in the memory of the Corsicans. They say he was just even to beasts. One day he heard the lambs of a flock in the Balagna bleating piteously; he asked the shepherds what was the matter with the lambs, and they confessed that they were bleating with hunger because the milk had been taken from the ewes; so Giudice commanded, that in future the ewes should not be milked till the lambs had been satisfied with drink.

I came first through Algajola, an old place by the sea, now quite decayed, and numbering scarcely 200 inhabitants. Many houses stand in ruins and uninhabited, battered by the shells of the English; for they have been allowed to stand as ruins till the present day in the state that the war reduced them to sixty years ago—a sad and palpable witness of the condition of Corsica. Even the inhabited houses are like blackened ruins. A good-natured old man, whom Napoleon's wars had once taken as far as Berlin, showed me the wonders of Algajola, and called a great pile of stones the *palazzo della communità*. In the time of the Genoese, Algajola was the central place of the Balagna; and being so situated that the inhabitants of every village in the Balagna could go thither and back home again in a day, the Genoese raised it to be the seat of one of the lieutenants of the island, and fortified it.

The greatest distinction of Algajola is the popular legend of two true lovers, Chiarina and Tamante. Tamante was condemned to death by the French, but his lady-love armed herself, and with the help of her friends delivered him from execution. The people every where honour the noble deeds of love, and immortalise them as legends: the story of Chiarina and Tamante is popular all over Italy, and I have seen loose leaves of it even in Rome.

Near the sea, at Algajola, a magnificent blue-greyish granite is quarried. I saw a column lying in the quarry which would do honour to an Indian or Egyptian temple, sixty feet long and twelve in diameter. It has lain for years on the field, forgotten and weather-beaten, and noticed only by the wanderer who sits down upon it, or the eagle who perches upon it. Originally intended for a monument to Napoleon at Ajaccio, it was left lying here because they could not raise funds sufficient for its transport. It will now probably be conveyed to Paris. Of the same splendid granite is the huge block that supports the Vendome column at Paris. With what fair pride, then, may the Corsican stand before that Austerlitz column, look down upon the French and say to them, " My country produced both, the great man up there, and the splendid granite he stands upon."

I now passed Lumio, an elevated *paese*, whose black-brown tower-like houses were not at a distance to be distinguished from the rocks. The green Venetian-shutters indicate, here and there, the abode of a man of rank. The descendants of the old Signori still live in all these villages; and men of the proudest names, and untold ancestors, live in the dingy Corsican *paeses*, in the midst of the people, and in company with them. Perhaps there is nowhere in the world such democratic uniformity of life as on this island, where differences of rank are scarcely perceptible, and the peasant associates with his master as a free man, as I have often witnessed. Above Calvi, in this district, lives Peter Napoleon, the son of Lucian, and the only Bonaparte who remained in his native island. The Balaguese are very fond of him, and praise him for being a good shot, for often mixing with the shepherds, and for having never forgotten that his ancestors were Corsicans. The election of Louis Napoleon naturally fills the Corsicans with pride and joy; I found his portrait every where, and heard his energy praised as Corsican energy. Some farther-seeing persons were not quite so prejudiced by their patriotism, and I heard, even from Corsican lips, the opinion expressed, that the Napoleons were tyrants, indeed the last tyrannizers over freedom.

Lumio possesses many orange orchards, and an astonishing number of cactus hedges, which I only found besides in Ajaccio in such profusion. The cactus here grows to the size of a tree. The view from the hills of Lumio, down to the valley and gulf of Calvi, is beautiful. Calvi lies on a tongue of land, at the foot of the mountains of Calenzana. With its dark-coloured flat-roofed houses, two domes rising high above the houses, and the walls of the fort, which stands at the extreme point of the tongue of land, its bears a striking resemblance to a Moorish town.

Calvi is the capital of the smallest Corsican arrondissement, which has about 25,000 inhabitants, divided among six cantons and thirty-four communes, and comprises nearly the whole north-western part of the island. Of this mountain and coast-land, not the half is cultivated; for the large coast-strip of Galeria is utterly waste, and only the Balagna is in good cultivation, and the most numerously peopled.

The little town of Calvi, now numbering about 1680 inhabitants, owes its origin to Giovanninello, Lord of Nebbio, the bitter enemy of Giudice della Rocca, and the adherent of Genoa. The town then gave itself to Genoa, and always remained faithful to that republic. The citizens of Calvi, like those of Bonifazio, received many privileges and immunities. In Filippini's time the town numbered 400 hearths, and he calls it a chief town, as well for its antiquity as for the beauty of the houses, to which he adds, "relatively to the capacity of the country." The Bank of Genoa, he says, built the fortress, and it cost, in the opinion of some, 1850 scudi.

Calvi is placed on the tongue of land in which one of the mountain ranges ends, which encircle the great valley around the gulf. These mountains consist of granite and porphyry ; they are bare, and form an imposing amphitheatre. Olives and vines thrive on their declivities, and their feet are covered by yew and various shrubs, myrtles, *albatro*, and *tinus*, from the blossoms of which last the bee sucks her honey. From this comes the bitterness of the Corsican honey, of which even Ovid and Virgil knew. Calenzana is especially rich in honey. A stream traverses this valley, and forms a morass with dangerous exhalations in the neighbourhood of Calvi, called *la vigna del vescovo*, the Bishop's vineyard. Of the origin of this morass one of those capital stories is told that delight the traveller in Corsica. The Bishop of Sagona, then, removed to Calvi, where he had a beautiful vineyard, and fell in love with a girl. In the vineyard he confessed to the fair one his love, and conjured her to reciprocate it ; then he caressed her, and covered her with kisses, and was as one bewitched. The girl, seeing the episcopal signet ring on the holy man's finger, said laughing, "Aha! what a fine thing a bishop's ring is! I will love you for this ring." The bishop heaved a deep sigh; but his passion burned, and he drew the sacred ring from his finger, and put it on the fair maid's finger, that she might be gracious towards him. But no sooner did she grant him the favour of an embrace, than the ring sprang off her finger, fell to the ground, and was not any where to be found. On the following day the bishop went again to his vineyard, to look for the ring ; but, lo and behold! there was no vineyard any more; it was gone, and in its place there was a morass.

CHAPTER V.

CALVI AND ITS MEN.

THE marsh air of the Borgo, or small suburb of Calvi, makes it
unhealthy: the air is better above, in the fortress which surrounds
the town properly so called. I went up to this old Genoese citadel,
the strongest in Corsica after Bonifazio.   Over the gates I read
the words, CIVITAS CALVIS SEMPER FIDELIS.   Ever faithful Calvi
was to the Genoese.   Faithfulness is always fine when it is not
slavish ; and Calvi was a Genoese colony.   That declaration
of faithfulness has become historical in more than one case.
When the republican general Casabianca had to capitulate in
the year 1794, after the heroic defence of Calvi against the
English, it was one of the articles of capitulation, that the old
inscription above the gate should not be touched.   Faithfully
has the condition been observed, as may be read above the gate.
    Only on one point are Genoa and the ever faithful Calvi at odds.
The Calvese maintain that Columbus was born at Calvi ; that
his family, though undoubtedly Genoese, had long ago settled
there.   A dispute actually arose about this birthright, as of yore
seven cities contended for Homer's cradle.   They assert that
Genoa took possession of the family registers of the Colombos of
Calvi, and rebaptized one of the streets of the town, called
Colombo Street, as the street *del filo !* I find also a record, that
the inhabitants of Calvi were the first Corsicans who sailed to
America.   I was also told that the name Colombo still exists in
Calvi.   Even modern Corsican writers claim the great discoverer
as their countrymen; and Napoleon, during his residence in Elba,
was thinking of having historical researches undertaken upon
this question.   Suppose we let the dispute rest upon its own
evidence.   Columbus calls himself in his will a born Genoese.
The world might be envious if, besides Napoleon, fate had given
to little Corsica a greater than Napoleon.
    Many brave men have adorned Calvi, and when one beholds
the little town enclosed by the fortress, and sees what a mere
heap of blackened and riddled ruins the English shells have reduced it to, one may read in this chronicle of desolation the

history of ancient heroes.   An extraordinary sight this—a town
bombarded almost a hundred years ago, and still lying in ruins.
Here in Corsica time seems to have stood still.   An iron hand
has held fast the past, with its old popular usages, the dirges of
the Etruscans, the family feuds of the middle ages, the barbarity
of blood-revenge, the simplicity of the life of old, and the
heroism of old: and as the people live in hoary ruins of towns,
so they still live in hoary conditions of life, that have become
fabulous to the men of civilisation.

   In the principal church of Calvi, the Moorish dome of which
is riddled by the English balls, they show the graves of a family
that bears the most precious and envied name in the world—
Liberty, Libertà.   It is the ancient heroic family of Baglioni
that bears this title.   In the year 1400, when some aristocrats
at Calvi set up for tyrants over the town, and were preparing to
deliver it over to the Arragonese. a young man, Baglioni,
roused himself, and with his friends fell upon the tyrants in the
citadel, as Pelopidas fell upon the tyrants of Thebes, put them
to the sword, and called the people to liberty.   From his cry
Libertà! Libertà! is derived the title given him by the grateful
people, and borne thenceforward by his family.   Among
Baglioni's descendants were three heroic brothers, Piero Libertà,
Antonio, and Bartolommeo, who were settled at Marseille.   This
town was in the hands of the Ligue, and alone defied Henry
IV. after he had entered Paris and received the homage of the
Guises.   Casaux, the consul of the Ligue, was the tyrant of
Marseille; he designed to deliver the place into the hands of
Andrea Doria, who commanded the Spanish fleet.   Then Piero
Libertà conspired with his brothers and other bold men of
Marseille to rescue the town.   He took them all into his house,
and as soon as they had laid their plan, they advanced boldly to its
execution.   They forced their way into the castle of Marseille,
and Piero Libertà with his own hand drove a lance through the
throat of the consul Casaux; and having cut down or disarmed
all the soldiers on guard, he closed the gates of the castle, and
rushed into the town with his bloody sword in his hand, crying
Libertà! Libertà! The people rose at this cry and took up arms;
and then they stormed the towers and redoubts of Marseille and
delivered the town.   The Duke of Guise then entered Marseille in
the name of Henry IV.; and the latter wrote an honourable
letter to Piero Libertà, dated from the camp at Rosny, March
6, 1596.   He made him supreme judge of Marseille, Captain

of the Porta Reale, Governor of *Nostra Donna della Guardia*, and loaded him with other honours. This happened at the same time at which another Corsican, Alfonso Ornano, the son of Sampiero, gained Lyon for the King of France. on which occasion Henry exclaimed, "Now I am king!"

Piero Libertà died a few years after the liberation of Marseille. He was buried most magnificently by the town, and his statue erected in the town hall, with the following inscription upon its pedestal:

𝔓etro 𝔏ibertae,

LIBERTATIS ASSERTORI,

HEROI, MALORUM AVERRUNCO,

ACIS CIVIUMQUE RESTAURATORI,

ETC.

A remarkable power of propagation distinguishes the Corsican families. Any one who has paid attention to the history of this nation, must have discovered that the father's powers are almost constantly transmitted to his sons and grandsons.

It is hard to pass from the graves of Libertà to the field of Calenzana, where are the graves of Schiavitù, slavery. They are the graves of. five hundred brave, but hired and sold, Germans, who fell at Calenzana.

I have told the story in the Corsican history. The emperor Charles VI. having sold to the Genoese a German auxiliary corps, they transported it to Corsica. On the 2nd February, 1732, the Corsicans, under their general Ceccaldi, engaged the German troops at Calenzana. The latter were under the command of Camillo Doria and Devins. The Imperialists were defeated after a terrible battle, and five hundred Germans were left dead on the field. The Corsicans buried the foreigners, who had come into their country to fight against liberty, on the beautiful hillside between Calvi and Calenzana. On foreign, but heroic, soil, rest the bones of our poor brothers. There is some dark blood-coloured porphyry rock in their vicinity, and the covering of their graves is verdant with myrtles and flowering herbs. And on every Easter Saturday, to the present day, the priests come from Calenzana to these graves of their foes—the *Camposanto dei Tedeschi*, as the field is called by the people— to besprinkle with holy water the spot where the poor hirelings fell. Thus the Corsican avenges himself on the foes who came to destroy his independence. It seemed to me as if I, who was

one of the few Germans who have stood upon the hirelings'
graves at Calenzana, and perhaps the only one who thought of
them, was bound to thank the noble nation of the Corsicans, in
the name of Germany, for this magnanimous and humane fellow-
feeling.   And I dedicate the following inscription to my countrymen:

EPITAPH

ON THE FIVE HUNDRED GERMAN MERCENARIES OF CALENZANA.

Five hundred wretched hirelings here we came,
To Genoa by our own Emperor sold,
The freedom of the Corsicans to slay.
For this offence we here lie in our blood,
And do sad penance in a foreign grave.
Not guilty call us, but for pity meet;
The foeman covers us with mercy o'er.
Revile not, wanderer, that dark age's sons;
Ye living shall make good our ignominy sore.

Those were dark ages, when our fathers were sold like an un-
thinking herd, these to serve against Corsica, and those against
America.   But then arose here Pasquale Paoli, and there Washington, and beyond the Rhine,the rights of humanity were proclaimed.   The ignominy of those times was cancelled, and the
ignominy of Calenzana too; for the grandchildren of these who
lie here in the graves of servitude, fought as free men for their
hearths and homes, and for the independence of their fatherland,
in great battles of nations and battles of freedom, and overcame
even the Corsican despot.

The sun sets, the gulf glistens, and the rocky mountains of
Calenzana are enriched by a glowing hue.   How enchanting is
the southern haze over the distance, and how delicate are the
gradations of colour!   Nothing so deeply impresses the human
soul as all transition.   On the border-line, whether in passing
from being to nothingness, or from nothingness to being, is the
fairest and deepest poetry of life.   It is no otherwise in the
history of nations.   Their most wonderful exhibitions are always
on the border where two periods of varying culture meet, and
the one is on the point of passing into the other, just as in
nature a season or a day displays the most glorious phenomena
when it is passing into another.   Methinks it is so also in the
history of an individual mind.   In it also there are many
transitions from one period of culture to another, or from one
form of educational influence to another, so full of charm and so

fruitful that there alone the germs of poetry or of creativeness can unfold themselves.

There is even at Calvi almost fabulous retirement from the world. The calm mirror of the gulf is unruffled; not a ship at a distance of miles; not a bird rises; yonder black tower stands up like the obscure figure of a dream on the snow-white shore. O, but here is an eagle perched, a magnificent creature, taking his rest solemnly and royally;—now he soars up with powerful stroke of wing and makes for the mountains: he has his fill of blood. Next I disturb a fox, the first I have seen in Corsica, where the foxes are remarkably large, and carry off the lamb like wolves. He was sitting enjoying his ease on the bank, and seeming to like the rose colour of the waves, for he was quite absorbed in the contemplation of nature, and so completely buried in his own thoughts that I stole up within five paces of him. All of a sudden Mr. Reynard sprang up, and as the shore was very narrow I had the pleasure of obstructing his road and putting him for a moment in a fix. He thereupon performed an evolution of decided genius, and ran off blithely to the mountains. He has a capital life of it in Corsica, where the beasts have made him their king, because there are no wolves.

As night came on, I got into a boat and rowed about in the bay. What delight, and what night-pictures! The Italian sky, dotted over with glittering stars; the air magical and transparent; far off on the point a gleaming lighthouse; lights in the castle of Calvi; shepherds' fires on the dark mountains above; a few vessels sleeping on the water; the waves sparkling round my boat, and the drops that fall from the oar, sparks; and in the deep stillness only the tones of a guitar, sounding across the water from the shore!

CHAPTER VI.

A FESTIVAL OF MASTER-SINGERS.

THE poetry of this evening was not yet over. I had hardly fallen asleep in my little *locanda*, when I was wakened by the sound of a guitar and singing in many parts. They played and sang for perhaps an hour in the still night, before my house. It was in honour of a young lady who lived there; they sang first a *serenata*, and then *voceros* or dirges. How strange! the song with which they serenaded a young girl was a dirge, and the very *serenata* sounded as mournful as a *vocero*. These psalm-like tunes, heard in the stillness of the night, enter indescribably deep in the soul, and excite powerful emotions; the tones are so plaintive, so monotonous, and so long drawn out. The first voice sang a solo, then the second fell in, then the third, and the whole chorus. The manner of delivery was recitative, in the manner of the Italian *ritornello*. And in the *ritornello*, too, a sentiment not in itself mournful is sung plaintively; but the *vocero* fills the soul with trembling, and attunes it to woe. I had heard such nocturnal music at other places in Corsica, but never so full and solemn as here. I can never forget the plaintive songs of that night at Calvi; I still often catch their echo; and especially the plaintive expression of the one word and the one sound, *speranza*, is often audible to me.

On the following morning I came by chance into the shop of an old shoemaker, who announced himself as the guitar-player of the night before. He was willing enough to bring out his instrument. The Corsican *cetera* has sixteen strings; it has nearly the form of the mandolin, only it is larger, and the sounding-board is not quite round, but a little flattened off. The strings are struck with a flat ram's horn tapering to a point. So I found the general experience confirmed here also, that the race of shoemakers are thoughtful, musical, and poetical all the world over. By my desire the Hans Sachs of Calvi fetched a few of the best singers. Shoes and lasts were shoved aside into the corner, and the little party of singers collected in the back-room, the flower-embosomed window of which looked out upon the gulf, and drew their chairs close to one another; the master-singer took his guitar, closed his eyes, and struck rich tones out of the strings.* But I will mention who the singers were. First and foremost was the old shoemaker as the master-singer, then his young apprentice, who learned from him how to make shoes and charming music, then an elegantly-dressed young man, a gentleman attached to the tribunal, and lastly, a silvery-grey old man of seventy-four. Old as he was, he

---

* "Drückte die Augen ein und schlug in vollen Tönen."—An almost involuntary allusion to Goëthe's beautiful song of the Harper, "Was hör' ich drauszen vor dem Thor," where it is said:—

> "Der Sänger drückt' die Augen ein,
> Und schlug in vollen Tönen ;
> Die Ritter schauten muthig drein,
> Und in den Schoosz die Schönen."

sang from his heart, if not quite so lustily as in his youth; and from the long extensions of the notes of the Corsican *voceros*, he frequently lost his breath.

Now began the charmingest festival of singers that was ever held. They sang whatever my heart desired, serenades and *voceradi*, or laments, but mostly laments, because the high originality and beauty of these charmed me most. They sang, after many others, a vocero on the death of a soldier; the subject was the following:—A young man from the mountains leaves his father, mother, and sister, and goes to the continent, to the wars. Returning home an officer many years after, he goes up to his *paese*, where none of his friends know him. He discovers himself only to his sister, whose joy is unspeakable. Then he says to his father and mother, to whom he has not yet discovered himself, that he would like them to prepare a splendid meal for the morrow, and he would pay handsomely for it. In the evening he takes his gun and goes out for some sport, leaving his knapsack, which contains much gold, in his room. The father sees the riches, and resolves to murder the stranger by night; and the dreadful deed is accomplished. So when day comes, and midday comes, and the brother never shows himself again, the sister asks after the stranger, discovering to her parents, in the anxiety of her heart, that he is her brother. They pass into his chamber, father, mother, and sister; there he lies in his blood! Now follows the sister's *lamento*. The story is true; and indeed all that the Corsican popular songs celebrate is real fact. The shoemaker told me the story very dramatically, and the old man seconded him with the most expressive gestures; then the former took up the guitar, and they sang the *lamento*.

The friendly singers, when I told them that I would translate their songs into my native language, and should long remember them and this hour, begged me to stay this evening in Calvi; then they would sing the whole night through, and amuse me. But if I was positively decided to go away, I must be sure to go to Zilia; there were the best singers in all Corsica. "Alas!" said the shoemaker, "the best of all is dead. He sang with a clear voice like a bird, but he went to the mountains and turned bandit; and for his beautiful singing the *paesani* long prevented the police from taking him. Yet they did catch him at last, and struck off his head at Corte."

Thus Calvi proved to me an oasis of song in these quiet unpopulous regions. Now it seemed to me worthy of note, that

two of the best Corsican poets were natives of Calvi; a sacred
poet, Giovanni Baptista Agnese, born in the year 1611, and
Vincenzo Giubega, who died in the year 1800, thirty-nine years
old, a judge of the tribunal at Ajaccio. Giubega is called, not
without justice, the Anacreon of Corsica. I read a few pretty
amatory poems of his, which are remarkable for grace and feeling.
There are but few of his poems in existence, because he burnt the
majority himself. As Sophocles says the memory is the queen of
things, and as the Muse of Poetry is a daughter of Mnemosyne,
I will here mention another Corsican of Calvi who once enjoyed
a world-wide fame, Giulio Guidi, who was the wonder of Padua,
in the year 1581, for his ill-fated memory. He was able to repeat 36,000 names after once hearing! He was called *Guidi
della gran memoria.* He produced nothing; his memory had
killed his creative powers. Pico of Mirandola, who lived before
him, did produce, but he died young. Thus it is with the precious
gift of memory as with all other gifts; it is a curse when the
gods give too much of it.

I have once already mentioned the name Salvatore Viale.
This poet, a native of Bastia, where he still lives at an advanced age, is the most fruitful poet that the island has produced.
He has written *La Dinomachia,* a comic poem in the style of the
Secchia rapita of Tassoni, translated Anacreon, and some things of
Byron. So Byron is actually in Corsica! Viale has deserved
excellently well of his country through his untiring scientific
activity, and also for his elucidation of Corsican customs. Corsica has also a translator of Horace, Giuseppe Ottaviano Savelli,
a friend of Alfieri, of whom I have already spoken. I might
mention many other names of Corsican poets, such as the song-
poet Biadelli, of Bastia, who died in the year 1822; but their
songs will not penetrate far into the world. The finest that
Corsica has produced, are and always have been the songs of the
people, and their greatest poet, affliction.

CHAPTER VII.

CORSICAN DIRGES.

THE character of the Corsican dirges is to be understood from the nation's rites with regard to the dead, which are very ancient. With a people among whom death moves more in the character of a destroying angel than elsewhere, presenting himself constantly in his most bloody forms, the dead must have a more striking ceremonial than elsewhere. There is something dark and striking in the fact, that the most favourite poetry of the Corsicans is the poetry of death, and that they compose and sing almost exclusively in the intoxication of grief. Most of these rare flowers of popular poetry have germinated in blood.

When death has entered a house, the relations stand round the bed of the deceased and tell their beads, and then raise a cry of lamentation (*grido*). The body is now laid on a table called the *tola*, against the wall: his head lies on a pillow, and wears a cap. To prevent the head and features losing their expression, a cloth or ribbon is bound round the neck and chin, and tied fast on the crown under the cap. If it is a young girl, they put a white grave-shift upon her, and deck her with flowers; if a married woman, she has generally a party-coloured gown, and an old woman a black one. A man lies out in a grave-shirt and Phrygian cap, and may then resemble an Etruscan corpse, such as I have found depicted in the Etruscan Museum of the Vatican, surrounded by mourners.

They watch and lament beside the *tola* often the whole night through, and a fire is kept burning. But the grand lamentation begins on the early morning before the funeral, when the body is laid in the coffin and before the funeral friars come to lift the bier. To the funeral come friends and relatives from all the neighbouring villages: and this assembling throng is called the *corteo* or escort, or the *scirrata*, a word that sounds like the German *schaar* (host, band), but whose origin can hardly be discovered. A woman, who is always the poetess or singer, which is here identical, leads a chorus of the female lamenters. So they say in Corsica, *andare alla scirrata*, where the women go in procession to the house of mourning; if the deceased has been slain they say, *andare alla gridata*, to go to the howling. As soon as the chorus enters the house, the lamenters greet the mourner, whether she be the widow, mother, or sister of the dead, and they lean their heads together for about half a minute; then a woman of the bereaved family invites the assembled women to lamentation. They make a circle, the *cerchio* or *caracollo*, round the *tola*, and perform their evolutions round the deceased, howling the while, expanding the circle or closing it again, and always with a cry of lamentation, and the wildest tokens of grief.

These pantomimes are not alike every where. In many places they are suppressed by the process of time, in others they are mitigated; but among the mountains far in the interior, especially in the Niolo, they exist in their old heathen force, resembling the funeral dances of Sardinia. Their dramatic vividness and furious ecstasy is agitating and awful. The dancing, lamenting, and singing are performed by women only, who, with hair dishevelled and shed wildly over their breasts, with eyes that dart fire, with black mantles flying, execute evolutions, utter a howl of lamentation, strike the flat of their hands together, beat their breasts, tear their hair, weep, sob, cast themselves down by the *tola*, bestrew themselves with dust:—then suddenly the howls cease, and these women now sit still like Sibyls on the floor of the chamber of mourning, breathing deep, and resting themselves. Terrible is the contrast between the wild funeral dance, with its howling laments, and the dead himself, who lies stiff and cold upon the bier, and yet rules this turmoil of Furies. On the mountains the female lamenters even tear their faces till the blood comes, because, according to an old heathen fancy, blood is pleasant to the dead, and appeases the shades. This is called *raspa* or *scalfitto*.

The nature of these lamenters has something of the demoniacal, and must appear fearful when their dance and lament are for a murdered man. They then become perfect Furies—the snaky-haired avengers of murder that Æschylus painted them. They swing themselves round in horror-inspiring evolutions, with hair loosened, striking their hands against one another, howling, and singing revenge; and so powerful is often the effect of their song upon the murderer who hears it, that he is seized with all the awfulness of horror and the pangs of conscience, and betrays himself. I read of a murderer who, shrouded in the

hooded robe of the funeral friars, had the boldness to hold the
funeral taper at the bier of him whom he had helped to murder,
and who, when he heard the song of revenge strike up, began to
quake so violently that the taper fell from his hand. In criminal trials, the declaration of a witness that a person has trembled
during the lamentations is held as a proof of guilt. Yea, many
a man in this island resembles the Orestes of Æschylus, and the
prophetess might say of him,*

> " On the navel-stone behold a man
> With crime polluted to the altar clinging,
> And in his bloody hand he held a sword
> Dripping with recent murder;
> And stretch'd before him, an unearthly host
> Of strangest women, on the sacred seats
> Sleeping—not women, but a Gorgon brood,
> And worse than Gorgons, or the ravenous crew
> That filch'd the feast of Phineas (such I've seen
> In painted terror); but these are wingless, black,
> Incarnate horrors."

A deathlike stillness reigns in the chamber. Naught is heard
but the deep breathing of the crouching lamenters, who sit
covered up by their cloaks, with the head dropped upon the
breast—expressing the deepest grief in the old Hellenic fashion,
as the artist represents *his* head as covered whose grief is above
measure great. Nature herself has given to man only two ways
of expressing the highest grief—the outcry of bursting feeling,
in which the vital power seems to unfetter all its energies, and
deep silence, in which the vital power dies away in impotency.
Suddenly one woman springs up from the circle of women, and
strikes up a song to the deceased, like an inspired seer. She
delivers the song in recitative, strophe by strophe, and every
strophe ends with a Wo! wo ! wo ! which is repeated by the
chorus of lamenters, in the manner of the Greek tragedies. The
singer is also chorus-leader, and either has composed or improvised the song. In Sardinia she is generally the youngest
girl present. Generally these songs—panegyrics, or songs of
revenge, in which the praise of the dead alternates with lamentation for him, or exhortation to revenge—are improvised upon
the spot.

What an extraordinary contrast to European civilisation we
have in a country which has preserved in life these scenes, which
would seem to be parted from our state of society by a chasm of
three thousand years ! Behold the dead man on the bier, and the

* *Æsch. Eum* 40.—*Blackie's translation.*

lamenters crouching on the ground ; a young girl rises, and with
countenance glowing with inspiration improvises like Miriam or
Sappho, composing verses full of unapproachable gracefulness and
the boldest imagery; and her ecstatic soul flows on inexhaustibly
in rhyme, with dithyrambs which melodiously tell the deepest and
the highest of human grief. After every strophe the chorus howls
out Deh ! deh ! deh ! I know not if a scene is to be found any
where in life, which combines the awful with the lovely into such
deep poetry as this, in which a girl sings before a bier whatever
her maiden soul inspires her at the moment to say, and in which
the chorus of furies accompanies her song with howls. And
again there is another girl who, with eyes flashing fire and
glowing cheeks, rises as an Erinys over her murdered brother,
who lies in his armour on the *tola*, demanding revenge in verses,
the wild and bloody language of which even a man's mouth
could not have made more awful. In this country, woman,
though low and subservient, holds her court of justice ; and before the tribunal in which her plaint is made the guilty is cited
to appear. So the chorus of maids sings in the Libation-pourers
of Æschylus : *—

> " Son, the strong-jaw'd funeral fire
> Burns not the mind in the smoky pyre;
> Sleeps, but not forgets the dead,
> To show betimes his anger dread.
> For the dead the living moan,
> That the murderer may be known.
> They who mourn for parent slain,
> Shall not pour the wail in vain.
> Bright disclosure shall not lack •
> Who through darkness hunts the track."

Some of these seers, whom I would compare with the German
Velleda, made themselves renowned for their inspirations ; so
in the last century Mariola delle Piazzole, the leader of funeral
choruses, whose improvisations were every where in request,
and so Clorinda Franceschi of the Casinca. In Sardinia the
lamenters are called *piagnoni* or *prefiche*, in Corsica *voceratrici*

---

* Æsch. *Choeph.* 322.—*Blackie's translation.*

Τέκνον, φρόνημα τοῦ θανόντος οὐ δαμάζει
Πυρὸς μαλερὰ γνάθος.
Φαίνει δ' ὕστερον ὀργάς.
Ὀτοτύζεται δ' ὁ θνήσκων,
Ἀναφαίνεται δ' ὁ βλάπτων.
Πατίοων τε καὶ τεκόντων
Γόος ἔνδικος ματεύει
Τὸ πᾶν, ἀμφιλαφὴς ταραχθείς.

or *ballatrici.* It is not always the usual chorus-leaders that sing, but frequently the relatives of the dead, the mother, wife, and especially the sisters. For a heart full of sorrow overflows in laments possessing an artless eloquence, and makes the language exalted, and the ideas happy, even without poetic talent. And moreover the form of the dirges is constant; so that when affliction comes, the Corsican woman must have already had frequent practice in the dirges, which go from mouth to mouth as other songs with us. Thus an atmosphere of gloom hangs constantly over men's heads here. When Corsican girls sit together, they are sure to strike up a *lamento,* as if they wished to rehearse for the heart-lament which, perhaps, each of them may have to sing at the *tola* of a brother, a husband, or a child.

That pantomimic dance of lament is called in Corsican the *ballata* (*ballo funebre*), the ballad. They say *ballatare sopra un cadavere,* to dance over a corpse. The lamentation is called *vocerare,* the dirge *vocero, compito,* or *ballata.* In Sardinia the ceremony is called *titio* or *attito.* They derive this word from the ejaculation of grief, Ahi! ahi! ahi! with which the chorus-leader finishes every strophe, and which the women repeat after her. The Latins ejaculated *atat,* and the Greeks, as we find in their tragedies, *ototototi;* and among us Germans, *ahtatata* obtains as an exclamation of violent pain, as any one can verify who notices what his outcry is when he has burnt his finger and snaps it in the air.

Finally, as soon the funeral friars come to the house to lift the bier, another ejaculation is raised, and then the train escorts the dead with *lamentos* into the church, where he is blessed, and from the church again with *lamentos* to the churchyard. The ceremony is concluded by the funeral feast, the *convito* or *conforto.* A meal, called the *veglia,* has been given preliminarily to those who watch beside the corpse, and every funeral friar is wont to receive a cake. The *conforto* itself is given to the relatives and friends of the deceased, either in the house of mourning, or at the abode of a kinsman, to which the guests are invited with pressing importunity. It honours the dead for the meal to be prepared on as large a scale as possible; and if he was in his lifetime a generally respected person, this is seen in the number of guests. Great expense is often run into for this funeral banquet (*banchetto*), and bread and meat are even sent out to the houses of the village. Mourning costume is black; and a mourner often lets his beard grow for a long time. The banquet is sometimes repeated on the recurrence of the anniversary of the funeral.

These then are the Corsican rites with regard to the dead, that are still kept up to the present day in the interior and south of the country, curious remains of ancient heathen usages in the midst of Christianity, and combined with Christian customs. How old this *ballata* is, and when and whence it was brought into this island, is difficult to say, nor will I venture upon any researches on the subject. But we will not omit to point out the relation in which it stands to some usages of other nations.

The expression of grief over the corpse of one beloved, is every where the same—weeping, lamentation, and spoken recollection of what he was in life, and of the love with which he was loved. The impassioned heart breaks out in violent, lively, and dramatic signs of grief. But the civilized man is restrained, by the force of culture, from allowing to his natural feelings unlimited freedom of gesticulation. Not so with man in a natural state, with the child, or with the so-called common folk, who in the midst of our civilisation, reflect the epic age of the human race. If we would convince ourselves that the epic men—kings, heroes, and national leaders—conducted themselves in grief quite as passionately as the Corsicans now in their *ballata*, we should read the poems of Firdusi, Homer, and the Bible. Esau cries aloud, and weeps for the stolen blessing.* Jacob rends his clothes for Joseph.† Job rends his mantle, and tears his hair, and falls down upon the ground,‡ and his friends do the same; they lift up their voice and weep, and rend every one his mantle, and sprinkle dust upon their heads towards heaven.§ David takes hold on his clothes, and rends them for Saul and Jonathan, and mourns and weeps;¶ so also he weeps on his flight before Absalom, and has his head covered, and goes barefoot.**

Still more passionate and unrestrained are the bursts of grief of the Homeric men. Achilles mourns for Patroclus; the black cloud of melancholy gathers round him, and he besprinkles blackish dust over his head with both hands:††

---

* Gen. xxvii. 34.   † Gen. xxxvii. 34.   ‡ Job i. 20.
§ Job ii. 12.   ¶ 2 Sam. i. 11.   ** 2 Sam. xv. 30.
†† *Iliad*, xviii. 26.   Given in Chapman's translation.

> " And himself he threw upon the shore,
> Lay, as laid out for funeral. Then tumbled round and tore
> His gracious curls : his ecstasy he did so far extend,
> That all the ladies, won by him and his new-slaughter'd friend
> (Afflicted strangely for his plight), came shrieking from the tents,
> And fell about him ; beat their breasts, their tender lineaments
> Dissolved with sorrow."

When Hector falls, Hecuba tears her hair, and Priam weeps and mourns piteously,[*] and tells Achilles later on, when he begs him for a couch to repose on, that he has been constantly groaning and brooding over his numberless griefs,—

> " Within the straw-yard of my court deep wallowing in the mire." [†]

Similarly in Firdusi, the hero Rustem tears his hair for his son Sohrab, roars with grief, and weeps blood ; Sohrab's mother casts fire upon her head, rends her clothes, is constantly sinking in a swoon, fills the room with dust, weeps day and night, and dies in a year. Passion finds its expression here on a gigantic scale, proportioned to the colossal nature of the heroes themselves.

In the Nibelungen, the greatest tragedy of blood-revenge, the passion of grief is expressed on a no less colossal scale. Chriemhild raises the cry of lamentation for the dead Siegfried ; blood flows from her nose, and she weeps blood beside his body, and all the women assist her with their lamentations.[‡]

In almost all these passages, we find the lament for the dead appearing as a lyrical outpouring of grief, and forming itself into a song. By way of comparison with the Corsican *lamenti*, we cite the noblest lament of all, David's lamentation for Saul and Jonathan :[§]

> The gazelle, O Israel, is slain on thy heights;
>   How are the mighty fallen !
> Tell it not in Gath, proclaim it not in the streets of Ascalon,
>   Lest the daughters of the Philistines rejoice,
>   Lest the daughters of the uncircumcised exult.
> Ye mountains of Gilboa, let there be no dew nor rain upon you, and
>   ye fields of offerings,
>   For there the shield of the mighty was cast away,
>   The shield of Saul, not anointed with oil !
> From the blood of the slain, from the fat of heroes
>   The bow of Jonathan turned not aside,
>   And the sword of Saul came not back empty :—

---

* *Iliad*, xxii. 405, 408.   † *Iliad*, xxiv. 640.   ‡ Nib. Nôt. Canto xvii.
§ 2 Sam. i. 19. As the authorized version is undoubtedly incorrect in several important grammatical points, I have given a revised one, mostly from Ewald.

Saul and Jonathan—who were beloved and gracious in their lives,
    And who are not parted in their death;
    Who were swifter than eagles, stronger than lions.—
Ye daughters of Israel, weep for Saul,
    Who clothed you in purple with delight,
    Who put ornaments of gold on your apparel!
How are the mighty fallen in the midst of the battle!
    Jonathan, slain on thy heights!
I am sad for thee, my brother Jonathan;
    Very dear wert thou to me;
    Thy love of me was more wonderful than the love of women.
How are the mighty fallen!
    And the weapons of war perished!

The lamentation over the body of Hector, in the last canto
of the Iliad, is quite dramatical, and may be perfectly compared
to a *ballata* at the *tola*. Let us listen to this *vocero* too:*

—" On a rich bed they bestowed the honoured person, round
Girt it with singers that the wo with skilful voices crowned.
A woful elegy they sung, wept singing, and the dames
Sighed as they sung. Andromache the downright prose exclaims
Began to all; she on the neck of slaughtered Hector fell,
And cried out, 'O my husband! thou in youth bad'st youth farewell,
Left'st me a widow; thy sole son an infant, ourselves cursed
In our birth, made him right our child; for all my care, that nursed
His infancy, will never give life to his youth, ere that
Troy from her top will be destroyed. Thou guardian of our state,
Thou even of all her strength the strength; thou that in care wert past
Her careful mothers of their babes, being gone, how can she last?
Soon will the swoln fleet fill her womb with all their servitude.
Myself with them, and thou with me (dear son) in labours rude
Shalt be employed, sternly surveyed by cruel conquerors;
Or, rage not suffering life so long, some one, whose hate abhors
Thy presence (putting him in mind of his sire slain by thine,
His brother, son, or friend,) shall work thy ruin before mine,
Tossed from some tower; for many Greeks have eat earth from the hand
Of thy strong father: in sad fight his spirit was too much manned.
And therefore mourn his people, we, thy parents (my dear lord,)
For that thou mak'st endure a wo, black and to be abhorred.
Of all yet thou hast left me worst, not dying in thy bed,
And reaching me thy last-raised hand, in nothing counselled,
Nothing commanded by that power thou hadst of me, to do
Some deed for thy sake: O for these will never end my wo,
Never my tears cease!'—Thus wept she, and all the ladies closed
Her passion with a general shriek. Then Hecuba disposed
Her thoughts in like words: ' O my son, of all mine much most dear;
Dear while thou liv'st too even to gods: and after death they were
Careful to save thee. Being best, thou most wert envied;
My other sons Achilles sold; but thee he left not dead.

        * *Iliad* xxiv. 719. Given in Chapman's translation.

Imber and Samos, the false ports of Lemnos entertained
Their persons; thine, no port but death; nor there in rest remained
Thy violated corse; the tomb of his great friend was sphered
With thy dragged person: yet from death he was not therefore reared,
But (all his rage used) so the gods have tendered thy dead state,
Thou liest as living, sweet and fresh as he felt·the fate
Of Phœbus' holy shafts'—These words the queen used for her moan,
And next her, Helen held that state of speech and passion.

"'O Hector, all my brothers more were not so loved of me
As thy most virtues. Not my lord I held so dear as thee,
That brought me hither, before which I—would I had been brought
To ruin, for what breeds that wish (which is the mischief wrought
By my access)—yet never found one harsh taunt, one word's ill
From thy sweet carriage. Twenty years do now their circles till
Since my arrival; all which time thou didst not only bear
Thyself without check, but all else that my lord's brothers were,
Their sisters' lords, sisters themselves, the queen my mother-in-law,
(The king being never but most mild) when thy man's spirit saw
Sour and reproachful, it would still reprove their bitterness
With sweet words and thy gentle soul. And therefore thy decease
I truly mourn for, and myself curse as the wretched cause,
All broad Troy yielding me not one that any human laws
Of pity or forgiveness moved to entreat me humanly,
But only thee; all else abhorred me for my destiny.'"

The Pelasgians, Greeks, Phœnicians, the Egyptians particularly, the ancient tribes of Italy, the Etruscans and Romans,
these have all had laments for the dead; so also the Celts, as the
Irish, and the Germans; and the same is true of the existing uncivilized tribes in Africa and America, as well as of the Indians.
In Italy also, besides Sardinia and Corsica, are found similar
usages with regard to the dead, especially in the kingdom of
Naples.

Even old Peter Cyrnœus finds a great similarity between
the Corsican rites regarding the dead, and those of the Romans,
which are undoubtedly Pelasgo-Etruscan. Whoever knows the
rites of the ancient Romans, will confirm this. They too had
their female lamenters, called then, as still in Sardinia, præficœ;
and they had the dirges called nœniœ. I have already communicated a Roman nœnia that the reader may call it to mind
here; namely Seneca's vocero on Claudius, which is, to be sure, a
parody. On occasion of the funeral of Germanicus, Tacitus also
speaks of the celebrations employed as ancestral customs; namely
eulogistic and memorial songs on his virtues, tears and excitation
of grief.* In the Laws of the Twelve Tables the ballata was

* Tac. *Ann.* ii. 73. Funus sine imaginibus et pompa, per laudes ac memo-
riam virtutum ejus celebre fuit.

called *lessus*, and punished as a barbarous custom, in the same way as it had been still earlier prohibited by the laws of Solon; " women shall not lacerate their cheeks, nor hold the *lessus* on occasion of a funeral."

The custom of celebrating a funeral *banquet* also dates from ancient heathen times. I deduce its origin from these circumstances : The need of refreshment after the exhaustion produced by the acts of mourning ; the honour conferred upon the dead by a last festive meal, of which he is as it were the giver; and lastly, the mystic religious symbol of eating, which is the return from death to life, to denote that the mourners now take part again in the world of the living. The funeral dish among the Phœnicians, Pelasgians, Egyptians, and Etruscans, consisted mainly of beans and eggs. Both these viands are mystic symbols of the active and passive generative and vital power, according to the old Oriental and Pythagorean mysticism. Even now beans and eggs are eaten in many places in Sardinia at the funeral repast; but I have heard of no similar custom in Corsica. The Romans called the funeral banquet, *silicernium.* The afflicted Trojans return from Hector's funeral to a solemn festive banquet in Priam's house.*

The Corsican *Voceri*, of which I communicate a few, are all composed in the dialect. Trochaic measure is the prevailing rule, which is however not unfrequently broken through. So also a triple rhyme is the rule, but it is occasionally modified. This measure, and the monotony of the rhyme, have a profoundly melancholy effect, and it would be hard to find a rhythm more appropriate to grief. The *voceri* themselves may be divided into two classes— the gentler complaint on the death of a person deceased, or the wild, fearful song of revenge. These songs cast a clear light on the nature of the Corsicans. They show how revengeful and hot-blooded the Corsican temper is, and how strong are their passions. When we consider that these songs are almost all composed by women, we are terrified at their violence, since woman is destined by nature rather to give utterance to the gentler sentiments of the soul, and to mitigate the raw force of the masculine nature. I know no example in the whole course of popular poetry, in which the horrible and fearful has to such a degree become the subject matter of the popular song; and here is displayed the wonderful power of poetry in general, which is able to mitigate even the most terrible with an air of

* *Iliad*, xxiv. 801.

melancholy beauty. For the Corsican nature is also in the highest degree capable of the tenderest sentiments. In these songs will be found the imagery of Homer beside that of the Psalms and the Song of Solomon. Artless as they are, they bear only the impress of improvisations, the limits of which may be extended at pleasure; and because they are improvisations, they catch the momentary genius of the intoxicated heart. The ineffable guilelessness and touching native simplicity of many *voceri*, remove us quite from our world to the world of children, shepherds, and patriarchs. No mere poetic *genius* can invent such sounds of nature. That among the "voices of nations," which we Germans have the art of catching,* the voice of lamentation may not be missing, I have translated a few of these Corsican *lamentos* with the utmost faithfulness both in form and tone. Beautiful songs, like tears wept in a noble grief, are often called pearls; I call these dirges blood-red corals from Corsica.

VOCERI: OR, CORSICAN DIRGES.

E come i gru van cantando lor lai
DANTE.

DEDICATION.

Call ye me, beloved twain,
Whose fresh tomb from earth emerges?
When the bard soft strikes his cithern
By the lonely island surges,
O how his lamento rouses
Then my soul's sad deep-felt dirges!

Spirits of my wanderings,
Swans that have before me flown,
On the mountains, on the ocean,
Greet ye me in gentle tone;
With the music sad of dirges
Greet me here on island lone.

What here my lament expresses
From my heart's depths it is wrung,
Echo is it of my feelings,
From my own affliction sprung;
To my dear departed, mourning,
I a Vocero have sung.

---

* Alluding to Herder's collection of the ballad literature of all nations, entitled, "Voices of the Nations in Songs," (*Stimmen der Völker in Liedern.*)

VOCERO.

ON THE DEATH OF A GIRL OF PIETRA DI VERDE.

Let me hasten to my daughter,
To my child let me come near;
For methinks that on the tola
I shall find her laid out here,
And that they a ribbon necklace
Round her neck give her to wear.

O Maria, mother's rapture!
O thou treasure of my joys!
O my child, thy father's blossom,
Thou, his eyes wont to rejoice!
Now today for ever part we,
It must be without our choice.

O how dost thou, Death, so cruel,
All my hopes so sudden blast?
Bruise the flower of my love,
Take my heart's pledge off at last?
And in floods of grief this morning
Dost my heart in sorrow cast.

Who, O daughter mine! could bear
This great wo, thy early death?
Ah! my heart forbears to beat,
And I, panting, gasp for breath!

(Pause.)

Never wilt thou now thy friends
Nor thy dearest playmates see;
How they stand in groups around thee,
Grieved to death for sake of thee!
Render them an answer, dear; •
Let them not uncomforted be.

Put thy clothes on, prythee, Mary,
Mother's joy, my darling lass;
See, the maidens all wish with thee,
On this early morn, to pass
To the church of Saint Elias,
There to hear the holy mass.

(A playmate of the deceased takes up the song.)

Let us go to holy mass,
For the lights are now displayed,
And the candles on the altar;
Quite in black it is arrayed.
To the church today thy father
With thy dower is gone, sweet maid.

In the church this very morning
We shall see a sight so splendid;

For Maria's dower has been
All in tapers bright expended.

(Another playmate takes up the song)

O my friend! thy malady's name
I would that I could hear it ever:
Shall I say it was consumption,
Or believe it was a fever?
Or was it a strange disease
Which besides has happened never?

O, where found he thee, dear maiden!
Death, the swift, the sorrow-bringer?
Thou didst alway sit in the arm-chair,
Or in the valley walking linger,
And thy mother at table let thee
Never e'en move thy little finger.

(The mother takes up the song.)

I this morn for St. Elias
Will a beauteous nosegay pull;
Flowers fairest, for a present,
Of the richest blossoms full;
Grateful will it be to him,
Such an offering beautiful.

To Maria I will pray,
To Lord Jesus I will speak;
For this morning I will go,
And my flowers I will break.
O Mari! thy mother's heart's love,
How my heart for thee doth ache!

(Pause.)

Thou of all fair maids the flower,
Who thy precious rings shall have?
Who shall own thy cherished treasures,
Which fond friends to thee once gave?
Brothers thou hast none, nor sisters;
All with thee goes to the grave.

Those bright rosy cheeks of thine,
Now how pale they are and wan!
Those bright roses, sunny-hued,
Whither, whither are they gone?
Death it is, the all-destroyer,
Who has this, sans pity, done.

Death, O deign to visit me!
To my sorrows put an end,
And have mercy; for I here
To thy hands my life commend;
That, united with my daughter,
I to-day from hence may wend.

(Pause.)

Now this day the village of Petra
Is thrown into dire despair;
All the people weeping stand,
Sadly sighing with grief and care;
And the fault of this, my darling,
Thou alone must singly bear.

Seest thou not how with caresses
Tenderly thee thy friends beset?
And how they thy darling face
With their tears of sorrow wet?
And thou thus canst leave them, dear,
Sadly, full of fond regret?

Some have gone to tie up flowers,
Some seek roses far and wide;
For a garland they are twining,
And they would crown thee as bride.
And thou now wilt leave us thus,
And in the coffin dark abide?

When thou went'st forth from the house,
Loveliness forth from thee did come;
Like a star shone forth thy kindness,
Spreading light amidst the gloom.
Death has taken thee away
In thy fairest, ripest bloom.

O, what lamentations will be,
From the deepest heart what sighs,
When our blood-relations all
Shall have heard this saddest news!

But now let us end our weeping;
We will cease henceforth to grieve;
For now our dear Marintscha
As the Lord's blest bride will live:
And to her this morn Maria
Will a place in heaven give.

(The Capuchin monks come.)

Ah, I hear, "Ora pro ea,"
Now they call unto Maria;
For the Capuchins already
Hither come—Ah me, Maria!
And they now will carry thee,
To the church of Saint Elia.

To the churchyard with the others
I had hoped to resolve to go:
But I scarce can upright stand,
So ye must leave me with my wo.
From my eyes a bitter stream,
Silent, constantly will flow.

VOCERO

OF A MAIDEN OVER THE BODY OF HER MURDERED FATHER.

(Dialect of the nearer side of the Mountains.)

(The girl comes with a torch.)

From Calanche I am come;
Midnight had just come and fled,
When by torchlight in the gardens
I did seek with anxious tread
Where my father was delaying—
In his blood I found him dead.

(Another girl enters, seeking a kinsman also slain; perceiving the deceased she takes him for her relative, stands still, and is going to strike up the lamento: *but the other girl says,)*

Further uphill thou must climb,
For there lies Matteo slain,
But this is my father here;
Mine 'tis for him to complain.

Take his apron and his hammer,
And his trowel homeward bear;
Wilt thou not to San Marcello,
Father, to thy work repair?
They have my own father slain,
Wounded too my brother dear.

Go and seek a pair of scissors,
Bring it me, and be not slow;
I would cut a lock of hair,
And with it stanch the blood's fast flow;
For my fingers are defiled
With the blood, a reddened row.

A mandile I will dye,
Redden it in my father's gore,
Which I'll wear when I have leisure
Mirth and laughter out to pour.

To Calanche I will bring thee,
To the church of Holy Cross,
Ever calling thee, my father;
Answer with thy loved voice!
They have crucified my father,
Like the Christ upon the cross.

VOCERO

OF NUNZIOLA ON THE DEATH OF HER HUSBAND.

(Dialect of the further side of the Mountains.)

O thou my Petro Francesco,
Thou whom I in sorrow mourn,
Thou my rose that bore me flowers,
Thou my rose without a thorn!
Thou from mountains unto sea
Wert a dauntless hero born.

I embrace thee with my arms,
And thy feet by mine are pressed;
Thou hast been my loving husband,
Star of hope, with loveliness blessed.
Yet of all my wo the source
Now thou art, of husbands best!

Thou my ship on ocean deep,
Striving hard to come to land,
Yet unable to reach the harbour
For waves high surging 'gainst the strand,
And with all its beauteous treasures
Driving straight upon the sand.

O my leafy cypress tree,
Bread from manna sweetly made!
O my vine of Muscatel,
With green vine-shoots overspread!
Ah! thy thunderbolt, O Fate,
Thou hast launched upon my head.

Come, O Griscio, my daughter,
Where in peace thy father lies,
Tell him that a happier lot
He must pray in Paradise,
For his only living daughter,
Than her mother now enjoys.

O thou wert my goodly pillar,
Wert my buttress full of power;
O thou wert my own dear brother,
Wert my fortress, my strong tower!
O thou wert my fairest treasure,
Thou my brilliant pearl, my flower!

O thou orange mine of gold,
Jewel carefully encased!
Thou my silver beaker blank,
Richly too with gold enchased!
Thou my lovely banquet-platter,
Shaft into my heart that passed!

O thou oil as crystal clear,
O thou vinous essence fine!
O thou lovely countenance,
Mingled pure with milk and wine!
Thou my bright reflecting mirror,
Ever bright with its pure shine!

Sooner into two salt streams
My poor eyes I will out-teem,
Than thy blessed memory
To forget I'd ever seem.
Thee, Francesco, thee with sorrow
I my own shall ever deem.

Thou hast been my sword so keen,
Weapon good, and coat of mail;
Thou my grievous fortune, ruin
'Whelming me beneath its fall.
To my eye thou hast appear'd
As within the port a sail.

I would have myself devoted,
Death from thee could I but ward;
But this has not been vouchsafed
To me, Petro, by the Lord.
O my husband, stalwart-hearted,
'Gainst all ill my screen and guard!

O my cock high-spirited,
Pheasant on a mountain-side!
Mirror of my happiness,
Bird 'mong flowery gardens wide!
Never more beneath thy wing,
Never more I now can hide.

O thou my Petro Francesco,
To the Lord our God I'll pray,
That his angels thee may carry
To 'mid-Paradise straightway.
After suffering thy loss
This will be my heart's best stay.

VOCERO

OF A GIRL ON THE DEATH OF HER TWO BROTHERS, BOTH SLAIN ON ONE DAY.

(Mixed dialect of both sides of the Mountains.)

O the boasting now of Pieru!
O the vaunting of Orazio!
They have made a desolation
Vast, extending to San Brancazio.
Satiated with our blood
Now is Michael and Orazio.

Death, O death, how black thou art,
Bringing to me all this wo!
For to thee a house its children,
Save the nest-egg, did forego.
How should I rejoice, an orphan,
Head of the house myself to know?

Of all women, I alone
Have sat by my fire bright,
And o'er all my brethren five
Domestic rule have held by right;
Yet is all my right of rule
For ever lost, forgotten quite.

I will don a black faldetta
Which no brightness shall enliven,
Since no breath of joy any longer
To my grieving heart is given,
For the fate of my five brethren
And my parents—in all they 're seven.

And to Asco I will send,
And will fetch me blackest pitch;
I will don that sombre dye,
Like the raven, in blackness rich;
And my life shall rise and sink
Like the rain-floods in the ditch.

See ye not how my poor eyes   .
Two salt streams do downward shower
For my sweet dear brethren twain,
Who both fell in one sad hour?
For the two deceased the bells
Now their funeral peals must pour.

Thou my ball of reddest gold,
Thou my ring of diamond-stone!
O Pieru, thou my rapture,
And Orà, for whom I moan!
In the church of Tallanu
None appears so fair—not one.

And now thee, O Sir Curate,
I must bitterly accuse,
Since to my poor house thou couldst
Such unthankful conduct use.
Seven in three short years thou 'st carried
Forth to burial from my house.

To the street-end I will go
With thee and my brothers' bier,
And with downcast weeping eyes
Homeward will betake me here
So the last sad journey's over
Of my five dead brethren dear.

VOCERO

OF MARIA FELICE OF CALACUCCIA ON THE DEATH OF HER BROTHER.

(Dialect of Niolo.)

I a clap of thunder heard
At my spindle as I spun,
Through my heart the din resounded—
'Twas a shot from out a gun.
And it seem'd to tell me clearly,
"Run, thy brother's fallen, run!"

Swift I sprang across the chamber,
To the window open wide;
In my heart the shot I felt,
For " He's hurt to death " they cried.
But for one reviving hope
I upon the spot had died.

I will buy myself a pistol,
And in breeches me attire;
I will show thy blood-stained shirt,
Since—besides this wo so dire—
I have none left to avenge thee,
And thereafter cut his hair.

Speak, whom wilt thou choose thee out
Thy Vendetta to execute?
Is't thy mother?—she is dying.
Sister Mary?—she will suit.
Were not Lariu in his grave,
He would not bloodless die, and mute.

Of thy kindred large remains
But a sister, an only one,
Without cousins of her own blood,
Poor and orphaned, young, and lone;
But to take Vendetta for thee,
Be assured, suffices one.

VOCERO

OF A HERDSWOMAN OF TALAVO, ON THE DEATH OF HER HUSBAND, A COWHERD.

On the sea-strand did he die,
Where the two great cork-trees be.
O Francesco, herdsman good.
Cruel 'tis thee dead to see!
How within dark forests lone
Shall I fare, bereft of thee?

I will now despoil the palo
Yonder of its branches seven ;
Never skin nor cap henceforward
To its keeping shall be given ;
And his ears he shall have cropped,
The dog by whom the sheep are driven.

Di, di, dih ! how mournful am I !
Raise your lamentations now,
Brethren mine and sisters all ;
Hard to bear is this my wo !
Dead is now the house's head !
O my God, thou layst me low !

*(When the herdsman has been buried, his wife returns to her cabin, and
describes the interment to the family and neighbours.)*

On the bier they laid him down,
To Prunelli him they carried.
Cows and lambs they all lamented,
With a bitter heart-sore worried ;
And the kids said *be, be, be,*
In their hurdles as they tarried.

In the church of St. Maria,
Sacred and parochial,
Sang the clergyman, the curate,
With his priests in chorus all.
Just as for a noble signor
Sang they all out of the missal.

When the service was completed,
Brisk and serving as they were,
They then opened deep a grave,
My Francesco to secure ;
And upon a bier the people
In great crowds his body bore.

Wo ! wo ! wo ! when I remember
To what next they did him doom ;
Down the grave I looked to see,
Light nor window has its room :
But I saw him by the men
Sunk into a darksome tomb.

VOCERO

ON THE DEATH OF THE BANDIT CANINO.

(Dialect of the Pieve of Ghisoni.)

The Sister sings.

Now would I that my weak voice
Thunderlike could boom abroad,
Through the gorge of Vizzavona,
That its echo should be heard,
Of thy cruel murderers
To the world to tell a word.

All they of Luco di Nazza
Vengefully together drew,
With yon grim-like company,
Bandits and the soldier-crew,
And marched forth in early morning
Suddenly, and not a few.

Suddenly they marched forth
To the sound of pipes, and sang,
As when murd'rous wolves do sally
Gainst weak lambkins, in a gang;
When into the pass they entered, ·
On thy throat they furious sprang.

When such news had reached my ears,
To the window ventured I,
And I cried, "What happens yonder?"
"O, thy brother is carried by;
By a murderer was he slain
In the pass most cruelly."

Naught could save thee, not thy musket,
Not thy trusty pistolet;
Not thy sharpened dagger's point,
Nor could save thee thy terzet;
Nor could save thee promised freedom,
Nor thy sacred amulet.

Cruelly my sorrows wax
On the aspect of thy wound,
Why, ah why! wilt thou not answer?
Death thy heart holds under bond.
Heart of thy dear sister, Cani!
Forth thy hue of life hath swooned.

O thou brother broad of shoulder!
O thou slender-membered brother!
Thou wert like a flowering branch;
Such as thou was never another.
Heart of thy dear sister, Cani!
They thy life in death did smother.

In the hamlet Mazza, a thorn
I will plant to my father's son.
Now that of my father's house
Living there remaineth none.
Since he had not three stout brothers,
'Gainst the seven he was but one.

To the thorn-tree I will carry
My poor bed, and there will sleep,
Since their daggers here, my brother,
In thy heart they buried deep.
I will lay my spindle down;
Arms will I take up and keep.

With cartouches will I gird me,
In my belt slip the terzetta ;
Cani, heart of thy dear sister!
And then I will take Vendetta.

VOCERO

ON THE DEATH OF ROMANA, DAUGHTER OF DARIOLA DANESI OF ZUANI.

The Mother sings.

See, she lies now on the tola,
Ah! my child, in her sixteenth year,.
Daughter mine, who has so long
Pain and sorrow had to bear,—
Ah! in this her fairest garment,
This the veilèd, white and clear.

Ah! in this her fairest garment,
She from hence e'en now will go ;
For the Lord no longer lets her
Sojourn on this earth below.
Whoso for an angel meet is
Needs not long earth's trouble know.

Ah! where are upon thy face
Now the roses, charming one ?
All its brightness, all its beauty,
Utterly in death is gone.
When I see it, to an eclipse
I must liken it, of the sun.

Ah, thou wert among the maidens
Of the fair ones fairest far ;
Like the rose among the flowers,
Or moon, the queen of every star.
Others' beauty did but heighten
Thine, my daughter, never mar.

When the young men of the village
Came before thy face to stand,
By thy beauty's fire enkindled,
Each then seemed a burning brand.
Kind thou wert to all ; but nearer
None might come, of all the band.

In the church at mass they all
Ever looked to thee askance,
From the first unto the last ;
But for none hadst thou a sense.
When the mass was over, straightway
Saidst thou, "Mother, let us hence."

Ah,' thou wert so highly honoured!
Ah, thou hadst of love full store!
Thou wert versed in holy lessons,
And in sacred heavenly lore ;
And from earthly cares retiring
Thou thy heart in player didst pour.

Who can give me consolation,
Thou my pride, now I'm alone?
Now the Lord has called thee home,
And that thou to him hast gone?
Why so warmly did Lord Jesus
Long for thee, beloved one?

But thou restest from thy labours
In the heavens, in blessed mirth.
Thy beloved face was surely
Much too fair for things of earth.
How much fairer now will be
Paradise on thy heavenly birth!

But to me of heavy toils
Full henceforth this earth will be,
And a day, by grief outlengthened,
Like a thousand years will be,
When I ask all people, daughter,
Whether they know aught of thee.

Death, why hast thou from my bosom
My beloved daughter torn?
Wherefore in this sore affliction
Leav'st thou me alone to mourn?
I have nothing left to live for,
Of her solace reft, forlorn.

Reft of love from my relations,
Reft of care from neighbours nigh ;
When I lay me down in sickness
Who my streaming face will dry?
Who will now give me to drink,
When in fever hot I lie?

Ah, thou dearly lovèd daughter,
Think upon my dreary lot!
When by help and love forsaken,
Old I be, and quite forgot;
When no solace can be given me,
Not a moment's peace be bought.

O that I could then have died,
When thou didst from earth remove!
Thou, my soul's fond hope, now taken
Grievously away, my love!
Oh then I should find thee yet,
Still live there with thee above.

Therefore pray the Lord Christ Jesus
That I may from hence be sent;
For I cannot bear it longer,
O, my soul's joy, since thou went;
And I cannot find an end,
Never, to my sore lament.

VOCERO

OF A WOMAN OF NIOLO, ON THE DEATH OF ABBATE LARIONE, 1740.

The baptismal gifts are come,
Ready made is now the cake;
For he said that me he wished
For his godmother to take.
Now—who dares to realize it?
Now we must his funeral make.

(*In the window of the opposite house she sees the mortal enemy of the deceased laughing at the vocero; so she sings to him the following verse :*)—

Laugh thou on at yonder window!
Scorn to fear, thy deeds to rue!
Go, forsooth, to Feliceto,
And to Muru go anew!
From the blood of Larione
On thy way I'll poison thee.

Of his blood a bitter drop
Inward to my heart has pass'd,
And into the village Muru
I a vengeance-spark will cast;
For his blood, so nobly born,
Earth has drunk up far too fast.

O my great high-hearted one!
O thou of my hopes the crown!
Ah! with spite they laid thee low,
Thou my Hector, thou *leone*,
Falsely, basely, strangled thee,
Thou my dearest Larione.

VOCERO

ON THE DEATH OF CESARIO AND CAPPATO.

(*This wild song of vengeance, which is still sung by the people, was composed under the name of a woman by an anonymous Frate (! !), a friend of Cesario. As the song predicted, the deceased were subsequently avenged by a certain Paolo, their kinsman : he then took to the bush, where, having lived as a bandit for a few years, he fell into the hands of justice.*)

Jesus, Joseph, and Mari,
And the holy sacrament
All ye now in company
Help me in my sad lament;
Every where the sound shall spread,
" Oh! our heroes twain are dead! "

Though ye go through realms untold,
Though through counties small and great;
To Cesaru a mate
Will ye never more behold;
None who ever was so choice
In the use of speech and voice.

But the murderer of Mastini
Like a dog his vengeance wreaked,
And into the thicket sneaked,
Goaded on by the Mastinis;
When he came unto his foe,
Felled him with a single blow.

He aimed at no distant goal,
But through Chinechinu's heart
Sent his foul and deadly dart,
Pistol or fusile ball;
That his heart the bullet must
Pierce, e'en as a dagger's thrust.

Up sprang Cappatu bold-hearted,
Like the lion wounded in strife,
On Tangone forward darted,
Who implored him soon for life.
He began repent with pain
That his foe he'd slily slain.

Dead are now the heroes both;
Paulu yet remains in life;
To the bush alone he goeth;
Soon his name's with vengeance rife.
Down into the plains he'll go,
And there many he'll lay low.

Wait awhile, till o'er the land
Melted is the winter snow;
Vengeance then in streams shall flow
From the mountains to the strand.
Vengeance is like flames of fire,
Catching all it meets, and dire.

Of the rich and of the lordly
Be a dozen murdered, then!
Yet a dozen murdered men
For his boots were vengeance hardly!
And for poor Cappatu's sake
He must bloody vengeance take.

My lamento I will close,
More I have not to complain.
Wo, thrice wo, unto all those
By whose wiles they have been slain!
Now for your escape take heed!
Else the priests your souls shall speed.

VOCERO

OF A YOUNG GIRL ON THE DEATH OF HER PLAYMATE AT THE AGE OF
FOURTEEN YEARS.

(Dialect of Vico.)

Decked my playmate is this morning
With a garb of fairest hues;
For she yet may be espoused,
Though her parents both she lose:
Is she now adorned and ready
For the bridegroom who her wooes?

All assembled is the pieve,
And they can do naught but mourn;
All the bells do peal so sadly,
And a flag and cross are borne.
But how could thy festival
Thus be changed to grief forlorn?

Now today my playmate leaves us,
Travels to a distant land,
Where our lost forefathers many
And my own dear father stand;
Where each one of us must tarry,
Where they wander hand in hand.

Wilt thou change thy home and clime,
Leave the country which thee bore?—
Ah! then is it much too early
To venture forth for evermore!
Hear thy playmate for one moment,
Once so dear, in days of yore.

I will forthwith write a billet,
And forthwith to thee will give,
And I will not seal nor close it;
For I in the hope will live
That thou then, on thy arrival,
To my father wilt it give.

And by word of mouth then tell him
News of his beloved ones all;
The little girl he by the hearth
Left weeping for her father's fall,
Has sprung up a comely maiden—
So they deem her—fair and tall.

And say that his eldest daughter
Found a husband here below,
And that him a son she bore,
Like a blossom-covered bough;
And that he his daddy knows,
And with his finger points out so.

That he bears his family name,
Which in honour high I hold;
And he has such pretty limbs,
Fair and tender, brave and bold;
All say, " O how like his father!"
Who the stripling wight behold.

And to my dear uncle say
That his village well has thriven,
Since by him at such great cost
That good well was to it given;
And that we all of him think
Every morning, every even.

Whene'er into the church we come,
To that spot our eyes we cast,
Near to yonder altar's base,
Where he found his rest at last;
Then our hearts feel pangs of sorrow,
And the loving tears flow fast.

See! to bless thee comes the curate,
With holy water from his hand;
With uncovered head the others,
A mournful company, do stand.
To the Lord in bliss departing,
Dearest, seek the heavenly land.

VOCERO

ON THE DEATH OF GIOVANNI OF VESCOVATO

(*A Woman sings.*)

From the bush a bird am I,
And tell a true and grievous fable;
Quick come down into the chamber,
For ye must put up the table.

(*Santia, the wife of the deceased, sings.*)

Now the tola is put up
For five hundred banquet-guests,
Sir Juvanni entreats ye all
That ye come to grace his feast!

Such a precious banquet-table!
Blithe the guests and of brave heart!
O Juvà, why hast thou on me
Thus inflicted such a smart?
Thus into my soul an arrow
Shooting through my midmost heart?

Nay, this is the stranger's room;
Now to go upstairs were well;
For thou knowest well, Juvanni,
Here we never used to dwell.
How has sunk thy house in ruins,
How into a wreck it fell!

Who bade thee no word to answer?
And my lot how shall I bear?
I my heart from out my body
With its deepest roots will tear;
Since in life thou bidst me languish
On throughout these days so drear!

Take thou back thy ring of diamond,
Which as pledge thou gav'st me erst.
Know'st thou not I am thy wife,
Thou to live my husband swar'st?
Ah, those pledges! clouds of mist,
In the air that form and burst.

Wilt thou live no more i' the hamlet,
To Bastia then come with me;
And there thy annunziata
Alway at thy side will be.
For may be that thou art angry,
And not glad thy wife to see.

Whither have our children, Felix
And Lilina, forth been hurried?
Be my heart within my breast,
By my own hand fiercely worried,
If that story can be true
Which to me the villagers carried.

(*A Woman of Venzolasca interposes.*)

Be resignèd, my Signora,
To Juvà farewell to say,
And the folk of Vescovato
Will lament him now for aye.
Early now to Vescovato
We will carry him today.

(*Santia takes up the song again.*)

But I fear that Vescovato
Will not let him go away.

O, three villages are come,
Thee unto thy grave to bear!
O Juvà, wilt thou not see,
'Gainst thee how they lay a snare?

O ye Lords of Venzolasco!
O ye victors, ye exalted!
Ye have taken my Juvanni,
Cast me into solitude.

I will now put off my veil,
In faldetta I'll go forth,
Wandering forth thus, even as wander
Other poor outcasts on the earth.

VOCERO

ON THE DEATH OF MATTEO.

(His Sister sings.)

Curses over ye shall come,
And o'er all your hated race !
Ye have killed my darling brother,
Who has gone to eternal peace !
Ye have caught him in your net,
Slain him there by treachery base.
But what sown is, soon or late,
Bears its fruit in its own place.

What he was I will not say,
Nor how now I found him killed:
To every one I leave his house,
Kindred, station, wife, and child;
Jesus, thrice exalted thou,
All into thy hand I yield.

I will hie to the blood-stained dust
There, hard by the river's brink,
Where my lovely darling dove
Lost his feathers and his wing.
Wandering on the road, a prey
He to falcons down did sink.
Death to all is common, true;
Sole and unmatched was he, I think.

I can speak no further now;
Grief doth me so deeply wound,
That, save two, my brethren five
All are laid beneath the ground.
The blood of Petracchiolo
So sweet, ye Powers! why have ye found?

By gens d'armes we are encompassed,
By sergeants who keep vigil good,
Grin at us and show their teeth,
While my brethren welter in blood.
When is come our time of action,
They will see our vengeful mood.

Who blew out that light of thine,
O my bright one, I would wis?
O that I could reach him now,
And pierce through that heart of his!

Thou wilt be, Matteju, ever
A leech, my wounded heart to drain;
More than twenty times I've told thee,
Brother, yet have told in vain,
That in their fell hearts there was
Naught but viperous poison-stain.

O thou heaven-cursed hatred! would that
Plague to thee could put an end!
Standing on the watch, they hinder
Us from out the house to wend.
Now the time is ripe for vengeance,
Down to hell we will them send.

O Mattè! what cruel tortures
In the night my heart enchain!
Nine times did they shoot their bullet
Ere they did their deed of bane.
Help me, help, O sisters mine!
My heart is throbbing full of pain.

VOCERO

ON THE DEATH OF MATTEO, A PHYSICIAN.

(This ancient lament, of the year 1715, was sung by a female relative of the deceased. Going as Chorus-leader at the head of the scirrata to the funeral lamentations, she comes to a bridge, where she meets the train of persons who are bearing the dead to his native village. Hereupon she strikes up the Lamento :)

When I came unto the bridge,
Throngs like clouds stood circling round;
Yet nor priests were there nor stola,
Nor the cross thereat I found.
Only merely the mandile
Round his neck in folds was wound.

(Refusing to greet, or to give any mark of friendship to the funeral procession, she continues :)

Here set down my dear Matteju;
I would take his hand, d'ye know:
I'll not give my hand to the others,
For such as him ye've none to show.
O Matteju, thou my dove!
Dead thou art from their foul blow.

Ah! arouse thee, dear Matteju!
Say, what sickness thy life-thread broke?
Thee no fever carried off,
Nor an apoplectic stroke.
Thy disease is called Negretti
And Natale, be it spoke.

When he, needing quick despatch,
Had his ink and paper ta'en,
If Italian was deficient,
Then he wrote in Latin strain.
Ah! that thou couldst go to Sorru
There to heal a wicked Cain!

(Another female relative of the deceased here comes up, and takes up the lament.)

When I think upon my cousin,
And remember he is dead,
The solid earth appears to totter,
I am torn by feelings dread.
Let us hasten home, dear neighbours,
And lay the corpse upon his bed.

He was like a turtle-dove,
Loved with all a brother's measure,
Solace to the poor and needy,
Craved by strangers as a treasure.
Where'er he went, he was observed
From doors and balconies with pleasure.

Fiercer than a dog, Natale,
Dog thyself, thou didst him slay,
Since, like Judas after supper,
Thy physician thou didst betray;
Thinking that the wage of murder
They would doubtless to thee pay.

But the blood of our Matteju
Unavenged it may not flow;
For his blood ye shall atone,
Whom guiltless ye have now laid low.
I'll become a Moorish heathen,
Sooner than unavenged him know.

.   (*The Chorus-leader takes up the song.*)

Yes, the vengeance for Matteju
Will not longer be delayed,
For the brothers and the cousins
Are aroused, and a vow have made;
And, if they be not sufficient,
All the clan has promised aid.

(*Whilst the train is passing through a village called Sorru, a peasant of this village comes and offers them all some little refreshments; but the Chorus-leader sings:*)

Nay, from you of Sorru's village,
We will never take our fill;
Naught we showed to you but kindness;
Ye have done us naught but ill.
Whom we gave you living, give ye
Back a corpse, all cold and still.

Eat up your own bread, and welcome;
Drink your wine alone, drink on:
For that is not what we crave for;
'Tis your blood we seek alone.
One of us as blood-avenger
To the woodland wild is gone.

Is not that the village yonder,
Where my cousin death hath tasted?
Would that fire would straight devour it!
May it desolate lie and wasted!

Y

(An old Woman takes up the song.)

O, be still, be still, ye sisters !
Cease, oh cease. your raving story !
For Matteju wills not vengeance ;
He is now in Heaven's glory.

Sisters, see this bier, and the banner
With the cross that o'er it flows.
Jesus Christ doth strive to teach us
To forgive our bitterest foes.
Goad ye on the men no longer ;
Enough has life of storms and woes.
Today we may have countless mercies,
And tomorrow loads of curses.

VOCERO

ON THE DEATH OF CHILINA OF CARCHETO D'OREZZA.

(The Mother sings.)

O ! already they sing Ave,
And I lie here by thy bier ;
And to see thee come the women,
Lying wreath'd for burial here.
O Chilina ! mother's rapture,
Beauty mine, as diamond clear !

Choicer than the rice thou wert,
Whiter than the mountain snow ;
But the tola has thy body, .
And thy soul to the Lord doth go.
O Chilina, mother's rapture !
Why must thou desert me so?

O my dove by morning's ray !
O my chicken in the night !
Never wilt thou wake to-day,
Thou my care and my delight !
O Chilina ! O thine eyes
Now have lost their radiance bright !

Never to the well she sent me,
Never to cleave wood she told ;
But she kept me like a lady,
And a daughter's place did hold.
Death, alas ! now all at once
Doth her tender wings unfold.

Where is gone thy beauteous hand,
Thy slender fingers quickly plying,
O'er the threads adroitly running,
Knots and meshes deftly tying ?
Death, alas ! hath taken her,
Death, the thief, on tiptoe flying.

Never could I this have thought,
Thus to be so soon alone.
How with joy will Annadea
Beam before the heavenly throne,
Clasping to her heart her sister,
O Chili! Chili my own!

O, why must thou, my Chilina,
Hie thee to that place so drear?
Never there a sun arises;
Never can they light a fire.
O Chilina! mother's rapture,
Never shall I see thee here.

Thou wilt never go to mass,
Nor to Ave, as of yore.
O Chilina! mother's rapture,
I shall never see thee more!
O! deserted thus to be
That in truth doth grieve me sore.

(A Girl enters the chamber of mourning, and sings.)

Now arise—arise, Chilina,
For thy pony is prepared;
And we travel to Carcheto,
Where the wedding peal is heard,
And the bridal train attends thee;
Be the moment not deferred.

Thou nor mov'st nor speakest aught.
Wilt thou, Chilli, no one see?
Thy dear hands are bound and swathed,
Bound and swathed are thy dear feet.
Sisters, loose her bands, for with us
She will go right willingly.

(A Woman interposes.)

Hush, be still, O Magdalena!
Ask her something now would I;
To me much rather than her mother
She will haply yield reply;
For her mother near her head
Weeps and sobs so piteously.

TEXT TO THE SECOND VOCERO IN THIS SERIES.

Eo partu dalle Calanche
Circa quattr' ore di notte:
Mi ne fulgu cu la teda
A circà per tutte l' orte,
Per truvallu lu mio vabu:
Ma li avianu datu morte.

Cullatevene più in su,
Chi truvarete a Matteju;
Perchè questu è lu mio vabu,
E l' aghiu da pienghie eju.
Via, pigliatemi a scuzzale
La cazzola e lu martellu.
Nun ci vulete andà, vabu,
A travaglià a San Marcellu?
Tombu m' hanu lu miò vabu,
E feritu u miò fratellu.

Or circatemi e trisore,
E qui prestu ne venite:
Vogliu tondemi i capelli
Per tuppalli le ferite;
Chi di lu sangue di vabu
N' achiu carcu le miò dite.

Di lu vostru sangue, o vabu,
Bogliu tinghiemi un mandile;
Lu mi vogliu mette a collu
Quandu avrachiu oziu di ride.

Eo collu per le Calanche
Falgu per la Santa Croce,
Sempre chiamanduvi, vabu:
Rispunditemi una voce.
Mi l' hanu crucifissatu
Cume Ghesù Cristu in croce.

I have published the text of this entire *vocero*, to enable the learned reader to form an estimate of the Corsican dialect, and compare it with the Italian. I notice no small affinity between the dialect of Corsica and the popular dialect of Rome spoken in the Trastevere. It is, however, a feature common to all the Italian popular dialects, to wear away or soften down the verbal terminations *are* and *ire*, and also to convert the *l* into *r*. The Corsican says *soretra* for *sorella*. The tendency of the Corsican dialect to flatten *o* into *u*, is universal. Linguists have declared it to be one of the purest of the Italian dialects; and it is especially commended by Tommaseo in his collection of Tuscan, Corsican, and Greek popular poetry, in which he has presented and elucidated the Corsican Voceri, though in a rather mutilated form. In this book, he calls the Corsican "a powerful language, and one of the most truly Italian dialects of Italy." It appears to me to be genuine gold compared with the patois of the Piedmontese and Lombards, and the dialects of Parma and Bologna. Even from the *vocero* communicated above, it will have been perceived that the Corsican language, although certainly a low dialect, is yet soft and graceful.

TRAVELS.—BOOK V.

CHAPTER I.

THROUGH THE BALAGNA TO CORTE.

I GAVE up a tour along the coast from Calvi to Sagona, where the bays of Galeria and Girolata, and the large gulfs of Porto and Sagone cut into the land. These districts are, in great part, uncultivated, and the roads frightful.

I set off by the diligence running from Calvi to Corte, to travel through the glorious, large, and excellently cultivated valley of the Balagna, which, as I have already mentioned, is called the garden of Corsica. It is enclosed by mountains, whose tops reach the clouds—snowy peaks, like the Tolo and the mighty Grosso, and eminences of the grandest forms, which would enchant a landscape painter. On the mountain sides are very numerous hamlets, which the eye can scan: San Reparata, Muro, Belgodere, Costa, Speloncato, Felicoto, Nessa, Occhiatana—all former abodes of the nobility and the caporali, and full of reminiscences of old times. The Tuscan marquises Malaspina, who were natives of Massa and the marches of Lunigiano, ruled here of old—a powerful family of Signori, whose fame is perpetuated by Dante in his " Divine Comedy." Finding Currado Malaspina in purgatory, Dante says to him :*—

> Oh, dissi lui, per li vostri paesi
> Giammai non fui; ma dove si dimora
> Per tutta Europa, ch'ei non sien palesi?
> La fama, che la vostra casa onora,
> Grida i signori, e grida la contrada,
> Si che ne sa chi non vi fu ancora.

The Malaspinas built the village of Speloncato in the Balagna. Five counts of their house, Guglielmo, Ugo, Rinaldo, Isnardo,

---

* Dante, *Purgatorio*, viii. 121.

Z

and Alberto Rufo, came to the island subsequently to the year 1019. Their numerous family is scattered in many branches over the Italian countries.

The barons subsequently lost their power in the Balagna by the democratic constitution of the Terra del Commune. The Corsican national assemblies (*veduta*) were frequently held here, as well as on the field of Campiolo. The Corsican historian relates a trait of heroism displayed on one of these *vedute* by the brave Renuccio della Rocca, well deserving our astonishment. Renuccio was just standing addressing the people at the veduta when his young son, fourteen years old, riding across the field on an intractable horse, was dashed on a lance which his squire, riding behind him, was incautiously holding out before him. They brought the dying youth to his father; but Renuccio continued his speech to the people without changing countenance, inflaming them to rise against Genoa. This Spartan characteristic, together with Gaffori's heroism, and that of Leoni of the Balagna near the tower of Nonza, at which his son had fallen, always reminds me of the unshaken manliness of Xenophon. While Xenophon was sacrificing, news was brought him that his son Gryllus had fallen. The father, stunned by the suddenness of the news, took the sacrificial chaplet from his brow; but on their telling him that his son had fallen fighting bravely, he immediately put it on his head again, and continued calmly sacrificing to the gods. But these Corsican heroes appear more Spartan than the Spartans themselves.

I found many corn-fields in the Balagna already reaped—a lovely sight on Corsican ground. There are every where, especially in the vicinity of habitations, perfect paradises of the most luxuriant chestnuts, walnut and almond trees, orange and citron orchards, and groves upon groves of olives. An excellent road leads all the way, skirting the base of the circle of mountains; and commanding at every point most charming distant views over the sea or up to the mountains. The most considerable places in the Balagna are Muro and Belgodere, the latter especially, which has its name from its beautiful situation. Around Belgodere extends an olive district, fit for the regular abode of Pallas.

It is asserted that there is no place in Italy where the olive-tree reaches such huge dimensions as in the Balagna. Its growth, its fulness of branches, and the abundance of its fruits, are perfectly astonishing. It is as mighty as a beach, and affords a shelter to repose under at burning noon. How attached people must grow to the olive-tree! It is not splendid to behold, as the plane-tree or the oak; its stem, and its long, narrow, greyish-green leaves remind one of our native willows. But, apart from the wealth it bears, which renders it literally the fat of the earth, the poetry of human culture is inseparably bound to it. Sitting beneath a grey olive at the seaside, we are transported to the sunny, religious Orient, where our imagination has been at home ever since our mother opened the picture-bible, and told us of the Mount of Olives at Jerusalem. How often have we fancied those olive-groves! And, again, there breathes through this tree the breath of the poetry of the Greeks and the wisdom of Minerva, transporting us into the sunny land of Homer, Pindar, and Æschylus, among the Muses and Gods of Olympus. A Christian and a Hellenic tree is this olive—a tree with a double home; its bough more precious than that of the laurel, presenting the fairest emblem of wealth and peace; and the first prayer man should put to the immortal gods should be, "Give me as a life-blessing a green olive bough." They give life-blessings of all kinds, the laurel-branch, the myrtle-branch, and the cypress-branch, too. Let man receive them with humility.

There are many kinds of olives in the Balagna, the Sabine (*Sabinacci*), the Saracen (*Saraceni*), and the Genoese (*Genovesi*), so called according to their pedigree, like noble families of Signori. The third kind is the most frequent; it is ascribed to the Genoese, who, under the rule of Agostino Doria, compelled the Corsicans to plant the olive abundantly. This is a beautiful peaceful monument of the Genoese dominion in Corsica. At what period the olive was generally introduced into Corsica I cannot say. In Seneca's epigram, complaint is made that the gift of Pallas is not to be found in the island; nevertheless it seems to me scarcely credible that the olive was not cultivated in Corsica before Seneca's time. The Corsican olive-trees enjoy the reputation of defying the changes of the seasons more boldly than all others in the world; a praise which the great Humboldt has bestowed upon them. They need but little attention. The gardener cuts off their oldest branches to give them strength, digs the tree round, loosening the soil about it, or manures round the stem. When the olives begin to fall off, they are collected. Twenty pounds of olives yield five pounds of clear oil, which is put into large stone jugs, in which it stands

till the month of May. The olive produces particularly abundantly every third year.

The birds come and scatter the olive-seeds, carrying them to
all four quarters of the compass. Thus the island is covered
with wild olive bushes, growing green and rank over hill and
dale, and only waiting for improvement by cultivation. An
attempt was made in the year 1820 to count them, and there
are said to be twelve millions. At the present day the richest
oil-lands of Corsica are the Balagna, the Nebbio, and the region
of Bonifazio.

I left the province of Balagna at the village of Novella.
Thence the road goes into the mountainous interior, and for
hours the carriage rolls through narrow glens, and between quite
unfruitful rocky hills, without the appearance of a single habi-
tation, till it comes into the Golo valley, at Ponte alla Leccia,
where the high-roads of Corsica meet, from Calvi, from Ajaccio,
and from Bastia. The drive now follows an agreeable valley
along the river Golo. To the right lies the shepherd-region of
Niolo, the modern canton of Calacuccia, a remarkable district,
enclosed by the highest mountains, in which the two lakes
Neno and Creno are situated. This district is a natural stronghold, opening out at only four points, towards Vico, Venaco,
Calvi, and Corte. A steep road, the *scala di santa Regina*, leads
to Corte. In this district live the strongest men in Corsica,
patriarchal shepherds, who have faithfully preserved the manners of their forefathers.

Several remarkable places lie on the road to Corte, as first of
all Soveria, the native place of the doughty family of Cervoni.
It was Thomas Cervoni who delivered Pasquale Paoli from the
convent of Alando, when besieged there by the enraged Matra.
It will be remembered that Cervoni was Pasquale's enemy, but
that his mother herself put arms in his hands and sent him to
the rescue of Pasquale, threatening to curse him if he would not
go. Cervoni hastened to the besieged convent, and Matra was
slain. It does one's heart good to travel through a land like
this island, where, from town and hamlet, from hill and dale,
deeds of heroism are every where pressing themselves upon the
traveller's attention.

Cervoni's son was the brave general, who, as an officer at
Toulon, carried off the first military honours after Napoleon.
He distinguished himself at Lodi: in the year 1799 he was
Commander of Rome. It was he who announced to Pope Pius

VI. the end of his sovereignty, and ordered him to leave Rome. He was the terror of Rome. Valery relates that this same Cervoni presented himself to Pope Pius VII. in the Tuileries, at the head of the generals, and paid him a compliment. His beautiful voice, and fine Italian pronunciation, astonished the Pope, and caused him to say something flattering about them. " Santo padre," rejoined Cervoni, " sono quasi Italiano"—" Oh!" —" Sono Corso"—" Oh! oh!"—" Sono Cervoni!"—" Oh! oh! oh!"—and at this terrible recollection the Pope retreated in horror to the fireside. A cannon-ball carried off Marshal Cervoni's head at Ratisbon, in the year 1809.

Near Soveria is Alando, renowned by the name of Sambucuccio, the oldest legislator and Lycurgus of the Corsicans, who established the democratic constitution. They point out some barely discernible vestiges of his castle on one of the rocks. One of Sambucuccio's descendants was vicar of the Corsican nation four hundred years after his time, in the year 1466. Some Caporali lived hereabouts, and especially in the neighbouring village of Omessa. Having been, in the first instance, tribunes of the people, and appointed in Sambucuccio's democratic system to defend the rights of the people, they subsequently yielded to the universal evil, which undermines and destroys the best of human arrangements, ambition and desire of rule; and they made themselves terrible dynasts on a small scale, just like the Signori. Filippini complains that even in his time the Caporali were the most frightful scourge Corsica had.

Around Alando chestnuts thrive; but the land is poor. On the mountain-heaths the black sheep and goats find their nourishment. Their wool is here worked up into the Corsican *pelone.*

As soon as we have passed over the mountain ridge of Alluraja, which rises high between the rivers Golo and Tavignano, we begin to descend by an excellent road to Corte.

CHAPTER II.

THE TOWN OF CORTE.

THE arrondissement of Corte, the central territory of the
island, contains 15 cantons, 113 communes, and a population of
55,000.   The little capital itself numbers about 5000 souls.

Corte is an inland town, in a situation no less imposing than
that of the Corsican seaports.   The panorama of brown mountains, in the middle of which it lies, and the citadel, perched on
a rugged inaccessible crag, lend to the town a sort of manly and
iron physiognomy.   Mountains rise on all sides, and in the most
varied forms.   Towards the north they are lower, and form mostly
dome-shaped hills, covered with bushes, or with corn-fields.
Summer has clad these hills in a deep brown, so that they give
a most sombre appearance to the country.   These hills are the
last declivities of the mountain-range which forms the water-
shed beween the rivers Golo and Tavignano, and divides the
two valleys of Niolo and Tavignano.   At the opening of the
latter, where the Tavignano is joined by the Restonica, lies
Corte.   The entrance into this mountain valley is commanded
by three lofty mountains, covered as with an armour of crags;
the two rivers, working their way through deep gorges, rush into another over a bed of crumbling rocks.   They are spanned
by two stone bridges.   •

The little town itself has only one main street, the so-called
Corso, which is new, and enjoys an extremely rural aspect
owing to an avenue of elms.   Even here, I was surprised to find
the out of the world stillness and the idyllic tone which gives so
peculiar an impress to places in Corsica.   One really fancies
oneself at the end of the world, and cut off from all possibilities of intercourse.

The town is venerable for its historical memories.   In the
time of Paoli it was the centre of his democratic government,
in the earliest times the seat of Moorish kings, and in all ages
important as the centre of the island ; and its fortress often decided the course of the events of war.

The aspect of the citadel is remarkable.   This fortress is the
Acropolis of Corsica.   It stands on a precipitous and jagged black

rock which rises up from the river Tavignano. Its walls and towers, and the old town surrounding it, all looks black, crumbling, awfully desolate, and battered by incessant strife. This citadel of Corte has been stormed and defended oftener than Belgrade. The foundation of its present form was laid by the brave Vincentello d'Istria, at the beginning of the fifteenth century.

They still show here the loophole in the wall, at which the Genoese hung out the young son of Gaffori, in order to cause his father to desist from the assault. If the locality alone is so awe-inspiring and so dizzy, how wild must that heroic scene itself have been! That is indeed one of the noblest episodes in Corsican history—a history which, as I have already said, is able to produce a parallel to every single classical instance of greatness of soul among the Greeks and Romans. This Corsican nation has verily been inspired by the same heroic soul that we admire in Brutus and Timoleon; but its deeds, especially many such individual acts, have lain buried in the obscurity of the age and locality.

Gaffori's name is the greatest ornament of Corte, and his little house, still riddled by cannon-balls, the brilliantest monument she possesses. But she preserves another heroic reminiscence, that of his heroic wife. The Genoese once availed themselves of Gaffori's absence to assault his house and get his wife into their power, agreeably to their frequent policy of using the families of formidable Corsicans as hostages, and combating the patriotism of husbands by means of their natural affection for their wives. But Gaffori's wife fortified herself instantly in her house; and having barricaded doors and windows, defended herself for days with the gun in her hand, by the help of the few friends who had rushed to her aid, against the Genoese, who overwhelmed the house with a perfect rain of bullets. But as the need grew more and more pressing, her friends advised her to capitulate. But she fetched a powder-barrel into a lower room, and, seizing a match, swore to blow up the house instantly if they stopped firing on the besiegers. The friends knew the desperate courage of Gaffori's wife, and again kept up their resistance till Gaffori came up with a band of Corsicans and rescued his wife. After the murder of Gaffori, this same woman made his young son, who had been hung out on that castle-wall, swear to hate the Genoese and avenge his father. So did Hasdrubal also with his son Hannibal in ancient times.

In this same house of Gaffori, Charles Bonaparte lived in the year 1768, with his wife Letitia: it was a worthy edifice to give being to a Napoleon.

Many reminiscences of Paoli are fastened upon a house bearing the name of the Palazzo de Corte, which was the seat of his government as well as his private house. There is the little room in which he performed his work, poor and mean, as well beseemed the legislator of the Corsicans. They have a story, that the great man, never secure from the bullets of an assassin, always kept the window of this room blocked up; and in fact the window frames, which remain now as they were then, are seen to be stuffed with cork. The National Assembly allowed him a body-guard of twenty-four men, as in olden times Greek democracies did to their popular leaders; and he always had in his room six Corsican dogs keeping guard for him. I cannot help being reminded of his contemporary and admirer, Frederic the Great, who was likewise always surrounded by dogs in his cabinet, but they were pleasure dogs—the charming Alcmene, the pretty Biche, and other greyhounds. The difference of the scene is characteristic. If an artist were to attempt to paint Paoli in his canine society, as Frederic has so often been represented in his, it would be rather a wild scene—the Corsican hero in his mean cabinet writing by the fireside, wrapped in a coarse woollen coat, behind a barricaded window, and grim shaggy wolf-dogs squatting on the ground: there is a regular Corsican historical genre-picture for you.

Another room, the former session-chamber of the state council of the Nine, preserves no less interesting a curiosity. There you may see the rods which were to support the canopy over a throne for Paoli. Paoli and a throne? Impossible! Did this great man of the people lust for royal emblems?· It is asserted; and the following story is told on the subject:—A throne was one day seen erected in the national palace. It was of crimson damask, decorated all over with golden fringe, and it bore a golden crown, so placed above the Corsican arms as to be over Paoli's head when he sat in the chair. To this throne were attached nine smaller crimson seats for the Council of Nine. When the council was assembled in the hall, they say that the door of Paoli's room opened, and he entered in a magnificent robe of state, with his head covered and a sword at his side, and advanced towards the throne. At this moment arose a murmur of astonishment and displeasure among the Nine, and then followed a deep silence. Paoli started; and he never sat upon the throne.

I find this story so often affirmed, that it would seem to me almost rash to doubt it. If there is any truth in it, it is a surprising feature in the soul of the great man; and at least a proof that human weakness steps in every where, and that no mortal is proof against the occasional insidious advances of vanity and love of show. Paoli and a throne! there could hardly be a greater contradiction. Surely the Corsican nation and freedom were the highest possible throne for the noble man; and never has mortal sat upon a more glorious one than the wooden stool occupied by Paoli, the legislator and deliverer of a nation.

His enemies have accused him of aiming at a king's crown, but they do him wrong; and the lie is given to the accusation by Paoli's own history. Perhaps by royal emblems he desired to lend an exalted external dignity in the sight of the people to his state, which had indeed always borne the old title of kingdom of Corsica? On no other occasion did he ever display any princely ostentation. He, like all other members of his government, went about in the costume of the country, attired in the woollen Corsican cloth, and lived in the simplest manners of the country. The heads of the state were distinguished only by their intelligence from the people; and only for the purpose of presenting to the French the external appearance of a well-ordered government, did Paoli decide on a distinguishing costume for the Council of State, namely, a green coat with gold stripes—the Corsican colours. He put on this robe of state himself, and caused it to be worn by the councillors, when the French officers came for the first time to Corsica: the governors of the country must appear in a worthy fashion before foreigners. This was a concession to French etiquette which is to be lamented, because here Paoli did not keep free from the love of semblance, and by a bit of gold lace destroyed that free democratic equality, which displayed itself outwardly in costume; and yet the Corsicans could wear their woollen blouses with juster pride than the French their showy uniforms. Unimportant as these things may appear in themselves, they afford matter for thought. For the age renders unessential differences essential ones, and converts the external into the internal. There lie in the age invisible influences for evil, which gradually sully all that is pure, demean all that is great, and abuse all that is noble. The human world is so constituted, that its grandest phenomena are only to be found where there is a real struggle for a noble end. It has often made me sad in Corsica to think, that all these heroic national efforts and these struggles for freedom have been fruitless, and that now in the land of Sampiero, Gaffori, and Paoli, the nation of vanity bears rule. But more painful still would be the discovery, that Paoli's state grew diseased in itself, and succumbed to human selfishness. I certainly believe it would not have escaped this universal fate: for true freedom lives only in Utopia, and humanity appears to be capable of it only in hallowed moments.

Paoli also once received a pompous embassy in this Palazzo Nationale. A ship of Tunis having stranded on the coast of the Balagna, Paoli not only caused all the property to be restored to the shipwrecked barbarians, which the inhabitants of the coast had carried off, but caused them to be hospitably treated and escorted home by two officers to the Bey of Tunis. The Bey consequently sent an embassy to Paoli, to tender his thanks, and assure him that he would ever remain the friend of Paoli and of his nation, and that no injury should ever be inflicted on a Corsican within his states. The ambassador from Tunis knelt before Paoli, and, raising his hand to his forehead, said in Italian, " Il Bey ti saluta, e ti vuol bene," The Bey salutes you and wishes you well. He brought him a present of a beautiful, splendidly caparisoned horse, two ostriches, a tiger, a sabre set with diamonds; and, after staying a few days at Corte, he returned to Africa.

In the immediate neighbourhood of Corte stands the old Franciscan convent, a majestic ruin. Here the Corsican Parliament assembled in Paoli's time, in the convent chapel, from the pulpit of which many a noble patriot launched forth his fiery words. Many sacrifices were made to freedom in this church, and the name of freedom sounded here as no unreal phrase: those who invoked her died for her too. In the year 1793, the Corsicans were assembled at a meeting on the open place before this convent; the times were stormy ones, for the French National Convention had cited the aged Paoli on a charge of high treason. Pozzo di Borgo, the inexorable enemy of Napoleon, and, like him, a citizen of Ajaccio, climbed into a tree, and held an inspiring speech to the people in defence of Paoli; and Paoli's accusers, the furious clubbists, Arena and the Bonapartes, were declared infamous.

When one wanders now through the dead stillness of the little town, where miserable-looking Corsicans are standing about

under shady elms, as if they were trying to dream away the day
and the world, one can scarcely conceive that, hardly a hundred
years ago, the most enlightened political wisdom had taken up
its abode in such an obscure corner of the earth.

Paoli also founded a university at Corte, and called into life
there the first Corsican printing-press, and the first newspaper.
From this academy, enlightenment and science were to be diffused as a flood of light over the mountains and into all the
valleys of Corsica, and the middle-age barbarism of the Corsicans was to vanish before its influence.   I have mentioned this
university in the History of Corsica, and said what a patriotic
institution it was.   Many capital men issued from it, mainly
able advocates, who in this island are the principal authors.
Charles Bonaparte also, Napoleon's father, studied there.   But
the young institution perished with the loss of freedom.   To the
purpose of reestablishing it, Paoli, on his death-bed, devoted a
legacy; and, by the help of this capital, a kind of university was
erected anew in the year 1836.   It comprises a director and
seven professors for learned and scientific subjects, but it enjoys
no great celebrity.   Perhaps an institution of an academical
kind is less adapted to the wants of Corsica than sound ele-
mentary schools.

I have met with many well-educated and learned Corsicans;
and in Corte I made the acquaintance of a man whose extensive reading in the Romanic literatures astonished me.   His
father was one of the brave captains who remained in arms after
the battle of Ponte Nuovo till the very last, and I have mentioned him by name.   His memory is so great, that he knew by
heart the best pieces from Italian, French, and Latin authors,
and made nothing of reciting whole pages of Tasso or Ariosto,
long passages from Voltaire or Macchiavelli, or from Livy,
Horace, Boileau, and Rousseau.   Once speaking to him on literature, I asked him, " Did you ever read any thing of Goethe?"
" No," said the well-read man, " of English writers I only know
Pope."

My friendly table-companions, among whom was the first
painter whose acquaintance I made on this island, took me to
the marble-quarries in the neighbourhood of Corte.   A rich
marble-quarry was discovered no long time since, on the rocks
above the Restonica.   The stone is of a bluish tint, with reddish-
white veins, and serviceable for architecture and ornaments.
They were occupied in the quarry with getting a great block

for a pillar down the mountain. They had put it on rollers, and were pushing it with the screw of Archimedes to the edge of the inclined plane, which led from the quarry to the place where the blocks are hewn into shape. The fine huge stone ran down the plane, hollowing itself a road as it passed, and enveloping itself in a black cloud of dust, and ringing forth with a sound clear and pure as a metal bell. At the foot of this marble mountain, the Restonica drives a mill, in which the marble is cut into slabs. Seven days are required to cut up a block into thirty slabs. In Corte, then, Seneca's declaration about Corsica is contradicted, that no precious stone is hewn there (*non pretiosus lapis hic cæditur*). With this exception, however, Seneca's words still retain their force, and the precious stones of Corsica have always been a dead stock.

CHAPTER III.

AMONG THE GOATHERDS OF MONTE ROTONDO.

—— Tomo un puno de bellotas en la mano, y mirando las atentamente solto la voz a semejantes razones: Dichosa edad y siglos dichosos aquellos a quien los antiguos pusieron nombre de dorados.—*Don Quixote.*

I HAD determined on ascending Monte Rotondo, the highest mountain in the island of Corsica, which lies half a day's journey south-west from Corte, and may be regarded almost as the centre of the island. Though the fatigue attending the ascent was represented to me as being very great, I yet hoped to have a clear day, and to be richly rewarded. But I was particularly desirous of getting a glimpse of the primitive natural life of the herdsmen.

I hired a guide and a mule, and, provided with a little bread and a few gourds full of wine, I rode early on the morning of the 28th July towards the mountains. The road, a herdsman's path, leads on through the glen of the wild Restonica, from its union with the Tavignano hard by the town, up to the summit of Rotondo, on which it springs. The bed of this fine mountain stream is a deep and awful ravine. In the neighbourhood of Corte the vale opens to a considerable breadth; and there chestnut and walnut trees thrive near the water. Higher up it becomes narrower and narrower; the banks become gigantic towering black walls on both sides, and are overshadowed by deep-green primeval forests of ancient pines and larches.

The mule climbed securely up on the narrowest shepherds' paths on the edges of precipices; and the view down into the abyss, through which the milkwhite Restonica foams along, was often beautiful and fearful. When the sun was up, a magnificent forest of pines and larches received me into its shade. Glorious and picturesque are these giant trees—the pine with its broad green shade, and the larch gnarled, and striving mightily upward with its many boughs, like the cedar of Lebanon. Their huge stems are covered round by a wild forest-garden of myrtles, sprinkled with white blossoms of high-shooting heath and box. Refreshing and balmy was the fragrance of all the medicinal herbs in which the mountains of Corsica are so rich.

My guide strode rapidly on. But often a shudder came over me when he cast a glance back at me, and I saw myself alone with him in this dark wilderness of rock and wood. He was an ill-favoured man, and no good appeared in his eye. I was afterwards to discover that blood clove to his hand—that he was a murderer. A year before, he had assassinated a Lucchese in the market-place of Corte with a single stab, as I was told.

Riding on for hours in this romantic mountain wilderness, one hears naught but the monotonous gurgling of the streams, the falcon's screams, and ever and anon the shrill whistle of a goat-herd calling his goats.

The herdsmen live dispersed in caverns or cabins, on the declivities of Monte Rotondo, up to the ridge of which their herds climb. The last herdsmen's hamlets are at a height of more than 5000 feet above the sea-level. Their curious stations have each its peculiar name.

After a ride of three hours, I came to the first herdsmen's station, the Rota del Dragone. Riding from the edge of the ravine down to the water's edge, I saw before me a sooty black hole, arched deep into the rock, and vaulted over with enormous granite blocks. A few steps before the entrance of it, the Restonica roared along, dashing away between fragments of rocks; all around, rocks above rocks, and dense wood. Round the entrance of the grotto, stones were piled as a fence. A fire burned in the cave, and round it squatted the herdsman's family. A wretched-looking woman was sitting there mending a gown, and by her side was a fevered boy, wrapped in a brown coverlid of

goat's hair, from which his pale face and twinkling eyes peered
wonderingly forth.

Meanwhile, the herdsman had come out of the cave, and in a
friendly way invited me to dismount and taste his new milk and
cheese. I thankfully accepted, and inspected the interior of the
curious black rock-cell. The grotto went deep into the mountain, and had room for a herd of two hundred sheep and goats,
which the herdsman drives in every evening to milk. It was so
exactly the cave of Polyphemus, that Homer's description might
seem to have been made from this; for I found every thing word
for word—the very rows of vessels full of milk, and more than
a hundred flat round cheeses, laid on a stand of fresh leaves.
Only Polyphemus himself I found not; for mine host, wild and
robber-like as he looked in his shaggy clothes, was hospitality
itself.

" Do the banditti ever come to you?" I asked the Troglodyte.
" Yes, to be sure they come," said the man, " when they are
hungry. See this stone here which I am sitting upon;—two
years ago, two banditti-hunters, on the track of Serafino, hid
here in my cave, but he slunk up to them in the night, and
silenced them both on this stone with two thrusts; then he
went back to the mountains."

The guide proposed to start. I thanked the herdsman for his
refreshment and rode away, not without a shudder.

The path, which now led through the Restonica to the opposite bank, became more and more steep and difficult. At length,
after two hours, wetted to the skin with the mist, and in the
midst of a grand thunder-storm, I reached the last herdsmen's
station, on the shoulder of Monte Rotondo, where I was to pass
the night. It is called Co di Mozzo.

I had heard much of the hovels on Monto Rotondo, and
pictured them to myself, with an idyllic fancy sufficiently original, as little cottages in a green fine forest, or on breezy Alpine
slopes in the most bucolic scenery. But, as I rode up in thunder
and lightning and drizzling rain, I saw nothing but a waste of
stones broken into Titanic fragments, and granite crags thrown
one over the other on the slope of a great grey desolate rock-
pyramid. From the stones rose a faint curl of smoke. The
grey of the rain-clouds, the faint lightning-flashes, the rolling of
the thunder, the rushing of the Restonica, and the deep melancholy of the grey mountains around, gave a mournful tone to
the soul.

Some larches, torn in pieces by the storm, stood on the steepest brink of a naked cleft, through which the Restonica foamed down in falls from block to block. Round about there was nothing to be seen but the barest crags, and a wide view into the mist-covered valley from which I had ascended. My eye long sought the hovels to which my guide pointed. At length I saw them before me among the rocks, forming the queerest community of herdsmen in the world, consisting of four dwellings erected in the style of architecture of the primitive world, or perhaps built with less art than termites and beavers are able to employ on their houses.

Each of these hovels consists of four walls of stones simply laid one above another. The walls are some three feet high. On these lies a gable-roof of blackened tree-trunks, and boards weighted by large stones. An opening in the front wall serves as a door. Here the smoke seeks an exit, and it issues from the roof or out of the walls, wherever it finds a chink. A fence of stones before the hovel encloses a small space, in which stand pots and pans. In the corner of this rises the *palo*, a stake with a few branches, on which hang kettles, clothes, and strips of goat's flesh.

A few shaggy dogs jumped up as I rode towards the hovel, and the men and ragged children of the pastoral community crept out of their cottages, and regarded the stranger with curious eyes. They looked picturesque enough on this waste of rocks, with the *pelone*, or shaggy brown mantle, thrown round them, and the red *beretto* on their heads, and with bronzed and dark-bearded faces. I called to the herdsmen : "Friends, give hospitality to a stranger who is come over the seas to visit the herdsmen of Co di Mozzo !" they raised a friendly cry of *"Evviva !"* and *"Benvenuto !"*

"Walk into the cabin," said one, "and dry yourself at the fire; it is warm within." I pushed in at once through the doorway, curious to see the interior of the cottage. I found a dark room of some fourteen feet in length and ten in breadth ;—there was no household stuff, no chair, no table, nothing but the bare black stone floor, the bare black stone walls, and a smoke from the pine fire, which was to me insupportable. At the wall burnt a mighty log, with a kettle hanging over it.

Mine host Angelo spread on the floor the rug which I had brought with me, and gave me the place of honour as near the fire as possible. Soon the whole family was squatting round it,

—the woman, three little girls, a boy, the host, I and my guide: the hovel was full. Meanwhile Angelo threw some strips of dried goat's flesh into the kettle, and his wife Santa fetched cheese and milk. The spread was in original herdsman fashion ; for the table consisted of a board three feet long, which was laid on the ground ; on this the herdswoman placed a wooden bowl of milk, a flat cheese, and a loaf. " Eat," said she, " and remember that you are with poor herdsmen. For supper we will give you trout, for my son is gone to fish them."

" Fetch the *broccio*," said the herdsman, " that is 'the best thing we have, and you'll like it." I was curious about the *broccio* ; for I had heard it praised even in Corte as the great dainty of the island, and as the flower of the herdsman's industry. Santa brought a round covered basket, which she set before me and untied : in it lay the *broccio*, white as snow. It is a kind of sweet curdled goats' milk, which, taken with rum and sugar, is undoubtedly a dainty. The poor herdsmen sell a *broccio* cake in the town for from one to two francs.

We fell to bravely on the broccio with the wooden spoons ;— only the woman and children might not eat with us. Cowering down on the ground at the fire in the narrow smoky cabin, with wild and curious faces around me, and the wooden spoon in my hand, the humour seized me, and I began to praise the life of the herdsmen on the mountains, who let the produce of their herds suffice for them, and know not the misery of mine and thine, and the golden cares of the palace.

But the honest *pastore* shook his head and said, " *Vita povera, vita miserabile !*"

And so it is in truth : these people lead a very wretched life. Four months long—May, June, July, and August—they dwell in these cabins, destitute of all that makes life human. In their world there is no other change than that of the elements, of storm, clouds, rain-torrents, hail, and warm sun ;—of an evening a melancholy song, a *lamento* to the shepherd's pipe, a banditti story over the fire, or a tale of the chase of the *muffro* and the fox ;—and high above them and around them the giant pyramids of the mountain, and the starry glories of the heaven ;—and in their breast, perhaps, despite the *vita povera*, a modestly contented, cheerful, resigned, and honest human heart.

In the grey of the morning these poor people rise from the hard floor, on which they have slept in their clothes and without covering, and drive the herds to their pasture. There they take their scanty meal,—cheese, bread, and milk. The old folk who remain at home lie round the fire in the hovel, or employ themselves with the merest necessities of house-work. In the evening the herd comes home and is milked; and then night comes on again, and it is time to lie down.

The rain-torrents and snow of September drive the herdsmen out of their mountain-cabins. They then descend with their herds to the coast and the *paese*. There they have generally their more habitable cottages, in which the women and children often remain through the summer also. My hostess Santa was the only woman in the pastoral community of Co di Mozzo, which consists of six families. "Why," I asked her, "did you come up from the *paese* to this gloomy cabin?"—"Oh!" Angelo fell in, "she is come up to refresh herself." I almost laughed out as he said this; for the smoke in the hovel brought tears into my eyes, and the atmosphere was infernal. So I was to regard the wretched heap of stones actually as a summer villa, to which a family was come for recreation! "Yes," said Angelo, when my countenance expressed scepticism; "below it is hot, and up here the mountain breeze blows, and the clear water comes down, which is as fresh and cold as ice. We live the life that God has blessed us with."—Methought, as Angelo spoke, and I saw the brown laughing faces of children around me, I was come to the wonderful mountain of the Brahmins, and Angelo was Jarchas, wisest of all Brahmins and philosophers of the mountain.* He spoke seriously and short, and was taciturn, as befits a philosopher.

Angelo possessed sixty head of goats, and fifty of sheep. Yet the produce of the milk is not great: in the summer it barely suffices to nourish the family. The broccio and the cheese are sold in the valley, and from the proceeds are procured the bread and the poor clothing. In the winter there is but little milk; for it is used up to nourish the young lambs and kids. Many a herdsman has some hundred head in his herd. When a division among the children takes place, then is the time to try for the luck of the patriarchs, and to multiply the herd. The dowry of a herdsman's daughter consists of twelve goats when she is poor; when she is rich, according to her means.

The mist had dispersed. I stepped out of the hovel into the fresh air, and drew breath. The herdsmen sat round on the stones, smoking their wooden pipes. They choose the eldest or

* See Philostratus, *Vit. Apollon. Tyan.* iii. 16—50.

most respected of them to be their president and justice of the peace. I was surprised by the observation made thus casually; for it gave me as it were, in this little democracy of herdsmen, an insight into the original condition of human society, and the beginnings of the formation of States. Thus six men cannot live by one another's side without their society becoming regulated, and laws growing up. I greeted the little *podestà* with reverence; and, as I contemplated him in silence, he seemed to me more venerable than Deioces, the first and wisest of all the Median kings.

Beside the cabins I observed smaller covered stone huts, of round or oblong form. These were the storehouses. Angelo opened a little door in his, and, creeping in himself, he beckoned me to follow. I contented myself with looking in. There lay the flat cheeses resting on green boughs, and balls of whitish goat's butter in little baskets.

I now sat down and sketched the cabins. The whole community surrounded me, and expressed their extreme pleasure. Every one now wanted to be drawn, in order to be printed afterwards in Paris, as they said; they stuck to it that I was from Paris, and I could not any how make them understand that there was besides Paris, another country called Germania. "So Germania is the name of your *paese*," said my host, "and this *paese* has kings, and belongs to Paris."—Here the matter dropped.

The afternoon sun shone warm, and allured me to the mountains. I took the herdsman's children with me, Antonio, a lad of thirteen years, who looked like a shaggy bear, Paola Maria, and Fiordalisa. Fiordalisa means lily. Imagine this lily of twelve years' growth of Monte Rotondo, in a dress falling to pieces, with her dark hair dangling wildly round her brown face, clambering nimbly as a chamois barefoot up the rocks. Her eyes were lively as those of a mountain hawk, and her teeth white as ivory. We botanized by the Restonica. I saw some beautiful red pinks on a ledge of rock that I could with difficulty have climbed, and pointed to them. "*Aspettate!*" cried the Lily, and, like the lightning, she was off and climbing to the top; and in a short time down again with a handful of them. The children now had climbing-matches, and danced on the perilous blocks of rock like goblins;—fearless, for they were children of the mountain. As we returned home, and had to cross the Restonica, the Lily sprang into the water, and in her mad joy

amused herself with giving me a regular baptism. I found on
the mountains our red foxglove in great abundance. The little
devils brought me a lot of it, and on our return we wreathed
the smoky cabin with a garland of the pretty poisonous flowers
—a decoration which surely it had never enjoyed before. And
this was to be the token of a feast-day in the cabin: for it is
always a feast-day for good people when a guest enters their
house.

The Lily had a foolish delight in the garland. "To-morrow,"
said she, "when you are on the top of the mountain, you will
find a blue flower, which is the most beautiful flower in all
Corsica."—"If you say so, Fiordalisa, it will surely come true,
and I shall find the blue flower to-morrow."

So came on the evening in the vast silent wilderness. Tired
with my day's work, I sat down before the cabins, and observed
the ever-varying spectacle of the formation of clouds. The mists
rose from the gorges, and, alternately drawn on or thrown off by
the mountains, they formed into a dense ball in the valleys, or
dissolved and dispersed into the clouds, which wound slowly
down over the mountain peaks. The flocks came home. I
regarded with pleasure these long trains of pretty black goats
and black sheep, to which the poor herdsmen are indebted for
their livelihood. Every herdsman drove or enticed them by a
shrill call into an enclosure beside his cabin, where he milked
them. This labour is performed with astonishing rapidity.
The herdsman sits among the herd, and catches one goat after
another by the hind-legs. All the animals he calls by their
name, and each he knows perfectly. Some mark, generally on
the ear, is the sign to whom the animal belongs. Forty of my
host's goats gave only a moderate-sized pailful of milk.

At night the herds remain in the enclosure. The shaggy dogs
guard them, not from the wolf, which is not to be found in
Corsica, but from the fox, which is remarkably strong and bold
on the mountains, and pounces upon the lambs like the wolf.
My host's Rosso and Mustaccio were a couple of splendid dogs.

In the meantime the eldest son had returned home with his
spoil of fine trout, and Angelo was dressing the evening meal.
It struck me as remarkable that the man always cooked, and not
the woman. Did he mean thus to honour his guest? For in
general, in Corsica the woman occupies the position of servant.
While I was pondering this, it occurred to me that in Homer
also the men do all this themselves—spit, roast, and serve up the

meat: and thus I had the man of the simple epic stage of culture
standing before me bodily. There are in Corsica men of Homer
and men of Plutarch.

There was a bread soup, cheese, and milk, and roasted goat's flesh,
in honour of the guest. The well-born and godlike goatherd*
took the meat from the *palo*, stuck it on a spit in primitive
fashion, and, kneeling before the fire, held it over the glowing
embers. The dripping was from time to time smeared on a
piece of bread, that the best part of the savoury loin might not
be lost. The trout were boiled in a broth of goat's flesh; and,
when they were done, he set them before me, helped me with
the large spoon, and gave me the same spoon to eat with to my
heart's content. I saw in the children's eyes that this was a
supper extraordinary; but I should have more thoroughly enjoyed it if they might have shared it with us.

Now for night in the cabin. I was impatient to see how we
should bestow ourselves in the narrow room. But it was soon
done; the rug was spread on the ground for me, and I stretched
myself out upon it along the innermost wall : the Son of Man
had not where to lay his head. I looked at Angelo : "Wise
and godlike Angelo," said I, "mayest thou hear these my words,
and ponder them well in thy heart. Never, I swear to thee, was
luxury habitual to me, but a pillow always. So, if thou wilt
give me something for a pillow, it will be one of the noblest
deeds of thy life." Hereupon Angelo the goatherd meditated,
and when he had meditated and weighed every thing maturely,
he gave me his goatskin, the *zaino*, and spoke the winged words,
"Now sleep, and *felicessema notte !*"

One after another the others lay down too, the woman and
children on the bare ground, with their heads against the wall.
Angelo lay next the threshold, with the youngest child Maria
next him, then his wife Santa, the Lily, Paola Maria, and I.
Thus we lay peacefully in company, all with our feet turned
towards the fire. It was not long before they had all fallen
asleep, and I contemplated with delight the Gymnosophist's
family happily slumbering, and thought of the profound Sancho,
how he began to praise the person who invented sleep,—"the
mantle that covers all human cares, the food that allays hunger,
the water that banishes thirst, the fire that warms coldness,
the coldness that mitigates heat, and, in a word, the universal
coin for which all things can be bought, the weight and the

* See note to p. 259.

scales that make the shepherd and the king equal." The red glow transfused the curious group with its light. I regretted that I was no painter. ˙But the intolerable heat and smoke of the resinous fire prevented me from sleeping; so I got up from time to time, and stepped over the sleepers and through the door-way out into the open air. I stepped from the cabin, I may say, straight into a cloud, which encompassed the mountain and the cottages; and thus I passed from hell to heaven, and back again from heaven to hell.

The night was cold and damp with mist; however, the clouds passed off, and the eternal heavens cast their myriads of lights down upon the mists, the rocky peaks, and the dark larches. I sat for long by the brawling Restonica, whose wild rushing broke in upon this grand, ethereal night. Never had the awful spirit of solitude come so near me as in this night, beneath black rocky mountains, by the headlong course of a boisterous stream, so high in the clouds, in nature's workshop, on a strange island forlorn in the middle of the sea. In such a moment the soul might be terrified by the feeling of isolation, and grieved by the sudden thought that man is after all but an atom—and perhaps, too, this spiritual atom might all at once lose its connexion with all its related atoms, and remain forgotten in empty space. But lo! the soul expands its pinions, and soars joyously from the lonely isolated mountain to its native air, and flies through the realm of spirits, and is never alone. I listen to the sounds of the mountains; sometimes they seem to utter wild laughter—it is the Restonica that rages so. These stones are silent witnesses of fearful ancient throes of creation, children of the ardent embraces of Uranus and Gæa.

The cold air drove me back to the fire. Having fallen asleep at last with weariness, I was suddenly waked by Santa's clear voice exclaiming several times, " *Spettacoli divini, spettacoli divini!*" She was laying her children straight, they having thrown themselves about into amusing attitudes. It was indeed a " divine spectacle:" the Lily lay entwined like a snake half across her mother, and little Paola had wound her arm round my neck. Perhaps the child had heard an owl in her sleep, or soon in her dreams the vampire that comes to draw the heart's blood.

I passed the rest of the night sitting up and gazing at the flame, and amused myself with picturing to myself the heretics whom the holy Romish church has burnt to the glory of God. But that is in truth an occupation that knows no end.

CHAPTER IV.

THE MOUNTAIN TOP.

THE grey of morning appeared. I went out and revived
myself by the waves of the sleepless Restonica, which leapt from
rock to rock in the freshness of its youth, and hurried into the
valley below. The young stream has a joyous life. After a
gladsome course of five-and-twenty miles through evergreen
woods, it dies in the waters of the Tavignano. I gained quite
an affection for the Restonica ; I know its whole life-history,
for I have followed it on a single day to the end of its course,
and it has presented me with many a delightful draught. Its
water is as clear, fresh, and light as the ether, and is renowned
far and wide in Corsica. I never drank better water; it
refreshed me more than the most generous wine. This incomparable well-spring possesses such keenness that it cleans iron
in the shortest possible time, and keeps it from rusting: even
Boswell knew that the Corsicans in Paoli's time put their
rusty gun-barrels in the Restonica to clean them. All pebbles
and stones overflowed by its water are rendered snowy white;
and its bed or its banks are garnished with these milk-white
stones as far as its conflux with the Tavignano.

When I summoned my guide to ascend the summit of Monte
Rotondo, he confessed that he did not know the way. Angelo
now became my guide up the mountain. We began the ascent
soon after three o'clock in the morning. It was less attended
with danger, but far more fatiguing than I had expected.

Several ridges of rock rise one above another, which must be
ascended before the Trigione, the last subordinate summit of
Rotondo, is reached. It is a huge natural staircase, with colossal
steps of splendid reddish primeval granite: heavy giants who
storm heaven, grasping masses of rock in their huge hands, might
stride up it. Here blocks lie upon blocks, huge and formless as
chaos, and as grey; so endlessly piled up that the foot of man
despairs. The granite has been often so smoothed by the autum-
nal rains trickling over it, as to present large surfaces which seem
permanently polished. The water flows in inexhaustible plenty
from thousands of rills. The growth of trees entirely ceases,

there being only alder bushes that indicate the bounding course of the Restonica.

Two hours afterwards we had climbed up the Trigione, and before us lay the snow-clad mountain top. Its rugged splintered rocks form a crater-like funnel, which is the cause of the mountain's name. Where this huge desolate amphitheatre of rocks opens, lies a little lake, the Lago di Monte Rotondo, darkly spread out amidst green meadows, an icy cold draught in a giant's granite drinking-cup. Fields of snow stretch from the lake to the summit, even in the scorching dog-days, and under the forty-second parallel of latitude—a rare sight and a curious feeling under a southern sky. They were coated with a crust of ice, and exhaled a cold air. But though I was in the region of eternal snow, the temperature continued pleasantly fresh and reviving, without ever becoming painfully cold.

The summit appeared to the eye very near, but yet we had to clamber over the rocks for two full hours, often on our hands and feet, before we reached it. The most difficult part was the passage over a streak of snow, on which the foot caught no hold. We managed by cutting steps one after another with a sharp stone, into which we could cautiously insert the foot. Thus we at length reached, in a very exhausted state, the extreme summit, which is formed of a grey rent obelisk of rock, and ends in a sharp pinnacle; so that by clasping it one holds one's-self on, suspended at a giddy height.

From this highest peak in Corsica, 9068 feet above the sea, I overlooked the greater part of the island, and the sea deep below on both sides—a view of unspeakable grandeur, such as it will be a joy for life to have been permitted once to behold. The horizon seen from Monte Rotondo is far grander and more beautiful than that from Mont Blanc. The eye wanders far over the island country to the beaming expanse of sea, and beyond the Tuscan islands to the continent of Italy, which in a clear air displays the white Maritime Alps and the entire arch of coast from Nice to Rome. On the other side emerge the mountains of Toulon, and thus the eye may span a grand and wonderful panorama, uniting in a magic ring mountains, seas, islands, the Alps, the Apennines and Sardinia. I was not quite so fortunate in my day; for the clouds and vapours which incessantly rose from the ravines, robbed me of part of my distance. Towards the north I saw the peninsula of Cape Corso stretching out long like a dagger ; towards the east, the plains of the coast descending in gentle lines, the islands of the Tuscan sea, and Tuscany itself; towards the west, the gulfs of Prato, Sagone, Ajaccio, and Valinco.   Ajaccio was plainly visible on its tongue of land in the beautiful bay—a row of little white houses, which looked like swans swimming on the sea.   The sea itself looked an ocean of light.

Towards the south, the view over the island is obstructed by the broad breast of Monte d'Oro.   Many peaks appeared around me, but little lower than Rotondo, and likewise covered with snow, as towards the north, the beautiful Mount Cinto and Capo Blanco, the summits of the land of Niolo.

The island itself appears to the comprehensive gaze like a huge rock-skeleton.   Monte Rotondo indeed lies not on the mountain chain which runs through the island from north to south, but on a branch range removed somewhat to the eastward.   But this station allows of a survey of the whole system and gigantic network of the range.   You see the principal chain right before you, and the mountain ribs running off parallel on both sides and forming the rows of cultivated and inhabited valleys.   Each of these valleys is traversed by a river, and from the main trunk of the range flow the three great rivers of the island, the Golo and Tavignano towards the east coast, and the Liamone towards the west.

Looking next at the immediate environs of the summit, the eye is terror-struck at the immense wilderness of rocks and awfully mighty mountain wrecks, silent as death all around. The desolate blocks lie here endless and huge, like a monument of the struggle between the spirit of the elements and the light of heaven.   Fearfully steep mountain-walls form a system of wild valleys.   In the midst of most of these lies a small un- troubled lake, which is of an azure, grey, or deep black colour, according as it receives light or shadow from the sky or from the rocks.   I counted several of these lakes all around me, the Rinoso, Mello, Nielluccio and Pozzolo, from which rills flow down to the Restonica, and the Oriente, from which the main source of the Restonica itself springs.   Further towards the north-west, lay before me the celebrated pastoral highlands of Niolo, the highest district in Corsica, and its black lake Nino, from which the Tavignano rises.

All these lakes are small and deep water-basins, and most of them swarm with trout.

Standing on the summit, one hears the constant gurgling of

the waters, which frequently find for themselves subterranean passages. Thus this rocky desert, though motionless and weather-beaten, overflows with living streams which pour into the valleys, and render cultivation and social life possible. Far below, on the declivities of these mountains, one sees here and there a *paese*, with its green orchards and streaks of yellow fields.

The clouds gradually gathered round the summits, and we were forced to descend. We now took a difficult path in the direction of the Lago di Pozzolo. There rises the mighty Frate, a colossal crag of Monte Rotondo, and the greatest granite pyramid of the mountain. He is surrounded by black peaks and pinnacles, and chaotic rocks, dashed and shattered into innumerable grey fragments covering his huge foot, which sinks down into the melancholy rocky glen of the Pozzolo. In the crevices of the rock grew the beautiful blue flower which Fiordalisa had told me I should find. Angelo plucked it, and called to me, " *Ecco, ecco lu fiore!*" I took it out of his hand; it was our forget-me-not. Camomiles, pansies, and ranunculi bloomed in great numbers in the rocks of the very summit, and the edges of the fields of snow were adorned by our violets.

It cost us great trouble to climb over the rocks of the Frate; and, when at length over, a patch of snow threatened to stop our passage, which the goatherd wished to avoid by going round it; but I, as a northern, should have been too sorry to miss this excellent slide, so I sat myself upon Angelo's *pelone*, and slid bravely down. So I had a slide in the heat of summer, and in Italy too, under the forty-second degree of latitude.

We had our breakfast at the foot of a peak, and then, strengthened by some bread and fresh water, continued our descent. I looked in vain for the wild animals that inhabit the rocks of Monte Rotondo, the muffro or wild sheep, and the bandit. Though Angelo assured me there were plenty in the cleft we passed, I could not discover any. I saw only a single wild creature on those heights, the pretty Alpine blackbird of Monte Rotondo, a beautiful grey bird, with red, black, and white feathers in his wings.

The Corsican wild sheep, the *muffro* or *mufflone*, is a remarkable production of the island. It is a fine animal with spiral horns, silky wool, and strong limbs, and of a brownish-black colour. He lives in the highest regions of eternal snow, and mounts higher and higher the more the summer sun dispels the snow

from the lower parts of the mountains. By day he roams about
the rocky tarns, where he finds green pasture, by night he again
seeks the snow. He sleeps upon the snow, and the ewe bears
her lambs upon the snow. Like the chamois, the muffro appoints sentinels. Sometimes in a hard winter, when their
pastures are covered by deep snow, these wild sheep come in flocks
among the herdsmen's goats, and they are often seen peacefully
grazing with the herd in the valleys of Vivario, Niolo, and
Guagno. The young muffro may be tamed and becomes tract-
able, but not the old one. They are often pursued; and when
the noise of the chase is heard up in the Corsican mountains,
and shot upon shot echoes from the rocks, people know that the
muffro or the bandit is being hunted. Both are brothers in
wildness, and mountain companions, and both climb to the
eternal snows.

After a descent of three hours I reached the cabins again; and
now, that my purpose was fulfilled, they appeared to me so
dismal, and their atmosphere, by comparison with the pure ether
I had just been breathing, so dreadful, that after an hour's rest
I had the mule saddled and set out on the road to Corte. I
bade the good folk of Co di Mozzo a friendly farewell, and wished
that their flocks and herds might multiply as those of Jacob, and
that their children might enjoy prosperity. They all escorted
me to the end of the hovels, and shouted an honestly meant
Evviva after me as I rode down the hill.

A few hours later I found myself again in the climatic region
where chestnuts and citrons ripen; and so I had traversed in
one day three climatic zones, from the eternal snows to the gardens of Corte, which is equivalent to a journey from the severe
winter of Norway to the countries of the south of Europe.

CHAPTER V.

VENDETTA OR NOT?

I WAS not destined to depart altogether in peace from the
peaceful Corte; and it was my guide to Monte Rotondo who
was to blame for this. I did not discover till after my return
to the town, what a passionate man I had confided myself to.
Although he had told me an untruth, and had forced me, from
his ignorance of the way to the summit, to take Angelo the

goatherd as my guide, I gave him the full sum originally stipulated. But he, in the most impudent manner, demanded half his payment over and above. His and my strong words drew some Corsican gentlemen to the spot, who took my side. "See," said one of them to the guide, "this is a stranger, and a stranger has always claims upon us." I replied to this good-natured pleader, that I laid my claim not as a stranger but as a man, and that I should instantly apply to the authorities of the town if the madman molested me any further. He threw his money on the table and went off in a passion, crying that he should soon find means of revenging himself on the German. Hereupon the landlady of the locanda came in and told me to be on my guard, for that the fellow was excessively passionate, and in the previous year had stabbed a man in the market-place.

In consternation at this news, I inquired the circumstances. "It was," said the hostess, "because the Lucchese had beaten the man's little brother for hanging on to his cart, as children do. The lad ran crying and complaining to his brother, and the latter instantly sprang after the fellow with his dagger, and murdered him with a single blow."

"How was he punished?"—"By five months' imprisonment, for there were no means of directly proving the crime against him."—"Now I confess, *la giustizia Corsa è un poco corta*. But, my good woman, you knew this man's choleric temper, and that he had shed blood, and yet you gave me this devil for a guide, and suffered a stranger to go up the lonely mountains unarmed, in the company of a murderer!"

"I thought, sir, you would see it in his face, and I gave you a wink too, several times. The fellow had offered, and, if I had been the cause of his rejection, I should have had an account to settle with him."

It occurred to me now for the first time, that the good woman had asked, when I set off with my guide, "When do you think you shall be back again?" and that on my answering, "In two days," she shrugged her shoulders, and seemed to say something with her eyes.

"Well, let it be," said I, "I shall not give the fellow a quatrino more than his claim, and there's an end of it." In the evening he came back, and merely fetched his due from the hostess. Yet, although he appeared to have acknowledged himself in the wrong, I deemed it necessary to be cautious, and did not go out of the town after dark.

On the following evening I took a walk in company of a Corsican officer, whose acquaintance I had made. Outside the town-gate I saw a small specimen of Corsican temperament. A lad of about fifteen years had fastened a horse to a fence, and was stoning it, quite beside himself with rage, and screaming, like a raving beast: the poor animal having probably been restive and disobedient. I stood still, and, exasperated at such bestial cruelty, cried out to the lad to stop stoning the animal. My companion instantly said to me, " For Heaven's sake, come away and be quiet !" I did as he said, and pondered long on the scene, and on the apprehensive manner in which my companion had said these words to me in an undertone. It was another glimpse into the condition of the Corsicans.

In a short time the lad dashed past on his horse, like a revengeful spirit, with his hair flying, his countenance burning, and his eyes flashing fire—the whole apparition passing by headlong, like an ebullition of rage.

At this moment the thought crossed my mind that I was after all among barbarians, and I felt a sudden craving for Florence and its gentle people.

But uncomfortable sensations multiplied during this walk. When we had walked barely half a mile further up the hills, I saw my guide with his gun on his shoulder, going off from the road to a neighbouring height, where he sat down on a rock, taking his gun on his knees. I could not tell whether he still cherished a grudge against me, and meditated any dark design; but it was possible. I pointed him out to my companion, and passed on quietly, not to display any appearance of fear ; but the air seemed rather oppressive. "He will not shoot at you," said my companion, "if you have not offended him in words. But if you have, I cannot answer for the consequences, for these men cannot put up with an offence."—Accordingly he did not shoot ; and this was a great kindness of this vampire, this poor devil I was going to say, who is to be accounted rather unfortunate than guilty. For nature is here more at fault than man. The blood shed on the Corsican mountains is seldom shed for common greed, gain, or worldly advantage, but most of all for a false sense of honour. The Corsicans engage in a knightly duel for life and death.

CHAPTER VI.

FROM CORTE TO AJACCIO.

THE road from Corte to Ajaccio rises for many miles as you go southwards, till you come to the mountain Monte d'Oro. It leads through a cheerful and well-cultivated undulating country, and glorious chestnut groves. Nothing can be brighter and more cheerful than the landscapes of the canton of Serraggio, which was the former *pieve* of Venaco. Brooks flowing from Monte Rotondo traverse a lovely green country, on the hills of which villages are situated, such as Pietro, Casa Nova, Riventosa, and Poggio.

Poggio di Venaco preserves the memory of the handsome Arrigo Colonna, who was Count of Corsica in the tenth century. One picks up in passing many a charming picture connected with some romantic tale, and this is always one of the great pleasures of travel. Arrigo was so handsome in form, and so fascinating in manners, that he was called the Bel Messere ; under this appellation he still lives in the mouth of the people. His wife, too, was noble and beautiful, and his seven children were all young and lovely. But his enemies wished to deprive him of his supremacy, and a ruthless Sardinian conspired with them against his life. The murderers fell upon him one day, and assassinated him, and threw his seven children into the little lake " of the seven bowls." Now, when the fell deed was done, there arose a voice in the air, which cried plaintively, " Bel Messere is dead ! Miserable Corsica, hope for no prosperity again!" All people began to grieve for Bel Messere. But his widow took up sword and spear, and marched with her vassals to the castle of Tralavedo, to which the murderers had retired, burned it down, and killed them all. On the green hills of Venaco nine ghosts are still often seen wandering by night ; these are the ghosts of Bel Messere, his wife, and the seven poor children.

It was Sunday. The people were strolling about in the villages, and generally sitting round the church, like their fathers in the days of old—a beautiful picture on a quiet Sunday, people celebrating the holy day, and keeping the Lord's peace. But even on Sunday, and before the church-door, a gunshot may be heard, and then the scene is changed.

Near Vivario, the country becomes wilder, and the mountains more considerable. Many a one pauses before the threshold of the little church of Vivario to remark a gravestone, on which is written in Latin the biblical verse, MALEDICTUS QUI PERCUS- SERIT CLAM PROXIMUM SUUM, ET DICET OMNIS POPULUS, AMEN. (Cursed be he that smiteth his neighbour secretly. And all the people shall say, Amen.—*Deut,* xxvii. 24.) The stone tells a story of revenge from the seventeenth century; beneath it the avenger lies buried. Blessed be the memory of the priest of Vivario, who took this saying from the Bible and wrote it on the stone! They say it is the talisman of Vivario; for it com- memorates the last case of blood-revenge in the village. Would that the hand that wrote it had been a giant's hand, and had written in giant letters over the whole of Corsica, *Maledictus qui percusserit clam proximum suum, et dicet omnis populus, Amen!*

There is a small guard-house, with a garrison of ten men, in a wild and lonely situation in the mountains of Vivario. The great valley of the Tavignano closes in here, and an elevated ridge forms the water-shed between it and the Gravone, which flows in the opposite direction, south-west to Ajaccio. On the confines of the two valleys are the two snow-covered mountains, the Monte Renoso and the Monte d'Oro, the latter of which is only a few metres lower than Monte Rotondo, and superior to it in the grandeur of its forms. One keeps the mountain in sight in front for many hours.

One next passes through the glorious forest of Vizzavona, be- tween the two mountains. This consists chiefly of larches (*Pinus larix*), which often attain a height of 120 feet, and a thick- ness of 21. Among all the pine tribe this mighty, broad-branch- ing, fragrant larch is surely next to the cedar in grandeur; not having seen the cedars of Asia, I may at least affirm the Corsi- can larches to be the finest of all the trees that I have ever seen. It was always an enchanting sight to me, to see it in its dark and silent majesty on the immense granite crags of those moun- tains. It well suits this royal tree to grow on granite : it rises high above the rocks, which are forcibly penetrated by its roots, and it stands gloriously and majestically in many places known only to the eagle or the wild sheep. There are in the forest, also, beautiful pines, red beeches, evergreen oaks (*ilex*), and firs. There is plenty of game concealed there, especially deer, which are small in Corsica ; the wild-boar is found more towards the coast, where he is eagerly hunted.

The forest of Vizzavona is the second in size, and comes next to that of Aitone in the canton of 'Evisa, which belongs to Ajaccio. All these forests are in mountainous regions : some belong to the state, but most to the communes. Here, too, great treasures are yet to be found. I saw a snake on the road, basking in the sun. Corsica possesses only two kinds of snakes, and no venomous animals, with the exception of a spider, called Malmignatto, whose bite brings on a sudden numbness of the body, and occasionally even death, and the venomous ant, Innafantato.

It was about noon that I passed the forest. The air was stiflingly hot, but the wood offered its cool and refreshing streams, which trickle down on every side towards the Gravone. Seneca can never have tasted Corsican mountain streams, since he says in his epigram that Corsica possesses no draught of water.

At length we reached the mountain ridge which forms the highest point on the road to Ajaccio, 3500 feet above the sea. This is the Foce of Vizzavona, which is mentioned in many a Corsican ballad.

The road now descends into the Gravone valley. This fruitful valley is formed by two chains of mountains, the northern issuing from Monte d'Oro, and ending in the Punta della Parata above Ajaccio, and parting the water system of the Gravone from that of the Liamone ; the southern running in a parallel direction from Monte Renoso, and separating the valley of the Gravone from that of Prunelli. On both sides of the Gravone are hamlets on the hills, which look more cheerful than· I have found them elsewhere in Corsica.

The first place in the canton is Bocognano, which is near the entrance of the wild defile of Vizzavona. It is surrounded by dark mountains covered with wood, and having snow-clad summits, and the whole district bears a solemn grandiose character. It is inhabited by poor herdsmen, a strong and brave population. Those who do not feed on milk, live on chestnuts. Many manufacture the *pelone*. Arms are here universal. The appearance of such strong men with their double-barrelled guns, their *carchera* and brown woollen coats, is quite in keeping with the gloomy Alpine mountains and pine forests all around. These Corsicans look iron, like the *fucili* they carry. The people seemed to me here to have remained stationary, and to have rusted since the dreary middle-ages.

The road constantly descends towards Ajaccio. At last we saw the magnificent bay. It was five o'clock in the afternoon when we approached the town. The more richly planted hills, vineyards, and olive grounds, and a fruitful plain called the Campoloro, in which the Gravone valley terminates near the bay, announced the capital of Corsica; which showed itself at length as a row of white houses running out into the bay, at the foot of a chain of hills, and surrounded by rural cottages. An avenue of elm-trees leads along the bay into the town : and so I entered with joyful emotion the small native place of the man who shook the world.

TRAVELS.——BOOK VI.

CHAPTER I.

AJACCIO.

AJACCIO lies at the northern end of a gulf which is reckoned among the finest in the world. Its two coast-lines are of unequal length : the northern one is shorter, and runs on in a westerly direction as far as the Punta della Parata, a point of land, opposite which are the Isole Sanguinarie, or Bloody Islands : the southern side of the gulf trends from north to south with many curves, as far as Cape Muro, sailing round which you come into the bay of Valinco.

One sees on the northern coast no villages, and on the southern but few, and several solitary towers and *fanali*. The northern end of the gulf is frowned upon by several high mountains, one of which is Pozzo di Borgo ; they are the mountains that confine the Gravone valley, which terminates in the fruitful plain of Campo di Loro. The situation of Ajaccio bears a surprising analogy to that of Naples.

They say that Ajaccio is one of the oldest towns in Corsica. The fabling chroniclers of the island derive it from the hero Ajax ; others from Ajazzo, the son of the Trojan prince Corso, who wandered with Æneas to the western sea, carried off Sica, a niece of Dido, and thus gave the island the name of Corsica. According to the statement of Ptolemy, the ancient town of Urcinium, which is said to be the Adjacium of the earliest part of the middle ages, lay on the gulf of Ajaccio ; and this town is always coupled with the oldest towns of the island, Aleria, Mariana, Nebium, and Sagona, which are decayed.

But ancient Ajaccio stood not on the site of the modern town, but on a more northern hill on the gulf, called San Giovanni.

On its summit are the ruins of an old castle, called Castello Vecchio, and there were formerly seen there remains of the old cathedral, in which the bishops of Ajaccio long continued to be consecrated. These ruins are gone, and nothing now betrays the former existence of a town upon the spot. But many old Roman ruins were found in the vineyards, and large vessels of *terra cotta* of an oval form, sepulchral urns, which always contained a skeleton and a key. They say, also, that the vaulted graves of the Moorish kings used to be shown there, but they have disappeared.

The new town, with the citadel, was founded by the Bank of St. George of Genoa, in the year 1492. It was the seat of a lieutenant or vicegerent of the governor of Bastia, and was not raised to the dignity of capital of the island till 1811, at the instigation of Madame Letitia and Cardinal Fesch, who wished by this exaltation to distinguish their own and the Emperor's birthplace.

From the above-mentioned hill of San Giovanni, the best view of the town and neighbourhood is gained. It presents the most cheerful picture that can be imagined, and no other Corsican town can compare with it. Its horizon is incomparable— mountains lost in the clouds far in the interior of the land, the majestic gulf bathed in azure light, a southern sky, and Italian vegetation—no finer combination can be conceived ; and there lies an idyllic, quiet, and harmless town of 11,500 inhabitants, concealed in the foliage of elm-trees, and bearing rule over a country that looks as if it were intended to contain an imperial metropolis.

Ajaccio is situated on a tongue of land, the point of which is occupied by the castle. Next to this follows the town, extending also in both directions along the gulf. The avenue of elms and plane-trees which leads to the town, is continued through its main street, the Cours Napoléon; for this is, in reality, a prolongation of the road from Corte. It has had to be partly blasted out of the rocks, of which there are two close by the houses and the entrance into the town. In this Corso the elms change into orange-trees of tolerable height, which give to the street a festive and rich appearance. The houses are high, but without any fine architecture. The grey Venetian blinds, which are preferred in Corsica instead of the bright green ones of Italy, are characteristic features; they give a dull and monotonous expression to the houses. All the more considerable houses of the Corso stand on the right hand side, and the little Gabriel Theatre, the neat Préfecture, and the Barracks.

I was surprised by the rural stillness in all these streets of Ajaccio; their names only appeal to the traveller, and tell the story of Napoleon. There may be read, Cours Napoléon, Rue Napoléon, Rue Fesch, Rue Cardinal, Place Létitia, and Rue du Roi de Rome, which calls up sad reminiscences. The memory of Napoleon is indeed the soul of the town, and one lounges from one street to another, buried in thoughts of the wonderful man and his childhood, and one has soon passed through them all. Parallel with the Cours Napoléon runs the Rue Fesch. The former leads on to the broad Place du Diamant, which lies on the sea-coast, and commands a fine view of the gulf and its southern shore; the latter ends in the market-place (du marché), and leads to the harbour. These are the two chief streets and the two chief squares of Ajaccio. Small by-lanes unite them, and traverse the tongue of land. The stillness invites one so charmingly to call up reminiscences, and the blue gulf also lies spread out so still and smooth, like a mirror, before one's eyes! The gulf may be seen in almost every street; and the eye is never imprisoned between walls, for the chief streets are broad, the squares large and planted with green trees, and the sea and the green olive-grounds that rise hard by the town, peep in wherever you may chance to stand. Ajaccio is a land and sea town at the same time—you live there in the midst of nature.

As evening came on, the Corso and the Place du Diamant were enlivened by promenaders, who wished to enjoy the coolness of the air. The military band played in the Place, and the people walked and stood about in blithesome groups. The women generally wore black veils, and those of the middle station of life were covered by the black *faldetta*. One might fancy one's-self standing any where on a Spanish coast.

The Ajaccines have really the most beautiful promenades in the world, whether on the square bearing so fabulous a name, or along the gulf, beneath avenues of elms, and in vineyards and olive grounds. I know few places that offer so fine a view as this rural Place du Diamant, of Ajaccio. Close by it roar the waves of the sea, and on the land side it is enclosed by cheerful rows of houses, among which are a stately military hospital, and an elegant seminary for priests, and it is backed by a green hill. A stone sea-wall protects it against the gulf; in a few steps one is on the shore, which is girt by a promenade.

I found nothing more delightful in Ajaccio, than to stroll in
the cool of the evening on that Diamond Square, when the west
wind blew over the gulf, or to sit on the sea-wall, and feed my
eyes on the enchanting panorama of sea and mountain around
me. The Italian sky beams at that time of day with a fairy
light; the air is so clear, that the Milky-way and Venus cast
long streaks of light over the gulf, and the waves reflect a mild
radiance. Wherever they tremble, or a passing boat furrows
the surface behind it, they quiver with phosphorescent sparks.
The shore right opposite is shrouded in night; the *fanali* burn
on the points of land, and at many spots on the mountains great
fires are seen blazing. They burn down the bush about August,
to gain cultivable land, which is at the same time manured with
the ashes. I saw these fires burning on for many days; by day
they roll volumes of white smoke over the mountains, by night
they shine like volcanos over the gulf, and then the resemblance
to the gulf of Naples becomes really surprising. Thus one may
enjoy a splendid illumination on the Diamond Square of Ajaccio
every evening.

The market-place is not less beautiful, if its view is not so
comprehensive. One surveys from it the secure and splendid
harbour, which is bounded by a granite molo, a design of
Napoleon's. A fine quay of granite terminates the harbour-side
of the market-place, which, planted as it is with trees, looks
quite rural and peaceful. At its entrance stands the chief well
of Ajaccio, a large cube of marble, from the sides of which the
water streams into semicircular basins. It is thronged from
morning till evening, and I could never look at these groups of
women and children drawing water, without thinking of the
well-scenes in the Old Testament. In a hot country, the well
of water is in truth the well of poetry and sociality: the hearth
and the well are the earliest consecrated centres of union of
human communities. The women no longer draw water here
as in Bastia, in those antique metal vessels, but in little barrels,
or stone pitchers of terra cotta, with a handle over the aperture.
These pitchers too are ancient; but they have also the stone
vessels with long narrow necks, which look quite Etruscan. The
poor people in the unfruitful island of Capraja, gain their livelihood partly by the manufacture of such vessels, which are sent
far and wide for sale.

On this same market-place behind the well, close before the
harbour and before the elegant town-hall, stands a marble

statue of Napoleon, on an extravagantly high, and by no means beautifully tapering, pedestal of granite. The inscription is as follows: "To the Emperor Napoleon, his native town (dedicates this statue). May 5, 1850, in the second year of the Presidency of Louis Napoleon." Ajaccio had long made exertions for a monument to Napoleon, and always without success. The arrival of a work of art in Corsica was no small event for the island. Now it happened that the family of Bonaparte was once sending a statue of Ganymede to Signor Ramolino. When the people saw it landed from the ship, they took the eagle of Ganymede for the imperial eagle, and Ganymede himself for Napoleon; so they collected in the market-place, and demanded that the statue might be at once set up on the cubic pedestal of the well, that they might at length have the great Napoleon in marble in the market-place. In converting the Trojan youth Ganymede into their countryman Napoleon, the honest Corsicans seem surely to have verified the chronicler's fable, that the Ajaccines are derived from a Trojan prince.

The beautiful statue of Napoleon by Bartolini the Florentine, was in reality intended for Ajaccio; but they could not agree about the price of 60,000 francs, and so Bartolini's work does not adorn Ajaccio. The statue of Napoleon on the market-place is only a mediocre work of Laboureur; but its position in the face of the gulf most advantageously enhances its local effect. It is a consular statue. The consul gazes from his pedestal out over the sea, turning from his diminutive native town to the vast element. He wears the Roman toga, and a laurel-crown upon his head; he has his right hand upon a rudder, which rests on the globe of the world. The idea is a good and happy one; for in sight of the gulf the rudder is a perfectly natural symbol, and doubly appropriate in the hand of the islanders. The contemplative mind here dwells on the history, not of the finished, but of the growing ruler, as he saw this little world of Ajaccio around him, in which he, the mightiest man in Europe, went about as a child and as a youth, not knowing what he was, and to what ends fate had destined him. Then memory roves again from the market-place to the sea, and sees the ship which brought General Napoleon from Egypt to France, anchor in this gulf here. He sat on board there by night, and hastily skimmed all the newspapers that they could beat up for him in Ajaccio; and here it was that he formed the resolution of seizing that rudder by which he was to govern, not France alone, but an empire and half the world, until it broke in his hands, and the man of Corsica was wrecked on the rocks of the island of St. Helena.

A few ships lie in the harbour, two or three two-masters and some sailing boats. Being not exposed to the *maestrale*, like the bay of San Fiorenzo, but sheltered by the coast against all storms, this gulf could receive the largest fleets on its splendid roadstead. But the harbour is dead, for all commerce is wanting. Once in the week, on Saturday, a steamer comes from Marseille, bringing news and articles of use from the external world. I often heard Corsicans lamenting that Napoleon's native town, though so eminently favoured by its incomparable position and happy climate, was no more than a petty town in any province of France. How small is the sale of wares, and how paltry is the native industry, one sees at once by a walk round the market-place, where most of the shops are on the lowest story of the houses. One sees not a single shop for articles of luxury, but only the most absolutely indispensable trades, especially tailors and shoemakers; and anything that smacks in any degree of luxury, has an antiquated and worn out appearance.

I found one single book-shop at Ajaccio, but even this is combined with a trade in small-wares; and soap, ribbons, knives, and baskets are sold together with books. Yet the town-hall has a library, considerable for Ajaccio, of 27,000 volumes. Lucian Bonaparte laid the foundation of it, and is said to have deserved better of Corsica for this collection of books than for his epic in twelve cantos, " La Cyrneïde." The préfecture also possesses a valuable library, the archives of which are especially rich in important documents for Corsican history.

In the town-hall is preserved also the collection of pictures which Cardinal Fesch bequeathed to his native town. They are a thousand in number, but the poor citizens of Ajaccio cannot display them, having no building suitable; so they have lain for years in the lumber-room. Fesch also designed his house to be given up for a public institution, first to the Jesuits, and then for a college, which now bears his name. It is composed of a principal and twelve teachers for various sciences.

The poverty of Ajaccio, in institutions and in public buildings, is great. Its greatest treasure is the house of Bonaparte.

CHAPTER II.

THE CASA BONAPARTE.

FROM the street of St. Charles you emerge on a small rectangular place. An elm-tree stands before an old-fashioned, yellowish-grey, stuccoed, three-storied house, with a flat roof, and a gallery on the roof, with six windows to the front, and worn-out looking doors. On the corner of this house you read the inscription, " Place Létitia."

No marble tablet tells the stranger who comes from Italy, where the houses of great men announce themselves by inscriptions, that he stands before the house of Bonaparte. He knocks in vain at the door; no voice answers, and all the windows are fast closed with grey Venetian shutters, as if the house was in the state of siege of the Vendetta. , Not a creature appears in the square. Every thing around appears dead, as if really extinct or scared away by the name of Napoleon.

At last an old man appeared at a window in the neighbourhood, and told me to come again in two hours, when he would procure the key for me.

Bonaparte's house, but little altered since his time, as they assured me, is, if not a palace, yet at any rate the dwelling of a family of rank and consequence This is declared by its exterior; and it may be called really a palace, in comparison with the village-cabin in which Pasquale Paoli was born. It is roomy, comfortable, and cleanly. But all furniture has disappeared from the rooms, the tapestry alone being left upon the walls, and that is worn out. The floor, which is inlaid with small red hexagonal flags in the Corsican fashion, shows itself injured in places. The rooms were rendered quite dreary and uncomfortable-looking by their bareness, and the darkness occasioned by the closed shutters.

This dwelling-house was brightened up of old, in the time of the fair Létitia, by the life of a large family and cheerful hospitality; now it looks like a burial vault, and one searches in vain for any object on which imagination might seize, to fill up the picture of the history of its mysterious inhabitants. The bare walls tell no tales.

I do not know when the house was built, but it can hardly be old. Genoa then governed the island, and perhaps Louis XIV. filled the world with the glory of himself and France. I thought of the time when the architect planned this house, and pronounced his wonted blessing upon it, and when, by hallowed custom, the family who had had it built were escorted into it by their relations;—little thinking that capricious fortune would shower imperial and royal crowns upon this roof, and that it would be the cradle of a race of princes who should swallow up whole countries.

The excited fancy seeks them all in these rooms, and sees them assembled round their mother—ordinary children, like other men's children, schoolboys toiling at their Plutarch or Cæsar, tutored by their grave father and their great-uncle, Lucian, and the three young sisters growing up careless and rather wild, like their neighbours in the half-barbarous island town. There is Joseph the eldest, then Napoleon the second-born, Lucian, Louis, Jerome; there Caroline, Eliza, and Pauline, the children of a notary of moderate income, who is incessantly and vainly carrying on lawsuits with the Jesuits of Ajaccio, to gain a contested estate which is necessary to his numerous family. For the future of his children fills him with anxiety. What will they be in the world, and how shall they secure a comfortable subsistence?

And behold! these same children, one after the other, take to themselves the mightiest crowns of the earth—tear them from the heads of the most unapproachable kings of Europe, wear them in the sight of all the world, and cause themselves to be embraced as brothers and brothers-in-law by emperors and kings; and great nations fall at their feet, and deliver their land and people, blood and possessions, to the sons of the notary of Ajaccio! Napoleon is European Emperor; Joseph, King of Spain; Louis, King of Holland; Jerome, King of Westphalia; Pauline, a Princess of Italy; Eliza, a Princess of Italy; Caroline, Queen of Naples. So many crowned potentates were born and educated in this little house by a lady unknown to fame, the daughter of a citizen of a small and seldom mentioned country-town, Letitia Ramolino, who, at the age of fourteen, married a man equally unknown. Her throes were really throes of the world's history.

There is not a tale in the Thousand and One Nights that

would sound more fabulous than the history of the family of
Bonaparte. That this tale, however, has become truth in the
sober days of our modern age, must be regarded as a great
achievement of history, and as a great boon. It has violently
broken through the course of human history, which was
becoming ossified by political routine, and deadened by a
kind of caste system; it has filled it with new motion and
a new spirit, and put man above political destiny. It has
violently delivered human powers and human passions from the
coercion of the traditionary class limits, and shown that the
individual, though born in the dust, may become every thing
attainable by man, since all men are equal. If the history of
the Bonapartes still seems fabulous to us, this is solely occasioned
by the middle-age state in which our life still moves, and by our
inherited ideas of the immutable distinctions of society. Napoleon is the political Faust. Not in his battles, but in his revolutionary nature, lies his greatness for the world's history. He
dashed to earth the traditionary political gods. The history of
this predestined man is therefore very simple, human, and
natural; but it cannot be written yet.

Even history is a part of nature. There is in it a chain of cause
and effect; and what we call genius or a great man, is always
the result of definite conditions, and necessary.

An almost unbroken contest of more than a thousand years,
between Corsica and her tyrants, had preceded, before the great
conqueror Napoleon was born, in whose nature this rock-bound
island, and this energetic and battle-proof island people, pressed
close on a narrow space of ground, produced for themselves an
organ whose law was boundlessness. This is the upward series,
—the Corsican bandit, the Corsican soldier, Renuccio della Rocca,
Sampiero, Gaffori, Pasquale Paoli, Napoleon.

I entered a little room with blue tapestry and two windows,
one of which looks on a balcony towards the court, the other
towards the street. One sees in it a cupboard in the wall behind
a tapestried door, and a fireplace bordered with yellow marble,
and decorated by a few mythological bas-reliefs. In this room
Napoleon was born, August 15, 1769. Is it not a curious,
indescribable feeling that possesses the soul on the spot where a
great man was born? It is surrounded by an atmosphere of
undefined sanctity and mystery; it is like catching a glimpse of
what is behind the curtain of nature, where nature silently
creates the incomprehensible organs of her actions. But man

354 CORSICA. [BOOK VI.

can perceive naught but the resulting phenomenon, and inquires in vain for the *how.* To stand still before the unsearchable mysteries of nature, and contemplate wonderingly the bright forms that rise out of darkness, is man's religion. Nothing surely takes a firmer hold on the thinking man than the starry heavens of the night, and the starry heavens of the world's history. They show other rooms too, the family dancing room, Madame Letitia's room, Napoleon's little bed-room, and his working-room. The two little cupboards are still to be seen in which his schoolbooks were kept. There are now books in them: I pounced upon them eagerly, as if they could have been the books of Napoleon; but they were old faded books of law, theological works, a Livy, a Guicciardin, and others, probably the property of the family of Pietra Santa, which is related to that of Bonaparte, and now possesses their house in Ajaccio.

In this house it does one good to represent to one's-self the youthful history of Napoleon, which has never been placed on an adequate basis. I will tell what I have either heard or read on the subject. I am indebted for much to the recent work of Nasica, a Corsican, " Mémoires sur l'enfance et la jeunesse de Napoléon jusqu' à l'age de vingt-trois ans." This book, dedicated to the nephew of Napoleon, is written insipidly and without discernment; but it contains undoubtedly correct facts and a few valuable documents.

CHAPTER III.

THE BONAPARTE FAMILY.

THE origin of the family of Bonaparte cannot be made out with certainty. Low adulation has brought up the absurdest stories, to find for Napoleon the most ancient and exalted ances-tors. A pedigree has even been constructed, commencing with Manuel II., the eighth Greek emperor of the house of the Comneni, and pretending that, after the fall of Constantinople, his two sons, emigrating under the name of Bonaparte, came first to Corfu, then to Naples, Rome, and Florence. From them the Corsican Bonapartes are then absurdly made to descend.

That the family of Bonaparte played a part in the middle ages among the Signori of Italian cities, is historically demon-strated. They were inscribed in the Golden Book of Bologna, among the Patricians of Florence, and in the Peerage of Treviso. When Napoleon had become son-in-law of Austria, the Emperor Francis caused eager investigations about the Bonaparte family in Italy during the middle ages to be set on foot, and transmitted to his son-in-law some documents to prove that the Bonapartes had long been Lords of Treviso. Napoleon thanked him, and replied that he considered himself sufficiently honoured by being the Rudolf of Hapsburg of his race. And on another occasion he pushed aside the ancient patents of nobility which some one had rummaged up for him, with the words, " I date my nobility from Millesimo and Montenotte."

When the Bonapartes came to Corsica is quite uncertain. Muratori has quoted a paper of the year 947, in which three Corsican Signori, Otho, Domenico, and Guido make a present, documentarily attested, to Abbot Silverio of Monte Cristo, of their possession Venaco in Corsica; among the witnesses who signed this paper at Mariana, occurs a Messire Bonaparte. The family, or a branch of it, must, according to this, have crossed to Corsica at a very early date. Perhaps others followed in the course of later centuries; for the Tuscan Bonapartes were partly Guelfs and partly Ghibellins, and were alternately expelled as the one or the other party was forced to leave the country. Some of them are known to have gone to Lunigiana and to Sarzana, and to have entered the service of the powerful Lords Malaspina, with whom I would maintain them to have gone to Corsica also. Another branch remained in Tuscany, and became quite permanently established there, first in Florence, and subsequently in the small Tuscan town of San Miniato al Tedesco, which lies on the road to Pisa. The family had their family vault in the church of San Spirito at Florence, and there, in the cloister of the convent, I read on a gravestone the following inscription, in the old orthography:—

S. di Benedeto
Di Piero di Giobuini
Buonaparte. E di sua Descendenti.

The arms upon it display a star both above and below the chevron; significantly enough, for the star has risen twice on the house of Bonaparte.

Members of the family remained in San Miniato down to Napoleon's time. After his Leghorn expedition, Napoleon found there the last of that branch of the Bonapartes, an old canon, Filippo Bonaparte, who made the young hero his heir, and died in the year 1799.

As to the Bonapartes in Corsica or in Ajaccio, they certainly ascend to Messire Francesco Bonaparte, who died 1567; the Corsican branch of the family had undoubtedly come over from Sarzana. For perspicuity's sake I give a little genealogical table:—

FRANCESCO BONAPARTE, 1567.

GABRIELE BONAPARTE MESSIRE,
(built towers at Ajaccio against the Barbaresques)

GERONIMO BONAPARTE EGREGIUS, PROCURATOR NOBILIS,
(Chief of the Elders of Ajaccio)

FRANCESCO BONAPARTE,
(Capitano of the town)

SEBASTIANO BONAPARTE   FULVIO BONAPARTE.

CARLO BONAPARTE NOBILIS   LODOVICO BONAPARTE, 1632.
                                        (Married Maria of Gondi)

GIUSEPPE BONAPARTE,
(Elder of the town)

SEBASTIAN BONAPARTE, MAGNIFICUS,   LUCIANO BONAPARTE,
(Elder of the town, 1700.)   (Archdeacon.)

CARLO MARIA BONAPARTE,
(born March 29, 1746, Napoleon's
father, married Letitia Ramolino.)

The Bonapartes played no part in the history of Corsica. Respected in their own town, and honoured with titles of nobility by the Genoese, to whom Ajaccio was obliged to be submissive, they limited themselves to taking a part in the civil government of Ajaccio. Not till Carlo Bonaparte does this name become respected, and in a certain sense historical over the whole of Corsica.

Napoleon's father, then, was born at Ajaccio, March 29, 1746, in stormy times, when the Corsicans were gathering up all their strength to shake off the hated Genoese yoke. Gaffori was the head of the Corsicans, and Pasquale was still in exile at Naples. It had become customary with the Bonapartes at Ajaccio to send their children to Tuscany for their education, and especially to let them study at Pisa: for the Bonapartes remembered their Florentine nobility, and never ceased to assert it. Carlo Bonaparte himself was styled Nobile and Patrician of Florence. However, young Carlo passed his first time of study at Paoli's newly founded academy at Corte, and then went to the university of Pisa, where he found many students his countrymen. He studied the science of law, and is said to have gained esteem by his knowledge, and affection by his liberality. Returning to his country after taking the degree of doctor of laws, he soon became the most popular advocate in Ajaccio.

Carlo Bonaparte, exceedingly handsome, eloquent, and of brilliant intellect, soon attracted the notice of Paoli, who generally had a correct eye for character. He took him into his service, and employed him in business of state. In the year 1764, the young advocate made the acquaintance of the most beautiful girl in Ajaccio, Letitia Ramolino, who was fourteen years old. An ardent affection sprang up between them; but the Ramolinos were of the Genoese party, and would not give their daughter in marriage to a Paolist. Paoli himself then mediated between them, and managed to gain over Letitia's parents, so that they gave their consent to the marriage. Letitia's mother, when a widow, married M. Fesch, captain in the Swiss regiment in the service of Genoa, and from this marriage was born the subsequent Cardinal Fesch.

So Paoli made young Carlo Bonaparte his secretary, and took him to Corte, the seat of government. Letitia accompanied him, though against her will. The catastrophe now came to the Corsican cause: the French had already entered the island after the treaty of Fontainebleau, and when the issue seemed to hang upon the edge of the sword, the people were convened to a parliament to deliberate upon the course to be taken. Carlo Bonaparte, in a fiery patriotic speech, gave his vote for war with France.

After the disastrous battle of Ponte Nuovo, when every one sought his safety in flight, and the French were already advancing upon Corte, some hundreds of persons of distinguished families fled to Monte Rotondo, among whom were Carlo Bonaparte and his wife, who was then pregnant with Napoleon. The mountain presented a sad sight of despairing, helpless men, and of women and children who feared that their last hour was come. Thus passed several days of anxiety and uncertainty in those wilds among the shepherds. At last there appeared French officers upon the mountain with a flag of peace, sent out by Count De Vaux, who had entered Corte. They announced to the fugitives that the island had submitted, and that Paoli was about to take ship for the continent, and that they had nothing to fear, and might come down from the mountain to their homes. The fugitives immediately sent a deputation to Corte, with Carlo

Bonaparte and Lorenzo Giubega of Calvi at its head, who, when they had received passports of security for all the fugitive families, returned to Monte Rotondo to fetch them away.

Bonaparte descended the mountains with his wife to the pastoral district of Niolo. To reach Ajaccio by this difficult road, they had to cross the Liamono; and. this river being swollen, Letitia was exposed to the danger of drowning, and was only saved from the stream by her courage and the promptness of her conductors. Carlo Bonaparte now desired to accompany Paoli, his friend and patron, into exile, considering it dishonourable to remain when their common country had fallen into the power of the French. But the entreaties of his uncle, Archdeacon Lucian, and the tears of his wife, prevailed upon him to relinquish this desperate idea. So he stayed in the island, returned to Ajaccio, and became assessor of the Royal Tribunal, then under French supremacy. Marbœuf treated him with great distinction; and it was by his influence that Carlo procured for his eldest son Joseph a place in the seminary of Autun, and for his second son, Napoleon, a position in the military school at Brienne. Thus it was Marbœuf, the conqueror of Corsica, who rendered possible the career of the young Corsican, Napoleon Bonaparte. He visited very frequently at the house of Bonaparte, and passed many a pleasant hour in the society of the beautiful Madame Letitia: this, and the patronage granted to her second son, prompted the enemies of the French Count to spread scandalous rumours to the disparagement of the fair mother of Napoleon.

Marbœuf was, however, under obligations to Carlo Bonaparte. When General Narbonne Fritzlar was intriguing against the latter with a view of gaining the command-in-chief in Corsica, Bonaparte had prevailed upon the French ministry, by his counsel, to retain Marbœuf in the government of the island. The Count requited this service by his friendship and good-will, and by the recommendation of the young military scholar Napoleon to the influential family of Brienne. Carlo Bonaparte showed his attachment to Marbœuf by every possible means. I have read a sonnet of his to the count, which I will not publish because it is not characteristic; every educated Italian ought to be able to make a pretty good sonnet in Italian.

In the year 1777, Napoleon's father, being elected a deputy of the nobility for Corsica, travelled by way of Florence to Paris. He repaired thither once more to terminate his lawsuit with the Jesuits of Ajaccio concerning certain estates. But he died on the way, at Montpellier, in February of the year 1785, in the thirty-ninth year of his age, of the same disease of the stomach which was to prove fatal to his son Napoleon. In his dying dreams he was always thinking of Napoleon, a proof that he had rested all his hopes upon that son; he exclaimed when dying, "Where is Napoleon? why comes he not to aid his father with his great sword?" He passed away in the arms of his son Joseph. He was buried at Montpellier. When Napoleon had become emperor, the citizens of this town proposed to erect a monument to his father. But Napoleon replied that they should let the dead rest in peace; for if he were to erect a statue to his father, who was so long dead, his grandfather and his great grandfather might with the same right claim the same honour. Subsequently Louis Bonaparte, King of Holland, caused his father's body to be disinterred, and buried at St. Leu.

Napoleon was at school in Paris when his father died. This is the letter of consolation which the youth of sixteen wrote to his mother:—

"PARIS, *March* 29, 1785.

"MY DEAR MOTHER—Time has today somewhat calmed the first outbreak of my grief, and I hasten to testify to you the gratitude inspired by the goodness you have always had towards us. Console yourself, my dear mother: circumstances demand it. We shall double our solicitude and our thankfulness, and be happy if we can in any degree make up to you by our obedience for the inestimable loss of a beloved husband. I conclude, my dear mother: my grief commands me to close, entreating you at the same time to calm your own. My health is excellent, and I pray Heaven daily to bless you with a similar gift. Offer my respects to my Aunt Gertrude, Minana Saveria, Minana Fesch, &c.

"P.S.—The Queen of France has given birth to a prince, called the Duke of Normandy, on the 27th March, 7 P.M.

"Your very devoted and affectionate son,
"NAPOLEON DE BONAPARTE."

If this laconic letter of young Napoleon is genuine, it has some value.

Carlo Bonaparte was a man of brilliant parts, a clear head, ardent eloquence, and patriotism; and yet, as we have seen, he yielded to the pressure of circumstances, and possessed a certain

2 c

political prudence. He loved splendour and profusion. On his death, Madame Letitia was only thirty-five years old, and had borne him thirteen children, of whom five were dead. Jerome was a child in the cradle.

The head of the family was now Archdeacon Lucian, who administered the family property with strictness. The Bonapartes possessed some landed estates, vineyards, and herds.

CHAPTER IV.

NAPOLEON'S BOYHOOD.

I myself also am a mortal man like to all, and the offspring of him that was first made of the earth.—WISDOM OF SOLOMON, vii. 1.

THERE is a great charm in picturing to one's-self an extraordinary man as a child, at the age when he is lost among his fellows, and is still untouched by destiny. One feels tempted to discover even in the child's physiognomy the greatness of the man: but childhood is a profound mystery; and who can discover in the soul of a child, the form of the angel or the demon sleeping there—who even detect the secret force that suddenly gives form to the mighty dormant powers, seizes upon them, and gives them an existence in Time?

I saw in the Uffizj of Florence a marble bust of a boy, whose innocent childish smile attracted me, and I regarded it with pleasure. On the base was written Néro.

Of Napoleon's early childhood but little is known. His mother, Letitia, was in the church at the festival of the Assumption of the Virgin, when she felt the pangs of labour. She immediately hastened home. She had not time to reach her own room, but was delivered in the small cabinet, and, as they say, on a carpet representing scenes from the heroic story of the Iliad. Her sister-in-law, Gertrude, performed the services of a midwife. It was eleven o'clock in the morning when Napoleon came into the world.

He was not christened till the 21st July, 1771, nearly two years after his birth, and then he was baptized together with his sister Maria Anna, who died soon after. They say he struggled violently when the priest besprinkled him with holy water; perhaps he wanted to baptize himself, as he afterwards crowned himself, taking the crown out of the hands of the Pope, who was going to put it on his head.

As a boy, he displayed a violent and passionate temper, and was constantly quarrelling with his elder brother Joseph. In the boyish battle-scenes Joseph was always worsted, and, when he ran to tell of his brother, Napoleon was always pronounced in the right. At last Joseph became quite submissive to his younger brother, and the family seems even at an early time to have regarded Napoleon as the head of the children. Archdeacon Lucian, on his deathbed, said to Joseph, "Thou art the eldest of the family, but yonder is its head; thou must not forget this."

We can readily believe that the boy Napoleon displayed an irresistible passion for every thing military, and that this born soldier liked nothing better than running along beside the military in Ajaccio. The soldiers were well pleased that the little fellow should exercise beside them, and many a greybeard lifted him up and kissed him, when he joined so zealously in the drill. He teased his father with entreaties to buy him a cannon; and long subsequently they showed in the Bonaparte house the little metal cannon with which this cannon-thunder and powder-cloud gathering Zeus used to play. Soon the respect for his commands extended over the youth of Ajaccio; and, like Cyrus with the Median shepherd-children, and Peter the Great with his playmates, he formed the children of Ajaccio into a military company, which bravely took the field against the hostile youth of the Borgo of Ajaccio, and engaged in sanguinary battles with stones and wooden swords.

In the year 1778, his father placed him at the military school at Brienne, where the subsequently renowned Pichegru was his teacher. Napoleon is known to have shown himself at the outset quiet, gentle, and industrious: only occasionally his passionate temper and irritable sense of honour broke forth violently. His quartermaster one day sentenced him, for a misdemeanour, to the ignominious punishment of taking his dinner on his knees and in a woollen dress, at the door of the refectory. This the young Corsican's pride could not brook; he was sick, and suffered a nervous attack. Father Petrault, however, instantly delivered him from the punishment, complaining that his best mathematician had been condemned to such ignominious treatment.

In the year 1783, Napoleon went to finish his studies at the military school at Paris, having already had an excellent training, and having his head full of heroic pictures from his beloved Plutarch, and his heart penetrated by the deeds of his great Corsican forefathers—a youth sparkling with genius, and a fully formed character. The world was then already in a state of fermentation, and the spirit of great events marched across the canvass of history. It was a powerful time, worth living in, full of the birth-pains of coming events, and of Titanic creative fury : it gave orders to nature to form great men in her workshop.

The young officer, Napoleon Bonaparte, went to Valence to his regiment, in the year 1785. His mind, internally and undefinably excited, was feeling after an expression for its ideas. He set himself to write the prize essay of the Lyon Academy : ".What are the principles and the training that must be given to men to make them happy?"—a favourite theme in that humanistic age, which Napoleon solved anonymously. He subsequently, when emperor, threw the manuscript into the fire, Talleyrand having rummaged it up from the archives of Lyon, to flatter the potentate. So the young beatifier of the human race had to pay tribute to the influences of his age, and sentimentality, too, was a feature of those times. What would have been said if Napoleon had created a *furore* as the author of a sentimental novel in the style of Richardson and Sterne? Having undertaken a journey with his friend Demarris to Mont Cenis, and having returned with his heart agreeably excited by some tender passage 'with Mademoiselle Colombier at Valence, with whom he planned stolen rendezvous and eat most harmless cherries, Napoleon sat down to write a sentimental journey to Mont Cenis. He did not get far in it; but the very idea itself is remarkable in the soul of Napoleon. And had he not the Sorrows of Werther with him in Egypt?

Corsican as he still was, body and soul, he actually wrote at Valence a history of .the Corsicans, a fine task for a young Napoleon. The unfinished manuscript is in the library at Paris, and will now be published. Napoleon sent the manuscript to Paoli, who was an object of his admiration, and who then lived in exile in London. The following is a portion of his accompanying letter to his great countryman :—

" I was born when our country died. Three thousand French belched on to our coasts, the throne of freedom sinking in waves of blood; such was the odious spectacle which first shocked my eyes. The cries of the dying, the sighs of the oppressed, the tears of despair, surrounded my cradle from my birth.

"You left our island, and with you vanished the hope of happiness; slavery was the price of our subjection. Under the accumulated weight of the threefold chain of the soldier, the legislator, and the tax-gatherer, our countrymen lived in contempt, contemned by those who have the power of government in their hands. Is not that the cruellest torture a man possessed of feeling can suffer?

"The traitors to our country, those venal souls who are biassed by the love of filthy lucre, have disseminated calumnies against the national government, and against your person in particular, in order to justify themselves. Writers adopt them, and transmit them as truth to posterity.

"I was fired with indignation on reading them, and resolved to dispel these evils, the children of ignorance. An early commenced study of the French language, a habit of observation, and notices derived from the papers of the patriots, enabled me even to hope for some measure of success. . . . I wish to compare your administration with the existing one . . . I wish to paint the traitors to the common cause black with the pencil of shame. . . . I wish to call the rulers before the tribunal of public opinion. I wish to paint their vexatious conduct down to the smallest details, to disclose their secret courses, and, if it be possible, to interest the virtuous minister who governs the state, M. de Necker, for the lamentable fate which so cruelly oppresses us."

Such are the sentiments and such the language of Napoleon, the young Corsican, the revolutionary democrat, and the devotee of Plutarch. He says in his History of the Corsicans: "When the fatherland no longer exists, a noble-minded citizen must die." These were at that time no phrases borrowed from Tacitus; they were the glowing language of a youthful soul capable of great things. There is surely scarcely any human being, whose rapid youthful development one could follow with such enthusiastic delight as that of the young hero Napoleon, till about the Peace of Campo Formio. An extraordinary man, a demigod flies past us, untouched as yet by the defiling hand of selfishness, till the beautiful human figure by degrees goes to wreck, and is classed by us with those who were vulgar despots. For no greatness is permanent, and Macchiavelli is right when he says, "There are none but ordinary mortals."—A few more

youthful works of Napoleon's are spoken of, which are now to
be published; among them are two novels, " Le Comte d'Essex,"
and " Le Masque Prophête," a dialogue on love entitled " Giulio,"
and other literary essays.

Napoleon came to Ajaccio every year, and then made his
influence felt on the education of his brothers and sisters. This
was simple, after the manner of the country, and possessed an
old-fashioned severity. " One would have fancied one's-self living
in a college or a convent," says the work of Nasica. " Prayers,
sleep, study, recreation, amusement, walking, all this was
regulated and measured out. The greatest harmony, a tender
and sincere affection, prevailed between all the members of the
family. It was then the pattern-family of the town, as it subsequently became its ornament and glory."

Archdeacon Lucian administered the family property with
economy, and it cost young Napoleon many an effort if he
wished to receive any more money than usual from his great-
uncle for his expenses. Nevertheless, he did receive it; the whole
family felt the young man's influence, and stood under the
supremacy of this born ruler. For rule he must, and it is very
characteristic that he, the second son, schools not only his
younger brothers and sisters, but also his elder brother, and
interferes in the determination of their education. It was soon
an understood fact that Napoleon was to be obeyed.

I find an authentic letter of Napoleon to his uncle Fesch, the
subsequent cardinal, dated July 15, 1784, from Brienne. The
lad of fifteen here writes with the clearest and most intelligent
perception of the circumstances of life, about the career which
his elder brother Joseph ought to adopt. The letter is well
worth reading, particularly if it be remembered that the Joseph
who is here discussed with such anxiety, was subsequently King
of Spain.

NAPOLEON TO HIS UNCLE FESCH.

" MY DEAR UNCLE,—I write to inform you of my dear father
having passed through Brienne on his journey to Paris, for the
purpose of taking Marianne (the subsequent Eliza of Tuscany)
to St. Cyr, and restoring his own health. He arrived here on
the 21st, with Lucian and the two *demoiselles,* whom you have
seen. He left Lucian here. He is nine years old, and 3 feet,
11 inches, 10 lines high; he is in the sixth class of Latin, and
will learn the various branches of the education; he displays

much talent and good-will ; one may hope that he will turn out
well (*que ce sera un bon sujet ;* Lucian was the only one who refused to be a king). He is vigorous and healthy, lively and
thoughtless, and they are satisfied with him for a beginning.
He knows French right well, and has quite forgotten Italian.
However he will enclose a letter in mine ; I shall not tell him
any thing, that you may hear his story from himself. I hope he
will write to you oftener than when he was in Autun . . . .
I am convinced my brother Joseph has not yet written to you.
How could you demand it ? He writes two lines at the most to
my dear father, if he even still does that. In truth he is no
longer the same. To me, however, he writes very often. He is
in the class of Rhetoric ; and he would do better if he would
work, for the master told my dear father that there was in the
college (at Autun) no student of physics, rhetoric, or philosophy,
who had as much talent as he, or made so good a translation.
Touching the profession which he should select, the clerical was,
as you know, the first that he chose. He kept to this determination up to this very hour, when he desires to enter the king's
service. In this he commits a mistake, for various reasons.

"(1.) As my father remarks, he has not sufficient boldness to
oppose his front to the dangers of a battle ; his weak state of
health will not allow him to bear the toils of a campaign ; and
my brother looks at the military profession only on the side of
garrison-service. Yes, my dear brother will be an excellent gar-
rison-officer ; good !—as he has a light heart, and is consequently
a dab in frivolous compliments, he will with his talents always
cut a good figure in society : but in a battle ! that is what my
dear father questions.

> ' Qu' importe à des guerriers ces frivoles avantages?
> Que sont tous ces trésors sans celui du courage?
> A ce prix fussiez-vous aussi beau qu' Adonis,
> Du Dieu même du Pinde eussiez-vous l' loquence,
> Que sont tous ces dons sans celui de la vaillance?'

"(2.) He has received an education for the clerical profession :
it is too late to forget it. M. the Bishop of Autun would
certainly give him a wealthy benefice, and he would be sure of
becoming a bishop himself. What advantages for the family !
M. the Bishop of Autun has used all possible influence to induce
him to remain, and promised him that he shall never have cause
to repent it. In vain : he is immovable. I am well pleased if
he has a decided taste for this, the finest of all professions, and

if the great Disposer of Events (*le grand moteur des choses humaines,*) in creating him, gave him, as me, a decided inclination for military life.

"(3.) He wishes to be placed in the military; that is all very well, but in what corps? or perhaps in the marine? (4.) He understands nothing of mathematics. Two years would be required to give him instruction in this. (5.) His health will not accord with sea-life. Or perhaps in a corps of engineers? then he would need four or five years to learn what would be necessary. Moreover I think it is incompatible with the lightness of his nature to be occupied, and to work hard the whole day. The same reasoning applies to the artillery as to the engineering, with the exception that he would need to work only eighteen months in order to become an *élève*, and as much to become an officer. Oh! that is not to his taste. Let that be : he is doubtless thinking of the infantry. Very good, I understand; he wishes to have nothing to do all day, but walk the pavement. All the more, what is a petty infantry officer?—a worthless fellow for three quarters of his time. And to that neither my dear father, nor you, nor my mother, nor my uncle the Archdeacon, will consent, for he has already showed some little specimens of levity and extravagance. Consequently, we must make a last attempt to gain him for the clerical profession; if that fails, my dear father will take him with him to Corsica, where he will have him under his eye. An attempt will then be made to give him a judicial secretaryship. I conclude with the request that you will continue your kind feeling towards me; to render myself worthy of it, will be my pleasantest and most urgent duty. I am, with the profoundest respect, my dear uncle, your very devoted and very obedient servant and nephew,

"NAPOLEON DE BONAPARTE.

"P.S.—Tear up this letter.

"Nevertheless, we may hope that Joseph, with the talents he possesses, and the sentiments which his education must have inspired him with, will change his mind for the better, and be the stay of our family. I wish you would in some manner place all these advantages before his eyes."

Should one not be justified in doubting that this letter, so clear, decided, and self-conscious, is the composition of a lad of fifteen? It has never been published hitherto by any writer upon Napoleon : I found it in Tommaseo's work, "Letters of Pasquale

Paoli," who explains that he is indebted for it to Signor Luigi
Biadelli, judge of the royal tribunal of Bastia. I think it is an
invaluable document. It allows one a deep insight into the
family counsels of the Bonapartes, and brings the little tribe
vividly before one's eyes. M. Fesch, when he received the letter
with the news of the frivolous Joseph, had his woollen blouse on,
and his wooden pipe in his mouth ; for so he 'has been seen by
many eyewitnesses. Subsequently he wore a cardinal's hat,
and the frivolous Joseph was King of Spain.

One may even in this letter see Napoleon as the future tyrant
of his family. As he here provided for his brothers, and thought
of their future, so he afterwards gave them king's crowns, and
demanded unconditional obedience. Only Lucian the civilian,
and Louis King of Holland, resisted his tyranny.

CHAPTER V.

NAPOLEON A ZEALOUS DEMOCRAT.

WHENEVER Napoleon came to Ajaccio on a visit, he was fond
of living and working at Milelli, a small country-house near
Ajaccio belonging to the Bonapartes, where the old oak-tree
may still be seen under which the youth Bonaparte used to sit
and dream, or meditate.

Then came the French Revolution, the assault of the Bastile,
and the downfall of the existing state of things.

Young Napoleon threw himself into the intellectual movement
with the whole passion of his nature. But fate had reserved
him for other things than to wear himself out early in the strife
of the revolutionary parties. He lived through the first storms
of the new period at a distance from Paris, and in his little island,
as if by way of preparation for what was to follow. Corsica
became his school.

We find him in Ajaccio a young ardent revolutionist, holding
speeches in the clubs, writing addresses, helping to organize the
national guard ; in a word, playing the great politician quite in
the fashion that we know from our own experience.

Ajaccio was at that time the centre of the Corsican revolutionists; the Bonaparte house soon became their place of meeting, and the brothers Joseph and Napoleon, decided leaders of
the democracy. The little town became wild with excitement

and uproar. Its agitation seemed very dangerous to General
Barrin, who then had the command on the island ; so he sent
Gaffori's son, Marshal Francesco Gaffori, to Ajaccio, to curb
the inhabitants. Gaffori met with no success; on the contrary
he was happy to find hospitality and protection in the house of
Bacciocchi, the subsequent prince of Lucca and Piombino.

Napoleon and Joseph meanwhile assembled the democratic
party in the church of San Francesco, and drew up a letter of
congratulation to the Constituent Assembly, in which at the
same time the bitterest complaints were expressed against the
existing government of Corsica, and the demand was made that
Corsica might be declared an integral part of France.

Napoleon perceived his time come ; renouncing his Corsican
patriotism, he became a decided Frenchman, and threw himself
into the arms of the Revolution.

In the month of November, 1789, he came back to Valence,
and was soon afterwards in Ajaccio, where the active Joseph was
exerting himself to obtain an officer's commission during the
organization of the national guard. Mario Peraldi, the richest
man in Ajaccio, and opposed to the Bonaparte family, was elected
colonel of the national guard, but Joseph was appointed officer.

In the mean time a proposition had been entertained in Corsica,
of recalling the exiles ; and on the instigation of the brothers
Bonaparte, and of Abbate Coti, the Corsican national assembly
appointed four deputies, who should meet Pasquale Paoli in
France, and escort him to the island ; one of these was Mario
Peraldi, and both Napoleon and Joseph attached themselves to
the deputation.

When Paoli came to Paris, the Constituante had already,
Dec. 1, 1789, decreed the incorporation of Corsica in France,
which decree had for ever put an end to her political independence. This motion was proposed by Mirabeau and the Corsican
Saliceti, who was a deputy of the *tiers état*, and subsequently
became noted as a statesman, and Murat's minister at Naples.

Napoleon himself hastened to welcome Paoli at Marseille, and
was witness of the tears of joy that the noble patriot shed when
he once more trod his native soil at Cape Corso. A national
assembly met at Orezza to deliberate upon and organize the
affairs of the island. Napoleon and his enemy, young Carlo
Andrea Pozzo di Borgo, here won their first spurs as public
speakers at the election meetings. Even for his father's sake
Napoleon could not fail to excite the interest of Paoli, who,

astonished at the sparkling genius and the brilliant judgment of the young man, is said to have predicted of him, " This young man will have a career; he only needs opportunity to become a man of Plutarch." They have a story, that Pasquale, stopping at a *locanda* and finding the rooms in disorder, received from the landlord the explanation of the circumstance, that a young man named Bonaparte had lodged there before him, who was always writing and tearing his papers up again, day and night, pacing restlessly up and down, and that he had then gone off to the battle-field of Ponte Nuovo.

Young Napoleon spared no machinations to aid his brother Joseph in obtaining the presidency of the district of Ajaccio; he traversed the localities in the district as a dexterous partisan, canvassed the voters and expended money.

In Ajaccio he was indefatigably active in keeping up the ardour of the Republican Club, and gaining a victory over the priests and aristocrats. There was a sanguinary contest in the town between the two parties, in which Napoleon was in danger of his life, and an officer of the national guard was killed at his side. He relates the circumstances of the affair in a manifesto drawn up by himself. The bloodshed lasted for several days, and Joseph's and Napoleon's lives were several times at stake.

Napoleon was the soul of the Ajaccio club. Like the young politicians of our most recent times, we see him hurling a fulminating address at an aristocrat. The latter was Count Matteo Buttafuoco, the same who had invited Rousseau to Vescovato, and, being in the French service at the time of the Corsican War of Independence, lent his arm to his country's enemy against his own countrymen. He was a deputy of the Corsican aristocracy, and had voted against the meeting of the Estates at Versailles, and in other ways rendered himself odious by his aristocratic votes. Against this person young Napoleon, in his country-house at Milelli, wrote a manifesto, which he had printed at Dôle and sent to the Ajaccio club. This pompous pamphlet, talented and poetical, but grounded on a firm basis of facts, is a remarkable contribution to the history of Napoleon. It has all the eccentric and ambitious flight of phraseology of the young revolutionists; and when I read it, in this out of the world Ajaccio, it vividly roused in me memories of the years 1848 and 1849. But it is more than a mere young demagogue's pamphlet; it is a rehearsal for the imperial edicts; it is the Emperor himself in his first flight. This manifesto cannot be dispensed with by any one who desires to learn Napoleon's growth and nature from the period of his youthful development.

" LETTER FROM M. BONAPARTE TO M. MATTEO BUTTAFUOCO,
" *Deputy for Corsica at the National Assembly.*

" SIR,—From Bonifazio to Cape Corso, from Ajaccio to Bastia, there is only one chorus of execrations against you. Your friends conceal themselves, your relatives ignore you, and even the intelligent man, who never allows himself to be tutored by the popular opinion, is this time drawn in to the stream of universal exasperation.

" What have you done? What are the crimes that can justify so universal an ill-will, so complete a desertion? This, sir, is what I now desire to sift to the bottom; and to do that I shall make use of the light afforded me by yourself.

" The history of your life, at least since you have been cast upon the stage of public affairs, is notorious. Your main features are there traced in characters of blood. Still, there are less generally known details; I may therefore commit mistakes, but I count upon your forbearance and your correction.

" Having entered the service of France, you came back to see your native country; you found tyrants put down, a national government established, and the Corsicans, inspired by grand sentiments, emulating one another in the sacrifices they daily offered to the public weal. You did not allow yourself to be seduced by the universal ferment; so far from that, you only heard with condescending commiseration this prate about Father-land, Freedom, Independence, Constitution, with which even the meanest of our field-labourers was puffed up. Profound meditation had taught you what value to set on these artificial sentiments, which are kept up only to the general detriment. In truth, the peasant must labour, and not play the hero, if he is not to die of hunger—if he is to bring up his family, and respect the constituted authority. As to the persons who, by their rank and their good fortune, are called to the position of governors, it is impossible that they should for long be so stupid as to sacrifice their convenience and their dignity to a chimera, and that they should stoop to pay court to a cobbler, that they may have the satisfaction of playing the part of Brutus. Still, when you lighted on the idea of fettering Paoli, you were forced to dissimulate M. Paoli was the centre of all movements of the body politic. We will not deny him talent, nor even a certain kind of genius; he brought the affairs of the island, for a time, into a good position; he founded a university, where those sciences which promote the development of our intellectual powers are taught among our mountains—perhaps for the first time since creation; he instituted an iron foundry, powder mills, and fortifications, which enhanced our means of defence; he opened harbours, which raised agriculture by encouraging commerce; he created a marine, which favoured our communications while it inflicted injuries upon our enemies. The rise of all these institutions was only a token of what he would have created in future. Unity, peace, and freedom were the harbingers of natural prosperity, if a badly organized government, built upon false foundations, had not been a still surer token of the evil fortune into which the nation might have been plunged.

" Paoli's dream was to play the Solon, but he copied his model badly. He put every thing into the hands of the people or their representatives, so that no one could exist without their good pleasure—a curious error, which subjects to a brutal day-labourer a man who, by his education, his distinguished birth, and his prosperity, is made for a sole ruler. In the long run, such a palpable inversion of reason cannot fail to induce the ruin and dissolution of the body politic, after involving it in anarchy by all sorts of evils.

" You succeeded to your heart's desire. M. Paoli, incessantly surrounded by enthusiasts and giddy heads, could not conceive that any one could possess any other passion than the fanaticism of freedom and independence. You gained certain French introductions to him, and hé did not take time to sift your moral principles more finely than your words. He caused you to be appointed to negotiate at Versailles, about the treaty which was in course of being concluded by the mediation of that court. M. de Choiseul saw you, and recognised your character. Souls of a certain stamp may be appreciated at a glance. Soon you were converted from the representative of a free people into the clerk of a satrap; you communicated to him all the instructions, the projects, and the secrets of the Cabinet of Corte.

" This conduct, which people have considered mean and shameless, I, for my part, consider perfectly simple; but in every kind of affair.it is important to understand and to pass one's judgment with *sang froid.*

" The prude condemns the coquette, and is quizzed on account thereof; that is your history comprised in a couple of words.

" A man of principle judges you in the most severe manner ; but you do not believe in men of principle. The ordinary man, who is constantly influenced by virtuous demagogues, cannot be appreciated by you who do not believe in virtue. One can pass sentence on you only through your own principles, as on a criminal through the laws : but those who understand *raffinement* say your actions discover you to be a great simpleton ; this then issues in what I have already said, that in every species of affair one should first understand, and then calmly pass judgment. Still, you can defend yourself no less triumphantly, for you have never craved the exalted dignity of a Cato ; you are satisfied with being on a par with a certain worldly society; and in that worldly society it is a received maxim, that he who can have money and does not use it, is a simpleton ; for money procures all gratification of the senses, and sensual gratification is the only thing to be prized. Thus M. de Choiseul, who was very liberal, allowed you to offer no opposition when your absurd country, with her amusing ways, paid you for your services by the honour of being permitted to serve her.

"When the treaty of Compiègne was concluded, M. de Chauvelin landed with twenty-four battalions upon our coasts. M. de Choiseul, who was greatly concerned in the promptness of the expedition, became so restless that he could not conceal from you his agitation. You advised him to send you hither with a few millions. You promised to subject all the country to him without let or hindrance, as Philip took cities with his ass. . . No sooner said than done; and you, hastening over the sea, threw off the mask, and, with your gold and your diploma of favour in your hand, entered into negotiations with those whom you deemed the most accessible.

" The Corsican cabinet could not conceive that a Corsican could love himself more than his country, and it had charged you with its interests. You, for your part, not conceiving that a person could *not* love money and himself more than his country, sold yourself, and hoped to buy all your countrymen in the same way. Reformed moralist, you know what every one's fanaticism was good for ; the varieties of character were shaded off in your eyes as a few pounds of gold more or less.

"Nevertheless, you deceived yourself; the weak were indeed shaken, but they were horrified at the dreadful idea of lacerating the bosom of their native country. Each fancied he saw his father, brother, or friend, who had fallen in the country's defence, raising his gravestone to stifle him with curses. These absurd prejudices were powerful enough to arrest you in your course. You sighed to think that you had to do with a childish people; but, sir, this refinement of sentiment is not given to the multitude, which lives thus in poverty and wretchedness, whilst the sagacious man knows how to rise rapidly as soon as ever circumstances are in any degree favourable to him. That is pretty nearly the moral of your history.

" On trying to account for the impediments that opposed the realisation of your promises, you made a proposal to send the Royal-Corse regiment hither. You hoped that its example would correct our too honest and simple-minded peasants, and that it would accustom them to a thing which they found so much repugnant to their ideas. In this hope, too, you were disappointed : for did not the Rossi, the Marengos, and some other fools, inspire this regiment with such enthusiasm, that the entire body of officers declared by an authentic deed that they would rather throw up their commissions than violate their oaths, or duties more sacred still ?

" You found yourself reduced to your own solitary example. Nothing daunted, you marched to Vescovato at the head of a few friends and a French detachment ; but the redoubtable Clement drove them out of the place. You retired to Bastia with your family and the companions of your adventure. This little affair brought you but small honour ; your house and those of your companions were burnt down. In your place of security you laughed at these sallies of impotence.

" They here boldly charge you with having intended to arm the Royal-Corse against their brothers. They likewise deny your courage, on account of the slight resistance you offered at Vescovato. These accusations are hardly well-founded ; for the first is only an immediate deduction, as being a means for the execution of your projects ; and as we have maintained your course of action to have been that of a simpleton, it follows that this collateral accusation is annulled. As regards the want of courage, I do not see that the action of Vescovato confirms that charge; for you did not go there to conduct a war in good earnest, but by your example to encourage those who were already wavering in their steadfastness to the opposite party. And then, what right had any one to expect that you would peril the fruit of two years' good conduct, and let yourself be killed like a common soldier? But surely you must have been

excited when you saw your house and the houses of your friends
becoming a prey to the flames ? Why, good God ! When will
these narrow-minded men cease to try to find a meaning in every
thing ? In allowing your house to be burned to the ground, you
compelled M. de Choiseul to give you an indemnification. Experience has confirmed the correctness of your calculation ; you
have been paid far beyond the value of your lost property. It
is true, a complaint is made that you claimed all advantages for
yourself, and gave only a mere trifle to the poor people whom
you had seduced from their country's cause. To understand what
you were justified in doing, it is only necessary to know whether
it could be done with safety : now, poor people, who stood in such
great need of your protection, were neither in a position to claim
compensation, nor even to perceive with clearness the injury
done to them; they could not play the part of malecontents and
revolt against your authority : odious as they were to their
countrymen, their return would not have been even safe. It
stands to reason then, that if you sent them a few thousand
dollars, they would not let them slip out of their hand ; that
would have been sheer stupidity.

" The French, defeated in spite of their gold, their patents of
nobility, the discipline of their numerous battalions, the lightness of their squadrons, the dexterity of their artillery, and
annihilated at Penta, at Vescovato, at Oreto, San Nicolao, Borgo,
Borbaggio, and Oletta, entrenched themselves extremely dispirit-
ed. The winter, the time of their repose, was for you, sir, the time
of greatest execution : and if you were unable to triumph over
the obstinacy of the prejudices which have taken deep root in the
mind of the people, you yet succeeded in seducing a few of their
leaders, whom you managed, though with difficulty, to estrange
from their honourable sentiments; and this, taken together with
the thirty battalions led by M. de Vaux in the following spring,
brought Corsica under the yoke, and forced Paoli and his most
enthusiastic adherents to retire.

" One portion of the patriots had fallen during the defence of
their independence ; another had fled a proscribed land, now the
loathsome nest of tyrants ; but a large number had been permitted neither to die nor to fly—they became an object of
persecution. Souls that had resisted all corruption, were of a
far different stamp from willing subjects. The French dominion
could be cemented only on their complete annihilation. Alas !
this plan was only too literally carried out. Some died as victims

of fictitious crimes ; others, betrayed by the hospitality and confidence they had appealed to, breathed out their last sighs upon the scaffold, suppressing their tears. Locked up in great numbers in the prison of Toulon by the agency of Narbonne-Fritzlar, poisoned by bad diet, tortured by their chains, overwhelmed with most ignominious ill-treatment, they lived for some time in the convulsions of the death-struggle, only to see death approaching with his slow march. . . . O God! witness of their innocence, why hast thou not constituted thyself their avenger ?

"In this universal misery, in the midst of the cries and sighing of this unhappy nation, you began, however, to enjoy the fruit of your labours. Honours, dignities, and pensions rained upon you; and your possessions would have multiplied at a still more rapid rate, if Mad. Dubarry, effecting the fall of M. de Choiseul, had not deprived you of a protector and appreciator of your services. The blow did not dishearten you; you appeared again in the service of the *bureaux;* you only recognised the necessity of being more active than ever. They felt flattered by this conduct; your services were so notorious! . . . Every thing was conceded to you. Not content with the pond of Biguglia, you demanded a portion of the lands of several communes. 'Why did you desire to deprive these of their own?' people ask. I for my part ask, what consideration could you be expected to feel towards a nation which you knew abominated you?

"Your favourite project was to divide the island among ten barons. What! not satisfied with having aided in riveting chains on your native land, you wished to subject it besides to the absurd feudal system? But I praise you for inflicting upon the Corsicans the greatest evil possible to you; you were in a state of war with them, and it is an axiom in war to do mischief that redounds to one's own advantage.

"But pass we by all these miseries; let us now come to the present time, and conclude a letter which will not fail to weary you by its terrible length.

"The state of things in France prognosticated extraordinary events; you feared a reaction in Corsica. The same madness that possessed us before the war, now began, to your great mortification, to put these amiable people beside themselves. You foresaw the possible consequences of this: if noble sentiments should rule public opinion, you from an honest man would be-

2 D

come a vile traitor, and even worse, if our warm-hearted fellow-citizens should have their blood got up by the influence of noble sentiments; for if a national government should ever result therefrom, what would become of you? So your conscience began to make you uneasy. Though alarmed and downcast, you did not give yourself up for lost; you resolved to stake every thing for every thing, but this you did as a man of intellect. You took a wife to strengthen the hold you possessed. A gentleman who, on the strength of your word, had given his sister to your nephew, saw himself outwitted: for your nephew, whose property inherited from his father was seized upon by you to augment an inheritance that ought to have been his entire, found himself with a numerous family reduced to distress.

"Having thus ordered your domestic affairs, you cast a glance at the country. You saw it reeking with the blood of its martyrs, covered with many a victim, and breathing nought but thoughts of revenge on every side. But you saw the savage soldier, the impudent writer, and the greedy tax-gatherer holding uncontested rule here; and the Corsican, pressed by the weight of these triple chains, not daring to think what he was, or what he might yet become. In the joy of your heart you said to yourself, 'Matters are going well; we have only to keep them in this state;' and you formed a union immediately with the soldier, the writer, and the farmer of the taxes. The problem was no other than that of managing matters so as to have deputies inspired by these sentiments; for, as concerning yourself, you could not imagine that a nation hating you would choose *you* as its representative. But you were destined to alter your opinion of your chance, when the papers of electoral qualification, by a possibly intentional absurdity, determined that the deputy of the nobility was to be elected in an assembly composed of only twenty-two persons. The only thing was, then, to gain twelve votes. Your confederates of the supreme council were active in the extreme—menaces, promises, blandishments, money, every thing was called in requisition; you succeeded. Your adherents were not so fortunate in the communes; one president lost his election; and two men, enthusiasts for their ideas—one was son, brother, and nephew of the stanchest defender of the popular cause; the other had seen Sionville and Narbonne, and, while he sighed over his own powerlessness, his soul was full of the horrors he had seen perpetrated—these two men were proclaimed, and they anticipated the wishes of the nation, whose hopes were fixed upon them. The secret ill-will, the rage, which took hold of every one on your election, does honour to your manœuvres, and the credit of your confederates.

" On arriving at Versailles you became a zealous royalist; in Paris you saw with evident regret, that the government which they were endeavouring to establish on the ruins of so much, was the very same which they had annihilated among us with such bloodshed.

" The efforts of bad men were impotent; the new constitution, admired by all Europe, has become the interest of every thinking being. There was only one means of escape left to you, and that was to get it believed that this constitution was not adapted to our island; although it was the very same which had worked out such good results, and which it had cost so much blood to wrest from us.

" All the deputies of the old administration, who naturally entered into your cabals, served you with all the warmth of personal interest. *Mémoires* were composed, the authors of which pretended to discover the advantages possessed for us by the existing government, and represented any alteration to be opposed to the wish of the nation. At this juncture the town of Ajaccio got wind of what was doing; it roused itself, formed a national guard, and organized a committee. This unexpected incident put you in a fright. The ferment spread on every side. You persuaded the minister, of whom you had the advantage in knowledge of the affairs of Corsica, that it was necessary to send thither your father-in-law, M. Gaffori, as a worthy precursor of M. Narbonne, who had the impudence to try by force, and at the head of his troops, to uphold the tyranny which his deceased father of glorious memory had, by his genius, defeated and prostrated. Innumerable blunders left the mediocrity of your father-in-law's talents no secret; he possessed only the art of making enemies. On all sides the people gathered against him. In this pressing danger you raised your eyes, and saw Narbonne. Availing himself of a favourable moment, Narbonne had formed the design of riveting the despotism which troubled his conscience, on an island which he had desolated by unheard-of cruelties. You seconded him; the plan is laid; five thousand men have received their orders; the decrees to augment the regiment of the province by one battalion, have been sent off; Narbonne has started. This poor nation, without arms and without courage,

is hopelessly and helplessly delivered into the hands of him who
has already been its executioner.

" O ye ill-fated fellow-citizens ! of what hateful intrigue were
ye the destined victims? ye would have seen it when it was too
late. What means were there of resisting, unarmed, ten thousand
men ? Ye would have subscribed the documents of your degra-
dation with your own hands, hope would have fled, or hope would
have been stifled, and days of disaster would have succeeded
one another without ceasing. Free France would have regarded
you with contempt, grieved Italy with anger ; and Europe,
astonished at this unexampled profound debasement, would have
expunged from her annals those virtuous traits that do honour
to your character. But your communal deputies fathomed the
design, and gave you warning in good time. A king who constantly desired only the happiness of his people, enlightened on
the subject by M. Lafayette, that stanch friend of liberty,
found means of annihilating the intrigues of a perfidious minister,
who was continually instigated by revenge to damage you.
Ajaccio in its address showed itself in earnest ; with so much
energy was the wretched condition there portrayed, into which
the most despotic government had brought you. Bastia, which
had slumbered till then, awoke at the sound of danger, and took
up arms with that resolution which has ever distinguished it.
Arena came from Paris to the Balagna, full of those sentiments
which render people capable of undertaking every thing, and
fearing no danger. With arms in one hand, and the decrees of
the national assembly in the other, he made his avowed enemies
turn pale. Achille Murati, the conqueror of Capraja, who had
spread despair even to Genoa, who only wanted circumstances
and a wider field to become a Turenne, reminded the companions
of his glory that it was time to gain it once more ; that in times
of danger the country needed not intrigues which it could not
understand, but fire and steel. At the sound of so universal a
shock, Gaffori relapsed into the nothingness from which intrigue
had drawn him forth against his will. He quaked with fear
in the fortress of Corte. Narbonne hastened away from Lyon,
to bury his shame and his infernal designs in Rome. A few
days after, Corsica is tied to France, and Paoli recalled ; and the
prospect, changed in one moment, now offers you a career which
you would never have dared to hope for.

" Forgive me, sir, forgive me ! I took up my pen to defend
you, but my heart has forcibly revolted against a system which

brought treachery and perfidy in its train. And how, son of
this same fatherland, have you never felt any feelings towards
it? And how was your heart then unmoved at the sight of
the rocks,' the trees, the houses, the districts which were the
scenes of the sports of your childhood? When you came into
the world, this country bore you on its bosom, and nourished
you with its fruits. When you came to years of discretion, it
rested its hopes on you, honoured you with its confidence, and
said to you, 'My son, thou seest the wretched condition to which
I have been reduced by the injustice of men, gathering myself
up with the force of passion, I am regaining the powers which
promise me a sure and infallible recovery; but I am menaced
anew—hasten, my son, hasten to Versailles, enlighten the great
king as to my state, dispel his suspicions, and pray him for his
friendship.'

"Well! a little gold made you a traitor to your country's confidence; and for a little gold you were soon seen, with a parri-
cidal sword in your hand, rending your country's inwards.
O, sir! I am far from wishing you any ill; but be apprehensive
. . . . there are stings of conscience that act the part of
avengers. Your fellow-citizens, whom you abominate, will enlighten France upon their cause. Your estates and pensions,
the fruit of your treacheries, will be taken from you. In the
decrepitude of age and misery, in the horrible solitude of crime,
you will live long enough to be tormented by your conscience.
The father will point you out to his son, the teacher to his pupil,
saying to them; 'Youths, learn to honour your country, virtue,
fidelity, humanity!'

"And you; whose youth, beauty, and innocence is thus prostituted. whose pure and chaste heart trembles at the touch of a
felon's hand! estimable and unhappy wife! . . . .

"Soon the chain of honour and the pageantry of riches will
vanish; the contempt of mankind will be heaped upon you.
Shall you seek any consolation in the breast of him who is the
author of all this—of him whom your gentle and loving soul cannot live without? Shall you seek tears in his eyes to mingle
them with your own? Will your quivering hand, laid upon
his heart, endeavour to tell him of the agitation of your own?
Ah! if you find tears in his eyes, they will be those of the pangs
of conscience. If his heart throbs, it will be with the convulsions of the wicked man who dies cursing nature, himself, and
the hand that guides him.

"O Lameth! O Robespierre! O Petion! O Volney! O Mirabeau! O Barnave! O Bailley! O Lafayette! see, that is the
man who presumes to sit by your side. Dripping with his
brethren's blood, defiled by crimes of every sort, he boldly presents himself in a general's uniform, the unrighteous wages of
his villanies! He dares to call himself representative of the
nation, he who has sold it, and ye suffer it! He dares to raise
his eyes to listen to your discourses, and ye suffer it! He never
had more than the voice of twelve noblemen, if *that* is called the
voice of the people. If that is the voice of the people, Ajaccio,
Bastia, and the majority of the cantons, should have done to his
effigy what they would have done to his person.

"But ye, who are seduced by the error of the moment, or
perchance by the abuse of the minute, to oppose the new changes,
can ye suffer a traitor, one who beneath the cold outside of an
intelligent man conceals the greed of a lacquey? I cannot
think it. You will be the first to expel him with shame and
ignominy, as soon as you shall have been enlightened concerning
the tissue of villanies of which he has been the artist.

"I have the honour, sir, to be your very submissive and
very obedient servant,

                                        " BONAPARTE.

"*From my Cabinet of Milelli, January 23,
            Year Two.*"

" From my Cabinet of Milelli!"—it sounds quite imperial. One
must confess this bold, unsparing, violent letter of the youth of
twenty-one—half a Robespierre, half a Marat—to be by no
means inferior to the best pamphlets of the revolutionary eloquence.

I will notice here, that of the six Corsican deputies at the
Convention, three voted for the detention of Louis Capet for
life, two for detention until the peace, and banishment afterwards,
and Cristoforo Saliceto alone for death.

CHAPTER VI.

NAPOLEON'S LAST ACTIVITY IN CORSICA.

IN the year 17,91, two battalions were to be formed in Corsica. The soldiers were to appoint their chiefs themselves. It is curious to observe how Napoleon, the subsequent Cæsar, esteemed it the highest honour, and an almost unattainable piece of good fortune, to raise himself to be chief of a battalion. The difficulties were very great, as was the energy of the young candidate. He was opposed by the most distinguished men of Ajaccio, Cuneo, Lodovico Ornano. Ugo Peretti, Matteo Pozzo di Borgo, and the wealthy Mario Peraldi. Peraldi made Napoleon appear in a ridiculous light, and scoffed at his figure, his stature, and his small prospects. Napoleon, quite enraged at this conduct, challenged him. Peraldi accepted the duel. His rival waited till evening for him at the beautiful little chapel of the Greeks, pacing impatiently up and down; but Peraldi never appeared, for his relations had prevented the duel.

When one now goes to the chapel of the Greeks, whence there is a very beautiful prospect of the town and the gulf, one perceives a small Ionic temple up on the hill near the shore, to one side. I inquired its meaning, and was told it was the monument of the Peraldi. Mario, Napoleon's rival candidate for a majority, lies buried there. His family has left behind it no other celebrity but that of being one of the wealthiest in Corsica.

Madame Letitia sacrificed half her fortune to procure for her beloved son the command of the battalion. Her house was always open to Napoleon's numerous party, and her table always spread. In the chambers and on the floor, mattresses always lay ready to give night quarters to the armed adherents. They lived there as in a state of defence against the Vendetta. The position was a dangerous one. Napoleon was never so highly wrought up as during that period; he slept not at nights, and by day he paced restlessly up and down in the rooms, or took counsel with Abbé Fesch and his partisans. He was meditative and pale; his eyes full of fire, and his soul full of passion. Perhaps he advanced with greater coolness towards the consulate and the empire, than towards the rank of a major of the national guard of Ajaccio.

The commissioner who was to preside over the election arrived, and lodged in the Peraldis' house. This was terrible. So, on the 18th Brumaire they determined on the execution of a little *coup d' état.* The Napoleon party armed themselves; the wild and insolent Bagaglino, a partisan of Napoleon, armed to the teeth, pushes by night into the house of the Peraldi, where they are sitting at table with the commissioner. " Madame Letitia desires to speak with you," cries Bagaglino in a menacing tone, " but instantly."—The commissioner follows him, the Peraldi not daring to withhold him: the Napoleonists carry off their guest, and force him to take up his quarters in the Casa Bonaparte, under the pretext that he was not free with the Peraldis. This *coup d' état* displays Napoleon all ready-made.

The Casa Bonaparte now held itself in a state of war, but Peraldi ventured to do nothing. Now came the day of the election. It was to be held in the church of San Francesco. There was a stormy scene, and Geronimo Pozzo di Borgo was pulled down from the speaker's chair, and with difficulty protected against violence. The result of the election was this: Quenza, of the Napoleon party, became the first commander, and Napoleon next to him, the second. The victory was almost complete, and the unattainable goal almost attained; Napoleon was second commander of a battalion!

From this time Napoleon lived entirely in his battalion, of which he was the soul. Here he passed through practical military studies before he ever went to the field, as he had passed through the school of a politician in the club of Ajaccio. The variance increased meanwhile from day to day, between the opposite party, that of the aristocrats and priest-ridden citizens, and the national battalion. From the present Corsican mountaineers one may form a tolerable idea of the appearance and the nature of the Quenza-Napoleon battalion. Not without reason must the Ajaccio citizen have feared this troop of mountaineers undergoing drill. On Easter-day of the year 1792, it came to a sanguinary battle between the people of Ajaccio and the battalion. This fell out on the Diamond Square, and lasted several days with much bloodshed, without either the civil authorities or the military commander, Maillard, interposing. Napoleon happily escaped all danger. When the storm was allayed, he composed a letter of justification in the name of his battalion, and addressed it to the department, to the minister of war, and to the legislative. Whereupon three commissioners made their appearance in Ajaccio, who gave a favourable report of the conduct of the battalion; but it was removed away from Ajaccio. Napoleon went to Corte, where Paoli received him with coldness.

In the May of the same year he travelled to Paris, to fetch his sister Eliza from St. Cyr. There he was surprised by the subversion of the existing state of things, which dashed the prospects of military promotion that he had hoped to realize in Paris. His passionate Corsican nature was so violently convulsed thereby, that. he is said to have entertained thoughts of suicide. He worked himself free of them in a dialogue on suicide. He left Paris soon after the terrible 2nd September, and returned to Corsica.

Thus at the time when Dumouriez was filling the world with astonishment at the first feats of arms of the young republic, the man who was destined to change the face of Europe was wearing out his strength in the wild island of Corsica, in keeping his ground against the cabals of his adversaries, and in forging cabals of his own, and was exposing his life daily to the perils of the dagger and the blunderbuss. Having again arrived at Corte, he was dismissed with severity by General Paoli. Their courses were henceforth completely divergent; for in the soul of young Bonaparte other wishes were now uppermost, than the desire of treading in the footsteps of the noble patriot. Had he done so, and had his heart retained its fire for the freedom of Corsica, then perhaps at this day a wild herdsman would have pointed out to me some place of terror on the mountains, and said, " See, here fell the great Corsican chief, Napoleon Bonaparte; he was almost as powerful a hero as Sampiero."

Paoli gave Napoleon orders to repair to Bonifazio, to attach himself to the expedition against Sardinia. Napoleon yielded a surly obedience.

He remained eight months at Bonifazio, to make the necessary arrangements, so far as they had been committed to him. On the 22nd January, one day after the execution of Louis Capet, Napoleon was near losing his life at Bonifazio. Some marines, a frantic rabble from Marseille, were come on shore, where they started a row with the Corsican battalion, and, when Napoleon hastened up to restore peace, they received him with roars of ça ira, and cried that he was an aristocrat; then, rushing upon him, they would have hung him up on the lamp-post, only the maire, people, and soldiers, succeeded in putting the noisy band to the rout.

The attempt upon Sardinia, commenced under Truguet's command, to terrify the court of Turin, was a complete failure. People affirm Paoli to have laboured to secure its ill-success. Although he had placed a thousand men of the national guard under the command of his most intimate friend, Colonna-Cesari, he said to Cesari, as the latter himself subsequently related, " Remember, Cesari, that Sardinia is the natural ally of our island; that she has provided us with provisions and ammunition under all circumstances; and that the king of Piedmont has ever been the friend of the Corsicans and their cause." The squadron commanded by Colonna at length left the harbour of Bonifazio, and sailed towards the island of Santa Maddalena. Napoleon was under the immediate orders of Colonna, charged with the artillery; he was burning with impatience, for it was his first feat of arms. He sprung ashore one of the first, and hurled a hand-grenade with his own hand into the little town of Maddalena. But his excellent dispositions had no result; the Sards made a sally, and Colonna instantly sounded a retreat.

Young Napoleon wept with rage, and remonstrated violently with Colonna; and on the latter paying no attention to his words, he turned to some officers and said, " He does not understand me." Colonna thereupon put him down, saying with authority, " You are an impudent fellow!" The young born soldier knew his duty, and silently betook himself to his post. " He is a horse for parade, and no more," he said subsequently. Thus, Napoleon's first deed of arms was unfortunate, unvictorious, and a retreat.

On his return to Bonifazio he heard that Paoli, who now found himself obliged to throw off the mask, had dissolved the Quenza battalion. This happened in the spring of the year 1793, at the time when the Convention sent Saliceti, Delcher, and Lacombe as its commissioners to the island. Lucian Bonaparte and Bartolommeo Arena had denounced Paoli. Napoleon, however, had no share in the denunciation; on the contrary, the memory of his father and his own generosity rather prompted him to defend his great fellow-countryman. He himself wrote Paoli's Apology, and sent it to the Convention;—an act which does him honour. This remarkable paper is extant, though imperfect in one or two places; in the form in which it lies before me, I

consider it as Napoleon's first rough draft, from which he would
have subsequently moulded an elegant whole.

" REPRESENTATIVES!—You are the true organs of popular
sovereignty. All your decrees are dictated by the nation, or
executed immediately by it. Every one of your laws is a boon,
and earns you a new claim to the thanks of posterity, which to
you owes the republic, and to that of the world, which from you
will date its freedom.

" A single one of your decrees has deeply dejected the citizens
of the town of Ajaccio; that which bids a feeble old man of
seventy to drag himself to the bar of your house, and puts him
for the moment beside the godless destructionist and the venal
aspirer to honour.

" And can Paoli be a destructionist or a selfish aspirer to
honour?

" A seditious agitator! and wherefore? Peradventure to
revenge himself on the family of the Bourbons, whose *perfidious
policy* loaded his country with misery, and *forced him into exile?*
But did not the former terminate with the tyranny, and have
not you satiated his resentment, if he still cherishes any, in
Louis's blood?

" A seditious agitator! and wherefore? Peradventure with
the view of restoring an aristocracy of *nobility* and *priests?*—he,
who from his thirteenth year . . . . . . he who immediately
upon coming to the head of affairs, *destroyed feudalism,* and
knew no other distinction than that of the citizen?—he who,
thirty years ago, fought against Rome and was *excommunicated*
[this is incorrect,] who seized upon the property of the bishops
to give it away, ... to Venice, ... in Italy . . . .

" A seditious agitator! and wherefore?—with the view of
delivering Corsica to England?—he who would not deliver it to
France notwithstanding the offers of Chauvelin, who was not
sparing of titles and favours?

" Deliver Corsica to England! what would he gain were he
to be living in the mud of London ? why then did he not remain
when he was actually exiled there ?

" Paoli a self-seeker ! If Paoli *is* a self-seeker, *what can he
desire more?* He is the object of the affection of his fellow
countrymen, who deny him nothing; *he is at the head of the*

army; and it is the eve of the day on which he will have to defend the country against a hostile attack.

" If Paoli was ambitious, he has gained every thing from the republic: and if he showed himself attached to . . . . . . since the Constituent Assembly sat, what must he do *now, when the people is all in all?*

" Paoli ambitious! Representatives, when the French were governed by a corrupt court, when there was no belief in virtue or patriotism, one must doubtless have said Paoli was ambitious. *We have made war on tyrants; this is supposed not to have been from love of our country, but from the ambition of our leaders !* In Coblenz, then, Paoli must be supposed ambitious; but in Paris, *in the centre of French freedom,* Paoli must, if rightly understood, be deemed the patriarch of the French Republic; *so posterity will think;* so the people believes. Follow my resolution, and let the calumny be silenced, and the fundamentally corrupted men who use it as a means. Representatives! Paoli is more than an old man of seventy; he is feeble, too! But for this he would have gone to your bar to confound his enemies. *We owe every thing to him,* even the happiness of being a French republic at all. He constantly enjoys our confidence. As regarding him, revoke your decree of the 2nd April, and restore joy to this whole nation." . . . .

Soon after, however, the young revolutionist fell out with Paoli completely, and to the most deadly extreme of hostility. The aged patriot found in the young man the most vehement opponent, not of his person, but of his ideas. They say Paoli at that time did not yet quite understand Napoleon, and that he hinted to him that he was engaged in a design for severing Corsica from France, and forming a connexion with England. Napoleon started up in a rage at hearing this, and Paoli was fired with passionate hatred of Napoleon. Pasquale's adherents were very numerous, and the fortress of Ajaccio was in the hands of his friend Colonna. Paoli and Pozzo di Borgo, then attorney-general, accordingly, cited before the Convention, bade defiance to the summons, and now lived under the ban of the Convention, and in open war against the French.

The three representatives now appointed Bonaparte inspector-general of the Corsican artillery, and entrusted to him the task of conquering the citadel of Ajaccio. He attempted; but all his efforts to force the fortress of his native town were frustrated.

Fortune had grown no laurels for Napoleon in Corsica. During this enterprise his life was in extreme danger. He occupied the tower of Capitello, on the gulf of Ajaccio, with a garrison of about fifty men, to carry on his operations by land from this centre, whilst the ships of war bombarded the citadel from the sea. A storm drove the fleet out of the gulf, and Napoleon remained alone in the tower, supporting life on horse-flesh, cut off from his fleet and reduced to the defensive, till some shepherds from the mountains rescued him from his position, and enabled him to regain the fleet by water.

Disheartened at his failure, he set out towards Bastia by land. But he learnt on the way that his life was threatened, Mario Peraldi having instigated the people to arrest him and deliver him to Paoli, who would have him shot as soon as ever he could get hold of him. At Vivario he was harboured by the priest, and at Bocagnano, rescued with extreme difficulty by his friends from popular violence; he concealed himself in a room, and escaped through a window into the road by night. He got off safe to Ajaccio. But being still more vigorously menaced here, he escaped from his house to a cavern near the chapel of the Greeks, where he held himself concealed for one night. His friends at length embarked him safely, and he reached Bastia by sea. The rage of the Paolists meanwhile was directed against Napoleon's family. Madame Letitia, alarmed at the indications of approaching danger, fled with her children to Milelli, attended by a few faithful *paesani* from Bastelica and Bocognano. With her were Louis, Eliza, Paolina, and Abbé Fesch; Jerome and Caroline remained concealed in the Ramolinos' house. Not secure at Milelli, the terrified family fled in the night towards the sea near the tower of Capitello, in hopes of being able to await there the arrival of the French fleet, which was announced. The flight through this difficult mountainous district was toilsome, there being no other roads there than those over the rocks, through the *macchia*, and across the mountain streams. Madame Letitia held pretty little Paolina's hand, while Fesch went with Eliza and Louis; before them marched a troop of their partisans from Bastelica, Sampiero's birthplace, and behind them the men of Bocognano, armed with daggers, guns, and pistols. Thus Napoleon's family wandered over the mountains; and after great exertions, climbing over rocks and wading through streams, they reached the shores of Capitello, where they all concealed themselves in the bush.

Just at this time Napoleon, embarking in a small vessel at Bastia, sailed at the head of the French fleet, which put to sea with the intention of landing at Ajaccio and taking the castle. Napoleon went ashore near the Bloody Islands, where many of the shepherds dependent upon his family had their flocks; and there, hearing that his family had fled, he sent out shepherds in all directions to search them out. He waited through the night in a state of eager anxiety for news. Morning came; he was sitting under a rock, thinking uneasily of the fate of his family, when a shepherd suddenly dashed up to him, exclaiming, " Save yourself!"—A troop of men, who had marched out of Ajaccio to find and bring home Napoleon and his family, was hastening towards him. Napoleon sprang into the sea; his little vessel, a xebec, kept the pursuers off by its fire, and the boat took him safely up.

On the same day Napoleon sailed into the gulf, and as he was cruising along the coast, he perceived some people on the shore who made signs to be taken in. It was Letitia, his mother, and her children.

The unfortunate family was now promptly transported to Calvi, where they found a hospitable reception. But the Bonaparte house was plundered and desolated by the enraged populace; and the family owed its rescue solely to the precautions of the Corsican Costa, to whom Napoleon left in his will the sum of 100,000 francs in acknowledgment.

Young Napoleon himself, after a vain attempt upon Ajaccio, sailed to Calvi, unsupported by the fleet, and ultimately himself recalled; and then, leaving Corsica, he appears again in Toulon.

Thus had Pasquale Paoli himself forced Napoleon upon the history of the world. Two men, opposed to one another as bitter enemies, Marbœuf and Paoli—that is, despotism and democracy—had indicated to Napoleon the direction of his career. When Napoleon became consul, and his constellation shone forth resplendent over the world, Paoli's star had long set. It deeply moves me to think of the noble old Pasquale, a long-forgotten exile, sitting solitary in his house in London, and to remember how he illuminated his house with unselfish joy on the news of Napoleon's appointment to the consulate, forgetting his resentment, and hoping that the great Corsican would be a rock and tower to humanity. He says in a letter: "Napoleon has accomplished our vendetta on all those who have been the cause of our fall. I only hope he will remember his country." He remained in banishment; Napoleon did not recall him, perhaps fearing to excite the jealousy of the French.

In the days of his prosperity, Napoleon forgot his little native land—ungrateful and weak like all upstarts, who do not like to be reminded of the obscure scene of their birth. He did nothing for his poor country; and this the Corsicans have never been able to forget. They cannot forget now, that once when a Corsican presented himself to the emperor, the latter asked him drily, "Well, how goes it in Corsica; do the people keep murdering one another still?"

Since his flight from Corsica he only once visited the island again; namely, on his return from Egypt. On the 29th September, 1799, his ship ran into the harbour of Ajaccio; with him were Murat (who was at a future date to leave this same harbour in another shape), Eugene, Berthier, Lannes, Andreossi, Louis Bonaparte, Monge, and Berthollet. During the night he sat up on board the vessel reading the papers, and far into the next day. He would not go ashore; but his companions being curious to see his native town, he no longer opposed their request and the entreaties of the citizens of Ajaccio. A man who had seen Napoleon's landing as a child, told me about it. "See," said he, "this square was covered with hurraing multitudes, and the roofs were crowded with people, who pressed to see the extraordinary man who but a few years ago used to go about among us a simple officer, and one of the leading democrats of Ajaccio. He dismounted at the Casa Bonaparte. He went to walk on the Place du Diamant. But here I must tell you a story which is honourable to him. When Napoleon was still at Ajaccio, the priests and aristocrats were very much embittered against him. One day as he was returning home, and was come just to the corner of this street, he saw a priest—my own relation—standing at the window of yonder house with his gun pointed at him. At the same moment Napoleon stooped, and the bullet passed over him into the wall—an instant sooner, and there had been no Emperor Napoleon in the world. Now Napoleon, on the occasion we were speaking of, met this priest on the Place du Diamant. The priest, remembering that he had once shot at him, crossed to the other side of the street. But Napoleon saw him, and going up to him, gave him his hand and reminded him gaily of the past. See, he was no Corsican in *that;* great men easily forget injuries." But Napoleon was quite a Corsican when he had the Duc d'Enghien shot. This was the act of a Corsican

bandit, and can only be truly comprehended when it is understood what is sanctioned by the custom of blood-revenge in
Corsica,—namely, the murder even of innocent members of the
hostile family. Not entirely could Napoleon belie his Corsican
nature, and so he was romantic, theatrical, and adventurous, as the
Corsicans frequently are. Egypt, Russia, and Elba, are points
in his history when he was nothing but a great and talented
adventurer.

At Ajaccio he went hunting with his companions, and passed
a day at Milelli, where in former days he had written the pamphlet against Buttafuoco. How many wonderful deeds now lay
behind him! how many princes and nations the power of his
sword and the thunder of his phrases had now laid prostrate!
He called his herdsmen to him, and he rewarded handsomely
that Bagaglino who had executed his first *coup d' état* for him.
He distributed his herds and his fields among them. His nurse,
Camilla Ilari, also came and embraced him with sobs; she
brought him a present of a flask of milk, saying in her simple
naïve way, "My son, I have given thee the milk of my breast;
take now the milk of my goat." Napoleon gave her a comfortable house at Ajaccio, and plenty of arable land, and when he
was Emperor he added a pension of 3600 francs.—After a stay
of six days he set sail again for France.

Since that time he never again visited his native island; but
fortune once showed it to his eyes, when he, a broken-down man,
shoved aside from history and used up for its purposes, stood
upon the little crag of Elba. Ironical fortune showed him the
obscure scene whence he had been drawn forth into the world
to try his fortune.

Later, in St. Helena, his thoughts were always recurring to
Corsica. Dying persons frequently retrace in thoughts the
journey of their life, and dwell most fondly on their childhood.
He spoke much of his native land. He says once in the com-
mentaries: "My good Corsicans were not satisfied with me at
the time of the Consulate and the Empire. They affirmed that
I had done little for my native land. . . . My enemies, and my
enviers still more, acted as perfect spies on my actions; all that
I did for my Corsicans was decried as robbery and as injustice
towards the French. This necessary policy estranged the
hearts of my countrymen from me, and cooled their interest in
me. I lament it, but I could not act otherwise. When the
Corsicans saw me unfortunate, when they saw me ill treated by

many an ungrateful Frenchman, and Europe conspiring against me, they forgot every thing, like men of firm and uncorrupted virtue, and declared themselves ready to sacrifice themselves for me if I had willed it. . . . What reminiscences has Corsica left me! I still think with delight of its beautiful scenes and its mountains; I still remember the fragrance its air exhales. I would have improved the lot of my beautiful Corsica, I would have made my fellow-citizens happy, but the downfall came, and I could not carry out my plans."

The first question Napoleon put to his Corsican physician, Antommarchi, when he entered his room in St. Helena, was, "Have you a Filippini?" Many of his island countrymen had accompanied him in his career; and many he had promoted. Bacciochi, Arena, Cervoni, Arrighi, Saliceti, Casabianca, Abbatucci, and Sebastiani. With the same Colonna, who had been Paoli's friend and had formerly opposed him, he stood on terms of intimate friendship until his death. They say Paoli had charged him to lay an ambush for young Napoleon, near Ajaccio, and to bring him alive or dead: well, they *say* so. Colonna refused. He continued a friend to both parties, Paoli as well as Napoleon, without hypocrisy, for he was a noble-minded man. He was the first who knew of Napoleon's flight from Elba, and to him Napoleon in his will confided the care of his mother. Colonna undertook this duty conscientiously, and remained with Letitia till her death, as her friend and major-domo. He afterwards retired to Vico, near Ajaccio.

From the hand of a Corsican, Napoleon, when dying, received extreme unction in St. Helena; this priest was Vignale, who was afterwards murdered in Corsica. Thus Napoleon died among his brother countrymen, who did not desert him.

CHAPTER VII.

TWO COFFINS.

Ah! where is now the greatest monarch's throne?
And where are all the mightiest heroes gone?
Thou goest hence—the world endureth on,
And its great lasting riddle solved has none.
Of lessons wise it hath for us full store;
Then why do we not hearken to it more?

FIRDUSI.

WHILST I pictured to myself the history of Napoleon, his brilliant empire, the nations and the princes whom this precipitate planet attracted to his court, and the flood of events and destinies that he cast over the world, I was overcome, in his now desolate and deathly silent house, by a feeling of sadness and of satisfaction at once.

All those immense passions, which insatiably devoured half the world, where are they now, and where is their influence still felt? They are like a dream, like a great fable told by nurse Time to·her children. Thanks be to Time! She is the silent, mysterious power that levels all again, even heaven-towering potentates. She is the salutary ostracism, the true potsherd justice.

Where is Napoleon? what is left of him?

A name, and a relic which is now openly adored by an easily dazzled nation. What has now been taking place beyond the Rhine, appears to me like Napoleon's funeral celebration of the year 1821. But the dead rise not again. After the gods came the ghosts, and after the world's tragedy comes the Satyric drama.—A cadaverous smell has gone out into the world since they have raised up a dead man there beyond the Rhine.

I went from Letitia's house to the chapel of her tomb.

The street of the "King of Rome" leads to the cathedral of Ajaccio. This church is a heavy building with a simple façade, above the portal of which an expunged coat-of-arms may be seen. Doubtless it was the arms of the extinct republic of Genoa. The interior of the church is gay, and rather rustic. Heavy pillars divide it into three naves; the dome is small, as well as the gallery.

On the right of the choir is a small chapel hung with black. Two coffins covered with black velvet stand in it before an altar, which is decked out quite in village fashion. At the head and foot of each coffin there are heavy wooden candelabra set up, and a constant lamp—extinguished, however—hangs above each. On the coffin to the left hand lies a cardinal's hat and a garland of everlastings.

These are the coffins of Madame Letitia and Cardinal Fesch. They were brought hither in the year 1851 from their Italian graves. Letitia died on the 2nd February, 1836, in her Roman palace on the Venetian Square, and her coffin stood from that time to this in a church of the small town Corneto, near Rome.

No marble, no work of art, no sepulchral pomp—nothing adorns the spot where a woman is buried who bore an emperor, three kings, and three princesses! ·

I was surprised by the unconscious irony, and the profound tragic significance embodied in this almost rustic simplicity of Letitia's sepulchral chapel. It resembles a princely grave composed of theatre scenes. Her coffin rests on a high wooden trestle; the inelegant candelabra are of wood too, and the gold is tinsel. The hangings of the chapel seem to be velvet, but they are of common taffeta, and the long silver fringes to them are of silvered paper. That golden Imperial crown on the coffin is of wood, with tinsel pasted over it. Only Letitia's garland of everlastings is genuine.

They told me this sepulchral chapel was provisional, and that a new cathedral is to be built, with a beautiful vault for Letitia. There will be no hurry about *that*, the Corsicans being so poor; and I should be sorry for it, too. The honest citizens of Ajaccio know not how deep a meaning they have illustrated. What a philosophy of life speaks from this chapel! . . . . What were the crowns, after all, which Letitia of Ajaccio and her children wore? For one short evening they were princes; then they hastily threw off the purple and the sceptre, and disappeared, as if nothing had happened. Therefore has history herself placed the tinsel crown upon the coffin of Letitia Ramolino, the citizen's daughter. Let it lie; it is not less beautiful though it be false, like the fortune of the bastard kings whom this woman bore.

Never since the world has been, has a mother's heart beaten more passionately than that of the woman in this coffin. She saw her children one after another on the high sunlit pinnacle of human glory, and one after the other saw them fall. She has paid the debt of destiny.

Yea, truly—one who stands by this coffin has difficulty to command his emotions; so painfully touching and so great a tragedy of a mother's heart lies buried in it. What an unmerited destiny! And how came it that, in the womb of such a cheerful, simple young wife, such world-wide, historical forces, such men and nation-absorbing powers, were destined to come to maturity?

CHAPTER VIII.

POZZO DI BORGO.

THE house in the Rue Napoléon in which the exile Murat lived, is transformed into a palace. The arms above the door tell that it belongs to the family of Pozzo di Borgo. Next to the Bonapartes the Pozzo di Borgos are the most celebrated family of Ajaccio, being of ancient nobility, and known in Corsica long before the former. In the sixteenth century they distinguished themselves in the service of Venice. The Corsican poet, Biagino di Leca, who celebrates the deeds of Alfonso Ornano, in his epic "Il D'Ornano Marte," extols at the same time several Pozzo di Borgos, and predicts immortal glory to their race.

The family at least gained a European celebrity through Count Carlo Andrea Pozzo di Borgo, the friend of Napoleon's youth, Paoli's friend, and the inexorable *Corsican* hater of the emperor. He was born March 8, 1768, at Alata, a village near Ajaccio. He studied law at Pisa, like Carlo Bonaparte, and then played a part in Corsica, first as a Democrat and Revolutionist, and subsequently as a Paolist. In the year 1791 he was the deputy for Ajaccio, and afterwards attorney-general, and Paoli's right-hand man. When Corsica attached itself to England, this dexterous man became president of the Corsican Council of State under Elliot's viceroyalty. They say that his diplomacy brought his patron Paoli into discredit with the English, in order to make his own influence solely felt. He subsequently left Corsica, and went several times to London, to Vienna, to Russia, to Constantinople, and to Syria; passing through the world and its courts, like Sampiero of old, this inexorable enemy unceasingly stirred up the hatred of cabinets against Napoleon. Alexander made him a Russian counsellor of state in the year 1802. Napoleon pursued him with equal hatred, and longed to get into his power this terrible foe, who crossed him in all his courses. After the peace of Pressburg, he demanded his extradition. Had he gained it, he would have done with Pozzo di Borgo as Charles XII. did with Patkul. An extraordinary thing is this hostility; it is regular Corsican vendetta, Corsican hatred transferred to the history of the world. Pozzo di Borgo it was who determined Bernadotte to act against Napoleon ; it was he who instigated the allies to a rapid march against Paris ; it was he who set aside the King of Rome, and who, at the congress of Vienna, urged them to 'banish Napoleon from the dangerous Elba to a far more distant island. At Waterloo he stood with arms in his hands against his great adversary, and was wounded. And when his gigantic foe was for ever humbled at St. Helena, the diplomatist, in the feeling of satiated revenge, spoke the proud and terrible words, "I have not killed Napoleon, but I have cast the last spadeful of earth upon him !"

Pozzo di Borgo earned the coronet of a Russian count, and the honour of being the permanent representative of all the Russias at the court of France. Living at Paris, he generally opposed the reaction, and was thrown into a position of difference with the courts in consequence. Notwithstanding his career, he' was and ever remained a Corsican. I was told that he never put off his national ways. He loved his native land. One might almost say that, even in withdrawing the gratitude of his countrymen from Napoleon to himself, he was carrying on his feud with Napoleon. Napoleon did nothing for Corsica ; Pozzo di Borgo a great deal. He instituted the publication of the two Corsican historians, Filippini and Peter, and Gregori dedicated to him a collection of the statutes. Pozzo di Borgo's name thus appears on the three greatest documents of Corsican history, and is indelible. His beneficence to his countrymen, in charitable institutions and alms, was great, as was his fortune. He died as a private citizen at Paris, Feb. 15, 1842, at the age of seventy-four, ill at ease with the world, internally worn out, and mentally diseased. He was one of the most skilful diplomatists and acutest heads of this century.

His immense fortune went to his nephews, who have bought large estates near Ajaccio. One of them was murdered a few years ago in the vicinity of the town. He was manager of the

charities distributed by Count Carlo Andrea, and had rendered
himself odious in this capacity. I was told that he had also
refused a certain high compensation demanded by the relatives
of a girl whom he had seduced. The parties aggrieved by him
resolved on his death. So as he was one day driving in his carriage from his villa to the town, they encompassed the carriage,
and cried out to him, "Nephew of Carlo Andrea Pozzo di
Borgo, descend!" The wretched man did so without delay. The
murderers perpetrated the execution with perfect *sang froid*, in
the light of day and in the open air, as an act of popular justice
against a criminal. The shots did not immediately kill him.
The murderers carried the dying man into the carriage, and told
the coachman to turn round, that Pozzo di Borgo's nephew
might die in bed. They then went into the bush, where they
were slain some time after in contests with the gens d'armes.

This is a specimen of terrible popular justice, such as is often
exercised in Corsica. I will here tell a second case. It is an
admirable but cruel history, which took place at the village of
Alata, the birthplace of the Pozzos, a few miles from Ajaccio.

*   *   *   *   *

THE CORSICAN BRUTUS.

Two grenadiers of the French Flemish regiment, which was
quartered as a Genoese auxiliary corps to garrison Ajaccio,
deserted. They fled to the mountains of Alata, and kept themselves concealed there in the wilds, where they claimed the compassion and hospitality of the poor herdsmen.

Sacred are the rights of hospitality. He who violates them,
before God and man is, by the time-hallowed usage of our fathers,
a Cain.

When spring was come, some officers of the Flemish regiment,
hunting on those mountains of Alata, came near the place
where the two fugitives lay concealed. The latter perceived the
huntsmen, and crouched down behind a rock, that they might
not be seen, and themselves be hunted down as game. A young
herdsman was pasturing his goats there; M. de Nozières, colonel
of the regiment, went up to him and asked him whether it was
possible that some fugitive grenadiers were concealed in the
mountains? "I do not know," said the herdsman, and appeared
embarrassed. M. de Nozières, gathering suspicion from his manner,
menaced him with the severe punishment of instantaneous confinement in the prison of Ajaccio, if he did not tell the truth.

Then Joseph was terrified; he said nothing, but he tremblingly pointed with his hand to the place where the poor deserters were hiding. The officer did not understand him. " Speak!" he thundered at him. Joseph would not speak, but again pointed with his hand. The other officers now let loose his hands, and hastened to the place indicated, perhaps expecting to find an animal that the simple mute had pointed out to them.

The two grenadiers sprang up and fled, but were overtaken and secured.

M. de Nozières gave Joseph four bright golden louis-d'ors for his information. The young herdsman, on holding the gold pieces in his hand, forgot, in a childish rapture, officers and grenadiers, and the whole world besides; for he had never seen pure gold. He ran into his father's cabin, and called together his father, mother, and brothers; and he behaved like one distracted with delight, and showed his treasure.

" How did you come by this gold, my son Joseph?" asked the old herdsman. The son told what had happened. At every word that he spoke his father's countenance became darker, and his brothers were horrified; and when Joseph had finished his story, the father was pale as death.

Sacred are the rights of hospitality. He who violates them, before God and man is, by the time-hallowed usage of our fathers, a Cain.

The old herdsman cast a terrible glance at his trembling son, and went out of the cabin. He called his whole kin together, and, when they were assembled, he laid the case before them, and called them to pronounce sentence on his son; for the latter appeared to him to be a traitor, and to have brought shame on his whole tribe and nation.

The court of kinsmen unanimously pronounced sentence that Joseph was worthy of death. " Wo's me and my son!" cried the old man in despair : " wo to my wife, that she bore me this Judas!"

The kinsmen went to Joseph, and led him to a lonely place near the city-wall of Ajaccio.

" Wait here," said the old herdsman; " I will go to the commander; I will beg the life of the two grenadiers. Let their life be life to my son also."

The old man went to M. de Nozières. He threw himself on his knees before him, and begged for the pardon of the two soldiers. The officer regarded him with astonishment, wondering at the compassion of a herdsman, who wept so bitterly for two strange soldiers. But he told him that deserters were worthy of death, for so it was ordained by the law. The old man rose and went away weeping.

He came back to the wall where the kinsmen stood with poor Joseph. "It is in vain," said he. "My son, Joseph, thou must die ; die like a brave man, and farewell !"

Poor Joseph wept ; but then he became tranquil and collected. A priest had been sent for, who received his confession, and gave him spiritual consolation.

It was the very hour when the two poor deserters were beaten to death with rods. Poor Joseph placed himself composedly against the wall ; the kinsmen aimed well, and Joseph was dead.

When he had fallen, his old father, bitterly weeping, took the four bright louis-d'ors, and gave them to the priest, saying to him, "Go to the commander and say to him, ' Sir, here is your Judas-wages back again. We are poor and honest men, and have executed justice upon him who received it from your hand.'"

Sacred are the rights of hospitality. He who violates them, before God and man is, by the time-hallowed usage of our fathers, a Cain.

   *   *   *   *   *

At Alata and Ajaccio they still cherish the memory of the magnanimous deed of a woman of the family of Pozzo di Borgo, in the year 1794.   Let this also be told here.

MARIANNA POZZO DI BORGO.

All the folk were merry-making at the carnival at Appietto, near Ajaccio. Agreeably to an ancient custom, which still subsists in the island, the carnival-king sat in the middle of the market-place surrounded by his ministers, with a golden crown on his head. Tables were set up full of wine, fruit, and viands of various sorts. For the king of the carnival had imposed extensive contributions ; and it is the law of the Corsican carnival that he is privileged to impose upon the families of the village, according to their property, the contributions in wine and victuals which they have to bring for the public good.

So they were drinking and feasting to their hearts' content. The guitars and fiddles struck up, and the young folk were whirling in the mazes of the dance.

All of a sudden, in the midst of the merriment, a gun-shot and a shriek were heard, and they all fled asunder in fright. A wild confusion arose on the market-place of Appietto. There lay the young Felix Pozzo di Borgo in his blood. An insult had been offered, and Andrea Romanetti had shot him. Andrea was off to the Macchia.

The dead youth was taken to the house of his mother. The women raised the *lamento;* not a guitar was heard any longer. Felix's mother Marianna was a widow, and had suffered great misfortunes. When the youth had been brought to the cemetery she wept no more, but only thought how he was to be avenged; for she was a high-spirited woman, and of the ancient house of Colonna d'Istria.

Marianna put off her woman's clothes, and put on the dress of a man. She wrapped herself in a pelone, put a Phrygian cap on her head, girded herself with the carchera, stuck dagger and pistols in her belt, and seized the double-barrelled gun. She perfectly resembled a rough Corsican man; only the scarlet girdle, a velvet edging on her pelone, and the ornamental handle of her dagger, bright with ivory and mother-of-pearl, betrayed her to be of a noble house.

She put herself at the head of her kinsmen, and restlessly pursued the murderer of her son. Andrea Romanetti fled from bush to bush, from cave to cave, from mountain to mountain; but Marianna was on his track. One dark night the fugitive took refuge in his own house, in the village of Marchesaccia. Here he was discovered by a girl of the hostile clan, who gave news of his hiding-place. Marianna hastened up; her kinsmen surrounded the house; Romanetti made a valiant stand, but when his ammunition was exhausted, and his enemies had already mounted the roof to break in upon him, he saw that he was lost. He then thought of nothing but the salvation of his soul; for he was pious, and feared God.

"Hold!" cried Romanetti from the house; "I will surrender myself, but promise that I may confess myself before I die." Marianna Pozzo di Borgo promised him this.

So Romanetti came forward, and surrendered himself voluntarily into the hands of his enemies. They led him into the village of Teppa, and stopped before the door of the priest, Saverius Casalonga. Marianna called the priest, and begged him for the love of God to receive Romanetti's confession, for he must die afterwards.

The priest entreated with tears for the life of the unhappy man, but his prayers were in vain. He received the confession; and whilst the murderer of her son was making it to the priest, Marianna knelt and prayed God to have mercy on his soul.

The confession was accomplished. The Pozzo di Borgos now led Romanetti out of the village, and bound him to a tree.

They raised their guns—suddenly Marianna rushed up— "Hold!" she cried; "for God's sake, hold!" and she ran to the tree to which he was bound, and clasped in her arms the murderer of her son. "In the name of God," she said, "I forgive him! Though he has rendered me the most afflicted of all mothers, yet shall ye do him no further injury, and rather shoot me than him." So she held him clasped in her arms, and covered him against violence by her own body.

The priest came up. There was no further need of his words. The men released Romanetti, and let him go free from that hour, and his head was a sacred one to the kin of Pozzo di Borgo, so that no one touched one of his hairs.

CHAPTER IX.

ENVIRONS OF AJACCIO.

I EXHAUSTED the environs of Ajaccio. Their extent is but small, and comprises strictly only three streets, a walk along the northern shore, one up into the country on the Bastia road, and one on the other side of the gulf, on the road towards Sartene. The fourth side is shut in by mountains. Country paths there lead between the vineyards, which adorn the immediate neighbourhood of Ajaccio on the north-east, in great abundance.

In these vineyards, those curious watchmen's boxes called Pergoliti, are frequently seen, which are peculiar to Ajaccio. They consist of four young pine-stems, bearing a little straw-thatched hut high in the air, in which the watchman can lie down. The latter bears the proud name, Barone. He is armed with a double-barrelled gun, and from time to time blows a conch or a shrill clay whistle to announce his presence, and scare away vine-robbers.

One evening, a friendly old man took me to his vineyard, on the hill of San Giovanni. He treated me handsomely to

Muscatel grapes, and plucked almonds, juicy plums, and figs, which grew variously twined together between the vines. He had seen me coming along the road, and therefore invited me into his orchard, as is the good hospitable custom. He was a good old grandfather, and a touching picture of old age, such as one sometimes finds it represented in poems of the age of Gleim, which, in their garrulous simplicity, often contain more human wisdom than the most read poems of our times. Is there a more gratifying picture of humanity than a cheerful old man in the garden which he planted in his youth, and whose fruits he now charitably distributes to the tired wayfarers who pass his gate? Yea, thus peacefully and beneficently should a human life end.

The old man was loquacious in the praise of this fruit and that, and told me what must be done to get them particularly juicy. The vines are here trained to sticks like beans, to a height of four or five feet, and four such vines generally stand together in a small quadrangular depression, and are fastened together by their top branches. The productiveness of the vines was great, yet the vine-disease prevailed in many places. The wine of Ajaccio is fiery, like the Spanish. I also found for the first time, in this *vigna*, the ripe fruit of the Indian fig, or cactus. When this plant has cast its flowers, the fruit ripens fast. Its colour is yellowish; you peel off the outside, and get at the pulpy and granulous part of the fig, which is unpleasantly sweet. Attempts have been made to extract sugar from it. The productive power of this species of cactus, which grows in astonishing profusion near Ajaccio, is wonderfully great. A torn-off leaf quickly strikes root in the soil, and converts itself boldly into a new plant. It needs only the very slightest nourishment and the least patch of dust to propagate itself.

A fine castellated villa, with Gothic turrets, and great stone Imperial eagles, stands near the hill of San Giovanni. It is the villa of Principe Bacciocchi.

The small fertile plain which extends on further at the end of the gulf, is called Campoluro. The spirit of a dismal event from the times of the Genoese wars broods over this rich plain. Twenty-one herdsmen from Bastelica had posted themselves here, —powerful men, Sampiero heroes. Against 800 Greeks and Genoese they made a brave stand, until, cut off in a morass, they were all killed with the exception of a single youth. The latter threw himself among the dead, and, being partly covered by them, pretended to be dead. But the Genoese came to cut off the heads of the dead, to plant them on the walls of the citadel. The young shepherd they brought into the presence of the Genoese lieutenant. Being condemned to death, this youth, the last of the twenty-one men of Bastelica, was led through the streets of Ajaccio laden with the heads of his companions, and then quartered and exposed to the ravens on the wall.

As the end of this field lies the Botanic Garden, which dates from the time of Louis XVI., and was, after its commencement, under the protection of Carlo Bonaparte. It was originally intended for the purpose of acclimatizing the exotic plants which were desired to be introduced into France. The garden, sheltered by the hills from cold winds and open to the south sun, contains the finest growths of exotic zones, which thrive luxuriantly in the open air in the warm climate of Ajaccio. You walk there beneath splendid magnolias, wonderful poincianas, tulip-trees, gledicias, trumpet-flowers, tamarinds, and cedars of Lebanon. On the immense Indian figs lives the cochineal insect, just as it does in Mexico.

This beautiful flower-garden quite transports one into tropical regions; and when one stands beneath one of those wonderful foreign trees, and one's gaze falls on the deep-blue gulf, over which the summer air is quivering, one might really fancy one were standing by some Mexican gulf. The garden is situated hard by the Bastia road, which is the most enlivened by passers-by. This is the case especially in the evening, when the inhabitants return home from the Campagna.

I often amused myself by sitting down by the gulf and observing the passers-by. The women are here well built, and have correct and tender features. I was often surprised by the gentleness of their eyes and the whiteness of their complexion. They wear the *fazoletto* or *mandile* wound round the head; that worn on Sundays is of white gauze, and looks extremely neat by contrast to the black *faldetta*. The peasant women here universally wear round straw hats, with a very low crown. They lay a little cushion on their hats, and then dexterously and lightly carry tolerable weights on their heads. The Corsican women, like the Italian, are distinguished for natural grace of demeanour. I often had occasion to be delighted at it. I one day met a young girl going with fruit to the town. I begged her to sell me some. The girl immediately set her basket down, and with a charming grace bade me to eat as much as I would. With equal delicacy of mien she refused to take any money. She was very poorly attired. As often as I met her afterwards at Ajaccio, she replied to my greeting with a grace that would have sat well on a high-born dame.

There comes a man dashing past us. His pretty wife it was perhaps who just went by, laden with a bundle of fagots or fodder for the cattle; but the lazy man comes down from the mountains, where he has been doing nothing but lie in vendetta. When one sees these half-savages going along in troops of threes, or sixes, or singly, riding or walking, all holding the double-barrelled gun before them, one might think one found them in a permanent state of war. The very peasant sitting on his hay-cart has his gun slung round him. I counted in one half-hour twenty-six persons armed with double-barrelled guns, who passed me going to Ajaccio. The people about Ajaccio are renowned in Corsica as the most warlike in the island.

These people often look bold and picturesque, often frightfully ugly, and even ridiculous. They are generally small men, of the stature of Napoleon, black-haired, black-bearded, and of a bronze complexion, and are seen riding their little horses; their jackets are brownish-black and shaggy, so also the trousers, and the double-barrelled gun hangs over their shoulders; by a strap on their back is attached the round yellow *zucca*, which is generally filled only with water, and by another strap at their side hangs the little goat or fox skin, into which bread, cheese, and other necessaries are crammed; round the body the leathern powder-belt is strapped, on which a leathern tobacco-pouch is commonly suspended. Thus is the Corsican rider equipped, and thus he lies all the day in the field while the woman works. I could never restrain my anger when I saw these furious men dash past with shouts, unmercifully urging on their horses, on one of which two persons frequently sat one behind the other, and when I then glanced at the beautiful shores of the gulf, on which not a village is to be seen. The soil of these shores would produce hundred-fold; now it bears rosemary, thorns, thistles, and wild olive shrubs.

Charming is the walk on the northern side of the gulf, along the strand. In a light wind the waves break on the granite reefs, and froth them over with their milkwhite foam. On the right rise the coast mountains, which near to the town are covered with olive-trees, and further on are bare and waste as far as Cape Muro.

On this coast stands the little chapel of the Greeks, close by the sea. They could not tell me why it bore this name, though dedicated to the Madonna del Carmine, and bearing the name of Pozzo di Borgo (*Puteo Burgensis*) on a tablet. It was probably given up to the Greeks when they came to Ajaccio. The Genoese caused the colony of Mainotes to settle at Paonica, far above Ajaccio. These industrious people were constantly threatened by the Corsicans. Full of hatred and contempt towards the intruders, who had raised their colony to a great pitch of prosperity, they fell upon the husbandman ploughing, and assassinated him, shot the vine-dresser in his vineyard, and wasted the fields and orchards. In the year 1731 the poor Greeks were driven out of their colony: they fled to Ajaccio, where the Genoese, to whom they had always continued faithful, formed them into three military companies. When the island became subject to the French, Cargese was given them as a possession. They brought the district into a flourishing state; but they had hardly made themselves comfortable in it, when the Corsicans again fell upon them in the year 1793, threw fire into their houses, destroyed their herds, trod down their vineyards, annihilated the produce of the fields, and forced the Mainotes to fly a second time to Ajaccio. General Casabianco led the exiles back to Cargese in the year 1797, where they thenceforward lived unmolested. The peculiarity of their manners has disappeared; they speak Corsican, like their troublesome neighbours. Among themselves, however, they speak a corrupt Greek. Cargese lies on the sea, northwards from Ajaccio, and to one side of the baths of Vico and those of Guagno.

On the same northern shore there are many small chapels scattered about, of manifold shapes—round, quadrangular, domed, in the form of a sarcophagus, in that of a temple, surrounded by white walls, and among cypresses and weeping-willows. The dead have here their country-seats: they are family vaults; their position on the coast in full view of the beautiful gulf among the green bushes, and their elegant Moorish form, produce a very cheerful and a very foreign picture. The Corsican is not fond of being buried in the public churchyard; agreeably to the ancient ways of the patriarchs, he desires to be interred in his own land, among his own dear ones. From this cause the whole island is dotted over with little mausoleums, which often enjoy the most charming situations, and enhance the picturesqueness of the landscape.

Wandering on towards Cape Muro, where a few red granite cliffs are situated close to the shore, called the Bloody Islands, possessing a lighthouse and several Genoese watch-towers—I found some fishermen occupied in drawing the net to the shore. They stood in rows of ten or a dozen men, and each row was winding up a long cable, to which the net was attached. These cables on each side are more than three hundred feet long; as much of them as has been toilsomely drawn up, in doing which the fishermen lean with their hands and breast against a coil of the cable—is skilfully and tidily heaped into a circular coil. In three quarters of an hour the net was on the shore, weighed down by riches, and like a well-filled sack. When it was drawn asunder, there was a swarm of poor sea animals, jumping, springing, and crawling about! They were mainly anchovies, and the largest fishes were rays (*razzi*), which resemble our Baltic *flinders*; they have a sharp goad on their long-pointed tail. The fishermen cautiously lays the ray on the ground, and cuts off its sharp tail with a knife. They were stout, active, vigorous people, these fishermen; the Corsicans are as clever on the sea as on the mountains. The granite mountain and the sea both determine the character of the island and its population, wherefore the Corsicans may be divided into two ancient and equally vigorous classes, the herdsmen and the fishermen. The fishery at Ajaccio is very important, as in all the gulfs of Corsica. In April the tunny passes along the coasts of Spain, France, and Genoa, into the Corsican channel. The shark is his sworn foe; he often appears in these seas, but does not come near the shore.

As I returned in the dark to Ajaccio from this coast walk, a gun-shot was heard in my vicinity on the mountains. A man came running up and asked in great excitement, "You heard the shot?"—"Yes, sir."—"Do you see any thing?"—"No, sir."— The interrogator disappeared again. Two *sbirri* now came up. What was it? Perhaps some one is weltering in his blood on the mountains. The walks here may have quite a dramatic interest. One is always surrounded by an atmosphere of death, and Nature herself has here the charm of a melancholy beauty.

TRAVELS.——BOOK VII.

CHAPTER I.

FROM AJACCIO TO THE VAL ORNANO.

THE road from Ajaccio to Sartene is rich in remarkable districts and peculiar views. For a time it leads along the gulf, passes the river Gravone, which flows out into the gulf, and then enters the valley of the Prunelli. The view of the great gulf is equally glorious from all sides; now it disappears from sight, and now it appears again, as the road runs spirally along the mountain sides.

At the mouth of the Prunelli is the lonely tower of Capitello, which we know from the history of Napoleon.

There are but few villages, such as Fontanaccia, Serrola, and Cavro. Cavro is a scattered *paese,* in a wild romantic mountain district rich in granite and porphyry, and surrounded by luxuriant vineyards. After going for ten minutes towards the mountains, one reaches the rocky glen in which Sampiero was murdered. The Ornanos had chosen the scene of the murder well. High rocks rise all round in a circle; a path winds its way along into the bottom of the valley, which is watered by a mountain stream; and the place is covered with oaks, olives, and wild shrubs. On a rock in the vicinity are seen the ruins of the castle of Giglio, where Sampiero had passed the night before he met his death. I looked about in vain for any monument to remind the traveller that in this awful place the greatest of all Corsican heroes fell. This too is characteristic of the Corsicans—their living memory is the sole monument of their wild tragical history. Every rock of this island is a memorial of their deeds; so they may easily dispense with memorial columns and inscriptions, so long as the events of history still

2 F

live as a part of their very nature. For so soon as a people begins to adorn its land with monuments, it offers a proof that its powers are already lost. All Italy is now a museum of monumental columns, statues, and inscriptions. In Corsica, the state of nature and living tradition has subsisted in this as well as in other respects; and the Corsican would not even understand the meaning of a statue, and it would have a curious effect among them. When a statue was voted to Pasquale Paoli, after his return from England, and he declined the honour, a Corsican said, "To erect a statue to a mere man is as much as giving him a box on the ear."

On the brink of the gloomy ravine of the murder, however, I found a group of living statues of Sampiero—peasants chatting in the sun, with the Phrygian cap of freedom pressed down over their foreheads. I went up to them, and we discoursed of the ancient hero. The people have given him the most honourable surname that the son of any nation can bear; for he is never spoken of otherwise than as Sampiero Corso—Sampiero the Corsican. Strikingly has the judgment of his countrymen declared itself in this surname—that Sampiero is the most perfect expression of the Corsican national character itself, and that he signifies his nation. The entire character of the island, as of its history, is comprised in this man of granite—wild valour, unshaken obstinacy, ardent love of freedom, patriotism, penetrating intellect, poverty and yet freedom from want, ruggedness and choler, volcanic passion, jealousy driving him to murder his wife like Othello the Moor; and that, in the history of Sampiero Corso, the one bloody trait may not be wanting, which even at this day renders the Corsican nationality psychologically so remarkable, blood-revenge was accomplished upon Sampiero himself. Living in an early age, he was able to preserve entire the national Corsican temperament. This temperament is, in Pasquale Paoli, rendered more general and cosmopolitan by the philosophical and humanistic character of his age.

Of Sampiero's sons we have seen the eldest, Alfonso d'Ornano, carry on the war against Genoa for a time after his father's death, until his banishment. In the year 1570, Catherine di Medici appointed him colonel of the Corsican regiment which she had taken into her pay. He distinguished himself by his valour in many battles and sieges under Charles IX. and Henry III. After the murder of this king, in whose name he governed Dauphiné, the Ligue used every effort to draw the influential

Corsican to their side; but Alfonso was one of the first who acknowledged Henry IV., and became one of his chief supports. The king appointed him marshal of France and requited his fidelity by his friendship. Henry writes in a letter to Alfonso:—— " My Cousin, through your despatch, which was transmitted to me by M. de Tour, I have received the first news of what you have brought to so happy an issue in my name in my town of Romans. God grants me the favour, that almost all these wicked designs have been frustrated; next to him, I know that no one has deserved so well of me in this matter as yourself, who have acted with all prudence and valour, as was to be desired, and I shall feel grateful to you. It is only the continuation of your wonted manner of action, and of the success that attends all your good designs." In the year 1594 Alfonso conquered Lyon for the king, then Vienne, and many towns of Provence and Dauphiné. He was the terror of the hostile party; and as he was feared and respected for his military genius, so he was venerated also for his justice and philanthropy. Many towns of France that were brought low' by war and pestilence, Alfonso alleviated out of his own pocket. He died at Paris at the age of sixty-two, in the year 1610, and is buried in the church De la Merci, at Bordeaux. By his wife, a daughter of Nicolas de Pontevèze Lord of Flassan, he had several children, one of whom, Jean Baptiste d'Ornano, likewise became marshal of France. He was ruined by court intrigues at the time of Richelieu; the minister threw him into the Bastile, where he died in the year 1626, poisoned, as was said, by his command. In the year 1670, Sampiero's family, which had passed over to France, in the person of Alfonso, became extinct.

His second son, Antonio Francesco d'Ornano, had a bloody end, like his father. It was he with whom his unfortunate mother Vannina had fled from Marseille to Genoa, and whom she had with her when the raving father murdered her. Antonio Francesco, like his brother, lived at the court of France. Being young and ardent, he desired to see the world, and accompanied the ambassador of Henry III. to Rome. A game at cards one day gave occasion to a quarrel between him and the French gentlemen of the embassy, especially M. De la Roggia. The violent Corsican offended the Frenchman by some hasty words; but the latter concealed his resentment, so that young Ornano suspected nothing. After this event the gentlemen took a ride to the Coliseum in company; Ornano remained alone with his servant after his Italian friends had left him; and with him were twelve Frenchmen, six on foot and six on horseback. M. de la Roggia asked him politely to dismount, to take a walk into the Coliseum. Ornano unhesitatingly followed the invitation; but no sooner had he dismounted than he was assailed by the insidious Frenchmen, both those on foot and those on horseback. Bleeding already from many wounds, the son of Sampiero · defended himself with heroic valour against numbers. Covering his back by a pillar of the Coliseum, he held his ground, defending himself with his sword till he fell. The murderers left him lying there in his blood, and escaped. Antonio Francesco was carried home mortally wounded, and died on the following day. This happened in the year 1580. He left no descendants, and was not married.

I have visited the grave of this youngest son of Sampiero in the church of San Crisogono, in the Trastevere of Rome, where he is buried among many Corsican lords; for San Crisogono is a Corsican church, having been given up to them at a time when many exiles settled at Ostia, and in the Tiber Borgo. Antonio Francesco is said to have been the living image of his father, and to have inherited with his face and figure also his undauntedness; and the latter virtue is praised as highly in Sampiero as the Romans praised it in Fabricius. As Pyrrhus endeavoured to terrify this general by the sudden appearance of an elephant, so the sultan Soliman made a similar attempt with Sampiero. Story tells that the grand Seignior wished one day to convince himself whether the accounts of Sampiero's fearlessness were exaggerated or not. So when Sampiero sat at table with him, he caused a two-pounder cannon to be fired off under the table, at the very instant when the Corsican raised his glass to his mouth to drink. The eyes of all were intent upon Sampiero; but he moved not a muscle, and the shot made no more impression upon him than the sound of a cup falling out of the hand of a slave.

Further to the north of Cavro lies the great canton of Bastelica, which is separated by a mountain-chain from that of Zicavo. This rugged mountain land, full of immense towering masses of granite, and wild valleys overshadowed by gnarled oaks, and overhung by gigantic mountain-heads, here and there crowned with snow, is the native land of Sampiero. In Bastelica, or rather in the small hamlet of Dominicaccia, they still show the black gloomy house in which he was born; for his own house was pulled down by the Genoese under Stephen Doria. Many reminiscences of him survive in this region, which is consecrated by fanciful popular memorials of various kinds. Now it is a footprint of Sampiero in the rock, now an impression of his gun, now a cave, and now an oak under which he is said to have sat. All the people of this valley are distinguished by a strong build and martial physiognomy; they are principally herdsmen, rugged men with the iron manners of their forefathers, and quite unaffected by culture. The men of Bastelica and of Morosaglia pass for the bravest of all the Corsicans,—most remarkably, they being the actual brothers of Sampiero and Paoli, both of whom were men of the people, without title, and without ancestry.

The mountain ridge of San Georgio parts the valley Prunelli from the great valley of the Taravo. When the pass called the Bocca has been surmounted, two beautiful alpine valleys spread out before the eye—the vale of Istria, and that of Ornano, watered by the river Taravo, which rushes through the rocks. I seek in vain for any well-known district of Italy to give an adequate idea of such Corsican mountain valleys as these. The Apennines would approximate to them in many places. But these Corsican mountains and valleys seemed to me far grander, wilder, and more picturesque, from their chestnut groves, their brown precipices, foaming torrents, scattered blackish villages; and quite incomparable is the picture, when the beaming ocean shows itself suddenly in the distance.

In these mountains abode, the ancient noble families of Istria and Ornano, which popular tradition derives from that Hugo Colonna whom I have named in the history of the Corsicans. Many a tower and ruined castle still tells its half unintelligible tale. The principal cantons of this district are those of Santa Maria and of Petreto.

The seat of the Ornanos was in Santa Maria d'Ornano. The *pieve* was originally called Ornano, but is now called Santa Maria. There is fine land all around, cheerfully diversified by green hills, pasture, and olive-groves. This was the native country of the fair Vannina, and there stands the high brown turreted house which belonged to her, picturesquely situated on an eminence commanding the valley. Near it are perceived the ruins of a castle built by Sampiero, and a chapel in its vicinity where he heard mass. He is said to have contented himself with looking out of the window of his castle when mass was said. He built the castle in the year 1554.

CHAPTER II.

FROM ORNANO TO SARTENE.

THE Taravo forms the boundary between the province of Ajaccio and that of Sartene, the most southern of the Corsican arrondissements. Close by the entrance into it is the beautiful canton of Petreto and Bicchisano, which extends down the Taravo as far as the gulf of Valinco. The prospect over this district and the bay far below, passes among the Corsicans themselves for one of the most glorious in their picturesque island All these districts beyond the mountains are in general on a grand and surprising scale, and bear the noble impress of primeval nature. Scattered in this canton lie the ruins of the castles of the Lords of Istria, miserably ruined however, and rarely with so much left standing as to render their black walls distinguishable at the first glance from the granite of the rocks.

On a hill above Sollacaro stand the ruins of a castle of that Vincentello d'Istria whose name is mentioned in history, buried deep beneath trees and creepers. With this castle is connected one of those wild legends which are characteristic of the Corsicans themselves, as well as of the terrible days of the middle ages. Formerly there stood here another castle, inhabited by a beautiful but unrestrained lady named Savilia. On one occasion she allured to her castle Giudice d'Istria, a powerful lord of the race of Istria, having promised him her hand. When he came, she had him cast into the dungeon. But every morning she went down to the prison, and, baring herself before his eyes at the grating of his place of confinement, jeered at him with the cruel gibe, "Look at me; are these charms made to be enjoyed by such an ill-favoured man as thou?" This game she carried on for a long time, till Istria at length succeeded in making his escape. He then marched with his vassals to Savilia's castle, burning with revenge, broke into it, and laid it even with the ground. The fair Savilia he then put in a hut at a cross-way, where he forced her to grant her favours to every passer-by; she gave up the ghost on the third day. Subsequently, Vincentello d'Istria built on the site of the destroyed castle that which now lies in ruins. The Colonnas are a still subsisting race in Corsica; indeed the Colonna family is perhaps the oldest and most numerous of all noble families in the world, and is dispersed over all Europe.

The next *pieve*, Olmeto, was entirely a fief of the powerful Istrias. High towering mountains enclose the principal place, Olmeto, on the one side; and on the other lies at its feet a splendid still olive valley, washed by the gulf of Valinco. Here also I was shown the ruins of a castle, which was of yore the stronghold of Arrigo della Rocca, perched on one of the steepest mountains, called Buttareto. The view from Olmeto, down into the valley and over the gulf, is enchanting and grand. The lines of the gulf are soft, and its shores brown and silent. Its extreme points are the cape of Porto Pollo to the north, and that of Campo Moro to the south. The name, "Moorish Camp," borne by the cape, by a small place situated close to it, and by a watch-tower, arouses lively memories of the Saracens, who so often landed here. From the Saracen conquest by the legendary Moorish king Lanza Ancisa, Corsica has derived her arms, the head of a Moor with a fillet round the temples. All the coast-land is here of a Moorish brown, breathing an indescribable summer stillness. When I came to the little port Propriano, on the gulf, that feeling of being out of the world came over me, which one cherishes so dearly on the lonely island. On the shore stood many fresh-coloured, dark-haired men, all with the double-barrelled guns over their shoulders, as if prepared to keep off the Saracens. The sight of these solemn martial figures, and the melancholy wildness of the coast-land, transported one completely into the legendary Saracen times. A Spanish romance comes into my head, which sings of the Corsair Dragut, known to us from the history of Corsica. We may hear it to advantage on this gulf among these martial figures.

DRAGUT BEFORE TARIFA.

Tarifa before, and distant
Little further than a mile,
Master Dragut, that bold Corsair,
Corsair bold by sea and land,
Of the Christians he discovered
And of Malta five good vessels.
Therefore was he then compelled
Loud and audibly to clamour:

"Al arma! al arma! al arma!
Cierra! cierra! cierra!
Que el enemigo viene à darnos guerra."

Master Dragut, that bold Corsair,
Fired off forthwith a cannon,
As a signal those should notice
Who were fetching wood and water.
Answer gave they him, the Christians,
From the shore and from the galleys,
And the bells too at the harbour
Dinned an answer to his challenge:
"Al arma! al arma! al arma!
Cierra! cierra! cierra!
Que el enemigo viene à darnos guerra."

And the Christian who was weeping
That his hopes were dead within him,
Now cheers up his mournful spirit,
Since for freedom now he hopeth.
Dragut with his captains all
Instantly holds council martial,
Whether yet to wait were better,
Whether should they hoist the sail:
"Al arma! al arma! al arma!
Cierra! cierra! cierra!
Que el enemigo viene à darnos guerra."

And the others thus they uttered:
"Wait, yet wait! let them draw near us;
When we reach the open ocean
Ours will be Victoria."
Dragut loud he cried and clearly:
"Up, ye rascals, up to battle!
Cannoniers up, one and all!
Load ye, shoot ye, load ye, cry ye,
'Al arma! al arma! al arma!
Cierra! cierra! cierra!
Que el enemigo viene à darnos guerra.'"

The burthen of this spirited song would be in English: "To
arms! to arms! to arms! Danger! danger! danger! For the
enemy is coming to give us battle." I have retained the Spanish
refrain, because it sounds so well.

On the 12th June, 1564, Sampiero landed in this gulf of
Valinco—another sound of steel and armour among these warlike reminiscences.

On the land side, the country rises towards the desolate mountains, whose sides are strewn with grey crumbling rocks. Stones,
shrubs, sea-sand, and a marsh, render this district particularly
cheerless. Yet the evergreen oak and the cork-tree grow here
in abundance, and the rugged land produces corn and wine. At
last I saw Sartene lying before me, a large *paese* in melancholy
isolation among melancholy mountains.

CHAPTER III.

THE TOWN OF SARTENE.

THE town of Sartene has only 3890 inhabitants. It is the chief place of the arrondissement, which numbers 29,300 inhabitants, comprised in eight *pievi* or cantons. Sartene appeared to me rather uncultivated, and to possess a less townish appearance than even Calvi and the small Isola Rossa; for it is nowise distinguishable from the large *paesi* of the island. Its style of building is the national rustic one of the villages, only somewhat embellished. All the houses, and even the tower of the principal church, are built of brown granite stones, laid one above another, and cemented with clay. The church alone is covered with a yellow wash; all the other buildings have a blackish-brown appearance. Many are wretched cabins, and some streets on the slope of the hill are so narrow that only two persons can stand abreast. Steep stone steps lead to the arched door, which is placed in the middle of the front wall of the houses. I strolled through these streets, which seemed worthy of being inhabited by demons; and such I fancy might be the appearance of Dis, the town of Hell, in Dante. But in the Santa Anna quarter, there are elegant houses of wealthy persons, and some look well enough in spite of their black building-stone. Original and picturesque they all are, and that is due to the obtuse-angled Italian roofs, which project far over the walls, and to the numerous chimneys in the Italian style, erected now in the form of pillars with fanciful capitals, now like little steeples, now in the shape of obelisks. Such a roof is a considerable adornment to a house; and if its walls are only composed of decently regularly hewn granite blocks, one is well enough satisfied with the effect. But I also found a repetition of my Monte Rotondo cabins in the middle of the market-place. These were some store-houses of the citizens. A curious effect is imparted by the pompous names of some of the inns, on which one may read "Hotel de l'Europe," "de Paris," and "de la France."

The name Sartene, reminds one of Sardinia, or of the Saracens.
They could not tell me its origin. In old times it was called
Sartino, and the town traditions tell that it was renowned for
its mineral waters. Many strangers came to use the waters.
The poor inhabitants of the wretched village were dying of
hunger, because the strangers ate them out of house and home.
So they earthed up the springs, deserted their houses, and built
themselves dwellings higher up on the hills. If this story is
true, it does not tell against the proverbial Corsican laziness.

Sartene suffered terribly from the Saracens. After repeated
incursions, the Moors surprised the town in the year 1583, and
in one day carried off four hundred persons into slavery, probably a third of the then population. After that event the
Sartenians surrounded their city with a strong wall.

At the present time one sees no trace in the quiet place, whose
inhabitants gossip peacefully in the idyllic market-place beneath
the great elm, of the grim passions that it has harboured within
its walls. After the July revolution, Sartene was for years the
scene of a horrible civil war It had been split ever since the
year 1815 into two parties, the adherents of the family Rocca
Serra, and those of the family of Ortoli. The former are the
wealthy, inhabiting the Santa Anna quarter; the latter the poor,
inhabiting the Borgo. Both factions entrenched themselves in
their quarters, fastened their houses, shut their windows, made
sallies upon one another, and shot and stabbed one another with
extreme rage. The Rocca Serras were the white or Bourbonists,
the Ortolis the red or liberals ; the former had denied their opponents entry into their quarters, but the Ortolis, being determined to force it, marched one day with flags flying to Santa
Anna. The Rocca Serras instantly shot from their houses, killing
three men and wounding others. This was the signal for a bloody
battle. On the following day many hundred mountaineers came
with their guns, and besieged Santa Anna. The government
sent military ; but although this to all appearance produced
tranquillity, the two parties still kept assailing one another, and
killed several men of their adversaries. The variance still continues, although the Rocca Serras and Ortolis have met amicably
at the festival of Louis Napoleon's election to the presidency, for
the first time after an enmity of thirty-three years, and allowed
their children to dance together.

These ineradicable family feuds present the same spectacle in
Corsica as the Italian cities, Florence, Bologna, Verona, Padua,

and Milan, offered to the world in the olden times ; and thus one sees the Italian middle ages reenacted at the present day in Corsica, with the same tumults which Dino Compagni depicts so graphically in his Florentine chronicle, and the same feuds of citizens, who, as Dante complains, are surrounded by one moat and by one and the same wall. But these family feuds are far more striking and terrible in Corsica, because they are carried on in such small places, in villages often possessing scarcely a thousand inhabitants, who are moreover indissolubly bound to one another by the bonds of blood and the rights of hospitality.

The good folk of Sartene are today solemnly assembled on the market-place, where a curious scaffolding is being erected for the 15th of August—Napoleon's name-day—for the display of fire-works. Perhaps the ceremony will excite the quarrel anew, and these black houses may be converted in a few days into so many small fortresses, from which each man finds means to aim at his enemy's head. Here politics occasioned civil war ; elsewhere this is produced by some personal injury, or by any the most trifling circumstance. For a dead goat there once died sixteen men, and a whole canton was up in arms. A young man throws a bit of bread to his dog, the dog of another man snaps it up ; thence arises a war between two parishes, and the consequence is murder and death on both sides. Occasions for quarrelling are not wanting at the public communal elections, at festivities, and balls. Sometimes the occasions are very ridiculous. In the year 1832, a dead donkey at Mariana was the cause of a bloody feud between two villages. In Easter-week, a procession going to a certain chapel stumbled upon a dead ass upon the road. The sexton was angry, and began to curse those who had thrown the beast on the road, and thus shown dishonour to the holy procession. A strife immediately arose between the people of Lucciana and those of Borgo, which parish the ass belonged to, and arms were seized forthwith, and shots exchanged ; the holy procession had suddenly converted itself into a battle. The one village cast the burthen upon the other ; each carried the ass to the other :—one while they of Borgo dragged him to Lucciana, another while they of Lucciana to Borgo, and this in the midst of constant shooting and wild battle-cries on both sides.

So fought Trojans and Greeks for the body of Patroclus. The men of Borgo once dragged the dead ass quite to the church of Lucciana, and threw him down at the church-door ; but those of Lucciana took him up again, and then having taken Borgo by storm, impaled him on the belfry tower. At length the podestà caused the *corpus delicti*, which was beaten into a pulp by its wandering, and was in a state of dissolution, to be seized and buried in peace. The poet Viale has composed a comic epic on this dead ass, after the manner of the Stolen Pail of Bologna.

A detachment of ten gens d'armes are stationed at Sartene. The same number are usually posted in every canton, or in such villages as are particularly disturbed. The officer of the gens d'armes was an Alsatian, who had lived twenty-two years in Corsica, and seemed quite rejoiced to meet with a fellow-countryman so unexpectedly. Every time I meet an Alsatian or Lorrainer—the latter speak very broken German—I feel historical regrets for lost German brethren. It is a lasting grief to us to know any portion of noble German earth in the hands of the French. The officer complained greatly of his dangerous service, and the guerilla against the banditti. He pointed to a mountain in the distance—the lofty Incudine—"See there," he said; "there is an arch-bandit, whom we chase like a mufflone. Fifteen hundred francs are offered for his head, but they are hard to earn. A few days ago we brought in twenty-nine persons who had carried food to him. They are confined in these barracks."

"What will be their punishment?"

"A year's imprisonment if the crime is proved against them. They are herdsmen, or other people from the mountains, friends and relations of the bandit." Poor Corsica! what is to become of thy agriculture and manufactures under such circumstances?

The sight of the gloomy mountain Incudine, on which I now knew the poor bandit to be lurking, and the family feud of Sartene, again gives rise to story-telling, drawn from the inexhaustible Corsican popular romance of Blood-revenge. So we will seat ourselves on a rock, from which we can see the great mountains and the gulf of Valinco, and hear a couple of the old gunbarrel's stories.

CHAPTER IV.

TWO STORIES OF THE GUN-BARREL.*

ORSO PAOLO.

THE people of the village of Monte d'Olmo were once celebrating a religious festival. The priests were already standing before the altar, and some of the congregation were already assembled for worship in the house of God, whilst others were still sitting in the churchyard gossiping on all subjects. Among them were the Vincenti and the Grimaldi, whose families had for generations been in constant hereditary feud. This day they ventured to look one another in the face, because the religious festival put a check upon all hostile actions.

Some one threw out the question whether the priests should be obliged to wear the cowl of their order during the procession, or not.

"No," said Orso Paolo, of the family of the Vincenti, "they shall not be obliged, for such was not the custom in the time of our forefathers."

"Yes," cried Ruggero, of the Grimaldi family, "they shall be obliged, for so the observances of religion prescribe."

And so they quarrelled about cowls or no cowls, and there was a noise and rage in the churchyard, much as if the matter of decision was Genoa or no Genoa. One took the word out of the other's mouth, one after the other jumped on the stone to do battle for his opinion, and the bystanders hissed or cried applause, hurraed or jeered, according as a Grimaldi or a Vincenti had said a word about the cowls.

Suddenly an insult was given. Instantly there arose a cry of rage, and pistols were snatched from their belts. The Grimaldis made an onslaught upon Orso Paolo, and the latter shot among his assailants. Antonio, the eldest son of Ruggero, fell, mortally wounded.   •

* See the explanation of this allusion, page 155.

The mass was interrupted in the church. The people rushed out, men, women, children, and the priests in their mass robes, with the crucifix in their hands.

The entire village of Olmo was a turmoil of flyers and pursuers, and echoed with cries of rage and gun-shots. The Grimaldi were crying out for Orso Paolo, eager to murder him.

Orso had dashed off with the speed of a stag to gain the bush. But his pursuers had seen him run off, and, furnished with the wings of revenge, they barred his road, and endeavoured to circumvent him.

He saw his furious pursuers rushing up on all sides, and their bullets whizzed around him. He could not reach the bush, and he had only a few minutes time to form his resolution. No escape was possible into the open country; only a single house stood near him on the mountain side, and this was the house of his mortal enemy Ruggero.

Orso Paolo saw this, and instantly darted into this house and bolted the door. He had his arms with him, his *carchera* was full of cartridges, and provisions enough were in the house; so he could hold out for days. The house was empty, all the inmates having gone into the village, and Ruggero's wife being busied with the wounded Antonio. Her second son, a child of a few years, was left behind alone in the house, and was asleep there.

Scarcely had Orso Paolo concealed and fortified himself there, than Ruggero made his appearance with all the Grimaldi; but the former pointed his gun out of the window, and threatened any one with a bullet who should dare to approach the door. No one dared.

They stood before the house in the extremity of rage, and knew not what to do; Ruggero was frantic that his mortal enemy had found a place of refuge in his own house. He roared as the tiger roars when he sees the prey that he cannot reach.

So stood the frantic band before the house, and the tumult was swelled every minute by those who joined the stream, and filled the air with their clamour. With this turmoil were mingled the lamentations of the women. They were carrying the seriously wounded Antonio into a kinsman's house. At the sight of his son, Ruggero's rage was doubled, and he rushed into a house and snatched a firebrand from the hearth, to hurl upon his own roof, so as to burn Orso Paolo with the house that sheltered him. As he was brandishing the brand in his hand,

and calling to others to throw fire upon his roof, his wife
threw herself in his way. "Madman!" she cried, "our child is
in the house. Will you burn your child? Antonio lies on his
death-bed, yonder sleeps Francesco in his chamber; will you
murder your last child?"

"Let it be burned with him!" cried Ruggero; "let the world
be burnt down, so that Orso Paolo be only destroyed with it!"

The wife cast herself howling at her husband's feet, and clasped his knees, and would not let him move from the spot. But
Ruggero shook her off, and hurled the firebrand into his house.

It set the house on fire. The flames ascended, and the sparks
flew with the wind. The mother had sunk down as one lifeless,
and been carried to where her son Antonio lay.

But Ruggero stood before the burning house, which the
Grimaldis had encompassed, that if Orso Paolo attempted an
escape he might not be missed by their bullets. Ruggero stood
before his house, and gazed fixedly into the flames with a grim
laugh on his face, seeing how they crept on till they met, blazing
and crackling; and when the beams crashed he screamed with
revenge, and with pangs of pain, for it seemed as though each
burning beam fell upon his own heart.

Often it seemed as though a figure was to be seen in the
flames, but it was perhaps a black smoke-cloud, or a curling
column of fire; now again he seemed to hear the voice of the
child crying in the house. Suddenly the roof fell in with a
crash, and smoke and blazing fire went up from the fallen ruins
to heaven.

Ruggero, who had stood mute and stiff, leaning forward with
his hand stretched out towards the house, and his eye fixed, fell
to the earth with a hollow groan. They carried him to the
house where his wounded son, Antonio, was lying. When he
came to himself, he had at first no knowledge of what had
. happened, but it dawned upon him immediately, and the glare
of his burning house shed the terrible light upon his soul,
informing him, to his horror, of the enormity of his deed. For
a minute he stood shut up within himself, as if struck to the
very marrow of his bones by the lightning of God's vengeance;
. then he started up and snatched the dagger from his belt to
bury it in his breast. But his wife and friends held his hands
and disarmed him.

What became of Orso Paolo? what of Francesco?

When the flames had gained the wood-work, Orso Paolo

sought for some place of refuge in the house—any hole or vault to keep him from the fire. He went through all the rooms. In one of them he heard the weeping and the cries of a child. He darted into the room; a young child was sitting on its bed, bitterly weeping, and stretching out its hand towards him, calling the name of its mother. Then Orso fancied he heard the evil spirit calling to him from the midst of the flames to murder the dear child, and so chastise his enemy's inhumanity. "Are not even the children of the enemy forfeited to the laws of revenge? Strike, Orso, destroy the last hope of the house of Grimaldi!"

Orso bent over the child with a horrible expression of revenge. The glow of the flames poured a purple light, like blood, over him, the child, and the chamber. He bent over the weeping Francesco, and suddenly snatched him up, pressed him to his breast, and kissed him with wild enthusiasm. He then rushed out of the room with the child in his arms, and felt his way on in the burning house, to see whether there was not a protecting place to be found any where.

Hardly had the house fallen in, than the horns of the Vincenti sounded through the village. The men of Castel d'Acqua, all friends and kinsmen of Orso Paolo, on receiving news of his distress, marched up to deliver him. The Grimaldi fled from the place of conflagration to the house where Ruggero, his wife, and Antonio were now assembled.

A fearful quarter of an hour passed by.

Then sounded on the market-place of Olmo a loud acclamation, and the cry, a hundred times repeated, of "Evviva Orso Paolo!" The mother of Antonio rushes to the windows; she utters a cry of joy and rushes out of the house, and Ruggero and the women after her.

Through the shouting multitude advanced Orso Paolo, beaming with joy, holding the child Francesco lovingly in his arms, covered with ashes, blackened with smoke, and with his clothes singed. He had rescued himself and the child under an arch of the staircase.

Ruggero's wife flew to Orso Paolo, cast herself upon his breast, and embraced him and her little son with unspeakable joy.

And Ruggero fell on his knees before his enemy, and, clasping his feet, prayed him and God with sobs for forgiveness.

"Rise, my friend Grimaldi," said Orso Paolo; "may God forgive us to-day, as we both forgive one another, and let us here, in the presence of the people of Olmo, swear eternal friendship."

The enemies fell into one another's arms, and the people exclaimed with exultation, "Evviva Orso Paolo!"

In a short time Antonio recovered from his wound; and pure joy reigned one evening in the village of Monte d'Olmo, when the Grimaldi and Vincenti celebrated the feast of their reconciliation. The houses were decorated with the olive-branch of peace, and naught was heard but Evvivas and the cling of wineglasses, joyful salutes from the guns, and the music of fiddles and guitars.

DEZIO DEZII.

At the time when the Genoese held dominion over the island of Corsica, the villages of Serra and Serrale, in the *pieve* of Moriani, were engaged in a desperate war. Two houses there were engaged in a sanguinary feud, the Dezii in Serra, and the Venturini in Serrale.

Wearied at length of their long and revengeful struggle, the two hostile families swore before the *parolanti* to keep the peace. Now, if you do not know, or have forgotten, who the *parolanti* are, I will tell you. The *parolanti* are the good people, the mediators, whom the hostile parties appoint in concert, to receive the written treaty of peace, and the oath confirmed by shaking hands, and to watch that neither breaks the peace. And whoever breaks it is godless, and suffers the scorn of all good men, and the wrath and condemnation of the *parolanti* falls upon his house, his field, and his vineyard.

Thus had the Dezii and the Venturini sworn peace, and there was charming tranquillity again in the *pieve* of Moriani. But as the wicked spirit of dissension cannot rest, but is always fanning the embers, endeavouring to rekindle a spark of the old vengeful resentment, it came to pass one day that he blew upon the grim heart of old Venturini in the market-place of Serrale. Nicolao was old in age, but as young in vigour as his sons. He had a wicked eye, an envenomed tongue, and a convulsive power in the hand that held his dagger. He met young Dezio Dezii, the pride and flower of the house of his enemy, in the marketplace. Dezio Dezii was handsome, and of agreeable manners, but his spirit was fiery and impetuous.

The old man with the wicked eye said a scornful and envenomed word to the youth; and no one knows how that was brought about, for Dezio had given him no occasion. The youth,

2 G

on hearing these words, was filled with shame and wrath, but he thought of the *parolanti*, of the sworn peace, and the grey hairs of Nicolao. So he smothered his feelings in his heart, and went away silent from the village of Serrale.

Now it happened that on the very same evening the old man and the youth met again in the fields. When Dezio saw Nicolao approaching unarmed, he quickly threw down his gun under a tree, that the evil spirit might not tempt him to assail an unarmed man, and went up to the old man and haughtily demanded an account from him of his reasons for insulting him.

The old man made a sneering rejoinder, and, words rising higher and higher, took hold of the youth and gave him a blow in the face. Dezio reeled backwards; in one moment he was off for his gun, and in the next a shot was fired, and the old man fell to the ground wounded to the heart.

Poor Dezio fled as if pursued by the avenging angel, and sprang from rock to rock, up to the peaks of Monte Cinto, where he threw himself down in a cavern weeping.

Upon the news of the deed of blood the *parolanti* hastened up. They denounced wo upon Dezio and his whole race, and proceeded to his house. Dezio's young wife was there. They told her she must leave the house, as it was put under a ban of outlawry; and, when she had gone weeping out of the door, they threw fire into it and burned it to the ground. Then they went to Dezio's chestnut plantation and olive ground, and barked every tree trunk, as a sign that Dezio had broken his oath and shed blood, and that the wrath of Heaven had cursed him and his estate. And this they did agreeably to the consecrated usage of their ancestors.

Dezio's kinsmen kept quiet, for they knew that justice had been done against him. But Luigione, the son of the murdered Nicolao, let his beard grow, as a sign that he would avenge his father's blood. He took his gun and roved over the mountains to hunt out Dezio, and not being able to find him, although he remained whole days and nights there, he took service under the Genoese, who held guard in the tower of Padulella. Peradventure he might thus be able to spy out his enemy with the help of the garrison.

But Dezio lived with the fox, the deer, and the wild sheep, and roamed about over the wilds, hiding his head at some new place every night, ever wandering and ever sad at heart, and full of terrors. So he one day took ship with some sailors who were his friends, to Genoa. He entered the Genoese service, and years passed over his head in exile.

After the lapse of a long time, the desire of seeing his country and his wife was aroused within him. So he took leave of his military life, and received in Genoa a letter of safe-conduct, by which he might live secure and unmolested in Corsica, and whoever did him any harm should be amenable to justice.

Perhaps Dezio hoped also that Luigione's resentment would have been lulled during such a length of time. So he came back to his village, found his wife again, and kept quiet in his own house. No one knew of his return; for he never showed himself in public, and only walked in the woods and in lonely places where he was sure of meeting no one. The shadow of old Nicolao attended him wherever he went.

So passed weeks and months, and no one knew or spoke of Dezio. One day Luigione, who was renowned on the mountains as a sportsman, said to his wife, "I dreamt that I was chasing a fox on the mountains; I will go a hunting; perhaps I may have good sport to-day." And he flung his gun across his shoulder, and went to the mountains.

A red fox came across his path, who ran into a thicket, and Luigione hastened after him. The place was lonely and melancholy. On entering the thicket he found a narrow shepherd's path, winding like a labyrinth, and leading deeper and deeper into the wilderness. Luigione suddenly stood still. Beneath a wild olive he saw a man lying buried in deep sleep. In the grass beside him lay his double-barrelled gun and his *zucca*. A long beard overshadowed his face. Luigione stood as stiff as a statue; his eyes only glanced feverishly, and eagerly devoured the form of the sleeper. His blood boiled and ran to his cheeks, and in the next minute his cheeks were deathly pale; his heart beat so loud that it might have awakened the sleeper.

One step he took forwards—another—he stared into the face of the stranger—yes! it was Dezio, the murderer of his father. A wild smile played over Luigione's countenance. He drew the dagger from his belt.

"God has given thee into my hands," he muttered, "that I may kill thee this day. The blood of my father be visited this day upon thee"—and he raised his two-edged sword. But a sudden thought stepped like an angel between him and the sleeper, and held his sword back. The angel said to him, "Luigione, thou shalt not murder sleep!"

He suddenly recoiled, and cried with a terrible voice:
"Dezio! Dezio! rise and arm thyself!"

The sleeper sprang up and felt for his arms.

"I might have murdered thee in sleep," Luigione said to him, "but that were the deed of a knave. Now, defend thyself; for my father's blood calls for revenge."

For one instant Dezio regarded the terrible man with mortal dread; then he hurled his gun far among the bushes, tore the pistol and dagger from his belt, and threw them both from him, and then he opened his breast, and said, "Luigione, shoot and avenge thy father! I shall find peace in my grave! kill me!"

Luigione regarded his ill-fated foe with astonishment, and both were silent for a while. Then Luigione put away his gun, went up to Dezio, and gave him his hand. "God," he said, "has given thee into my hands that I may forgive thee. Peace to the blood of my father! Now, come and be my guest!"

The two men entered the village arm-in-arm, and they continued friends. And, a child being born to Luigione, he asked Dezio to stand godfather as a sacred token of their reconciliation. And this he did, agreeably to the usage of their forefathers.

Dezio soon grew weary of the world, and took the cowl. His conversation was so pure and godly that he was loved by all men till the latest period of his life, and the blessing of his piety produced peace far and wide over the mountains.

When he fell asleep in the Lord, all the villages of the neighbourhood attended him to his grave; and they say to the present day in the *pieve* of Moriano, Dezio the Worldly, Dezio the Murderer, Dezio the Bandit, Dezio the Monk, Dezio the Priest, Dezio the Saint.

CHAPTER V.

ENVIRONS OF SARTENE.

THERE are desolate mountains about Sartene, among which the Incudine and Coscione raise their heads towards the north. The Coscione is renowned for its pastures, which are watered by the charming streams of Bianca and Viola. Hither the herdsmen of Quenza drive their herds in the summer, and in the winter they descend to the coast of Porto Vecchio. One of these mountains near Sartene is a curiously-shaped rock, in the form of a giant raising his uncouth head to the clouds. It is called the Man of Cogna. In the district of Sartene are also some remains of *menhirs* and *dolmens*, those ancient mythical stones which are found in the islands of the Mediterranean and in Celtic countries. They consist of columnar stones erected in a circle, and are here called stazzone. Sardinia is as rich in these architectural relics as Corsica is poor. I regret exceedingly having been unable to see the *stazzoni* of Sartene.

On the mountains round about are many ruins of castles belonging to the brave Renuccio della Rocca and the celebrated Giudice della Rocca. The fief of these ancient lords was round Sartene. The canton of Santa Lucia de Tallano especially preserves the memory of Renuccio by its old ruined Franciscan convent, an institution founded by this lord, with whom the power of the Corsican barons sank, never again to rise. In the church they show the grave of his daughter Serena, who lies there in marble with a rosary in her hand, from which depends a purse, as a symbol of her liberality.

In the rocks of Santa Lucia is found the remarkable kind of granite peculiar to Corsica, called *orbicularis*. It is of a greyish-blue ground colour, but there are many black, white-margined eyes sprinkled over the stone, which appear on the surface wherever the rock is split. I saw capital pieces of it; polished, this fine granite looks extremely beautiful, and may be employed for all sorts of furniture and ornaments. It is one of the most interesting *lusus naturæ*, and a jewel in the richly stored mineralogical treasury of Corsica. This orbicular granite of Santa Lucia de Tallano has found a place in the Mediccan Chapel at Florence, which is inlaid with the rarest stones.

In the valley of the Fiumiccioli, to the north east of Santa Lucia, lies the celebrated old canton of Levie, extending as far as the small gulf of Ventilegne. It is covered by mountains and considerable forests. Here also abode some ancient noble families, especially that of Peretti, to which belonged Sampiero's friend Napoleon, the first of this name mentioned in Corsican history, not however an ancestor of the Bonapartes. He met his death in a battle against the Genoese.

To Levie belongs San Gavino de Corbini, a place mentioned in Corsican history as being the chief seat of that extraordinary sect the Giovannali, those ancient Corsican communists, who made such rapid progress on the island, and were in a manner forerunners of the St. Simonists and the Mormons. Exciting causes of the rise of such a sect must needs be present in a wild land, still subject to the natural, uncivilized state of society, where the natural equality of man was the prevailing principle of the nation, and in the bloody times of universal misery. It is much to be regretted that the chronicles of the country have not preserved more particulars of the nature of this community. Its existence seems to me a remarkable train in the physiognomy of Corsican history: fleeting and transient as it appears, it is still to me a well-marked line in the portrait of the Corsican people.

Before taking leave of Sartene, I will most heartily praise the hospitality of its inhabitants. I experienced it in the kindest fashion, and felt quite at home in simple and friendly intercourse with good people. They absolutely would not let me go, but I must hunt the wild sheep with them up to the highest mountains, and above all go into their orchards to refresh myself with fruit to my heart's content. And when I wished to depart again in the early morning, all these good people who had been friendly to me, escorted me on my way, and one of them—he was a cousin of the unfortunate Vittoria Malaspina—handed me on parting a piece of paper.

On unfolding the paper I read the following words :—

"To Signor Ferdinando.—Should you ever be in want of anything, or should any unpleasant circumstance happen to you in our country, remember that you have a friend in the town of Sartene.

"ALESSANDRO CASANOVA."

I have carried this paper about with me as a talisman, and as a token of the excellent Corsican ways, according to which my friend of Sartene was not satisfied to assure me by words, and a shake of the hand, that he had taken me in a manner under his protection as a guest for all future time, but actually also confirmed this by a special document.

CHAPTER VI.

THE TOWN OF BONIFAZIO.

At eight o'clock in the morning I set off on my drive from Sàrtene to Bonifazio, the most southern town and fortress in Corsica, I traversed a desolate coast region, where the mountains gradually sink down to the sea. There is not a place on the whole road, and I should have half perished of hunger and thirst if my travelling companion had not taken bread and wine with him. Who ne'er his bread with rapture ate, or o'er the wine-cup 'neath an olive sate, he knows ye not, ye heavenly powers!

We passed through the Ortoli valley—barren hills every where, and no fruit. The olive ceases, and only shrubby cork-trees and strawberry-trees now cover the land. We approached the perfectly barren southern coast. Not far from the mouth of the Ortoli stands a solitary post-house, and opposite it a ledge of rock, on which the tower of Roccapina stands. An oddly shaped block of stone rises near it on the sharp edge of rock. It bears a striking resemblance to a colossal crowned lion, and the common people call it *il leone coronato*. Upon this coast, the first occupied by Genoa when she wrested Corsica from the Pisans, this extraordinary rock looks like a monument, or like the arms of the Republic herself •

From this eminence I first perceived the coasts and mountains of Sardinia afar off over the sea, but not very distant. There is a glorious distant view. The sight of a strange land suddenly unfolding itself to the eye, and displaying, here only its outlines, there objects full of character, arouses the most agreeable sensations of expectation, longing desire, and uncertainty. These sensations most recall the fabulous fancies of childhood.—It is quite an island. So I stood a long time on one of the barren masses of rock, in a high wind and the heat of noon, looking longingly over the straits at the twin sister of Corsica. She was completely enwrapped in the most ethereal blue veil, and the waves excited by the *maestrale* foamed around her with white surge.

After a two hours' rest we proceeded along the coast, which

is interrupted by arms of the sea, and melancholy. Small rivers creep through morasses into the sea, upon the coast-cliffs of which grey towers hold guard. The air is foul and unhealthy. I saw a few small hamlets on the side of the hill, and was told that they were empty, for that the inmates do not return to them from the mountains till the month of September.

The sea here forms two small gulfs, that of Figari and that of Ventilegne. They resemble fiords, and their coasts are frequently of the oddest conformation, rising like rows of ashen-grey obelisks.

Crossing the last point of land in Corsica towards the south-west, namely Santa Trinita, the tongue which ends in Capo di Feno, the white chalk cliffs of Bonifazio then come into view, and this most southern and most original town of the island itself, snow-white like the coast, placed high up on the rocks;—a surprising prospect in the midst of the wide and depressing solitude.

The coast-land round about is stony and bushy. One drives however for half an hour amongst olive-groves and orchards up to the town, and is astonished to find such fertility, which man, here compelled to industry, has forced from the chalky soil. The district of Bonifazio produces an abundance of olives, which are said not to yield in goodness to those of the Balagna. The traveller now drives downhill between chalk-cliffs to the *marina* of Bonifazio, which extends along the gulf. Into the town itself he can come only on foot or on horseback; for he has to climb up the steep chalk-cliff on a broad path cut into steps. Passing over two drawbridges and two old gates, he then enters Bonifazio. The whole town is within the fortress, on the plateau of the rock.

Bonifazio hails the wanderer with a welcome greeting as he enters through the gloomy old gate: for upon one of its towers parades the great word Liberty. I have often read it upon towers and town-halls in Italy as the most pitiable irony upon their present state, and upon many a banner has this word paraded; but here it makes a proud figure upon the old tower, which has such brilliant deeds of arms to tell of; and thus I entered the town with the joyous sensation of coming among brave and free men. For even at the present day the Bonifazines have the reputation of being the most republican, as well as the most laborious and religious inhabitants of Corsica.

The situation of Bonifazio is most remarkable. Fancy a whitish colossal rock-pyramid with horizontal strata, inverted with the base upwards, set down by the seaside, and upon the

base fortress, towers, and town high up in the air, and you will
have a picture of this Corsican Gibraltar. The façade of the
rock is moreover excavated into huge caverns. The rock is
connected with the land; on two sides it is lashed by the surges
of the straits, on the third it is washed by a narrow arm of the
sea, which forms gulf, harbour, and fortifying moat at the same
time, and is enclosed by most precipitous, indeed inaccessible,
hills. The force of the water has crumbled away the shores all
round, and produced the most grotesque forms. Seen from
below, that is, from the sea, which in many places has no edging
of shore at all, from the rock sinking quite precipitously into the
waves, this rock is most awe-inspiring. I descended and looked
up it: the waves broke in surges, and clouds were driving across
the sky, and it seemed as if the rock were tottering and would
fall down upon me—an illusion which is the more natural because
a part of its base has actually been torn off, and the chalk strata
blackened by the storms are here and there exposed freely to
the air. When I saw Bonifazio, I well understood that Alfonso
of Arragon could not take the town.

It numbers 3380 inhabitants, comprising no communes in its
insular position. Its houses are of Pisan and Genoese origin.
Old and worn out as they are, they are more like ruins than
dwellings. The rocks upon which they stand generally furnish
their building-materials. They are all white, and the city-walls
and short towers being also white, there is enough of this contrast to the Corsican national colour. It would be hard for me
to give a clear picture of the town itself; for the medley of
narrow lanes cannot possibly be described, in which draughts or
the sea-breeze are always whirling the dust about, and in which
one strays now uphill, now downhill, in astonishment at the
novelty of the situation, where the eye, wherever it finds an
outlet into the open world, discovers the sea deep below, not less
blue than the heaven above. Beams are often thrown across
from one house to another, and there are frequently dark passages
leading from one narrow lane into another.

The wind whistles and the sea-waves are surging: one
feels ill at ease. The feeling of *space*, a most beneficial one to
the soul, is here banished. The solitary sentinel on the round
tower there paces up and down, quite surrounded by a whirl of
chalk-dust I will try to find a *piazza*, to come among men
again. But there is no *piazza*: the want of room allows of no
such extension; but the main street is here curiously called the

Piazza Doria, for the Bonifazines must have felt the necessity of
having a square or forum, without which a town is like a house
without assembling-rooms. So they called the main street their
square. The want of extent compelled them to build the houses
high; and, from the want of depth, the staircases are exceedingly
steep. On many houses I saw the arms of Genoa, the crowned
lion rampant holding a ring in his claws. This old token rouses
proud reminiscences, as does the name Doria, which has preserved itself here alive, there being still in Bonifazio a family
called Doria, or more correctly d'Oria. This is the proper form
of the name of the celebrated Genoese lords, who were of the
great family of Oria. The Corsicans hated Genoa with a mortal
hatred; whenever I spoke to them of the old republic, I found
the same rooted hate. All the misery that has befallen Corsica
—its moral as well as its physical wilderness—they ascribe to
the Genoese. But with the Bonifazines Genoa stands in the best
possible odour; and this is intelligible from their history.

It is not agreed what the tract upon which the modern Bonifazio is built was called in antiquity. It is held to be either the
ancient Syracusanus Portus, or the ancient town of Pallae, which
is the last enumerated by the Itinerary of Antoninus in his list
of the Corsican stations. Bonifazio itself was founded by the Tuscan marquis whose name it bears; and we know that he planned
it in the year 833, after a naval victory over the Saracens, to oppose a dam to their piratical incursions, as they were wont to land
from Spain, Africa, and Sardinia, on this side of the island. Of
the fortifications erected by the marquis, the great old tower
called Torrione, is still standing. Three other towers besides
are erected upon the rock: Bonifazio carries them all in its
armorial bearings. The town, as well as the island, subsequently
came under the Pisans; but the Genoese deprived them of
Bonifazio as early as the year 1193. It was during a wedding
that they assembled and gained the city. They treated it with
great liberality, gave it very free statutes, and allowed it to sub-
sist as a republic under their protectorate. In the Red Book of
Bonifazio, the instrument is preserved which Brancaleone d'Oria,
the procurator of Genoa, signed on the 11th February 1321, and
solemnly swore to upon the Testament. By this instrument
perfect free trade with Genoese ports without imposts, was
secured to the Bonifazines; furthermore, the privilege of governing themselves. They elected their elders, called Anziani, in
their popular assembly; to their decrees the Genoese podestà,

who was annually sent to the town as syndic or commissioner,
was to conform. He could not impose any tax or make any
innovation without the will of the Anziani; and he was not
competent to hold in arrest any citizen of Bonifazio who could
offer bail, except a murderer, thief, or traitor. When a new
podestà came to Bonifazio, the possession of the town could not
be granted him till he had solemnly sworn an oath upon the
sacraments, to observe inviolably all the treaties and statutes
of Bonifazio. This instrument is subscribed, "Per Brancaleonem
de Oria, et per Universitatem Bonifatii, in publico Parlamento"
—"by Brancaleone d'Oria, and the entire community of Bonifazio,
in public parliament assembled." This sounds sufficiently
pompous for a little town which had then no more than 1000
inhabitants.

Thus these brave people gained for themselves freedom without stint, which they found means upon their rock to preserve
for many centuries.

The Genoese honoured the Bonifazines in every possible way.
If one of their ships came to Genoa and declared its native port,
they used to ask, "Are you from the territory of Bonifazio, or
from Bonifazio proprio?" Hence the popular saying has been
derived, which may still be heard, "He is a Bonifazino proprio."
Many Genoese nobles and citizens, glad of such immunities and
privileges, removed from their glorious city to this rock, and
Bonifazio thus became in language, manners, and sentiments, a
Genoese colony. This may be seen at the present day, not only
in the old armorial bearings, but in the people themselves.

Like Calvi, Bonifazio always kept faith inviolably with the
Genoese. These two towns occupy, in virtue of these sentiments,
a peculiar historical position; and it is remarkable to find, on
the terrible ocean of Corsican hatred, two little islands, as it
were, in which the tyrannical Genoa was loved. Let us not be
hard upon the manly Genoese, and envy them this advantage:
their old and sinful, yet ever great and glorious Republic, has
long paid its debt to history, and no longer exists.

A Bonifazino, Murzolaccio, wrote a small separate history of
his town in the year 1625. It was published at Bologna, and
is extremely rare. I have not been able to beat up a copy,
which I regret, because I grew so attached to Bonifazio. But I
will here relate the memorable siege of the town by Alfonso of
Arragon, according to Peter Cyrnæus; for the heroism of the
Bonifazines well deserves to live in the memory of man beside

that of Numantia, of Carthage, and of Saragossa in modern times.
I give Peter's description, not always imitating verbal peculiari-
ties, nor entire, as it is too long.

CHAPTER VII.

THE SIEGE OF BONIFAZIO BY ALFONSO OF ARRAGON.

ALFONSO of Arragon, having reconnoitred the position of the
town, occupied a high hill towards the north, and threw stones
from his bombards by night and day from thence and from
the sea, into the town. The Spaniards had come with eighty
ships, twenty-three of which were triremes; after the fall of two
towers they advanced into the harbour. Now when a large
portion of the defensive works and walls had already fallen in, and
it seemed possible to break into the town, King Alfonso called
his generals to a council of war. He was young and fiery, and
eager for great exploits. "When Bonifazio has fallen," he said,
"all Corsica will be in my power, and I will then set sail against
Italy." He proclaimed rewards for the first man who should
scale the walls and plant his banner on them, and for the second,
and so on to the tenth. The Spaniards heard this with great
delight, and prepared for the assault. The people of Bonifazio
suffered greatly from missiles and arrows, but they threw back
the scaling parties with stones and long lances into the sea, and
held out bravely. Suddenly the tower called Scarincio fell with
a tremendous crash ; the ships immediately stuck close to the
breach, and the Spaniards leapt upon the wall and planted the
banner upon it. And through the king's army went the cry,
"The town is stormed." Then the marines were seen hastily
climbing the walls by help of the masts and yards, and throwing
firebrands upon the roofs when they came near enough to the
houses. Now arose a great tumult of fliers and opposers and
stormers. But Orlando Guaracchi, the heroic Margareta Bobia,
and Chiaro Ghigini, threw themselves in the way of the assailants,
and from their posts came Jacopo Cataccioli, Giovanni Cicanesi,
and Filippo Campo, and they cut down to the last man all the
enemies who had pressed into the town. Then they threw fire
into the ships in the harbour, and so the king was driven back
with great loss.
The struggle had lasted for three days, with conflagration and

bloodshed without end. Every age and sex now put their hand
to the wheel, to make the walls strong again, and to stop the
breaches with beams. But the corn magazine was unfortunately
burnt down. Alfonso meanwhile threw into the town arrows
with letters attached, which promised a reward in gold to all
who would desert to him. Two deserted, Galliotto Ristori, a
Bonifazine, and Conrado, a Genoese, and these excited the confidence of the king by telling him that those in the town suffered
want of both bread and arms. So the king occupied another
hill near the town, and having drawn a double chain obliquely
across the harbour, to cut off the Bonifazines from all Genoese
aid, he resolved to force the town to submission by a long siege.
This came to the ears of the doge, Thomas Fregoso, who equipped a fleet of seven sail; and in these preparations September
came to an end. And during the whole of October, November,
and December, the sea was so terribly stormy, that the fleet
could not leave the harbour of Genoa. But the Bonifazines
were reduced to such extremity by the hurling of bombs and
missiles, that they had to go out of the town into the grove near
San Antonio, and conceal themselves in the convent of St.
Francis, as the majority of their houses were reduced to ruins;
only on the military posts they still remained.

The king, now reinforced by supplies and ships from Spain,
still wished to try the way of negotiation, and gave a solemn
promise to those in the town, that they should live free and according to their own laws, if they would submit themselves to
him. The Bonifazines protracted as long as possible the negotiations with the ambassadors; and as they looked wretched,
pale with hunger, and starved, and the Arragonians scoffed at
them for their hunger, and thought it must soon force them to
surrender, it is said that, to give the lie to this calculation, they
threw bread from many parts of the walls among the enemy's posts,
and made the king a present of a cheese made of women's milk.
The king then advanced all his storming machines against the
town by means of ships, each pair of which carried the besieg-
ing towers. The assault began anew from the hills as well as
from the seaside. To protect themselves against the naval machines, the Bonifazines had likewise posted engines at various
parts of the walls; upon the more distant ships they hurled
stones of enormous weight, upon the nearer ones stones of lesser
weight, and missiles as thick as hail. Although they were now
themselves overwhelmed by the hail of the bombs and arrows,

untasted, roots and wild-fruit as well as bark, and animals never
eaten before. And, despairing of succour, many, weeping and
wailing, put a voluntary end to their life, and many, wounded
and helpless, would have been carried off by hunger, had not the
compassion of the women offered them relief; for the kind-
hearted women of Bonifazio actually offered their breasts to
their brothers, children, blood-relations, and sponsors, and there
was no one during that terrible siege of Bonifazio who had not
sucked the breast of a woman.

Now when no ray of hope appeared to them in such terrible
need, the Bonifazines concluded a compact, that they would
surrender if the Genoese did not come to raise the siege within
forty days. They gave as hostages two men and thirty children
of the noblest families. But the Bonifazines were full of
apprehension, because the King of Arragon would not allow them
to·send messengers to Genoa. They therefore built a small
vessel in haste, and let it by ropes down the rock fronting
Sardinia, and most distant from the enemy, and then similarly
let down the young men, twenty-four in number, who were to
be its crew, and their messengers to Genoa. The magistrates
had given them letters. to Genoa, and a great multitude of
citizens attended them as far as the rock, and followed them
with their good wishes. The women by turns offered them
their breasts, for food they could take none with them. After
many perils by sea, and long detained by winds, the courageous
messengers at length arrived at Genoa, and informed the senate
how Bonifazio was reduced to the last extremity.

In Bonifazio the people meanwhile resolved to implore God
in a solemn procession to deliver them from the pressure
of the enemy, and to forgive all their sins. The procession
marched from the cathedral of St. Mary to St. James's, then to
St. Dominic, and all the other churches; and, though the winter
was severe, they all walked barefoot, and sang hymns with great
fervour. Prayers were said in the churches from early morning
till late evening, and the minds of all were constantly fixed upon
the hope of relief, and upon the possibility of at length receiving
news of their messengers.

These returned at length to Bonifazio in their little vessel on
the night of the fifteenth day, gave the signal, and were drawn
up by ropes. The joy in the town was so intense that the
people seemed to be out of their mind. When the messengers
went to the church of St. Mary, where the senate was assembled

by day and night, all the people streamed after them to hear
their message. They gave the Doge's letters, which were read,
and after this they were introduced to the assembly of the
people. Picino Cataccioli, the chief messenger, here gave a full
account of his errand, and tendered the assurance that the
Genoese fleet was ready, and only waiting for a favourable wind
to set out. The senate of Bonifazio now ordained a public
thanksgiving of three days; and the joy in the town knew no
bounds when the little corn was distributed which the messengers
had brought with them from Genoa.

In the mean time the day of surrender was approaching without
any sign of the coming of the Genoese fleet; the ambassadors of the
king already urged upon the senate the fulfilment of the compact.
"If the Genoese do not make their appearance in the following
night," the Anziani declared, "we will surrender." Then began
a wailing and lamentation of women and children, and all were
possessed by a terrible despondency. But the senate convened
the assembly of the people to hear their opinions. Guglielmo
Bobia urged persistency, and conjured the shade of Count
Bonifazio, who built the town, to fill the Bonifazines with his
spirit, that none might relinquish their freedom. So they
resolved to hold out to the last possible moment. Suddenly in
the night the cry was raised that the Genoese were coming.
All the bells began to peal, fire signals were seen on all the
towers, and a cry of joy without end rose to heaven. The
Spaniards were astonished, seeing nothing of the Genoese; and
their ambassadors came without delay to the gate by break of
day, and demanded the surrender of the town according to stipulation. But the people of Bonifazio rejoined that they had in
the night received the Genoese succour; and lo! there appeared
armed men, bearing the Genoese banner at their head, passing
three times round the walls, which dazzled with lances and
glittering arms. For all the women had in the night put on
armour, so that the numbers of the Bonifazines appeared to
be tripled. When Alfonso of Arragon saw this, he exclaimed,
"Have the Genoese wings, that they can come to Bonifazio
when we are holding all the points strictly invested?"—And
he caused all his engines to advance once more to the assault.

But at length the Genoese really appeared, on the fourth day
after the expiration of the stipulated time, and anchored over
against the channel. Angelo Bobia and a few other brave men
swam in the night to their ships, and horrified them all by their

famine-worn figures. But the Genoese captains declared that they could not venture an attack upon the Spaniards. Then Bobia, as if thunderstruck, laid his finger to his lips and said, " We have hoped in God and you alone ; you must venture it, and we will help you ! "—the Genoese hesitated.

Alfonso immediately turned a portion of his ships against the Genoese, and directed his bombards against the harbour to cut off the relief. The Genoese ships did not venture to attack the Spaniards, until the young Giovanni Fregoso, Rafael Negro, and other captains in the council, carried the motion that battle must be risked. Jacopo Benesia, the bravest and the boldest, especially voted for battle. For seven hours the contest lasted in the harbours and before the rock,—a horrible one, because ship was jammed against ship, and unable to move in the narrow channel, whilst the Bonifazines were hurling missiles and fire-brands from above. But the Genoese burst the chain which closed the harbour, and forced their way to Bonifazio ; and un-speakable was the rapture of the famished townsmen, when seven Genoese corn ships came to shore and landed their cargo.

Then Alfonso of Arragon saw that he could not take Boni-fazio, and raised the siege, and set sail for Italy, taking the hos-tages with him, deeply humiliated and exasperated, in January of the year 1421.

CHAPTER VIII.

OTHER REMINISCENCES OF BONIFAZIO, AND A FESTIVAL.

OPPOSITE my *locanda* stands an old gloomy house, whose mar-ble door-cornice attracted my notice. There are old sculptures upon it, the arms of Genoa and Gothic initials. My delight was great when I was told that the Emperor Charles V. stayed two days and a night in this house. I felt as if I had, all of a sudden, found a fellow countryman and a good friend on this strange rock. The house speaks to me in German, broad Fle-mish German ; and when I contemplate the window at which Charles V. stood, it overwhelms me with German history, and suggests many a well-known name—Luther, Worms, Augsburg, Wittenberg, Maurice of Saxony, Philip of Hessen, and tells me of Schiller and Don Carlos, of Goethe and Egmont. Charles V.

is a striking phenomenon. He was the last emperor in the full sense of the word ; for against the emperor in whose dominions the sun never set, a small man in a grey cowl arose, and let fall a word which shattered all the glory of his empire like a bomb. Yet those are foolish who reproach Charles V. with not comprehending the Reformation, and putting himself at the head of the movement. The fact is precisely that he *was* emperor. Before his end he grew weary ; and the man whose stirring life had been an incessant battle with the powers that were causing the fall of Germany, France and the Reformation, gave away his dominions, and, acknowledging the force of the great innovator Time, became a hermit, and laid himself in his coffin. I am very glad to have seen Titian's splendid portrait of Charles V. My neighbour at the window here is now no mere idea to me, but a person of flesh and bone.

It was chance that brought Charles V. to Bonifazio. My friend Lorenzo told the story thus. Charles returned in the year 1541 from his unsuccessful expedition against Algiers ; a storm compelled him to anchor in the gulf of Santa Manza, in the vicinity of Bonifazio. He went ashore with his escort, and, curious to see the manners of Corsica, which then, as now, had the reputation of being barbarous and warlike, he entered a vineyard. Filippo Cataccioli, the possessor of it, happened to be there at the time. He offered the emperor some of his grapes, and in conversation excited in the latter a desire to see the extraordinary town of Bonifazio, which Alfonso of Arragon had not been able to take. So the Corsican offered to accompany him, and to receive him as a guest into his house, and promised to respect his incognito. He gave him his horse, the emperor mounted, and the little procession began to move. But Cataccioli had sent a messenger forward, and sent word to the Anziani, that "Charles, King of Spain, and Emperor of the holy Roman Empire, would this day be the guest of Bonifazio." So, as Charles came towards the town, the cannon suddenly thundered a salute, and the thronging people cried, "Evviva Carlo di Spagna !" Charles turned surprised to Cataccioli and said, " Friend, thou hast betrayed me after all."—"No !" replied the latter; " this is the nature of the cannon of Bonifazio, that the sunbeams let them off when a prince like you approaches."

So Charles took up his abode in Cataccioli's house, where he was treated with great attention and respect. On taking leave, he called his host and said to him, "Friend, as you have treated.

your guest handsomely, you may ask three favours for yourself."
Cataccioli asked three privileges for the town of Bonifazio, which
being conceded, the emperor bade him to demand another favour,
but this time a personal one for himself. The Corsican considered for a long time, and then said, "May your Majesty deign
to command that when I am dead my body shall be interred in
the most holy part of the cathedral; for, as that pertains to no
layman, it will be the highest possible honour and distinction
that has ever been granted to a citizen of Bonifazio."

The emperor accordingly commanded this to be done, and
Cataccioli escorted him again to the harbour, and after the embarkation of his guest, took the horse on which the latter had
ridden, and shot it upon the spot.

Cataccioli's house is not quite finished; some gaps are observed
in the wall. During the progress of the building, the Anziani
had interdicted its completion, in consideration of the fortifications. Cataccioli promised to build a lighthouse at his own
expense, if they would allow him his house. The magistrates
entertained the proposition, and it was stipulated that Cataccioli
was not to complete his house till he had brought the lighthouse
to completion. So he built both at the same time, but brought
the lighthouse no further than the foundations, whilst he got his
house roofed in and completed, with the exception of a few gaps
which he left in the wall.

Cataccioli was tall and handsome of figure, and was therefore
called by the people Alto Bello. His family was one of the
wealthiest and noblest in the town, and is frequently mentioned
in its history.

The eye which glances past this abode of Charles V. falls upon
the island of Santa Maddalena, which is off the skirts of Sardinia.
I clearly see the tower upon it, and see the young artillery officer
Napoleon spring out of the vessel to take it. Napoleon lived
about eight months in Bonifazio, opposite Charles V.'s house.
This proximity of two great emperors is remarkable; for it was
Napoleon who dashed in pieces the ancient and glorious imperial
crown of Charles V.

Bonifazio had of old, in the time of its glory, some twenty
churches and convents. The convents are secularized, and only
three churches remain, the cathedral church of St. Mary of the
Fig-tree, San Domenico, and San Francesco. Santa Maria is a
large heavy church of Pisan architecture, buried in the midst of
narrow alleys. Its roomy vestibule is the place of assembly and

promenade of the townspeople, who walk about in it like the Venetians in the verandas of the Place of St. Mark. In the olden times, the senate of Bonifazio assembled in the cathedral to deliberate upon the affairs of the city.

Further on towards the brink of the rock stands San Domenico, a fine church of the Templars, whose triangle is still visible upon the wall. The building is gracefully executed in the purest Gothic proportions, and only wants the decorated façade to produce an agreeable impression externally also. It is incontestably the most beautiful church in Corsica, after the Canonica of Mariana, which is in ruins. Its snow-white octangular tower, commenced by the Pisans, resembles an embattled fortress tower; it is unfinished. I found in the church many gravestones of Templars and Genoese nobles, that of a Doria among the rest. Cardinal Fesch presented some pictures to the church, which however are of no value. Far more interesting are the little *Ex votos*, the votive pictures on wood, which citizens of Bonifazio have dedicated to the Madonna and St. Dominic after a deliverance. There is many a picture among them which gives a right spirited representation of pirate scenes.

The third church, San Francesco, is small, but possesses a great curiosity, as it contains the only living spring in Bonifazio. The Bonifazines drink besides only rain water out of cisterns, and are supplied especially by the great deep cistern, into which they descend by stone steps—a meritorious work of the Genoese.

Most of the former convents of Corsica were of the order of Franciscans. These priests settled in great numbers in the island, and their saint himself is said, by tradition, to have been in Corsica. He was in Bonifazio; and, as the citizens of this town pass for the most religious in the island, I will tell a legend of my friend Lorenzo's.

The deserted convent of San Giuliano is observed situate on the opposite side of the gulf; St. Francis himself gave the following occasion for its establishment. He once came to land, I know not on what voyage, in the harbour of Bonifazio, and went ashore. As it was night, he knocked at a door, and requested admission and a night's quarters. But he did not meet with so good a reception as the Emperor Charles V. The door was shut in his face, because he looked quite wild and hairy, and just like a Corsican bandit. St. Francis went away sorrowing, and lay down to sleep in a cave near the house, and fell asleep after commending his soul to God. A servant-girl soon came out of

the house to throw her slops into the cave, as was her wont.
But on approaching it she saw something shining in it, and in
her fright was near pouring the contents of her bucket over St.
Francis; for it was he who emitted a light in the cave. St.
Francis, I think, then rose from the ground and said, with his
mild smile, "Friend, do the same that you always do, without
minding me, for I have lived in a pigsty for a whole year, as all
the world knows." The foolish maid ran screaming to the house,
and exclaimed that she had seen in the cave a man who possessed
the faculty of being luminous on some parts of his body. The
news flew through Bonifazio; the Bonifazines hastened to the
spot, and, on finding the holy man, caressed him, and begged
him to leave behind him a memorial of his presence. So St.
Francis said, "My friends, let us then erect a convent as a permanent record of this day." The Bonifazines instantly fetched
stones, and St. Francis laid the foundation-stone with his own
hand, and after so doing took his leave, and embarked on his
vessel. But the convent was not called by his name, because
he was not then canonized, but by that of St. Julian. The
Bonifazines subsequently built the church of St. Francis in his
honour. Near it, upon the rock, stood in the olden times a
grove of pines, myrtles, and, box—a perfect miracle to be produced upon the bare limestone. It was forbidden, on pain of
losing the right hand, to fell a single tree in the wood. Holy
bushmen, hermits, dwelt in a mountain cell in it, praised God,
and sang pious hymns high above the straits and near to heaven.
Now the wood and the hermitage have both disappeared, and
the sentinel marches up and down in his red breeches, and
whistles a military air.

On the 15th August, I was awaked by the firing of cannon
under my window. In my sleep I fancied Alfonso of Arragon
and the Spaniards were making a horrible cannonading and
assault against the rock; but I soon collected my senses, and
remembered that this firing was for the birthday of the old
Napoleon, and in honour of the divine Virgin Mary. For
Napoleon was born during the festival of the Assumption of the
Virgin, and both have now the honour of being celebrated
together through the whole of France. The cannonading rolled
and echoed mightily over the waters, and aroused Sardinia from
her sleep. How beautiful and solemn was the morning—heaven
and sea blue, and bedizened with red flags, and the air still and
cool !

The people of Bonifazio swam this day in a sea of bliss. They were bustling about the whole day long in the streets, in which national banners were paraded, displaying the proud devices, "République Française," " Liberté," "Égalité," "Fraternité."— " Believe me," a Bonifazine said to me, " we have ever been true republicans." I saw many groups playing at draughts in the streets, and in the great gateway too, they were sitting at this old knightly game. Others were promenading in their best clothes and in high glee, in the Piazza.

I always take pleasure in seeing a holiday crowd; one feels oneself then for once to be upon a happy earth. And I felt quite joyous here, where this out-of-the-world population rested for once from its labours upon its rock, and from its scanty means prepared a childlike holiday. These poor people have so absolutely nothing that varies and enlivens life—no theatre, no society, no horses or carriages, no music, and newspapers only few and far between. Many are born and laid in their limestone grave here without ever having seen Ajaccio. They live here high up in the air on their dry rock, having nothing but air and light, and the one great prospect over the straits and the mountains of Sardinia. It may therefore be easily imagined what a holiday must be here.

The population of the country round also came to Bonifazio to see the great procession, and it was a curious contrast to see so many gaily dressed people walking about in the dreary streets, and the girls laughing merrily at the worn-out old windows, dressed in white and with flowers in their hair, for today I think all the girls of Bonifazio were angels in honour of the procession.

The beginning of the procession was proclaimed by the sound of cannon. It issued from St. Mary's of the Fig-tree, which was dazzling with lights, and proceeded to the church of St. Dominic. Crucifixes and old church banners, which looked as if they were Genoese, preceded; then came the train of men, women, and girls, with tapers in their hands, and last of all the Holy Virgin. She was carried by four strong men upon a litter, on each corner of which stood a smart wooden angel with a bunch of flowers in his hands, and in the middle of which was Mary herself, sitting upon blue wooden clouds; she herself was also of wood. A silver glory hung above her head, and on her neck was a precious chain of coral, which had been fished near Bonifazio and offered up to her by fishermen. Half Bonifazio joined the procession, and there were many pretty girls in it with white dresses and pale faces, looking as if they were formed of the gypsum of Bonifazio. They all carried tapers; but the sea breeze also walked in the procession—a great tall fellow made of white lime, and quite enveloped in a white mantle of lime dust. He blew out the taper of one pretty plaster figure after another, and, before reaching San Domenico, had won his game of *moccoli*, and extinguished the last taper. I too went with the procession as far as San Domenico. When any one asked me how I was pleased with the procession, I saw in his delighted eyes that it was very fine, and said, " Signore mio, ella è maravigliosa." I was touched by their childlike simplicity and delight in the festival. In the evening they erected a large bonfire in the narrow street before the town-hall, and illuminated the streets with it. When I asked what the great fire was kindled for, I was told, " This fire is kindled in honour of Napoleon." Thus Bonifazio celebrated its great festival, and was happy and joyous, and long after nightfall I heard merry singing in the streets and the twanging of the guitar.

CHAPTER IX.

THE STRAITS.

In the evening before dark it is my delight to go through the old fortress-gate, and sit on the high brink of the rock. There I have the most original picture all round me—Bonifazio on the rock hard by me, on a dizzy steep above the sea, the beautiful straits, and Sardinia not far distant. There is an old book which, among the wonders of the world, counts this rock of Bonifazio as the seventy-second ; my good friend Lorenzo has read it. Looking down from this stone bench to the shore, I have a survey of the entire flight of steps leading down to the Marina. There are people constantly coming and going in and out at the gate, and riding up from below in a zigzag course on their little asses, or driving these animals up laden with melons in a zigzag; for so they can easier climb the brow. I never remember to have seen such small asses as at Bonifazio, and could not conceive how a man could ride on such a beast. I noticed no one coming with a *fucile*—and guns, one sees none at all here.

When I sat on that bench by the little chapel of San Rocco, I was soon surrounded by curious strangers, who often seated themselves confidingly by my side, and inquired whence I came, and what I came for, and whether my country was civilized or not. The latter question was very frequently put to me, as soon as I said I was from Prussia. A gentleman who seemed to be of quality sat down one evening beside me, and when we got into a political conversation upon the present King of Prussia, expressed his surprise that the Prussians spoke Italian. On subsequent occasions, also, I have been often asked in good earnest whether Italian was the language of Prussia. My friendly companion next asked me whether I spoke Latin, and on my answering that I understood it, he said that he also understood Latin, and began to speak thus : "Multos annos jam ierunt che io non habeo parlato il latinum." When on the point of answering him in Latin, I made the discovery that my Latin would turn into Italian, and that I was in danger of expressing myself, if possible, more egregiously than my Bonifazine acquaintance. Two related languages mix themselves directly on the tongue, if one has been in the daily employment of one only.

This gentleman, too, quoted correctly Rousseau's prophecy about Corsica, which one cannot fail to encounter in conversation with a cultivated Corsican.

The view of the straits becomes more and more beautiful in the evening light. Sailing-boats glide past, battling against the waves, and lit up with a golden glow; some cliffs rise black out of the water, and the mountains of Sardinia are dyed with violet. Exactly opposite are the beautiful mountains of Tempio and Limbara, yonder the heights that conceal Sassari, to the left a magnificent pyramidal mountain, the name of which I cannot learn. The evening sun falls brightly only on the near coast, and full upon the nearest Sardinian town, Longo Sardo. A tower stands at the entrance of it. I distinctly discern the houses, and would fain fancy yon streaks of shade wandering Sardinians. On a still night I was told the beating of the drum could distinctly be heard. I counted six towns on the coast. Castello Sardo and Porto Torres, the nearest towns on the coast in the direction of Sassari, I could not discern. My hospitable Lorenzo had studied at Sassari, for three years, and was able to tell me many stories of the Sardinians, and knew their dialects.

Silent gaze we down and pensive
On the coasts so foam-besprinkled,
On the azure straits of ocean
    Which two sister islands part.

Oh how fair thou art, Sardegna,
Thou by sea-shells bright-bejewelled,
Myrtle-chapleted, brunette-like,
    Sister wild of Corsica!

As with coral necklace costly,
Dizened is she round with ruddy
Island cliffs and rocky ledges,
    And with many a sea-lashed cape.

"Friend Lorenzo, yonder mountains,
Exquisite and azure-tinted,
Wake in me such ardent longings,
    Fondly craves my heart to see."

"Beauteous mountains of Limbara!"
Spake Lorenzo, low replying,
"Yon blue mountains are but phantoms
    Fair and false, like human life.

"Sapphires from afar thou think'st them,
Crystal domes to heaven aspiring;
But if thou draw near them, then they
    Cast the azure mantle off.

"Barren crags they then discover,
Menace thee with thorny creepers,
With their stones and precipices,
    Even as human life, young friend."

"Yonder plain, my friend Lorenzo,
Smiling greets me, golden-gleaming;
Fain I would but wis how liveth
    In that fairy land the Sard.

"Far the forest rises inland,
Yellow towers in trees are bosomed,
And his mule with bell sonorous
    Drives the Catalonian.

"On his crown *sombrero* bearing,
Dagger, pistol in his girdle,
Thus he hums a Latin ballad,
    Marching truly to its tune.

"To the coast he southward wanders,
To the bays of Cagliari,
Where the hamlet-dwelling Moor strikes
    Castanet and tambourine.

"Moors they are of Algesiras,
Lisping forth a language barbarous,
Round the fan-palm dancing, leading
    Brunette lasses by the hand."

How plainly one remarks even in Bonifazio the vicinity of the
third great Romanic nation, the Spanish! My room is covered

with pictures of Columbus which have long Spanish explanations; and here and there one meets Sardinians who speak the Catalonian dialect. The two islands, united in primeval times, but now rent asunder, have a smuggling commerce with one another. The advantageous position of Bonifazio must have raised it to a rapid prosperity if the trade had been free. There is a very strict control kept; for even the banditti of the two islands have a mutual intercourse. But Sardinians do not often escape to Corsica, because they cannot maintain their ground there; many Corsican avengers of blood, however, fly to the mountains of Sardinia. The police at Bonifazio is extremely vigilant. I was never asked for my passport in all Corsica, except at the two southern towns of Sartene and Bonifazio. A proprietor had been my companion all the way from Cape Corso to Bonifazio, and on his kindly offering me his boat, which lay at anchor at Propriano, for my return-journey to Bastia, and inviting me to take up my abode in his house on Cape Corso, I received him into my spacious lodgings, as he was in uncomfortable quarters. So he had the honour of being supposed to be a bandit who was endeavouring by specious appearances to escape to Sardinia.

On the approach of evening the lighthouse of Bonifazio hangs out its light. The coast of Sardinia is shrouded in darkness; but from Longo Sardo comes the answer of the red light of a *fanal*, and thus the two islands converse by night through the sign-language of their revolving lights. The lighthouse-keepers on either side lead a lonely life. Each of them is the first or last inhabitant of his island. He of Bonifazio is the southernmost Corsican I ever saw, and he of the opposite cape the northernmost man in Sardinia. They have never seen or spoken to each other. But every day they wish one another good-evening, and *felicissima notte*, the greeting in Italy when the woman enters the chamber with the bed-candle. The Corsican lighthouse-keeper first looks out into the night with his light and says *felicissima notte*, and then the Sardinian replies and also says *felicissima notte;* and so they go on night after night, and will go on their life long, until the light on one side shall fail for a time. And then the other light-keeper shall know that his old friend opposite is dead, and shall weep and say, *felicissima notte!*

1 visited this most southern Corsican on his tower. It stands a couple of miles distant from Bonifazio, on the low cape of Pertusato. The southern end of Corsica here terminates in a

truncated triangle, on the two points of which are to the west Cape Pertusato, and to the east Cape Sprono, a narrow craggy point nearest to Sardinia. One may be in Sardinia within half an hour with a good wind. The little lighthouse is surrounded by a white wall, and resembles a fort. The keeper received me in a friendly manner, and set a glass of goat's milk before me. He lives in the wind, like Æolus. It is curious to think that the long years of a man's life should be used up by an oil-lamp, and that a human being is employed to burn lamp-wicks by night on a lonely cliff. There is nothing more insatiable, and also nothing more modest than human life.

My light-keeper took me on to the balcony of the lighthouse, where the strong wind compelled me to hold fast by the railing, and he showed me from the pinnacles of his roof all his island kingdom and subject population, which consists of thirty head of goats and a vineyard; and when I saw that he was contented, and possessed enough of the good things of this world, I forthwith declared him happy even before his end. He showed me the glories of Sardinia, the islands and *isolotti* that swarm around it—Santa Maria, Santa Maddalena, Caprara, Reparata, and the smaller islands. The western mouth of the strait is strewn with island-crags, but the eastern one is broader; and there lies, opposite to the Sardinian cape Falcone, the picturesque and mountainous island of Asinara.

To Corsica belong a few small island crags of the oddest forms, lying scattered about in the strait quite near, and called San Bainzo, Cavallo, and Lavezzi. They are composed of granite, and the Romans established stone quarries upon them to procure columns for their temples and basilicas. One distinctly perceives the places of their labour, and their very charcoal in the old Roman forge has left traces. Huge half-hewn columns are still lying about, on these rocks, two especially on San Bainzo, and other blocks already worked with iron tools. No one knows for what building in Rome they were intended. And what panic fear can it have been that drove away the artists and stone-masons so suddenly from this lonely workshop in the midst of the sea, that they left the result of their labours here unfinished? Perhaps they were overwhelmed by a flood; perhaps slain by the wild Corsican or grim Sardinian. I wonder no story of a Roman ghost's-workshop arose here. For I myself, at any rate, saw the dead artists rise from the sea by moonlight, grave men in Roman togas, with broad brows, aquiline noses, and hollow eyes. They all silently set to work upon the two columns, and began to clip and chisel in a ghostly way. But one stood upright, and pointed with his finger, as though commanding the rest. I heard him say in Latin, " This column will be one of the finest in the golden house of Nero. Brisk, lads, and get on! for, if you have not finished in forty days, we shall all be thrown to the wild beasts." I was just going to exclaim, " O Artemon, and ye other dead men! the house of Nero has long vanished from the earth; how will ye even now build columns for it? Go to sleep in your graves." But as I was on the point of saying this, the words suddenly became Italian upon my tongue, and I could not. And to this circumstance alone it is due that the old Roman ghosts are still busy at the pillars in the workshop; every night they rise up, and begin to chip and chisel in restless haste, but as soon as ever the cocks crow at Bonifazio, their white forms spring back into the sea again.

Another long last gaze I cast upon the far-stretching coast-line of Sardinia, upon the land of Gallura, calling to mind the beautiful Enzius, son of the Emperor Frederick. He too was once alive, and was a king on yonder coast. A few months ago I stood one evening before his prison at Bologna; a puppet-theatre was set up there, and over the quiet large square loud echoed the voice of the Pulcinella.

The world is round and history a globe, as is the individual life of man.

CHAPTER X.

THE CAVES OF BONIFAZIO.

'Ρόχθει γὰρ μέγα κῦμα, ποτὶ ξερὸν ἠπείροιο
Δεινὸν ἐρευγόμενον· εἴλυτο δὲ πάνθ' ἀλὸς ἄχνῃ.
Odyss. v. 402.

ONE beautiful morning I went out at the old Genoese gate, on the wall of which the arms of the Bank of Genoa, the lion rampant, and the dragon killing the saint, are chiselled; descended to the Marina, and called the boatman and his boat. This day the sea permitted a sail into the caves of the coast, though it was still agitated by the *maestrale*, and played roughly enough with the boat.

In the deep narrow harbour however, the securest in the world, there is a complete lull, and the few sailing-boats and the two two-masted traders of Bonifazio—the Jesus and Mary, and the Fantasia—reposed in it as in Abraham's bosom. Fantasia is the best name a ship has ever borne; that every one will allow, the vessel of whose fancy has ever sailed upon the sea, and come to port with its treasures, or been thrown upon the sand. Jesus and Mary, too, is a beautiful name upon the sea.

The lime rocks straiten the harbour so much on both sides, that its issue into the sea remained long concealed. The narrowness of this channel renders it possible to close it by a chain across, as Alfonso of Arragon did. They showed me an immense iron ring still existing, driven into a rock on the coast. To the right and left, and further on the open sea-coast, the force of the water has formed both large and small caves, which are well worth' seeing, and would be celebrated all over the world, did not Corsica lie, as it were, out of the world.

In the immediate vicinity of Bonifazio there are three parti-cularly beautiful caverns. You first come to that di San Bartolomeo. It is a narrow cavernous passage, allowing just sufficient room for the boat to push in. It resembles a cool Gothic chamber. The sea enters almost to the upper end, so far as that is visible to the eye, and overspreads the bottom with its still clear water. It is a social grotto for the fishes, who pay their mutual visits here, secure from the shark. I found a charming happy family of fish in it, consisting of *muggini* and *loazzi*. They were not at all disturbed, but swam merrily round the boat. The cavern extends much further into the rock of Bonifazio.

Rowing on past this cavern, one comes into the open sea after a short time, and has a surprisingly grand view of the sea side of the rock of Bonifazio, which, rising mightily out of the water, stems the floods with its double breast. This gigantic façade is a glorious piece of architecture of the great artist Nature. On both sides it has columns propping it up, immense buttresses of lime and sandstone strata, deeply fluted by the waves. One of them is called Timone. Between them springs a colossal arch, high up on which stand the white walls of Bonifazio, and in the middle of which a magnificent grotto opens like a portal to the building. I was quite taken by surprise at the grand and original building, which was like a model for human works, temples and basilicas. The agitated sea threw up its waves against the walls of the grotto; but within it was calm. This cave does not go far into the rock; it is only a grand niche of rock, or a gallery, surrounded in semicircles by clustery garlands of stalactites. One might set up a colossal figure of Poseidon in this niche. It is called *sotto al Francesco*.

Sailing to the east, or right hand side, one sees the coast extensively undermined, and observes curious formations of vaults, into which the sea penetrates. I sailed into one of these grottoes, called by the fishermen Camere. In its vicinity is the most splendid cavern of Bonifazio, the Sdragonato, which I despair of finding words to describe. I have never seen any thing similar, and perhaps this cavern may stand alone as the only thing of its kind in Europe. The entrance to it, as to San Francesco, is a gigantic stalactite niche, which, however, opens out into the interior of the mountain, and leads through a small gate into the entire inner cavern. It was a beautiful but anxious task to steer through the narrow throat; the enraged waters surged up against the sides, threw up their white foam to the rocks above, recoiled, were swallowed by the succeeding waves, and rolled forwards again. To hear such a wild sound of many waters, is a perfect elemental delight; their sound is happily expressed only by the Italian language, which calls it *rimbomba*. The bark was safely washed through the jaws of hell, and glided along all at once in a glorious vaulted temple of immense circumference, on a sheet of water, here green, there dark-brown, here azure-blue, and there rose-coloured. It is a wonderful natural pantheon. Above, the dome gapes asunder, and the light of heaven shines In ; a tree bends and hangs suspended over the edge, green bushes and plants lean over into the cleft, and wild pigeons flutter into it. The walls of this beautiful cavern are almost regularly vaulted; the water oozes down from them, and covers them with a coating of stalactites, which have not, however, the strikingly odd forms seen in the cavern of Brando on Cape Corso, or in the Harz caves. They hang in knobs, or line the rocks as with lapis lazuli. One can row about in the grotto or step out of the boat as one pleases; for nature has formed seats and steps of stone, which are free from water except when the floods of a tempest cover them. Hither come the sea-dogs of Proteus, and encamp in this hall of pleasure. I unfortunately saw none of them ; I only scared wild pigeons and cormorants. The bottom is deep and clear; the shells, fishes, and seaweed are all visible. It might be very rewarding to fix one's summer abode here from time to time, to read the Odyssey, and watch for the entrance of the creatures of the mysterious sea-depths. Man understands neither the plants nor the animals that live on the land and are his friends; how much less those dumb and wonderfully formed creatures of the great watery element! They live and have their laws, their understanding, their joys and sorrows, their love and hatred. Not bound to the glebe, like the land animals, they roam about in the boundless element, and live in the clear crystal depths, form powerful republics, and have their revolutions, migrations, and Corsair-like inroads, and charming water-excursions whenever they will.

The coast from Cape Pertusato to Bonifazio is worn by the sea, and rent into curious forms. Many remarkable petrifactions are found there, and the curious kind of spider which builds houses. This spider makes a minute sand-house in the sand of the shore, and a little door in it, which she can open and shut at pleasure. When she wishes to be alone, she shuts the door; when she wishes to go out, she opens the door and goes out, and takes her daughters a walk beside the beautiful straits, namely, when they have been industrious, and have spun long enough at their portion. This excellent building spider is called Mygal pionnière, or Araignée maçonne of Corsica.

I also saw the Scalina di Alfonso, the King of Arragon's staircase, which he cut in the rock, according to the story, close under the walls of the town. As he could not force the town, he lighted upon the excellent idea of secretly cutting a passage into the rock. The Spaniards landed by night at a point which could not be seen by the citizens, where a cavern extends into the hill capable of harbouring three hundred men, and containing fresh water. Here the Spaniards cut a flight of steps up the rocks, and actually reached the walls of the fortifications, when they were seen by a woman, who gave the alarm, and were driven down again by the citizens, who hastened up. The story is a fable; for it appears incredible to me that the Spaniards should have hewn this narrow winding staircase without being seen by the Bonifazines. The monks of San Francesco, however, had hewn another rock-staircase of the same kind, to reach their sea-bathing place; it also is in great part destroyed.

I was unfortunate; for they do not now catch tunny in the straits, and the coral-fishers do not put to sea, on account of the *naestrale.* The straits are rich in coral, but the Corsicans leave this prize to the Genoese, Tuscans, and Neapolitans. These come in April, and remain till September. I saw beautiful red coral in the possession of a Genoese. It is sold by weight, for three francs an ounce. Most of the corals which are worked up in the manufactories at Leghorn, come from the straits of Bonifazio. Since the French, however, have found better and more abundant corals on the coasts of Africa, the coral fishery in the straits has diminished. They are now taken principally on the coast near Propriano, Roccapina, Figari, and Ventilegne, where the tunny-fish are also particularly numerous.

Having now gained a knowledge of both the land and coast of Bonifazio, I prepared for departure from this remarkable place. I found the people of Bonifazio as Lorenzo said. They are no real Corsicans at all. " We are poor," Lorenzo told me, " but we are industrious, and have enough. The olive grows abundantly on our lime soil, the vine yields enough to supply our houses, and the air is healthy. We are cheerful and contented, and accept with thankfulness the days that God sends us on our rock. When the poor man returns in the evening from his field, he always finds his wine ready for him to mix with water, his oil to season his fish, perhaps also a bit of meat, and in the summer always melons."

I shall remember the hospitality of the Bonifazines as thankfully as that of the Sartenians. On the morning when I started before sunrise to travel to Aleria, Lorenzo was already waiting at the fortress gate to wish me once more a pleasant journey, and to accompany me as far as the Marina. Descending the rock at dawn, I took leave of the extraordinary town with one of those scenes, the image of which, however small it be, impresses itself ineffaceably upon the memory. On the brink of the rock below the gate, is the small unroofed chapel of San Rocco, built upon the spot where the last victim of the plague in the year 1528 perished. Now as I descended from the gate, I beheld this chapel straight before me: the doors stood wide open, and the priest was officiating at the altar, upon which the candles were burning; before him pious women were kneeling in two rows, and men and women were kneeling also upon the rock outside. The view from above of this quiet pious congregation, in the glow of the dawn, high above the straits, was a profound surprise to me, and methought I here beheld a picture of true piety.

2 I

TRAVELS.—BOOK VIII.

CHAPTER I.

THE EASTERN COAST.

THE tracts along the eastern coast, after leaving Bonifazio, are
barren and lonely. The road leads past the beautiful gulf of
Santa Manza to Porto Vecchio, which is reached in three hours.
Near the little hamlet of Sotta stands Campaña, the ruined castle
of an ancient Signor, close by the road ; and it tells an extraordinary tale. In hoary times of old there dwelt here Ors'
Alamanno, the German Bear, who imposed upon his vassals the
terrible seignorial right of the first night (*jus primæ noctis*).
Any one who married a wife must take her to the castle that
the German Bear might enjoy her first favours, and must besides
bring his finest horse into Orso's stable for him to ride upon.
So from year's end to year's end the Bear's chamber and his
stable were never empty. Now a young man named Probetta
wished to wed a beautiful maiden. He was a desperate rider,
and could throw the lasso dexterously. He secretly put his
lasso under his coat, mounted a fine horse, and rode to the
Signor's castle to display the animal to Orso, and show him what
a beauty it was. The German Bear came out of the gate and
laughed for joy that he was to kiss the fairest maid and ride the
finest horse. So as he stood laughing and looking at Probetta,
the latter dashed suddenly past, and had thrown the lasso round
him in a trice, and then scoured down the mountain like the wind,
dragging Orso along over the stones. They destroyed the castle
and buried the German Bear at an obscure place. But a year
afterwards some one wondered what had become of the dead
Orso, and they ran to the place where he was buried and dug
him up. A fly flew out, which flew into all the houses and

stung all the women; and it grew bigger and bigger, and was at last as big as an ox, and stung every one in the whole neighbourhood. Then they knew not how they should get rid of the ox-fly. But some one said that in Pisa there were wonder-doctors who could cure away all sorts of things. So they went to Pisa and fetched a wonder-doctor who could cure away all sorts of things.

When the doctor saw the great fly, he began to rub plasters, and rubbed six thousand Spanish fly-plasters, and rolled a hundred thousand pills. Then he put the six thousand fly-plasters on the fly, and gave him the hundred thousand pills to take. Thereupon the fly grew smaller and smaller, and, when he was reduced to the size of an ordinary fly, he died. Then they took a large bier and covered it with a snow-white sheet, and upon the sheet they laid the body of the fly; and all the women assembled, tore their hair, and wept bitterly, that such a fine fly was dead, and twelve men carried the fly upon the bier to the churchyard, and gave him Christian burial. Then they were delivered from harm.

This pretty story I have told in accordance with the Corsican chronicler, except that he makes the doctor from Pisa simply kill the fly; so I have added the rest.

Porto Vecchio is a small walled town of about 2000 inhabitants, situate on the gulf of the same name, the last and only gulf on the entire eastern coast. It is large and glorious, and might become of extreme importance, lying as it does opposite the continent of Italy. The Genoese founded Porto Vecchio to keep off the Saracens from these coasts. They gave the colonists many privileges to induce people to settle there. But the district being unhealthy on account of the many marshes, and fevers beginning to rage, Porto Vecchio was three times deserted and desolated. Even now that entire great canton is one of the least cultivated and populous in Corsica, and is mainly inhabited by deer and wild-boars. Yet the land is uncommonly fruitful. The neighbourhood of Porto Vecchio is rich in olives and vines; the town itself is built on porphyry rocks, which crop out at the surface. I found it almost desolated, as it was August, and half the population had taken refuge on the mountains.

To the north of the beautiful gulf the coast runs along in an even line, and the mountain-chain is still near on the left hand, until, in the district of Salenzara, it recedes towards the interior, and leaves free those great plains which give to the eastern coast of Corsica so different an appearance from the western. The entire west of the island is a continuous formation of parallel valleys; the mountain-chains there descend into the sea, ending in capes and encircling the magnificent gulfs. The east has not this prominent valley formation, and the land sinks down into levels. The west of Corsica is romantic, picturesque, and grand; the east gentle, monotonous, and melancholy. The eye here roves over plains many miles in extent, seeking for villages, men, and life, and discovers nothing but heaths, with wild shrubs, and morasses and lagoons extending along the sea, and filling the land with melancholy.

The constantly level and excellent road leads for almost a day's journey from Porto Vecchio to the ancient Aleria. The grass grows a foot high upon it. People are afraid of travelling on it in the summer. On the whole journey, I met not a living creature. Not a single hamlet is passed, and only here and there a village is seen afar off on the mountains. There only stand solitary abandoned houses on the seashore, at such points as possess a small seaport, a Cala or landing-place, such as Porto Favone, the place to which the old Roman road led, Fautea, Cala di Tarco, Cala di Canelle, Cala de Coro, which is said to be called Cala Moro—Moors' landing-place. Here also stand Genoese watch-towers.

All these houses were abandoned, and their windows and doors shut; for the air is bad along the whole coast. The poor Lucchese here performs the slight field-labour for the Corsican, who does not venture down the mountains. Yet I did not suffer from the bad air; however, I followed the precautions of my travelling companion, and snuffed camphor, which is said to be a good preservative.

Being provided with very scanty provisions for the journey, we were suddenly overpowered by hunger, which persecuted us during this day and half of the following, for we nowhere found either an open house or an inn. The pedestrian would starve here, or be forced to seek refuge on the mountains, and to wander about for hours till he should find a footpath leading to some herdsman's cabin. It is a *strada morta*.

We crossed the river Taravo. From thence commences the series of lagoons, beginning with the long narrow Stagno di Palo. There are in succession the Stagno di Graduggini, the lagoon of Urbino, of Siglione, del Sale, and the fine one of Diana, which has retained its name from the Roman times. Sandbanks

separate these fish-swarming lagoons from the sea, but most of
them have an entrance. Their fish are celebrated; these are
large fat eels and immense *ragnoli.* The fishermen catch them
in nets of rushes.

Far northwards from the Taravo extends the most glorious
pianura, which is the Fiumorbo, or canton Prunelli. Crossed
by rivers, and bounded by lagoons and the sea, it resembles, as
seen from a distance, an endless luxuriant garden by the seashore. But there is hardly the scantiest arable land to be dis-
cerned, but only boundless plains covered by ferns. It is quite
melancholy to find such a splendid plain desolate and uninhabited. It is inexplicable why the French government does not
colonize these districts. Colonies would more certainly prosper
here than in the man-and-gold-devouring sands of Africa.
There is room here for two populous towns of at least 50,000
inhabitants. Colonies of industrious cultivators and artisans
would convert the whole district into a garden. Canals would
destroy the morasses, and make the air healthy. There is not a
finer strip of land in Corsica, nor any with a more fertile soil.
The climate is milder and more sunny than that of southern
Tuscany; it would bear even the sugar-cane, and corn would
yield a hundred-fold. Only by means of colonization and manufactures, which enhance competition in production at the same
time that they increase the demand, could the Corsican mountaineers be compelled to come down from their black villages
into the plain, and to till the fields. Nature offers every thing
here in the most profuse abundance which can create a brisk
industrial system; the mountains are regular storehouses of valuable stone; the forests yield pines, larches, and oaks; there is
no want even of mineral waters worth sending to a distance;
the plain yields the fruits of the field, and nourishment for a
large live stock; and the close connexion of mountain, plain,
and the fishy seas of Italy, leaves nothing more to be desired.

The state in which the coast now is, is strikingly illustrated
by the picture which Homer sketches of the coast of the Cyclo-
pian island, which was uncultivated, but in the highest degree
capable of tillage.*

> No worthless isle is that; all fruits would it in season bear:
> For meadows near the shore there are, beside the hoary sea,
> Well-watered, soft; the vine might there imperishable be.

----

* Odyssey ix. 131.

Light were its unworked soil to plough; and they might alway mow
At harvest-time a heavy crop; for fat the earth below.
There too a harbour safe and wide, where ships ne'er need a chain,
Nor throw out anchor-stones, nor must their sterns with ropes detain.

On seeing this glorious plain I could not but praise the correct judgment of the ancient Romans, who established their only colonies in Corsica precisely at this spot.

CHAPTER II.

SULLA'S COLONY, ALERIA.

ON approaching the river Fiumorbo some solitary palace-like houses are perceived; some of them are settlements of French capitalists who have been bankrupted because they commenced indiscreetly; others are wealthy estates, perfect counties in extent, such as Migliacciaro in the canton Prunelli, which belongs to a French company, and was formerly a revenue of the family of Fiesco of Genoa.

The Fiumorbo, which springs from the highest mountain-trunk in Corsica, disembogues itself above the Stagno di Graduggino. It has its name, "Blind River," from its course; for it falters about through the plain like a blind man, till at length it feels its way out into the sea. The land between it and the Tavignano is said to be the most fruitful in Corsica.

When evening came on the temperature changed, with striking rapidity, from the driest heat to damp misty cold. In many places the air was impregnated with corruption. A monument at the wayside caught my eye. Erected as it was in this solitude, it appeared to point out some memorable spot. It was a monument to a road-contractor, who had been shot by a peasant, for an attachment to a girl whom the latter was courting. Nothing, after all, attracts human interest so much as the romance of the heart. A simple love-tragedy exerts the same power on the fancy of the multitude as a heroic deed, and is retained often for centuries in the memory. It is beautiful that the heart has its chronicles. The Corsicans are demons in jealousy; they avenge love as well as blood. My companion told me the following incident:—A young man had forsaken his lass, and turned his attentions to another. One day he was sitting in an open place in his village, playing draughts. Up came his abandoned mistress, overwhelmed him with a flood of imprecations, drew a pistol from her bosom, and sent a bullet through his head. Another forsaken maiden once said to her lover, "If you take another you shall never enjoy her." Two years passed, and the youth led a maiden to the altar. As he was passing out of the church door with her, the forsaken mistress felled him to the ground with a shot; and the people cried, "Evviva, hurra for thy countenance!" The justices sentenced the girl to three months' imprisonment. Youths sued for her hand, but not one desired the young widow of the murdered bridegroom.

The Corsican women, who sing such bloody songs of revenge, are also able to carry pistols and *fucili*, and to fight. How often did they fight in battles as well as any men! It is said that the victory of the Corsicans over the French at Borgo, was at least half due to the heroic valour of the women. They also fought in the battle of Ponte Nuovo; and the bold wife of Giulio Francesco di Pastoreccia still lives in the memories of all her country people. She fought in that battle by her husband's side, and came into close combat with a French officer, overcame him, and took him prisoner; but when she saw that the Corsicans were falling into the disorder of flight, she gave him his freedom, saying to him, "Remember that a Corsican woman overcame thee, and gave thee back thy sword and thy freedom."

These Corsican women are the living female forms of Ariosto and Tasso.

Beyond the Fiumorbo commences the water-system of the Tavignano, which flows out near Aleria, below the lagoon of Diana. I wished to leave the *vettura* there, as I had a letter of introduction from a citizen of Sartene for Casa Janda, a rich estate near Aleria, possessed by Captain Franceschetti, son of the general known to us from the history of the last days of Murat's life. Signor Franceschetti was unfortunately on the continent, and I was disappointed of the pleasure of making the acquaintance of this energetic man, and gaining instruction from him on many points. It had meanwhile grown dark, and we had approached near to Sulla's colony of Aleria. We perceived the dark row of houses, and the fort on the hill by the road-side; and in the hope of finding a locanda in the little town, though far from certain of it, we stopped the vehicle and walked thither.

The scenery around seemed to me truly Sullanic;—a night as still as the grave, a barren plain full of feverish air at our feet, dark night-shrouded mountains behind the fort, and the horizon reddened as with the glow of burning towns; for the thickets were on fire all round; the town dead, and without a light. At last a dog gave the alarm, and gave us some hopes, and soon the whole population of Aleria came out to meet us—namely, two Doganieri, who were the sole inhabitants of Aleria. The people had removed to the mountains through fear of the malaria, and every door was closed except that of the fort, in which the soldiers of the coast were stationed. We begged them for a lodging for this one night, as the horses were done up, and there was no place in the neighbourhood that could receive us. But these good followers of Cornelius Sulla refused our request, fearing the captain of the *dogana*, and because they would have to go on guard in an hour. We conjured them by the holy Virgin not to force us out into the feverish air, but to give us shelter in the fort. They stuck to their refusal, and so we returned not knowing what to do, my companion angry, and I but little pleased at being shown the door at the first Roman colony that my foot had entered, in spite of two great Cæsars who are my particular friends. The Sullans, however, began to feel some human compassion, and came running after us, exclaiming, "Entrato pure!" We joyfully entered the little fort, a quadrangular building, without any bulwarks or rampart or moat, and felt our way up the stone steps into the soldiers' quarters.

The poor soldiers soon slung their guns over their shoulders, and went out with their dogs to the lagoon of Diana, to be on the watch for smugglers. Their service is a dangerous one; they are changed every fifteen days, as they would otherwise succumb to the fever. I lay down on the floor of the room and tried to sleep, but the sultriness was dreadful. I preferred to return to the *vettura* and imbibe the bad air, which was at least cooling. I-passed a truly *Sullan* night at this Aleria, in front of the church at which Peter Cyrnæus was deacon, in meditations on the causes of the greatness of the Romans, and of their decline, and on those luxurious Sullan· banquets, where there were good fish-liver pasties, and fountains of costly sauces. It was a diabolical night, and I sighed out more than once, "Aleria, Aleria! chi non ammazza vitnperia!" "Aleria, Aleria! who does no murder must revile thee;" for that is the lampoon the Corsicans have made upon the place, and I think it suits excellently a colony of Sulla.

The morning broke; I sprang out of the carriage, and tried

to get a notion of the locality of Aleria. This is excellently
selected. The plain is commanded by a hill, from which there
is a splendid view of the lagoons of Diana and del Sale, of the
sea and islands. Fine mountain cones enclose the panorama on
the land side. The morning was charmingly refreshing; air
and light were in a delicate transition-glow; the view free and
extensive; the soil Roman, and, still more, ancient Phœnician.

The present Aleria consists only of a few houses attaching
themselves to the Genoese fort. The ancient Aleria occupied
several hills, and stretched far down both sides of the Tavignano
into the plain, where ancient iron rings on the lagoon of Diana
still betray the site of the harbour of the town. I wandered to
the ruins in the vicinity. The hills all about are strewn with
stones and ruined walls of houses, but I found not a single piece
of decoration, neither capitals nor frieze, nothing but rough
materials. Here and there are seen the remains of arches, a
few steps of a circus, and a ruin which the people call Casa
Reale, and which is supposed to be the house of a Prætorium, I
know not with what reason, for from the ruins nothing at all
can be inferred, not even the epoch. To judge by its extent,
Aleria must have been a town of about 20,000 inhabitants.
Vases and Roman coins have been found in the fields; I was
told by goatherds that a golden coin had been picked up three
days ago. A returning soldier, however, strained my curiosity
to the highest pitch, by telling me that he had found two marble tablets containing an inscription which no one was able to
decipher. The marble tablets were locked up in a house, but he
had taken a copy of them. He thereupon fetched his pocket-book;
they were two Latin inscriptions, which this excellent antiqua-
rian had copied in such a truly Phœnician fashion, that I made
out with difficulty that one was a votive inscription from the
age of Augustus, and the other a sepulchral inscription.

This was all that I found of the ancient Aleria.

CHAPTER III.

THEODORE OF NEUHOFF.

Abenamar, Abenamar,
Moro de la Moreria
El dia que tu naciste
Grandes senales avia.

MOORISH ROMANCE.

IT was at Aleria that Theodore of Neuhoff landed on the 12th March, 1736, a man who was to commence in Corsica the series of upstarts who give to the modern history of Europe a romantic middle-age character.

On that morning at Aleria, accordingly, I saw the image of that fantastic knight of fortune, as I had seen it portrayed in an unpublished Genoese manuscript of the year 1739 : "Accinelli, historical, geographical, and political memorabilia of the kingdom of Corsica." This manuscript is in the possession of Signor Santelli at Bastia, who readily granted me a sight of it, but would not permit me to copy from it some original letters, which I have nevertheless since discovered elsewhere. With what sentiments the Genoese composed his work, is declared by the motto upon it, which thus describes the Corsicans : "Generatio prava et exorbitans. Bestiæ et universa pecora,"—"A perverse and erring people, beasts, and all brutes." This motto is taken from the Bible. In his manuscript he has painted Theodore in water-colours to the life, in Moorish costume, with a perruque and a small hat, a sabre and cane. He is standing gravely by the sea, out of which an island is seen rising.

Theodore of Corsica may also be seen well portrayed in an old German book of the year 1736, which was printed in Frankfort, with the title, "Account of the Life and Acts of Baron Theodore of Neuhoff, and of the Republic of Genoa injured by him; published by Giovanni di San Fiorenzo." (Nachricht von dem Leben und Thaten des Baron Theodor von Neuhofen, und der von ihm gekränckten Republic Genoa, herausgegeben von Giovanni di S. Fiorenzo.)

The vignette exhibits Theodore as he was in life, in Spanish

costume, and with a very small beard. In the background is
seen a walled town, probably Bastia, and in front of it three
men most amusingly depicted—one of whom hangs on the gallows, another is impaled, and the third is going to be quartered.

Theodore's appearance in Corsica, and his romantic election to
be King of Corsica, then engaged the attention of all the world.
This is evidenced from this very German book, which appeared
during the course of the same year, 1736. As it is at the same
time the only German book that I have used for my studies
about the Corsicans, I will communicate some extracts from it.

This is the description of the island at that time :—

"Corsica is one of the largest islands of the Mediterranean
sea, lying over against the island Sardinia. It is about twenty-
five German miles long, and twelve broad. In point of atmosphere it is not considered particularly healthy ; but the land is
tolerably fertile, although it is mingled with many mountains
and stony tracts. The inhabitants have the reputation of being
courageous and hardy in arms ; but it is also said against them
that they are very malicious, revengeful, cruel, and addicted to
robbery. Besides this character they have the reputation of
being called gross Corsicans, which I will not indeed contest."

The account of Theodore's landing was thus given in the book,
on the authority of letters from Bastia of the 5th April :—

"At the port of Aleria arrived lately an English ship, said
to belong to the consul of that nation at Tunis, and in this a
very exalted personage, to judge from his appearance, whom
some announced as a royal prince, others as an English lord, and
others as the Prince Ragotzy. So much we have means of
stating, that he is of the Romish confession, and bears the name
of Theodore. His costume is after the manner of the Christians
who travel in Turkey, and consists of a long scarlet-lined coat,
a perruque, and hat, as well as a stick and sword. He has a
suite of two officers, a secretary, a priest, a lord-steward, a
steward, a head-cook, three slaves, and four lacqueys with him ;
also, he has had disembarked 10 cannon, above 7000 muskets,
2000 pairs of shoes, and a great lot of all kinds of stores, among
which are 7000 sacks of flour ; likewise several chests of gold
and silver specie, one of which is a strong lead-cornered one with
silver handles, full of whole and half sequins from Barbary, and
the treasure is reckoned at two millions of pieces of eight. The
Corsican leaders have received him with great demonstrations
of reverence, and conferred upon him the title of Your Excel-

lence and of Viceroy; whereupon he then appointed four of the Corsicans colonels, with a monthly salary of one hundred pieces of eight; he next created twenty companies, and caused a gun, a pair of shoes, and a sequin to be given to each common soldier; but a captain receives henceforward eleven pieces of eight every month, and, when the companies shall have received their full comple-ment, twenty-five. He has taken up his residence at the episcopal palace at Campo Loro, before which house four hundred men with two cannon keep guard. It next transpires that he is going to repair to Casincha, near St. Pelegrino, and that he awaits some more large ships of war, which are to arrive about the 15th of this month, to assail the Genoese with all his force by land and sea; to which end he will raise many more compa-nies. We are assured that he has been deputed by some Catholic European potentates, who will second his enterprise in every way; wherefore the Genoese are thrown into the extreme of alarm, and regard their cause in this island as good as lost. Some more recent accounts add, that the above-mentioned foreigner is appointing his court with greater and greater magni-ficence, and is always attended by a guard from one church to another, and has appointed one named Hyacinthus Paoli to be his treasurer, and made one of the most distinguished citizens of Aleria a knight."

Now people were eagerly occupied in investigating the circum-stances of Theodore's life and genealogy. His adventures and connexions pointed principally to the romantic land of Spain and to Paris. But here is a letter, extracted from our little book, written by a Westphalian nobleman to his friend in Holland, concerning Baron Theodore.

*   *   *   *   *

YOUTHFUL ROMANCE FROM THE LIFE OF THEODORE OF CORSICA.
Exhibited in a Letter.

"Sir,—It is so great a pleasure to me to satisfy you in every thing that lies within my power, that I cannot refuse to let you know what is known to me of the life of a man who begins to make a noise in the world.

"You have read in the papers, sir, that Theodore of Neuhoff, to whom the Corsicans have offered a crown, was born in West-phalia, in a district appertaining to the King of Prussia. This is true, and I can the more readily add my testimony to this, as he and I studied together, and lived for some years in intimate friendship. We have almost forgotten those examples which antiquity presented to us of persons of the middle station who ascended the throne; but Kuli Cham in Persia, and Neuhoff in Corsica, revive these examples in our times. This latter was born at Altena, a small town in Westphalia, whither his mother had repaired to stay at the house of a nobleman of her acquaintance, after the early loss of her husband, who left her a widow, and pregnant with Theodore.

" His father was a captain of the body-guard of the Bishop of Münster; and his grandfather, who had grown grey in military service, had commanded a regiment under the great Bernhard von Galen. At his father's death his domestic affairs were much embarrassed, and, but for the good cousin who took charge of them, they would have been in a deplorable condition. When he was ten years old, he was entered at the Jesuits' College at Münster, to enter upon his studies, where he made good progress in a short time. I came to the same college a year after him; and, as his maternal estates bordered on mine, so were we linked together even from the earliest childhood in a friendship which was subsequently most closely confirmed. He had a figure surpassing his years, and his lively and fiery eyes testified to his courage and stout-heartedness. He was very diligent, and our teachers constantly held him forth as an example for us. That which excited ill-will in other scholars gave me pleasure, and aroused in me the desire of following him in his diligence. We remained six years together at Münster; and, when my father learned of our close intimacy, he proposed, in order not to separate me from my friend, to make him my travelling companion, and to give him means to prosecute this plan handsomely.

" We were sent to Cologne, to continue there our studies and exercises. We seemed to be in a new clime, as we were now set free from the restraint of school tyranny, and began to taste the sweets of freedom. Perhaps I might have abused this freedom, if my discreet companion had not wisely kept me from all the forms of a dissolute life. We were boarded by a professor, whose wife, although rather far gone in years, was of a sprightly disposition; whilst her two daughters, as sprightly as beautiful, combined these two qualities with a very discreet deportment. After supper we amused ourselves for some hours with games, or went to walk in a garden which they had near the gate of the city.

"This delightful intercourse had lasted nearly two years, when it was disturbed by the arrival of the young Count of M——, who was placed by his father in the same house where we lodged. He had a tutor who was a native of Cologne; and the latter, having had for years his own acquaintances and haunts there, often deserted his pupil to follow his own amusements. When we saw that the time often hung heavily on the young Count's hands, we were unfortunately the first to propose to him that he should enter our society—which offer he accepted with joy.

"Theodore had always had his place between the two sisters, and I mine between the youngest and her mother. We were now necessitated to make a different arrangement, and, in deference to the rank of the Count, to resign to him the place which the Baron of Neuhoff had hitherto occupied. I often perceived that my companion looked with eyes of love on the elder sister, and that, when their eyes met, the fair one changed colour from modesty. She was a pretty brunette, her eyes were black, and her complexion of a rare whiteness. It was not long before the Count became deeply in love with her; and, as the eyes of a lover see much sharper than other people's, Theodore soon found out that he was endeavouring to make himself agreeable to Mariana (so this charming girl was called); and he thereupon fell into deep pensiveness.

"'What ails you, most valued friend?' I asked him one evening on going to bed; 'I have found you for some days quite buried in your own thoughts; you have no longer that sprightly nature which made your conversation so pleasant; you must certainly be assailed by some inner vexation.'—'Ah, my dearest friend;' he answered me; 'I am born under an unhappy star! I have never known my father, and there is no one but you to lighten the course of my life, which would be far unhappier without you.'

"'But why do you now make these sad contemplations?' I rejoined. 'My father will insure you wellbeing, and you yourself are competent to supply the want of all that fortune has deprived you of. Confess it, Theodore, it is something of quite another nature that agitates you; if I am not very much mistaken, the beautiful eyes of Mariana have done the work of the spoiler in your heart.'

"'I cannot deny it,' was his answer; 'and I am quite induced to confess to you all my weakness. You know with how much pleasure we have passed these two years with these charming girls. My heart at once inclined towards Mariana; and whereas, I thought to have no more than a tender respect for her, I now perceive that she has inspired me with the most vehement love. The arrival of the young Count causes me to make this discovery. I perceive only too plainly the addresses that he pays her; and the advantage of his birth above mine, causes me to fear that he will maintain this superiority, even in the affections of the fair Mariana. By the jealousy I feel, I discover how passionately I love her; for her I forget eating and drinking; I pass the night without sleep—and this, with the fire of love that consumes me, will quite be the death of me.'

" 'But, my dear Theodore,' said I, 'how can you, who are otherwise so prudent, allow yourself to be overmastered by a passion which can have none but melancholy consequences? Mariana is not of such a rank as to make it possible for you to marry her, and she has too much virtue to commit herself to you in any other way. Let us change our abode; on the removal of the object that inflames your passion, you will gradually lose your memory of it.'—'All that you say is well founded,' replied Theodore; 'but when have you heard of love listening to reason? and know you not that in this case, as in those that concern honour, one takes counsel of no one but one's own heart? I cannot withdraw from Mariana without forgetting myself; the wound is already so deep, that it cannot be healed.'—'But what will your friends say,' I continued, 'if you enter into such a close connexion with her, that no means will avail to frustrate it? Your fortune rests with them; they will not fail to withdraw their helping hand from you, and to deprive you of the inheritance that you expect from them.'

" 'They may do what they will for me,' he said; 'I shall never cease to love the adorable Mariana.'

"We then said good-night, and I fell asleep; but Theodore did not pass the night so quietly. I found him in the morning so altered and worn out, that I did not like to return to our conversation of the evening before. We returned to our studies and exercises, and met in the evening, according to custom, in our little social circle. They rallied him a little about the confusion of his thoughts, and he accounted for it by the pretence of a headache, and begged to be excused from playing. During the game, he observed the eyes of Mariana and the Count, and fancied he discovered a certain amorous mutual understanding, which brought him into absolute despair. We took our departure, and, on entering our room, he said, ' Well, do you yet doubt the love Mariana and the Count feel for one another? They exchanged a hundred amorous glances, and he said something into her ear on taking leave; my unhappiness is only too certain.' —' I have observed nothing of all this,' I replied; ' your jealousy perhaps showed the affair to you in a different form from what met my eyes.'

"Two or three days passed with such conversations. Our professor gave a dinner to us and some other persons, in his garden, on occasion of Mariana's name-day. The Count, acquainted of this, had in the morning presented her with a bouquet, and a costly diamond rosette. Nothing more was wanting to put Theodore quite beside himself; he fell into a dejected silence, and ate next to nothing during the whole dinner. His headache had to come to his aid again; we rose from table, and, after a few turns in the garden, began the ball. The Count opened it with Mariana, who was of necessity queen of the ball. Theodore would not dance, but walked about in the garden the whole evening. The ball lasted till morning, when we returned home.

"I went into my room; my companion remained below in the court, and, meeting the Count there, forced him to draw his sword. I heard the clash of swords, and ran down with all speed, but I came too late; he had already given the Count a mortal thrust, and sought safety in flight through the back-door. You may judge of the pain and astonishment which this event produced in the whole house. The poor Count was laid upon his bed, where he expired two hours after. Neither I nor his friends could learn where Theodore had escaped to; and we should never have heard it but for the letters which he wrote us, a few months ago, from the island of Corsica."

*   *   *   *   *   *   *

All that transpired of the life of Theodore before he came to Corsica, and that is of course, from the very nature of this man, uncertain and contradictory, displays him to us as one of the most prominent and successful of the series of adventurers of the eighteenth century. The exhibition of such men as Cagliostro, Saint Germain, Law, Theodore, Casanova, and Königsmark, forms a most characteristic contrast to their great and *positive* contemporaries, Washington, Franklin, Paoli, Pitt, and Frederick the Great. Whereas the latter lay the foundation of a new

order of things in society and state ; the former, like fluttering
storm birds, announce the great elemental agitation of minds.

It is related that Theodore of Neuhoff became a page to the
celebrated Duchess of Orleans, and was educated into a finished
and dexterous courtier.   His Proteus-nature drew him into the
most contradictory careers.   In Paris, the Marquis de Courcillon
procured an officer's commission for him.   He became a desperate
gambler; then he fled to Sweden, to save himself from his creditors, to Baron von Görtz; and by turns formed connexions
with the adventurous and intriguing ministers of that age—with
Ripperda, Alberoni, and lastly with Law, who all more or less
transferred to political life the character of soldiers of fortune.
Theodore became an intimate of Alberoni's, and gained such
influence in Spain, that he amassed a considerable fortune, until
Alberoni fell, and the vessel of his fortune was grounded again.
He now clove to Ripperda, and married a maid of honour of the
Queen of Spain.   Elizabeth Farnese, of Spain, a mistress of all
kinds of intrigue, had played a high game to procure for her son,
Don Carlos, a kingdom in Italy.   All this went on in the most
extravagant gambling way.   The world was then a great society
of knights of fortune, and full of upstarts, aspiring pretenders,
fantasts, and fortune-hunters.   A whole series of them can be
counted up in the political world alone—Don Carlos of Spain,
Charles Stuart, Rakotzy, Stanislaus Leszcinski, the creature of
the great adventurer Charles XII. of Sweden; and, besides the
already mentioned statesmen, the Russian upstarts, a Menczikoff,
a Münnich, a Biron; Mazeppa and Patkul also belong to the
beginning of the great series.   At the same time, it was the age
of decided petticoat government in Europe.   We see then on
what soil our Theodore of Neuhoff stood.

His wife was Spanish, but, as it would seem, of Irish or English
descent, a relation of the Duke of Ormond.   She appears not to
have been a paragon of beauty.   Theodore abandoned her, and,
it is asserted, not without taking possession of her jewels and
other treasures.

He went to Paris, where he managed to worm himself into
Law's good graces, and got a quantity of money by help of the
swindling concern of Mississippi shares.   A *lettre-de-cachet*
again started him on his travels, and so he moved about through
all countries of the world, trying every thing in turn, in England, and particularly in Holland, where he set speculations on
foot, gambled, and made debts.   How he came to Genoa I have

already told in the history of Corsica: perhaps his immense burthen of debt made a crown very desirable to him. And thus we have the amusing spectacle of seeing a man suddenly stand out before us as a crowned ruler, who a short time before, perhaps, numbered his tailor among his creditors. Such things are possible in times when the pillars of political and social orders are undermined at their foundations ; then the breezes of romance are immediately felt to blow in the world, and the most impossible things may become real.

We know that Theodore came to Genoa, formed connexions with the exiled Corsicans there and at Leghorn, took up the idea of becoming King of Corsica, and went to Tunis. In Barbary he was taken prisoner, wherefore he subsequently included a chain on his royal coat-of-arms. His inexplicable genius not only delivered him from bondage, but procured him the resources, provided with which he suddenly landed in Corsica. No sooner had he escaped from a prison than he became king.

From Corsica he wrote the following letter to his Westphalian cousin, M. de Drost; this, as well as all other documents which I communicate, I read in the manuscript of the Genoese Accinelli, and found printed as authentic documents in the third volume of Cambiaggi. The little German book gives them also; so I will give the letter according to its text, and not in a translation from the Italian, because it may quite possibly be the German composition of Theodore himself:—

"SIR, AND MOST HIGHLY HONOURED COUSIN,—The kindness and esteem which your excellence has borne towards me from the earliest youth, give me hopes that you still honour me with a share of your memory and good-will. Although, on account of the disorder and disarrangement that has been occasioned by some evil-minded persons, and perhaps also through my natural desire and inclination to travel incognito, to the end that I may at some future time be useful to my neighbours according to my intentions, I have omitted for so many years to report to you on my affairs ; yet I beg you to believe that you have been constantly present in my memory, and that I have had no other ambition than to return to my country in the desirable conditoin of being able to be grateful to my benefactors and friends, and to annihilate the unjust calumnies spread abroad against me. But at last, as a sincere friend and good kinsman, I cannot omit to discover to you that, after many persecutions and adversities, I have succeeded in coming in person to this kingdom of Cor-

sica, and accepting the offer of the faithful inhabitants thereof,
who have declared and received me as their sovereign and king:
so that because, after many large disbursements made on their
account during the last two years, and after suffering captivity
and persecution, I have not been in a condition to take any more
journeys to deliver them at last from the tyrannical government
of the Genoese, I have at length repaired by their desire to this
country, and been acknowledged and proclaimed king ; and I
hope with the Divine assistance to maintain my position.   I
should esteem myself happy, my worthy cousin, if you would
rejoice and console me by sending hither some of my friends,
that I may employ them to their satisfaction, and give them a
share in my good fortune : which good fortune I hope, by the
advantages gained on my travels, and by the Divine help, to make
yet more glorious, to the honour of God, and to the great gain
of my neighbour.   It will probably be unknown to you that I
had the misfortune last year to be taken prisoner on the sea, and
taken to Algiers as a slave : from which condition I nevertheless
found means to deliver myself, but still suffered great loss thereby, etc. I must, however, put off to another period the mention
of what I have gained through the grace of God: and at this
present only request you to count upon me as surely as upon
yourself, and to be assured that I have inscribed in my heart the
sincere tokens of friendship manifested towards me in the richest
measure ever since early youth, and that I will exert myself in
every way to give you substantial proofs of my sincere devotion,
with which I shall ever be attached to you ; remaining with my
whole heart yours, and a true friend and Cousin,

" THE BARON OF NEUHOFF,
" <i>King-Elect in Corsica, with the title of Theodore the First.</i></div>

" <i>March</i> 18, 1736."

" P.S.—I entreat you to give me a report of your doings, and
to greet all the worthy family and friends from me ; and, as my
exaltation redounds to their glory, so I hope they will all
together help to contribute to my good, and come to me, to assist
me with their counsel and their actions.   Since also in many
years no letters have been received from my friends in the Brandenburg dominions, permit me to transmit to you the enclosed
letter, with the request that you will forward it to Bungelschild,
and will send me news whether my uncle is still alive, and what
my cousins at Rauschenberg are doing."

CHAPTER IV.

THEODORE THE FIRST, BY THE GRACE OF GOD AND THROUGH THE HOLY TRINITY, KING-ELECT IN CORSICA.

No sooner had Theodore arrived in Corsica, and made himself known in the world, than the Republic of Genoa, "injured by him," published a manifesto, in which it declared its sentiments relative to his person; "and the Genoese," says the above quoted German book, "describe Theodore very odiously in an edict."

They do indeed describe him very odiously, as the following may show :—

" We, DOGE, GOVERNORS, *and* PROCURATORS *of the Republic Genoa*—On the receipt of the news, that at the port of Aleria, in our kingdom of Corsica, the English Captain Dick's small merchant ship has landed stores of war, and a certain notorious orientally attired person, who has unaccountably succeeded in rendering himself popular to the leaders and the common people; and whereas this foreigner has distributed to them as well arms, powder, and some coins of bullion, as other things, and further-more, with a promise of a more than adequate assistance, gives them various counsels tending to the disturbance of the public peace, which we are solicitous to restore to the good of the sub-jects of our above-named kingdom; we have been informed, by means of credible testimonies, of the real quality and life of this person. It is hereby known to us that he is a native of the Westphalian marches, that he passes for the Baron of Neuhoff, that he boasts a knowledge of Alchemy, the Cabbala, and Astrology, by the aid of which he has discovered many important secrets; further, that he has made himself notorious as a vagrant and vagabondizing person of small fortune.

" In Corsica he is called Theodore. In the year 1729 he came under this name to Paris, where he deserted his wife, a person of Irish birth, whom he had married in Spain, when with child.

" During his rovings over the world he repudiated his sur-name and the place of his birth. In London he passed for a German, in Leghorn for an Englishman, in Genoa for a Swede;

and called himself now Baron Von Naxaer, now Von Smihmer, now Von Nissen, now Von Smitberg, as may be seen especially by his passports and other authentic papers, dated from various towns, and preserved.

"By thus changing his name and his country, he succeeded by his impositions in living at the expense of others ; and it is well known that in Spain, about the year 1727, he squandered the monies advanced to him for the levy of a German regiment, and then raised himself out of the dust ; and that he has at many other places defrauded Englishmen, French, Germans, and people of other nations.

"At the places where he practised such frauds, he endeavoured to remain in concealment. But when he was away he made himself notorious by the knaveries he practised, as is especially proved by a letter, written Feburary 20th of this year, 1736, by a German cavalier.

"That he has been wont to live after such fashion as this, is proved by the following fact :—A few years ago he borrowed 515 pieces from the Leghorn banker Jaback, with the promise of remitting them to him in Cologne. When the latter found himself defrauded, he caused him to be arrested. To regain his freedom he made use of a shipmaster, whom he seduced into giving security for him ; and when his release from confinement was published in an instrument engrossed by the Leghorn notary Gumano under date of the 6th September 1735, and as he was in ill health during the period of his arrest, he was received into the Bath-hospital of the above-named city, to be cured as one requiring the use of the waters.

"About three months ago he betook himself, with letters of recommendation, from Leghorn to Tunis, where he acted a medical man, and had several secret conferences with the heads of that infidel land. There he afterwards procured arms and stores of war, with which he repaired to Corsica, in the company of Christopher, brother of Boungiorno, the physician at Tunis, of three Turks, one of whom is a certain Mohamet, who has been a slave on the Tuscan galleys, of two Livornese runaways from their paternal abodes, by name John Attimann and Giovanni Bondelli, and of a Portuguese ecclesiastic who was compelled, not without reason, by the missionary fathers in Tunis, to withdraw from that city.

"Under such circumstances and such undoubted testimonies, as this person has put himself into the position of ruler of Corsica, and has maliciously presumed to seduce our subjects from the allegiance due to their natural sovereign; and as it is to be apprehended that a person of such infamous designs may be capable of causing yet more confusion and commotion among our people, we have resolved to make all public and notorious, and to proclaim, as we herewith do by the present ·edict, that this so styled Baron Theodore of Neuhoff, as actual author of new seditions, seducer of the people, and disturber of the public peace, is pronounced guilty of the crime of *læsa, majestas*, and has accordingly incurred all the pains and penalties therefore prescribed by our laws.

" We accordingly forbid all persons to have conversation or commerce with the person in question, and we declare all those who shall render him aid and assistance, or who shall otherwise take his part, in order to the greater embroiling and excitation to revolt of our people, guilty *læsæ majestatis*, and disturbers of the public peace, and liable to the same pains and penalties.

" *Given in our Royal Palace, May 9, 1736.*

　　　　　　　　(Signed)　　" JOSEPH MARIA."

The injured Republic had no success from this manifesto. Even in her own city of Bastia, the people wrote beneath it " Evviva Teodoro I. Re di Corsica;" and Theodore, far from being ashamed of being an upstart, said with manly humour, " Since the Genoese decry me as an adventurer and charlatan, I will soon set up my theatre in Bastia."

He published meanwhile, a counter-manifesto to the Genoese one, and this is very rich:—

" THEODORUS, *King of Corsica, to the* DOGE *and* SENATE *at Genoa, his Greeting and Long-suffering.*

" It never occurred to me that I was guilty of a sin of omission, in not communicating to your august house my resolution of going to Corsica; to say the truth, I deemed such a formality useless, since I thought that rumour would in any case have preinformed you of it. Therefore I considered it a work of supererogation to inform you of the same thing of which your Corsican ministers had previously informed you in pompous narratives.

" But as it still appears to me that you have complained of my having concealed my intentions from you, I find myself necessitated by the duty of a citizen—as every one who removes notifies the fact to his neighbour—to notify to you that I have

changed my lodging. I must remark on this head, that being
tired of the long and extensive wanderings, which as you know
I have had, I have at length come to the determination to
choose myself a place of settlement in Corsica; now, as this is in
your neighbourhood, I take the liberty of herewith paying you
my respects by this letter. Your commissioner in Bastia, if he
does not deceive you like his predecessors, will be able to assure.
you of my especial exertions to send to the said city a sufficient
number of troops, to give it unmistakeably to understand this
our new position as neighbours.

"But as change of residence often creates strife between
neighbours about boundaries, right of way, or otherwise, 1 will
therefore abstain from further compliments, and speak at once
with you of our affairs, the more as I am assured from various
quarters that our new position as neighbours is very disagreeable to you, and that you bitterly repudiate it, and even, with an
utter forgetfulness of your duties towards us, absolutely refuse it.
The declaration given by you, that your neighbour is a disturber
of the public peace and a seducer of the people, is the most
evident lie, put forth, not here and there, but before the
whole world, as truth; although every body knows that peace
and tranquillity have for the last seven years been banished from
Corsica, and that it is you alone who have disturbed it by your
administration, and then banished it through your cruelty.
These state maxims, under the appearance of promoting peace,
have thrown the poor Corsicans into a river of blood.

"This was your behaviour, and thus you have banished peace
and tranquillity from Corsica, after it had been restored again
with so much pains by the emperor. Your guilty and obstinate
Pinelli seduced the people, and in such a condition I found the
country when I came to live here only a few days. But wherefore is the guilt of your own crimes put upon my shoulders? In
what law has it been read that so harmless a neighbour as I am
can be guilty of high treason? Treason presupposes a breach of
friendship, accompanied by the coarsest guilt, committed under
the guise of friendship. Supposing now that you were most
coarsely injured by me, what manner of friendship has subsisted
previously between us? and when have I been your friend?
Heaven preserve me from ever thinking of being the friend of a
nation that has so few friends!

"But it is attempted to prove by dint of force that I have
committed the crime of *læsa majestas*. The very idea of such a

horrible accusation terrifies me. But, after earnestly investigating from what source your *majestas* is derived, I have comforted myself again by the fact, that notwithstanding my most serious investigations I have never discovered that source. Pray tell me, have you inherited such a *majestas* from your Doge, or made prize of it on the sea when you left your city to the Mohammedans · as a place of refuge, and from cupidity attracted so many Turks thither, that they would have been amply sufficient to overpower all Christendom? Perchance you brought this *majestas* on your shoulders from Spain; or it must have somehow come into your country from England, by a ship which was sent by an English merchant to one of your countrymen who had just been elected Doge, and brought a letter with the address, 'To Mr. ——, Doge of Genoa, and dealer in miscellaneous wares.'

" But pray tell me, in the name of God, where you picked up the dignity of a monarchy and the title of sovereign, when your republic was formerly nothing but a guild of gain-seeking pirates? Have, then, any other persons sat for many hundred years in your council-chamber, but such as administer civil offices, and is it they from whom you received your majesty? Is not the name of Duke, which you give to your Doge, a very unseemly title? I am convinced that the laws and fundamental articles of your republic are so ordained that no one can be a sovereign but the law itself, and that you, as executors and administrators of it, indecorously arrogate to yourselves the appellation of sovereign, and with equal want of justice call the people your subjects, whereas they ought by rights to govern together with yourselves, as is indeed actually the fact. Now although, in your own country, to which you have no right, you still remain for the present in peaceful undisturbed possession, yet I cannot see that you are likely to fare equally well in Corsica, where the people, having their eyes open, take their stand upon their legitimate demands, and are forced to shake themselves free of the yoke. I for my part am firmly resolved, to hold to that party to which reason and love of justice may attach me. And whereas you have decried me over the whole world as a defrauder of each and every nation, I now purpose by my acts to demonstrate the contrary to one nation, namely the oppressed Corsicans. As often then as I can cheat you, by helping you out of this lie, I shall be only too glad to do so, and will leave you to find out where you can do the like to me.

" However, you may confidently rely on this, that my credi-

tors will duly receive payment from your estate, since your possessions, which the Corsicans have in due form made me a
present of, are more than adequate to liquidate my debts.   But
I should be sorry if I could not adequately requite to your republic the severity practised by it in this realm, especially seeing
that no money-payment can appear too large in retribution for it.

"I will not forget also to announce to you herewith, that my ·
party makes rapid strides, at the same time that you will have
heard that I have as many troops in my pay as is essential to
show, that I am not only capable of living from the purses of
others, but also clever enough to maintain 10,000 men at my
own cost.   Whether these receive their full pay and provisions,
may those heroic soldiers attest who keep themselves shut up
in the walls of Bastia, because they have not the courage to
submit to a closer inspection in the open field.

"I assure you, however, that, much trouble as you give yourselves to asperse my good name before the world, I have no fears
of your making the impression intended upon these men, nor of
the ducats they receive having a lesser influence than all the
calumnies you are incessantly inventing against my person.   One
favour I have still to beg of you, namely, to take care that, in
the skirmishes possibly occurring between my troops and yours,
at least one of your countrymen may be visible holding the
command over yours, since the true heroism cherished by honest
men for their country is undoubtedly to be found among such
men.   But I am quite ready to believe I shall not attain the
fulfilment of my request, as you are all so much engrossed by
your bills of exchange, your usury and commerce, that the spirit
of valour can find no room near you.   Therefore I am as far as
possible from supposing you will ever reap honour from your
troops, since those who ought to lead them have neither time
nor valour enough to lead them into the field, after the example
of other valorous nations.

"*Given in the Camp before Bastia, July* 10, 1736.

                                   "THEODORUS.
      "SEBASTIANO COSTA,
"*Secretary of State and Chancellor of the Realm.*"

This envenomed, scornful letter, of course, could not but most
deeply offend the republic of Genoa.   But such is the course of
events; the proud mistress of the seas was now fallen, a small people before her very doors terrified her by the force of their arms,
and a foreign knight of fortune cast his taunts at her unchastised.

The elective capitulation was consummated in Alesani, April 15, 1736; Theodore was elected king for life, and after his death the crown was to pass from him to his male issue, according to the claims of birth and age, and, in default of male heirs of his body, to his daughters. In default of heirs of his body, his relations were to mount the throne. But the Corsicans only gave their king his title; they preserved their constitution.

I never heard that the new king ever thought of giving a queen to his country; perhaps time pressed too much. He arranged his abode in the bishop's house at Cervione in kingly fashion, so far as circumstances would.permit, surrounded himself with guards and princely ceremonial, and played the king as well as if he had been born in the purple. We have already heard that he introduced a grand-sounding court-system, and, as behoves a generous king, created counts, marquises, barons, and dazzling court functions. Men and their passions are every where alike. A man may feel himself a king quite as well in the gloomy rooms of a village house, as in the splendid saloons of the Louvre; and a Duke of Chocolate or Marmalade at the court of a negro king, will bear his title with scarcely less pride than a Duke of Alba. In Cervione people were also seen pressing for admission, who wished to warm themselves at the beams of the new sun, and coveted titles and favours; in the dirty mountain village, in a black tumble-down house now called a palace, ambition and intrigue played their game as well as at any other court in the world.

One of Theodore's acts of royal plenipotency was the foundation of an order; for a king must have orders to distribute. As already related, this order was termed that of Liberation. The knights cut a very handsome figure. They wore an azure-blue dress and a cross; in the middle of the cross was a star in .enamel and gold, having in it the figure of Justice with the scales in her hand. Beneath the scales was seen a triangle with a T in the middle of it; and in her other hand Justice held a sword, beneath which was seen a globe with a cross upon it. In the corners of the sign of the order, the arms of the royal family found their place. Every knight of the Order of Liberation had to swear allegiance to the king by water and by land. And he had to sing two psalms every day, the forty-sixth, "God is our refuge and strength," and the seventy-first, "In thee, O Lord, do I put my trust." ●

Theodore's gold, silver, and copper coins, which have become very rare, display on one side his bust, with the inscription, THEODORUS D. G. UNANIMI CONSENSU ELECTUS REX ET PRINCEPS REGNI CORSICI; and on the other side the words, PRUDENTIA ET INDUSTRIA VINCITUR TYRANNIS. On other coins is seen a crown supported by three palms, with the letters T. R., and on the reverse the words PRO BONO PUBLICO CORSO.

To the executioner also Theodore gave the necessary royal employment, and caused the execution of many a one who appeared dangerous to him. But he lost ground with his subjects, especially after the execution of a distinguished Corsican named Luccioni de Casacciolo; and he was besides accused of having tempted the virtue of some Corsican maidens, in a manner not to be justified by the terms of the elective capitulation. But for a few years the Corsicans clung to him with great fidelity. This poor nation had in its despair longed for a king, as the Jews desired a king to deliver them from the Philistines. When he went away for the first time, they remained true to him, and published this manifesto:—

"*We*, DON LOUIS, MARCHESE GIAFFERI, *and* DON GIACINTO, MARCHESE PAOLI, *Prime Ministers and Generals of his Majesty* KING THEODORE, *our Sovereign.*

"No sooner had we received the letters of King Theodore I., our sire, than, in obedience to his commands, we summoned all people of the provinces, towns, villages, and castles of the kingdom, to the town of Corte, to hold a general assembly touching the regulations and commands of our above-named sovereign. The assembly was general, from one side of the mountains as well as from the other. All received with satisfaction and submissiveness the commands of his majesty, to whom, as their legitimate and supreme sire, they unanimously renewed the oath of fidelity and allegiance. They likewise confirmed to him and his descendants his election as King of Corsica, as had been inviolably stipulated in the convention of Alesani.

"To this end we make known to all whom it may concern, and to the whole world, that we shall always observe an inviolable fidelity towards the royal person of Theodore the First, and that we are resolved to live and die for him as his subjects, and never to acknowledge another sovereign than him and his legitimate descendants. Once more we swear upon the Holy Gospel, in all points to keep the oath of fidelity in the name of the here assembled people.

"And to the end that the present document may possess all due validity and authenticity, we have caused it to be registered in the Chancery of the realm, and have subscribed it with our own hands, and confirmed it with the great seal of the realm.

"*Given at Corte, Dec. 27, 1737.*"

Similar declarations were repeated in the year 1739, when Theodore again landed in Corsica amidst the acclamations of the people. On this second landing he was near being burnt alive. A German captain, Wigmanshausen, who commanded his ship, was bribed by the Genoese to blow it up. In the night Theodore awoke several times with a presentiment of being burnt alive. So it occurred to him to go with three of his attendants into the cabin of the captain, whom he found actually occupied in preparations for kindling the powder-magazine of the vessel. King Theodore sentenced him on the spot to death by fire, but subsequently commuted the sentence to that of being hanged on the mast of his ship; and the sentence was immediately put in execution. Thus Theodore experienced, even in his short career of royalty, an attempt on his life.

With Theodore's subsequent history we are already acquainted. After a vain attempt to regain his island-crown, he retired to England. He left behind him a wonderful life-dream, in which he had seen himself on a wild island, with a crown on his head and a sceptre in his hand, and surrounded by marquises, earls, barons, knights, chancellors, and keepers of the great seal. He now sat beggared and sad in the London debtor's prison, into which he had been cast by his creditors, and thought over the royal romance of his changeful and wandering life; and complained no less bitterly and feelingly that he must languish as a martyr in captivity to English merchants, than Napoleon at a later date in his English prison at St. Helena. And Theodore 'too had been a king; he was a fallen potentate, and a tragic personage. The minister Walpole opened a subscription for the benefit of the poor Corsican king, and delivered him from imprisonment; in gratitude for which, Theodore made him a present of the great seal of his kingdom. He too, like Paoli and Napoleon, died on English soil, in the year 1756. He was buried in the cemetery of Westminster.* He was an extraordinarily dashing man, of a fantastic genius, inexhaustible in projects, more

* "He was buried in an obscure corner, among the paupers, in the churchyard of St. Anne's, Soho." For this correction we are indebted to an article in the *Athenæum*, No. 1427, Mar. 3. 1855.

persevering than his curious fortune, and of all adventurers the most praiseworthy, because he manfully employed his head and hands for the freedom of a brave people. He bitterly experienced in his own person the sharpest contrasts of human life—royalty, and the debtor's prison, in which he wanted for bread. We Germans will gladly give the poor man a place among the brave of our nation ; and this slight memorial token I have raised to my valiant countryman, to revive his memory among us.

CHAPTER V.

MARIANA, AND RETURN TO BASTIA.

> Era già là ora che volge il disio
> Ai naviganti, e intenerisce il core
> Lodì che han detto ai dolci amici a dio.
>
> DANTE, *Purg.* viii. 1.

THE *paese* of Cervione lies northward from Aleria on the side of the mountains. I am now punished for not having visited it, by my present wish to be able to say I have been there ; for although it contains nothing worth seeing, it was Theodore's royal residence. However, the traveller is sometimes weary of travelling, and passes many an object worthy of consideration with his eyes shut. I saw Cervione on the hill above me, and gave it up for the sake of the ruins of Mariana.

To the north of Cervione the river Golo flows out, the largest vein of water in the island, watering many villages. The summer drought had almost dried it up. The stream has formerly overflowed the broad plain of Mariana, or Marana as the Corsicans now say. Here stood the second Roman colony, on the left bank of the river, founded by Marius. It is remarkable that to this bloody land of Corsica the two blood-avengers and mortal enemies, Sulla and Marius, were destined to send colonies.

Their terrible names, which suggest the most awful horrors of civil war and revolutions, enhance the sultriness of a Corsican atmosphere.

I searched for the ruins of Mariana. They lie an hour's walk off from the road, towards the sea-coast. Here, as at Aleria, I found extensive tracts strewn with stones of walls, covering the whole ground. One wanders sadly over such a

field, when one considers that these stones were once a human
town, and that the life of centuries dwelt within them.   One
would fain take up Amphion's lyre, harmonize the stones together
again, and take a glance at the town and people.   For of what
kind were they? to what epoch did they belong?   The ruins of
Mariana are yet more insignificant than those of Aleria.   No
judgment can be formed from them as to their age.   The Corsican is glad to see people try to find in those stones the remains
of Roman buildings; and the wanderer may sit down in self-de-
ception on one of those heaps of ruin, and think of Marius himself sitting on the ruins of Carthage, and lamenting the fall of
the great city.

Two ruined churches alone attract attention; they are the
most prominent ruins from the middle-age period.   The first
and smaller one was a beautiful chapel, the long nave of which
has been well preserved.   It has a pulpit decorated outside by
six pilasters of the Corinthian order.   Sculptures of very simple
work are placed above the cornice of the side entrance.   A
mile farther stand the beautiful ruins of a larger church, of
which likewise the nave remains erect.   It is called the Canonica.
The building is a basilica of three naves, with rows of pilasters
of the Doric order, and a pulpit constructed like a Gothic chapel
on both sides.   The niche on the outside has likewise pilaster
decorations of the Doric order.   The length of the nave amounts
to 110 feet, and its breadth 50.   The façade is half destroyed,
and displays the Pisan style.   On the portal-arch are seen
sculptures—old men, dogs hunting a stag, and a lamb, of such
rough workmanship that it might belong to the eighth century.
This Canonica has been styled a Roman temple which the Saracens converted into a mosque, and the Christians into a church
again, when Hugo Colonna won back Mariana from the Moors.
One readily perceives that the building has been restored, but
nothing speaks for its having been Roman.   On the contrary, it
appears in every respect like a basilica of the Pisans.   Its forms
are excellently pure, noble, simple, and of the best symmetry;
and this, as well as the beautiful closeness of the Corsican marble
with which the church is faced, certainly gives it the appearance
of ancient architecture.

On passing into the interior of the church, I was surprised at
the devout congregation that I found kneeling in it.   These were
high-shooting wild plants, quietly luxuriating in rows, one behind
the other, across the nave.   A bearded goat just stood in front of

the pulpit, apparently indulging in moral rather than in gluttonous
meditation.   The herdsmen were pasturing their herds of goats
beside the Canonica.   I asked them in vain about coins; yet here,
as in other places in Corsica, have been found a considerable
number of imperial coins, with which half the world is blessed.
From this former colony of Marius, which was founded before
Aleria, and cannot, like Sulla's colony, have been a military but a
civil colony, the only Roman road in Corsica led by Aleria to
Præsidium, Portus Favoni, and Palæ on the straits of the
modern Bonifazio.   So the island was in those times yet poorer
in roads than it now is; and into the mountainous interior the
Romans never penetrated.

Here Bastia shows itself again, and I will close the circle of
my wanderings.   To the left rise the blood-drenched hills of
Borgo, where many a battle was fought, and where the Corsicans
gained their last victory over their French oppressors.   Farther
on gleams the still picturesque lagoon of Biguglia, and above it
stands Biguglia itself, once the residence of the Genoese governor.
The old castle is cast to the ground.   The last place before
Bastia is Furiani.   Its grey castle is in ruins, and the black walls
are clothed by the ivy and the white clematis in most luxurious
green.   Once more the eye wanders hence to the lovely Golo
plain, and to the ethereal blue mountains, which nod farewell to
me from the interior of the island with their veils of clouds.   A
salutary and beautiful journey is now accomplished.   And here
the wanderer stands still in joyous contemplation, and thanks
the kind powers that have attended him.   Yet the heart finds
it hard to take leave of the wonderful island.   It has become
like a friend to me.   The still valleys with their olive groves;
the enchanting gulfs; the ethereal mountains with their well-
springs and crowns of pines; towns and villages, and their
hospitable inhabitants—have given many a hospitable gift of
permanence to my intellect as well as to my heart.

Once more the picture of a Corsican, who, lying beneath an
old olive, endeavours to give me an idea of the land and people.

THE STRANGER.

WILD mountain Corsican, what dreamest thou,
Here idly lying 'neath the olive's bough?
Outstretch'd with double gun upon thy arm,
Forth staring through the air, so sultry warm?
In yon grey tower doth weep thy hungry child;
Thy wife spins on, and sings her dirges wild,
Complaining that unceasing is her care—
No fire on the hearth, the chamber bare.

Yet thou art perched, a falcon, on this stone,
And scorn'st to let the golden grain be sown,
Nor plantest vines, nor scatterest seeds to earth,
Nor keep'st a comfortable home and hearth.
Look here, how stretches out the plain to view,
So blithely following yonder mountains blue,
And sinking down unto the sea with smiles,
A paradise o'erflowed by teeming rills.
Yet only myrtles thrive on every side.
And stunted albatro extending wide;
And fern, and cytisus, and heath is there,
The summer food of goats with darksome hair.
The Golo river creeps down 'mong the weeds,
To marshes overgrown with sedge and reeds,
Where heavy is the air, with fever rife,
That, slow and sure, consumes the fisher's life.
And as the wanderer passes o'er the plain,
Moor-birds alone pour in his ear their strain;
He there meets ruins only, walls down-tumbled
Of Roman towns which into dust have crumbled.
Up, Corsican! away with thy base rest,
And get thee down, and grasp the axe in haste;
The spade and mattock seize, and till thy ground,
Until a fruitful garden teems all round!

THE CORSICAN.

Thou foreigner, whose sires I met of old
Near Calenzana, and in death's sleep did fold,
Why troublest thou my peace? Two thousand years
I have been fighting, full of strife and tears,
And wrestling for so long have made my stand
Against the foe who overran my land.
On Col di Tenda erst I forced to yield
The Romans whose footprints are on this field;
I conquered Hasdrubal off my sea-coast,
And scattered forth like seeds th' Etruscan host.
For booty pressed the Moor into my bay,
And bore my wife and children far away,
And hurled into my house the fiery brand;
I clenched him, wrestled, gained the upper hand.
Again I heard the conch-horn loudly blow,
When overran my land anew a foe,
First Lombard, and then Turk, and Arragon.
And though my blood in reddened streams flowed on,
And though I saw my roofstead burnt to dust,
I wept not—for no foe my freedom crushed.
Then came the Genoese—O curse most bitter!
For her own child would Italy enfetter!
Dost thou complain, so waste is now my land,
The fields a wilderness, and bare the strand,
The hamlet ivied o'er and half destroyed?
Then know—the Genoese hath made this void.
If by the sea the mandolina's tones
Thou hearest, or vocero's long plaintive moans,
And wonderest thou that aye the strain is sad,
Then know, that by the Genoese 'twas made.

2 L

Hear'st thou the gun-shot o'er the hills resound,
See'st thou the bleeding victim fall to ground,
And shudderest for our vengeance never cooled;
Then know, that by the Genoese we're schooled.
Know now what we've endured with none to save!
But I have dug for Genoa her grave;
And when thou see'st her, then say, "I saw
The Corsican isle, the grave of Genoa!"
Fell was the strife and endless cruel; my land
The merchant gave into the Frenchman's hand,
Like an estate that one may buy for gold;
Yet calmly did a coward world behold.
Thou stranger, hear! on Ponte Nuovo's bank
I yielded to the freedom-killing Frank;
And wept and dragged me, like a bleeding stag,
Forth from the battle field, up rock and crag.
Such battling wears one out—I'm weary now;
Then let me rest beneath the olive-bough.

THE STRANGER.

No bitter word would I 'gainst thee rehearse,
But only feeling grieve thy fortune's curse,
Thou champion-warrior, bleeding, battle-worn.
Thou son of Death, thou of a Fury born.
Then rest! since thou through Europe's age of night
Alone wert wakeful on thy rocky height;
Alone for man's estate hast stoutly fought,
When its mere name seemed by the world forgot.
Of thy forefathers I have heard the glory
Of Pasqual Paoli the solemn story.
I thought new life could by my living word
On rusty hero-memories be conferred.
And what though they were bloody horrors dark,
Or else soul-harrowing grievous cares and cark,
That oft have touched my homeless heart while here;
It yet hath breathed a hero-atmosphere:
It yet from all thy tuneful death-laments
Hath caught the fairest, clearest of accents.
And as I sat beneath the giant rock,
And saw dash down through clouds the torrent-brook,
Her glories nature poured out o'er my head,
And o'er my soul the love of light did shed;
I in the land of death have been a guest,
Yet home return with branch of olive blest;
The pilgrim glad that cherished sign displays,
Which kindly spirits gave to cheer his ways.
Then, Corsican, adieu! and fare thee well,
Whilst o'er the restless wave my ship's sails swell,
Heaven's blessings on thee for those fruits of thine,
For nightly shelter and for generous wine!
May thy fat olive teem year after year,
Thy orchard never fail a crop to bear!
Ripen upon the lea enough of maize!
Thy vengeance be burnt up by sun's bright rays,
That by his glow, of hero-blood the stain
Be dried up on thy hero-soil again!

Tall grow thy son, e'en as his fathers stern,
Thy daughters pure, e'en as the mountain-burn!
Between her and the vice refined of France
Thy granite mountains ever put a fence!
Island, farewell! may never wane thy fame,
Be fathers' virtues and their sons' the same!
Lest haply a stranger on thy hills deplore,
"Sampiero's hero-mind is now no more!"

NOTE.

I will give at the conclusion of my book a slight literary notice of the works that have been of essential service to me in its composition. Even here the usual experience is verified, that any subject, however insulated it be, draws a continent of literature after it. The historical works I have already named, such as Filippini, Peter of Corsica, Cambiaggi, Jacobi, Limperani, Renucci, Gregori, &c. To these I will add, " Robiquet, Recherches Historiques et Statistiques sur la Corse. Paris, 1835 "— a book which is very rich in matter, and has supplied me with some valuable notices. Of the works of Niccolo Tommaseo I was enabled to consult his " Lettere di Pasquale de Paoli. Firenze, 1846 ;" and the " Canti populari Corsi," in his collection of Corsican, Tuscan, and Greek popular poetry. The Corsican dirges published by me are taken from the "Saggio di Versi Italiani e di Canti Popolari Corsi. Bastia, 1843." The subjects of the Corsican stories, which all relate actual occurrences, I have gathered from a collection of such stories, by Renucci, Bastia, 1838 ; the treatment is my own. The work of Boswell, " Journal of a Tour in Corsica, with Memorabilia of Pasquale Paoli," (London, 1769), is worth reading, because the author was personally acquainted with the great Corsican, and wrote down his actual words. Lastly, I owe various remarks to Valery's book, " Voyages en Corse, à l'île d'Elbe et en Sardaigne. Brussels, 1838." I need not mention other books not specially relating to Corsica.

INDEX.

ERRATUM.

Page 172, line 17, for *get*, read *bear*.

THE END.

M'CORQUODALE AND CO., PRINTERS, LONDON—WORKS, NEWTON.

TOUR ON THE CONTINENT,

BY RAIL AND ROAD,

IN THE SUMMER OF 1852,

THROUGH

NORTHERN GERMANY, AUSTRIA, TYROL, AUSTRIAN LOMBARDY, &c.

BY JOHN BARROW, ESQ.

" CELER EUNDO."

LONDON:
LONGMAN, BROWN, GREEN, AND LONGMANS.
1853.

TO THE MEMORY OF

LIEUTENANT-COLONEL HENRY SAMUEL DAVIS,

WHO DIED, IN COMMAND OF THE 52ND LIGHT INFANTRY,

ON THE 23RD SEPTEMBER, 1851, IN THE PRIME OF LIFE,

THESE PAGES ARE AFFECTIONATELY INSCRIBED,

BY HIS FRIEND,

JOHN BARROW.

PREFACE.

In submitting to the readers of the "Travellers' Library" the following brief Notes, taken during a Summer's Tour on the Continent in 1852, I indulge the hope that they may, perhaps, prove useful to future travellers; and possibly be the means of inducing some to go abroad for amusement, for relaxation from business, or for the benefit of their health, who might otherwise have remained at home. If any should be tempted to do so upon this recommendation, and return benefited either in body or mind, it will afford me as much pleasure (should it chance to reach my ears) as I remember deriving, some years ago, on reading the following passage in the preface of a prettily written book, entitled, "Journal of a Tour to Moscow, in the Summer of 1846, by the Rev. R. B. Paul, M.A., late Fellow of Exeter Coll. Oxford, author of Grecian Antiquities," &c.—a gentleman with whom I was wholly unacquainted, and have never since had the pleasure of meeting with him, or of even exchanging communication: "Why I have troubled the public with a Journal of my

Tour to Moscow," Mr. Paul says, "is a question which
I find no small difficulty in answering. I believe it
was the perusal of Mr. Barrow's little book that first
inspired me with a taste for travelling in the north
of Europe; and the recollection of the pleasure which
that book afforded me, has made me hope that my own
personal narrative will not be entirely without interest
to the public." Mr. Paul then proceeds to say, that
his health had been a good deal shaken by different
causes, and that he was glad to embrace an opportunity
of recruiting his strength by an excursion, which promised so much of interest and excitement. "How
completely the proposed object was attained, I acknowledge," he says, "with feelings of the deepest gratitude
to Him, in whose hands are the issues of life and death."

I have thought it best to give my notes very nearly
as they were written off at the time, retaining the dates,
and even the hours of arrival and departure, which may
prove useful to others on their journey. In fact, this
little volume is only meant to be a pocket-companion, a
Vade Mecum, touching very slightly at the several spots
visited; it pretends to nothing more.

The Hand-Books of my excellent friend, Mr. Murray, are indispensable. No traveller should be without
them, and all travellers know and appreciate them; but
two or three of his octavo volumes are necessarily re-

quired, to embrace the countries travelled through in this Tour.

These pages, then, can claim no other title than to be considered as a brief Itinerary, chiefly of dates and distances—a species of *avant courier*, to Murray—with a few observations made on the rail and road, *en passant*.

I recommend every one to obtain a passport from the Foreign Office (the regulations for which I annex), and to get it *viséd* in London by the foreign ambassadors of those countries through which they may contemplate passing.

To all families travelling abroad (not intending to reside), I strongly recommend the employment of a courier, and particularly so if they are limited in their time, as we were. His services are almost indispensable on an extended tour; but I would also recommend them to keep a sharp eye upon his accounts. Some of them, no doubt, are thoroughly honest; but many of them are not altogether to be trusted. In either case, one cannot err by being upon his guard, which is due both to the courier and to the employer. Gentlemen travelling by themselves scarcely require a courier.

The several hotels at which we rested are mentioned. They were generally considered the best; and, with one or two exceptions, we found them all that could be desired.

I have now only to remark, that this somewhat extensive tour occupied about two months, the time to which my duties limited me, and that our sole object was to vary the scene as much as possible, and not to dwell long (however much we might have wished to have done so) at any one spot.

REGULATIONS RESPECTING PASSPORTS.

1. Applications for Foreign Office Passports must be made in writing; and addressed to Her Majesty's Secretary of State for Foreign Affairs, with the word "Passport" written upon the cover.

2. The fee on the issue of a Passport is 7s. 6d.

3. Foreign Office Passports are granted only to British subjects, including in that description foreigners who have been naturalized by Act of Parliament, or by Certificates of Naturalization granted before the 24th day of August, 1850: in this latter case, the party is described in the Passport as a "Naturalized British subject."

4. Passports are granted between the hours of twelve and four, on the day following that on which the application for the Passport has been received at the Foreign Office.

5. Passports are granted to persons who are either known to the Secretary of State, or recommended to him by some person who is known to him; or upon the written application of any BANKING FIRM established in London, or in any other part of the United Kingdom.

6. Passports cannot be sent by the Foreign Office to persons already abroad. Such persons should apply to the nearest British Mission or Consulate.

7. Foreign Office Passports must be countersigned at the Mission, or at some Consulate in England, of the Government of the country which the bearer of the Passport intends to visit.

8. A Foreign Office Passport granted for one journey may be used for any subsequent journey, IF COUNTERSIGNED AFRESH by the Ministers or Consuls of the countries which the bearer intends to visit.

FOREIGN OFFICE, 1853.

*** The Countersignature or *visa* of the Bavarian, Prussian, or Sardinian authorities in London, is not required.

TOUR ON THE CONTINENT.

LONDON TO OSTEND.

Monday, July 12, 1852.—Left London, with my mother and sister, by the 4.30 p.m. Express, for Dover.

Embarked at 7.30 in H. M. steam-vessel Vivid, for Ostend. The Vivid being ordered on some special service, we had the vessel almost to ourselves, and received much attention and kindness, as every one does, from Captain Smithett, who commands her. Sir John Hamilton (Captain Smithett's father-in-law), who is now eighty-eight years of age, and who commanded the "Active" cutter at Camperdown, went across with us. This noble specimen of a British seaman commanded one of the Harwich packets during the whole of the last war, and was for many years afterwards on the Dover station. Sir John Hamilton, I presume, is as well known to every one, who has been in the habit of crossing over to the Continent, as he is to myself. He is an old acquaintance of mine, and the last time I had the pleasure of seeing him was in command of his own vessel, the Widgeon, in 1840, when I was at Ostend, waiting for a gale of wind to moderate, to enable the packets to put to sea. He was at that time verging on fourscore—his age "frosty but kindly." I thought him then one of the most extraordinary men I had ever met with, and of course think him more so now. His memory is wonderful. We had a long chat together, and one to me of deep interest. He knew each of our great naval heroes of the last war,—Nelson, Collingwood, St. Vincent, Howe, Duncan, Keith, Duckworth, Sir Sidney Smith, &c.,—all were familiar to him, and he was full of anecdotes respecting them.

In allusion to so distinguished a man, I am sure my readers will peruse, with pleasure, a brief history of his public career, which I have obtained from him for the express purpose of placing it on record, to be read on the Rail, and with his own permission to do so. It will be found in the Appendix.

Eagerly listening to an unusual and agreeable conversation with so remarkable a public character as Sir John Hamilton, time, as may be supposed, soon passed away on board the Vivid, and the end of our voyage was at hand. We reached Ostend at 12 p.m.—exactly four hours and a half, the distance being sixty-two miles. The shortest passages to the Continent are from Dover to Calais, which is only twenty-two miles and a half, and from Folkestone to Boulogne, which is twenty-six. Ours, to Ostend, was a tolerably quick passage, being at the rate of about fourteen miles an hour. The shortest passage the Vivid ever made to Ostend was, I believe, three hours fifty-one minutes. She is certainly a fast boat, and of a beautiful mould : like all other fast boats, however, necessarily wet, at least we found her so, with a fresh breeze and a little sea up. The Vivid is a paddle-wheel boat, built by Oliver Lang,* assistant-master shipwright of Chatham-yard, the builder of the "Nankin" —to my mind one of the finest frigates that was ever laid upon the stocks. The length of the Vivid is 150 feet, breadth 22 feet, depth of hold 11 feet 4 inches; with engines of 160 horse power. Her speed, after several trials at the measured knot, in Long Reach (light draught), was ascertained to be above seventeen statute miles per hour. The average speed of the Vivid in service, at the load-line, may be stated at about sixteen miles an hour.

The night we crossed to Ostend was beautiful, the stars shining bright over head. At a considerable distance we saw the Revolving Light at Dunkerque, which shows like a meteor every minute, and, being 194 feet high, may be seen from a still further distance than that from which we had seen it.

There was luckily just water enough to enable us to enter the harbour at Ostend, which Captain Smithett skilfully contrived to do, notwithstanding the light-keepers had omitted to show the usual light at the pier-head. At dead low-water there is only a foot or two over the bar. Sir John Hamilton was quite on the *qui vive* on entering the harbour. I watched him standing on a bench near the paddle-box, looking over the side of the vessel, and to the man at the wheel, with a sharp experienced eye, which, I warrant, would have

* This talented officer, on the death of his distinguished father, has just been promoted to the rank of Master-Shipwright of Pembroke Dockyard.

carried us in safety into the harbour, if it had depended upon him. Farewell, thou good and brave old man!

Ostend is strongly fortified, and the works upon which they were so busy when I was last there, are now completed. Independent of the fortifications which surround the town, there is on either side a fort, and there are separate batteries facing the sea. I did not, however, observe many soldiers at Ostend. The *present* Peace Establishment of the Belgian army is, I learn, only 60,000 men of all classes, now under arms; but this number could be readily augmented in case of war, from 110,000 to 120,000, and it would require only a few days to raise it from its present number, of 60,000 to 80,000, by calling out the reserved battalion of each regiment.

The army is at present composed as follows, viz.—

			Battalions.	Men.
12	Regiments of Infantry		3	36,000
3	Do.	Chasseurs	3	9,000
1	Do.	Grenadiers	3	3,600
1	Do.	Engineers (Genie)		1,200
7	Do.	Cavalry	(800 each)	5,600
4	Do.	Artillery	about	3,400
		Gendarmerie		1,200

Landed, and proceeded to the *Hotel des Bains*, where we had to knock up the inmates, who had all retired to rest, not expecting any one at that time of night, the several Packets having arrived at their usual hours. Nothing, however, could be more good-humoured than the people, although disturbed in their sleep at so unseasonable an hour. The waiter told us that he thought the house was on fire.

There is not much to attract attention at Ostend, and

few, I imagine, who have been there before, would wish to remain any length of time.

In 1840, I was detained at Ostend three days by a gale of wind, when none of the Packets could venture to put to sea, and I found it dull enough; but fortunately was able to pass some hours very pleasantly in Sir John Hamilton's society on board the Widgeon, the vessel of which he was then in command, and which was also detained in the harbour. Ostend is, however, the resort of many visiters, as a watering-place, during the summer months, and the bathing is considered good. They come from all parts of Belgium, Germany, and the North of France, and many Russians also frequent it. Several reigning dukes and persons of distinction, likewise pass two or three months of the season at Ostend. Almost every house lets out apartments, and the visiters generally are, I believe, of the most respectable class of society, lodgings being high for that period.

There are considerably more than a hundred bathing carriages every morning busily employed, and the stone "Digue de Mer"—a noble esplanade of great length fronting the sea—may be seen at certain hours filled with well-dressed ladies.

I am told that there are several good English families resident at Ostend, and that provisions are moderate.

It has also a Protestant Church, well conducted; which may help to recommend it as a place of residence.

I must not omit to mention, that King Leopold has a house at Ostend, which is called the Palace, and that his majesty was in the habit for several years of resorting thither in the summer months, with the royal family, for the sea-bathing, until the death of the queen, which sad event took place at Ostend, in October, 1850.

The Palace is still kept ready for any of the royal family passing to or from England, and even so recently as last year was occupied by the king, on the occasion of his visiting our own sovereign during the Great Exhibition.

ANTWERP.

Tuesday, July 13.—Took our departure from Ostend by train, at 12 a.m., and arrived at *Antwerp* at 5½ p.m. Having myself more than once gone through this level line of country, I felt but little interest in it. It was intensely hot too all day—a broiling sun, and a dry easterly wind, a sort of *Sirocco.* The crops were every where remarkably fine, and the people already gathering in the harvest.

We went to the *Hotel St. Antoine,* and arrived there just in time for the Table d'Hote, at which, as might be expected, were more English than foreigners.

Wednesday, July 14.—Remained at Antwerp. Visited the several churches and the cathedral, where I again saw the magnificent painting of the Descent from the Cross, by Rubens. The carvings in all the churches still struck me as most beautiful, and not any where to be surpassed. The heat was very great. I took a boat to the opposite side to look at Antwerp once more from the river; I wished also to make a sketch, and to compare the view in my mind's eye, with a beautiful painting by my beloved brother-in-law, the late Lieutenant-Colonel Batty, whose memory I shall ever hold dear, for his amiable qualities and high accomplishments. His painting of Antwerp is now in my possession, together with many others which I have met with, and have purchased from time to time, being the originals from which the engravings were published, in his well-known work of " The Principal Cities of Europe."

Antwerp still, as regards its shipping, seems to be dull, and neglected as ever. It was in former days a great commercial city, one of the chief, in fact, of the north of Europe, and much still remains in its fine old buildings which bespeaks the opulence of its merchants in bygone times. The fatal blow, however, that Antwerp received to its commerce, was unquestionably in the last revolution.

There was something mournful to me in viewing the Scheldt denuded of shipping: nothing, indeed; but a few barges were passing up and down this noble river, and one solitary steamer was lying alongside the quay. The aspect was the same when I was last here; every thing wearing the same marks of desertion. No one who has entered Antwerp by the rail, should omit to take a boat to look at the city from the river.

The lofty spire of the cathedral is here seen to great advantage, pointing to the skies in all its beauty and elegance. From no other spot can a better view be obtained of its general character.

Of the many spires I have seen, there is none, I think,

not even that of Strasburg, which equals in the exquisite symmetry and lightness of its architecture, that of the cathedral of Antwerp. I would advise all young people to ascend the spire of this cathedral. I confess, I did not this time, being less ambitious now of attaining giddy heights; but it has heretofore been a rule with me, to go up to the *highest* point of view in all large towns, to ascertain their position, and many a beautiful panorama have I enjoyed by so doing.

At Antwerp, the view on a clear day would be extensive, over a flat country; and if it should happen to be somewhat obscure, a passing visiter might possibly be gratified with a sight similar to that described from the tower of the cathedral, by Evelyn in his Memoirs. " The sun," he says, " shone exceeding hot, and darted its rays without any intermission, affording so bright a reflection to us who were above, and had a full prospect of both land and water about it, that I was entirely confirmed in my opinion of the moon being of some such substance as the earthly globe consists of; perceiving all the adjacent country at so small a horizontal distance, to represent such a light as I could hardly look against, save when the river and other large waters within our vision appeared of a more dark and uniform colour, resembling those spots in the moon, supposed to be seas there, according to our new philosophy, and viewed by optical glasses."

We dined again at the Table d'Hote, and went to the Zoological Gardens (which are prettily laid out), and to some other gardens in the neighbourhood, belong-

ing to the Harmonic Society, where a splendid band
played some beautiful pieces of music during the evening.

LIEGE.

Thursday, July 15.—Heat very great.

Off by rail to Liège, where we arrived at 1½ p.m.,
having left Antwerp about 9½ a.m. The descent into
Liège, which is situated in a deep valley, is accomplished by an inclined plane, down which the train
passes, checked by ropes.

To the *Hotel d'Angleterre.* Took a delightful drive
in the evening to some gardens known as the Casino,
from which there is a charming panorama of the surrounding heights, Liège being beautifully situated
among the hills, at the junction of two rivers, the Meuse
and Ourthe. It is a busy manufacturing town; every
one well employed. They are a very early people at
Liège; and at six a.m. I found the shops open (as I
noticed when last here), and made a purchase at that
early hour of a clever bronze figure of a Capuchin
friar, with a book and torch in his hands—a lucifer-
match holder—to which I had taken a fancy. Liège is
famous for its manufactures, which are carried out
on an extensive scale; and there are large founderies,
in which heavy cannon are cast. The great Lion, on
the mound at Waterloo, was cast here. The surrounding hills abound in metal, as well as in coal, so that
every thing is close at hand; and Mr. Cockerell, the
English engineer, has taken advantage of these products, and turned them to good account.

COLOGNE.

Friday, July 16.—Intensely hot. By rail at 7 a.m. to Cologne, where we arrived at 12½ p.m., and remained at the opposite side of the river, at the *Belle Vue Hotel,* till four in the afternoon. Thermometer 84 in the shade at three p.m. The king was dining at the Belle Vue. Though we did not see his majesty, we got a glimpse of some of his generals, decorated with orders.

In passing through Cologne we remarked the great progress which had been made, since last year, in the building of the cathedral; when finished, it bids fair to be one of the grandest and most imposing pieces of architecture in the world. I have often been at Cologne; but, besides the cathedral, the bridge of boats across the Rhine, and the view of the town from the river, I never discovered any thing very attractive. The portion of the town on the river is, perhaps, the next best sight.

Cologne is strongly fortified, and could not, I think, be taken without some difficulty. It is strange, that a place so famed for its delicious perfume, which finds its way to all parts of the globe, should be so abominably ill-savoured in itself. There are not many places abroad more filthy; and it is totally inexcusable, with a rapid river rushing through, which would carry off all the offensive matter and vile odours of Cologne, with very little trouble, and at a trifling expense.

DUSSELDORF.

Continued our journey to Dusseldorf, which we reached at 5½ p.m., a fatiguing day's work owing to the intense heat; but we took a pleasant drive in the cool of the evening.

Dusseldorf is an agreeable town on the banks of the Rhine, with a beautiful park close adjoining, with many pleasant and shady walks. It is also a garrison-town.

We put up at the *Breidenbacher-hof,* an excellent house. Music and the Fine Arts are much cultivated here. Early in the morning I heard some beautiful church music, which some youths were practising in an adjoining institution.

HANOVER.

Saturday, July 17.—Weather still sultry in the extreme.

> ———"Distressful nature pants :
> The very streams look languid from afar."

A long journey by rail, first to Minden, situated on the Weser. At Minden we were received at the station with fixed bayonets, which seemed strange to peaceably disposed persons like ourselves. For my own part I should shudder to see, at the Great Western terminus, a row of police with their truncheons displayed. The fixed bayonets were more formidable. Stopped half an hour, and got a hurried dinner at the station.

We arrived at Hanover at 8 p.m., having left Dusseldorf at 9 a.m. It continued intensely hot all day. Went to the *Hotel Royal.*

Sunday, July 18.—To church in the morning. In the afternoon we drove about to the gardens and to the park, which is prettily laid out, and where the fountains were playing very pleasantly; one of them throwing up a fine volume of water to a height of some fifty or sixty feet, which looked somewhat imposing, and reminded me, "parvis componere magna," of the Geysers, those magnificent hot springs in Iceland, which it has been my good fortune to visit, and which throw a dense column of water, far exceeding these *jets d'eau* in diameter, to an ascertained height of eighty feet and upwards, accompanied with dense volumes of steam—one of the grandest sights in the creation. Hanover is one of the most interesting old towns, as regards its buildings, of any I have seen on the Continent. Many of the houses are of great antiquity. There is indeed a strange and motley group of ancient and modern architecture throughout the town; and some of the buildings are of the most quaint and fantastic description. Notwithstanding the beautiful park, and the variety of architecture which engages the attention, Hanover appears to me to wear a dull, deserted appearance; yet it is one of the capitals of Europe, and well repays a short visit, and particularly to an Englishman. One peculiarity I noticed, viz.,—paper blinds, generally blue or green; and as most of the modern houses have adopted them, and the blinds are generally drawn down to keep out the sun, the effect is simply—peculiar. In

the afternoon we were visited with a storm and heavy
rain, which to my great delight cooled the air considerably, and in a short space of time.

Monday, July 19. — Weather much cooler to-day.
The heat has hitherto been intense beyond any thing I
ever experienced. We went through the Palace, which
is handsomely decorated, and into the plate-room, where
there is a large collection of plate, made by the late
king, some modern, and some of considerable antiquity,
but all very beautiful. The floors of the Palace are
prettily inlaid. The room in which the king died was
pointed out to us: I believe he was very much beloved
and respected at Hanover. That he was a kind-hearted
man there can be no doubt; and I cannot forbear
reminding my readers of the generous manner in which
his Majesty transmitted £500 for the relief of the
family of poor Theodore Hook, at a time when few
—"very few of those," as the reviewer in the Quarterly remarks, "who had either profited as politicians
by his zeal and ability, or courted him in their lofty
circles for the fascination of his wit, were found to
show any feeling for his unfortunate offspring." With
Theodore Hook I was myself personally acquainted.
I never met with one more full of the " milk of
human kindness." He might have been a happier
man if he had "minded not high things," but had
been satisfied with " condescending (as he ever did)
to men of low estate," to whom his charity literally knew
no bounds.

The present King of Hanover is generally beloved:

his character may, I believe, be summed up in a few
words—amiable, virtuous, kind, and accomplished. His
"Ideas and Reflections on the Properties of Music,"
written when Prince George of Hanover, is a work of
acknowledged merit, and has been favourably noticed in
the Quarterly Review, " as incontrovertibly establishing
his claim to rank as the most accomplished amongst
contemporary scions of royalty."   In the square fronting the Palace is the Waterloo Memorial, a handsome
pillar, 160 feet high.

BRUNSWICK.

Departed by train at one o'clock for Brunswick, and
arrived there at three : put up at *Das Deutsche Haus*.
Brunswick is a remarkably quaint old town, with innumerable gables, high pitched roofs, and overhanging
stories, one above another, the tops of the houses ap-
proximating each other on either side, in the narrow
streets.   We took a carriage and drove about the town
and environs.   A fine obelisk is erected to the memory
of the two Dukes of Brunswick, father and son, who
nobly fell at Jena and Quatre-Bras.   The first Duke of .
Brunswick was mortally wounded in the battle of Jena,
in 1808.   He was Commander-in-Chief of the Prussian
army in that terrible conflict, when no fewer than twenty
thousand Prussians were killed or taken ; a grape-shot
wound in the face compelled him to be carried off the
field, and his hurried retreat to Altona (where he was to
have embarked for England) brought on inflammation,

which terminated his career. His son (it is said) vowed eternal revenge; and certain it is, that nine years after, that son fell gallantly on the field of battle at Quatre-Bras, whilst charging at the head of a regiment of lancers. Harassed by the fire of the enemy's batteries, attacked by columns of French infantry, and a large force of cavalry advancing upon them, it is little to be wondered at, that the Duke of Brunswick's corps should have fallen back as it did, in confusion, at Quatre-Bras. Putting himself at the head of a regiment of lancers, the Duke gallantly charged the French infantry; "but these received him with such a steady front, that no impression was made, and the lancers retreated in confusion on Quatre-Bras. The Duke, perceiving that the enemy was too strong for him, desired his infantry to fall back in good order upon the same point. They tried to do so, but failed; for the French artillery struck with terrible effect among them, and the tirailleurs closing in, supported by clouds of cavalry, the troops so assailed lost all self-possession, and broke. They fled in confusion, some by Quatre-Bras, others right through the English regiments, which had formed on the left of it, and all the Duke's exertions to stay them failed. It was at this moment that the gallant Duke of Brunswick, while striving to arrest the flight of one of his regiments of infantry, received the fatal shot which terminated his existence. "Thus, in the forty-fourth year of his age, the Duke of Brunswick died, as his father had died before him, on the fatal field of Jena.* *

* Gleig's Story of the Battle of Waterloo.

The Palace of Brunswick is a handsome modern building, but has nothing else remarkable about it.

In the evening we went to the Opera, a neat little theatre, about the size of our " Olympic," with an unusually large orchestra. The opera was " Fidelio," and was well performed—over at nine. The chief attraction —a young lady from Stuttgard, who sang sweetly. We were received at the Opera with fixed bayonets, as we had been at the Railway station at Minden; but our nerves were not particularly affected by it, either at one place or the ether.

HARTZBURG.

Tuesday, July 20.—To Hartzburg in the morning by rail (about two hours). Got rooms at the *Hotel de Brunswig,* close to the railway. Hartzburg, a small pretty village, with a pleasant little trout stream flowing through. Lost about two hours in getting a conveyance to look at the surrounding scenery of the Hartz mountains.

An agreeable drive eventually brought us to the foot of the Ilsenstein, a precipice about 420 feet high. Thence . to the village of Ilsenburg, which is a pleasing little spot, where we had lunch at the "Rothe Florellen," or, *Red Trout*—of which, however, we got none.

We proceeded in the carriage some distance further up the ravine, where the river Ilse falls, in many charming little cascades, from rock to rock. On the road from Hartzburg a good view is frequently obtained of the Brocken, which rises about 3500 feet above the level of the sea, but has no appearance of grandeur in its outline.

The scenery immediately about it, from all accounts, and from the little that we saw, is of a pleasing description. I regretted that we could not devote a day or two to ramble in the neighbourhood, ascend the summit, and watch for the *Spectre of the Brocken;* but this was not at present our object.

MAGDEBURG.

Wednesday, July 21.—We started at 10, *en route* for Magdeburg, where we arrived at 4½ o'clock; having waited an hour and a half at an intermediate station, near which was a Café, in the shape of a Turkish kiosk. Here we had some refreshment, and came in for some good music, as a rehearsal was going on in the Summer Theatre, in the gardens. Very hot all day. Put up at Magdeburg at the *Stadt London.* Drove out in the evening to look at the fortifications, and at the river Elbe, which flows in three different branches through the town.

Thursday, July 22.—I saw a regiment exercising this morning between the hours of 7 and 8 a.m., at which time I generally get a walk before breakfast. The men are quicker in all their movements than our troops, and go through their exercise with greater energy, and more spirit. Our soldiers appear to me to move more mechanically, which gives the appearance of a want of life

and animation in all they do. I speak chiefly of the *parade*
work, and am ready to admit that in point of steadiness
they are perfect, and in the field not to be surpassed. The
Prussians, on the contrary, however, seem to feel *indivi-*
dually interested, and are full of animation. The helmet
and the short cut frock look remarkably well in line. I hope
one day to see our Dockyard Brigade dressed like them,
and adopt for their motto, *Pro Aris et Focis.* That
brigade is a fine, useful body of men, and makes a creditable appearance, considering all the disadvantages
under which it labours. The extra cost of the helmet
would be provided for by the saving in the cloth of the
coat, which would be considerable. For the organization
of this valuable corps, the country is mainly indebted
to Captain Baillie Hamilton, R.N.

We walked to the cathedral, a splendid building; the
interior of which is truly magnificent. The capitals of
the columns are elaborately and beautifully carved;
and there are several interesting and highly finished
sculptured monuments. The beauty and magnificence
of the cathedral of Magdeburg, would alone repay a visit
to the town.

BERLIN.

Off by 11¼ Express train for Berlin, where we
arrived at 3 o'clock, passing Potsdam (which we
hope to visit). Obtained rooms at the *Hotel du Nord*, in
Unter-den-Linden, a noble street, with avenues of lime-
trees down the centre. The principal buildings and

statues being all concentrated here, the effect is grand.
I strolled about, and got a general idea of the principal
parts of the city, which lies on the left bank of the Spree,
—a very insignificant river, flowing through a level plain,
on which the town is built, and eventually joining the
Havel, which discharges itself into the Elbe. The effect of
the "West End" is so grand that I am forcibly reminded
of St. Petersburgh; but it is not to be compared with
the "Admiralty Quarter" of Petersburgh, which eclipses
Berlin " as daylight doth a lamp," both in grandeur
and in the extent of its noble edifices.   The equestrian
statue of Frederick the Great, erected recently by
Professor Rauch at Berlin, and inaugurated with great
military pomp, may vie with that of Peter the Great at
Petersburg; though they can scarcely be compared,
being so entirely dissimilar.   That at Berlin is, perhaps,
the finest bronze group in the world; the pedestal,
which is twenty-five feet high, having four equestrian
statues at the angles; and each side of it embellished
with figures the size of life in alto-relievo, representing
the distinguished generals and most eminent statesmen
of the period intended to be marked, which I believe
is that of the Seven Years' war, each in their respective
costumes, and all supposed to be likenesses.

The statue of Frederick the Great, seated on horseback (which is exceedingly characteristic), is said to be
upwards of seventeen feet in height; so that the whole
group is not less than forty-two feet from the ground.

It is an imposing ornament to the capital of Prussia,
which owes all its splendour to *Frederick* the Great; just

as St. Petersburgh does to the Czar, *Peter* the Great.
There is also at Berlin a fine bronze statue of Blucher,
not far from that of Frederick the Great. At the entrance to the museum is the beautiful bronze statue of
the Amazon, by Professor Kiss; a copy of which was
in the Great Exhibition at the Crystal Palace. The
original is indeed a most exquisite work of art; as
are also two equestrian statues on the opposite side
of the square in front of the palace, one of which was
presented by the Emperor of Russia. They represent
horses in a rearing position, reined in by the figures
which hold them. At one end of the palace is a handsome polished marble pillar with bronze capital, surmounted by the Prussian eagle in gilt.

Friday, July 23.—Visited the palace, which is magnificently fitted up in the interior. The throne-room and
ball-room surpassed any thing of the kind I had seen,
more especially the latter, which is most elegant. Thence
to the museum of sculpture and paintings, on the opposite
side of the square. In front of the building stands a vase of
polished granite, some sixty feet in circumference, worked
out of a large block brought to Berlin from the neighbourhood. Here, too, is grandeur combined with great
taste. When the new part of the museum is finished,
it will be one of the finest in Europe. No expense is
spared to render it so. I sigh for England, when I see
how the fine arts are every where encouraged abroad,
at Paris, Munich, Berlin—but the Great Exhibition
of last year has given us a stimulus, and the effects
of that vast and successful undertaking are now *be-*

ginning to be seen and felt in different parts of the metropolis. Under the colonnade of the museum at Berlin, are some frescoes which I could not appreciate: perhaps some will think them very superior who better understand them. We had the luck to see the king step into his carriage at the Academy of Arts, and to get very near to his majesty, who is a stout, pleasant, good-humoured-looking man. We went to the Opera, to hear Der Freischutz. The music was fine, and the incantation scene, the perfection of *Diablerie.* The Opera is a splendid house, and beautifully decorated. The king's box occupies a large space in the centre, projecting in a semicircle beyond the box tier. At the Opera at Brunswick, the duke's box was on a similar plan. The performance began at 6½, and was over at 9. I wish we could adopt the same rational hours.

Saturday, July 24.—Drove through several of the streets of Berlin, and to a rising piece of ground in the suburbs, where a handsome bronze monument, about sixty feet high (somewhat similar in form to Sir Walter Scott's monument at Edinburgh), commemorates the various battles fought by the Prussians. The view of the city from this monument is imposing, and makes it on that account alone worthy of a visit. An old Prussian soldier who had passed through six battles unscathed, but lost his leg at Waterloo, attends at the monument. He is a good specimen of "a fine old" Prussian soldier, "one of the olden time."

CHARLOTTENBURG.

Drove to Charlottenburg, and walked through the grounds, which are pretty; and to the Mausoleum, where rest the bodies of the late King and Queen. Two exquisite marble statues, reposing at full length, representing their Majesties, are placed within the building, the roof of which is supported by handsome marble pillars—and the side walls are also of marble, obtained in the neighbourhood. It is a spot of great interest, and reminded me of the mausoleum near Paris, in which lies the body of the Duke of Orleans, consigned to an early grave.

Both are sanctuaries of simple grandeur, designed with judgment, feeling, and refined taste. The marble figures of the late King and Queen are by Professor Rauch, and are very chaste and beautiful.

On our way, we observed on the road two or three storks' nests with the birds sitting on them, keeping a sharp look-out. Perched at the very top of the trees in the avenue, they looked odd enough, and reminded me of my friend Captain Penny's "Crow's nest" on the topgallant mast-head of the "Lady Franklin," when in the Arctic Seas. We dined at the Table d'Hote, and in the evening went to some gardens not far from the Brandenburg Gate, where there were performers vocal and instrumental. Many young people were present, and officers of various regiments in their different uniforms. The gardens belong to M. Kroll, and are much frequented. The house has

several saloons, one of which I think surpasses in size
and splendour any saloon of the description I have ever
seen. It would hold many hundreds of people; and
when filled with company, and lit up, must certainly
look remarkably fine. The Brandenburg Gate is a
triumphal arch, on the top of which stands a war
chariot drawn by four horses, the same which Buonaparte took to Paris, where it remained many years;
but was afterwards recovered by the Prussians, and
replaced on the gateway where it now stands. This,
it will be remembered, was the chariot on which
the celebrated pun was made upon Napoleon,—"Où
est Napoleon? le Charlatan—*l'attend*," it having been
intended to place a statue of the Emperor in the
car.

Sunday, July 25.—We attended church. It is
entered directly from the hotel at which we were staying. The Bishop of Jerusalem preached an impressive
sermon.

POTSDAM.

In the afternoon we went by rail to Potsdam (being
limited to time), and saw the Palace, fitted up in the
old style, just as it was left by Frederick the Great.

Some of the fountains were playing, but not to their
usual height. Still they were pleasing; and the sun
shining bright on the spray formed a beautiful rainbow,
which we gazed upon with our backs to the sun—a
sight I have often enjoyed, by placing myself in a simi-

lar relative position when viewing large falls of water in mountainous countries. The gardens of Sans Souci are neatly laid out. There is not much to see in the " New Palace" (as it is still called), except a handsome vase presented by the Emperor of Russia, one or two fine pictures, and a saloon fitted up with shells and specimens of mineralogy. There is also a bath-room, supposed to be in exact imitation of the one at Pompeii, and in it are two statues, said to have been found among the ruins of the latter place. We dined at the station, and returned by train in the evening. The journey occupies about three quarters of an hour each way. Upon the whole I was disappointed with Potsdam : so much is said about it, that I certainly expected to see something not to be surpassed either in elegance or in grandeur; in my opinion it can boast of neither one nor the, other, and, if it were not for its interesting associations, would not repay the trouble of a visit. But there is a fine church in Potsdam, which gives an air of great importance to the place—the dome being of the most beautiful proportions.

So much for Potsdam. And now we shall speedily quit Berlin *en route* for other cities, which I trust may prove less noisy than Berlin; for any thing to equal the incessant rattling of vehicles, day and night, I never experienced : the noise of Piccadilly, Oxford Street, or Holborn, is nothing to it. The former is bad enough at night. A friend of mine, a sailor, who hired a lodging in Piccadilly, told me he was constantly jump-

ing out of bed at night as the cabs rattled by, dreaming it was coming on to blow fresh, and that he would
have to take in sail ! He had, however, but just
·returned from an unusually lengthened cruise in the
Pacific, and up into Behring Straits.

DRESDEN.

Monday, July 26.—Left Berlin by 7 a. m. train for
Dresden, the capital of Saxony, where we arrived at
12¾, and went to the _Victoria Hotel._ On approaching
Dresden the country begins to undulate a little. Before
this all had been a dead level. Indeed the whole surface we had traversed, from Ostend to Dresden (except
about Liege), may be called one vast plain of many hundred miles in extent, stretching to the Baltic, and
broken only by the Hartz range of mountains.

We visited the gallery of pictures—one of the finest
collections I have seen; but, of course, could only glance
over them. It would take weeks to study them, which
would not have answered our present purpose. We
drove through the town. It contains nothing remarkable in the way of buildings, though many are of great
antiquity. But there are one or two large and handsome churches. The theatre is likewise a fine building,
and a new museum is in progress, which will be handsome when completed; and the gallery of pictures
in Dresden will hereafter be removed to it. A pleasant walk surrounds the town, commencing with a
flight of steps on the left bank of the Elbe, over

which are two bridges, one of them being quite modern.

In our drive we passed the palace of Prince Puckler Muskau, who became notorious in England for a book · of travels he published—no one, I believe, having heard much of him before or since. I observed at Dresden a marked difference in the appearance of the soldiers, who have very little martial look about them.

In Prussia, and particularly at Berlin, every thing of course is military; the town is filled with troops. I sometimes pitied both officers and men, especially the former, as they could not walk fifty yards through the streets without having to return as many salutes.

Tuesday, July 27.—We visited the armoury, which contains an extensive and beautiful collection of ancient armour, with groups of grim warriors, "fierce and strong," armed *cap-a-pie*, and mounted on their war-horses, some in tilting attitude, with their heavy lances pointing at each other's breast, scorning

> "To yield a step for death or life ;"

and waiting only for the signal:—

> "Forward, brave champions, to the fight !
> Sound trumpets ! God defend the right."

From thence we went to the Green Vaults (as they are called); for what reason I know not. They contain a charming collection of works of art of the last two or three centuries; some of the most exquisite gems of *vertu* imaginable, and each with a room set apart for them—one for carvings in ivory, another for wood, a third for silver ornaments, &c., and the jewel room, with the king's jewels. Any description of such things would be next to impossible—suffice it to say, that they are both "rich and rare." We went into the church formerly belonging to the Roman Catholics. It is a fine building; but the inhabitants of Dresden are Protestants, and the church therefore is empty on most days. I regretted that time did not admit of our visiting any of the porcelain manufactures in the neighbourhood of Dresden; but having inspected them at Sévres last year, and more than once gone carefully through the earthenware operations at Worcester, I consoled myself by thinking I should not have acquired any more knowledge, however much I might have been amused and gratified. By rail at one o'clock to Potzscha. The rail runs on the left bank of the Elbe, just above the river. The formation of the sand cliffs, lying in horizontal layers, is well seen on the opposite side, and affords a good study for the geologist.

SAXON SWITZERLAND.

At Potzscha crossed the river Elbe, which cuts through the chain of mountains dividing the kingdom of Saxony from Bohemia, and called Das Erz Gebirg and Riesen Gebirg. Took a delightful walk through what may be called the heart of Saxon Switzerland, to the Rock of Bastei, from which a splendid view is obtained, not to be surpassed in any scenery of a similar nature. Rocks of every kind, with abundance of wood, and the Elbe winding its serpentine course at a depth of some 800 feet below us. Many of the rocks we passed in our walks through the Ottowalder Ground, much resemble those at Tunbridge Wells in their general character, though higher and more grand. Passing the "Devil's Kitchen," we walked as far up the ravine as "Das Thor" (the gate), where some large fragments of rock have formed an arch overhead.

From Bastei (where we dined) we took a carriage, and after a drive of two hours, through scenery of a beautiful description, arrived at half-past eight at Schandau in light marching order, having sent on our heavy baggage by rail to the station, on the opposite side·of the river. Got rooms at the Post-house, *Forsthaus*. Some of the views obtained were extremely fine, especially on the road from the Bastei to Schandau, from the highest point of which a most extensive prospect is obtained, embracing in point of fact—in a bird's-eye view—the whole of Saxon Switzerland. Among the many remarkable rocks rising into the air, and clad with pines, the Konigstein (on which stands a fortress) and Lilienstein are pre-eminently conspicuous. On our left was a long range of rock called the Brant, I believe on account of its having been once on fire, when the timber was to a great extent destroyed. I must not omit to mention another point of view—that from the Wahl Rock, which it would be difficult to describe properly. It looks into a valley of huge

rocks, of all imaginable shapes, many entirely denuded.
From hence is a fine echo, almost equal to that at
the seven churches at Glendalough :—

> " By that lake whose gloomy shore
> Skylark never warbles o'er."

Verses which the celebrated guide, Winder, is wont to re-
cite line for line, and each of which is distinctly echoed
from the opposite mountains. My friend, Mr. Weld, tells
me that he passed three or four weeks in Saxon Switzerland this last summer, and that it quite repaid him.
He describes the walks and rides as most enchanting and
the country abounding in trout-streams for the dis-
ciples of Isaac Walton. I, too, should have liked to
dwell upon this lovely spot; but rigid are the rules of
office, and two months was all I had to call my own.
My object now was to amuse myself as I best could, and
to see as much as possible in a short time, by rail and
road. To explore the beauties of Saxon Switzerland,
dive into the recesses of the Hartz mountains, and climb
the Brocken, is one thing; but to take a great sweep
round the continent of Europe, to visit most of its
capitals, and to get a superficial glance of the whole, is
another. The latter was *solely* my object; and having
previously visited many of the localities through which
we passed—some more than once—and being familiarly
acquainted with them, it was only when I came to such
spots as Saxon Switzerland and the Brocken range—
and to such cities as Vienna, Venice, &c.—that I felt
regret to take at present but a cursory glance, in-

dulging however in the fallacious hope, that I might one day be my own master, free from the trammels of office, to go where I please, and stay as long as it might suit me.

Wednesday, July 28.—Up early, recrossed the Elbe to the station at Krippen on the opposite bank, and off by the train at 8 a.m. for Prague, stopping at Bodenbach in Bohemia, on the Austrian frontiers, for about half an hour, to examine luggage, which was done in a civil courteous manner, and occasioned but little delay. Here the scenery undergoes a change, the hills receding, and losing their precipitous character, but still very beautiful. The rail continues to run along the left bank of the Elbe, and it is really a pleasing railway trip; the river being enlivened with numerous boats and lengthy rafts floating down the stream. The rail follows the winding of the river nearly the whole journey to Prague, where we arrived at about 2 p.m.

PRAGUE.

Prague is remarkable for the number of its sharp, needle-pointed spires, and is beautifully situated on the river Moldau, which, taking its rise in the chain of mountains that separate Bohemia from Bavaria, flows with many tributaries into the Elbe through Saxony. We got rooms at the Hotel de Saxe with some difficulty, drove about the town and environs in the evening, and visited the Museum, where there is an excellent collection of minerals, birds, &c., and of natural history in general. There is also a collec-

tion of paintings at Prague, but they were undergoing
re-adjustment in the rooms, and we could not see
them. I have no hesitation in saying, that (with the
exception of its beautiful situation) I was greatly
disappointed with Prague, the capital of Bohemia;
and, as it may be considered heresy to say so, I am
rejoiced to learn from so good an authority as Mr. Weld
that he was no less so.

Thursday, July 29.—Went out for a morning walk,
and saw a regiment of Hungarians (Austrian army),
with their tight blue pantaloons and high-lows, which
they usually wear. They were returning from exercise. The place, being in a state of siege, was filled
with troops, whose presence appeared to create no
discontent. I took a walk on the ramparts, which
surround a great part of the town and form a pleasant
promenade; and in the afternoon we visited the Jews'
synagogue, a most curious and interesting old building, said to have been erected in the sixth century
—also their burial-ground, which is a very singular spot,
with innumerable solid head-stones heaped together.
I think I never saw so many hustled one upon another—a perfect forest; and it is curious to reflect
upon the countless thousands whose bones have found
their last resting-place in that small spot. I remember once being much struck with the register of
deaths and burials in a very small churchyard,
in a small village, in Oxfordshire. Being desirous
to ascertain the interment of a somewhat celebrated
character in English history, some hundred years ago

(the Earl of Rochester), I inquired if they had
the registers. The books were placed in my hands.
Hundreds upon hundreds had gone to their rest
in that sacred spot, enclosed by a few stone walls,
which, with a few mounds, were all that marked the
little acre which held them.

> " I like that ancient Saxon phrase, which calls
> The burial-ground God's Acre."——

No one should omit to visit the Jews' synagogue
and burial-ground. I learn from Mr. Drach, with
respect to the synagogue of Prague, that the Jews,
having fought the heathens under Boleslaus II., were
rewarded with permission to build their synagogue soon
after the public adoption of Christianity in the year 996.

In the burial-ground we were struck with the number of small stones, pebbles, pieces of tiles, &c.,
placed on the tops of the head-stones, just as children
might lodge them in our own churchyards—but these
were so numerous, and so carefully deposited, that
there was evidently some religious feeling connected
with it. On referring the question to Mr. Drach, I
find that the custom of placing a stone at the grave
of a friend, parent, &c., is merely a memorial of their
survivors having visited the sacred spot. This gentleman
further observes, that persons who committed suicide, or
had died before incurring legal punishment to which they
had been sentenced, had stones *thrown* on their coffin
or grave as a sort of expiation, in a country where
stoning was a capital punishment; but that *throwing*
stones under any other circumstances was condemned

by the Jews as Paganism, it being customary to throw
stones at the image of Hermes, of Mercury—"Ha-sorch
Eben l'merkules so he abodato,"—He who throws a
stone to Mercury worships him. In the Jewish *Ritual*
a singular practice exists to this day, of burning a
candle in the room where a corpse has been laid, and
that for many days; and placing a basin of water and
a towel, under the strange supposition that the *Manes*
of the departed may wish to purify. I need not say
that any thing so outrageously absurd is scouted by
the intelligent Jews of the present generation, and
some effort has been made by the public to expunge
so gross an absurdity from their *Ritual,* but with no
effect, as many still hold to the superstition, and
delight I suppose, " *stare super antiquas vias.*" It is on
a par with the untutored savages, who place spears
and armour beside the bodies of their dead, thinking
they may require them in the chase. The synagogue
at Prague is in the Jews' quarter of the town, but
difficult to find. Kings have visited both, and the
Emperor Nicholas was the last who did so.

· There are some good streets in Prague, but few public
buildings to attract notice. We proceeded by rail towards Vienna, starting at 3 p.m. for Böhn Trübau, where
we proposed remaining the night to break the long
journey. It was a single line of rails: we travelled
fast, and the stoppages were few and short. The day
before we had not fared so well. The carriages are
constructed with a passage through the whole of them,
and are entered at the ends instead of the sides, after.

the American plan.   We arrived at Böhn Trübau at
9 p.m.   The few last stages took us through some
beautiful scenery of fine fir-clad hills, through which
the rail winds its course in more curves than I had
ever seen, and consequently we went at a slow pace.
At Böhn Trübau we emerged, to our disappointment,
from the beautiful scenery which we had been enjoying
so much.   There is a junction at this spot, and it
is a convenient place to select to divide the long
journey.   Single line all the way.

Friday, July 30.—The next morning I took an early
stroll, tracing a charming little trout stream to its
source, where the water bubbles up, clear as crystal, at
the foot of a hill.   It was a very hot day, the sun
shining brilliantly, with its piercing rays darting from
a clear blue sky, unbroken by a cloud.

I passed two young women at their morning toilet in
the stream: washing and arranging their hair, which they
fastened up, all wet as it was, with a silk handkerchief
soaking wet.   The sun would doubtless soon dry their
handkerchiefs—and their brains too, I should have
thought; but the peasantry expose themselves to the
fiercest rays of the sun with no other covering than a light
handkerchief, and I have often seen the men with nothing
to protect their heads.   Walked through several fields,
where beautiful winged butterflies were settling on
the wild-flowers in great numbers, enjoying the glorious
sun, which shone, as I have said, without a cloud to
intercept its splendour.   The weather was, in truth,
very fine, though intensely hot; indeed we have had

nothing but the finest weather since starting on our
tour.

BRUN.

We left Böhn Trübau by train at 11 a.m., and
stopped at Brun (which we reached at 2½ o'clock) for
half an hour, and had some luncheon. Brun appears
a place of some importance, and a manufacturing town.
Latterly, I observed we had a double line of rail.
Women in great numbers were working on the rail,
and doing the hard work of *navvies*. (This happens,
I suppose, from keeping up a large army.) They
were also employed building houses, &c. I never saw
this in any other country I have visited. Whilst at
work in the broiling sun, they cover their faces with
handkerchiefs, leaving nothing visible but the eyes
peeping out—a great advantage to some who have
nothing but bright eyes to attract one; a pair of which,
I remarked, were very piercing; but I have no idea
what the remainder of the young "navvy's" features
were like. I observed that the Prussian and Austrian
employés on the railways salute the trains as they pass
tout au militaire, both being under military government. These Austrian railway porters are uncommonly
well set up, and really have a soldier-like look. They
all wear fierce moustaches.

The crops every where in the countries we have passed
through appeared remarkably fine, and the greater part
of the harvest was already cut, and carried.

VIENNA.

We arrived at Vienna at 7½, and proceeded to the *Golden Lamb.* On approaching Vienna a railway bridge crosses the Danube, which is here a noble river. It seems strange that the city should not have been built nearer to that spot.

Saturday, July 31.—Drove about the town sightseeing. Vienna is a splendid city, giving the idea of great opulence, although in point of fact it has but one fine street of great width. Every thing is, nevertheless, in grand style. The principal objects of attraction we saw were the tombs of the emperors, which are in vaults. The monumental sarcophagi, in which their bodies are now "quietly inurned," are most beautiful, being elaborately worked in bronze. Some statues by Canova—one, a monument in one of the churches, very grand; another, Hercules slaying the Centaur, in a temple in one of the gardens.

There is at Vienna a splendid gallery of paintings by the old masters, and some by modern artists. Paid a visit to the Emperor's stables, which, when full, will hold six hundred horses. There were several in the stalls, and all fine animals, well kept, well fed, and well groomed; state carriages and other vehicles innumerable: the whole display being quite equal to that in our own Royal Mews.

The cathedral at Vienna is an ancient building, very grand, inside and out. The Treasury is another place we visited, where, amongst other valuable things, the crown jewels are kept; but there was such a mob of people, and it was so hot, that we were soon satisfied, and glad to quit the place without setting eyes upon one-third part of the treasures.

In the afternoon we took a drive to the Prater, the Hyde Park of Vienna, which in the month of May is thronged with equipages, horsemen, and pedestrians. But now all the fashionable world were absent from the town.

In the evening went to the Opera. *The Prophète* was performed—as splendid a spectacle as I have ever seen on the stage. One or two of the scenes were magnificent. They could not well be excelled in scenic representation. The music and singing, as might be expected, first rate; the whole indeed is as grand an Opera as it is possible to conceive. No *habitué* at Her Majesty's Theatre, or at Covent Garden, could have desired better performance. The orchestra is unrivalled.

Sunday, August 1.—Opposite our hotel, in front of a café are numerous oleanders in full bloom, and many people seated at their little tables sipping their coffee, reading the paper, and perhaps settling the affairs of the nation.

I was generally up at 6 a.m., and on looking out of my window, the seats at the café were always occupied. They are a very early people at Vienna, as every where else on the Continent, and the vehicles are rattling about at 4 a.m. Yet they do not appear to be particularly early in going to bed. We attended morning service at the ambassador's, and in the afternoon drove to

SCHOENBRUN,

the Versailles of Vienna, and the summer residence of
the Emperor.   The gardens are very pleasant to walk
in, and the esplanade of the palace is perhaps one of the
finest in Europe.   On a rising slope of ground stands a
sort of temple called the Belvidere, from the top of which
a magnificent panorama presents itself, and Vienna is seen
to much advantage, extending over a great surface of
ground.

Close to the palace is a café, where we dined.   Numerous well-dressed parties were there, and some of the
elite.   An excellent band played many pleasing airs.
At about 8 o'clock we came away.   The road was literally swarming with one moving mass of human beings;
some on foot, and some in vehicles of every description,
each on their way home, like so many bees to their
hives.   The whole town go *out of town* apparently on
the Sunday, and all the cafés on the roadside are
thronged.   It had the appearance of a great fair.
Mounted police kept the road clear.   Every one appeared
to be orderly and well conducted, and all to be enjoying
themselves.

Monday, August 2.—Took a long drive to-day, first to
a spot called Brühl, where we walked to a fine old ruin
of a castle, and afterwards to Laxemburg, a summer
residence of the Emperor, where there is a modern-built
castle, on the plan of one of those of ancient times, and
into which have been collected many remnants and relics from the old ruined castles in that neighbourhood.

They are both beautiful spots, especially the former, where the scenery is lovely.

On an elevated spot south of the town, stands a stone cross, from whence a fine view is obtained of Vienna. We found every thing tranquil at Vienna; nothing to indicate discontent. The streets were filled with people, all apparently intent upon their usual vocation and pursuits, and the shops well stored with goodly merchandise. The art of dress is evidently not neglected here; and probably there is no city in Europe where there will be seen ladies more elegantly attired. It is altogether a fascinating place.

THE DANUBE TO MELK.

On *Tuesday, August* 3, we were off at 5 a.m., and started by the steamer at 7, up the Danube. She was absolutely *crowded* with people, not less than five or six hundred persons on board; the fore part of the vessel being the most crammed. There was a motley group and a variety of costume, as may be supposed. Some poor fellows, labourers, were lying on the deck fast asleep, and nothing seemed to disturb their repose—not even the sun, which was scorching them, nor the passengers who walked over them. In the after part of the vessel the passengers were fortunately not so numerous. They were apparently of all nations except our own; we seemed to be the only English on board. There was but one person in the after part in any way remarkable in his appearance. This was a gentleman with a pair of

D

fiery-red mustaches, which, I do not exaggerate in
stating, hung from six to eight inches down, on either
side, from the upper lip, and were very bushy into the bargain. He was further remarkable for having an infinity of
rings on every finger. I was disappointed with the
scenery on the banks of the Danube, which only becomes
attractive on approaching a place called *Melk,* where we
landed at 5 p.m. There is here a very large monastery
of Benedictines, and one of the finest churches attached
to it that I have any where seen on the Continent.
It is worth a long journey to visit it; and the view
from the monastery, which stands on a rock rising
immediately above the "dark-rolling" Danube, is one
of the most beautiful that can be imagined. The first
part of the voyage, as I have said, possesses little or
no interest; but the latter part, towards Melk and
beyond to Linz, as I am informed, is uncommonly
fine, the river contracting considerably, and the rocks
rising precipitously, well clad with firs.

There were numerous rafts descending the river,
which flows with fearful rapidity, even now, low as it
is—and on some of them were several horses embarked.
As the steamer passed these rafts, the waves, knocked up
by her, set them rocking, and the horses too. These
rocking-horses not being of wood gave the boatmen some
trouble, as might be judged by their angry gestures and
loud gesticulations on passing. The river is at present
unusually low, and in many parts entirely dry, and the
navigable channel shallow and intricate.

Wednesday, August 4.—Having left the steamer, and

slept at Melk, we proceeded by the road to Linz at 6½ a.m.
Scenery beautiful; on our left a fine range of mountains,
rising in many shapes in the distance to a height, perhaps,
. of about 3000 or 4000 feet. The road was in good order.
We stopped at Amstein to lunch. The whole of the
country we are now passing through is Austria *proper*.
Dined, at Enns, a small town, with a curious old tower
in the centre.

I observed that at sunset here, as elsewhere in these
parts, " the curfew tolls the knell of parting day," and
every person takes off his hat during the few minutes
the bell is sounding, and utters, I presume, a prayer.

LINZ, ON THE DANUBE.

Arrived late, 10 p.m., at Linz, and had some difficulty
in getting housed; but we found rooms at last at the
Baireschen Hof. The range of mountains which we had
seen on our left, present a noble appearance between
Enns and Linz. It proved a long journey from Melk;
any thing is better than passing a night in a steamer
with 500 or 600 persons on board, and with no accommodation. We lost, however, some of the fine scenery
of the Danube, but saw Melk, and the scenery on the
road in exchange; and consoled ourselves by thinking,
that as the evening was drawing in, we should not have
seen much of the fine scenery of the Danube, and we
were, moreover, too tired to enjoy it.

Landing at Melk was an experiment, and it was
questionable whether the postmaster could supply

either carriage or horses, and whether we should be able to get them further on, as the road is seldom travelled. We fortunately succeeded in getting a vehicle that held together, which is all I can say of it, and horses to drag it.

Thursday, August 5.—Linz is prettily situated on the Danube.

It has no other attraction, that I could discover, than its site. The town is dirty and disagreeable. The river is crossed by a wooden bridge, of frail construction, which shakes much as vehicles pass over. The head-dress of the peasant girls, at Linz and in the neighbourhood, struck my fancy—a black silk handkerchief drawn tight over the head, and streaming down over the shoulders, with a pretty face under it (and there are many to be seen), has a pleasing appearance. The old saying, is almost a proverb, " Linz formosa puellis,"—a place remarkable for pretty girls.

There seem to be but few of our countrymen at present travelling in this part of the Continent. During the whole of our journey we scarcely met with any, and found none either at Vienna or Linz—not even one, as I have said, could I detect in the crowded steamboat. The same remark applies to Hanover, Brunswick, and Prague. The north of Germany, in fact, did not appear to be a frequented route this summer. The stream, I suppose, is chiefly setting towards Chamouni; Mr. Albert Smith having probably turned the current in that direction, and filled them with the ardour of an *ascent of Mont Blanc*—a matter of more fatigue than risk, as I have learned from several who have gone up, the dangers being generally somewhat exaggerated. For the turn of the tide we owe him a debt of gratitude; not liking to encoun- . ter the stream, as I have frequently done on the Rhine, where Regent Street may be said to be let loose in the summer months, and where one has to rush from house to house to get rooms. I am better pleased to meet the natives of the countries we are passing through, who are, for the most part, affable, courteous, and of good manners.

At 10½ a.m. we started from Linz, *en route* towards Ischl. There is a tramway part of the distance, and passenger-carriages are drawn on rails by horses; but we preferred a carriage and the road. Nothing can be more beautiful than the range of mountains towards which we are approaching. The forms are very fine, and parti- cularly that of an abrupt rock called Traunstein.

Lunched, *sub tegmine fagi*, at the small village of Lam- bach—through which the river Traun flows in a beautiful stream. On nearer approach to the mountains, I consi- dered them from 2000 to 3000 feet in height. On the road to Gmunden we passed the Falls of the Traun, which is a fine shoot of water on a small scale. The river is diverted from its course through a narrow channel, to turn some mills, and also to enable boats to shoot past the falls. We saw one pass down, just as a canoe is steered down the rapids in America—every thing de- pending upon the skill and steady nerve of the steersman: the slightest indecision would be immediate destruction. The shoot of water I estimated at about ten or twelve

·miles an hour, certainly not less. The latter part of
our drive to Gmunden was most beautiful.

GMUNDEN.

Arrived at Gmunden at about six p.m., and got rooms
at the *Golden Ship.*

Gmunden is a small village, prettily situated at the
end of the small lake, Evensee, where the river Traun
flows out of it. The lake is eight or ten miles in extent,
hemmed in by the rocky hills and mountains, the base
of which is partly clothed with verdure, and some of the
hills to their very summit.

EVENSEE: ISCHL.

Friday, August 6.—Left Gmunden at seven a.m., in the
steamboat which traverses the lake, and in an hour
reached the opposite end, and landed at the village of
Evensee. The lake, however, besides bearing that
name, is called the Gmundensee, and the Traunsee; the
latter being the more appropriate, as the river Traun
flows through it. Nothing can exceed the beauty of this
lovely little lake. I have always considered small lakes,
with high hills or mountains on either side, far more
beautiful and picturesque than those on a grander
scale.

· We took a carriage, and in two hours reached Ischl,
following the Traun the whole way, through charming
scenery.

We only remained an hour at Ischl, a spot famed for its mineral waters, and in which there is nothing worthy of note except its site; but the excursions from it, in all directions, must be delightful. We proceeded on our way toward Salzburg, continuing to pass through the finest scenery; and along the side of an azure lake, blue as the Rhone as it flows out of the lake of Geneva, we reached St. Gilgen, at the head of it, in three hours. The lake bears the name of St. Gilgen. Continued our journey to Salzburg, skirting the lake of Fuschl, which is the last of these beautiful sheets of water. The roads are excellent, but hilly.

SALZBURG.

Arrived at Salzburg at eight p.m. Our driver drove well, and exerted himself to the utmost in jumping up and down incessantly, to fix the drag. I never saw a man go through greater exertion; it was painful to witness it. We went to the *Archduke Charles Hotel,* Erzherzog Carl. I was at Salzburg in 1840 with Mr. Graham, twelve years ago, although it seems but the other day that we were there together.

Saturday, August 7.—It rained nearly all night, and is pouring down this morning—the first wet morning we have had. There is little to be seen at Salzburg. Its situation on the Salza, which flows into the Inn at no great distance from where the river enters the Danube, is certainly beautiful; but there is not much to admire

in the town, except the cathedral, which is a noble
building.   The fountain, with four sea-horses spouting
water from their mouths and nostrils, is fine.   There is also
a statue erected to Mozart worth looking at.   The rain
prevented our going to the bishop's garden, and crossing
the bridge, from whence there is a splendid view,
which I saw on my former visit.   The fortress rises finely
above the town, on a precipitous rock.

UNKEN.

Started at 11 a.m. towards Innsbruck.   On leaving
Salzburg the road passes through a tunnel in the rock,
at each end of which a handsome gate is hewn out
of the stone.   We stopped at Reichenhalle.   There
are some salt-works stretching across the valley, which
is surrounded by lofty mountains.   The weather having
cleared up, we greatly enjoyed our drive through several
mountain gorges and much sublime scenery, continuing
all the way to Unken, a small village in the midst of the
mountains, where we arrived in three hours, and took
up our quarters.

Sunday, August 8.—I enjoyed, as usual, my early
morning walk before breakfast, and met many of the
peasantry on their way to church, strangely dressed—
the long-skirted, short-waisted coats, numerous buttons,
and knee breeches, strongly reminding me of the Norwe-
gian peasantry.   The women have generally hats, much
the same as those worn in Wales; and both men and
women rejoice in crimson umbrellas.   For the last two

or three days I have noticed many a "*memento mori,*" in the shape of little paintings on boards, representing accidents. These are common in all Roman Catholic countries, but particularly so in the Tyrol. There was one yesterday in a little chapel, which the parents had erected to record the loss of their son, who perished in an avalanche. The figures are often represented in purgatory, and the passers-by are invited to pray for them. As specimens of the fine arts, they are not brilliant by any means. In the afternoon we took a delightful walk in the beautiful valley and on the hill-sides, and obtained a fine view of the majestic rocky mountains which surround the village of Unken. In this locality there are some of the best views for a landscape painter that can be imagined; and it would, I think, repay Mr. West to take a run into these parts, though the scenery is not, of course, on so grand a scale as that of Norway; his faithful and beautiful representations of which have ranked him amongst the first artists in Europe.

RATTENBERG.

Monday, August 9.—We left Unken at 6½ a.m., having had a good day's rest in a clean neat post station, and enjoyed the beautiful scenery of the locality. Went as far as Rattenberg, a curious old town upon the river Inn, which flows rapidly through. There are two ruins of castles on the heights immediately above the town. A good bridge of three arches (the piers of stone) is thrown across the river. The whole of the drive to-day has been through fine mountain ranges.

INNSBRUCK.

Tuesday, August 10.—Again started at 6½ a.m. for Innsbruck, where we arrived at two p.m.   The morning was wet, but it cleared off in the afternoon.   The clouds, which were low, and enveloped the sides of the mountains, gradually lifted, and enabled us to obtain a view of the rich valley and sloping sides, dotted with numerous houses, villas, and hamlets, together with spires of churches all white as snow, rising out of the rich verdure, and forming a pleasing contrast.   Twelve years ago I was at Innsbruck with the friend whom I have already mentioned—it has been greatly improved since then.   The river Inn is now crossed by a handsome suspension bridge; the best sort of bridge for rivers which overflow their banks, and sweep every thing before them, as frequently happens with the Inn, and which I experienced in some spots on my former visit to the Tyrol, and last year at Interlaken.   A handsome building has been erected for the museum, which we went through.   It contains an interesting collection of various things, but chiefly of pictures.   These, however, are of no great merit, except some very spirited cartoons by a Tyrolese artist.   There are also specimens in natural history, mostly of a local character—such as the minerals of the Tyrol, birds of the Tyrol, butterflies, botanical specimens, &c.; also a few of the guns used by the

Tyrolese in the war, mounted on their carriages, which were strapped on the backs of the peasantry, and so transported over the mountains—the weight being about 80 lbs.

A handsome new street has been built, and public walks have been laid out, which I do not remember to have seen on my former visit. Revisited the Emperor Maximilian's tomb, and was again charmed with its exquisite marble tableaux by Colin. It is impossible to conceive any thing more beautifully worked, more artistically designed, or more elaborate. On either side stand several large statues in bronze, one of which (Arthur, king of England) is exceedingly fine. I well remember being enchanted with it when here before. It is one of the most graceful statues I ever set eyes on. There is also a fine monumental statue of Hofer, whose memory is justly cherished throughout the Tyrol. This remarkable man, who fought so gallantly in defence of his country, and forfeited his life for it, was an innkeeper in one of the valleys of the Tyrol; and at the age of forty took up arms against the united forces of France and Bavaria, himself taking command of the brave mountaineers, assisted by two chiefs—Speckbacher and Haspinger—the latter a Capuchin friar, a man of large stature, and who is still, I believe, living at Innsbruck, at a very advanced age. It was in the year 1809, that Innsbruck was in the actual possession of the French, Bavarians, and Saxons.

The Tyrol had long been appended to Austria—and was satisfied to be so, shewing at all times loyalty and

attachment (as they do to this day) to the Crown of
Austria.

The Archduke John of Austria, had for some time
placed himself in communication with Hofer, and a day
having been previously fixed upon for a popular insurrection at Innsbruck, the French and their allies were
entirely routed, and compelled to surrender the town. A
great number of the allied army were killed and wounded; several officers of their staff taken prisoners;
together with ·from three to four thousand artillery,
cavalry, and infantry. This splendid achievement occurred on the 9th of April, 1809; and on the 29th of
May following another great battle was fought, and a
·second time were the French driven out of Innsbruck.
An armistice having been agreed upon between Austria
and France, the Austrian troops were withdrawn from
the Tyrol, and the brave peasantry were invited to lay
down their arms. Indignantly rejecting the offer, they
placed themselves under the command of their gallant
'leader, Andrew Hofer.

On the 13th of August the terrible battle of Issel-
berg was fought, when the Duke of Dantzig was entirely
defeated at the head of 25,000 men by 18,000 Tyrolese,
who drove him out of Innsbruck; and the French army
evacuated the Tyrol, while Hofer made his triumphal
entry into the capital. The French, however, having
beaten the Tyrolese at Malck, again occupied Innsbruck, and Eugene Beauharnois besought the people to
lay down their arms, with a promise of peace and pardon. The brave peasantry still steadily refused, and

for a length of time nobly defended their mountain passes, till overwhelmed by a constant succession of fresh columns of the enemy, who pressed in upon them.

A Saxon major, who was in Lefebre's army in the Tyrol, in August, 1809, and was taken prisoner, has written an interesting account of their passage over the Brenner, extracts of which are given in my former publication of a tour in Austrian Lombardy and the Tyrol, where there is also given a summary of the war, of which this is but a meagre outline. "Our entrance into the passes of the Brennen," observes the Major, "was only opposed by small corps, which continued falling back after an obstinate though short resistance. Among others I perceived a man, full eighty years old, posted against the side of a rock, and sending death amongst our ranks with every shot. Upon the Bavarians descending from behind, to make him prisoner, he shouted aloud, hurrah! struck the first man to the ground with a ball, seized hold of the second, and with the ejaculation, in *God's name!* precipitated himself with him into the abyss below. Marching onwards, we heard resound from the summit of a high rock, ' *Steven!* *shall I chop it off yet?*' to which a loud '*nay*' reverberated from the opposite side. This was told to the Duke of Dantzig, who, notwithstanding, ordered us to advance: at the same time he prudently withdrew from the centre to the rear. The van, consisting of 4000 Bavarians, had just stormed a deep ravine, where we again heard over our heads, ' *Hans! for the most Holy Trinity;*' our terror was completed by the reply, ' *In*

the name of the Holy Trinity, cut all loose above,' and ere
a minute had elapsed were thousands of my comrades
in arms crushed, buried, and overwhelmed by an incredible heap of broken rocks, stones, and trees, hurled
down upon us. All of us were petrified : every one fled
that could; but a shower of balls from the Tyrolese, who
now rushed from the surrounding mountains in immense
numbers, and among them boys and girls of ten or
twelve years of age, killed or wounded a great many of
us." Overpowered by continual fresh reinforcements of
the enemy, the Tyrolese were at last obliged to submit
to Eugene Beauharnois, and their leader was compelled
to seek refuge in the mountain fastnesses.

Hofer remained concealed for a month in a wretched
hut close to the glaciers, in the middle of winter, hoping
for better times, and to renew hostilities ; but his abode
was discovered, his person seized, and he was dragged in
chains to Mantua, where he was tried by court-martial,
and, by a telegraph message from Milan, was ordered to be
executed in twenty-four hours. He received the intelligence with his characteristic firmness. On reaching the
place of execution, a corporal and twelve privates stepped out from the ranks, and stood before him. A white
handkerchief was given to him to bind his eyes, and he
was told to kneel. He threw away the handkerchief,
and peremptorily refused to kneel, observing, " that he
was used to stand upright before his Creator, and in
that posture would deliver up his spirit to him." Having cautioned the corporal to take good aim, he gave the
word " fire " in a loud voice, and fell to the ground. Of

all the acts of Napoleon, this appears to have been one
of the most harsh.

Across the main street of Innsbruck stands a handsome triumphal arch, which had slipped from my memory. There is nothing else to be seen or noticed at
Innsbruck—the attraction of which rests in its site,
perhaps the most remarkable of any town in Europe.
Placed in the valley, through which flows the Inn, and
stretching across it, the majestic mountains rise precipitously over the town, some thousand feet above it.
These were now capped with recent fallen snow.

PASS OF THE BRENNER.

Wednesday, August 11.—We started from Innsbruck at seven a.m. The clouds were hanging low down
in the valley, which was consequently obscured in a thick
fog ; but as we mounted the height, we were soon
above the clouds, which were now rapidly dispersing
themselves, and we obtained a most beautiful view of the
summit of the lofty range which enclose the valley—
the crisp white snow making the tops of the mountains
stand out in glorious relief against an azure sky, while
the fleecy clouds hung about two-thirds down the sides.
The ascent from Innsbruck affords one of the most
splendid scenes that can be witnessed ; and when the
valley is clear the view would doubtless be still more
striking. A fine road leads to the summit ; and far below flows the river Sill, twisting like the coils of a snake.
In one part it is spanned by a noble arch, which we de-

scended to look at. Through this arch a fine view presents itself of the snow-capped range, which long
remains in sight from various parts of the road; of course
with infinite variety of foregrounds to the landscape.
At the second post station at Steinach, the pass of the
Brenner is approached.

In nearly all the houses in the Tyrol, paintings on the
walls are common, generally representing religious subjects, and the windows and doors are festooned with
various devices. They are observable here, as elsewhere.
The ascent of the Brenner commences at a small village,
called, I believe, Kreis. It is easy, and the summit soon attained. The total height above the sea is not
more than 3300 feet. The scenery is of a pleasing character, but of no pretension to grandeur. The descent
is perhaps the finest, and the road constantly crosses and
recrosses a rapid mountain torrent, which foams over its
rocky bed. We travelled post, procuring such carriages
as we could, and some queer ones, but always excellent
drivers and good horses, which enabled us to get quickly
on.

The little town or village of Sterzing, is at the foot
of the Brenner, and is one of the neatest I have seen in
the Tyrol. From Sterzing the road is very beautiful to
Mittewald, following the course of a river. Mittewald
is a small village, which stands prettily among the hills.
The mountain-ash, with its bright red berries, is every
where abundant; and the many wild-flowers in the
hedges by the roadside, give a great charm to the journey, and are a constant source of delight; as are also

the numerous butterflies, which are of great beauty ; and in some places I noticed some beautiful dragon-flies, which would have captivated my friend, Mr. Curtis, or any entomologist.

BRIXEN.

Proceeding to Brixen, we passed the fortress of Franzensfeste. It is amazingly strong, and so completely commands the mountain defile, that no army could, I think, ever attempt to pass. It was built by the Emperor Francis, in 1830. ' On approaching Brixen we entered the country of vines, which are grown in terraces on the slopes of the hills. The descent into Brixen affords a pretty view. Brixen is a small town, in the very midst of the hills. An agreeable view of it is obtained, by ascending a little way up the hill close to the hotel (the *Elephant*,) which is the post station. I saw some Hungarian soldiers in the guard-house, amusing themselves with dancing a peculiar sort of national dance.

DESCENT OF THE BRENNER.

Thursday, August 12.—We started from Brixen at 6¼ a. m. The road follows the river Eisack, a tributary of the Adige, through a rich valley, in which the vines grow luxuriantly on the several slopes, trained on trellis-work, with large clusters of grapes hanging from them, which, with the beautiful Spanish chestnut, walnut, and plum trees, indicate an approach to a more genial climate. Near the little town of Klausen, the first post

E

station, stands a convent, perched on a precipitous rock, and forming a prominent object. The narrow street through which we drove reminded me of Wexford; for in both one might, without any great stretch of the imagination, or of the arm, shake hands out of the window. The Eisack now begins to contract, and foams over its rocky bed. The road is occasionally carried to an elevation of about 100 feet above the river. The whole drive to Unter-Atzwang is beautiful. The river flows over large fragments of rock (the debris of the mountains, which rise in solemn grandeur above the river,) presenting one uninterrupted series of cascades, the continual roar of water adding greatly to the wildness of the scene. The scenery continues much of the same description until approaching Botzen, a town of considerable size, situated in a valley of vines.

Passing through the market-place, I noticed the women's baskets filled with peaches, plums, &c.; the latter are growing every where, and the trees full of fruit. On either side of the road acacia shrubs are plentiful.

BOTZEN.

Arrived at Botzen at 11 a. m. During the morning's drive we passed one or two castles perched on the rocks. We met many carts laden with casks of oranges and lemons. On leaving Botzen, the scenery undergoes an entire change, and we lose sight of the river, and with it of much that is romantic in its character, but there is enough remaining to admire.

The afternoon turned to wet, and heavy clouds hung in dense masses on the mountain sides—clouds such as I have never seen, resembling light but dense smoke, and the air saturated with moisture, indicating a more southern latitude than I had yet visited, my excursions hitherto having been chiefly confined to the rude north.· We now come upon the Adige, flowing through a broad valley, with a grand range of mountains on the right bank.

SALURN.

At 3½ we reached Salurn, which is on the bank of this fine river. A little lower down, below Salurn, the mountains rise very precipitously, and with much grandeur, on either side of an extensive valley of weeds and willows, all under water. At Salurn we stayed an hour to rest the horses, which were to carry us on to Trent. The vines are every where most luxuriant, and full of large bunches of white and red grapes hanging in clusters, and quantities of convolvulus growing about them. The Indian maize now attains a higher growth, frequently not less than six or seven feet, and quite obstructing the view. The hedges were filled with beautiful flowers; the white convolvulus mixed with clematis, large branches of red barberries, and the purple phlox, forming a most charming mixture of colour, amongst the brilliant and verdant green. In one part of the road ·we passed through an avenue of weeping willows, which were remarkably fine, the pendant boughs borne down by the wet, and hanging like plumes. The alteration in the features of

the peasantry is most marked, and certainly not for
the better.   The clear complexion, bright eyes, and
cheerful face, is changed for the dark, swarthy, and
somewhat sullen look.   The good-humour, civility, and
good feeling of the people of that portion of the
Tyrol through which we had been travelling, was delightful to witness.   They rarely passed without a
salute, and when walking in the morning or evening, I
was always greeted with a good wish from old and young,
male and female, uttered sometimes by the smiling lips
of a pretty face.   The part of the country we were now
passing through may be termed the Italian Tyrol. One's
ideas are carried back to a remote period on seeing the
women in these parts sitting at the doors with their
spinning-wheels.   All the houses in the town are in a
dilapidated, dirty, slovenly state, and as a necessary consequence the people are in much the same condition.

TRENT.

At eight p.m. we arrived at Trent, where I was glad to
find some cleanliness, in the hotel at least (the *Kaiser's
Krine*), which is excellent, and kept by Germans.   It·
rained heavily the greater part of the afternoon.

Friday, August 13.—It continued to rain heavily all
night, with lightning and loud thunder, and had not
ceased in the morning.   It was fortunate we had got on
so far; for the roads would certainly become impassable
in the Tyrol, and broken up, as I have seen them before.
Trent is prettily situated on the banks of the Adige,

which is here a navigable river; but the town has no attraction. It has a dirty, neglected look. I took a walk down to the bridge, from which a good view of the old walls round the town is obtained, and of the river sweeping finely at the foot of the houses. I also went to the church, which is handsome in the interior, and hung with rich crimson damask. In this church is a good organ; but, the organist—*non est inventus.*

The best part of the town seems to be that in which the Dome Church stands—a square—in the centre of which is a handsome fountain. In one street, the Contrada Larga, the grass was growing richly, forming a complete and beautiful green carpet on either side of the pavement. And now adieu to Trent.

At 9½ we started, and, in the course of an hour or two, came upon the banks of the Adige, passing on our left a large castle on the heights belonging to the Emperor, but not used as a fortress, though a strong one if needed. There is nothing to admire on the road thus far, but the mountain range.

Passing through Roveredo, a town of no interest, and dirty as all others in the Italian Tyrol, the road traverses a scene of great desolation. Enormous fragments of rocks scattered about in all directions, as if some terrific earthquake had shaken the foundations of the mountains, and hurled the rocks from their lofty summits, which has, probably, at some period been the case. Such scenes as these repay the toil of travel. Some of the happiest hours of my life have been passed in the wildest spots,—

> "Along those lonely regions, where retired
> From little scenes of art, great Nature dwells
> In awful solitude !"

The road occasionally skirts the Adige, which is hurry-
ing into the Adriatic in a muddy stream. On leaving
Ala, a dirty town, the form of the mountains is remarkably grand, particularly one, from the summit of
which rises a vast amphitheatre of rock. High walls
on either side of the road, were to-day a great nuisance
to us.   Shortly after leaving Ala, we quitted the
Italian Tyrol, and entered Italy.

A remarkable monastery, stuck upon a prominent
rock below the summit of the mountains, is seen on the
right; and, on approaching Rivoli, a fortress is observed
on the left, begun in 1849, and finished last year. A
great battle was fought at this spot in 1848, when the
Austrians repulsed the Piedmontese.

The river now took a serpentine course through some
rocky cliffs, and the road passed altogether out of the
mountains, among which we had enjoyed so much
beautiful scenery.

VERONA.

Passing two or three new fortresses, we entered
Verona at 6½ p.m., much pleased with its appearance
under a glorious sunset, which gave us " token of goodly
day to-morrow."

Verona stands upon the banks of the Adige, now a noble

stream, which flows through the town towards its outlet in the Adriatic.

Outside the town, there was an encampment of about 2000 men under canvass; but, during these heavy rains, their situation is not agreeable. They were to be out in their tents for a month.

We put up at the "Two Towers" hotel, or the *Albergo Imperiale delle due Torri.*

Saturday, August 14.—Close to the hotel stands the St. Anastasia Church, the interior of which is magnificent, and the columns very grand, springing from a square pedestal. Figures seated on the two pedestals carry fonts on their backs. One on the right is said to have been sculptured by the father of Paul Veronese. All are of marble; indeed every thing here is marble—the very roads are made of it. Outside the church, and close to it, are some quaint old monuments.

The Cathedral is beautiful; and the entrance door, of Byzantium architecture, curious and interesting.

St. Firmo Maggiore, has a splendid roof of wood, and is a fine church.

The Tombs of the Scalligiers, the ancient Dukes of Verona, are of great interest. Rose, in speaking of the Gothic monuments of Verona, observes, that there is often an odd kind of poetry in these monuments, which speaks strongly to the imagination.

"These reflections," he says, "were awakened by a view of the sepulchre

> —— 'of the Lombard,
> Who bears the Holy Bird upon the ladder.'

To say nothing of the architecture of the several tombs of the Scalligiers, two of these struck me as saying more than any sepulchral monuments I ever saw; they give you an image of the life and death of the man whom they commemorate. On the top, the Capitano del Popolo is represented on horseback, with a sword by his side, and a wand in his hand. On a lower stage, he is stretched on the bed of death, with his hands folded in prayer."

The house of the Capulets is also very interesting to see. I well remember, at Elsinore, the delight I felt in going through, what the Danes are pleased to call, " Hamlet's Garden;" and the reverential awe with which I looked at, what I imagined might *possibly* have been, the platform before the castle, where, in days of old, was wont to stalk—

> "In the dead waist and middle of the night,"

that

> —— "fair and warlike form
> In which the majesty of buried Denmark
> Did sometimes march."

So, at Verona, did I lovingly gaze upon the balcony, pointed out to us as that which Romeo scaled through Capulet's garden; but where the moon no longer

> " Tips with silver all the fruit-tree tops,"

but shines down the centre of the street, over which the balcony projects.

This, too, is all that now remains of the legend at Verona, and the inference may be drawn thence. Montague failed to fulfil his pledge to raise a statue, (now not so difficult to accomplish)—

—— " in *pure gold;*
That, while Verona by that name is known,
There shall no figure at such rate be set,
As that of true and faithful Juliet."

The chief sight, however, at Verona, is the amphitheatre, said to be the most perfect in the interior of any in existence. We went up to the top of it. All the seats are entire, rising in steps one above the other.

There are two or three bridges across the Adige. One of them has an arch of great span, through which the town is seen, forming a pleasing picture.

There is much to see and admire at Verona. Many of the houses have fine pieces of ancient sculpture about the door-ways, and some of the old palaces are beautiful. We left Verona by the rail, and in three or four hours reached Venice, arriving at four o'clock.

VENICE.

Venice is approached by the rail, which somewhat destroys romance; yet, but for the rail, I never should have seen Venice. All honour, then, to the immortal Stephenson! The bridge which has been carried across the lagoon is a splendid work. It consists of a great number of arches;

nearly all the piers being built upon piles. It was constructed by the Lombardo-Venetian Railway Company —the first stone having been laid in 1841, and the whole completed in 1845.

We got rooms at the *Hotel Royal Danieli.* Often, from boyhood, have I wished to visit this spot, and to be able to say,

> "I stood at Venice, on the Bridge of Sighs."

In 1840, when at Milan, I had intended to do so, but was stopped by the excessive heat of that year, to escape from which we crossed the Stelvio, and were soon in a snow storm. And *now* my wish is accomplished; and here—thanks to the rail—I am writing this at Venice.

August 15.—We made the most of our time yesterday, and were sculled about in a gondola. To one unaccustomed to the sight of these boats, there is a somewhat triste, funereal look about them. Nearly all are painted entirely black, within and without, with canopies of black cloth, relieved only by an occasional small brass ornament on the sides of the door—a dolphin, or a shield for a crest, or a coronet; and these bright pieces of brass only tend the more to remind one of what, in England as elsewhere, has no very agreeable association. It is difficult to know why this sombre colour is adopted so universally, unless it be that intrigues, political or otherwise, may be the better carried on, where one gondola is the counterpart of another :

much in the same way, and for the same cause, that in Vienna, *on dit,* the gentry drive about in fiacres, with numbers upon them, in imitation of the public vehicles—a fact I cannot vouch for, and considerably doubt. There are, however, a few gondolas which have coloured canopies, and there are some painted white, of a larger size, with the familiar and (*horresco referens*) plebeian word, OMNIBUS ! painted upon them.

The gondola is a boat most admirably adapted for the purpose to which it is applied, and they are very skilfully handled. Being of so light a construction, and the bow and stern so much out of water, that they can be turned almost upon a pivot by the slightest motion of the paddle. They are propelled by two men (gondoliers) standing up, one at the bow and the other at the stern, who, with their feet, and a forward inclination of the body, keep time to the stroke; and on approaching the several windings and turnings round the sharp corners of the houses, all of which are built upon piles, call out lustily which way they are coming, whether to the right or to the left, and by this means collisions are avoided. The turns are quite sharp round the corners, so that it is impossible to see whether any thing is in the way or not; but, if no answer is given, the passage is assumed to be clear. There are many hundreds of these boats ; indeed it is only by means of the canal that persons can conveniently go from place to place. There are a few streets in Venice, or, more correctly speaking, a few courts, narrow and paved for foot passengers, but there is not a horse or vehicle of any

description. Gondolas supply their place. Lord Byron's
description of them is inimitable :—

> "Didst ever see a gondola ? for fear
>   You should not, I'll describe it you exactly :—
> 'Tis a long cover'd boat, that's common here,
>   Carved at the prow, built lightly, but compactly,
> Row'd by two rowers, each call'd gondolier.
>   It glides along the water, looking blackly,
> Just like a coffin clapt in à canoe,
> Where none can make out what you say or do.

> "And up and down the long canals they go,
>   And under the Rialto shoot along,
> By night and day, all paces—swift or slow—
>   And round the theatres, a sable throng,
> They wait in their dusky livery of woe,
>   But not to them do woful things belong:
> For sometimes they contain a deal of fun,
> Like mourning coaches when the funeral's done !"

We passed through several of the narrow streets of
Venice, which we found swarming with people, and I
was particularly struck with their pallid and enfeebled
look; even the soldiers quartered at Venice partook of
the same appearance.

It really was sad to see the naturally healthy bronzed
countenance of the Hungarian soldier, to which we had
every where been accustomed since leaving Prague,

> ——"brown with meridian toil,
> Healthful and strong ;"——

now "sickly o'er with the pale cast"—of Venice. Can
it be otherwise, notwithstanding the tide which now

rises and falls a foot or two?—a narrow crowded city, in-
tersected with canals, into which all the filth finds its
way, and which, under a summer's sun, comes reeking
up into the gondolas, enough to stifle one in some spots.
On looking over the "Livre des Etrangers," at the *Hotel
Royal*, at Milan (on our arrival there,) I saw that the
parents of two young men, both under age, had been
suddenly summoned from the north of England to that
city, in consequence of the dangerous illness of their
sons, brought on by malaria, caught at Venice. They
arrived only to find both dead, and to follow their
remains to the grave. There may be some romance in
cruising about in the gondolas, and I quite delighted in
them; but it must be admitted there is a good deal to
destroy the romance; and I find (being an old traveller)
no small advantage from carrying with me, as I usually
do, a good supply of Eau de Cologne; but at Venice
I should recommend otto of roses,—eau de Cologne
not being strong enough to overpower the odours.
If Venice "offers many conveniences as a winter residence, it is insufferable in the summer months," as
Mr. Rose observes (in his Letters from Italy;) "the
small canals (to borrow a phrase I once heard from an
English lady's-maid,) have not at any time a *pretty*.
smell with them." Possibly a little of Sir William Bur-
nett's chloride of zinc might prove an antidote. In
England, fortunately, we can generally do without having recourse to these expedients.

I must not omit to mention that the gondolas have,
for the most part, a prow, formed of a sharp piece of

steel, something in the form of a battle-axe; it is merely ornamental.

The Grand Canal runs through Venice something in the form of the letter S inverted, and is, I think, about two miles in extent. From this other canals branch off in all directions, just like so many streets, and numerous bridges are thrown across them. The most remarkable is, of course, the Rialto. They are all of single arches.

The churches at Venice are very grand, the principal one being that of St. Mark's, the locale of which is known to every one as the chief spot of attraction in Venice.

> " On this spot of earth, the work of man,
> How much has been transacted! Emperors, Popes,
> Warriors from far and wide, laden with spoils,
> Landing, have here perform'd their several parts,
> Then left the stage to others. Not a stone
> In the pavement but to him who has
> An eye, or ear, for the inanimate world,
> Tells of past ages . . . .
> The sea, that emblem of uncertainty,
> Changed not so fast, for many an age,
> As this small spot. To day 'twas full of masks;
> And to the madness of the Carnival
> The monk, the nun, the holy legate mask'd.
> To-morrow, came the scaffold and the wheel,
> And he died there, by torchlight, bound and gagg'd,
> Whose name and crime they knew not."

Familiar as every one must be with this, and other parts of Venice, from the paintings of Canaletto, and much as these had raised my expectations of Venice, I

was in no way disappointed with the reality. True
it is, all seemed familiar to me as if I had visited
the spot before—I fancied the very gondolas of Canaletto, with the men propelling them, were before me;
but I was now looking upon a living picture, and on one
which I can never forget—and which must be seen
to be appreciated. No description can convey to
the mind a hundredth part of what Canaletto's
paintings have rendered so well known to all the
world, of

> "Venice, that strange place, so stirring and so still,
> Where nothing comes to drown the human voice
> But music, or the dashing of the tide."

The church of St. Mark is very beautiful, of which
Mr. Rose truly says, there is no wonder in Venice
superior to it. "*Canaletto* may show you what it is
without, but a *Rembrandt* alone could give an idea of
its interior . . . . . if I could have visions any
where it would be here." Beautiful, too, is the stately
tower which rises opposite to it—the Campanile of St.
Mark; and the buildings on either side of the square,
which is neatly paved with flagstones. There stands
the ancient palace of the doge, and the very chamber in which the grand council sat. Who can attempt
to describe the thrilling interest with which the prisons are visited—those gloomy dungeons, where the
light of day never pierced through the massive iron bars,
which warned the prisoners in their close and solitary
confinement, "Lasciate ogni speranza voi ch' entrate."

To this hour

> ———"the secrets
> Of yon terrific chamber are as hidden
> From us . . . .
> As from the people . . . . .
> ———Save the wonted rumours
> Which (like the tales of spectres, that are rife,
> Near ruin'd buildings) never have been proved,
> Nor wholly disbelieved."

The Bridge of Sighs, which separates one prison from another, and which is all enclosed, but from which the lagoon is seen through the close fretted stonework of a beautiful window in the side, is a spot of deep interest; and I may be pardoned for again quoting Lord Byron, and for saying, as every one has before me, and will continue to do so, as long as the Bridge of Sighs exists:—

> "I stood in Venice, on the Bridge of Sighs,
> A palace and a prison on each hand :
> I saw from out the waves her structures rise,
> As from the stroke of the enchanter's wand.
> A thousand years their cloudy wings expand
> Around me, and a dying glory smiles
> O'er the far times, when many a subject land
> Look'd to the winged lion's marble piles,
> Where Venice sate in state, throned on her hundred isles !"

This palace of the doge is altogether a place of great interest. The magnificence of the rooms, the beautiful paintings on the ceilings and walls—every thing, in fact, is full of interest ; not the least so is a splendid collection of statues, and busts, and Roman antiquities. In the hall of the grand council hang all the portraits of the dukes; but there is a vacant space left for that of Marino Faliero,—" Locus Marini Falieri decapitati pro criminibus." The unfortunate Marino Faliero having, in the fourteenth century, as the story goes, been elected one of the Dukes of Venice, and being an ambitious man, sought to make himself Lord of Venice. It chanced on the occasion of some great festival, he ordered one Steno, a gentleman of poor estate and very young, to be forcibly removed from the scene of festivity, for presuming to pay his addresses to one of the ladies attached to the suite of the duchess. Incensed at the insult, the young man watched his opportunity, and wrote on the chair of the duke words of a nature to give offence, touching the characters of himself and the duchess. The words were as follows:—" Marin Falieri, dalla bella moglie, altro la gode, ed egli la mantiene." Steno was detected, and tried by the council, who sentenced him to one year's banishment from Venice—which greatly provoked the duke, who considered that he should have forfeited his life.

From this moment Marino Faliero sought by a conspiracy to be proclaimed Lord of Venice; but failing in the attempt, was tried before the council, and judgment given, " that his head should be cut off, and that the execution should be done on the landing-place of the stone staircase where the Dukes take their oaths when they first enter the palace." And now, reader, follow the poet Rogers and—

F

"Enter the palace by the marble stair,
    Down which the grizzly head of old Faliero
    Roll'd from the block—pass outward thro' the hall,
    Where among those drawn in their ducal robes
    But one is wanting—where, thrown off in heat,
    A brief inscription on the Doge's chair
    Led to another on the wall as brief."

In the place of St. Mark's we observed that numerous
pigeons were flying about perfectly tame. No one
molests them, and they come between your legs and fly
close to your face. It is forbidden to touch them.

But now for the churches. St. Mark's, with its fine
dome, and exquisite mosaic-worked ceilings, and tesse-
lated marble pavement, which a traveller, whose name I
know not, thus beautifully describes :—"Who can forget his visit to St. Mark's church, where you see nothing,
tread on nothing, but what is precious ? The floors all
agate and jasper, the roof mosaic, the aisle hung with
the banner of the subject Citus, the font and its five
domes affecting you as the work of some unknown people ? Yet all this will presently pass away; the water
will close over it; and they that come row about in
vain to determine exactly where it stood."

"Oh Venice ! Venice ! when thy marble walls
    Are level with the waters, there shall be
    A cry of nations o'er thy sunken halls,
    A loud lament along the sweeping sea."

It is indeed to be hoped that it will be a long time yet
ere this happens; but certain it is, that even now the
floor of St. Mark's has considerably sunk in many

places. The beautiful church of Fabri, in which is a fine monument to Canova by that artist, and one now being placed to Titian (by Canova,) is well worth visiting. The church of Santa Maria della Salute is also a fine church, and so are many others which we did not visit. We made the entire circuit of the Grand Canal, passing under the Rialto, and returned home by the Lagoon, round the other side of the island upon which stands the Salute. By this means we saw all the principal houses of the old nobility, the house in which Lord Byron lived, the palace of Taglioni! &c.

We had already been once or twice up the Grand Canal, but never entirely along it. I think it is, as I have said, about a mile and a half or two miles long. Numerous gondolas were flitting up and down. "We were no sooner in the middle of the great Lagoon which encircles the city, than our discreet gondolier drew the curtain behind us, and let us float at the will of the waves. At length night came, and we could not tell where we were—'What is the hour?' said I to the Gondolier, 'I cannot guess, sir; but if I am not mistaken it is the lover's hour.' 'Let us go home,' I replied; and he turned the prow homeward, singing as he rowed some verses of the sixteenth canto of *Jerusalem Delivered*." *

Opposite all the great houses are large wooden posts to which visitors attach their gondolas, and some of these posts are surmounted with swans, or any ornamental device that may be fancied.

* Goldoni.

In the evening the band of one of the Austrian regiments played in the square of St. Mark's, and hundreds of people promenaded up and down. The whole square was filled with them, and crowds of people were also upon the mole facing the square, enjoying the sea breeze. Venice, being in a state of siege, patrols were about the streets, and passing through the crowd with fixed bayonets; but nobody seemed to give themselves any concern about them. Every one appeared to be happy and contented. A few fieldpieces were also drawn up in front of the guard-house at the entrance of St. Mark's.

Monday, August 16.—At 7 a.m. I ascended the campanile di San Marco, the tower or belfry of St. Mark's, which is opposite the church, and was the study of Galileo. It is a great height, three hundred and thirty feet from the ground, and from the summit a good bird's-eye view is obtained of Venice, once " Queen of Ocean," now " Lady of Lombardy," as beautifully designated by Lord Byron. Unfortunately it was low water, and the view not seen to advantage, as many sand-banks are uncovered when the tide is out, and a large extent of flat shelving sand may be seen stretching towards the sea—which, however, is visible beyond ; and for the first time I now . gazed upon the Adriatic.

The lagoons of Venice are approached from the Adriatic by two or three navigable channels, each more or less intricate, the principal entrance being, I believe, that of Malomacca. The Austrians have now strongly fortified all the approaches, and it would be no easy matter to run the gauntlet of the formidable batteries they have recently constructed. Venice might, in fact, be almost considered impregnable from the seaward, unless these forts could first be carried, were it not for the modern invention of shells (" devil's eggs," as the Chinese appropriately called them) which may be thrown in at a distance of three miles. During the late occurrences I believe that no attempt was made by the Austrians to attack Venice from the Adriatic. The Piedmontese had their ships there to protect the entrances to the lagoons; but she was vulnerable inland, at the head of the lagoons, and suffered from the fire from the fort of Malghera. Nobly did she stand the siege, holding out to the last, notwithstanding the cholera within the city was a more deadly enemy than the foe without. Reduced almost to a state of famine, Venice at last surrendered to the Austrians. It would have been well for her had she never taken part in the revolution of 1848, which swept over so large a portion of Europe; but she fell at the feet of a mighty conqueror, the octogenarian Radetzky, who sought her submission, and nothing more, and who had the magnanimity to spare the city from rapine and bloodshed. The republic of Venice was at an end, and although still in a state of siege, every one appeared to us to be happy and contented; so much so indeed, that it was said the siege would shortly be altogether removed.

On the land side a vast plain, dotted with houses, villages, and towns, extends to the foot of the mountains of the Tyrol—some of which were towering above the rest, capped with snow. The haze was in this direction

also ; but in clear weather, *and at high water*, I am sure
there must be a superb panorama from the campanile of
St. Mark's, probably embracing the range of the Julian
Alps, the highest of which (Mount Terglou) rises to a
height of nearly eleven thousand feet, and is distant, in a
direct line, not more than ninety miles.

The belfry is easily ascended by a continuous series
of inclined plains which lead up the four sides of the tower.
A watch is kept all night, to ring the bells in case of fire.

At the end of the square of St. Mark's is a clock
similar to that at St. Dunstan's of old, near Temple
Bar ; and the figures strike the hour on a bell.   I happened to see them beat the stroke of seven a.m. from the
top of the Campanile.   Proceeding to the Mole on either
side of which stand two granite pillars, brought from
Greece in the 12th century—the one with a winged lion
on its summit—the well-known "Lion of St. Mark's,"
the ancient device of the republic of Venice—the other
the Patron Saint.   We crossed in our gondola to the
Isola Maggiore and visited the church of St. Giorgio
Maggiore, which is a fine building, with a grand dome.
It contains one or two good pictures.   In a column
at one of the altars a small figure (resembling our
Saviour) is carefully pointed out—said to be in the veins
of the marble, but I strongly suspect it has been concocted with a little scagliola.

Thence to the Accademia di Belle Arti, where there
are some fine paintings, ancient and modern, and some
sculptures, the best of which, I think, was a lion
couchant. We visited also the Gallerie Mamfriere, which

is a private collection with many fine paintings, and went
to the church of St. Roche, where they were celebrating a
fête to their Patron Saint. The music was fine, but
somewhat operatic (according to our more sober ideas,)
like much of the church music on the Continent. Another "swim in Gondola" was very agreeable.

To describe Venice would be an endless task, but the
foregoing are some of the many spots of attraction.
Almost every house, however, has something worthy of
notice, and the many beautiful palaces of the nobility
(some now used as barracks !) give a continued interest
to the scene.

> " There is a glorious city in the sea—
> The sea is in the broad, the narrow streets,
> Ebbing and flowing ; and the salt seaweed
> Clings to her marble palaces.
> No track of men, no footsteps to and fro
> Lead to her gates. The path lies o'er the sea
> Invisible, and from the land we went
> As to a floating city, steering in
> And gliding up her streets, as in a dream,
> So smoothly, silently, by many a dome
> Mosque-like, and many a stately portico,
> The statues ranged along an azure sky."

It is sad, however, to see the palaces going to decay,
and converted to such purposes. It interferes, too,
somewhat, with one's sentimental ideas, to look up
from a gondola at these ancient ducal palaces, richly or-
namented with elaborate and most beautiful designs in
architecture ; and to see (as I often did see) a numb

of soldiers leaning out of the windows *en deshabille,* smoking their pipes and cleaning their accoutrements, side belts, &c., leaving marks of pipe-clay on all the fretted parts of the building. In 1848 the property of many of the nobility was confiscated, and Venice, like Vienna, still remains, as I have said, in a state of siege, and is filled with troops.

And now adieu to Venice. The gondola will shortly convey us to the railway, and I shall quit this fairy spot, in all probability for ever; but it can never be effaced from my memory, and will be looked back to with many a pleasant reminiscence. *Hæc olim meminisse juvabit.* The railroad will soon see us far away from Venice, and out of Italy, and so I say :—

> ———"farewell to Italy! perhaps
> For ever! yet methinks I could not go;
> I could not leave it, were it mine to say,
> Farewell for ever!"

If my readers think that I have drawn too freely from the several fountains whence flow the beautiful streams of poetry which adorn these pages, I can only exclaim, with the poet Rogers, from whom I have quoted largely, "Happy should I be if by an intermixture of verse and prose, of prose illustrating the verse, and verse embellishing the prose, I have furnished my countrymen in their travels with a pocket companion."

VERONA.

We arrived at Verona at eight p. m., having left by rail
at four, and were fortunate enough to obtain the same
apartments as we had previously occupied at the *Due
Torri*, a most excellent hotel, admirably arranged. Learnt
from the head waiter, Louis Bellini, an agreeable, intelligent, and very superior man, that he had been thirty-
five years with Bernadi, his former master, and that his
father, Antonio Bellini, was seventy-two years (all the
days of his life) at the same hotel. The hotel is now
kept by Paul and Auguste Barbesi. I have never been in
a better conducted hotel in any town on the continent.

BRESCIA.

Tuesday, August 17, *en route* for Milan. Shortly after
the first post station the road comes upon the Lago da
Guarda, and passes the head of the lake at Degenzano.
It is a fine expanse of water, and the waves roll in upon
the pebbly beach with a noise like the waves of the sea,
on a calm day, on a shingly coast.

In the first part of the journey a fine view is obtained
of a lofty range of mountains on the right, running parallel with the road, and ever and anon beyond them is
seen the lofty snow-capped peaks of some of the mountains of the Tyrol. With this exception the road is
without interest, and dusty to an unusual degree.
Starting at nine we arrived (travelling post) at three at
Brescia, where we intended to remain the night.

Brescia is a place of considerable interest.   It is a large and fine town, and an improving one.   Most of the streets have excellent pavement on either side, and a paved causeway for the carriage wheels to run upon. There are new streets and new houses, but the attraction of Brescia is in its antiquities.   Some twenty years ago, a temple of Vespasian was discovered, and by digging round and removing the earth, the remains of a vast and beautiful temple have been exposed to view, as in the case at Herculaneum and Pompeii, but it is difficult to say by what process this temple became imbedded, with its massive columns.   A large number of Roman antiquities found on the spot, and in other parts of Brescia and the neighbourhood, are here collected together.   The whole forms a museum of great interest.

The cathedral of Brescia is a splendid building, and there are paintings by Tintorretti, and a beautiful one by Titian.   It represents the Woman taken in Adultery.   The picture is chaste, and the story well told.   I think, without pretending to be a *connoisseur*, it is as finely conceived and pleasing a painting as I have ever seen.   Adjoining the cathedral (which is modern) stands a church of great antiquity.   It is entered by a flight of steps leading down from the cathedral.   One part is said to be the most ancient building standing in the town, and to have been in former days a temple of Diana.

We also visited a private gallery of paintings and sculptures, the Gallerie Tosio, which contains a good collection of paintings belonging to a nobleman of that name, who has given it, or bequeathed it after his death, to the town of Brescia.

A fine view is to be obtained by going up to the ramparts, but I had not the opportunity before dusk.

We got apartments at the "*Due Torri*," which appears to be a favourite sign in these parts. The town of Brescia is well fortified.

Wednesday, August 18.—The Emperor's birthday was announced at three a.m., by a discharge of artillery, which lasted some time, and must have effectually awakened every one in the town.

I saw in the books at Brescia, the names of Frederick Graham and Coore, my travelling companions in 1840, on which occasion we parted at Munich, they to extend their travels, and I to return to my duties. It is very cold here in winter, I am told, and the snow lies two or three feet deep on the ground, shewing that temperature does not altogether depend upon latitude, and that it may possibly be warmer sometimes at the Pole (as some assert) than many degrees to the southward of it.

MILAN.

Starting at eight, and posting, reached Milan at four p.m., and in good time for the Table d' Hôte, at the *Albergo Reale*, Signor Bruschetti, where we got rooms: an excellent hotel, well conducted in all respects. The road is on a level the whole way, very dusty, and of little interest.

From Treveglio there is a rail into Milan, but it did not
answer our purpose to shift baggage, wait for train, &c.
There are numerous fine mulberry-trees on the road:
these and the Acacia most prevail. We observed between
Verona and Milan a large number of persons affected
with goitre, but no cretinism. Why is the goitre common
here? Scarcely, I should think, from drinking snow
water, though doubtless it may be so, as the rivers take
their rise in the adjoining mountains.

In travelling through Italy paper will be found a
common substitute in all the villages for glass in the
windows, generally much torn and in holes, giving a
wretched appearance to the houses.

Entered Milan by the Porta Orientale into the Corso
Orientale, and Corso San Francisco, which is a splendid street; indeed I know of none equal to it in any city
on the continent, and I consider Milan one of the finest.
Nowhere is there anything to compare with its glorious
Cathedral. Walked carefully round several times, admiring its great beauty as a whole, and its exquisite
workmanship in detail. I was at Milan in 1840; it
is now under martial law; and patrols are in the
streets as at Venice, marching up and down day and
night with glistening bayonets. In the evening the
band of one of the Austrian regiments played in
the square facing the Cathedral, the Piazza del Duomo,
but few persons were present besides the Austrian
soldiers. The Milanese are evidently not pleased,
and this was marked on the Emperor's birthday.

There was no rejoicing here. Never was the face a more true index to the mind than in the present aspect of the Milanese.

Thursday, Aug. 19.—At seven a.m., went on to the roof and upper platform of the Cathedral, which I well remembered. No description can convey any idea of the beauty and magnificence of this superb structure, which is entirely of marble, inside and out, and filled with statues, and rich sculptured pinnacles, canopies, and bas-reliefs innumerable, many thousands in all. The view from the summit of the highest spire (which I ascended when last here) is extensive and grand. No one who is able to climb to a great height should omit to ascend to the highest pinnacle, when the weather is clear and promises a fine view.

On one side lie the Apennines, and on the other the Alps; and whilst " talking of the Alps and Apennines," I may briefly mention that all the high passes of the Alps and loftiest mountains are distinctly seen on a clear day— Mont-Blanc, the Great St. Bernard, Monte Rosa, the Simplon, the Jungfrau, Finster-Aarhorn, St. Gothard, Splugen, &c. It was too obscure to day to define any of these; but the great chain of mountains, with many clear outlines, capped with snow, was distinctly seen. The Cathedral at Brescia I also plainly saw with a glass.

Dr. James Johnson, in his charming book, called " Change of Air, or the Pursuit of Health," (published in 1831,) remarks, that the panorama from the Duòmo, including a fine bird's-eye view of Milan itself, impresses on the memory " a splendid image, a gorgeous and

majestic picture of nature and art, of desolation and cultivation, of everlasting snow and perennial verdure,
which time only can efface, by breaking up the intellectual tablet on which it was engraved by the delighted
senses."

The interior of the Cathedral is grand, and elaborately finished. We visited all parts of it, and I
distinctly remembered most of what I had seen on
my former visit. We saw the statue of St. Bartho-
lomew, and the tomb of Carlo Borromeo, to which we
had to descend, but declined looking at the decayed and
disgusting face of the poor saint. The netted grating
over the tomb, with money scattered plentifully upon
it, from those who could ill afford to throw it there,
still filled me with pity for the poor deluded people, who
thus submit to have it wrung from them. Went up again
to the roof at 10 o'clock, but the view was no better.

Revisited the Palazzi di Brera and Bibliotheca Am-
brosiana, in both of which are fine collections of pictures
and sculptures; and, in the latter, a splendid library.
Also, the Scala, which is the finest opera-house in the
world. We saw it of course to great disadvantage—
empty, and by the glimmering light of a few lamps.
Went on the stage, which is also greater than any
other. In a saloon of the theatre is a monument to
Malibran—(poor Malibran!)—surmounted by her bust.
There is also a bust of Bellini.

Passed through the "Gold and Silver-smiths'" Street,
which, as may be inferred from the name, is occupied
on either side chiefly by jewellers' shops, just as at

Lisbon, where they have a street for each. It is generally supposed that "two of a trade never agree;" but here, although at close quarters, it is to be hoped they seldom fall out. Revisited the Triumphal Arch, or Arco della Pace, which is a beautiful gateway—a marble arch surmounted by a war-chariot, and horses in bronze, and a horse at each corner, with a figure, I suppose, of Peace, seated on each. Also, the Arena, a large open amphitheatre made by Buonaparte, in imitation of the ancient amphitheatres.

Then to the old church of St. Maria delle Grazie, in the refectory of which is the celebrated painting, by Leonardo da Vinci, of the "Last Supper," said to have been greatly injured by the French troops firing at it— which I do not believe to be the fact. It seems as if it were but yesterday that I was admiring it, yet it is twelve years past.

COMO.

Friday, August 20.—Wet morning. By rail to Como, starting at 10, and arriving at 11½. This rail has been opened since I was last here. It avoids a tedious level road, which I then found two or three inches thick with dust, and very hot, shut in with acacia-trees. These were, however, in full blossom, and very beautiful.

Although it was raining, we took a covered boat for an hour, and rowed out a short distance. Notwithstanding the heavy clouds, the lake looked pretty, and a good view is obtained of Como, which is situated at its foot. When I was here in 1810, having crossed the Splugen, I came down the whole length of the lake in the steamboat, and it was very beautiful.

We visited the Cathedral at Como, which is a fine building; and then engaged a voiture with three horses to take us to Vevay, across the Simplon. The only drawback to voiturier travelling, is the delay of two or three hours in the middle of the day, to rest the horses, when one can only loiter about and lunch.

VARESE.

Started at about three p.m. for Varese, where we arrived soon after six, and got rooms at the *Albergo del Angelo*.

The latter part of the drive is extremely beautiful, and a splendid view is obtained of the snowy Alps, rising in great grandeur, piercing to the skies.

Varese is a small town of no interest, but prettily situated on the slope of some hills; but there is a favourite resort in the neighbourhood to the Sacro Monte, where there is a temple to the Madonna, to which pilgrimages are made. We had no time to make the pilgrimage ourselves; nor, for my own part, any great inclination, except for the view.

LAGO MAGGIORE.

Saturday, Aug. 21.—We started from Varese at eight for the Lago Maggiore, and were delayed at Sesto Calende, as the passport of the voiturier was not *en règle*, and they would not allow him to proceed. The difficulty was got over by a man coming on with the carriage, and the voiturier remaining behind till his passport could be corrected by sending it to Milan; and as we purposed to stay at Bavéno on the morrow (Sunday,) we hoped to get him back again in time to proceed on Monday to D'omo D'Ossola. The Austrians are very particular about passports here, as elsewhere. I was once turned back at Lavéno (which is opposite to Bavéno,) on account of some irregularity in my passport. Travellers should be very careful. Yesterday, some English had to go back to Turin on reaching Sesto Calende. Many complaints have been made by our countrymen of incivility on the part of the Austrian authorities. We met with none: on the contrary, nothing could be more courteous than they invariably were; and our passport being *en régle*, we experienced no trouble or delay of any description; but as it is known that they are strict, it is the traveller's own fault if he does not conform to their regulations.

The drive from Varese to this spot, where the river Tecino (the outlet to Lago Maggiore) is crossed in a ferry-boat, is in parts very beautiful, a magnificent view being obtained of the snowy peaks of the Alps—the Great St Bernard, St Gothard, and Monte Rosa, as I supposed them to be. Nothing can be finer, and we saw them to perfection, with the sun shining bright upon them, and not a cloud resting upon the summits. We missed our road, and went a considerable distance out of it; but had no occasion to regret this, as we obtained some splendid views of the Alps. The women were all particularly neat in dressing their hair, and wore at the back of the head the usual tiara,—resembling silver salt-spoons, or something of that shape.

On crossing the ferry, we entered Piedmont, and proceeded to Arona, where we remained a couple of hours to rest the horses; and took the opportunity of visiting the colossal statue of St. Carlo Borromeo, which stands 108 feet high, including the pedestal. The interior may be ascended, and a view obtained from a trap-door which I observed between the shoulders; but I was satisfied without going up. The road now follows the margin of the lake to Bavéno; and it is a beautiful drive. Arrived at Bavéno at six p.m., and got housed at the post station. The sun was shining bright upon the islands, and lighting up the several villages and houses on the opposite shores of the lake. It was a lovely sight, and in truth "a glorious eve," as the song says.

BAVENO.

Sunday, August 23.—I was on the sick list all day; seldom more unwell. The diet is every where bad, and this possibly had something to do with my being so completely *hors de combat*, which is rarely my case. Took a quiet stroll in the neighbourhood, and enjoyed, so far as my state allowed me, the view of the lake, and of the Borromean Islands, which from the shore have a pleasing effect.

Well do I remember this spot when here with my brother some years ago.

Numerous lizards were basking in the sun on the stone walls and on the top of the stones which mark the

road; and, judging from the way they would dart like
lightning to their recesses, on a near approach, I conclude they must be very acute in sight or hearing.

BORROMEAN ISLANDS.

We took a boat to the Isola Bella, and went over the
Palace of the Count Borromeo, which has many good
paintings and fine apartments; but the great attraction
is the artificial garden or terrace, with trees of tropical climes, and flowers, and orange trees, and lemon, full
of fruit. We rowed round the Fisherman's Island, but
did not land. On a mountain rising immediately above
Baveno a fine view is said to be obtained of the Alps;
but we had no time, and not feeling well, I had no inclination to go up, the weather, moreover, was cloudy, and
no view could have been obtained.

SIMPLON.

Monday, August 23.—Started this morning at 7½ a.m.,
for the Simplon, went with our three horses as far as
Domo D' Ossola, and there took post-horses to carry
us up to the village of Simplon, leaving our own to follow.
In the first part of the road, after quitting the Lago
Maggiore, we twice crossed the river Toce in ferry
boats. From the second ferry (shortly after) a splendid view is obtained of Monte Rosa, with its summits
covered with snow, and looking very beautiful, as seen
through a gap in the mountains, the verdure of which
forms a charming contrast.

The ascent of the Simplon begins at Domo D'Ossola, and not far from the next post station, Iselle, we entered Switzerland.   The pass of the Simplon, its galleries cut through the rocks, its bridges, and skilfully constructed road, are too well known to need any attempt at description on my part, and equally familiar must be its towering precipices, with innumerable cascades pouring down their sides, the mighty rush of water between the large fragments of rocks, and the snow-clad summit of one of the mountains which is constantly seen during the ascent. The whole indeed is magnificent.   Nature and art combine to fill the mind with delight, on crossing this splendid passage of the Alps.   In one part, not far from Iselle, I noticed the largest piece of detached rock I had any where seen : what a splendid pedestal it would make for an equestrian statue of Napoleon, facing the pass of the Simplon from the Italian side !   David's picture of Napoleon crossing the Alps, has doubtless given me the idea.   A clever sculptor would manage this by working the stone on the spot; and it should be modelled from that celebrated picture.

We reached the village of Simplon about five p.m., and got rooms at the clean, well-conducted little inn, placed at this high elevation, where we found the air fresh and invigorating after all the heat we have endured of late. The village consists of a few houses, some dozen or eighteen, perhaps, (and a church,) surrounded by high mountain-peaks and ridges, on some of which the snow lies deep. Approaching the village of Simplon, we observed beautiful pasturage, and houses scattered on the sides of the mountains, reminding me strongly of the Sœters in Norway.

Tuesday, August 24.—Started about seven a.m., and continued the ascent of the Simplon to the Hospice, and thence descended to Brigue, at the foot of the pass, which we reached in about four hours.

The air was keen at so high an elevation as the Hospice, on approaching which a marked difference is observable in the vegetation.

The firs gradually become few and far between, and of stunted growth, and no shrub but the rhododendron is to be seen amidst the naked rocks.

We went into the Hospice, a large building, with many comfortable and well-furnished sleeping apartments, and with a handsome chapel attached to it.

This and the several houses of refuge we passed, which are all numbered refuge No. 1, 2, &c., and placed at certain intervals from the summit, afford asylums for the travellers caught in snow-storms; so that few lives are ever lost, but occasionally passing travellers are brought in, in the last stage of exhaustion.

The highest point of the road seems to be a few yards beyond the Hospice, and is marked by a cross.

We were particularly fortunate in the weather both yesterday and to-day; for even in midsummer, snow, hail, thick fogs, and high winds, are frequently encountered, and delay travellers on their journey.

The Swiss side of the Simplon is not so striking as that of Piedmont; the galleries are fine, but the mountain pass is not so contracted, and the rush of water in

all directions is far less; yet there is much grandeur,
and the high summits, covered with eternal snow,
are very imposing, and particularly the view of the
glacier of the Simplon, which is best seen on approaching Brigue.   And now having crossed this magnificent pass, " whose gentle ascents up the face of a
mighty Alp scarcely tire either horse or man—whose
windings along the brinks of yawning precipices alarm
not the eye, whose descents into the most frightful
chasms and profound abysses, scarcely require a drag on
the carriage wheels"—let me ask, with Dr. James Johnson,
whose tour in pursuit of health I have already noticed,
" Can we fail to extend our admiration of the route to
the great man whose comprehensive mind designed and
executed a gigantic task,

> " Beyond all Greek, beyond all Roman fame ?"

BRIGUE.

From this little town there is another glacier, seen to
greater advantage than on the descent of the Simplon—
the glacier Aletsch.   At Brigue we remained a couple
of hours to rest the horses, not having been able to get
post-horses at the Simplon to carry us to the summit.

For want of something better to do, we visited the
College of Jesuits, in which there is nothing to interest
one that I could discover ; but a good view is obtained
from their garden of the two glaciers to which I have
alluded.

On passing through the town, we went into a church

adjoining a house which had fallen in on Christmas-day
last; it was used as an hospital, in which some poor people
had been crushed under the ruins. From the way they
are rebuilding it, I should think a similar catastrophe
not unlikely to happen. The road now follows the
valley of the Rhone, and runs nearly level the whole
way.

Shortly after leaving Brigue a splendid mountain is
seen on the left, with its summit covered with snow, upon which the sun was glistening, showing it off to great
advantage against a bright azure sky. This I imagined
to be Monte Rosa. On the right of the valley an occasional glimpse was caught of the snowy summit of the
Bernese Alps. The mountains on this side of the valley are of much grandeur, and particularly at a spot
looking up a fine gorge which leads to the baths of
Luisk. At Tourtmain, which we passed on our left, is a
cascade. We did not stop to look at it: I had seen it,
however, on a former occasion; but, proceeding on to
Sierre, arrived there about five o'clock, and obtained
rooms at the *Hotel du Soleil.*

SIERRE : SION.

Wednesday, Aug. 25.—We started at seven a.m. from
Sierre, and proceeded to Martigny, where we arrived in
about four hours, continuing our road through the valley
of the Rhone : many glimpses are caught of snowy peaks
towering over the mountains which enclose the valley.
On approaching Martigny there are some fine sharp

peaks, and serrated ridges, covered with eternal snow, which are seen to great advantage on the left of the valley. There is also a remarkably fine peak of rock, rising far above the rest, on the left, and reminding me from some points of view, of the drawings of the Devil's Thumb in Baffin's Bay. On the right of the valley, also, the rocks rise precipitously, and with much grandeur, their outline being very sharp, and tipped with snow. This against a bright blue sky looked beautiful. The valley of the Rhone has no other interest than the mountain scenery. It is frequently under water, and we found a great part to be so now. We passed through Sion, a small town, where one or two castles stand on the pinnacles of some rocks which rise abruptly from the valley.

MARTIGNY.

Martigny is a small place of no attraction in itself. I was here with my brother, when we crossed the Col de Balm, from Chamounix. At Martigny the valley of the Rhone strikes off to the right. The river shortly finds its way through a fissure in the rocks, and
· is here crossed by the road. The pretty cascade of Sallenche is now seen, and the road passes close to it. I have little doubt it varies much; but as we saw it there was a considerable body of water, and it was a fine fall. Looking back upon Martigny, a splendid mountain is seen in the distance, buried in snow, which was, no doubt, the Great St. Bernard.

LAKE OF GENEVA : VILLENEUVE.

A four hours' drive brought us to Villeneuve, at the head of the lake of Geneva, passing on our way through St. Maurice and Bex. At St. Maurice the river winds prettily, and is again crossed by a bridge of a single arch span. The lower part of the valley greatly improves, and is in parts well cultivated. The mountain ranges which enclose it are remarkably fine, especially on the left of the valley. Those which finish the range of the valley, are the same as are seen to such great advantage from Lausanne, and other parts of the lake, giving a fine bold character to the head of the lake. The Dent du Midi, with its snow-covered peaks, is a grand object in the panoramic view of the latter part of the drive through the valley.

We procured rooms at a little hotel, the *Hotel du Port*, close upon the head of the lake of Geneva, where the Rhone enters the lake. This hotel is one of humble pretension; but we found it well conducted, and were content to remain the night there instead of proceeding to the *Hotel Byron*, which stands at a short distance from the lake—a stately mansion recently erected, where families may pass the summer months.

Villeneuve is a small place, charmingly situated, and the front windows of the *Hotel du Port* look directly upon this noble sheet of water, with the castle of Chillon jutting out into the lake close at hand. We arrived just in time to see a beautiful sunset on the hills immediately opposite. The sky was of a splendid red and

orange tint, which was strongly reflected on the water.
Two or three large boats, with lateen sails, came to
anchor close up to the shore of the lake.   They appeared to be laden with wood, limestone, slates, flour,
&c.   The steamer also anchored within a stone's throw
of the shore.

CASTLE OF CHILLON.

Thursday, Aug. 26.—Started at seven a.m., and visited
the Castle of Chillon.   The dungeons of the castle are
the most interesting part.

> " There are seven pillars of Gothic mould
> In Chillon's dungeon deep and old."

There are

> —— " seven columns massy and grey,
> Dim with a dull imprison'd ray.
>
> *   *   *   *
>
> Lake Leman lies by Chillon's walls ;—
> A thousand feet in depth below
> Its massy waters meet and flow."

Some years have elapsed since I visited Chillon, yet all
was fresh in my recollection.   We proceeded on to

VEVAY,

Which stands prettily on the lake, and is a favourite
resort.   Here, too, is a grand hotel.   These noble

buildings, almost palaces, have all sprung up of late years.

From the terraces of the church, above the town, is an excellent view of the lake, I think the best to be got without ascending the heights. Part of Mont St. Bernard and the Dent du Midi are best seen from this spot, and are grand objects in the scenery. We embarked in the steamer at two p.m. for Geneva, and arrived there at six. I met a friend on board very unexpectedly; he had come from Malta for a change of air, his health having suffered from cholera. Such meetings are always very agreeable, and this was particularly so, being with one to whom I had always felt attached.

Geneva was full of people, and we had great difficulty in obtaining rooms. We tried in vain at the hotel where we were lodged last year, *L'Ecu*, but were more successful at the *Hotel des Bergues* on the opposite side, across the bridge, where every thing was excellent but the attendance, and that was bad. However, we were at the top of the house, which may account for the bad attendance, and were thankful to get there under all circumstances. It is a fine establishment. On the arrival of the boat at Geneva, numerous porters came on board to carry off the luggage, and many disputes arose in consequence. Two fellows seized each other by the throat, and were fixed in deadly grasp; one turned black in the face, and in another moment would have lost his life, when one of the police rushed up and separated them, just as I had myself sprung forward to use my best endeavours to do so, or "perish in the attempt," as the saying is. The English mode of settling disputes with the fists is certainly better than this; and the "noble art of self-defence" after all has its advantages. So long as that is in practice, we need have no fear of fellows tearing each other by the hair, kicking, strangling, or stabbing with knives. There were numerous bulky porters standing by, quietly looking at these men amiably strangling each other. All the passengers had quitted the vessel but ourselves.

THE JURA.

Friday, August 27.—At nine a.m. started *en route* for Dijon, travelling post. The ascent of the Jura begins shortly after leaving Nyon on the side of the lake, and the view from the highest part of the road is splendid. We missed it last year on account of the rain, but were more fortunate this time. The whole extent of the lake is seen, and the rich plain at the foot of the Jura.

At Les Rousses, near the summit, the baggage is examined as we enter France. They were very civil about it, but it occasions a tiresome delay. We went on to St. Laurent, where we slept last year at the same comfortable post-house, the *L'Ecu*, where every thing is good, and the people most attentive, and desirous to please. There is a pleasant little garden at the back of the house. Before we arrived, some dark clouds, which had been gathering, poured down their contents upon us most unmercifully in our open carriage, and we were not sorry to get shelter.

ST. LAURENT.

Saturday, August 28.—A heavy storm passed over the little village of St. Laurent last night, with much thunder and lightning. There was one loud burst of thunder which quite shook the house, and the flashes of lightning were unusually vivid. To one unused to it, there was something awful in such a storm; but I was surprised to learn in the morning that it is so common in this mountain abode as to be scarcely noticed by the inmates, who slept through it with quiet consciences, whilst mine was all on the stretch. I enjoyed a morning stroll in the garden, and saw a rich coloured rainbow, which is at all times a beautiful and impressive sight. As Wordsworth says—

> "My heart leaps up when I behold
> A rainbow in the sky;
> So was it when my life began;
> So is it now I am a man;
> So be it when I shall grow old."

DIJON.

We started at seven a.m. for Dijon, which we reached at seven p.m., travelling post, and very rapidly, without any stoppages, and through a country of little interest. Some of the postilions in the early part

" Gallop'd apace their fiery-footed steeds."

Much of the scenery of the Jura, about the summit, forcibly reminded me of some parts of the Höllenthal in the Black Forest, which it much resembles, being thickly planted with firs on broken ground, with pasturage between, which is remarkably fine, and quantities of cattle are seen grazing upon it. The descent of the Jura to Poligny, which lies at the foot, is a constant succession of pleasing scenery, and many pretty waterfalls are passed; they were seen to great advantage after the heavy rains, which we heard had fallen for the last six weeks, and had swelled the mountain torrent. We certainly have been most fortunate in our weather, having had almost continued sunshine during the whole of our journey, although at many of the places we have latterly passed through, we are told they have had nothing but wet all the summer through until now; so that we have just come into their fine weather. Whenever we have had rain I have mentioned it, and that has been seldom.

On descending to Poligny, an extensive view opens out over a fine tract of country. Poligny stands prettily at the entrance of the mountain gap, through which the road across the Jura is carried.

Last year we took the road from St. Laurent to Chalons. Our present route was through Champagniol, Dole, Auxiens, a strongly fortified town, to Dijon. These towns are mostly situate on the banks of rivers. On ascending the hill above Dole, a vast extent of

country lies stretched out like a map, with many towns
and villages scattered over it. It is a long dull road to
Dijon ; and the harvest being all cut and carried, there
was no one working in the fields. We met few persons
or vehicles on the road, with the exception of a few
carts laden with cotton or wool, and the diligence. Our
arrival at Dijon, however, was enlivened by a charming
sunset. We were just in time to see the glorious orb of
day dip behind the hills which lie beyond Dijon.

There is a feeling of satisfaction in reaching the end
of a journey just at sunset, after having started a little
before sunrise, in companionship with the Sun, "who
rejoiceth as a giant to run his course."

We got rooms at the *Hotel de la Cloche,* a good and
well-managed hotel.

Dijon is a large town, with fine well-paved streets, the
residence, I believe, of many of the better class of society.
It appears to me a good specimen of a French town.

Sunday, August 29.—We went to the large church, a
fine building, and heard high mass. They have a good
organ. There is also a Protestant church; but the
minister, who is a Swiss, was ill. He is a man greatly
respected.

In the afternoon we went to the cathedral, the exterior of which is of great interest, and of ancient date.
The façade possesses much beauty and elegance of architecture. The interior is not remarkable.

The Hotel de Ville is an extensive building, with
several quadrangles, in one of which is a museum of
painting and sculpture. It was open for a few hours;

but we went in too late to see much, and were speedily turned out with the rest of the visiters.

The tomb of one of the Dukes of Burgundy is a fine monument.

We walked to the Jardin des Plantes, just outside the town. It is a pleasant garden, and among the trees is a magnificent old Italian poplar. The stem is about 25 feet in circumference. In the garden there is a very creditable museum of natural history, cleverly managed, and containing much to interest.

Near the Jardin des Plantes, and just facing the arch entering the town, is a neat little fountain, and a small planted plot of ground for a promenade; also, a handsome stone reservoir, from which the water is supplied to the town. . I believe it is brought a distance of fifteen miles from its rocky bed, and by this means the town is furnished with most excellent water.

I observed nothing else worthy of notice at Dijon. A few soldiers were quartered here, who enlivened the place, and some, as they marched under our windows, were amusing themselves by singing in chorus. They reminded me of my poor friend, Henry Davis, of the 52nd, to whose memory I have dedicated these pages. He took great pains to teach several of his men to sing, and had as many as sixty who could sing well together on the march. He was one of the best specimens of an officer of the British army that ever I met with; very talented, and without any self-conceit; always studying to promote the happiness of every one around him. With truth it might be said of him that he possessed

"The courtier's, soldier's, scholar's eye, tongue, sword."

No officer ever had more of the *esprit de corps* about him. The 52nd was all in all to him. He entered it as an ensign, and rose to the command of the regiment. Sickness seized him, and in less than a year after obtaining the command, working on a constitution already injured by service in the West Indies, where the regiment suffered greatly, he passed away from this life, about a twelvemonth since, beloved and regretted by all who had the happiness of his acquaintance.

We dined at the Table d'Hôte, and I amused myself, as I have often done, by observing the infinite variety of the cut of beard—the cut Henri Quatre, the thick mustache blending into the short cut beard, with the rest of the face carefully shaved, and the hair of the head cut close. Then there is the mustache with whiskers and beard of a goodly length; the mustache and pointed beard, generally known as the *Charlie*, being identical with that worn by Charles the First; and, occasionally, alone in its glory—if it be a remarkably fine cut—such as that worn by the individual on board the steamer on the Danube, whose mustache I have already recorded, as being not less than six inches long from the corner of the. mouth, on either side, and red into the bargain! For my own part, I rather like this liberty of the shaving brush, which allows many Englishmen of amiable countenance to wear a fierce mustache on the Continent, and beard of the severest cut. There is a pleasure, perhaps, in doing as one pleases, and in an escape from the thraldom

H

of fashion, who, after all, is but a fickle jade. Who would have believed, fifty years ago, that pigtails would vanish from the face of the earth, and men cease to powder their hair?—that all bishops, and many judges, would lay aside their wigs, and that only a few coachmen of the nobility should now be seen in them. The judges had some reason for leaving off theirs, as a man in court once told a judge, not very respectfully, that "he was not to be scared by an owl in a bush." We may yet live to see every one wearing the mustache in England as they do abroad.

PARIS.

Monday, August 30.—Left Dijon by the express, at eight a.m., and arrived at Paris at four p.m. We passed through a great extent of country, covered with vines, which were beautifully cultivated on the slopes of the hills and in the valleys. Dijon was visited with a very heavy storm a night or two ago, and the vines in the neighbourhood are said to have suffered greatly.

On arriving at Paris, we found rooms at the *Hotel Chatham*, in the Rue Neuve St. Augustine, running out of the Rue de la Paix.

Tuesday, August 31.—I passed the morning at the Louvre, and amongst many other paintings feasted on Canaletti's Views of Venice. They might have been painted yesterday, as regards the buildings, gondolas, &c.; the only difference being in the dress of the people.

In the afternoon we strolled about the Champs Elysées and along the quays, and went on board the School Frigate, lately moored off one of the bridges, in which young gentlemen are to be taught preparatory to their entering the navy. A monstrous eagle, well carved, was displayed as the figure-head.

Wednesday, September 1.—Took an early walk before breakfast, and a last look at the Tuileries, and at the wonderful improvements in progress in the Rue Rivoli, and quadrangles of the Louvre.

AMIENS.

By train to Amiens. We started at 11 a.m., and did not reach Amiens till near four p.m.—the train being an hour late. Obtained rooms at the *Hotel de France et d'Angleterre*, clean and well conducted. Dined at the Table d'Hôte at five, afterwards walked about the town, which is not very clean, or agreeable to the olfactory nerves, and visited the Cathedral—a splendid building, of exquisitely beautiful architecture, both in the exterior and interior design. A visit to it would well repay any one who may stop at Amiens; and yet how many thousands (masters of their own time) rush on to Paris without seeing it! Its proportions are so beautiful, and the building so elegant, that at a short distance no one would imagine it to be so large. The interior is seen to greatest advantage by standing with the back against the centre division of the doorway, and looking directly up the centre of the cathedral.

Viewed from this point it is as fine an interior as any I know.

CALAIS.

Thursday, September 2.—We left Amiens by the 10 o'clock train, and reached Calais about 3½—an hour beyond the time. We found the " Princess Maude" (a very fine sea-boat, built by Ditchburn & Co.) belonging to the South Eastern Railway Company, waiting with her steam up, and, soon after four o'clock, steamed out of the harbour, and landed at Dover in less than two hours; just in time to save the tide. We had a calm passage. The average service speed of this fine vessel is thirteen statute miles an hour, and her greatest speed fifteen miles.

The "Princess Maude" is not so long as the "Vivid" by nine or ten feet, and two or three feet less in breadth. She is built of iron, with paddle-wheels, and engines of 120 horse power (the Vivid 160.)

I have before crossed in the boats belonging to this company, and can speak in the highest terms of them; they are as fine boats as can put to sea, and are admirably managed. We had seventy passengers on board; but the vessel is so roomy that I could not have supposed there were half the number, had I not ascertained the fact. By the company's tidal steamers to Boulogne passengers walk on board and on shore, and small boats are never used.

. DOVER.

On landing, we were met by a friend, who announced to us that Mr. and Mrs. Croker were at the hotel, Mr. Croker having come over from Folkestone to see the Duke of Wellington. We had an agreeable meeting on landing, and a pleasant welcome to the shores of Old England. Obtained apartments at the Ship Hotel.

Friday, September 3.—Went up to the Castle this morning, not forgetting the "poor debtors' box" (as I hope no one will,) and afterwards left by train to Folkestone, to see my brother and his family, and Mr. and Mrs. Croker; Captain George Hathorn, Royal Navy (the harbour-master and superintendent of the South Eastern Railway,) accompanied us, and saw us off per train, at two o'clock. From him I learnt that the previous day the great and immortal Duke had been over at Folkestone to see Mr. Croker. Even this visit was not a little characteristic of the duke, from the details he gave me. I little thought, when Captain Hathorn was narrating to me the event, that in a fortnight's time one who had filled so vast a space in this little world of ours, would have passed for ever away from us.

We reached London at six, and were home to dinner, all safe and well, after an agreeable run upon the Continent, and having, in the short space of two months, gone over a large extent of ground, through several countries, and enjoyed a constant and varied change of scene and circumstances, sometimes in the midst of large and populous cities, in the centre of the arts and sciences, and not unfrequently far away from the haunts and habitations of man, and in the midst of the mighty works of the Creator of the universe—the Lord of all things—" who has so done His marvellous works that they ought to be had in remembrance."

APPENDIX.

MEMOIR OF THE SERVICES OF SIR JOHN HAMILTON.

SIR JOHN HAMILTON joined Admiral Macbride, in command of the " *Charlotte*," armed cutter, in the Downs, in 1792, and served on the expedition with the Duke of York at the siege of Dunkirk. In 1794, he was appointed to command the " *Active*," armed cutter, and was ordered to attend King George the Third at Weymouth. Thence to join the grand expedition from Cowes, under Lord Moira, to Cancalle Bay, with the emigrant army; and was put under the orders of Sir John Warren and Sir Edward Pellew, with a squadron of frigates, to cruise off the Channel Islands. He was then ordered to join Commodore Payne, and in the spring of 1795 went to the river Elbe, up to Stadt, in Hanover, and embarked the Princess Caroline ; put her on board the " Jupiter," lying off Cuxhaven, and sailed for the Thames. Her Royal Highness was then put on board his Majesty's yacht, which Captain Hamilton escorted to Greenwich. Whilst serving in the " *Active*" cutter, under the orders of Lord Duncan in the " Venerable," with the North Sea fleet, blockading the coast of Holland in the year 1797, Captain Hamilton in the " Active," and the " Speculator" lugger (under the orders of Captain Halkett, of the " Circe" frigate), were left to watch the movements of the Dutch fleet in the Texel, his lordship having sailed on the 1st of October, with the fleet, for Yarmouth Roads, to refit.

During a cruise inshore, on the 6th of October, Captain Hamilton received information from the master of a galliot he had boarded, that the Dutch fleet were to sail the next morning. He immediately communicated this intelligence to Captain Halkett, who desired him to watch inshore. Captain Hamilton went in, and succeeded in sinking the red buoy at the mouth of the Texel, in order to annoy the enemy coming out.

The Dutch fleet did put to sea on the morning of the 7th, as was expected, when Captain Hamilton sailed along their line to ascertain the force of each ship, which he then communicated to Captain Halkett. The Dutch chased him about thirteen leagues from the Texel, when he fell in with the "Russell," Captain Trollope, and two frigates. At midnight he went on board the "Russell," and related to Captain Trollope, at his bedside, the intelligence of the Dutch fleet being at sea.

On the morning of the 8th, as soon as Captain Trollope had made out the force of the enemy, he sent the "Vestal" frigate to Yarmouth Sands, to call out Lord Duncan's fleet, and the "Active" cutter was ordered with despatches to the Admiralty (Lord Spencer being the First Lord); but Captain Hamilton finding, on arriving near the English coast, that the "Active" had beaten the frigate out of sight, and being doubtful if she could possibly get up in time to call the English fleet out, decided *on disobeying his orders*, and worked the "Active" up at the back of Yarmouth Sands, making signals "*to call out the fleet.*" On going on board the "Venerable," Lord Duncan's ship, and giving his lordship this intelligence, Captain Hamilton was ordered to lead the fleet; and when off the Texel, on the morning of the ever-memorable 11th of October, they saw the enemy's fleet to leeward,—which ended in the glorious victory off Camperdown. When we first saw the enemy's fleet, the Dutch admiral, De Winter, having carried away his main topsail-yard, formed his fleet in close line. Admiral Duncan, in the "Venerable," then led the van, and in running down received a tremendous fire from the centre of the enemy's ships; but passed through their

line in a most gallant style, setting a noble example, if he had
been well supported. Captain Hamilton was on the quarterdeck
of the "Venerable," when the Dutch admiral, De Winter, resigned
his sword, and accompanied Lord Duncan to Walmer Castle,
where his lordship made known his important services to Mr.
Pitt. He continued to serve under Lord Duncan, until his lordship resigned the command of the North Sea fleet in 1800.

Lord Duncan then obtained for him the command of one of
the government packets, for which he had been noted by Lord
Auckland, then postmaster-general, whose desire was to shew
" every attention in his power to the *glorious and important services to which Captain Hamilton had contributed*."

Sir John Hamilton continued to serve in the command of one
of H. M. packets on the Harwich station, and at the termination
of the war was ordered to the Dover station, where, from time
to time, he had the honour of conveying many high and distinguished personages across the Channel,—amongst them King
Leopold, on the occasion of his marriage to the late Princess
Charlotte. He also accompanied his Royal Highness Prince
Albert across the Channel, on the occasion of his marriage to our
beloved queen, and was constantly selected for various important
services.

After *fifty years* of public service, Sir John Hamilton retired
honourably into private life ; received the highly merited order
of knighthood in 1845 ; and is a chevalier of the order of Leopold.

Such is a brief history, extending over half a century, of the
remarkable career of no ordinary man, and, I am sure, I need
make no apology for having inserted it ; still less for the following deeply interesting anecdotes, relating to the action off Camperdown, which I give in the very words in which I received
them from Sir John Hamilton :—

" As soon as the action was over in the rear, I went on board
the 'Monarch,' and was received by Admiral Onslow, who said
he was very happy to see me, and if I went with dispatches, and

landed at Yarmouth, would I call on Mrs. Onslow, and say that
he was quite well, but that he had 148 men killed and wounded,
and that all his best forecastle men were gone. I found him so
much affected he could not speak another word; and when I
said, 'Admiral, this is a great proof of the discipline of your ship;
after losing so many brave fellows, the last broadside you fired
was equal to any you had fired in the whole of the action, for it
went off like a flash of lightning, and brought down the Dutch
admiral's mainmast in three pieces.' He did not speak another
word; but I saw the tears run down his cheeks. I went into the
cabin, when he asked me what was such a ship about? 'Hove
to, to reef topsails,' I said. He repeated the question with regard
to another ship. I replied, 'She was doing the same.' I found he
was much displeased with the conduct of those ships, when I said,
'Now, admiral, allow me to go on board the Dutch ship, as the
admiral has struck his colours.' He said, 'Do so, and return and report to me.' I said, I could not do that, for as soon as the action was
over in the van, I must go on board the commander-in-chief; and
I made my bow and went to the quarterdeck, where I met Captain Edward O'Brien. I observed to him the beautiful style the
'Monarch' went into action,—passing through the enemy's line,
she gave a broadside into the Dutch admiral's stern, and another
into the next ship's bow,—brought to close under the admiral's
lee, and opened the most tremendous fire I ever saw. Captain
O'Brien said, 'They will give me the credit of that, for you know
Dickey has not got a good name (meaning the admiral); but I can
assure you he went to the quarter-master at the wheel, and said,
You will pass through the enemy's line, close under the Dutch
admiral's stern, and bring the ship to as near under his lee as
possible. He took command of the ship himself, and fought her
through the whole of the action; and a more brave or gallant
man never stept than Admiral Onslow. There is not the smallest
credit due to me; and now, sir, I beg you will mention this
wherever you have an opportunity.'

"I was on the quarterdeck of the 'Venerable,' when the Dutch admiral (commander-in-chief) was brought on board by Lieutenant Richardson (the late Rear-Admiral Richardson).

"I went to Ormes's, in Bond Street, to sit for my likeness, where I met Lord Nelson, who said, 'Why, Hamilton, the admiral took you down to Walmer Castle with him—what did Mr. Pitt do for you?' I replied, 'That as the admiral wished me to stop with him whilst his flag was flying, he promised to do something for me afterwards.' Lord Nelson said, 'Pitt ought to have done something better for you than a promise; but don't mind, it will always be of service to your family hereafter : don't depend upon that, however, as John Bull is ungrateful, and your services may soon be forgotten.' I served under the admiral till he struck his flag, and lived with his family at Yarmouth, by the whole of whom I have always been treated with the greatest kindness. I last served under Admiral Thornborough, of the 'Leda' frigate, Captain Honeyman. The Honourable George Cadogan, the present earl, was then lieutenant of that ship ; and I was afterwards appointed Captain in H. M. Packet Service."

The following is a copy of the letter received by Lord Duncan from Lord Auckland, who was at the time Postmaster-General, intimating that he had noted Sir John Hamilton for the command of one of the Dover Packets.

Sir John received the medal and clasp for the battle of Camperdown.

"GENERAL POST-OFFICE,
February 11, 1800.

"MY DEAR LORD,

"Lord Gower has concurred with me to-day, in ordering a minute to be made on the Office books, of your lordship's recommendation of Mr. John Hamilton for a Dover Packet ; and our personal respect for your lordship, as well as our desire to show every attention in our power to *the glorious* and *important services* to *which Mr. Hamilton contributed*, will make it a real gratification to us, if, on an eventual vacancy upon the station in question, we should be able to comply with your wishes. I have, &c.

(Signed)   "AUCKLAND."

"Lord Viscount Duncan."

INDEX.

THE END.

M'CORQUODALE AND CO., PRINTERS, LONDON.
WORKS—NEWTON.